Praise for BILL CLINTON

"[D]istinguished biographer Nigel Hamil... ...
of Clinton in a sustained and unflinching ...
act. But, for the most part, Hamilton succeeds. . . . ιчо шаιισι ....
in biography might be, there is no mistaking that *Bill Clinton* is a bold, highly
readable interpretive study of the man from Hope in which no aspect of his
inner or external life is off-limits."
— DOUGLAS BRINKLEY, *Boston Sunday Globe*

"Nigel Hamilton traces the threads of Clinton's personality to their origins, in
this superbly researched work. . . . His adventures are so breathtakingly dangerous that this biography has the feel of a thriller. Americans may or may not
be proud of Bill Clinton, but I applaud a society in which a talented man from
the humblest origins can journey to the summit of political office."
— MICHAEL PORTILLO, *The Sunday Telegraph* (London)

"Biographers usually find it difficult to learn much meaningful detail about a
subject's parents, childhood and adolescence. By conducting large numbers of
interviews and locating documents in unlikely places, Hamilton has overcome
the hurdle impressively. He supplements the facts, rumors and gossip with frequent psychological analysis. Hamilton is especially strong when reporting and
ruminating about the role of social class in Clinton's rise from small-town
Arkansas to the White House. . . . At times, the psychological insights seem
downright brilliant." — STEVE WEINBERG, *Baltimore Sun*

"Hamilton has brought it off with some success. He has done a prodigious
amount of research. . . . He certainly presents the most complete portrait yet
of the formative years that led to the creation of perhaps the most gifted, if
also the most flawed individual ever to occupy the Oval Office."
— ANTHONY HOWARD, *The Sunday Times* (London)

"Nigel Hamilton's study is written on the grand scale. . . . [It is] a gripping account of the rise of one of the most charismatic politicians of our age. . . . This
first volume of Nigel Hamilton's fascinating and fluidly-written biography,
reading at times like a modern morality play, ends just as Clinton realizes his
dream of entering the White House."   — GRAHAM STEWART, *The Spectator*

"The story of Bill Clinton's rise to power is one of the great narratives of modern American life. . . . [He is] the only Democratic president since Franklin D.
Roosevelt to win two terms. Hamilton does produce some amusing and revealing insights into Clinton's character and psyche. . . . There is doubtless a sizable
audience of the already converted who will embrace Hamilton's screed, in an
era whose remaining shreds of grace and decorum Clinton sometimes seemed
to do his best to fray."   — TODD PURDUM, *New York Times Book Review*

ALSO BY NIGEL HAMILTON

Monty: The Battles of Field Marshal Bernard Montgomery
The Brothers Mann
Monty: The Making of a General
Master of the Battlefield: Monty's War Years
Monty: Final Years of the Field Marshal
JFK: Reckless Youth

BILL
CLINTON

An American Journey

GREAT EXPECTATIONS

BILL CLINTON

An American Journey

GREAT EXPECTATIONS

NIGEL HAMILTON

BALLANTINE BOOKS   NEW YORK

Grateful acknowledgment is made to the following for permission to reprint
previously published material:

MARGARET JONES BOLSTERLI: Excerpts from *Born in the Delta* by Margaret Jones
Bolsterli, copyright © 1990 by University of Tennessee Press, copyright © 2001 by
Margaret Jones Bolsterli. Reprinted by permission of Margaret Jones Bolsterli.

ALFRED A. KNOPF, A DIVISION OF RANDOM HOUSE, INC.: Excerpts from *The Good Life*
by Loren Baritz, copyright © 1988 by Loren Baritz. Reprinted by permission of
Alfred A. Knopf, a division of Random House, Inc.

RANDOM HOUSE, INC.: Excerpts from *All's Fair* by Mary Matalin and James Carville,
copyright © 1996 by Mary Matalin and James Carville; excerpts from *Hillary's
Choice* by Gail Sheehy, copyright © 1999 by G. Merritt Corporation. Reprinted by
permission of Random House, Inc.

REGNERY PUBLISHING, INC.: Excerpts from *Boy Clinton: The Political Biography* by
R. Emmett Tyrrell, Jr., copyright © 1996 by Henry Regnery Publishing; excerpts
from *On the Make: The Rise of Bill Clinton* by Meredith L. Oakley, copyright © 1994
by Henry Regnery Publishing. All rights reserved. Reprinted by special permission of
Regnery Publishing Inc., Washington, D.C.

STERLING LORD LITERISTIC, INC.: Excerpts from *Behind the Oval Office*
by Dick Morris, copyright © 1997 by Richard S. Morris. Reprinted by permission
of Sterling Lord Literistic, Inc.

Library of Congress Cataloging-in-Publication Data

Hamilton, Nigel.
Bill Clinton: an American journey / Nigel Hamilton.
p.   cm.
Includes bibliographical references and index.
Contents: [1] Great expectations
ISBN 0-812-97054-3
1. Clinton, Bill, 1946–   2. Clinton, Bill, 1946—Childhood and youth.
3. Presidents—United States—Biography.   4. Governors—Arkansas—Biography.
5. Interviews—United States.   I. Title.
E886.H36   2003   973.929'092—dc21   2003046804
[B]

Book design by Carole Lowenstein

For Emily and David Stavis-Polstein,
and their sons, Gus and Harry—
with love and gratitude

ACKNOWLEDGMENTS

The genesis of this book goes back to the spring of 2000, when I came over to America to discuss with a number of academic, literary, and personal friends my plan to write a biography of President Clinton.

I wish to thank, right up front, the new literary agent I chose to represent me, after the sad death of Claire Smith of Harold Ober Associates. The agent I selected was Owen Laster, executive director of the William Morris Agency, who felt it was by no means too early to embark on such a work (President Clinton was still in the White House). Owen was convinced that my intention—to recount Bill Clinton's life not only as an individual's life saga but as a mirror to the many changes that have taken place in our own generation's cultural history since World War II—would be useful to an American public. I mapped out my vision of the book on a single sheet of paper. Owen did the rest.

The "rest" boiled down, in the end, to Random House and Bob Loomis, the editor of my previous biography of an American president, *JFK: Reckless Youth.* As executive editor of Random House, Bob is the doyen of publishing gurus in America. A heavily accented British writer, I am prone to misunderstand certain aspects of American culture, also to the sin of inveterate repetition. I owe enormous gratitude to Bob for seeing the merit of my proposal, then seeing the work through the various stages of research and composition, after which there followed six months of iteration, from first to final draft. That Bob asked, given the ever-mounting size of the manuscript, if Random might publish the work in two parts, was the answer to this author's dream. That he had the patience to guide me through the preparation of this first volume was equally so.

To Owen Laster and to Bob Loomis: *merci infiniment*—as to my stalwart and loyal British agent, Bruce Hunter of David Higham Associates, and my British publishing editor, Mark Booth of Random Century.

I owe, also, a great debt of gratitude to my adopted family in Newton, Massachusetts: Emily and David Stavis-Polstein, and their two sons, Gus and Harry, who took me into the bosom of their household—or rather, their attic suite!—and nurtured me like a prodigal (if overgrown) son, or friend, until I was firmly on my feet and ready to move into my own quarters in Cambridge, not far from Harvard Yard. In that Newton attic I had brought work on my revised life of the British World War II general, *The Full Monty,* to near completion in the spring of 2000, and it was in those mansard quarters, having finished the Monty manuscript, that I began work on *Bill Clinton: An American Journey* in the late fall of that year, as well as in their beautiful old Maine farmhouse. It is to them that I dedicate this book.

Simultaneously, as Professor of Biography on leave from De Montfort University, Leicester, England, I was welcomed back to America with open arms by the director of the John W. McCormack Institute of Public Affairs at the University of Massachusetts, Boston, Professor Edmund Beard. It was as a John F. Kennedy Scholar and a fellow of the McCormack Institute that I had researched and written my Kennedy volume. Once again as a visiting fellow of the McCormack Institute, I am indebted, a decade later, to Ed and his colleagues for their rocklike support, help, and encouragement. To Dr. Beard and to Sandy Blanchette, the McCormack's indefatigable administrator, my heartfelt thanks. Also to my McCormack postgraduate research assistant, Katie Griffin, who helped set up my office and website, arranged my interview schedules, and assisted in scrupulous footnote checking and copyright clearing, my lasting gratitude. The staff of the Institute—most of all Candyce Carragher, Jamie Ennis, Mike MacPhee, and former staffer Maureen Mitchell—deserve especial mention, as do those McCormack colleagues who have encouraged, listened to, debated with, criticized, and cajoled the "damned Brit" into producing a (hopefully) better book, including Dick Hogarty, Lou DiNatale, Ian Menzies, Sheila Gagnon, Padraig O'Malley, Donna Haig Friedman, Carol Hardy-Fanta, Erica White, John McGah, Carol Cardozo, Robert Wood, Margery O'Donnell, Phyllis Freeman, Charles Cnudde, Mary Grant, Joe McDonough, Elizabeth Sherman, Elaine Werby, Ajume Wingo, Consuela Greene, Erika Kates, Michelle Hayes, Miranda Hooker, Michael Stone, Carrie Peters, Tatjana Meschede, Charles Ndungu, Jennifer Raymond, Mary Stevenson, Jain Ruvidich-Higgins, Pat Peterson, and Julia Tripp. Professor Al Cardarelli was my early—and unrelenting—sociohistorical mentor, while Matt Vasconcellos created the original McCormack website for the work, and Andi Sutedja provided technical assistance.

I must thank, alongside the staff and fellows of the John W. McCormack Institute, I must thank the staff of the Healey Library and Computer Services department, UMass Boston, most especially Bill Baer, as well as Professors Clive Foss (now at Georgetown University), William Percy, and Paul Bookbinder of the UMass Boston history department, and Lois Rudnik of American studies. Former chancellor Sherry Penney was most encouraging, as were colleagues in many disciplines in the Faculty Club. All surviving errors of understanding and scholarship are, I hasten to emphasize, my own.

Outside UMass Boston I have been privileged to enjoy the company, companionship, intellectual and interdisciplinary encouragement, and constant critical sparring of a number of friends who have added enormously to my understanding of the United States and the cultural issues of twentieth-century America. They include the distinguished author Larry Leamer, and his wife, Vesna, who helped start me on my new biographical journey; my distinguished fellow biographers, Lt. Col. Carlo D'Este and his wife, Shirley, and Edmund and Sylvia Morris; Dr. David Chanoff, veteran collaborative author, and his wife, Liisa; history professors Claudia Liebeskind and Rafe Blaufarb; Dr. Mark Schneider, historian, and Professor Judith Beth Cohen, English teacher and writer; Dr. Paul Hans, psychiatrist, and Alexandra Vozick-Hans, counselor; Dr. Sam Rofman, psychiatrist, and Elaine Rofman, nurse-educator; Richard Feldman, photographer, and Judy Rosenberg, bakery tycoon and author; Captain Ilya Schneider, member of the Ancient and Honorable Artillery Company, and his wife, Rachel, computer consultant; Raynel Shepard, educator; psychologist Katherine Reeder; architect Janice Ann Crotty; Sam Pitroda, IT entrepreneur and philanthropist; and many, many others over the past two years whose insights have contributed to my cornucopia of American lenses. For the remaining misperceptions and misinterpretations, I take complete responsibility.

In Arkansas I was privileged to make a new set of friends and acquaintances—indeed without them this work would be immeasurably poorer. First, Dr. George and Gail Hamilton invited me to stay at their Little Rock home, overlooking the Arkansas River, while conducting my interviews in the state—even flying me, on one occasion, to Hope, in George's plane. Author and attorney Griffin Stockley also welcomed me into his life and home. Dr. Bobby Roberts, director of the Central Arkansas Public Libraries in Little Rock; Tom Dillard, director of the Butler Center; and Dr. John Ferguson, the director of the State Historical Commission at the capital, and his staff, were enormously helpful and generous with their time, while Rod Lorenzen of Lorenzen & Co. helped supply the many books I needed. Audrey Burtrum-Stanley not only showed me around the city but consented to read the manuscript for factual and other errors—a task she has fulfilled far beyond the call of friendship, as did Jane Kirschner, a Georgetown classmate of Bill Clinton. Kerry Kirschner, mayor of Sarasota, also furnished me with a video record of Georgetown classmates and kindly consented to be interviewed.

Meanwhile, Ernie Dumas, Burl Rotenberry, the late governor Frank White, David Watkins, Skip Rutherford, Jim Morgan, Joe Purvis, David Leopoulos, Paul Greenberg, John Brummett, Dr. Paul Root, Professor Joycelyn Elders, Professor Cal Ledbetter, Professor Gene Lyons, Jim Johnston and his wife, Virginia, Glenda Cooper, George Fisher, and a number of others privileged me with their memories and insights, in interviews without which this book would not have been possible.

In Hope, Arkansas, I was privileged to meet the then director of the Clinton Birthplace, Beckie Moore, who not only illuminated President Clinton's early years and family background in Hope but arranged a number of important interviews for me, including those with Floris Tatom, Wilma Rowe Booker, Mary Nell Turner, Donna Taylor Wingfield, Falba Lively, and Roxie Lawrence, who held a memorable coffee morning in her home to help and discuss my research in the area. To all of them, my humble but heartfelt thanks.

In Fayetteville, I was fortunate to be helped by Michael Dabrishus, then the director of the University of Arkansas Special Collections, and his staff, especially the head of Research Services, Andrea Cantrell, and her colleagues Betty Austin and Cassandra McCraw. Interviews with Professor Al Witte, Roy Reed, Ann Henry, Lt. Col. Billy Geren, Milt Copeland, and Cliff Jackson were particularly valuable. I was also privileged to meet and interview one of Bill Clinton's closest Arkansas friends, Jim Blair, and Mr. Clinton's longtime chief of staff while governor of Arkansas, Betsey Wright. Again, my deep gratitude for their trust and frank recollections.

All history and biography is necessarily selective, and brief extracts from an interview often run the risk of supporting an author's conscious or unconscious agenda rather than the intention of the speaker. I hope my sources will feel I have used their generous help wisely, and have painted a balanced portrait of my subject and his times.

In the absence of any currently accessible primary Clinton documents in Arkansas or elsewhere, historians and biographers are, beyond interviews, largely dependent on secondary sources, including newspapers, journals, and books. All sources are given in the endnotes to this volume, but I would particularly like to record my gratitude to the authors of the primary works on which any prepresidential biography of Bill Clinton will always have to draw heavily, both for material and biographical insight: Robert Levin's *Bill Clinton: The Inside Story*, 1992; Charles Allen and Jonathon Portis's *The Comeback Kid*, 1992; Ernest Dumas's *The Clintons of Arkansas*, 1993; Meredith Oakley's *On the Make*, 1994; David Gallen's *Bill Clinton: As They Know Him*, 1994; John Brummett's *Highwire*, 1994; Virginia Kelley's *Leading with My Heart*, 1994; David Maraniss's *First in His Class*, 1995; Gennifer Flowers's *Passion and Betrayal*, 1995; Emmett Tyrrell's *Bill Clinton: The Political Biography*, 1996; Martin Walker's *The President We Deserve*, 1996; and Roger Morris's *Partners in Power*, 1996. For the biography of Hillary Rodham Clinton, I have drawn heavily—and gratefully—on Gail Sheehy's *Hillary's Choice*, 1999, and Joyce Milton's *The First Partner*, 1999. The sources of all quotations have, hopefully, been correctly noted, and I would like to acknowledge and thank the authors concerned most sincerely.

A final word regarding my subject: President William Jefferson Clinton, né Blythe. President Clinton, when I approached him to request an interview before he left office and afterward, was elusive, and eventually I understood why. He had contracted to write an account of his own life for another (sister) publisher. I was therefore especially delighted to meet him in person at a dinner in Little Rock, Arkansas, in the summer of 2002.

The dinner—held on July 23 to raise funds for an extension to the Governor's Mansion—was a grand affair, attended by every living governor of the state and his wife. Unfortunately, Senator Clinton, the former First Lady of Arkansas, could not be present, owing to her duties in Congress. The former President gave an excellent speech, however, and I was afterward introduced to him by the former director of the Clinton Birthplace Foundation, Beckie Moore. It was for me, as a simple citizen, writer, and teaching historian, a great honor. As Mr. Clinton's biographer, however, it was also a tantalizing opportunity to interact "in the flesh" with the subject of my biographical study (about whom I had had a series of extraordinary dreams when beginning my manuscript).

The meeting did not take place without a certain psychological melodrama—indeed, as biographer of Thomas Mann, I thought afterward how Mann, the great German ironist of the twentieth century (*Lotte in Weimar* is one of my favorite novels), would have been profoundly intrigued by it.

President Clinton, I had been told, knew my previous work, having devoured my biography of John F. Kennedy, his hero, whose life holds certain parallels with his own. Such relish for nonfiction had not, unfortunately, extended to helping Mr. Clinton's own biographers (David Maraniss and John Brummett, especially) in the past. It did not do so now.

At first, having heard my name, the President appeared, as we shook hands and posed for a photograph, not to make any connection between my name and my impending biography, despite my correspondence with him. Instead, taking the beautifully embossed menu card from my hand, he began to autograph it for me, in the manner of a star—which, indeed, he has remained, out of office, wherever he goes.

It was then, as the President's pen began the inscription, that it faltered. The *g* in my first name stopped halfway through its curlicue. From being only a few inches from my face, beaming jovially and an instant friend, the President pulled back at least a yard. He stared at me. His blue eyes narrowed. The blood drained from his face. He looked, at that moment, as if he might strike me.

To try and defuse this tension, recalling how in his podium speech he'd made reference to his years at Oxford, I made a joke about being English and having attended university at "the other place" (Cambridge, England).

It was as if, at that instant, a lightbulb went on in the President's head.

"Cambridge?" Mr. Clinton queried. Bearing back in on me, and raising himself to his full height, he asked if I had read *Wittgenstein's Poker*.

Wittgenstein's Poker? I confessed I hadn't—at which he started immediately to enlighten me. The book, he explained, describes the brief but historic meeting in Cambridge, England, of the two greatest philosophers of the twentieth century: Ludwig Wittgenstein and Sir Karl Popper. Both were men of Jewish birth, both from Vienna—but from contrasting social and economic backgrounds. In the chilly rooms of a Cambridge don in King's College, in the winter of 1946, and under the chairmanship of the legendary philosopher and activist Bertrand Russell, the two eminent Viennese émigré philosophers, meeting for the very first time in their lives, faced off in the presence of approximately forty members of the Cambridge philosophical debating society. It was a clash of philosophical titans, and of their competing philosophies of philosophy. The one was a suffering homosexual, a millionaire émigré in a time when homosexuality was still outlawed in Britain, an athlete who was a mountain climber and educator devoted to the study of philosophy as an abstract mathematical engagement with "puzzles" or brain twisters. The other was a married émigré from lower-Viennese-middle-class Jewry, devoted—in the train of Hegel and Karl Marx—to the ethical aspects of democracy versus totalitarianism in twentieth-century society, but a man who would never be given a post at the elitist academic institutions of either Oxford or Cambridge. Tempers had immediately risen as Wittgenstein challenged Popper's approach to philosophy, and, seizing a red-hot poker from the fire, he began to brandish it in Popper's direction. Lord Russell, alarmed for the safety of the university's distinguished visitor, had felt compelled to call out: "Put down that poker, Wittgenstein!" Whereupon Wittgenstein, snarling, had done so—thereupon abruptly leaving the room . . .

The President's account was spellbinding. *"Now, you read that book, Nigel!"* was Mr. Clinton's final injunction to the bemused author, accompanied by a famously wagging finger as he withdrew into the crowd of Arkansas well-wishers, leaving me speechless—and without any promise of a biographical interview.

Mr. Clinton had got away from me. In a discussion at the JFK Library in Boston on May 29, 2003, he later remarked that there is "a whole lot of difference in writing a retrospective biography when all the records are in, than just essentially feasting in them under the guise of trying to enlighten the public when it has nothing to do with enlightening the public—it's a grab for power, or ratings, or position." In short, he distrusts the motives of biographers.

Having withheld all his gubernatorial papers, and under no obligation to release his presidential records for five years after leaving office, Mr. Clinton has, of course, hardly made it easy for the records to "come in" to serious researchers, nor has he helped biographers struggling to chart and understand his life's course. One day, when the Clinton Presidential Library is opened as part of the National Archives of the United States, the full documentary record of President Clinton's life and career will, I hope, finally be accessible. In the meantime, perhaps this tentative account of his life will, despite Mr. Clinton's natural reservations about current biography, shed some light on his extraordinary journey, and in a balanced manner that, for all his high intelligence and learning, Mr. Clinton himself—impelled and constricted by his own agenda—will not be able to do.

It remains for me to thank only my family: Olive, Lady Hamilton, my mother; Outi, my wife, in London; and my four sons—Alexander in Australia, Sebastian in London, Nicholas in California, and Christian in Massachusetts—for their patience and understanding while the aging scribbler squirreled away these acorns for himself and for all those who are as fascinated by presidential history and biography as I am.

NIGEL HAMILTON
McCormack Institute
University of Massachusetts Boston
May 2003

POSTSCRIPT

Paperback publication of the first volume of *Bill Clinton: An American Journey—Great Expectations* has given me an opportunity to correct factual errors and revise certain passages that seem, in today's environment of war, terrorism, and widespread insecurity, inappropriate in tone or emphasis. What *is* important, I hope, in understanding Bill Clinton's fate in the White House in the 1990s, is the domestic, historical, political, and cultural context in which he was born, grew up, and embarked on his extraordinary journey. From the humblest of roots he rose to be the forty-second president of the United States for eight years—years that are the subject of my concluding volume.

NIGEL HAMILTON
May 2004

CONTENTS

CHAPTER TWELVE: RHODES SCHOLAR

CHAPTER THIRTEEN: AVOIDING THE DRAFT

CHAPTER FOURTEEN: THE FUGITIVE

CHAPTER FIFTEEN: THE END OF THE SIXTIES

CHAPTER SIXTEEN: ATONEMENT

CHAPTER SEVENTEEN: BILL AND HILLARY

CHAPTER EIGHTEEN: LIVING IN SIN

CHAPTER NINETEEN: ON THE TEXAS *TITANIC*

PART THREE: A CAREER IN ARKANSAS

CHAPTER TWENTY: LAW PROFESSOR

CHAPTER TWENTY-ONE: CAMPAIGN FOR CONGRESS

CHAPTER TWENTY-TWO: THE WEDDING

CHAPTER TWENTY-THREE: STRIKE TWO

CHAPTER TWENTY-FOUR: ATTORNEY GENERAL

CHAPTER TWENTY-FIVE: YOUNGEST-EVER GOVERNOR OF ARKANSAS

CHAPTER TWENTY-SIX: RECOVERY

CHAPTER TWENTY-SEVEN: THE COMEBACK

PART FOUR: BORN-AGAIN GOVERNOR

CHAPTER TWENTY-EIGHT: ON THE A TEAM

CHAPTER TWENTY-NINE: A BAD APPLE

CHAPTER THIRTY: HEART OF DARKNESS

PART FIVE: TO BE, OR NOT TO BE

CHAPTER THIRTY-ONE: THE MEETING THAT NEVER HAPPENED

CHAPTER THIRTY-TWO: SAYING NO

PART SIX: THE TEMPER OF THE TIMES

CHAPTER THIRTY-THREE: TELEVANGELIST PREVIEW

CHAPTER THIRTY-FOUR: THE FACE OF AMERICA'S FUTURE

CHAPTER THIRTY-FIVE: THE SPECTER OF DIVORCE

PART SEVEN: THE TURNING POINT

CHAPTER THIRTY-SIX: MOMENT OF TRUTH

CHAPTER THIRTY-SEVEN: PRIMARY TIME

CHAPTER THIRTY-EIGHT: FIVE TIMES GOVERNOR

CHAPTER THIRTY-NINE: THE PERILS OF RUNNING FOR PRESIDENT

PART EIGHT: DEMOCRATIC NOMINATION

CHAPTER FORTY: DECLARING

CHAPTER FORTY-ONE: RETURN OF THE GENIE

CHAPTER FORTY-TWO: THE DRAFT

CHAPTER FORTY-THREE: ENTER PEROT

CHAPTER FORTY-FOUR: NOMINATION

PART NINE: THE 1992 ELECTION

CHAPTER FORTY-FIVE: ON THE CAMPAIGN TRAIL

CHAPTER FORTY-SIX: VICTORY

PART ONE

ARKANSAS

Virginia Clinton and her two sons, Bill and Roger

CHAPTER ONE

THE WALLS
OF HOPE

Arkansas Beginnings

Few American presidents have had so little idea of their family's past as William Jefferson Clinton. On his father's side—well, the many questions that surround his paternity we must defer until later. On his mother's side, however, he had reasonable cause to believe he was a sixth-generation southerner, able to trace his Cassady forebears back through Alabama to South Carolina in the early nineteenth century. Then, in the late nineteenth century, he was told, a certain James Monroe Cassady left Alabama with his wife, Sarah Lou, and his Russell parents-in-law, in a traditional covered wagon. They migrated across the Mississippi River, moving to an area known as the New Hope Community and settling beside Ebenezer Primitive Baptist Church in Bodcaw, Nevada County, Arkansas, a group of extended families numbering perhaps a hundred souls, 110 miles southwest of Little Rock, the state capital. There, in 1886, they built a wooden house, became Arkansans, and began cotton farming.

Whatever had been the motive for the Cassadys' move, however, it did not bring prosperity for the family. Arkansas was, at the end of the nineteenth century, a backward, landlocked state, the twenty-fifth in the Union, some 55,000 square miles in size, bordering the Mississippi on its eastern side and abutting Indian territory on its western frontier. In between, spread out not only across its lowland, delta landscape but up high into its hinterlands, which stretched across the Ozark and Ouachita Mountains to the northwest, the state boasted almost one million people, almost no industry, the worst schools in the nation, and widespread poverty among whites as well as blacks—who, in the wake of slavery and the Civil War, made up more than a fifth of its population.

James Eldridge Cassidy

The Cassady family seemed to go in for presidential names—though none can seriously have imagined that one of their descendants would actually become a U.S. president. William Jefferson Clinton's great-great-grandfather had been baptized with the names George Washington Cassady—though why James Monroe, his eldest son, left Alabama, several years after getting married in 1880, nobody knows. It was on the small cotton farm in Bodcaw, Arkansas, however, that James Monroe's third son, James Eldridge Cassady—William Jefferson Clinton's grandfather—was born on August 19, 1898, the youngest of their five children.

James Eldridge Cassady's childhood was marred by poverty and death. He was orphaned at eight, when his father died of pneumonia on a train trip to the old family home in Alabama. The family farm was sold two years later, in 1906, and, moving with his mother to her widower brother's home, he was thereafter raised by his uncle Bill Russell, alongside Bill's ten children, on whose cotton farm he was expected to work once he left school. This he did at age thirteen, after fifth grade.

Had cotton been financially profitable or had they been able to obtain credit to switch to other forms of farming, the life of small Arkansas sharecroppers might have held out the prospect of economic progress after the ruinous years of civil war. However, without access to banking credit, small farmers in Arkansas had come to rely on cotton as their sole cash crop in order to survive—and the decline in the price of cotton in the latter part of the nineteenth century had resulted in white penury on a gigantic scale. "The debt-ridden, one-crop economy consigned the majority of Arkansans to subsistence on an annual income well below what would have been reckoned the poverty level in the growing American cities," one historian summarized.

It was in rural poverty in Bodcaw, then, that young James Eldridge Cassady worked as a half orphan—and at age twenty-three, having changed the spelling of his name to Cassidy, he got married on January 3, 1922, to Valerie Edith Grisham, the nineteen-year-old proverbial girl next door, whose family was also "eking out a living raising cotton" on her family's "hardscrabble farm."

Opting for Change

"Edie" Grisham was a short, handsome, feisty girl who was somewhat better schooled than Eldridge, having reached eleventh grade. The following year, on June 6, 1923, Edie gave birth to a child, indeed their only child, a daughter whom they named Virginia—Virginia Dell Cassidy.

Poverty in rural Arkansas made for a difficult domestic life. Virginia later characterized her mother as a woman subject to uncontrollable rage—an anger that welled from somewhere deep inside her. Edie had been dealt, Virginia reflected, a cruel hand: born in south Arkansas in rural poverty, growing up on the land, and marrying on the land. In those days, Edie had no option—a person's life mirrored the relentless pattern of nature and the seasons.

With Virginia's birth, Edie did, however, opt for change. She insisted at the end of 1923 that she, her husband, and the infant leave the land and move twelve miles away, to the local market town of Hope.

Hope had a population thirty times larger than Bodcaw, having expanded around a major cotton-market station on the Cairo & Fulton Railroad, effectively displacing the old Hempstead County town of Washington. Her childhood, Virginia later recalled, was punctuated with the whistles and bells of heavy locomotives, since her home was always by a railroad track. The segregated town's main roads had only recently been paved for whites, in 1920, and boasted several expensive residences on "Cotton Row"—but the Cassidys were far from wealthy. They were "country poor," as the town historian Mary Nell Turner put it, and lucky to find employment at the bottom of the proverbial white ladder.

One town resident later recalled that it was "a rough, busy, dirty, smelly town—in the damp, still air of evening every privy contributed its quota of perfume—but you couldn't help but love it." Eldridge eventually found work in the Ivory Handle Company factory—which would ruin his health, thanks to its boiling furnaces, dyes, and tanning chemicals. It did, however, permit him in time to purchase his own four-room house on Foster Street, on a mortgage.

Edith, meanwhile, decided to carve her own career and proceeded to take a correspondence course in nursing, gaining a certificate as an auxiliary, or private-duty, nurse without having to attend college. It was just as well. In the wake of the Great Crash, a long drought, and the worsening economy, as Virginia recalled, money would become "extremely tight"—so tight that when Eldridge lost his job, he was unable to keep up the payments on his mortgage. The Great Depression had arrived.

The Depression Strikes

The Depression hit Arkansas as hard as or harder than any other state in the Union, largely because of its overdependence on cotton. "Cotton remained king for the first half of the twentieth century," the Pulitzer Prize–winning newspaper editor–turned–historian Harry Ashmore related—and the cost, in the 1920s and '30s, was ruin. After a brief rise in the price of cotton during World War I, the price began to slide until it fell lower than the cost of production: down to 16 cents per pound in 1928, even before the Great Crash—and to a mere 4 cents four years after that.

In a state where, in 1930, 63 percent of Arkansas farmers worked someone else's land, the quasi-feudal system of sharecropping spelled, in the Depression years, disaster and starvation. Attempts to unionize tenant farmers proved a failure, and cooperative farming also failed, since few but a handful of farmers, in the traditionally individualistic land of "hillbillies," were interested in cooperating. Only God could provide.

The Depression, in other words, hit Arkansas like a long affliction, vitiating any hopes that the state would ever raise itself from its reputation as one of the most backward, uneducated, and fraudulent in America. "The state government remained insular and corrupt," wrote Ben Johnson in his history of modern Arkansas, while the rapidly declining market price of cotton dragged down a region that had set its face against agricultural diversification and lacked sufficient credit—state or private—to invest in alternative crops. As Johnson pointed out, the average Arkansas cotton farmer owned only $137 in equipment in 1929, but the average rice grower required almost twenty times as much. Without federal, state, or commercial programs, cotton sharecroppers in the state found themselves simply too poor to make the switch. They had already racked up a 150 percent rise in indebtedness in the 1920s, following World War I—and they could not withstand the triple onslaught of flooding (which in 1927 affected more than 13 percent of arable land), a crippling drought in 1930, and the financial catastrophe resulting from the collapse of the Wall Street stock market and banking system the year before. With four out of every five of the state's residents living and working on farms and plantations—compared with only 20 percent working on the land in America as a whole—Arkansas was bound to suffer in the Depression, and it did, grievously.

No politician came forward on the state scene who was capable of mitigating the effects of the meteorological and financial drought. Fraud, intimidation, localism, and racism had long characterized Arkansas politics, leaving the state prostrate in the face of the economic debacle. The state's roads were the worst in the country, much highway spending having gone into the pockets of officials rather than into paving. Public education was probably the poorest in the United States, with schoolteachers licensed through a feeble county examination that required only four years of high school. The public debt, meanwhile, was the highest in the country. In a state of dirt roads, "dirt poor" became a reality, not a metaphor.

Between 100,000 and 200,000 white and black families—in a state of less than 2 million inhabitants—soon required Red Cross relief. "Barefoot and without decent clothes, no meal, no flour in the bin, ragged children crying from hunger . . . nothing but hunger and misery," one aid worker described rural Arkansas as the Depression took hold. Strikes and protests were beaten down with a ruthlessness that shocked the nation. Attempts by federal officials, journalists, or outsiders to assess the economic, educational, social, and racial problems of Arkansas were met by vigilante violence that would have done justice to a banana republic—erstwhile slavery having been transformed into a peonage system that seemed little better. Visiting journalists described Arkansas, as the state historian Ben Johnson commented, "as a benighted land almost without parallel in the world."

Coming in succession to a series of floods, drought, and bankruptcies, these events appeared to many to be a biblical prophecy being fulfilled. Certainly no politician ever came forward to speak for the dispossessed or against cruelty toward and intimidation of blacks. For decades fear had underlain the psyche of a male white population too uneducated to ask questions before resorting to shooting, murder, and lynching—even live "roasting." "The Ku Klux Klan had a strong following throughout the state," wrote the historian of black civil rights in the period after World War I, Mark Schneider. "By 1924 it felt strong enough to contest the governorship in the Democratic primary"—making Arkansas a "dangerous place for African Americans," one in which lynchings demonstrated "the impunity with which racist terrorists acted in Arkansas." Will Turner, accused of attacking a white woman, had been seized from a sheriff's posse, hung, and burned before a crowd of thousands in 1921 in Helena. The *Arkansas Survey,* one of the state's few black newspapers, noted in an editorial that Helena was "a seething cauldron of hate, when the least indiscretion meant death." Barely a week later Robert Hicks was hung by a public highway near Lake Village for simply sending a note to a white woman. In Little Rock the next year, a suspected armed robber was openly lynched in front of the Como Hotel in the downtown center. "No official action against the lynchers is expected," *The New York Times* commented. Although the Klan's power had declined thereafter, the tinderbox of race relations had remained easy to strike. When John Carter, a black, was suspected by a mob of raping two white women, in 1927, he was riddled with bullets and his body then towed around the black neighborhoods of the capital and finally set on fire on a pyre constructed of wooden pews ripped out of a black church—with no one indicted by the subsequent grand jury.

A century before, Arkansas had proudly advertised itself as an "asylum for the emigrant"; indeed, the "last asylum," as one group of proponents in Little Rock had stated, drawing white immigrants from Virginia, Kentucky, Alabama, North Carolina, Tennessee, and Louisiana. Mark Twain, however, had pictured it as a land of cowardly lynch mobs and "lunkheads," the state becoming a symbol of much that was wrong, even evil, in America—symbolized in its political machinations. The Civil War had made an end of slavery, but the subsequent secret ballot, for example, had simply been used, in tandem with the notoriously backward and segregated public education system, to disenfranchise blacks, who, if illiterate, had to declare this at the polling precinct and submit to being intimidated, often at the end of white men's guns. Poll tax requirements had also militated against blacks' voting, so that between 1890 and 1894 the black vote had *decreased* in Arkansas by a staggering 65,000! Fearing a coalition between Republicans (the victors in the Civil War) and agrarian reformers, the Democratic Party in Arkansas had retrenched to become the party of reactionary conservatism and segregation: "Dixiecrats." In a move that contradicted the very meaning of its party name, the Arkansas Democratic Central Committee had even changed the nomination procedures for state primaries. Official Democratic Party candidates had to be chosen by a "popular" vote, it had determined—but with the proviso that only whites could cast those votes!

As C. Calvin Smith noted in his history of modern Arkansas, by the 1930s the state of Arkansas in the mind of most Americans had become synonymous with "watermelons, the unshaven Arkie, the moonshiner, slow trains, malnutrition, mental debility, hookworms, hogs, the big fat lie, shoelessness, illiteracy, windy politicians, and hillbillies with paddlefeet who could not pronounce correctly the name of their state."

With Arkansas politicians indifferent or powerless to improve conditions in the worst areas of rural poverty, revolution had become a looming possibility. In January 1931, white Arkansas farmers made national radio news history by marching on England, a small town south of Little Rock, in a strange repeat of Wat Tyler's fourteenth-century peasants' revolt in old England. "When we get to town, we'll ask for food quiet-like," their organizer declared, "and if they don't give it to us, we'll take it, also quiet-like."

Some on foot, some in buggies, some on horseback, the rest in rusting trucks, they made their way toward the banks that had failed them, in despair of being helped by the Red Cross, which was now refusing even to give out provisions. "Red Cross headquarters at St. Louis was called by phone and advised of the situation," the *Arkansas Gazette* reported as the men—more than half of them armed—shouted, "Our children are crying for food and we're going to get it!"

In fear of looting, England's local merchants handed out enough food for 1,500 white mouths, hoping the Red Cross would reimburse them. But the march became symbolic, nationwide—and a further nail in Herbert Hoover's approaching presidential coffin.

Thanks in large measure to Hoover's successor, Franklin D. Roosevelt, and his new administration, America survived the Depression, but the experience for Arkansans was grim. Roosevelt's revolutionary New Deal measures to help farmers proved of little immediate assistance to poorer folk in Arkansas. The administration's agricultural initiatives worked through grants to landowners, not tenants or sharecroppers—who were thus the last to benefit.

Rightly or wrongly, the Depression further cemented an image of poorly educated hillbillies clinging to outdated, pretractorized forms of agriculture and using obsessive, die-hard racism and hatred of the North as their calling cards. When one of Roosevelt's administration officials sought to speak at a meeting in Birdsong, Arkansas, in 1935, the Southern

Tenant Farmers Union official who began the convocation with the words "Ladies and gentlemen" was interrupted by a group of riding bosses from nearby plantations, "There ain't no ladies in the audience," they shouted, "and there ain't no gentlemen on the platform. We don't need no Gawdamn Yankee bastard to tell us what to do with our niggers"—and they ran the Roosevelt official out of town.

Religious fundamentalism also gained ground during the Depression. "Fundamentalist Christianity always assumed a close relationship between this world and God's," wrote the Arkansas historian Michael B. Dougan. "The economic disaster overtaking the nation was viewed by some as a punishment for sin." With the "double whammy" of the drought of 1930 and falling farm prices, churchgoers were treated to apocalyptic and Pentecostalist visions of the end of the world. Fundamentalist preachers viewed the Rooseveltian notion of WPA community work to alleviate the ravaging effects of drought, cascading cotton prices, and bankruptcy as northern heresy. Southern Baptists and Methodists remained wedded to prayer, Bible study, and stalwart domestic morality as the answer to all earthly problems.

In this struggle between biblical-minded traditionalists and modernists calling for more responsive government and change, the frontier spirit of Arkansas proved, yet again, to be a dead end. Arkansas became the only U.S. state in the Depression to default on its debts—suspicion of Roosevelt and the federal government remaining endemic despite federal assistance programs. Administration "handouts" would be taken, greedily, but the state itself would do little or nothing to emulate Roosevelt's public works program; indeed, it even refused to pay its own teachers when the education exchequer ran dry, assuming the federal government would pay for such things. Ordinary Arkansans could either starve or leave, state politicians and administrators reckoned.

Many left. "I have traveled over most of Europe and part of Africa," wrote the novelist and educational reformer Naomi Mitchison, "but I have never seen such terrible sights as I saw yesterday among the sharecroppers of Arkansas." Given the poverty sweeping the land—a land in which no more than 1 percent of farms had the benefit of electricity—migration was often the only recourse. As Ashmore wrote, "Hundreds of thousands of white and black Arkansans joined the forced migration that began in the depression years and continued for three decades, taking those called Arkies to California and dumping the others, black and white, in the inner city ghettoes of the East and Midwest. For many of these it was a pilgrimage not much less cruel than the Cherokees' trek across the Trail of Tears."

The Cassidys, however, stayed—and lost their home.

Foreclosure

Foreclosure became commonplace not only in Arkansas but across America. Already by 1930 the number of foreclosures had trebled, and by 1932 it reached a quarter of a million. By 1933, it was reckoned that more than half of all mortgages in the entire United States were technically in default, with foreclosures proceeding at the rate of a thousand per day. New Deal emergency legislation sought to soften the blow by offering refinancing assistance, but 40 percent of the mortgages thus "saved" in time fell prey to the continuing grip of the Depression.

Eldridge Cassidy's demise was not uncommon, but that did not make it any less humiliating. In Edie's eyes, it was Eldridge's fault—regardless of the millions of other Americans losing their jobs and homes. Told she would not be getting a new Easter dress, Virginia forgave her father, but her mother did not.

One particular scene, after the Cassidys moved to rented accommodation on Elm Street, on the south side of Hope, remained etched on Virginia's mind. There being no money to order groceries, Edie decided to buy them nevertheless, despite the cost. Virginia would never forget the sight of her father breaking down and sobbing. It was one of the "cruelest acts" she ever saw—and symbolic of her parents' deteriorating marriage. Night after night she was unable to sleep for the sounds not only of the thundering trains but of her mother's screaming fits, directed at Virginia's father.

The Depression seemed to be ravaging Arkansas inside as well as out. Watching her mother hit her father or throw things at him, Virginia wondered why he never sought to defend himself or retaliate. Why didn't he draw the line, even hit her back, instead of tolerating her bullying rages? As she later reflected, wife abuse would become, thanks to feminism, exposed as a scourge of patriarchal society—but as a child she had witnessed the other side of that coin.

This was a story that misogynists, even the great novelist William Faulkner, simply overlooked: namely, a new domestic war, occasioned this time not by the North or the South or by slavery but by the Depression. The Depression brought misery to millions—8 million people jobless in

1931, 13 million in 1932, and 15 million and rising when in March 1933 Roosevelt took office. Its domestic effect, however, was to bring the battle between the American sexes, despite the recent emancipation of women, to a new pitch of civil bitterness; and in that cruel struggle the Cassidys were no exception.

The Myth of the Strong Woman

Revolution, civil war, or even foreign wars are often a displacement for men, distracting them from domestic, social, and economic troubles. The United States, however, had pulled out of the League of Nations in the 1920s and was largely opposed to radical European-style solutions—especially socialist or Communist ones of the kind being carried out by Lenin, Stalin, Mussolini, Hitler, and Franco.

For the moment Americans simply swallowed the country's Great Depression without significant protest. Strikes proved largely ineffective, hunger marches were suppressed, and 25 percent of American families endured less-than-adequate nutrition. Everything slowed, even the rates of marriage, divorce—and procreation. Women working, one sociologist noted, "proved to be the most effective contraceptive yet discovered." Forced into the labor market by the unemployment of their fathers and husbands, women sometimes "had better chances for employment than men," wrote the pioneering historian of the American middle class Loren Baritz—but the shame for such men was often debilitating, since the notion of women working "collided with the attitude that the male who was not a breadwinner was less than a man."

Here was a major social and cultural problem, one that characterized the Cassidy household as it did so many American homes during the Depression. After the dreams and excesses of the 1920s, the Depression became a matter of survival of the fittest—the fittest, in this case, being women.

"Families whose emotional relations were strong and resilient not only withstood economic crisis but drew closer together, circled the wagons," Baritz recorded. With penetrating insight he analyzed what went on within those wagons, however. The heroic struggles of the Depression "redefined ideal womanhood as a particular kind of moral strength. Throughout the culture of the depression, this rediscovered symbol of strong woman, also a feature of earlier pioneers as well as immigrants, helped people to think about the depression, find an emotional anchor and grounds for hope. Her radiance would warm the cold, protect the weak, and guard the only sphere that now truly mattered—the home." The result was a "flourishing mythology of the strong woman in whose competent hands the future of men, children, and the nation rested safely. She was to provide a center and structure to lives in chaos."

Edith Cassidy certainly performed this role—at a price.

The Failure of Men

"The major obligation of the domesticated male was to earn money to support his dependent loved ones, who would respond with respect and, if he had secondary virtues, love," Baritz recorded. If the male did *not* earn enough money, however, and if his secondary virtues were inadequate, love was often withdrawn. "Prolonged unemployment often meant that the man of the house lost authority as a husband, a father, and a man. He was rejected not only by the marketplace but by his loved ones, and not only by them but by himself."

Impotence was one consequence, but there were others, including drink and ill health. Worst of all, "as Americans they were culturally required to blame themselves for what they thought was their failure as men. Otherwise they would have relinquished the right to take credit for their past and future successes," Baritz noted. "In a perverse way they were defending the legitimacy of their status by this self-flagellation."

Uneducated and unskilled, Eldridge Cassidy was certainly a typical victim of the Depression and its social consequences. The very culture of the 1920s that had caused Edith Cassidy to insist that she, Eldridge, and their baby move to town after generations in the country now went into reverse, extolling tradition and strong women. Skirts dropped—but only in length. "The need for an anchor in perilous times resulted in a matronly look: more feminine-looking, longer hair, emphasized hips and breasts, a marked waistline—in short the woman as mother not eternal girl. . . . The goal was to appear responsible, not chic," Baritz commented.

The exotic, erotic, lingeried heroines of the twenties cinema screen were soon almost redundant—indeed, radio now eclipsed film as the popular entertainment medium of the nation. While 150 million hours a week might be spent, nationwide, watching movies, some 80 percent of the entire American population could receive radio by the end of the thirties, including 5 million listening in their cars. Daytime soaps, aimed at women, soon dominated the airwaves—rising from three a day in 1931 to sixty-one in 1939. Most followed a basic requirement: strong, ordinary women, such as Ma Perkins, set in small-town America. "The soap's characteristic message," Baritz chronicled, "was the necessity of a return. Return to the time-tested values of yesteryear, of dear papa's wise advice. Hold on to what you know to be true. The world is evil. Ignore it. Change is bad. . . . Men are dangerous and must be housebroken. Sex is a snare. Be strong."

Edith Cassidy certainly followed this prescription. She was, as one family friend remembered, "what we call 'the strongest cat food.' She was a very forceful, a very strong woman, domineering; Eldridge was a very soft-spoken man and was probably what we would call today 'whipped'—'p-whipped.' "

Those men who avoided p-whipping did so, Baritz noted, out of female range—and Eldridge Cassidy was not among them. *The Lone Ranger*—which reached its one thousandth episode in June 1939, shortly before the outbreak of war in Europe—for example, saw its radio star operating far from the reach of dominating women. Such escapism was, however, a sign of women's escalating domestic power. How long, Baritz questioned sarcastically, could "even this classic American male have avoided paper-training?"

The writing was on the wall—and it was in a woman's hand. The Lone Ranger was "lucky to be responsible only for enforcing justice in seven western states, where, in his life, women did not count," Baritz sneered—adding, "The Lone Ranger could be strong, manly, and free, as Huck Finn knew perfectly well, only at great distances from the modulating and castrating civilization of good women."

It was, in other words, war—between men and women, with freedom the prize. In the "myth of the sexes propagated by radio culture," Baritz chronicled, "the freedom of each sex depended on the eradication of the other's."

It was against this "strong woman–weak man" civil war backcloth in Hope, Arkansas, then, that Virginia Cassidy, the only child of Eldridge and Edith Cassidy, spent her childhood and adult years.

A Born Rebel

Eldridge, laid off by the Hope Handle factory, eventually found work in a small liquor store that had been opened after the repeal of Prohibition, on

North Hazel Street—until it, too, was forced to close when Hope went dry. He then began working as an ice-delivery man.

Despite the blue-collar nature of his trade, Virginia was proud of her father. In the days before refrigerators he would wear a black leather overall that covered not only his front but also his back, as he swung the blocks of ice over his shoulder. After work he would drink and play cards at home with his buddies: Lone Ranger in a mock saloon presided over by Ma Edie, who was often out, tending the sick.

Virginia Cassidy, their only child, had little choice but to meld quietly into this working-class scenario. She was, however, a born rebel—and once she reached her teens, rebel she did.

Common People

Segregation in the South was endemic, but it was a segregation of class as well as race. In recalling her childhood, Virginia was deliberately and literally covering her tracks. In truth Hope's color bar excluding blacks was replicated in a sophisticated white middle-class structure that excluded working-class people: a caste system in which Virginia was seen to be a girl from the wrong side of the social tracks, the daughter of "country poor"—folks who were "common."

In her memoir *Born in the Delta: Reflections on the Making of a Southern White Sensibility,* Margaret Jones Bolsterli gave an unforgettable description of white southern class distinction at this time. Plantation culture had given "the practice of patriarchy in the South a distinctive flavor that it lacked in other parts of America," she recalled—and its rules were absolute. The "place of a woman in the Deep South" was "on the highest pedestal her men could afford." Delta belles were brought up not to work but to be protected *from* work, indeed from dirt of any kind, recalled Bolsterli—who was not even allowed to feed her own horse lest it diminish her pedestal status, and thus her father's stature. For the protectors of southern belles, the most potent threat, after poverty, was rape by "The Drunken Sex-Crazed Negro" of southern white male imagination. "The effect of this protection," Bolsterli explained, however, "was to isolate them in what were, metaphorically speaking, harems that included all of a man's women. His mother, girlfriend, sisters, wife and daughters, if not indeed all 'decent' women, were to be given his special protection if they in turn would 'behave,' thereby protecting his name and ideals. . . . The need for this protection made it imperative that southern women be well-trained in the skills necessary to secure a husband, and, since a man's worth would be compromised by a wife who worked, it follows that the most valuable wives of all were the most useless."

What Bolsterli also learned, once she went to school and mixed with other Arkansas girls from the Delta, was that the "stratified caste system" of the South was based upon everyone knowing and accepting "your place on the ladder." Nor were the rungs defined solely by wealth. As Bolsterli pointed out, the "connection between the concept 'common' and money was complex and tenuous. Not being common implied having manners, and having manners frequently, but not always, implied that a family had had leisure at some time. . . . You could be dirt poor and landless and still not common, while common people could get hold of both land and money."

Sadly, in Hope society, Virginia—who admitted to being attracted by gaudy, "bright-colored clothes" from an early age—was seen as common. "Common people," Bolsterli explained, "draw attention to themselves; they have loud voices, wear loud colors, admit to having feelings, and do not know any better than to mention bodily functions. Common women let their slips show and their stocking seams remain crooked . . . common people were the ones who got drunk and swore and stole and murdered and went to jail. The daughters of common people were welcome to come to our house if I invited them, but I could not go to theirs. When I made a new friend, I would wait cringing for Mother's quiet assessment. I did not want it to matter and would swear that it would not, but when she murmured 'common' about the family of a new acquaintance, it affected me. The friendship could never be what I was always looking for, a partnership between equals. I could never spend the night at my new friend's house, and knowing that Mother felt the way she did, I could never see her with unbiased eyes. I hated it with every fibre in my soul, but I could not ignore it."

Virginia Cassidy was a typical victim of such white snobbery. She would never forget the moment when a girl in grade school wouldn't play with her because she was from the country. Country poor was country common.

White Trash

Explaining Virginia's exclusion, another of Virginia's schoolfriends recalled more than fifty years later how Virginia, by virtue of her parents, was simply not considered good enough to be visited—even though her house was painted, which raised her above the rural poor. For one thing, Virginia's parents "played cards"—which to Southern Baptists was anathema. Moreover, they "drank." On top of that, neither Eldridge, a Baptist, nor Edith, a Methodist, attended church regularly. One might feel sorry for their daughter, but that did not mean one could allow one's daughter to go to her house, let alone stay overnight. The very fabric of white southern society depended on maintaining appearances and manners, and the Cassidys were so far down the ladder as to be considered by some to be "white trash"—a term too common for "nice" women to say aloud. But the unspoken label stuck—and was irremovable.

If the Cassidys were not good enough, there were others even more unfortunate: blacks, universally referred to as "niggers"—though Edith Cassidy, to her credit, seems to have objected to this, giving Virginia a beating she would never forget when she dared call out "Hi, Nigger" to an old black lady walking past their house.

According to Virginia, if she misbehaved, it was not her father but her mother who whipped her, often using a tree shoot she fetched from outside for the purpose and which, when applied to Virginia's bare legs, made her bleed.

Violence was not confined to the Cassidy household. In such a hothouse of unspoken southern rules, as Margaret Bolsterli noted, violence was "the peculiar quality" that lay "just under the surface of even the most civilized parts of southern society." Poverty, fear of poverty, and fear of losing one's social position all bred insecurity on a pervasive scale—"the fear of rape" being "one of the strongest forces shaping the lives of southern girls and women during my childhood," Bolsterli recalled, while the men of her class, ready for all eventualities, kept loaded guns in their pickup trucks, ready to dispense their own justice when called upon or provoked.

It was in this fear-filled, hierarchical southern society that Virginia Cassidy had to determine her destiny. Her relationship with her mother was one of clashing wills and a refusal on Edie's part to communicate other than by insisting upon more rules, followed by beating when these were infracted. Simple and strong, Edie could neither forgive nor explain. When her menstruation began, at only eleven, for example, Virginia bled profusely but inexplicably—her mother unable, Virginia recalled, to bring herself to elucidate the business, despite being an auxiliary nurse!

It was at high school, though, as the 1930s came to a close, that Virginia decided she had had enough bullying at home and social exclusion at the hands of Hope's "society" outside her home.

"The House of Prostitution on Wheels"

Some, indeed most, of Virginia Cassidy's contemporaries simply gave in to the social exclusion system, unwilling or afraid to confront their parents. Virginia, an only child, was different. She had, she later recognized, inherited her mother's forceful will, even obstinacy. She also recognized that she had to stand up to her mother's "tyranny," or she would be crippled for life, as her father had been. She started smoking—and faced down her mother when Edith challenged her. But it was over boys that Virginia declared real battle.

Once she began dating, Virginia found herself being watched by her mother with eagle eyes. She was undeterred—in fact, emboldened by her own burgeoning sexuality to strike a "major and lifelong blow" against her mother's tyranny. She was determined not only to date boys, but on her own terms. She wasn't jealous if they dated other girls, and she expected the same permissiveness in return. Otherwise, she candidly explained, she would simply drop the boy—a feminist approach that was ahead of her time and that was to have profound repercussions on her own children.

Virginia claimed that her "steady" boyfriend, in her later high school years, was Richard Fenwick, whose brother owned a car—"a house of prostitution on wheels" as a local judge referred to the automobile's effect on popular morals. Virginia agreed. The object of having a car "wasn't necessarily transportation," she recalled candidly; it was to be somewhere private. What you did in it was neither your parents' nor a judge's business.

A Social Pariah

Here, for the white children of Hope, was an English-style, class-ridden society, based in the American South upon white-guarded safety and opposed to change, whether that change were economic, social, educational— or carnal.

The upside of such protective policing was that white girls could walk to the swimming pool outside the town and back home without ever feeling threatened or nervous, just as they could after a movie or returning from an evening at the Checkered Café, the popular hangout of Hope's young folk. The downside was the price paid for such security: namely, a punitively restrictive moral code that not only put people into social and racial boxes but kept them there for life, much as if times had not changed since Jane Austen's day in England. As the only daughter of working and working-class parents—parents who never went to church, and who played—Heaven forbid in the pre–World War II Bible Belt!—cards, and perhaps gambled too, when playing, and who certainly drank alcohol—Virginia was, through no fault of her own, a social pariah. She might be allowed to sleep over at a pajama party—but no middle-class daughter would ever be permitted to go to her home, let alone stay there overnight.

There was no getting away from such a sentence of social exclusion. "Everybody here knew everybody else" one contemporary recalled—and everybody watched his and her neighbor, not only to gossip but to police exclusion zones. "We knew each other's faults and sins and slippings," the contemporary remarked. No one could get through the barriers.

For Virginia this was a double curse: her mother subjecting her to punitive restrictions at home in the hope that Virginia might grow up "pure" and do better than her parents, while Hope's middle-class parents beat her down again.

Nowhere was this better illustrated than by the story of the pajama party given by the sheriff of Hope for his daughter, to which some seventy local girls were invited—Virginia among them. The girls were allowed to date boys in the evening but by 10:30 P.M. had to be back at the new jailhouse, where they were given meals on tin plates and locked up in the cells by the sheriff's wife for the night. "Virginia liked to sing. She would have liked to have a good solo voice and sang all night long in her cell—keeping us all awake!" one of the girls later recalled.

Virginia longed to belong—but if she couldn't, she would at least stand out. Among middle-class "goody-goodies," in an age before drugs, smoking cigarettes was one symbol of young people's bid for independence. She smoked. Then there was petting, much like the practice of "bundling" in the Middle Ages. "You'd get in the car and go off into the country. That was the big sin! And in church, on Monday evenings in what we called Training Union, the big subject would be whether or not to pet—and whether or not to kiss a boy."

For the teenage Hope pioneer Virginia Cassidy, however, this was all too tame. She was not by nature a wallflower or a goody-goody. Determined to make her mark and burst the middle-class lock on social acceptability, Virginia became determined to beat the system: not by playing the southern virgin and attempting to marry into a higher class—the traditional path for would-be southern belles—but by defying convention: debelling as well as rebelling. In other words, going with boys.

The Walls of Hope

It was in this way that Virginia Cassidy became, as her contemporaries recalled, a law unto herself, playing "fast and loose": not only heavy petting but going further with boys, a step that damned her soul not only in the eyes of a church she only intermittently attended but in the eyes of the watchful Hope "society" as well.

Having willfully decided on her plan, Virginia threw herself into her new role as high school *fille fatale,* beginning a lifelong affair with provocative clothing and megamakeup: bright lipstick, false eyelashes, false eyebrows (as her own, by a quirk of nature, were almost nonexistent), and heavy mascara. "Oh yes, she started this before the war came, while we were in high school—she was not only rebelling against Edith, her strict mother, but against the walls of Hope: the social class divisions that separated social classes in the community," one contemporary reflected. Enticing as many boys as she could was Virginia's own particular way of "getting even." She loved dancing, and, though not a classic beauty in terms of her natural looks, she made herself into a quasi beauty queen, with her curvaceous figure, her exaggerated makeup, and her fun-loving, adventurous, and ambitious character.

What Virginia could not have known, as the 1930s came to an end and world war approached, was that her personal, instinctive defiance would come to characterize the rise of Western women in the latter half of the twentieth century. As Margaret Bolsterli remarked, before World War II "common people could get hold of both land and money" but only with a great deal of additional effort and aping of "nice" people's manners might they be able to "eventually transcend their condition and not be common anymore." Such a transformation took generations—indeed, not even the Civil War and its aftermath had altered the southern class structure that had been developed and maintained since the early nineteenth century.

Commonness, however, was a-comin'—and a great deal faster than most southern folks imagined. The war and its aftermath would undermine the "walls" of Hope in a way no one in those days could have dreamed possible. As Bolsterli quoted an older southerner, at the end of the twentieth century, as saying, "Honey, *everybody's* common now."

The glue that had held "the social ladder together," as Bolsterli put it, had finally come unstuck—and in helping loosen it, Virginia Cassidy would pave a way for her own offspring to storm the once sacrosanct citadel.

CHAPTER TWO

TUG-OF-WAR

The End of Adolescence

Like so many kids of her time, Virginia Cassidy took for granted the educational revolution that had taken place in America—at least, white America. In public high school, white children of all backgrounds, all abilities, and both sexes joined in an educational, cultural, and social community experience that would shape American democracy—and thus world democracy—in the latter part of the twentieth century.

In many southern states and towns, however, there were bitter fights over issues such as creationism. Moreover, high school education was provided within a national system of apartheid, or Supreme Court–approved racial segregation, involving separate schools for blacks and, in the South, separate restaurants, separate seating on public transport, and even separate drinking fountains.

Within the segregated white mainstream, however, comprehensive public education offered American high school students a social forge: nurturing and advancing predominantly middle-class values, respect for knowledge, and self-empowerment. The ideal was not necessarily to produce high-scoring examinees, as in Europe, or industrial robots, but confident middle-class American citizens, whether or not the students went on to college. Virginia remembered with pleasure her time at the newly constructed, purpose-built building that cost $150,000 in 1931, situated "way out on Main Street in an old cornfield." It boasted the first intercom system in any high school in the state and a nationally lauded new vocational building in 1937. She joined the Dramatic Club, the Science Club, Music Club, Library Club, Art Club, and Press Club. She performed in class theater productions, worked on the class newspaper, was elected class secretary, and was a member of the National Honor Society, she recalled.

This was light-years from the education her parents had enjoyed—or not enjoyed—despite the way Virginia fought at home with her mother. Shrewd and naturally intelligent, Virginia did well. College, however, never even occurred to her, she recalled, given the cost. She considered herself practical and self-sufficient. If her mother had achieved a measure of female independence through auxiliary nursing—practicing private day-and-night care in Hope, as she did in her distinctive whites with red nursing cape and cap—then Virginia would do the same. Indeed, she decided, she would aim one higher. Without further thought, Virginia enrolled in 1941 at the Tri-State Hospital in Shreveport, Louisiana, ninety miles away. She would become a fully qualified nurse.

No More Students from Arkansas

Graduating from Hope High School, Virginia was about to enter the same adult war zone within which her mother had fought: the battlefield of the sexes. Able-bodied young men might leave, from December 1941, for boot camp and combat against Japanese, Nazis, and *fascisti* around the globe, but Virginia's struggle, like that of so many millions of fellow American women, would be with the expectations of a traditionalist, male chauvinist society. One of her boyfriends, Richard Fenwick, had given her a ring. But, as Virginia reflected later, the ring betokened a wish, not a guarantee.

Virginia had seen her father emasculated, almost literally (the Cassidys had no further children after Virginia). The days of men as society's overlords were numbered, she knew; but at work, as in so many southern homes, men still had power of possession, which was nine tenths of the law. It was difficult, if not impossible, to displace them.

The next battle began on Virginia's arrival in Shreveport. Dr. Willis, the owner of the Tri-State Hospital, was a martinet. He brooked no backtalk—so much so that when Virginia spoke up on behalf of a nurse Dr.

Willis was berating, he told his assistant to remind him, in the future, not to accept trainees from Arkansas.

Sex and the Single Nurse

Sadly, the senior female nursing staff colluded in this male monopoly; indeed, they behaved in the manner of sexually repressed, punitive nuns, beating out their resentment upon their female students, a quarter of whom dropped out. "If I ever catch you crying again, you won't finish nurse's training here," warned Nurse Frye, Dr. Willis's right-hand woman, when Virginia wept over the death of a young mother from postnatal complications.

Under hospital rules Virginia was not permitted to go home for the first six months. When she called her father at the end of six months and he took her home for a couple of days, she neglected to inform Nurse Frye. On Virginia's return there was a note on her dormitory bed. It was brutally sarcastic. "You know, I just didn't realize how important it was for you to go home," Nurse Frye had written. "Now you can go home and stay."

Virginia was suspended for a month.

The only way out, apart from resignation, was, once again, coquetry as protest. Virginia was soon dating and went not only into town in the evenings but, in terms of makeup, really to town. She not only liked bright colors but loved people to notice her. They did. On December 7, 1941, the night of the attack on Pearl Harbor, for example, she had a date with a captain at Barksdale Field. The pilot was soon posted away, however, while many of the nurses, too, gradually left Shreveport, joining either the armed services or their servicemen husbands. The once stable world of American life in the Depression, tight in terms of money and even tighter in terms of sexual license, was over.

Meanwhile, eighteen months into her training as a nurse in Shreveport, twenty-year-old Virginia met personal trouble on a megascale: Bill Blythe.

In the Wake of Pearl Harbor

In the wake of Pearl Harbor, the United States had not only prepared for war with Japan in the Far East but had mobilized for war in Europe too, once Hitler, on December 11, 1941, also declared war on America. Arkansas agriculture and its still meager industrial base, especially bauxite mining, would be profoundly affected—indeed, with increased production and a price-guaranteed market, the war would signal the end of the depression in the state, as in the rest of America.

The chief change for Arkansans, however, would be change itself. Two hundred thousand Arkansans would don uniforms or serve in the American armed services—entailing a massive change in public spirit, national identity, social attitudes, education—and intimacy.

One night in July 1943, Virginia's number came up. At the end of the evening shift an emergency case was admitted—a woman with severe pain in her side, suggesting appendicitis. Virginia was assigned to take the patient's details—and found herself looking up into the eyes of a wickedly handsome man who at that moment was holding the patient's hand. As she later recalled, she literally went weak at the knees—indeed, she imagined everyone in the ward could see her confusion. It was the proverbial *coup de foudre.* Virginia remembered the man as markedly tall, though as he was five feet, nine inches, this was not the case. Nevertheless, what she felt was what too many young women felt about the stocky, broad-shouldered, sandy-brown-haired Texan still in his twenties, Bill Blythe. The fact that he was married four times over, with a number of children born in and out of wedlock to boot—indeed was still married—was not a fact that Bill Blythe vouchsafed, either then or later, to Virginia. "We're not married" was his reassuring comment when Virginia referred to him by the same surname as his companion, the anesthetized patient.

She had never been so relieved in all her life, she later confessed—blissfully unaware, however, that he *was* still married, but to a different woman!

A Serial Bigamist

Intrigued by Virginia's personal question, Blythe returned the compliment. Halfway out the door he stopped, turned around, and asked the twenty-year-old about the engagement ring on *her* finger.

Blushing, Virginia said it signified "nothing."

Whatever Blythe thereupon told Virginia, sadly, turned out to be more lies. How he subsequently managed to convince Miss Virginia Cassidy that he was so smitten that he was going to stop in Shreveport, find an apartment, and get himself a job selling Cadillacs was in part a tribute to his persuasiveness and also in part a measure of Virginia's gullibility—and arousal. She kissed him, she later confessed, on their first "date"—

which began immediately after they left the appendicitis-stricken patient in the operating theater! As she recalled, she knew the moment she laid eyes on Bill Blythe "that all the rules were out the window." The next day he called her, and the next night they saw each other again. Thereafter they saw each other day and night.

Sex was and remained central to the Blythe-Cassidy agenda. When Virginia's roommate called to speak with her, Blythe responded, "Yes, she's lying right here beside me." As Virginia later reflected, had he still been alive, she would have slapped him for such outrageous candor, but that was Bill.

When not in bed they went out to the movies and dancing. Bill had only an eighth-grade education, but then, Virginia's father had had less, and Virginia loved him nonetheless. He took her to nightclubs, where they would dance to "String of Pearls." Or they'd go to Cross Lake in Bill's "house of prostitution on wheels," where, with its fine leather upholstery and reclining seats, he'd dip her to other music on the car radio.

Virginia was "so in love" that she was, in telling Bill that she wanted to get married, willing to give up on the career for which she'd spent two years training—for Tri-State did not permit married students. Bill tried to talk her out of it, Virginia recounted years later—forgetting, or being unwilling to believe in retrospect, even when she knew the facts, that Blythe's reluctance had stemmed from the fact that he was still married!

Blythe explained that he was about to be called up, when—according to incontrovertible military records—he had already entered the military two months before he had met her, in May 1943, in Shreveport itself, after being inducted in Louisiana under Selective Service regulations. He would, however, be posted overseas, he now told her, truthfully. Virginia recalled his added reason for not getting married: she'd inevitably get lonely on her own and want to make new friends. She was, after all, only twenty, whereas Bill was five years older and more experienced "in the ways of the world."

Bill certainly had more experience than Virginia—a very great deal more. For one thing, he was illegitimate: one of nine children born to a poor farmer, "Willie" Jefferson Blythe II (genealogists disagree about whether an earlier uncle counted in the numerical sequence, but most now consider Bill to have been William Jefferson Blythe III). For another, although only twenty-five, Bill was already committing adultery outside his *fourth* marriage! He was far from clever; had been brought up with his natural father in an unpainted three-room, wood-frame house without water or electricity. He had a single year of high school education. His father had died when he was sixteen, the forty-acre farm had been foreclosed and sold in the Depression, and when his mother moved to Sherman, Texas, he'd taken a series of salesman's jobs, selling auto parts and equipment. He'd begun a pattern of pointless, whirlwind romances, followed by whirlwind rejection of the very women he'd courted and married. He'd married his first wife, Virginia Adele Gash, for example, when only seventeen, lying about his age to get the license in Medill, Oklahoma. When "Adela" traveled to visit an aunt in Dallas, he'd sent on to her a parcel containing her clothes—for in his view the marriage was already over. They were divorced before he was nineteen. This did not stop him continuing to have sex with her whenever he was in Dallas, however, with the result that he fathered an illegitimate son by her, born in postwedlock in January 1938: Henry Leon Blythe. Nor did it discourage Bill from marrying again, in August 1938, when he took a twenty-one-year-old, Maxine Hamilton, for his second wife. Within two weeks, the subsequent divorce papers stated, he had "refused to recognize her as his wife" and had not only "abandoned and deserted her in Los Angeles, California" but even refused to pay for her return trip to her parents' in Oklahoma! According to Adela Gash, his first wife, Blythe then agreed to marry her sister Faye in 1940, supposedly "to keep from having to marry [another] girl who was pregnant." This third marriage also lasted only a few months, and in May 1941—two years before he met Virginia Cassidy—he married a fourth time, this time another girl he'd made pregnant, Wanetta Ellen Alexander, who gave birth to a daughter, Sharron Blythe, eight days after the wedding in Kansas City, Missouri. Blythe would not officially and secretly divorce Wanetta until March 1944—seven months *after* his bigamous wedding to Virginia Cassidy, in Texarkana, Arkansas, on September 3, 1943.

Here, then, was "white trash" of a dangerously unreliable kind: a sexual vagabond of low intelligence, a serial bigamist and "traveling man"—but one, Virginia hoped, who would rescue her from Hope.

The Impact of War

Whether by accident or design, Bill Blythe III was almost instantly called to base in Sherman after his wedding to Virginia and posted overseas in a vehicle maintenance battalion stationed in Egypt. After the successful Allied landings at Salerno, he was then moved to Naples and Caserta in southern Italy. There, way behind the fighting in the Mediterranean theater, he worked to repair tanks and trucks and recondition their engines. Whether he availed himself of the local womenfolk is unknown, but he certainly kept his 1944 divorce from his fourth wife a secret from his fifth, Virginia; conversely, Virginia kept from him the fact that she was dating other men and living high first in Shreveport (thanks to World War II and the shortage of nurses, the hospital had accepted her back as a married student, the first in its history), then in New Orleans, where at the Charity Hospital she completed her advanced training in pediatrics and obstetrics.

By day a nurse, Virginia went out as often as possible at night. "She loved to get all dressed up and, shod in the clunky high heels of the day, go dancing and drinking until dawn," one biographer chronicled. "When we had time off we would go to the French Quarter and hear Dixieland jazz or big-band music, and I would embarrass my friends by getting up and singing with whoever was up there," Virginia recalled her love of karaoke.

Virginia had visited with Bill Blythe's parents and even stayed with Bill's brother Earnest in Sherman, but had been spared the truth about her husband's checkered marital and procreative career. Had she known, however, would she have minded? The "strong woman" of the Depression was now about to become the "good woman" of World War II in Loren Baritz's retroanalysis: the "angel" to whose uplifting—and uplifted—bosoms fighting soldiers would hope one day to return. This media angel was largely, however, mythology, as Virginia knew best. Millions of young women like her were now joining the workforce, and, behind the patriotic icons propagated by wartime movies, radio, and advertising, they were now asserting outside the home the dominance their mothers had begun to achieve within it during the Depression. Angels might be the way innocent boys, going off to war, preferred to see them, but in reality America was taking one more lurch toward the modern world that artists and writers had been predicting since the 1920s—and the statistics for sexual diseases and unwanted pregnancies, after a national decline in the Depression, now shot up to record levels. Women were enjoying "new and daily association with other men and women on their jobs"—and that enjoyment was often intimate. As older women found wartime employment in the defense industries, they left their jobs "as waitresses, barmaids, and carhops for teen-age girls who, due to poor wages, often turned to prostitution to supplement their meager incomes." "The infection rate was so high around army installations," wrote the Arkansas war historian C. Calvin Smith, "that military authorities threatened to declare nearby cities off limits to their personnel." "Victory girls" became the name given to young women "who performed 'patriotic' sexual favors for men in uniform"—and by 1943 the Arkansas Health Department was reporting almost 13,000 new cases of syphilis and 3,500 of gonorrhea.

The tide of behavioral freedom could not be turned back. Behind the phalanx of male warriors going forth to serve their country, a social revolution among women was taking place, especially in the South. As Smith summarized, "the war's impact on the structure of the traditional Arkansas family would be permanent," with population shifts unseen for more than a century. Almost twenty thousand families had already deserted their farms by 1943, halving the number of people working the land—indeed, more than 10 percent of the state's population simply left "home" and moved to other states offering more work, less racial oppression, less traditional morality, and less class division.

For Virginia Cassidy it was significant that the man she had chosen to marry should be a stranger, his past unknown: a mystery man met on the arm of another woman, a man whom she had successfully seduced and used, consciously or unconsciously, as a means to free herself from the constraints both of her Cassidy home and snobbish Hope society. Her parents—though she claimed they had met and taken a liking to Blythe—had not attended the wedding, nor had anyone from her hometown. She was, literally, home free. And with a ring on her finger—bigamous or not—she had no need to play the virgin: She could assert her rights to both lovemaking and, once her husband returned from the war, eventual maternity as a modern woman.

Registered Nurse

Returning to Hope a registered nurse, Virginia began to work in one of Hope's two private hospitals, where her relations with doctors soon gave cause for considerable gossip.

Given her reputation as a "loose" woman, "a wild one," Virginia had been lucky to avoid pregnancy. As a nurse, however, she knew how to be careful. Hope had become "a bustling city almost overnight." In the month after Pearl Harbor the town's population had doubled, increasing from 7,000 to 15,500, thanks largely to the army's new, $15 million Southwestern Proving Grounds, a five-mile-wide, fifteen-mile-long tract of land north of Hope where, using a permanent workforce of more than a thousand but many times that number to construct and maintain the site, aerial as well as artillery shells were tested. Hope was thus no longer a boondocks rural backwater market Delta town but part of a burgeoning new wartime economy fueling America's might in the Pacific and Europe.

Virginia's husband continued to write from Italy and she to him—but neither of them had any intention of staying in Hope once Bill returned from war. Early in May 1945, the Germans surrendered in Italy and northern Germany, and on May 7, peace in Europe was declared: VE Day. Three months later, on September 2, 1945—after atomic obliteration of Hiroshima and Nagasaki—Japan gave up the unequal struggle too. America, so long an isolationist democracy, had become the most powerful and interventionist nation on earth.

Virginia had known Bill Blythe for only two months in 1943 before their marriage. They had been separated for two years thereafter, thanks to the war. Blythe had never been to Hope, nor did he wish to stay there more than a few days, he informed her, having lined up a job in Chicago. He would, he promised in a letter, come to collect her sometime in December 1945, once he got home from Italy, obtained his discharge papers, and collected his civilian clothes from his mother in Texas.

The Soldier's Return

How Sergeant Blythe felt about his young bride on his return is difficult to know. Bill had changed: had seen the Middle East and Europe and the devastation of modern war—"had been through hell," as his colleagues at the Manbee Equipment Company of Chicago later embellished—if no actual fighting. But Virginia had also changed—as had so many millions of women on the home front. A century before they had been but men's chattels, legally; even in 1939 and 1940 some twenty-four American states had laws restricting the right of married women to work. Now, in the long sequence of women's suffrage, then the Depression, and finally World War II, women had at last become coadults; in fact, in the operating theaters of Shreveport, New Orleans, and Hope, Virginia had seen far more blood than her husband had.

For many men, however, this latest challenge to traditional patriarchal supremacy, following the dark years of the Depression, was bad enough; worse still, it coincided with the growing challenge to white supremacy on the part of blacks who'd served in the armed forces or who had obtained significant new employment in war industries alongside whites.

The divorce rate soared.

The problem here was women's raised expectations: economic, social, and sexual. Sixteen million male Americans had entered the military during the war, but nineteen and a half million women had worked to support the war effort. In the South, especially, there was a renewed call to arms against any relaxation of Jim Crow laws over segregation—for blacks, empowered by the war, might get ideas above their station, as might women, too.

The white men's answer, after their wives, fiancées, and jobs had been reclaimed, was to impregnate the mythic angels and make them into mothers. "The non-sexual female—mother and daughter—rose again as the icon of cultural stability," Loren Baritz noted. "As defined by men, the asexual angel, like the Virgin Mary, always forgave and comforted; she embodied hearth, home and manners, not passion or adventure. She led the way to higher, finer things, to abstract, solemn, and uplifting ideals, not to flesh and blood or fire in the belly."

Even among men, this idealization caused problems, since it posited responsible males as good fathers: masculine, yet with no lewd thoughts. Macho masculinity, however, was already in decline. A full third of rejected recruits in World War II had been, one psychiatrist considered, "emasculated males" who wanted to be protected by women rather than to protect them. For many soldiers the experience of combat had been equally complicated, involving the bonding of men as buddies, with whom one learned to communicate better than with women and whom one could not let down. As Baritz saw it, "in war and peace, American men were struggling to define their masculinity, and consequently to recognize the kind of woman who could support their hopes and alleviate their fears. The choice was between the 'pure girl,' whose domination and love would prove a man's virtue, and a 'real woman,' whose subordination and love would prove a man's manhood. This conflict intensified throughout the 1950s," Baritz recorded; indeed, it "deformed the psychology of the middle-class American male."

It also deformed the psychology of the female, who was forced back into not only tight corsetry but the kitchen. As Baritz added, "Her cooking mattered much more than her 'braininess,' and her figure was more important than her face."

Whether Virginia Cassidy's marriage would have survived this postwar repackaging of women is speculation. Honorably discharged as auto mechanic in the rank of Army Tech, Third Class, with good-conduct medals for the European Theater of Operations and a World War II Victory Medal, as well as $203.29 back pay in his wallet, William Jefferson Blythe III—having been home to Texas to collect his personal belongings—duly met his young wife in Shreveport sometime in the second week of December 1945 before he set off to Chicago to resume his job and look for a place to live. Virginia joined him a few weeks later, and they shared his hotel room while they hunted for, and eventually found, a brick home in Forest Park, a suburb outside the city.

In Chicago, Virginia was deafened by the noise, confused by the bustle, and frozen by the cold of a northern city she considered to be as alien a city as she had ever encountered. However, she did her best to be optimistic—especially when later that same month, with alarm, she began to feel sick. With growing anxiety, only two weeks after her reunion with Bill, she realized she was expecting.

Pregnancy and Death

It was "before Christmas 1945" when Virginia first began to feel morning sickness, she later confided. She was a trained nurse and knew precisely what the symptoms portended. She was pregnant. Wisely, she waited another month. Then, one night after he came home, she broke the news to her husband. Bill was, she recalled, ecstatic—and soon every relative and friend from Chicago to California to Texas had been told.

Virginia was not alone. Studies would show that anywhere between 4 and 10 percent of births in those years had not been occasioned by the legal father. As long as the baby did not sport features incompatible with Bill Blythe's as father, Virginia had to hope all would be well. At least, she reckoned, the move to Chicago would obviate close questioning by family or relatives. Meanwhile, on February 14, 1946, Virginia flew in an airplane for the first time to be with Blythe's mother, who'd had a stroke, in Sherman. She was by her mother-in-law's side when she died, before Blythe could join them. Back in Chicago, after the funeral, they found that the purchase of the house they'd found in Forest Park was going to take even longer than they'd anticipated. Together with her morning sickness, she claimed, this led to the decision that she should return to Arkansas and stay with her parents for awhile.

Whether this version was entirely honest is unclear. Certainly in March 1946 Virginia was back in Hope. How well the marriage was working, however, was questionable, for Virginia veritably hated being home with her mother, with whom she was continually at loggerheads. Whatever the truth, in May 1946, having moved in some furniture and redecorated the Forest Park house, ex-Sergeant Bill Blythe drove down with a caseful of bourbon to collect Virginia in his maroon Buick sedan. Halfway there, on Highway 60 in Missouri, three miles outside Sikeston, a tire blew while he was traveling at high speed. The car ran off the road and rolled over twice in a cornfield. Blythe was either thrown clear or managed to crawl out, semiconcussed—only to drown in three feet of water in a drainage ditch, his hand clutching at a bush by which to pull himself out. He was twenty-eight.

Of Dubious Paternity

The funeral of William Jefferson Blythe III was held at the First Baptist Church in Hope, and the burial was performed in the nearby Rose Hill Cemetery, less than forty-eight hours after the accident—contradicting local newspaper writers' assumptions that Blythe's body would be taken either back to Chicago or to his family in Sherman. No Blythe relatives came. In this way at least the cruel truth of Blythe's multimarital past was withheld from Virginia.

Equally, three months later, without Blythe or his family present in Hope, there were no formal questions raised when Mrs. Virginia Blythe's baby was born at 9 A.M. on August 19, 1946, in the Julia Chester Infirmary—a bare eight months since Bill Blythe's reunion with his wife. According to the nurse who delivered the baby, it was "full-term": a big, bouncing, healthy infant weighing in at seven and a half pounds.

William Jefferson Blythe, the farmer's orphan son, army sergeant with only an eighth-grade education and a confused history of five marriages and multiple offspring, would lend his posthumous name to the child; but to those who watched the brilliant boy grow up in the years that followed, Blythe's supposed paternity seemed at best dubious. When questioned on tape half a century later, most relatives and friends of Virginia's simply shrugged or went silent, wishing to speak no ill of the dead. Not a single one, in confidence, believed Bill Blythe to have been the child's father. Even Jim Blair, the child's best friend in later years, considered that, in "my own opinion, Blythe is not his father"—indeed, he recalled an "incident" when a man in Louisiana "insisted that his dad had been out with Virginia about nine months before Bill Clinton was born and that Bill Clinton was a dead ringer for his brother"—a story which Bill Clinton "believed might be true."

Only DNA could resolve such a question. Both by rumor and by instinct, however, Bill Clinton would know there was a problem, and in due course he would insist upon surrendering his Blythe surname in order to adopt another that would one day become known the world over: that of his mother's second husband, a car dealer and alcoholic: Clinton.

Hot as Holy Hell

The weather in Hope had been stormy, Virginia recalled many years later, shortly before she passed away. There was a big electrical storm the night before the birth, with the temperature in Hope exceeding 100 degrees—the hottest day of 1946. Then it cooled to 71 overnight and began to heat up as the sun rose on August 19.

Wilma Rowe Booker, who came from nearby Washington, eight miles away, was the duty RN. More than fifty years later she recalled finishing up her training at Charity, the Jewish hospital in Hot Springs, where she heard how Virginia's husband had been killed—"small-town gossip, we knew all about that.

"I come to work in Julia Chester hospital, in Hope, just after graduation. Now, I had not met Virginia till she come into the hospital to have the baby! But I knew her mother, and I knew some of the relatives, that I'd worked with. But the gossip was . . . you feel sorry for somebody so young, and having a baby and whose husband was not alive. . . .

"I come in June, and Virginia's mother, Mrs. Cassidy, worked there as a nurse. She did private-duty nursing for patients when I first went there. She was not a registered nurse—she got her qualification through mail order or something. We had two or three women who just sat with patients and we called them nurses—I guess like a nurse aide. She was outgoing, laughing, loud. . . . Everything was funny to her, whatever it was, she had a smile and a laugh to it.

"And then I was called to surgery to help deliver the baby! I worked that end of the floor, of the house: surgical, labor, delivery, nursery—just three RNs in the hospital, so we had a big job to do.

"It was a cesarean section. We'd had hot weather, there was no air-

ARKANSAS · 35

conditioning in the hospital, no fans—big cotton scrub dresses and scrub pants, nothing paper—now it's all paper! Dr. Luther Lyle performed the surgery, and Sagey May was the instrument nurse, and I was the RN on duty.

"Mrs. Cassidy and the relatives were in the hall. The double door went out of surgery into the hall—and the hall was full of people! I think most of my fellow employees were there! Of course, there were so many of them who were related to Virginia!

"Dale Drake was one of the relatives there—she was a short, red-haired, very attractive lady in those days. 'Well, Wilma,' she said, 'I bet it's hot as holy hell in there.' I said, 'It is!' And told 'em: 'It's a boy!'—and went back in to do my work."

To those who asked how the birth had come a bare eight months after her husband's return from military service, Virginia simply claimed that the baby was a month premature. Few, looking at the size of the infant— weighing seven and a half pounds—were taken in. "He was a big, large baby—he wasn't premature at all," Wilma Booker recalled emphatically.

Whoever the father was—and rumors circulated about one of three doctors in Hope, as well as one man from Louisiana and another from Arkansas—the child's intelligence would become legendary among his teachers and contemporaries, making him arguably the most intelligent president in recent, possibly all, U.S. history. Clearly, unless some rogue gene had surfaced in the Blythe family, the baby's brains did not owe their genesis to Bill Blythe III.

The Battle for William Jefferson Blythe IV

Virginia's trials were only just beginning. The birth certificate recorded the infant's name as William Jefferson Blythe, after Virginia's late husband. After ten days' recuperation, she left the Julia Chester Infirmary and made her way home with her baby. The lease on the Chicago house had been torn up, but since neither she nor the army could find a record of recent payment of Blythe's army life insurance premium, she found herself nearly destitute. As a single mother she would have to fend for herself and the infant on her own.

Virginia's parents, by contrast, were happy for her to live with them in the rented house on Hervey Street, Number 117; indeed, the little infant literally brought new life to their staid marriage, thirty yards from the

Cairo & Fulton (later Missouri Pacific) railway tracks. Given the history of warfare between Virginia and Edith, however, it never promised to be an easy time—and it wasn't. Almost immediately a new battle or tug-of-war began between the widowed Mrs. Blythe and her mother, Mrs. Cassidy: this time over William Jefferson Blythe IV.

Edith Cassidy meant well, Virginia allowed, but it soon became clear who was the boss; indeed, Virginia began to feel she was a student once again as her mother took charge of the infant's daily and nightly schedule, every activity from eating to sleeping being carried out by the clock. Falba Lively, a much older second cousin to Billy, was "just a poor country girl" who "didn't come into Hope except for funerals and the like," but she seconded Virginia's description, indeed would never forget "Aunt Edith, who was an extraordinary woman. I don't think enough credit has been given to Edith—she didn't have much money, worked at hospital and nursing homes, yet managed to bring up 'Billy,' as she called him. She was so concerned he might get dirty," Falba recalled, "that she wouldn't allow him to go out. Very, very strict as regards training—mealtimes." In fact, Billy slept so contentedly as a small infant—up to sixteen hours a day—that Virginia became anxious, for she wanted, she later confessed, the infant to wake up and play with her.

Virginia's brazen self-centeredness would become legendary in the family and fodder for psychoanalysts. One professor in particular deplored her "pursuit of her own pleasure" over the "identity that could have been provided by her work" and motherhood. Such pursuit could, however, be seen as an understandable reaction to the driving force in her household: her mother. Her father, Eldridge, was affable, well-meaning—and completely dominated by Edith. "He always seemed to be so quiet," recalled one of Virginia's contemporaries, "and he'd come from the farm, so he'd had a hard time making a living—delivering ice, downtown, to restaurants, and companies. Edith, now, she was outgoing—never saw a stranger—loved everyone—'Just let me hug ya,' she'd say—and was a nice-looking lady. She didn't wear so much makeup as Virginia, but lots of it."

The women thus wore the pants on Hervey Street, Hope, Arkansas—but women, sadly, at loggerheads with each other. Liquor, in the battle between the sexes and among the sexes, had not been legally available in Hope since 1944, but it was at least above board in the privacy of one's home: an essential requisite to soothe frayed nerves. Edith's temper could be volcanic. As a nurse she might show unstinting patience with her charges—indeed, she would become legendary for her abilities as a carer—but with her husband and errant daughter she was often explosive. Crockery flew and china broke, according to Virginia.

The first few years of little Billy Blythe's life were not, therefore, an easy time—and his life would get harder before it grew easier.

Real Life

Were such stories and conditions unusual after World War II? "This was probably the world's first generation of mothers who were told—and believed—that they did not know what they were doing," Loren Baritz related. Virginia was a prime example. Yet the fact that both Edith Cassidy and her daughter, Virginia, were professional nurses, with their own modest but independent incomes, was also a sign of changing times in a South where, as Margaret Bolsterli put it, people like her mother were "locked in a tradition that forbade women to be independent or teach their daughters to want independence." Feminism was almost unheard of in the South—and not at all in Arkansas. "Arkansas was a state with a strong family tradition in which the role of women was generally limited to the home and to the rearing of children," wrote war historian C. Calvin Smith. "The majority of women in Arkansas accepted that role with little or no complaint."

Edith Cassidy and Virginia Blythe did not. They might fight each other over baby Bill, but in the new, postwar American world neither mother nor daughter deferred to men—or to convention.

Woman power—based upon behavioral as well as financial independence—thus characterized the Cassidy home in the aftermath of World War II. "Mrs. Blythe will be remembered as the former Miss Virginia Cassidy," the *Hope Star* had added to its announcement of little W. J. Blythe's birth, reminding readers of Virginia's maiden past—but there seemed little chance of returning that genie to its bottle. A group of former friends, including her former high school demifiancé Richard Fenwick, had trooped upstairs to see Billy in his crib shortly after his arrival. The sight of mother and child had not, however, inspired a rush of marriage offers. This time, Virginia noted, "it was all so different."

Virginia Blythe, then, was not a war widow but among the first of the postwar, single, working mothers. "I'm sure there was a good deal of ostracization," one family friend reflected. "I'm not sure Hope had a whole lot of single, eligible men in their late twenties to early thirties who would have been willing to date Virginia, much less willing to date a woman who already had a son! That was one of the downsides of it being a fairly small town."

Certainly no southern gentleman stepped forward to fill the breach.

Single Mother

Virginia Blythe, in many respects, was the archetypal new single mother. To the tut-tutting disapproval of the community, she made no concessions to the old southern ways. She did not attend church, just as Edith (a Methodist) and Eldridge (a Southern Baptist) declined to attend. Among the outraged churchgoing folks of the little town, Edith had always been reputed to be a flirt—a reputation confirmed, even exacerbated, by the loving care with which she looked after her patients. Virginia, half her mother's age, seemed in this respect a chip off Edie's block—in fact, even more brazen. Her yearbook at high school had already recorded her future as one of "magnetic attraction" exercised upon men. "Magnetic attraction," however, was a euphemism for sex appeal—and that appeal only seemed to increase postpartum.

The truth was that in a world where traditional mores had been challenged by the changes and vicissitudes of war, Virginia had no intention of returning to the old, prewar days. To Edith Cassidy's chagrin, therefore, the young widow began to date men—but not the sort of men Edith saw as prospective fathers to little Billy, her beloved grandson. Moreover, the man Virginia took up with in earnest was, as Bill Blythe had been when she met him, still married, and "a pretty wild critter, by all accounts," as one family friend recalled.

A Place Apart

Roger Clinton, age thirty-six at the time, was a big spender—"pretty wild and woolly" as the family friend recalled; indeed, his great-uncle had actually thrown Roger out of his rooming house in Hope as a miscreant: "a kind of loud, boisterous, drinking, womanizing, skirt-chasing fella who liked to party and gamble, and a lot of things that are probably not always appreciated in a small southern town, where most people go to church on Sunday."

Roger hailed not from Hope, however, but from the legendary town of

Hot Springs—the "sinful city" as it was known at the time, "set like a jewel between two mountains in a clearing at the heart of a woods that stretched (and still stretches) two hundred and fifty miles or more from east to west in central Arkansas," as the writer Shirley Abbott, whose father was a well-known bookmaker in the city, later described it.

Bookmaking, in the midst of the Bible Belt, was a strange anomaly—but then, the healing waters of Hot Springs had always been an anomaly since European gold seekers and settlers had first chanced upon them in the sixteenth century: a "certified miracle," as Abbott later described it, where hot water poured forth from the ground replete with scores of minerals. "Buried deep in the earth is a fiery furnace, a geologic heating system that sends waters to the surface bubbling and seething, cascading out over your hands at 140 degrees Fahrenheit," Abbott proudly described. With its nearby lakes, forests, creeks, valleys, and mountains, Hot Springs had in fact become, in the nineteenth century, "the American Carlsbad," as one writer called it, much like the spa cities of Baden-Württemberg to which the sick and exhausted went for cures and recuperation. Far from the civilities of the East, however, the town had married frontier morals with healing minerals—the outcome of which had been a community similar, yet quite, quite different, from the spas of Europe. Dostoyevsky's *The Gambler,* set in a fictional Roulettenberg, had brilliantly captured the roué elegance and immorality of resorts like Baden-Baden, but in the German Palatinate gambling was at least legal and prostitution practiced in a demimonde of high Victorian fashion. Hot Springs was different.

In Hot Springs, Arkansas, the scalding waters spurted out of the ground in a setting of fabled beauty (it had been selected as America's first national park), yet the town itself was situated in the epicenter of a Bible Belt state in which gambling was considered morally evil as well as being illegal. Thus the town was, in many respects, the very antithesis of the South—or rather, an escape valve for southern hypocrisy. The feuds, violence, and lawlessness that had made Hot Springs "a haven for Mississippi riverboat gamblers and Confederate veterans and scoundrels disguised as such" in the nineteenth century had gradually given way to a "spot known to everybody in the United States who was either sick or on the make or both."

This duality—the coexistence of convalescents and hoodlums—had led, in the 1920s, to a strangely modern, twentieth-century American amalgam, incorporating almost every aspect of American postindustrial entertainment, half a century before Las Vegas. Attracting some of the most notorious gangsters of the time—men such as Al Capone, Owney Madden and Frank Costello, Bugs Moran, Charley Lucky, "Boo Boo" Hoff, and Bugsy Siegel—Hot Springs had become a favored recreational paradise for gangsters of the 1920s—yet once there they had miraculously set aside their guns to enjoy the delights of thermal baths, sitz baths, steam rooms, soothing massages, and good-time girls. Madden, a gangland killer from Harlem, was typical: having evaded New York justice, he had married the Hot Springs postmaster's daughter—and now controlled the town's wire service! Others concentrated on gambling or bootlegging. But instead of dispensing the rough gangland justice of Chicago and New York, such gangsters agreed to an amazing sort of *pax piranis,* in which their law-exempt status was guaranteed by the Hot Springs mayor, Leo McLaughlin, in return for peaceful coexistence in the frontierlike town. Thus there arose a fantastic compromise or contradiction: a wealthy, cosmopolitan community in which thieves from across America mingled with medical pilgrims seeking cures for every ailment from rheumatism to syphilis and gonorrhea and in which state laws against gambling, prostitution, and drinking were broken with impunity—all the while its infamous residents observing unofficial local laws of self-restraint and nonviolence.

Gradually a sort of legitimization had taken place. By 1933, Prohibition had been ended by Congress; in 1934, horse racing had been permitted once again at Oaklawn Park, on the edge of Hot Springs; and in 1935, pari-mutual betting, after a gap of twenty-three years, was also permitted again.

This, however, was but the tip of the gambling iceberg. Roy Reed, Arkansas biographer of the infamous governor Orval Faubus, described how McLaughlin had built new streets and sewers and a fire department from the very money levied on gambling violators and prostitutes, who were encouraged to continue their illegal occupations immediately after their weekly court appearances. The city had been substantially rebuilt and services improved after McLaughlin's election as mayor in 1927. Then the mayor took care of the mayor. "He liked expensive clothes and the high life," Reed recorded. "Every day at the same hour, dressed in a suit and red tie, a red carnation in his lapel, the brim of his straw hat turned up, he drove his sulky from his big old house on Malvern Avenue down the main thoroughfare, Central Avenue, past the bathhouses and the swank Arlington Hotel where big-name gangsters from the North, come to take the waters, were often in residence. The sulky was drawn by a costly pair of horses. Even their names were an affront to the Baptist ethic that lapped at the shores of the town. He called them Scotch and Soda."

"We had glamour, and depth, and a wicked soul that few outsiders understood," wrote Shirley Abbott of her hometown. It was an understatement. Certainly outsiders in the rest of Arkansas for the most part saw it as a den of iniquity: an almost biblical Sodom. As "Justice Jim" Johnson, a leader of the notorious White Citizens Council in the 1950s, later remarked, thanks to its strange history Hot Springs became over time an asylum for sinners, right in the heart of Arkansas. "On the farm, in the barnyard, there's always a corner where you put the dung. And everybody knows it's over there, they just don't step in it unless they're going for the dung!" The city was, in his view, the dunghill of Arkansas—"a place apart, that we all knew was there, and we all tolerated it, and the Governors [of Arkansas] tolerated it and got their rake-off from not letting the state police go in and raid it, and enforce the law."

The rake-off was at the heart of the "southern way" of doing things. "The police were always in cahoots and on the take, a system so convenient that it continued well into modern times," Abbott wrote, describing the pirates' covenant with the authorities.

Once while in high school before World War II, Virginia Cassidy had spent a "whirlwind day" in Hot Springs—capped by winning what, for a high school student, seemed a prodigious sum at the Oakland racetrack. She had put down "two crisp dollar bills on the daily double" and had won $84.

As a "place apart," Hot Springs' impact on Virginia's life might have ended just there. But with the advent of Roger Clinton, "the dunghill" of Hot Springs, eighty miles from Hope, would become the epicenter of the young widow's life—and that of her offspring.

The Dude

Nurse Wilma Booker had met Roger in Hot Springs, as a trainee, before Virginia had. "He was in business with some relatives in Hot Springs. They had an automobile agency. And you know, when a man had a car, that was something! I never dated him, but some of the girls, my roommates and friends, did. And then, after he'd come to Hope, I didn't see him."

Virginia did, though. She later remembered thinking he was attractive, "and a lot more dashing, in a dangerous sort of way, than most of the men in Hope," Virginia later recalled. He was known to all as "The Dude"; she could see why, she commented. As psychoanalyst and political science professor Stanley Renshon sniffed, "appearance rather than substance seems to have played a major role in her life."

With money from his elder brother Raymond, Roger was setting up his own Buick dealership in Hope, capitalizing on the postwar demand for cars. Roger put great store by clothes; indeed, he saw himself as a lady-killer in his blazer, knife-edged pants, and two-tone footwear. He was flirtatious and flashy. He gambled and gamboled, spent money like water, and drove women wild. When he asked Virginia for a date, she accepted.

In Hot Springs, such dating would have caused no concern. But their soon openly adulterous affair—since Clinton was married—cut straight through Hope's sin-watching small-town southern moral code. For Virginia, of course, as in high school, this was part of the attraction.

In Arkansas, for the most part, selling alcohol and gambling were illegal, so Roger would drive her to nearby Texarkana, on the Texas border, or they'd go to Roger's place. There, in his apartment, Virginia got to know a gallery of companions that would have done Raymond Chandler proud—characters such as Van Hampton Lyell, the young owner of a Coca-Cola bottling plant in Hot Springs and an amateur pilot who daredeviled under road bridges in his plane, and Gabe Crawford, married to Miss Hot Springs and the owner of a chain of drugstores in Hot Springs and Hope—where he ran an illegal betting operation in the back—as well as a powerful motorcycle on which he tore around the countryside, fueled on Coke and whiskey.

Roger's apartment doubled as a gambling den. Virginia had never seen so many dollar bill denominations, she later recalled of one evening's game of crap on the upturned coffee table, with Roger almost blind drunk.

After a year of home cooking and shared bringing-up of the baby in Hope, Virginia had been enthusiastic when her mother suggested she return to nursing school, out of state, to get an advanced qualification. Having been accepted as a nurse-anesthetist trainee at the Charity Hospital in New Orleans, however, she found it hard to give up the good life she was enjoying with Roger.

For Edith, by contrast, Virginia's departure had seemed more and more urgent, indeed essential, since Edie was a great deal "less enthralled" by Roger Clinton "than Daddy and I were," Virginia admitted. Contemporaries seconded this impression. As one recalled, "Any mother, regardless of what she herself has done with her life, wants her daughter to do better than that—to avoid her mistakes and maybe, as we say around here, 'marry a little higher than that.' " The fact that Roger was still a married man was, in such people's eyes, a scandal. "That was why the mother did not approve of Roger!" Virginia's contemporary Roxie Lawrence confided. "You wouldn't want your daughter mixed up with a married man—that would have been her thinking."

There was another concern, however: Edie worried about little Billy. Suppose Roger married Virginia—and took away Edie's beloved, only grandson? Edie was therefore doubly determined her daughter should go—not only to break the budding relationship but to gain and keep, as Virginia saw things, "total control" of little Billy.

Double Trouble

If Edith Cassidy hoped that distance would bring Virginia to her senses, she was to be deeply disappointed. Virginia's scandalous affair with Roger Clinton failed to fizzle out with distance, as Edith had hoped—Roger paying for Virginia to fly the 330 miles to Hope twice and visiting her on numerous occasions in New Orleans in 1947–48.

Edie was vexed and ashamed—the more so since it was Edie's husband, Eldridge, who had first introduced Virginia to Roger. Others, however, felt that like was meeting like. For the most part the matrons of Hope were relieved; mothers had often been heard to warn their sons not to get too close to Virginia. "Stay away from that Cassidy woman!" had been a frequent injunction—and similar warnings to their daughters were now being issued with regard to the wealthy, still married car dealer from Hot Springs.

In this respect, then, Virginia and Roger seemed well matched: two daredevils who went out with other partners when apart but partied the harder when together. For Roger, New Orleans offered nearly as much entertainment as Hot Springs, and though Virginia was seeing both medical students and doctors, her status as single mother gave rise to no romance—leaving her free to pick up with Roger where they had last left off.

As Virginia increasingly consorted and cavorted with Roger, however, the tug-of-war between mother and daughter escalated. "In essence," one family friend recalled, Edith "had been mother to the child for the first three or four years, while Virginia was off at nursing school, and there was a strong clash. Because Virginia was very strong-willed herself, the two of them had some pretty good disagreements. Virginia was never shy about voicing her opinion on something! And she got that in part from her mamma—there were some pretty good disputes!"

Most of the disagreements centered on Roger Clinton. Edith had brought up little Billy in loco parentis since birth, taking him everywhere with her and at home teaching him—by age three—to learn numbers, using playing cards pinned to the window curtain, as well as to read, using flashcards she made herself.

Watching this, Virginia was both proud and alarmed. She had been an only daughter. Now Edie had an only grandson—and centered her ambition on him, as Virginia saw it, recalling grandmother and grandson seated at the kitchen table, grandmother drilling him "to count and read. I was reading little books when I was three," Billy later recalled, humbled by his grandparents' commitment to learning when they themselves "didn't have much formal education." They had "really helped imbed in me a real sense of educational achievement"—but as Virginia pointed out, Bill didn't dare *not* learn if that's what his grandma wanted; "you didn't cross her."

The Go-Between

As little Billy Blythe grew from infancy to toddler, he became not simply the go-between but a sort of prize in the battle between Edith and Virginia: a conflict now moving onto a new battlefield as on the one side Edith attempted to instill the traditional values in which she believed—however little she had herself been able to abide by them—while on the other Virginia countered by further extending the boundaries of the modern, independent woman: single mother, trainee nurse-anesthetist, and party girl in New Orleans.

Between these two poles, bright, pudgy little Billy Blythe tried his hardest to satisfy both constituencies. As his high school friend and daughter of a Baptist minister Carolyn Staley later remarked, Bill would be fated to "wear good on one shoulder and bad on the other"—and nowhere was this better illustrated than in the fight between grandmother and mother as Edith enrolled Billy at the local Baptist church, even though she herself disliked organized religion, involving subordination to a male minister, and was in any case a Methodist. She simply left Billy at the church door to be indoctrinated in the "good," as opposed to the "bad" that Virginia and Roger personified.

Everything in the little boy's life, Edie determined, was to be orderly—and as far as possible under her control. When he played in the garden, near the main Missouri Pacific railway track, no neighbors' children were allowed to play with him, nor was he encouraged to go to their houses. As a result he was, people recalled, a lonely child—socially inferior and, even where socially of the same class, nobody daring to brook Edith's wrath by interfering with her regime.

Edith's strict raising—the one kid who was brought up strictly by the book, neighbor Dale Drake recalled—and her possessive, quasi-parental love, were inevitably difficult for the child to understand or, at times, to cope with, given his natural attachment to his mother. After accompanying Virginia to the station at the end of Virginia's trips home to Hope, little Billy would race upstairs and fling himself on his cot bed overlooking the yard and railway line, crying his heart out.

Only Billy's grandfather Eldridge—"Pappaw," as they called him—seemed to understand. Some days, if Edith was working, he'd take Billy with him to the new store opposite Rose Hill Cemetery that, with financing from a wealthy local businessman, he'd begun to run on the edge of the community's black neighborhood, selling cigarettes, cigars, food, candy, and stockings over the counter—as well as liquor under it, now that his days as an ice-delivery man had come to an end. There he let little Billy stay and talk with the customers, who included both blacks and whites.

This, in segregated Hope, was unusual, as it would have been in every southern town at that time—yet it would form, some maintained, a defining experience in little Billy's life. His second cousin Falba, seventeen years older than Billy and growing up in the countryside, remained deeply skeptical of integration for blacks, who, she felt, "became confused when they changed the rules. They didn't want to worship in white churches, they were much happier separate—and the same was true in education." Billy's grandfather, however, refused to make a distinction in his store. Blacks were real people, real customers, real friends. Billy was taught to be courteous to them and "never to be ugly to anyone," of whatever creed or color, recalled his neighbor Dale Drake.

Why blacks were free to come into the store yet not permitted to enter white churches, drink from the same water fountains, sit with white folks in restaurants, ride in the same compartments on trains, step on the same sidewalks, sit alongside whites in buses, or learn with white children in schools—none of this was immediately clear to the plump, curious, obser-

vant little boy, with his blue eyes, chubby cheeks, and obedient tempera-
ment. But he did not question it. He wanted always to please, and without
a father alive or even a mother present in his life, the lonely, precocious
grandchild identified not with the segregated, all-white middle-class characters, heroes and heroines of the books he got from church or as gifts, but
with the characters who peopled his grandfather's store. They were an extended family to him, a community: one that formed the sole intersection
between whites and blacks, where—unknown to the little child—illegal
liquor formed the central transaction underpinning the commercial enterprise, under the proverbial counter—in this case, in a back room, wrapped
in brown paper bags. And it was Roger Clinton, driving regularly to Hot
Springs to pick up more cars for the dealership in Hope, who supplied, as
Virginia later learned, the liquor. "Roger"—she shook her head—"was the
supplier and Daddy handled sales."

Caught in the Divide

Eldridge Cassidy's little Hope store, with its outward face of propriety and
inner shadow of illegality, was considered in traditional, Bible Belt Hope,
Arkansas, to be transgressive: a place of illegal trading of "evil" alcohol, a
substance that was abhorred by Southern Baptists and Methodists in particular and that, when taken to excess, could and did ruin people's lives. Beyond alcohol, however, there were other transgressions—as Virginia,
determined to forge her own identity as a postwar modern woman, was il-
lustrating.

This conflict between traditional values and modern mores would color
Billy Blythe's entire life, as it would color the lives of hundreds of millions
of his baby-boom contemporaries across the Western world. Whatever people at church might say, however, the little boy knew better than to question
his grandmother and grandfather—"Mammaw" and "Pappaw"—who had
raised him like an orphan. He was the quintessential model child, repaying
their loving care and instruction by being precisely the little boy they
wanted him to be: bright, cheerful, helpful, caring, and precocious.

But when, in the summer of 1948, his mother graduated from Charity
Hospital in New Orleans and returned to Hervey Street, Hope, and rein-
troduced domestic conflict, involving wars of words between mother and
daughter, rows, shouting, and flinging of objects in the little house by the
railway tracks on Hervey Street, little Billy Blythe was inevitably caught in
the divide.

The Tug-of-War

Roger Clinton remained the chief bone of contention. With Virginia living at her parents' home and seeing more and more of him, Edic came to hate Roger with all the passion of a mother animal, sensing a marauding male who threatened, via her daughter, her grandchild. "Mother remained amazingly immune to Roger Clinton's charms," Virginia recalled, missing the point. She countered by saying that Roger was wonderful with children— but it was this very skill that struck terror into Edie's grandmaternal heart. Eldridge, depending on Roger for his supply of liquor, welcomed him to the house on Hervey Street. Edie, however, refused to speak to Roger when he came to deliver his "groceries," nor would she acknowledge his presence— and the antipathy was reciprocated. The effect, however, was to drive Virginia out of the house—with little Billy, too. Increasingly, Virginia spent her free time at Roger's place.

Whatever Edith did to discourage the relationship—she even burned Virginia's beloved white leather jacket with western-style tassels, given to her by Roger—only backfired. Neither his married status nor even his open infidelity could dampen Virginia's spirits. In fact, when she learned from a friend that Roger was entertaining an airline stewardess from Kansas, she simply took little Billy in his stroller and invaded Roger's apartment, to which she had her own key.

Virginia and little Billy arrived to find signs of a veritable bordello. Exotic ladies' lingerie littered the place, from silk stockings to garter belts, lacy bras and gossamer slips draped across the bed. The woman, Virginia snorted in retrospect, was not only a tart but a messy one—oblivious to the fact that this might be what attracted Roger. There was also the fact that she herself was classed as a tart by a number of the citizens of Hope. Virginia was too infuriated to care, however. Seeing so much underwear strewn about, she was tempted to wonder what the stewardess was currently wearing under her blouse and skirt. As her mother had burned her leather coat, so she in turn tore up and flushed her rival's air ticket down the toilet and hung out the lingerie on the washing line, where the entire neighborhood would see it. Many did—indeed, the incident became part of local folklore. "Everybody in town saw that Roger Clinton was seriously in the doghouse."

Conversely, Virginia was not above going out with other men, as she and Roger were not exclusive. Gradually, though, the crowd thinned—leaving Roger and Virginia. The omens, in Edith Cassidy's eyes, were grim: an only daughter, way out of control, neglecting her child. Virginia's growing determination to marry the Buick dealer from Hot Springs became a bitter new battleground. Roger Clinton did not deserve to breathe the same air as little Billy, Edie felt—and she girded herself to fight such a possibility.

For little Billy, the battleground was now becoming as scary as it was for Virginia. When Edith threatened to go to court to keep Billy, Virginia saw red. She had seen her mother angry and vindictive, she recalled, but going to court to gain custody would destroy the family. The blackness inside Edie, Virginia felt, had finally consumed her, and there was nothing left "but the blackness itself. I screamed that the only way she was going to get my child was over my dead body." Eldridge argued, but to no avail. Virginia, meanwhile, hung on to her little boy, appalled. He was only four—too young to be damaged by all this, she hoped. As she later recognized, she was profoundly mistaken.

Virginia's naiveté was breathtaking. Far from being too young, little Billy was the one who most felt the pain of such dissension, since he himself was the cause or object of it. His mammaw's reluctance to let him go into that dark night, after her years of iron tutelage, could not fail to make him blame himself; it was a waking nightmare in which he was torn between two primary loyalties to two powerful and determined women, a human toy over which willful adults were fighting. His bedroom—situated off the passage leading to the corner room occupied by his grandparents and the big room occupied by his mother—was only too emblematic of his strange, fought-over status, as well as the intergenerational battle being waged. Edie and Eldridge's room was small and cottagy, with a double bed against one wall and another double bed for visitors and relatives against the opposite wall: intimate, homey, cosy, nonsexual, as in a fairy tale; his mother's room, on the opposing side of the corridor, the opposite: a room that stretched almost the width of the house, with multiple windows overlooking the main road and in between the windows, against the wall, Virginia's wide makeup console and mirror, like that of a film star. There she would sit each morning for at least twenty minutes, dolling herself up to face and wow the world—a world that did not really include Billy but centered all too often on the smirking, mischievous figure of The Dude: Roger Clinton.

"Uncle Buddy," Grandma's brother, spoke for all the Cassidys when he told Virginia to her face that she wasn't fixing to marry Roger Clinton, she was "fixin' to marry a bunch of Buick cars!"

Easy Money

Prophetically, "Buddy" Grisham warned Virginia that she'd "have hell on," and for the rest of her life, if she went ahead and married Roger. Obstinacy was, however, Virginia Blythe's second name. Indeed, the very tension at 117 Hervey Street seemed to drive her toward disaster—especially when Edith not only threatened legal action to try to keep Billy but actually went to see an attorney.

The battle between mother and daughter was degenerating into not only family war but total war, with Billy the innocent prize. What made it all the more tragic was that, in her heart of hearts, Virginia knew that "Uncle Buddy" was right, that Roger Clinton was a poor choice of partner: unreliable, weak willed, ineffective in his job, prone to rob his own till, a heavy drinker, and inveterately unfaithful. His divorce finally came through in 1948—but, unknown to Virginia, it was granted on the basis of persistent wife abuse, including bodily injury! Roger Clinton, car dealer and gambler, was a big, unintelligent, spoiled "good ole boy," a southern chauvinist, the "baby" of his family—indeed, still called "Baby" by his mother, even as he approached his forties.

Virginia didn't love Roger Clinton, she confessed later—at least, not in the romantic way in which she'd fallen for the equally charming and much-married Bill Blythe. Moreover, Virginia had certainly never dreamed she might marry Roger when she began to fool around with him. But the fact was that in little Hope she could not find better. She had deliberately, willfully placed herself in the "fast" crowd and could only hope to throw in her lot with one of them. Roger's prosperity and status had, she later acknowledged, made her head swim. Also, Roger seemed actually to care for little Billy, and his generosity in paying for her to fly home from New Orleans to see her son was something she would never forget, even after the disastrous years that followed.

As Edith knew instinctively, the relationship was a disastrous mistake—for easy money went just as easily as it came. But Virginia's mind was made up in the implacable Cassidy way. Nothing, but nothing, could dissuade her.

The Wedding

Later it would be easy for snobs to look down on Virginia: to despise her for her insufficient education, her imperviousness to high literature, classical music, history, and art; her loose morals, inattentive mothering, love of money, costume jewelry, excessive makeup, tawdry, bright-colored clothes, glitter, partying, drinking, horse racing, and gambling. But if Virginia offended the sensibilities of judgmental, traditional white southern citizens, it was perhaps because she so well represented—as would her son—the changing face of Western society as a new generation left the land and adapted, or did not adapt, to modern, latter-half-twentieth-century urban culture. Eloping one day in the summer of 1950, at the cusp of a new half century, the widowed Virginia, aged twenty-seven, decided, at any rate, to defy her mother: to marry The Dude.

The runaway wedding took place on June 19, 1950, at "a little white house serving as a parsonage for the church, across and a few blocks from the racetrack" in Hot Springs. There were only two witnesses: Roger's best friend, Gabe Crawford, and Gabe's wife, also named Virginia. No member of Virginia Blythe's or Roger Clinton's family attended. Even little Billy stayed home in Hope.

Virginia's parents were furious—as were the parents of Roger Clinton, given that he was already in legal trouble for not keeping up alimony payments to his former wife and children.

For Mrs. Virginia Clinton, as she became, it was an inauspicious beginning to a second marriage, however: the "triumph of Hope over Experience," as Dr. Johnson had famously quipped. The best that could be said was that it was at least legal this time. Thus, wearing her outsize false eyelashes, painted eyebrows, and copious lipstick, the fun-loving, irreligious, twenty-seven-year-old mother, returning from her honeymoon to Hope, was determined to make her second marriage work—if she could.

CHAPTER THREE

FROM HOPE TO HOT SPRINGS

Nuclear Family

As a new bride, Mrs. Roger Clinton could now move out of Hervey Street and live with her husband in a small house on East Thirteenth Street, on the other side of Hope. For the next three years little Billy Blythe thus lived in the white-painted, timber-framed, one-story bungalow.

Number 321 was a modest home. The path from the sidewalk led up to a concrete porch supported by simple white uprights on either side. Inside the front door was a small living room with a tiny dining room on one side, a kitchen on the other. Further inside, a corridor led to a bathroom, master bedroom, and, opposite that, two small bedrooms—the back one of which was for Billy. In the other Billy set out the Lionel train set given him by his stepfather and with which Roger would play for hours alongside Billy.

Little Billy Blythe now had a mother and a stepfather: a classic American postwar baby-boom nuclear family in the new nuclear age.

A Real Obnoxious Little Kid

Despite the move across town and the ring on her finger, life for Mrs. Virginia Clinton did not improve materially or socially. Hope remained as class-conscious as before, and though there were more children on the residential block than on Hervey Street, they too had their own issues with the precocious, lonely, little fat boy whom they found irritating, indeed sometimes downright sickening, in his desire to be accepted as a playmate.

Donna Taylor, for example, was the same age as Billy Blythe. Her mother was one of Virginia's best friends, but that did not endear Billy to Donna, who, as a wildly pretty five-year-old, resented him. "He loved to be wanted—always wanting to be included, involved! He was a most obnoxious child, to another child," she recalled. "I remember feeling 'Get back, get back!' He always wanted to be right in the middle of it. We all got mad at him.

"One day we were down at Rosie's, down the street, playing—we'd got mad at him for something—and here he came, saying he had a new swing seat in his garden. Well, we decided he wasn't so bad after all, but we still didn't want to play at his house."

So obnoxious was the little boy that at Miss Marie Purkins' School for Little Folks—Miss Mary's Kindergarten—resembling a scaled-down one-room schoolhouse, complete with steeple and school bell and run by a Miss Marie and a Miss Nannie Purkins—the other children tripped Billy deliberately and broke his leg.

"We had a jumping rope, and he had his little boots on, and his pants rolled up—they didn't come in different lengths at that time, and they were too long," Taylor recounted. "Well, he wanted to get involved in this jump-rope game; we called it 'hot peppers'—and he fell and broke his leg! We all hated that, once we realized, but truth was, we were picking on him because he was this real obnoxious little kid."

Conflict-Averse

For Billy's mother, things were little better. Virginia still had her circle of wild friends, still worked at the hospital, and even—thanks to Roger's Buick agency—drove a smart Buick convertible with the top down. Marriage to Roger Clinton, however, although it raised the family's income level to that of the prosperous middle class (Roger earned $10,000 a year as owner-manager of the Buick dealership, apart from fringe and other benefits), did not make her more liked by the matrons of Hope. She was seen by traditional town society as a "flamboyant mother, a little loose" and a member of the "fast crowd," as one contemporary recalled.

Virginia had wanted, most of all, to separate herself from her mother, Edie, and to run her own life without her mother's interference—or possessiveness in terms of little Billy. In moving to East Thirteenth Street, however, Virginia was trading her dedicated mother, who worshiped little Billy, for a part-time black maid and an errant white husband.

Billy was understandably perplexed. His mother took him to Sunday school and Sunbeams now, but she herself never stayed. Dressed in "white short pants, buttoned onto the shirt, and the tucks and the Peter Pan collar, and white top shoes" he was well-behaved amid the big congregation. But at Sunbeams on Monday evenings at First Baptist, where the four- and five-year-olds learned about Jesus and Baptist missions around the world, one of the volunteers found herself being attacked by the little boy. "He didn't have his way that day, and he kicked her," a friend recalled. The volunteer was "such a lady, she didn't complain, she just said, afterwards, 'he's so accustomed to getting his own way at home, he's with a maid most of the time.' "

In the new world of middle-class working mothers, Billy Blythe was a quintessential latchkey kid. A neighbor, Brack Schenk, recalled how once Roger Clinton had bought Billy a cowboy suit while away (supposedly) on business. "Bill nearly always had his cowboy boots and cowboy hat on, and he would be on that little bicycle, leaning over like he was riding a racing bike or a wild bronco, churning down the sidewalk as fast as it would go." Speed excited him, but not violence—indeed, he seemed almost unnaturally conflict-averse. George Wright, a kindergarten buddy, recalled how Billy was the "biggest child in our age group" but far from domineering; indeed, most saw him as clumsy. He was also brainy. "I remember he was pretty smart," Joe Purvis, another kindergarten contemporary, recounted. "As much as anything he was a peacemaker. I remember at kindergarten kids would be getting into fights or having disputes as kids very often do, and he would be the one that would broker the peace, be the peacemaker. That's always been his nature."

Such precocious peacemaking, as far as his contemporaries could see, went hand in hand with an unusual concern—in a boy, at least—with being liked. "It upset him if someone in any group that he went into didn't seem to like him," George Wright recalled. "It would trouble him so much that he seemed to be asking himself, 'What have I got to do to make this person like me?' I can remember that from when I was six years old."

To Wright and others, not knowing what went on in the inner sanctum of the Clinton home on East Thirteenth, it was a puzzle.

Racial Prejudice

From kindergarten Billy moved, in 1952, to first grade, Brookwood Elementary School, on South Spruce Street, under Miss Wilson, who had only one arm.

Billy, having only one usable leg following his accident—he spent weeks in hospital with his limb broken in three places, hanging in a splint, suspended from the ceiling, while his playmates were brought to see him and appreciate what they had done—sympathized with Miss Wilson. He also seemed to love the schoolwork she made the children do and at which he could shine—he could learn anything from first sight or sound, thanks to a "phenomenal memory." Indeed there was something strange about Billy Blythe, so bright and so anxious to please in a world of small-town social snobbery—and, perhaps worst of all, racial distinction.

Donna Taylor—who would be credited by Billy as having been the first girl who ever let him kiss her—was brutally frank about racism in Hope as a child. Billy had a black maid and had even played on occasion with the black children a couple of blocks away, "but you always knew the difference in Hope, Arkansas," Taylor pointed out. "If he'd stayed right here," she added with deliberate understatement, "he'd probably have been a little more prejudiced."

But Billy didn't stay.

The Shooting

As Billy Blythe prepared to enter second grade in the summer of 1953, his parents decided to leave Hope—forever.

At the time, Virginia gave her relatives and friends a variety of reasons for the move. There was little work for her personally, so that she found herself often being employed as a private nurse, instead of practicing as an anesthetist. Hope, it was clear, was *not* expanding—indeed, the population of the town, which had peaked at almost 16,000 during the war, had slipped back to 9,000 and below with the phasing out of the Proving Grounds at the end of World War II and as the military cut back still further, following peace in Korea. With the easing of war restrictions there was certainly a greater demand for private cars, but there were also more cars being produced in Detroit—and more competition in selling them in the South, making Roger's task at the Buick agency more difficult. The good years, for Roger, were over.

Yet the deeper truth underlying the Clintons' move was that, behind The Dude's clothes and the genial ole-boy manner, "Baby" Roger Clinton was never cut out to be a successful businessman. Virginia, for example, recalled Roger's secretary at the dealership saying that Roger "kept stealing from himself"—simply opening the cash box and taking as much as he required in spite of his $10,000-a-year salary, which was a considerable income in those times. Thanks to his gambling, there was never enough. Falling needlessly behind with his alimony payments to his first wife and children, Roger had turned increasingly to drink. His bouts became worse, and Virginia, who was hardworking and seemed to have no problem with her own self-image, was forced to take note, for one day, as she prepared to take Billy with her to the hospital, where her maternal grandmother was now dying, Roger, drunk and whining, forbade her to leave the house. When she ignored him and made to leave regardless, he simply shot at her.

Spousal abuse was southern behavior of a traditional kind; every white man was authorized to keep guns in his house and his pickup truck, not only to shoot the potential black rapists of southern mythology but to compel obedience on the part of his "harem," as Bolsteri called it. Roger had hit her before, but when he shot at her, Virginia related, it was no joke.

Fortunately, Roger's aim was unsteady, thanks to the drink. "I heard a gunshot and a bullet smacked into the wall next to me, about two feet up from the floor," Virginia vividly recalled. Grabbing her little boy by the hand, she fled across the street and called the police from the neighbor's house. A cruiser promptly arrived, Roger was locked up for the night in jail, and though his brother Raymond raced over from Hot Springs to avert a scandal that might reflect on the Buick dealership, not even he could persuade the Hope sheriff to release Roger. As Virginia recollected thankfully, not even an act of Congress would get Roger freed before the next day—and keep him out of the newspaper.

Unfortunately, Roger was not alone in his addiction. The couple's next-door neighbor, Mr. Williams, a retired railway employee, also had a major drinking problem—indeed, despite its supposedly "dry" status and the hymn singing in Hope's churches, the little town seemed to seethe, behind its lace curtains, with hidden problems. At the back of the town drugstore owned by Roger's friend Gabe Crawford, for example, a bookie operation had been set up, as well as several slot machines. The phrase "running down to the drugstore" came to have a fresh meaning, Virginia chuckled. She also recalled another occasion when Raymond Clinton was compelled to come from Hot Springs and rescue his younger brother, who had not only rigged a game of craps but invited a town official to participate.

Between embezzlement at the Buick dealership and drunken violence and illegal gambling at home, it was high time to move before things got further out of hand. To his credit, Roger—on his brother's advice—now bit the bullet. Suddenly Roger announced that they would be moving to Hot Springs, Virginia recalled of the summer of 1953. He had, he told Virginia, sold the agency to Sid Rogers, a local businessman, and with the money they could uproot themselves and try their fortunes in the more clement commercial and social environment of Hot Springs.

Virginia was not altogether surprised—or disappointed. The years in Hope were, finally, over.

Moving to Hot Springs

Moving to Hot Springs was, for the Clintons, a move away from the prying eyes and asphyxiating, restrictive rules of a Bible Belt southern town—rules that seemed made to be broken. Virginia favored the idea. She worried that Roger's increasing drinking problem would become public—shaming her in front of her parents, especially.

This was silly. Edith and Eldridge knew exactly what was going on; indeed it was exactly what Edie had always feared, from the time she'd first met Roger Clinton. As grandparents, however, they were mortified by the move on Billy's behalf. The little boy was now turning seven. For all its social snobberies and hidden vice, Hope was a real southern community in which everyone knew everyone and people helped one another in time of need—however much that need might be the result of the sin-obsessed values of the community.

For Virginia, Hope might represent a social prison, a community that hated change. But for little Billy it had offered, like all communities with strong religious congregations, security. Leaving Hope would mean, for him, leaving the certainties and verities of a traditional southern township, dominated by its vast First Baptist Church on Third Street as well as the Missouri Pacific railway trains thundering through the town up to a hundred times a day. It would mean leaving behind the Double Dip ice cream parlor at Cole's, and the baseball games on the Hope Legionnaire's field on the corner of Main and Second, and the Rialto and Saenger cinemas with their flickering screens. Most of all, it would mean leaving behind his beloved "Mammaw" and "Pappaw" on Hervey Street.

As the electric train set was boxed up for the move from Hope, it was clear that a chapter of Billy Blythe's life was ending—one he would not reconstruct for another fifty years, in a way that would transform him from an unknown contender into the elected president of the United States of America.

Rotten to the Core

Hope and Hot Springs were, Virginia knew, not simply eighty miles apart, they were like day and night. Indeed, the contrast and contradiction between the two towns in the molding of the life and character of Billy Blythe IV would be incalculable. In the view of many Arkansas observers, Billy Blythe's personality was beaten out on the twin anvils of the two towns and in the struggle between their two ethoses: the one puritanical, moral, decent, "good," hiding its sins; the other thermally cleansing but openly corrupt and corrupting: a place where "good" meant "bad"—delightfully bad.

"In Arkansas, Hot Springs enjoyed the reputation of being the neutral ground for the mobsters of the world," "Justice Jim" Johnson recalled with retrospective wonder, yet alongside the gangsters were convalescents of culture and wealth. "The town had *sophistication* that Arkansas was not noted for! I mean, you could get caviar, you could get whatever there was— *they really had it!*

"I used to have a friend that had a newspaper over there, a maverick. He called it *The Hot Springs Rubdown*. And the second name, under the heading, was 'We Scald the World!' "

Hot Springs certainly scandalized the Bible Belt world. "It's an attitude, a *state of thought,*" Johnson explained, his voice mixing fascination and contempt. The people of Hot Springs, "they're lovin', en'ertaining people— they are *charmin'* people. But they don't have the basic conviction that ordinary people have. They're *hollow! And it's not their fault!* It's kinda like these kids that's raised on the streets, that they just got hatched, and nobody has ever told 'em different! Just whatever is necessary to survive, do it!"

Though Johnson was not a preacher, his view had the patronizing, excoriating qualities of a Pentecostalist's. "The people of Hot Springs lived in this little area that has been exclusive to them, that we outsiders have an awful time understanding! *And it's all on the surface.* In other words, the foundations of the community have been based on *illegality.* Now, that makes it pretty rotten to the core, when you talk about *morality,*" he explained, emphasizing the operative words.

"It's hard to explain," he allowed, cocking his thin, bony head with its sharp, angular nose. "In other words, to do something illegal wasn't repulsive to them. It wasn't that offensive! To them, to make a story come out right is just not an offensive thing, it just makes it a better story! Even if you have to supply some facts that's not there!"

Looking back, Johnson—archetypal white supremacist, lawyer, former elected member of the Arkansas Supreme Court and even more notorious leader of the White Citizens Council—saw Billy Blythe as his nemesis: a "nigger-loving" product of Hot Springs, trained and able to use his skills in illegality and amended storytelling to personal advantage. "I equate it to having a liar on the witness stand. He's the most dangerous witness on earth, because he's not hemmed in by the truth! He's a perjurer. He's not hemmed in by the truth, and he can make the story fit whatever will benefit the side he's on!"

Whatever the truth about the acculturating effects of the Arkansas "dunghill," as Johnson pictured it, it was to the legendary city of Hot Springs that the Clinton family moved in the fall of 1953. Taken out of second grade at Hope's Brookwood Elementary School, little Billy Blythe would now have to begin life afresh. His stepfather had already moved their furniture and worldly goods, though not to Hot Springs proper. Instead they settled on Gabe Crawford's four-hundred-acre mixed farm just outside the city, where Roger Clinton intended to set himself up as a "gentleman farmer."

It was not a wise decision.

Awash in Sin

The traditional life of a farmer—whether plantation owner, gentleman farmer, or working farmer—was prized in the South. Roger Clinton's attempt at agriculture, however, was as doomed as his attempt to be a car dealer. When he dressed in the morning, putting on his best clothes and shoes instead of overalls and boots—to check on the animals—Virginia could only shake her head. Often, she recalled, he turned for "expert" advice to Van Hampton Lyell, owner of the local Coca-Cola bottling plant.

A trained nurse-anesthetist, dealing every day with matters of life and death, Virginia merely waited for the first frost to kill the plants, the animals—and the notion. As one of the only three anesthetists in Hot Springs, a lodestar for the sick and convalescing, she herself had no shortage of work at St. Joseph's and Ouachita hospitals. Each day she drove off to earn real money—indeed, once the other two anesthetists went on strike (over Virginia's willingness to work Thursdays, their traditional day off), Virginia became for a time the town's *only* anesthetist.

Virginia loved Hot Springs—indeed, she would stay there the rest of her life. The gambling town's "state of thought," as Johnson classed it, might be considered immoral, but if so, it was the "thought" of America's future: vibrant, cosmopolitan, open to change, devoted to entertainment, and above all classless. Southern class, as a social construct involving moral standards in the *noblesse oblige* vein—of "nice" people versus "common" people, of southern belles—simply did not exist in Hot Springs, where the prosperity of the town rested upon its medicinal properties, its natural beauty, its visitors from across the nation—and the lure of gambling, horse racing, and nightlife.

For Virginia's husband, Roger, too, the return to Hot Springs was a relief, for he was moving back closer to his "darlin'" mother, Eula, or "Mama" Clinton, in whose thrall, according to Virginia, he remained. He was also returning to the protection of his older brother, Raymond, who lived on Lake Hamilton and directed the growing fortunes of his Buick dealership in the town. Raymond could not, however, protect Roger from his gambling buddies—the group, as "Justice Jim" put it, "that would also be at the various gambling casinos at night. And there's not any real distinction between the owners and the gamblers, because they usually have the homes around the lake and they go for the high rolling in the casinos. There's no class difference, you just bet!"

For good or ill—and in the minds of puritans it was definitely the latter—seven-year-old Billy Blythe was in any event now moved from the safe haven of small-town, moralistic Hope, Arkansas. The little boy would have to make his way in a world awash in sin; would have to learn to survive without traditional "morality."

Like Fishes to Water

Hot Springs in 1953 had a population of 36,807—four times that of Hope. More important, the town had an annual tourist population of half a million, which made it more cosmopolitan than any other town in the state, including the capital, Little Rock.

Residents of and visitors to Hot Springs were served by two airlines, two railways (Missouri Pacific and Rock Island), and seven bus lines. There were two daily and two weekly papers; eight theaters (including three open-air drive-ins); five golf courses; sixty-three churches, temples, and synagogues catering to all religious faiths and denominations; four radio stations; four parks totaling more than a thousand acres; two federal banks; three hundred hotels; five hospitals (including the Army and Navy General, dating back to 1887) with 1,500 beds; and three rest homes. It boasted the largest alligator farm in the United States and eight "bathing palaces" in its famous, magnolia-lined Bath House Row: the Maurice, built in 1912 ("capacity 1,000 daily"); the Ozark, built in 1922; the Buckstaff, built in 1912 ("the entire force of the Buckstaff is composed of experienced WHITE persons"); the Fordyce, built in 1915 (boasting a library, music room, and two bowling alleys); the Superior; the Hale, built in 1893; the Quapaw, built in 1922; and the Lamar, designed by Mann and Stern in 1920. Colored bathers had to go to the Crystal Bath House on Malvern Avenue. In addition, there were spectacular horse-riding trails, first-rate fishing, incomparable hiking, and a new public library with more than ten thousand volumes.

Hot Springs' nightlife was provided by a host of large and small private clubs—in which casinos could be operated—as well as by the hotels. These included the Southern Club, the Belvedere Club, the Tower Club, the Palms, the Black Orchid Lounge, the Vapors, and the Arlington and Majestic hotels. Since the state collected almost $1.5 million a year from pari-mutuel betting at Oaklawn Park and the city raised its own taxes, as well as levying fines on "illegal" gambling and prostitution that could be used for the improvement of roads, streets, lighting, education, cleaning, and sewage, it was considered wisest for the governor of Arkansas, forty-five miles away in Little Rock, not to interfere with the mayor's administration or attempt to police the widespread gambling that continued. Mayor McLaughlin had been unseated in a reformist coup in 1947, but the supposed reforms had never come—and in many ways the next twenty years would prove the heyday of the spa town: a mini–Las Vegas.

Within the Bible Belt culture of Arkansas, then, Hot Springs was truly a "place apart"—and Mr. and Mrs. Roger Clinton took to its healing waters like proverbial fishes.

A Head-Butting

Little Billy Blythe (in view of Roger's closet drinking problem, Virginia had refused Roger's repeated offers to formally adopt the boy and give him the Clinton surname) was driven into town each day to the first private, parochial grade school he had attended in his life: St. John's School, next to St. Joseph's Catholic Church on West Grand Avenue.

St. John's had been started in 1908 for white children and by the 1950s boasted 250 pupils—all still white. Classes were conducted by the Sisters of Mercy, and it was they who, in their spinsterly but dedicated way, were the first to recognize the precocity of the little Baptist boy in their midst: attentive, bright, and competitive to the point of nuisance.

Virginia found herself too busy, as she later related, to attend parents' meetings or events, but when she received Billy's first report card, which showed an A in every single subject except deportment, where he'd been given a resounding D, she feared that the emotional disturbance at home and the sudden move to Hot Springs had had some terrible effect on Billy's behavior at school. She shot off to see the sisters.

"Why there's no real problem," Billy's teacher assured her: "it's just that . . . he is so sharp and he's so alert . . . he knows the answer immediately and will not give the others a chance." Relying on the fact that "he is so competitive he will not be able to stand this D," the nun had marked him down not for misbehavior but for overachievement!

While Billy Blythe was being urged to control his urge to outshine all others, his stepfather was attempting to adapt to ranch life, though with less success.

Worked off her feet as an anesthetist—as well as having to drive daily to help tend to her sick father in Hope—Virginia was right. The farm plan was a disaster—symbolized when one of the rams went wild and began butting little Billy in front of his stupefied parents, until Roger's father picked up a rock and rushed to intercede, stunning the animal with a blow between the eyes. Little Billy never forgot the experience—or nightmare. "I was too young, fat, and slow to run," he later recounted, "even after he knocked me down the second time. He must have butted me ten times. It was the awfullest beating I ever took and I had to go to the hospital for stitches." The near tragedy, Virginia recalled, almost cost Billy his life; the scars on his head never completely erased.

Appalled by the incident, Virginia called a halt to the agricultural experiment. The farm was abandoned, and the Clintons then did what they should have done from the start: they moved into town.

1011 Park Avenue

Settling into another of Gabe Crawford's properties, the Clintons unpacked their things in an old two-story wood-frame house: 1011 Park Avenue, next to the Perry Plaza Motel on the steep slope to the left of the main road leading out of Hot Springs to the north. Roger claimed he was buying the house, but as Virginia would later discover, it was Roger's brother Raymond who had struck a deal with their mother to buy it, to help save Roger. Raymond would then employ Roger—who had lost all the money he'd received from the Hope dealership to gambling—in his Buick agency in Hot Springs, as parts manager.

For Roger the offer from his older brother was a financial godsend but a humiliating comedown after running his own Buick dealership in Hope. He had little option but to accept the proposal, however. He was now forty-three, remarried, and—unknown to Virginia—penniless.

For the next fifteen years, till he died of cancer, Roger would order, store, sell, and reorder spare parts for his brother's dealership—drinking away his sorrows.

Married to an Alcoholic

Roger's alcoholism seemed to mark his despair—the once high-living, free-wheeling, party-going Dude reduced to being a clerk in his brother's garage. Every night he'd get drunk, leading to perpetual fights and threats, by Virginia, of leaving him. He was, however, as Virginia later reflected, just as miserable when not drinking. Despising himself, he became more and more jealous of Virginia: of her status as an anesthetist, her *joie de vivre,* of her love for and pride in her son—by another man . . . He even became "insanely jealous," Virginia recalled, of her women friends. She became aware of him following her after work, stalking her when she was out. Humiliated by his failure in the workplace (his elder brothers all either owned their own prosperous businesses or were senior managers in large companies) and without children of his own, Roger was vainly attempting to keep control of all that was left of his empire: his second wife. And this Virginia would not allow.

Paradoxically, the more Virginia succeeded in her own profession as an anesthetist, the more Roger's confidence and personality fell apart. Every third night, Virginia was off call and would party. Her taste might be tasteless in terms of high art, but it was utterly self-assured. She liked to wrap her Christmas presents in aluminum foil, the better to gleam under the tree, but it was the glittering decorations and glitterati of the town's nightclubs that exercised a magnetic attraction. She liked the Vapors, a club that was every bit as ostentatious as the clubs of Las Vegas. She adored its big crystal chandeliers, the plush red velvet upholstery, the dance floor, and, in the back, the gaming tables—slot machines, blackjack dealers, roulette wheels, crap tables. It drew some of the biggest names in popular music and entertainment, and in that carefree ambience, after the stress and pressure of the operating room, she was in her element: her face painted, her hair coiffed, her pumps polished, her dress bursting, her energy inextinguishable. When Roger would emerge from the gambling tables, having lost more money and seeing his wife dancing with abandon with other men, his temper would fray and at home he would launch a litany of drunken accusations—much as Virginia's mother had done unto her father. Once he beat a dance partner of Virginia's "to pulp," but gradually he began to do without specifics. Sitting in the kitchen with Billy, Virginia and her son would "tense up" at the sound of Roger's car coming up the steep drive. The door being slammed, the swearing aloud, the entrance of a bitter, vengeful man . . . "At times like that, I knew we were in for a night of it," she related.

Bedlam

As Billy reached his teens, Virginia reflected at the end of her life, he was in all likelihood disgusted by the goings-on in Hot Springs.

Virginia meant the gambling; but for little Billy gambling at the Vapors was as nothing compared to the vapors emanating from his stepfather. When Roger was on the alcoholic warpath, the house was "just bedlam," Virginia recalled, from dusk until dawn, when Roger finally passed out—the nights punctuated by his hurling "accusations of infidelity, pitiful rants about where-was-I-at-a-certain-time-when-I-was-supposed-to-be-somewhere-else."

Victims of alcoholism would recognize such patterns of dysfunctional tyranny. The fact that in the 1950s violence and domestic abuse had, at all costs, to be concealed from "the neighbors" only made the tension in the home more unbearable, reinforcing Billy's aversion to confrontation in an attempt to keep the peace at any price. "I couldn't wait to get big enough to know there would be peace in my home," he later confessed. Violence at home was something that left "a strong emotional burden. It always made me ambivalent about the imposition of my will in other places."

Typically for an alcoholic, Roger would, in his rages, accuse Virginia of all the misdeeds he himself was guilty of. Mortally wounded in his own self-esteem, he knew just how to wound Virginia in hers. He would deride her for her faults, such as Virginia being despised by her friends, who, he claimed, considered her vulgar and a show-off. Meanwhile, his ability to present a front of good-ole-boy bonhomie and sobriety to others—as, for example, when called to the telephone by members of his family in the very midst of his drunken fits—never ceased to amaze Virginia. How he managed to drag himself to the Buick dealership each day, after his nights of mayhem, was equally extraordinary. On occasions when he felt he was falling completely apart, he would simply leave town.

Roger's hypocrisy was staggering. Most of their married life, Virginia recalled, with retrospective disbelief, she had no knowledge of where he might be—whereas Roger reserved the right to know precisely where she was, day or night. Often he would take one-day "business trips" and return days later with cock-and-bull stories that deceived no one, including himself. But Virginia merely shrugged, for in truth, she no longer cared, as long as he left her and Billy alone. Once she had hung the evidence of his promiscuity on his washing line for all the world—certainly the neighbors—to see. Now, as his wife, she was indifferent and showed not the remotest interest in his extramarital or extracurricular activities. "Let carousing dogs carouse," was her attitude when enjoying herself with her friends. There seemed no way Roger could win back her attention or respect other than by reforming himself—and this he could not or would not do.

Fifties Facade

Was Virginia exaggerating in her later description of her husband's carousing? Certainly, on the night that Roger Clinton's own father passed away, as his family congregated around the dying man's bedside, Roger was nowhere to be found. The next morning he was located, drunk, in another woman's bed by Lake Hamilton, at the edge of town.

The truth was, the neighbors all knew what was going on—but in the manner of the decade, it was the neighbors' children who were not allowed to know. In this respect the 1950s were a last, vast conspiracy to keep from middle-class children the truth about real life and real lives; an era of rabid conservatism (personified in the McCarthy witch-hunts) after decades of New Deal Democratic programs; a period of sexual and moral retrenchment after the briefly glimpsed feminism of World War II; a time of cold war; a decade of conformity, continued racial segregation, and denial. The American economy was prospering as never before, with living standards increasing by leaps and bounds. After the bitter years of Depression, then of national sacrifice during World War II, nobody was allowed to rock the boat—or be seen to.

As social, cultural, and biographical historians now know, however, this front was for many only a facade, and behind the curtains of 1011 Park Avenue, Hot Springs, little Billy Blythe, listening to his stepfather's drunken ravings over infidelity and promiscuity, knew it too.

A Look at American Life

How typical was the domestic drama being enacted at 1011 Park Avenue in the context of the 1950s?

One problem faced by cultural historians and sociologists is that the work done by social scientists in that decade was so punitively circumscribed, thanks to the leading moralists of the era. In the 1950s, for example, Professor Alfred Kinsey, a distinguished entomologist, was vilified by conservatives, who then, as later, saw him as "a corrupter of morals, a godless scientist, or, worse yet, a charlatan and a fraud" for his survey work on human sexuality. In particular the eminent evangelist the Reverend Billy Graham claimed to be outraged by Kinsey's publications: *Sexual Behavior in the Human Male,* published in 1947, and, more controversial, *Sexual Behavior in the Human Female,* published in 1953. Of the latter the Reverend Graham warned in 1953: "It is impossible to estimate the damage this book will do to the already deteriorating morals of America."

Henry Pitney Van Dusen, head of the Union Theological Seminary, went even further, insisting that Kinsey's painstakingly researched findings would contribute to "a prevailing degradation in American morality approximating the worst decadence of the Roman Empire."

If Billy Graham and Van Dusen hoped that oral sex, masturbation, premarital sex, extramarital sex, and homosexuality would somehow go away if funding was withdrawn from Kinsey's Indiana University research institute in the 1950s, they were mistaken. Funding *was* withdrawn—but the decline in Western morals continued. The decadence of the American Empire was neither Kinsey's invention nor his creation. His was simply a courageous look at modern American life, based upon tens of thousands of one-on-one interviews and one hundred percent statistical sampling of diverse groups. As James H. Jones remarked in his life of Kinsey, the sexual behavior that Kinsey painstakingly counted, chronicled, and even tested out for himself (including gay sex, wife swapping, and group sex) was not a precept but a record of changing reality as America cast off the stultifying, lingering repressions of Victorian middle-class society—changing behavior that was "driven more by social and economic changes than by the work of sex researchers. What Kinsey did accomplish," Professor Jones reflected, "was to bring intimate matters into the open so that people could discuss them with unprecedented candor. This cultural dialogue, in turn, helped shape what followed."

In other words, the work of Kinsey and others did not, and could not, change people's evolving behavior patterns—only how people might see that behavior.

The Cultural Pressure Cooker

The truth, as Professor Kinsey had long suspected, was that the variety and diversity of sexual behavior were as rich in the human as in the natural world. Adultery was no perversion but something bred into human beings as part of human evolution—the product of sexual competition and selection. Moreover, women were as adventurous as men, though with their own agendas.

The Victorians had attempted to ignore and deny this, channeling extramarital sex into vast underworlds of vice and prostitution, especially child prostitution. But the repressions of the past century were wearing increasingly thin by the 1950s. In a postwar age of increasing affluence and prosperity, things—whatever the Reverends Graham and Van Dusen might warn—would change.

The cultural pressure cooker was about to burst, and the explosion would be not only in the field of sexuality. For little Billy Blythe, plump, superintelligent at school, a voracious reader of newspapers and books at home, and an avid watcher of television once the family acquired a set in 1955, it was as if he had a ringside seat as America's modern destiny unfolded before him.

CHAPTER FOUR

DOMESTIC STRIFE

Moms Loving Dads

Each day on the small black-and-white television screen in the living room, a portrait of middle-class family life was prepared for the national diet. It was "a wonderfully antiseptic world of idealized homes in an idealized, unflawed America," as David Halberstam described it in his cultural history *The Fifties:* a safe place where, in family sitcoms such as *The Adventures of Ozzie and Harriet,* there were "no economic crises, no class divisions or resentments, no ethnic tensions, few if any hyphenated Americans, few if any minority characters." There was definitely no divorce. Indeed, there was "no serious sickness, particularly mental illness. Families *liked* each other, and they tolerated each other's idiosyncrasies. Dads were good dads whose worst sin was that they did not know their way around the house and could not find common household objects. . . . The dads were, above all else, steady and steadfast. . . . Above all else, the moms loved the dads, and vice versa, and they never questioned whether they had made the right choice. . . . Moms and dads never raised their voices at each other in anger. . . . No family difference was so irreconcilable that it could not be cleared up and straightened out within the allotted twenty-two minutes."

But 1011 Park Avenue was not such a home.

Mad Money

Part of the problem, perhaps *the* problem, was that Virginia had a profession. As Halberstam noted even of situation comedies such as *Ozzie,* in such an idealized world "the moms never worked." By contrast, Billy Blythe's mom did—and Roger Clinton, his stepfather, resented it.

Women's magazines of the 1950s—owned and edited by men—were justifiably nervous about the issue and depicted feminism as "a deep illness": a threat not only to male hegemony but to the togetherness of the American family. Mrs. Dale Carnegie remarked in April 1955, "Let's face it, girls. That wonderful guy in your house—and in mine—is building your house, your happiness and the opportunities that will come to your children." In return, it was the manifest duty of a woman to tend the home, stand by her man, and ensure her husband's "success in HIS job."

For Virginia, who had HER job, such admonitions were, as to millions of American women, irritatingly unreal. Virginia worked because the modern American economy needed her to work. Moreover, having been trained as an anesthetist, Virginia enjoyed her profession and the empowerment it afforded her. If Roger Clinton could not handle that, then that was his problem.

Roger Clinton's problem, however, increasingly became Virginia's problem, as his drinking and gambling spiraled out of control. In the end, standing by her man became impossible. As Roger floundered in another drunken stupor, shouting imprecations and knocking pictures off the walls, Virginia gathered some clothes together and, taking Billy to her car, drove him to safety.

Once on the road, however, she realized she had no idea where she was heading. She had no money, not even access to her own account at the bank, since Roger "controlled the checking account."

Staying in the apartment of some people she knew, Virginia recognized this as the key to feminism in the twentieth century. Women were, by their natures, locked into responsibility for the welfare and well-being of their offspring, whom they could never desert. However, they were powerless to desert abusive, failing husbands unless they had money—a thought that caused her to recall the emergency funds given to girls in the old days lest they be stranded on a date that turned nasty or didn't work out. Such funds were called "mad money"—for girls who got mad at their dates.

The result, a decade before Betty Friedan, was a momentous personal decision made by Virginia: "As Bill slept soundly next to me that night, I made a vow to him and to myself: *Never again will I be without money to protect us.*"

Though she went back to Park Avenue and to Roger Clinton, spare parts tyrant, Virginia began to salt away a portion of her income. When the time came to leave Roger, she would be in a position, she determined, to buy her *own* home. Once again she would become a single mother—but this time by her own volition.

Peyton Place

Brought up in infancy by his grandmother Edie and taught by a succession of women at kindergarten and elementary school—the strict nuns of St. John's replaced by other teachers once he transferred to Ramble Elementary School, Hot Springs, in fourth grade—Billy was spoiled for choice in terms of female role models but got no help in the male role-model department. The absence of a real father and the presence of weak men such as his grandfather (who would pass away in 1957) and his stepfather Roger Clinton—men who were either cowed by strong women or got drunk, cussed, and resorted to violence in a sort of vengeful impotence—was unfortunate.

None of this was to be seen on NBC, CBS, or ABC television, nor to be found in books of the period; indeed, when Grace Metalious wrote *Peyton Place,* her famous exposé of small-town American life, in 1955, no respectable publisher would touch it. It was eventually published in paperback in 1957—by a woman—and sold 10 million copies in three years!

Grace Metalious was no angel. Nor were the women in her books. As one publishing historian noted, her characters might have come right out of the Kinsey report on women but the men in her books were even worse: "unreliable and childish." Yet, as publishing historian C. K. Davis put it, for perhaps the first time in popular fiction "a writer was saying that women wanted sex and enjoyed it but they wanted it on their terms. They were not passive receptacles for dominant men. To a generation fed on Mickey Spillane, for whom women counted as little more than animals, or Erskine Caldwell, whose Southern women were for the most part sluttish trash, the women of Peyton Place presented a new image."

To millions of readers, Metalious's women were a welcome antidote to the mythology promulgated by men. "Independent, self-fulfilling, strong yet capable of love and desire, they were far from the perfect exemplars of the shining new woman that eventually followed with the onset of the feminist movement," Davis pointed out, "but they were a breakthrough, a first faint glimmering that women were preparing to break out of the mold carefully prepared for them by centuries of male domination."

Such a woman was Virginia Clinton—and little Billy Blythe adored her unreservedly.

The Need for God

If Virginia Clinton was a heroine to her son, Roger Clinton was a villain, increasingly. Both witness to and victim of his stepfather's worsening domestic abuse, Billy suppressed his fear, confusion, and anger, channeling them into a growing determination to be his own master: to be independent, if not in body then in mind. His physical ineptitude and his strange background as the son of the exotic anesthetist from Hope gave him an outsider status—but at least he was an outsider in a town where half a million other outsiders arrived annually, bringing a richness of ethnic, religious, and cultural backgrounds unknown in Hope or indeed any other village or town in Arkansas.

White supremacists such as "Justice Jim" Johnson might mock the Hot Springs of the 1950s as the "dunghill of Arkansas," but the town was, in its way, a quintessential melting pot: a pre–Las Vegas gambling city where races, cultures, religions, traditions, and views came together and mixed in extraordinary harmony. Whatever might be going on in the great American battle between the sexes and however quickly Roger Clinton might be moving toward "self-destruction," as Virginia termed it, little Billy Blythe was reading the newspaper from cover to cover, listening to the radio, watching television, and conversing with the people—residents and visitors—of his adopted hometown. Domestically he might be a prisoner, given the war between Virginia and Roger; intellectually, however, he was a citizen of a freer world than Hope, empowered by his high intelligence and his growing ability to interact confidently with other children—and with adults. He not only loved school and did brilliantly in class because of his high motivation, but on Sundays he walked to the palatial redbrick First Baptist Church, down Park Avenue, Bible in hand and without either parent accompanying him.

Some might later question Billy's religious faith, considering it the sham religion of one who was patently not among The Saved, but for himself Billy Blythe *did* feel saved—and saved from a far more oppressive domestic reality than most of his contemporaries or teachers were aware of.

Billy's devout baby-sitter, Mrs. Walton—who had watched over him since the move to Hot Springs—predicted a career as a preacher, given Billy's precocity and way with words, and certainly in church Billy Blythe was entranced by the lyrical and musical beauty of the services. The actual historical basis for a belief in Christ's divinity could never be proven, but it could be appreciated, indeed believed in *as gospel truth:* good news from another place, in another time, set to great choral music, emotionally reaffirming, and, however naive, the idealistic, hope-filled product of a religious culture that offered the little boy sanctuary from the frightening violence and abuse of home; a place of spiritual peace, human community, and idealism. It was still there when he pinched himself or wept at the war being waged between his parents; a place with a real preacher who was delighted to see him, real gospel songs sung by a real congregation of adherents, and real love, or goodwill, in the air.

His grandmother—who had taught him his ABCs but who had become a morphine addict in the state mental hospital in Benton after her recovery from a stroke—his grandfather Eldridge, his stepfather Roger, even his mother, Virginia, on occasion, might let him down in the struggle for psychological survival. Jesus, however, was a divinity who could never be compromised. He had existed for almost two thousand years, and He continued to exist, in exactly the way Montaigne had described: a supernatural father who would have to be invented were He not to really exist, because people *needed* Him.

And little Billy Blythe, walking to church and Sunday school on his own from the age of eight, had a special need.

JFK on the Screen

For Billy Blythe, the advent of a brother, born on July 25, 1956, certainly seemed a godsend: the answer to a prayer. He was no longer home alone and would no longer be the sole brickbat between fighting parents. Thus, instead of seeing a rival for parental love, as so often occurs, Billy Blythe felt deeply relieved by the new arrival—intuiting also, when his stepfather went out to get drunk that night, leaving him on his own, that he himself might be called upon to act in loco parentis.

There was another birth that summer, too: that of a new national political hero. Virginia had bought a television set the year before, and though much of the programming was pap—"the Age of Golden Syrup" as one critic dubbed it—televising of the national conventions brought the drama of political selection to tens of millions of viewers, including ten-year-old Billy Blythe at 1011 Park Avenue.

Television thus provided the beginning of a lifetime love affair with politics, as Billy later acknowledged. "I think it sort of came home to me in a way on television that it wouldn't have otherwise," he reflected. The grand, televised challenge "left a lasting impression on him," another chronicler maintained, as the 1956 Democratic Party contest for the vice presidential nomination became an open contest between the civil rights battler Estes Kefauver and a young, handsome, Catholic senator and Cold War warrior from the East Coast, John F. Kennedy. Billy was enthralled, indeed "loved it"—something that, for a child still so young, astonished Mara Leverett, who later became a senior editor at the *Arkansas Times.* Clinton and Leverett were the same age. She later recalled the impact of the convention— but not in the same way. To her, it was a travesty, allowing national politics to crowd out children's television programs, and the notion that Bill, aged ten, found politics interesting was "pretty weird to me."

But it wasn't weird to Billy Blythe compared to the weirder things that went on at night in his home. Politicians were fighting for power—and power was something he sorely lacked.

The Head of the Family

The only male power figure little Billy Blythe could unashamedly respect was his stepuncle: Roger Clinton's older brother Raymond, head of the Clinton family, president of the Clinton Buick Agency, and a political as well as commercial operator in Hot Springs. If Roger Clinton was an example of the rotten apple, Raymond was the opposite. Raymond's "family was good to me," Billy later remarked gratefully; indeed, it would be his respect for Raymond that would persuade him, several years later, to change his name to Clinton, after Virginia finally divorced Roger.

While Roger Clinton was hot air beside strong women, Raymond Clinton thrived on the political battles and campaigns that took place in Hot Springs. This group of politicos had been successful in overthrowing Mayor Leo P. McLaughlin. Meanwhile, thanks in part to his successful automobile business, Raymond took over the role of head of the Clinton family. He sold cars to some of the wealthiest visitors and residents from his business at 319 Market Street. There, in the Clinton Buick dealership, he held court with the big shots of the city, who would come by for a cup of coffee and to gossip, drawing on their fat cigars and debating the ills of the world, Virginia recalled with a trace of contempt. But for ten-year-old Billy, watching them quietly after school or during the holidays, this was the real world—the nexus of power and influence, one he would never forget.

Poor Roger, by contrast, would be in the back, counting spares. It did not take long for his precocious little stepson, himself abused and a witness to his mother's almost nightly verbal and sometimes physical battering, to figure out the relationship between power and money and the difference between leadership and impotence. His second-grade teacher at St. John's Catholic School had said he had the talent to become anything he wanted—including president of the United States. That might have seemed a long way from the backwoods of Arkansas, but in an America that was growing economically stronger by the day, it was not impossible. Uncle Raymond, with his big cigar, big billfold, big connections, and big heart, was an icon in a world of little men losing out to big women and the challenges of a new America.

Unconsciously, then, a personal die was cast in Hot Springs in 1956, as the chubby little stepchild, spurred on by watching the Democratic National Convention, surveyed the Clinton family and decided on new role models. Times were changing, and new models were emerging in every arena of human life and affairs, not only in the showrooms of the Buick dealership. Nikita Khrushchev, leader of the Soviet Union, had denounced the memory of Stalin; Colonel Gamal Abdel Nasser had scandalized the Western world by nationalizing the Suez Canal, challenging the European powers as well as Israel to take military action. Yet it was on the small screen in the living room at 1011 Park Avenue that another, in some ways more improbable figure or role model would catch Billy Blythe's ten-year-old imagination: Elvis Presley.

Forbidden Fruit

Billy's mother was the first to be smitten. Virginia was simply "dumbstruck," she later recounted, when she finally saw Elvis Presley on television.

Elvis's records had begun selling by the million, and in the Ouachita Hospital the staff and nurses were already talking about him, as Virginia recalled—an *echt* southern boy making it big on the national music charts. The czar of American television, Ed Sullivan, refused, however, to have Presley on his Sunday-night show, *The Toast of the Town.* Sullivan liked being deferred to and hated to be upstaged. He abhorred Elvis's overtly sexual "gyrations" in performance and saw no reason to invite him. But when a competing program, *The Milton Berle Show,* asked Elvis to perform and Berle's television ratings subsequently topped those of *The Ed Sullivan Show,* Sullivan relented. Reactionaries and horrified church ministers would have to swallow their venom. "It was one thing to guard public morals for the good of the nation and the good of your career," as David Halberstam neatly summarized; "it was another thing to guard public morals at the cost of your career."

Elvis's first appearance on Sullivan's show, on September 9, 1956, as Britain, France, and Israel prepared to invade Egypt to prevent nationalization of the Suez Canal, was seen by almost 83 percent of all Americans watching television that night—some 54 million people. "He's just one big hunk of forbidden fruit," one female fan remarked of the dark-haired twenty-one-year-old guitarist and singer as he belted out "Hound Dog" and crooned "Love Me Tender." Virginia Clinton, watching in Hot Springs, felt the same. This was epiphany time for a woman whose marriage had gone disastrously wrong. She was certain that Roger, sitting drinking beside her in front of the television screen, had no idea what had taken place in her heart, indeed, her spirit. Virginia, however, was unashamedly moved, claiming later that she'd never heard such a sweet and spiritual sound as Elvis's renderings. Nor did she hide the fact that she found him a hunk—in fact, she confided to her girlfriends that if she hadn't had children and a job, she'd have become an Elvis groupie. She accepted that many people disliked Elvis, "but he's my taste, the way horse racing and Vegas and bright makeup and leather boots are my taste."

So bombarded by parental complaints were the producers of Sullivan's show, meanwhile, that, for his second appearance, they recorded Elvis only from the waist up. Little Billy Blythe, however, observing his mother's sudden obsession with Elvis—"whenever Roger gave me problems, I would go listen to my Elvis 45s," she later recalled—absorbed another lesson in the contradictions and competing ideologies of real life.

While his Baptist minister deplored the "lewd" and "vulgar" antics of Elvis Presley, Billy's mother adored them. What was going on?

Elvis the Pelvis

The truth was, Elvis's rhythms came directly out of black music—"jungle music," as southern white conservatives called it. This was a major problem in the South. Racial segregation precluded any crossover between white and black culture; any break in that southern line was to be immediately and virulently denounced, even set upon, white conservatives insisted. The day before Elvis's appearance on *The Ed Sullivan Show,* for example, state police and the National Guard had had to be summoned when a mob of five hundred white people sought to stop twelve Negro students from attending Sturgis High School in Tennessee.

Elvis, however, proved even more threatening to the status quo. His first record producer, Sam Phillips, had listened to the sounds coming out of a neighboring black Methodist church while sitting inside his own white Baptist church—and had been forever affected by the rhythm and power of black singing. "If I could find a white man with a Negro sound I could make a billion dollars," he'd boasted. In Elvis Presley he had found one.

Phillips's discovery was mutual. At age eighteen Elvis had learned to play the "Negro sound," joining the Songfellows, a local gospel group drawn from his hard-core segregated, white fundamentalist Christian Pentecostal church, which had co-opted the black beat into its white music. Though Elvis could not read a note of music, he had perfect pitch—and ambition. He had thereafter developed a personal style that infuriated older white folks but, in the manner of his own movie idol, James Dean, made him into a rebel-hero for the young.

Presley's huge success first on the Milton Berle, then on the Ed Sullivan, shows in 1956, demonstrated that he was hitting a chord in the younger white American cultural psyche. As Halberstam noted, it was a matter not only of race but of class. Elvis was, to all intents and purposes, white trash, his parents living in federal housing in Memphis without even a phone and his father working in a can factory in Tupelo, Mississippi, before the success of their son raised them out of abject poverty. Elvis himself had been driving a truck for the Crown Electric Company at $35 a week until his first vinyl recording in 1954.

Hitherto records had been for people with enough money for phonographs, and their taste, traditionally, had run to classical and swing, leaving those who liked country and black music to listen to the radio. Prosperity and television, however, were now changing this social divide,

abetted by a new consumer class: the young. By early 1956, it was estimated, there were 13 million teenagers in America, each with a weekly disposable income of $10.55—as much as that of a whole family fifteen years
before. Teenagers now bought phonograph players and their own vinyl
records, as well as other items that advertisers wanted to sell. Reaching the
youth market was therefore a necessity—as Sullivan, in deference to his advertising sponsors, had ultimately accepted.

Instinctively, Virginia sensed Elvis's revolutionary appeal—thus tying
herself to her son's generation, not her husband's. "I never once discussed
Elvis with Roger Clinton," she later noted; "he wouldn't have understood
and he would've been jealous." Instead she discussed Elvis with Billy, who
was also won over by Elvis's powerful rhythmic genius, performance energy, and animal magnetism on stage. It was a passion they could share.

When Virginia heard "Jailhouse Rock" the following year, she was even
more enamored. She might have come from the wrong side of the Hope
tracks, have lost her first husband, Sergeant Blythe, in an automobile accident, be discriminated against by male doctors in the medical fraternity of
Hope and in Hot Springs, and be married to an abusive alcoholic who had
failed in his professional life and was destroying himself through alcoholism, but she was not going to give in or up. Driving her Buick convertible down Park Avenue or Central, "I'd start slapping time on the
dashboard so hard," she recalled of Elvis's new song, "I thought I was
going to have to drop the car off with Roger to get me a new dash."

For little Billy, this was cool: his own mother strangely, feistily in tune
with the changing times and the rebel culture of the young. Virginia might
be tasteless in the snobbish middle-class sense, but like Elvis she was a
rebel, a woman with attitude, a free spirit, a fighter for her rights: women's
rights. She had no class—but then, neither did Elvis. And Elvis was the idol
of millions.

Fanatics

Thus, alongside his awakening of political interest, even ambition, while
watching the Democratic National Convention in 1956, little Billy Clinton
experienced another childhood epiphany. No longer would he model himself on Hopalong Cassidy, despite his grandparents' and his mother's
maiden name. Henceforth he'd style himself after the boy from the wrong
side of the tracks in Memphis, Tennessee: a young man who wore pink

shirts and blue suede shoes, made love to his guitar on stage, yet loved his mamma. As Billy's bosom pal David Leopoulos, son of the local Greek restaurant owner, remembered, as boys they would do the usual "stuff" that kids do—go up into the forest, hike, play ball, hang out, play Monopoly—but the rhythm and beat of their world were altered irrevocably by Presley's music. A Cincinnati car dealer had promised to smash fifty Elvis records for every car he sold to discerning customers, but Elvis was now smashing different records, selling 7 million in 1956 alone. "We had most of Elvis's records memorized and would hum them during our dog touch football games," Leopoulos recalled, remembering how "fanatical" they were about the King. "He was the cultural rage of my childhood," Billy himself recalled, remembering how he had even grown his sideburns long in tribute to his hero.

Billy and his friend were not alone. "Elvis Presley is the greatest cultural force in the twentieth century," Leonard Bernstein would later say. "He introduced the beat to everything and he changed everything—music, language, clothes, it's a whole new social revolution—the Sixties comes from it."

John Lennon, who would himself help to revolutionize popular music in the sixties, was even more emphatic. "Before Elvis," he would later remark, "there was nothing."

CHAPTER FIVE

LEARNING RIGHT FROM WRONG

The Gathering Black Revolution

The year 1957 would prove a decisive one in the rise of Elvis Presley and his rock-'n'-roll music, music that had been stolen from black culture: "thievery in broad daylight," as David Halberstam noted.

Elvis himself had been unconcerned, for whites' attitudes toward blacks had always been exploitive. But if times were changing, making Elvis's black-beat music acceptable in white culture, they were also changing in what blacks would accept from white exploiters and segregationists. President Harry Truman had already desegregated the armed services by executive order in 1948, and in 1954 the Supreme Court had ruled segregation in education unconstitutional, yet almost nothing had been done to integrate schools in the South. How long would blacks wait?

In 1860, Arkansas had been swept into the reactionary camp of American history, joining the Confederacy after the attack on Fort Sumter. Almost a century later, the little state joined the reactionaries once again, this time led by a governor who was not a plantation owner, indeed was the opposite: a child of rural poverty. His name would go down in Arkansas history as the longest-serving governor of the state but in the annals of race history as one of the great American villains: Orval Faubus. It would be Faubus's confrontation with the federal government over the integration of

schools in 1957 that would become the great moral issue of the time—
watched with awe by eleven-year-old Billy Blythe.

The Southern Manifesto

In response to the Supreme Court's *Brown v. Board of Education* ruling of
1954, a "Southern Manifesto" had been drawn up, similar in its way to the
statements drawn up by the southern states before the Civil War. This declaration pledged its signatories—senators and congressmen at their head—
to "use all lawful means to bring about a reversal" of the Supreme Court's
decision and any federal moves—especially "the use of force"—to back it.
Even the liberal internationalist senator from Arkansas William Fulbright
was coerced into signing, to the consternation of his staff—guaranteeing
his reelection to the U.S. Senate, like his colleague Senator John McClellan, but adding fuel to the gathering racist fire in Arkansas.

By the summer of 1957 the situation in Little Rock was becoming "so
explosive," the Arkansas congressman Wilbur Mills, second-ranking Democrat in (and later chairman of) the House Ways and Means Committee,
later claimed, that any sign "that indicated that you weren't on their side in
maintaining segregation" spelled electoral death.

"Their side" meant the racist coalition of White Citizens Councils and
other Arkansas white conservatives. Men such as "Justice Jim" Johnson
were permitted to pursue anti-integration propaganda of the most inflam-
matory kind, arousing fear and racial hostility among whites with impunity. Any prominent citizen who spoke out against such tactics was
targeted and inexorably ruined. Challenged by Jim Johnson in the Democratic Party primary in the summer of 1956, Governor Orval Faubus, citing
his work in traveling to Washington and getting the congressional team's
signatures for the Southern Manifesto, won renomination—but with
80,000 votes cast for his antisegregation opponent, the writing was on the
wall. In a state in which gubernatorial elections were held every two years,
his own renomination might, Faubus recognized, be short-lived.

Faubus had hoped, once reelected, to straddle the civil rights fence and
judge the temper of the times as they unfolded—but the fence itself proved
unstable. In a state where more than 80 percent of whites were resistant to
the notion of desegregation, great moral leadership was required if violence and intimidation were to be avoided. To the consternation of liberals,
however, President Dwight D. Eisenhower refused to set an example, de-

clining to comment publicly on the 1954 Supreme Court decision when it was made and turning silent again three years later, as the issue became volatile in the South. Instead the President traveled north to a golfing holiday in Rhode Island.

If Eisenhower hoped the issue of school desegregation would simply go away, however, he was mistaken. With tragic inevitability, it now caught fire not in Louisiana or Alabama or any of the larger southern states or cities but in diminutive Little Rock, Arkansas.

Integration by Stealth

Why Arkansas? Why Little Rock?

Governor Faubus had not been known to be a bigot during his career up to that time; indeed, as governor of Arkansas since 1954, he had appointed blacks to a number of committees and Democratic Party positions in the state. Desegregation in the state's distinguished law and medical schools had taken place without problem, even in the formerly white high school in the state university town of Fayetteville. How, then, was the tragedy of Little Rock's Central High School allowed to take place in 1957, destroying business confidence and investment in Arkansas for almost a generation and scarring the state's good name forever? "What went wrong?" Professor Anthony Badger—a specialist in post–World War II southern political history—asked in a symposium forty years afterward.

As Thelma Engler, the chair of directors of the Arkansas Council on Human Relations and state president of United Church Women, later related, part of the problem was the place. Integration of the high school in her Fayetteville area, in the northwest corner of the state, had gone seamlessly because, in a predominantly middle-class, reasonably well educated white community where there were virtually no blacks, the admission of a handful of Negro children in 1956 had posed no perceived threat either to local white residents or to Jim Johnson and his fellow firebrands in distant central and eastern Arkansas. Little Rock, however, was different; it was the state capital, a symbol to all citizens in the state, a city where more than 20 percent of the population was black—twice the percentage of Jews in Poland when Hitler undertook his extermination program.

The Little Rock school superintendent, Virgil Blossom, and the Board of Education had chosen to integrate Central High in the summer of 1957—after a failed attempt the previous year—by stealth. They would introduce only a tiny number of black kids to the school, with a minimum of information or publicity, as befitted the fifties. "He did not want one word of this broadcast," Mrs. Engler recalled forty years later. "He wanted to have these kids show up without anybody knowing anything about it. Well, we warned him that that would be nothing but trouble and asked him to investigate the Louisville [Kentucky] integration process, which went smooth as silk, because the Louisville school board held prior meetings with teachers, the public, and what have you, and they all knew what was going on, and they did not feel threatened. But Blossom said, 'No, we cannot do that.' He said if we let it be known before the day that this happens, we'll have trouble. We told him he was doing it exactly backwards."

As an old-fashioned educator, Blossom remained convinced that integration by stealth was the best policy: that once the seventeen (later whittled down by intimidation to nine) black children were at the school and accepted by their peers, Jim Johnson and his White Citizens Council cohorts would be seen as disrupters of education if they attempted to object *post factum*.

But Blossom had, as Mrs. Engler and her Arkansas Council on Human Relations warned him, misread the wiliness of his foes and the fatal ambivalence and ambition of the Arkansas governor, Orval Faubus.

Inviting Disaster

"Integration in Little Rock was to be a one-man show," wrote Faubus's biographer Roy Reed of the crisis. "Teachers and students expressed interest in preparing for the big change; Blossom rebuffed them repeatedly." Similarly, the advice, views, or help of parents was not solicited. "Several civic leaders discussed bringing in a law enforcement expert to help prepare for any disturbances. Blossom told them he needed no outside help. The Parent-Teacher Associations volunteered to help. He told them to stick to PTA programs and stay out of integration." When black and white church ministers asked about making public statements, Blossom told them, "Keep quiet. Do nothing."

This was inviting disaster—and disaster soon obliged. Central High School prepared to open its doors for the new academic year over Labor Day weekend 1957. Even the elite patrician Harry Ashmore, editor of the *Arkansas Gazette,* had misread the governor and had not done his homework on the streets around the school. Daisy Bates, the coordinator of the

National Association for the Advancement of Colored People, had—though even she could not believe Faubus would use armed force to *stop* rather than ensure integration. From the beginning, however, she'd feared that Blossom and the school board were making a critical mistake in choosing Central High School. The tan-colored brick Gothic Revival building, called "one of the most beautiful schools in America" when opened in 1927, served a predominantly working-class school community—and, as Adolf Hitler had demonstrated in Germany and Oswald Mosley in the streets of London, without ethical leadership working-class people respond easily to tabloid journalism and simplistic slogans of hate and fear. Poorer whites were, in certain respects, less educated than many blacks; certainly they felt more threatened. For them integration, even of only nine young students in a school of two thousand, represented the thin edge of a black wedge: a wedge that would push them even further down the social scale until as whites they would be on a par with, or lower than, blacks—while middle-class schools in prosperous areas remained completely segregated.

Thus arose a great irony: the black children whom Blossom had specially selected, after months of vetting, were of aspiring middle-class black background, motivated to learn and succeed, while the parents of many of the white children were of blue-collar background, with little interest in education—and certainly no interest in the notion of black children becoming educated to the point of competing with their children for jobs. Without real dialogue between Blossom and the school board, such parents were easily inflamed into a kind of peasants' revolt.

Governor Faubus was himself from a background of rural poverty. As an adult he had spent his summers earning extra cash picking strawberries—where for the first time in his life he had encountered a black person. He had shown no particular racial bias in his career thereafter; in fact, as aide to liberal governor Sidney McMath in the early fifties he had shown himself well disposed to blacks and concerned to get their vote, in the cases where they were permitted to register. Intelligent and able, an infantry officer during the Battle of the Bulge, Faubus was nevertheless a leader in the mold of many populist dictators, seeking to placate rich backers when he rose as a politician. In the history of the state only one Arkansas governor had ever been elected to serve three terms. Faubus would not only match that record, he would beat it. A man of little principle—it was reckoned he took more than $100,000 in cash per annum from Hot Springs casino rake-offs—Faubus thus decided, to the dismay of his moderate supporters, to play the race card in the fall of 1957: with catastrophic consequences for his state and for the standing of the United States in the world.

An American Passion Play

For Billy Blythe, turning eleven and attending junior high school in Hot Springs, the drama that unfolded forty-five miles away in Little Rock in 1957 proved more extraordinary even than John F. Kennedy's fight the previous year with Estes Kefauver or Elvis Presley's electrifying performances on *The Ed Sullivan Show*. Suddenly, each evening on the network television news was a morality play, in his own state, more vivid and more compelling than any school lesson or even the Sunday school stories of punitive mob violence in biblical times that had led to the crucifixion of Jesus Christ— for now, on black-and-white television, the thirty-year-old news reporter John Chancellor nightly introduced the American passion play, the little state of Arkansas becoming the humanitarian focus not only of the nation but of the entire civilized world.

On the morning of Wednesday, September 4, 1957, chanting, hate-filled white mobs filled the streets of Little Rock to stop any black children who had the temerity to try to attend a white high school. "The anger and ha-tred that had been smoldering just beneath the surface in the South since the enactment of *Brown v. Board of Education* had finally exploded," David Halberstam chronicled in his study of the fifties, "and now because of tele-vision, the whole nation and soon the whole world could watch America at war with itself."

As "Justice Jim" Johnson later confessed, he had organized a Nazi-style campaign of telephone harassment to put relentless pressure on both Vir-gil Blossom, the Little Rock school superintendent, and Orval Faubus, the governor. "We were dedicated to hustling him," Johnson confessed. "Our people were phoning him from all over the state. Orval hid out, but our people in Little Rock got through to him"—giving Mr. Blossom the same message: namely, that blood would flow if the governor permitted or forced integration to take place. "We had Blossom climbing the wall," Johnson congratulated himself in retrospect, taking special pride in having invented a story of a vast caravan of armed men who would descend on the capital to halt integration unless the governor stopped it himself. "There wasn't any caravan. But we made Orval believe it. We said, 'they're lining up. They're coming in droves.' " In truth it was a hoax. "The only weapon we had," Johnson admitted, "was to leave the impression the sky was going to fall."

The impression worked, if only because Faubus was, as governor of Arkansas, convinced it could work to his personal advantage. "Jim," he telephoned Johnson, "I'm going to do something that ought to please you very much, and it may be that you'll want some of your friends to be here, be present, when school opens on Monday, or Tuesday, morning." He was going to use military force to stop the black children from entering the school.

Johnson had his friends there on Tuesday and again on Wednesday. The mob chanted racial insults, threatening to lynch any black children who approached. Without an order from the governor, the fire chief refused to use his hoses to hold back or disperse the white crowd, but there were insufficient police to keep order. On instructions from the governor, therefore, 250 uniformed soldiers of the Arkansas National Guard fixed bayonets—but not to control the mob! Instead they told the black students, when they arrived, that they could not pass. "What are your orders?" someone asked a soldier. "Keep the niggers out!" he responded.

One black girl, fifteen-year-old Elizabeth Eckford, had not received notice of where to assemble and had gone alone to Central High, in bobby socks and a pretty frock with a pinch-waisted white top and a wide, checked gingham skirt that she'd made herself at home. "Here she comes! Here comes one of the niggers!" shouted the crowd. "Lynch her! Lynch her!" they screamed after the soldiers refused to protect her or to let her into the safety of the school. "Go home, you bastard of a black bitch!" people screamed. And as the crowd surged around the terrified girl: "No nigger bitch is going to get into our school!"

A white teacher's wife shielded Eckford and eventually managed to get her onto a bus, but in the late-summer heat of Little Rock, Arkansas, death seemed to be in the air, waiting—death orchestrated as a prank by Jim Johnson and his segregationist brethren.

Recalling the "unforgettable episode" years later, Bill Clinton confessed that it had had "a profound personal effect on me." Watching the drama, he "felt somehow personally connected to those brave boys and girls as they marched through a mob right up to the front steps of Central High." Indeed, thirty years later it would be one of the "proudest moments" of Bill Clinton's life and of his time as governor of Arkansas to greet the same nine students back to Central High and invite them to recount, openly, their terrifying experiences at the hands of his predecessor Governor Faubus.

Whether Faubus foresaw, in the fall of 1957, the level of hate and poisonous racism his decision would inflame is unclear, but the intimidation he caused, the lives he ruined, the suicides he triggered, and the legacy of bitterness he created would redound upon his memory for all time: the most popular and most reelected governor of Arkansas in the state's history, yet, in terms of the suffering, the wanton brutality, and the sheer inhumanity he promoted for his own personal political ends, an unmitigated disaster for Arkansas's reputation. Firebombing, arson, shootings, beatings, window smashing, physical and psychological intimidation, withdrawal of commercial business, harassment, telephone threats, company dismissals, and a campaign of fear invited comparisons with Hitler's Germany—the very Reich Faubus had fought to topple a decade before. As the Little Rock mayor lamented in the opening phase of the crisis, "I am sure a great majority of the people in Little Rock share my deep resentment at the manner in which the Governor has chosen to use this city as a pawn in what clearly is a political design of his own"—a "disgraceful political hoax" that appealed to the basest of human instincts. Even the governor's own father, Sam Faubus, would disavow his son's segregationist politics, claiming that "they are trying to do the same thing in this country old Hitler did for Germany. It will be the Negroes here instead of the Jews," he warned his other children.

Man of the Hour

Faubus's refusal to protect the rights of the nine black children to enter Central High School was, as Bill Clinton later described, "a microcosm of the South": a South inflamed by "the forces of division and hate." Having successfully excluded, by means of his troops, the nine black students for the foreseeable future, Faubus had gone on to bask in national prominence and the enthusiastic, congratulatory company of the Southern Governors Conference; but, as Daisy Bates recorded, he left behind him a state capital in more turmoil than it had ever known in its history. "After the attack on Elizabeth [Eckford], hysteria in all of its madness enveloped the city. Racial feelings were at a fever pitch. Every day new recruits for the hate groups poured into the city from all parts of the State," Bates recalled, "and the effectiveness of the local police in dealing with these groups steadily diminished." Having used armed soldiers to circumvent the Supreme and federal courts, in accordance with the Southern Manifesto, Faubus was, however, the man of the hour—invited to fly up to Rhode Island on September 14 to meet the President of the United States, on his golfing vacation, and discuss the national crisis with him.

There, in the segregated white Newport Country Club, the former infantry major "double-crossed" his former wartime Supreme Commander in Europe, agreeing to use his National Guard forces to facilitate integration in accordance with the Supreme Court's ruling but reneging on his word as soon as he was home. "Just because I said it doesn't make it so" became his most cynical southern quip when taxed about his behavior.

The result, on September 23, 1957, was even more sickening than on September 4. In pursuance to a renewed federal court ruling (Faubus's lawyers having walked out of court in order to avoid hearing it) and still in accordance with the Little Rock Board of Education's official integration plan, the nine black children tried once again to enter Central High, outside which an even more vicious mob was assembling. Instead of summoning the National Guard to protect them, as he had given President Eisenhower to believe he would, Faubus had withdrawn the National Guard completely. Vastly outnumbered by a mob armed with knives, guns, and lead-filled pipes, the city police were wholly unable to keep order, especially when the fire chief again refused to permit his men to use fire hoses to move back the baying, taunting, hate-filled crowds. "Just let those niggers show up! Just let 'em try!" they screamed. "We won't stand for our schools being integrated. If we let 'em in, next thing they'll be marrying our daughters."

For Daisy Bates, whose mother had been violently murdered by three white rapists, the sexual subtext of segregation was revolting: sadism masking profound sexual fear. Michael Dougan, the historian of Arkansas, noted that "Extremists often were rabid Negrophobes, and running throughout their rhetoric was a concern about sexual relations between the races. Hot Springs journalist Curt Copeland claimed integration was a plot to 'put a nigger into your bedroom.' Arch segregationist Jim Johnson, who had lost to Faubus in the 1956 Democratic primary, stated at Hoxie, Arkansas, 'If I send my child to an integrated school, I might see the day when I'll be bouncing a half-nigger on my knee and have him call me "Grandpa." ' "

Eisenhower, dismayed at Faubus's blatant betrayal, had previously shown little interest in public education or in southern integration. He certainly had no desire to bounce a "half-nigger" on his lap any more than "Justice Jim" Johnson did, but the five-star general was infuriated by personal insubordination, just as he had been when having to discipline General George Patton or Field Marshal Bernard Law Montgomery in World War II. Pictures and reports of the violence in Little Rock—where the nine black pupils, having been smuggled into the school through a back entrance, had to be smuggled out again before midday, when the violence reached fever pitch—were being flashed across the world, placing in jeopardy not only the children's lives but the prestige and good standing of the American nation. To Faubus's shock and chagrin, the President therefore decided to retaliate with an iron fist.

Walpurgis Night

On the night of September 23, 1957, as another mob numbering a thousand people assembled outside Central High School chanting, "Two, four, six, eight: we ain't going to integrate!," orders went to the U.S. Army to take charge. While television news programs documented the rising level of white supremacist hate in Little Rock—"I hope they bring out eight dead niggers!" one white leader was heard to shout—the President finally acted. Not only did he federalize Faubus's 10,000-strong National Guard, putting it under his own command as commander in chief of America's armed forces, he now ordered up an integrated battalion of black and white soldiers of the country's most famous airborne division, the 101st Airborne Division, or "Screaming Eagles," which had parachuted into Normandy on D-Day, over Arnhem, and again across the Rhine. It was the first time federal troops had been sent south in anger since the Civil War and Reconstruction.

The arrival of U.S. airborne troops completely altered the terms of the conflict. Faubus had expected federal marshals to appear, thus permitting him to paint a picture of local Arkansas police and state soldiers ranging themselves against plainclothes "outsiders" acting on behalf of a distant attorney general in Washington: the states against the federal government, as in the Civil War—or "War of Northern Aggression" as it was widely known in the South. Eventually, Faubus knew, the rule of federal law would probably have to prevail—but in the meantime he'd be able to delay integration, garner more votes, and in his governor's mansion south of the city center, near where General Douglas MacArthur, World War II commander in chief in the Pacific and later in Korea, had been born, he'd be able to sit pretty, subsidized by cash pickings from Hot Springs and other sources of extraneous gubernatorial income. Instead, he now found himself outmaneuvered as governor, his capital resounding with the boots of armed U.S. airborne troops acting on presidential orders to ensure the safety of nine black children in their desire to be educated at a desegregated public high school, according to a plan drawn up by Little Rock's own Board of Education, in conformity with the U.S. Supreme Court's ruling. As one of the children—fifteen-year-old Minnijean Brown—said later that day, "For the first time in my life, I feel like an American citizen."

Faubus now had but two choices: to fight the President and Supreme Court or, as governor of Arkansas, to extricate himself from a pit of his own making, by accepting federal force majeure and educating the citizens of Arkansas in the need for gradual compliance, given the Supreme Court's rulings—even though it might well temporarily end his governorship the following year, given the level of hate he'd unleashed. His wife, Alta Faubus, besieged by Little Rock voices of reason and anxious for their own safety, begged him to listen and to respond to the need to change: to understand that by supporting the rights of children and putting down white mob violence, he would be able to build a course and constituency for the future, not a rampart to hold back the future.

Having ushered in the forces of extremism, however, Faubus was hoisted by his own petard. He had no intellectual courage; indeed, he suffered from the same feelings of inferiority as the majority of Arkansans toward the wider, better-educated, more sophisticated world. As his biographer Roy Reed noted, he had—unlike his socialist father—no deep inner convictions. "I can probe him and probe him to find what the core is here, and I'm not finding any core," Congressman Brooks Hays—who would soon be voted out of office by segregationists in his district—once complained.

Faubus had become Faustus—and the moderates of Arkansas, such as former governor Sidney McMath and *Arkansas Gazette* editor Harry Ashmore, quickly faded from his radar picture. "The governor's weak spot," Reed chronicled, "was that he seldom reached out for advice from knowledgeable people outside his administration"; he merely waited for people to call him. "Thus it was that the people who got the governor's ear, to their good fortune," Reed related, "were the leaders of the Capital Citizens Council and their far-ranging network."

Having made his pact with evil—with men of powerful, if misguided, conviction, such as the Reverend Wesley Pruden, Amis Guthridge, and Jim Johnson—Governor Faubus could not climb down. He might proclaim to the world that Little Rock was an "occupied" city, like Budapest—which Russian troops had overrun with tanks when putting down the Hungarian uprising the year before—but it was, he knew as a former major in the U.S. Army, a ridiculous analogy, when the entire world could see nine unarmed students simply trying to get an education. More apposite, in Faubus's tormented conscience—a conscience that kept him "tossing and squirming" so much at night that his wife took to sleeping in a different room—was the irony that he had himself once fought the Nazis to overcome arrogant, extreme Aryan racism. Now he was opposing his former comrades in arms: soldiers sent to Arkansas as he had once been sent to Nazi Germany, to ensure that racist evil not be permitted to reign unchecked.

Epiphany on Park Avenue

Years before, Billy Blythe's grandfather in Hope had "tried to explain to me why it was that a young black boy I played with couldn't go to school with me, or why the streets in the black neighborhood were not paved like the streets in the white part of town." Thereafter, neither Virginia nor his stepfather had concerned themselves with the rights or wrongs of civil rights, nor had the preachers at the Baptist church he attended. However, in the fall of 1957 Bill Clinton was exposed to a new moral tutor: the mother of his best friend, David Leopoulos.

Leopoulos's father was Greek and owned a real as well as proverbial Greek restaurant in Hot Springs. His staff was for the most part colored, but it was his wife's views on integration that were considered unusual. Mrs. Leopoulos came from New York and was a deeply religious Episcopalian. Faubus's stand against integration and the poisonous racism he was inflaming were anathema to her. Taking Billy Blythe aside one day, she told him a truth that shamefully few preachers or priests in Arkansas were willing to articulate in public: that segregation and racism were morally wrong and offended the basic tenets of Christianity, whatever sect one belonged to.

Mrs. Leopoulos's words did not fall on stony ground. As David recalled, the "Battle of Little Rock" became the "defining event" of their lives as youngsters: the first occasion when a national moral dilemma, facing the entire American nation, "came home" to them personally and in the most vivid way, challenging their young consciences as no other issue until Vietnam. "I felt then the way I felt the first time we bombed Iraq, later!" Leopoulos reflected, remembering the mob scenes in front of Central High and the pictures of the 101st Airborne's arrival. "I was hearing the stuff on the radio, watching the TV, and looking at the newspapers and seeing those awful things happening—it just scared me to death! I mean, I was petrified! I thought—you know, you're eleven years old, twelve; you don't know if they're gonna come marching into your house, the army." It was, in all senses, a trial of conscience. "You know, the army's coming into Arkansas!

"Now, my dad was an angel; he treated his staff like gold," Leopoulos recalled. "If they got into trouble, he'd help 'em. My mother didn't have a prejudiced bone in her body." Listening to Faubus spouting on the radio and television about Communists and troublemakers and the need to defy federally ordered integration at any price, Leopoulos's mother was a beacon of moral conscience. "She taught us, 'That's all bullshit: you don't want to do that!' And she sat Bill down one time, and she told him how wrong it was! I never knew anything about it—Bill told me this in '92, the day before I left for the inauguration. He'd met with some of the people from Central High—Ernest Green and others—and he was still on a high, being around those guys. And he said, 'Look, I never told you about how much your mom meant to me about this.' He told me how my mom had helped him to see what was right"—a lesson that was crucial to Billy Blythe's growing up, since, although his mother was a tremendous role model as a protofeminist, she was not initially open to ideas of integration. "I don't remember any conversations about segregation or anything around Virginia," Leopoulos recalled.

Leopoulos was right—as Virginia was the first to admit. Billy's stance, as an eleven-year-old, stunned her. "He is the one who taught me about civil rights," Virginia later recalled with amazement, thinking of the time he'd first challenged her views on segregation—as also the time, in junior high school, when Billy had asked her a leading question. Reading the paper on the couch and seeing a graph showing a national league table for educational performance in which Arkansas had once again come in at the bottom, he'd questioned why kids in Arkansas fared so badly. Weren't they born with the same brains as the children at the top of the table? Poor education was one thing, however; segregation, as a system that compounded poor education, was another. The precocious little boy's concern about blacks at such a young age first appalled, then moved her. Bill was, she told Jim Morgan, the co-author of her autobiography, the one who had first taught her about integration. "You're right," she'd responded, but had asked, too, that Bill be "very, very patient" with her, for it was just not the way she'd been brought up.

Billy *was* patient—and the moving picture gallery of hate-filled white faces, coupled with the calm courage and stoicism of the nine black students in the fall of 1957, proved indelible. In years to come, Billy would be called by the writer Toni Morrison "the first black president" of America. He would be perhaps proudest of that epithet, knowing that his epiphany had come in the late summer of 1957, as Governor Faubus made Arkansas a byword for racist obstinacy and his best friend's mother had helped him, at age eleven, to see through the rhetoric of his segregationist relatives, "neighbors and friends." Whatever else would happen in his life, racism would never be a sin laid at his door. Even his cousin Falba was amazed. "He's just different," she would later say, shaking her head. "Billy didn't recognize any differences in the people he met, they were just people to him. That was his magic. Unique."

CHAPTER SIX

DIVORCE

The Darker Side of Life

Though Hot Springs was spared the fate of Little Rock (violence, intimidation, hatred, and all public schools closed for a year), Billy Blythe's home life reflected other tensions threatening the American fifties idyll.

"When I was a small boy, I was taught, as so many of my generation were, that I had to get a good education and work hard so that I could do better than my parents and grandparents had done," Billy later recalled of his upbringing—an upbringing in which the move to the sinful city had reflected the growing affluence of middle-class America. "When I was small my stepfather married my mother they moved to Hot Springs, they both worked, we had a comfortable living," he added gratefully. There were, to prove it, two new(ish) Buick convertibles in the carport, as well as Roger's older, cut-down Henry J. Their friend Van Hampton Lyell arranged for their Coke box to be topped up regularly from his Coca-Cola tankers. It seemed to outsiders an idyllic existence for the nuclear family, and to the insiders, too, it was—as long as Roger Clinton was not at home.

At school or playing with his friends, Billy maintained the same facade—though he never perhaps realized how much the phalanx of mother-and-supersmart-son-and-new-baby served to reinforce Roger's drinking habit, deepening the former car dealer's growing sense of failure. Coming home to a family who tolerated but increasingly despised him for a weakness he could not control was a cross he could not bear—either blotting it out through alcohol, running away, or both. "It really was a painful experience to see someone you love, that you think a lot of, that you care about," Billy later remarked, "just in the grip of a demon. I think most people who are alcoholics, or who are drug addicts, or who have some other compulsion suffer from at least bouts of low self-image, self-esteem. There's some fear, some demon they can't get rid of."

Such compassion—and the recognition that the demon was not so much the drink but the emptiness in Roger Clinton's soul—was a tribute to Billy's sympathy, given the devastating scenes he witnessed at home. "But at times it was really tough," he once confessed, lowering his guard. "I had to learn to live with the darker side of life at a fairly early period."

Avoiding a Spanking

That Billy *did* learn to live with the darker side was psychologically remarkable. Terrorized by his drunken father, his younger brother, Roger Jr., would cling to his mother for protection yet become, in his turn, a spoiled, wayward addict like his father; indeed, he would eventually be imprisoned for drug dealing. By contrast, Billy's response to his stepfather—as his response had been to the tension at the Hervey Road home in Hope when he was an infant, torn between grandmother and mother—was to become brilliantly "good."

As Virginia perceptively recalled, her Billy the Kid was not cut out to be a rebel. As a child he had done "everything in the world to avoid a spanking—and he never needed but one—because that was an insult to his dignity." Lacking a real father, the little boy was, from infancy, determined to placate, not to confront, if possible controlling situations and people so that he would never be defenseless. By doing well at school and by behaving in a sensible, responsible, quasi-perfect way at home, he maximized his domestic scores while giving no license for punishment or humiliation.

Billy wanted to please; he hated to displease. Worst of all, he hated to be disliked. Confrontation, with the prospect of dislike, was anathema to him; instead, he used his high intelligence to avoid it. If he had to get even—if getting even was necessary—he would do so in other ways. His adult life would bear out these basic childhood patterns.

Sadly, this overcompensation would lead to a trait where Billy Blythe, as an adult, would become almost pathologically unable to admit wrongdoing or even his own mistakes, as his chief of staff in the governor's office in Little Rock, Betsey Wright, would recall. Yet in the context of a "tough" domestic situation as a kid, where the neighbors' children were not supposed to know what was going on and he had to remain silent for his entire early life about his experience of domestic alcoholic abuse, such control-freakishness, such desire to please everyone including enemies, such outward perfectionism through overachievement, and such unwillingness to shoulder blame for his own mistakes—indeed, unwillingness to accept *he* could make mistakes rather than others make them—were perhaps the sole psychological methods by which little Billy Blythe could survive and prosper in an abusive world. And, unlike his younger brother, survive he would, in the most spectacular way.

Feminine Instincts

Almost from the start of school, as his friend from kindergarten Joe Purvis noted, Billy Blythe was a "peacemaker"—behavior that continued throughout his school years. Given the escalating experience of violence at his home, violence at school disturbed him. Though he had, in frustration at not getting his way, kicked his Sunbeams teacher at the First Baptist Church in Hope, he quickly found a better way to sublimate his own anger and resentment: by seeking inclusion, not exclusion; acceptance, not rejection; popularity, not unpopularity or notoriety. His size and ungainliness might cause other children to mock him, but his megaintelligence and competitive determination in class made him a formidable intellectual adversary, as they would in later life. Here, he recognized, was the real high ground: great grades and yet a feminine desire to be liked rather than feared.

Years later, in a documentary investigation of masculine and feminine traits associated with hormonal levels in fetal development, researchers would characterize standard male social behavior in childhood as inherently aggressive, selfish, and bedeviled by short attention span, while girls of standard disposition seemed to have a built-in propensity to want to share and be accepted by their peers. In documented cases where exposure to hormones was radically at variance with the norm for the gender of the fetus—as in enhanced estrogen levels for a male fetus or higher-than-normal exposure to testosterone of a female fetus—the result would often be a girlish boy or a tomboyish girl. While such research would never be more than indicative, Billy Blythe certainly fell into the category of feminine boy, even if his tough domestic background stamped him increasingly in a leaderlike mold, irrespective of gender. His stepfather was continually beating up on—and occasionally physically beating up—his mother. Each blow was a rod upon not only Virginia's but Billy's back.

More and more Virginia came to rely upon Billy, not Roger Sr., as the man in the household: a teenage boy with amazingly high intelligence and self-discipline—yet a desire to please. Although he avoided trouble as best he could, Virginia recalled, he was by no means a coward. As Roger Sr. went downhill, Bill became "father, brother, and son" combined, as she put it.

Roger Jr. was devoted to his older, protective brother, whom from infancy he called "Bubba." However well Billy behaved, though, and however much responsibility he took for peace and goodwill in the family, he could not be Virginia's lover—would in fact be condemned to a lifetime's philandering in search of Jocasta-like substitutes. In the meantime he concentrated on his grades, as well as his dignity: the Responsible Male at home and at school.

The Jerk

Such precocious peacemaker leadership and high intellectual ability, along with his affection-seeking side, made Billy a distinctive boy. Indeed, it would be hard to find a close contemporary, whether student, neighbor, or adult, who did not feel, from an early age, that Billy Blythe was going to achieve significant things in his life. Ramble Elementary, which he attended from fourth grade, led to seventh grade in junior high school on 215 Oak, one block off Central Avenue via Orange Street, next to the town's high school, which followed in tenth grade. At every level Billy was in the top handful of students in virtually every subject from math to English. Thanks to the citywide grade school band program under George Gray, he'd begun to play his tenor saxophone in public—and as a member of the Trojan Band, he played numerous concerts in the field house behind the school. During basketball games, especially, he would lead the "wild-'n'-crazy" Trojan Pep Band. Meanwhile, at the town's Masonic Temple at 311 West Grand, he joined the Masons' junior or DeMolay order, where, under the "advisorship" of adults, he learned "leadership skills, civic awareness, responsibility, and character development" through a "variety of self-directed, real world applications and activities"—becoming, over time, a Chevalier, the order's highest distinction.

More significant, despite or because of the fact that he had no sisters, Bill's preference was to mix with girls on the playground rather than with boys. With boys he could give free rein to his responsible leadership style, based on his size, intelligence, and energy; with girls, however, he could indulge his sharing quality. Soon he was a sort of star, especially to younger females—females who all knew him as "Billy." Kathy McClanahan hated to hear them calling to win his attention, asking him to throw the ball to them, so obviously infatuated with him. Schoolgirl crushes were one thing, but his delight in playing this field irritated her to no end. In fact, before reaching her teenage years, Kathy would remember the contempt she felt for him: "Oh, what a jerk."

The "jerk" seemed to lack the athletic ability of most boys and, when thrown a football, would fumble and drop it, without fail. Impressed with the way Kathy caught the ball on their first encounter, Billy was swift to compliment her, however. Her tomboy ego was flattered; a friendship started. She claimed, once she got to know him, that he wasn't really interested in the girls who had crushes on him, or the way, as Maura Aspell recalled, girls played at trying to "make each other jealous" through "boy-girl stuff, fun stuff, kissy face at parties." Kathy became a friend, and found they shared a number of interests, especially music. They'd sit outside and even in eighth or ninth grade, Bill was, she recalled, talking national and international politics, gauging the strategy and motives of the Soviet Union, and the direction of economic development in America. Even the tomboy Kathy found this too much at times—telling him to leave politics to the politicians and statesmen, and just dance to their record player.

Kathy was both right and wrong. Billy was amazingly undiscriminating, liking girls of *all* types—or rather wanting to be *liked by* them. Thus he would deliberately fashion himself, chameleonlike, to fit their expectations, their good books, or rather, their good looks and conscious, even semiconscious, desires. Like a master dater, little Billy Blythe—the boy who had once conformed to being the infant idol of his tough grandma Edie in Hope—was making himself into the Good Companion, even hero, of his contemporaries. As if in some subliminal way, he seemed to read or be able to tease out the personalities of his colleagues—even of their parents. It was as if he'd missed out on a real childhood and was an adult in child's clothing, with an almost messianic agenda: to charm with his intelligence and empathy every individual, male or female, child or adult, dog or cat, into liking or at least respecting him.

The Drama of a Gifted Child

Years later Billy Blythe would confess to a girlfriend that throughout his childhood he had been deceiving himself and others. All children are, however, prisoners in their home-life drama, and in Billy Blythe's case, the domestic tableau was immutable and unavoidable—even when his mother took the momentous, long-threatened step of divorcing Roger Clinton.

In her famous book on narcissism, *The Drama of the Gifted Child,* the psychoanalyst Alice Miller pointed out the penalties of "grandiosity" in talented patients. As gifted children they had often been either abandoned by a parent or parents or been subjected to a mother's molding of her child as a love object—molding undertaken largely to replace the mother's own impotence as a child.

Responding to such control, gifted children would often lose out on their own childhoods, casting themselves in the expected mold of high achievers and, on behalf of the mother, achieving extraordinary results— yet forfeiting the benefits of natural development and individuation in an endless pursuit of motherlike acclaim.

Billy Blythe certainly conformed to Alice Miller's stereotype; indeed, he did so with a charismatic aplomb that was literally bewitching.

One young student who found herself impressed by Billy in ninth and tenth grades was Glenda Cooper, whose father was in the military and who, having traveled the world as an "army brat," could barely credit the myopia, hatred, and violence that the drama of Little Rock Central High had engendered among so many whites in Arkansas.

"My mother was from Hot Springs," she recalled, "my father was from Kentucky. I spent all my early life moving around. After my mother died when I was six, we moved to Little Rock for about four years, then France, then Virginia for two years, and then my father went to Vietnam for the first time and I went back to Hot Springs because I had a grandmother there. And lived there while in the ninth and tenth grades, which was how I originally knew who Bill Clinton was, in junior high." Coming from outside Hot Springs, indeed from outside Arkansas, she felt she had a "perspective that the others didn't because they always lived there!"

Though not in Bill's closest "circle of friends" at that time, Glenda found him "always kind" and "generous," too. What appealed especially to Glenda and made a lasting impression on her own life and friendships was the fact that Hot Springs was spared the southern social exclusivity and racism that so poisoned the rest of the state, indeed much of the South. Arkansas, overall, was bigoted and inward-looking—"a fairly homogeneous population in terms of culture and beliefs and just the general sociology of it—much more rigid socially than anywhere else in the world I'd been, very class-oriented—you know, people were always taking into account 'who are your people?' " In Hot Springs, by contrast, she found a different atmosphere from the rest of the state. "A lot of it has to do with the gambling, the horse racing, and the people who came to town. It was— there were a lot of people you'd find in Hot Springs you wouldn't find in other parts of the state, people from Chicago and New York and other cities. It meant there was a different flavor to Hot Springs—certainly different from that of Little Rock, where I'd lived for a while and which was a much quieter place, culturally speaking, with a population just from Arkansas."

Hot Springs, in other words, was a multicultural oasis in which the tenth-grader felt immediately at home. "I was accepted, as an outsider in a way, but accepted! Comparing that to Little Rock, it was a totally different world! It was a lot more fun!"

Even though Glenda's grandmother didn't permit her to go to nightclubs such as the Vapors, other parents, such as Virginia Clinton, allowed their children to go. "It's a toleration of diversity," Glenda reflected—one that was epitomized in the way Virginia Clinton was accepted as an eccentric, not frowned upon. "She was quite a character. Well, anybody who gets out in a tank top, sunbathing and gardening, in Arkansas has to be! She could do it—she lived her life, I don't think she cared much what other people thought, she wanted to have fun—though she did tell me, later, how much she had to struggle. She was a pioneering sort of woman. A woman who really was devoted to her children—she was very proud of them both. I thought she was very shrewd, very tolerant. She was very startling, when you would see her, you know, with the eyebrows and eyelashes, and the white streak in her hair. She listened. But she was a woman who knew what she wanted and could stand up for herself, which was a very hard role for a woman in Arkansas, back then—even today! She was a key figure in Bill Clinton's life, absolutely! He adored his mother!"

In terms of racism, the year 1957 had "marked us out—well, I don't know that it marked *everybody,* but certainly it marked me and anybody like Bill, who became politically active. It drew the line between the reactionaries and the progressives. It was an event that was still pretty early in your life—but then, together with [the election of] JFK in '60, that was it! People who were interested in the social scene, I suppose, were politicized by '57—and certainly by '60. So that was that!"

It was the dawn of the sixties.

A Passion for Doing Things

John F. Kennedy's victory in the November 1960 election galvanized American liberals—and his inauguration speech, in January 1961, sent a frisson through the entire nation, Democrats and Republicans alike. America's idealism, dormant during the long years of McCarthyism, rising prosperity, and consequent materialism, raised its head again.

Like the excessive nostalgia for antebellum society and reverence for the Confederacy, racism was backward-looking. At Hot Springs Junior High, which was segregated, there was, as in the rest of Arkansas, "a lot of racial talk, you know, the 'N' word—just all those jokes," Glenda recalled. But it was at least nonviolent and easy to reject. "That was one part of the culture that I always despised. I always made myself clear: 'Don't talk to me about that, I don't find those jokes amusing! I'm not going to participate, I don't use that word. That word is so hateful to me I just can't—I don't ever say it.' And Bill was the same way, for his own reasons: that was always the sense that I got. Perhaps from his grandparents in Hope, in the store."

Perhaps. But then again, perhaps Billy Blythe's refusal to go along with southern racism came from a deeper part of his psyche, Glenda reflected. Intelligent, traveled, and sensitive, she came to recognize in Billy's refusal to participate in racist bigotry—even during the worst excesses of Faubus-inspired white supremacism in Arkansas—a more personal agenda than merely a moral lesson learned or experienced; recognized that racism, in its anxious, exclusionary virulence simply ran counter to Billy's *character,* which even in his early teens became surprisingly confident and loving, not hating and insecure. "You know, that's another sort of thing that you can't always attribute to external circumstances. Some people are just more aware, empathetic, or sympathetic—it's just who you are! It's genuine, and people can sense that," she remarked of Billy.

For Glenda, the amazing thing about Bill Clinton was that he could combine such empathy or compassion for people less advantaged than himself with so much personal poise, even in ninth and tenth grades. "I was aware of his charm, his ability to be involved in student politics, his self-assurance, his confidence. I think he was a student representative in the tenth grade. I do remember his coming up, shaking my hand, 'I'm Bill Clinton, I'm running for this and that.' " Yet it was the wholeness, the certainty that he had so much to share with people of his own age, that stunned her. "He had such a presence! In the tenth grade most people are just full of insecurities and anxieties, you know, 'Am I good enough to face the world?' That sort of thing. He didn't seem to suffer from that. He just had a passion for doing these things, for volunteering."

False Self

Billy Blythe's self-confidence was extraordinary for a boy of his age, but did it emanate from a "false self," as psychologist Alice Miller classified the construct? Was it, in its goody-goodness, "a substitute for their own missing structures," as Miller put it: a false self in which "real" emotions, such as hate, jealousy, and despair, were not permissible? Even had he been able to cast off his "false self," though, would it have helped? "I was raised in that sort of culture where you put on a happy face," he would later explain, "and you didn't reveal your pain and agony. Those were not things you shared with people."

Billy Blythe, after all, had known no real father and in infancy had been abandoned by his mother when she had gone to New Orleans without him; had necessarily become dependent on his proxy mother, or grandmother, whose iron determination to mold him—whether in his eating habits or in learning his letters and numbers—had reached the point of family meltdown when Edie had threatened to go to court rather than surrender him to his returning mother and stepfather-to-be.

Finding a way to placate his rejected grandmother and his new but violent stepfather, as well as his feisty, hardworking, but often absent mother, Billy had drawn on the mantle of churchy goodness, charm, precocious sociability, and a striving for excellence at school. Once assumed, the mantle of goodness, he found, became him, inspiring widespread approval; indeed, it became a second skin rather than apparel, since he could never take it off again: never lower his guard, cry like other children, rail against his fate, or run away—or even tell his friends what was going on. By the age of sixteen he was having to act forty, he later reflected. "I never felt like I got to complete my childhood."

The effort was certainly taxing, if effective. Almost to a man or woman, all his contemporaries would later remark on how steadfastly Billy concealed his vulnerable self, his abused self. Never, ever did he speak a word of condemnation or reveal anything of his stepfather's violence or alcoholism to anyone; instead, he internalized the experience completely. The most he would admit later was that there had been "a lot of adversity in our life when I was growing up"—adversity he felt his mother had "handled real well" and that "gave me a high pain threshold, which, I think, is a very important thing to have in public life. You have to be able to take a lot of criticism—suffer defeats and get up tomorrow and fight again. And I think that my childhood had a lot to do with that."

It did—though it produced a stoicism that ensured survival more than psychological maturation or self-understanding.

Meanwhile, however, Billy Blythe did excellently at school; indeed, he seemed a remarkably able, responsible, polite, and well-balanced kid, more and more liked and admired by his school contemporaries and his teachers. In the Park Place Baptist Church at 721 Park Avenue he had been ceremonially baptized by being immersed in water at age ten, on October 17, 1956. In 1957, aged only eleven, he had begged a Sunday school teacher to take him to Little Rock to hear the Reverend Billy Graham preach—and had sent him a contribution from his allowance. He was a Hot Springs Key Club member, he was a DeMolay highflier. "I spent most of my life being a boy wonder," he later reflected bitterly, "and it was much overrated"—for behind that facade his biggest domestic trial had already, at age thirteen, begun.

The Beginning of the End

Roger Clinton, Sr.'s self-destruction was proving unstoppable. At a dance he had become "violent," Virginia recalled; at home he was no better; indeed, he had "actually beaten me on a couple of different nights, and Bill had to call my lawyer, Bill Mitchell, who summoned the police."

A thirteen-year-old having to call a lawyer and bring in the police to protect his mother? By March 1959, Virginia had felt she could stand it no longer and separated from him and filed for a divorce—but then returned to Park Avenue and withdrew the application.

Violence, separation, reconciliation? Dimly Virginia could see, in retrospect, what all this might be costing her children. She was, she later maintained, "ashamed" of what she herself had tolerated—although glad that her own father, Eldridge, never knew how bad it was. But the climax was coming. The year 1960, she later reflected, "was the beginning of the end for Roger and me."

Oedipus Rex

Eldridge Cassidy had been a weak man but not blind, and Virginia had been fooling herself if she thought she could hide such marital abuse from her own family.

One night in 1960, Roger's reign of terror came to a head. Perched on the steep hillside above Park Avenue, the two-story mock-Tudor house looked more imposing from a distance than it really was. Its lower half was faced in fieldstone, above which was simple white stucco intersected by half-timbering painted an unusual, bright seafoam green. Walking or driving up the steep driveway, the Clintons, like most visitors, would enter by the side, via the carport and kitchen door. A bay area on the south side accommodated an eating area. All the living quarters were on the first floor (the second floor, under the eaves, was used only as a games and party area). The kitchen led into the dining room. Beyond that was Bill's bedroom, located opposite the master bedroom, where Virginia had her boudoir, every bit of makeup and every perfume bottle as she had had on South Hervey Street in Hope while living with her parents: a bedroom-cum-actress's dressing room, with lights around her dressing table mirror, her rows of eyeliners, lipsticks, and other cosmetics in neat order. Her radio blared out the popular songs she loved and that entertained her for the thirty minutes it took to apply her war paint for work or the Vapors.

Coming home that particular night, Roger had decided he was not going to be ignored or treated as a second-class citizen any longer. He had been drinking heavily and was now going to teach his errant wife a lesson—in no uncertain way. He entered the house bawling at the top of his voice, ignoring the children. Roger Jr. began screaming in terror as his father moved toward his mother in the kitchen, forcing her backward into the bedroom, where he locked the door.

The scene befitted a Tennessee Williams script. This time, Roger Clinton would *make* his wife listen. His dander was up: he would beat her, make her submit, draw blood, force her to acknowledge who was boss. "I kept moving, kept dodging him," Virginia recounted, "kept pushing chairs in his way." Immediately opposite their bedroom, she recalled, was "poor Bill," who, after listening to the shouts and screams, could tolerate such tyranny no more. Roger's abuse had been going on for years—years of pretending to the neighbors and the world that everything was fine domestically. It was not. His little brother was screaming with fear, while behind the marital door, "what sounded like bloody murder was taking place."

Murder, rape—or just the mating game? It was an Oedipal confrontation of almost classical dimensions. "I just broke down the door of their room," as Bill later confided.

Exhausted by his own screams of abuse and accusation, Roger had temporarily paused, drunk, and was slumped in a chair by the game table at the foot of the bed.

Bill told his stepfather to get up.

"And of course Roger couldn't," Virginia recalled. "He mumbled and snarled and slurred and stumbled, but his legs wouldn't lift him."

At thirteen, Billy was already an inch taller than his stepfather. Though opposed to violence, he could no longer watch while Roger, a brainless, drunk buffoon, intimidated the family and continued to abuse his mother.

" 'You must stand up to hear what I have to say to you,' Bill told him. 'Daddy, I want you on your feet.' "

Roger looked stunned. "If you can't stand up, I'll help you." Bill lifted under his arms and held him there while he looked him in the eyes. "Hear me," he said to Roger. "Never . . . ever . . . touch my mother again."

Touch? Make love to? Hit? Beat?

Drink, violence, and carnality were, in the South, intertwined, and it would have needed a trained psychologist to disentangle them. How seriously Roger took the threat in his alcoholic stupor is uncertain, since it was not the last time the scene would be staged. On this occasion, however, Virginia called the police, and once again Roger—who had stripped to his shorts to have sex with her—was hauled off to the police station in his underwear and made to stay the night there.

It was a night to remember. Yet of all the haunting images, Virginia later confessed, it was not Bill's epiphany that most affected her. It was the sight of her little four-year-old, Roger Jr., going to the backyard for a stick, almost as large as himself, with which to defend his mother. For Virginia, that was the turning point. *I may be married,* I thought, *but I'm a single mother nevertheless. And this is no way to bring up my children.*

Sanctuary for a Bruised Heart

How Billy Blythe managed to keep the saga of domestic violence from his friends was to them a cause for admiration later on. Bill's high school guidance counselor, Miss Irons, acknowledged later that there were family issues Bill kept completely to himself, and which she knew nothing about—a sign of character in a boy who had "courage, ambition and determination" as she would write in his *Old Gold Yearbook*. Not even Carolyn Yeldell, next door, was privy to Bill's domestic secrets. "Billy never said a single thing to any of us about his father's drinking or the violence that he witnessed. Nothing. Billy went out of his way to lead us to believe that his life was pretty much picture-perfect. That was his reputation in the community, after all."

Psychologists, even Billy himself, were less sure about this later, during the grim business of family addiction therapy—though at the time Billy saw it as a matter of survival. Looking back, though, he wished he'd been able to share more of the burden and the suffering, for it was the necessity to become, at thirteen, Oedipus Rex rather than Oedipus Filius Regis that really ended all vestiges of childhood. "I was raised in a time and a culture where I was never supposed to talk about myself or my own problems—my own pain or my own ambivalence," he later confided. "I didn't have anybody I could talk to about it." Later he felt this repression—or suppression—to have been a mistake, though a typical one in "an alcoholic family," as he put it. "Like most families of alcoholics, you do things by not confronting problems early"—as a result of which "you wind up making things worse. I think that the house in which we grew up, because there was violence and trouble, and because my mother just put the best face on it she could—in later years a lot of the stuff was dealt with by silence."

The positive result of such suppression would be superachievement. The negative, though, would be a deep well of blocked-off, repressed anger and a disturbing level of resentment—resentment in which Billy constantly saw himself as a victim, yet one who could not bring himself to blame his stepfather.

The fact was, breaking into his parents' bedroom and confronting Roger Clinton, his stepfather, had not truly led to psychological freedom. Though that night would be a defining moment in Virginia's own marital story, it did not seem so to Billy later—at least in terms of his own journey. "That was a dramatic thing. It made me know I could do it if I had to," he later confessed with great candor. "But it made me more conflict-averse. It's really a painful thing, you know, to threaten to beat up your stepfather."

It was. The truth was, as Billy knew all too well, that the rhythms of alcoholic family life were not linear or simple; they were—as Garry Wills once brilliantly described them—"reconciliations, relapses, pretences of reform and urgent maintenance of façade for the outside world." For every step forward, his mother and stepfather would take one, even two, steps back, which left Billy holding the bag, one that became increasingly heavy. It was "intermittent hell that we all put up with," he later confided. "I guess I suppressed a lot of that stuff." He never protested, never complained, never shared, never even told his pastor—though he did pray and seek weekly guidance and spiritual, as well as musical, sustenance in the worship of God. "I came to see my church as a place not for saints but for sinners, for people who know they're weak," people who do "not pretend to be strong," he later revealed his symbiotic relationship to the Almighty and the sanctuary that church had offered his bruised heart.

Physical Abuse

Why would his mother not cut her tie to Roger Clinton? Why in heaven's name did she always go back, take Roger Sr. back, endure repeated pregnancies and repeated miscarriages by him, on top of her one fully formed (and beloved) child by him? Why did she go on *forgiving* him?

God, presumably, did so (even though neither Roger nor Virginia attended church), but why, Billy Blythe wondered at thirteen, did his adored mother, as an ordinary human being, have to do so? Virginia was *not* God; she was simply his mother, whom he loved not as a saint but as the embodiment of life—and of absence, from the beginning.

He blamed himself: he had not loved her enough to cause her to stay at home; ergo, he was unlovable. On the other hand, she *had* taken him with her when she remarried, even though—like his beloved grandmother—she had of necessity to go out to work. But why choose Roger Clinton? Why *marry* such a jerk: a clown, a failing poseur? Love was a mystery. Did Virginia love Roger Sr. more than she loved him, Billy Blythe, if she was willing to continue in a marriage that was clearly abusive, destructive, and largely joyless? Did her little boy, Roger Jr., represent some invisible psychological chain to Roger Sr.? Was Billy burying, in his own love of his brother Roger and his tremendous desire to protect and defend the little boy, almost as a father, his own uncertainty, his own fear of taking second—even third—place in his mother's affections? Virginia was certainly immensely proud of her "Bill" and his great achievements, *but was pride love?* And if she still loved Roger Sr. despite all his failings, why the continual fireworks between them? Was real love fireworks? Or was there a sexual component he still didn't, as an innocent, prepubescent teenager, really understand?

In truth the fights were not continual. Often Roger would be sober, indeed almost placid, certainly inoffensive. Sometimes he could even be funny. "Gawd dang it!" was his favorite expression. Another that always made Billy laugh was "You can't tell which way a frog'll jump until you punch him"—a witticism that seemed to typify the hillbilly dueling mentality of Arkansas. Inevitably, however, these periods of calm would preface volcanic eruptions. "I grew up," Billy later reflected, "in an environment in which either nothing happened or all hell broke loose." There was "either repression or explosion," not the normal "day-to-day workings of life"—a pattern that left him at a loss to know what represented what, particularly after he had, as it were, revealed his hand to his stepfather: that he hated him for abusing, touching, having sex with his mother and would if necessary fight him—at least, when Roger was drunk and less than capable of fisticuffs. As a result their nondrunken relationship could never be quite the same thereafter—and it wasn't. The boy was now having to be a man: a man facing a once-man, now a child: "his mother's baby," as Virginia mocked her abusive husband, "Raymond's little brother."

Shamed and ashamed, Roger did attempt to reform, aware that he was pushing at the boundary of marriage and might end up out in the cold. He had, on his side, southern patriarchy, the license as a man to be domestically violent. But divorce was becoming more common, even in the South. He was, after all, himself divorced from his first wife, whom he had also physically abused. Without self-respect or the lineaments of real character, however, Roger Clinton was unable, for all his attempts at reform, to grow up. His bouts of drunkenness merely increased in frequency. "For the last four or five years," fifteen-year-old Billy would give testimony for his mother's divorce filing, "the physical abuse, nagging, and drinking has become much worse. On one occasion in the last month I again had to call my mother's attorney because of the defendant's conduct causing physical abuse to my mother, and the police again had to be summoned to the house." With a mixture of pain and childlike horror he added, "The last occasion on which I went to my mother's aid, when he [Roger Clinton] was abusing my mother, he threatened to mash my face in if I took her part."

The fact was, the effect of so much domestic violence, threats, intimidation, and emotional chaos in the inner sanctum of his family would be reflected in Billy's later professional life: as if, alongside his own manic overachievement, he *needed* such repeated moments of disorder, indeed dysfunction, to feel at home, to know where his traditional role lay: in rescuing his family from chaos.

Meanwhile, by the spring of 1962, as on the national scene President Kennedy cut off all trade with Cuba and Senator Barry Goldwater began to emerge as the Republican answer to JFK's improving poll numbers, Virginia made up her mind yet again. Bill was having to "protect me when he was too young to have to," she later lamented. She could "stand it no longer," as she put it in her petition for divorce. Roger did not wish her to go out on her own, but he did not wish to go out with her himself, either, in effect keeping her a prisoner in their own home, subject to endless disputation and quarreling, leading inexorably to physical abuse, whether she ignored him or stood up to him: "bodily harm" inflicted not only on her but on Roger Jr., together with threats to "mash" Bill if he interfered. "I am afraid of him when he is drinking because of the physical abuse that I have received at his hands in the past," Virginia stated in her deposition. She wanted out.

Divorce

On April 9, 1962, Virginia announced her decision to Roger, who had "sat down warily" in the kitchen to hear what she had to say.

Ever the male chauvinist, Roger Clinton refused to accept Virginia's decision. She was, after all, only a damned woman. Virginia, however, was past caring. The following day she packed for herself and her two boys, and they left the Park Avenue house.

The fugitives went to a motel owned by some friends—the Capri on Central Avenue—and over the following three weeks Virginia househunted. Eventually she found a new house: a rabbit hutch of a home at the end of a new street of suburban, one-story houses on Scully Street, not far from her beloved Oaklawn racetrack. She had never had "taste" in any cultivated middle-class sense of the word, and the house and its furnishings duly reflected this: "a wonderful new brick ranch-style house," she boasted, with glitzy bathrooms, and all the "latest amenities. They were show houses, essentially. I bought the very first Gold Medallion house in Hot Springs," she proudly related, "bought it all by myself, with the money I had been rat-holing out of my paycheck."

This was the crunch, in all senses. The house might be modern suburban mediocrity par excellence, set in a low-lying, flat Hot Springs neighborhood of equally charmless mediocrity—but this was to see home as architecture and architecture at its least architectural. For Virginia it was home, pure and simple: *her* home at last.

It was also the end of an era, and the beginning of a new one. A lone American astronaut, John Glenn, had orbited the earth three times in *Friendship 7,* a Mercury spacecraft launched into the stratosphere from Cape Canaveral, in Florida, to rival Russia's sputniks, and the prelude to a race to the moon. President John F. Kennedy, thirteen months in office, had proudly congratulated Glenn, as had Congress and the people of New York in a ticker-tape parade unknown since the end of World War II. As Kennedy—the first president to be born in the twentieth century—had promised in his memorable inauguration speech the year before, scripted by Theodore Sorenson, a high-minded Nebraskan, the torch was passing to a new generation of Americans whose common enemies were "tyranny, poverty, disease and war."

For Virginia, at last, divorce offered liberation without poverty. The days of Roger Clinton's tyranny and alcoholism, as well as domestic abuse and strife, seemed finally over; the New Virginia could start afresh, with her two wonderful boys.

The one would in time become President of the United States; the other, a convicted drug dealer.

CHAPTER SEVEN

THE SIXTIES

A Change of Name

Billy Blythe IV could have become a doctor—joining the medical fraternity of his adored mother—a musician, an educator, a diplomat, a writer, or a corporate lawyer. In none of these areas would his sexual (mis)behavior have presented a problem in terms of his efficiency or professional success. But fatefully, in the early sixties young Bill Clinton chose, for reasons we shall now examine, the profession of politics: the one area of American life where traditional Victorian attitudes would *not* be successfully challenged and modernized. Instead of going down in history for his political achievements, he would go down—in every sense of that verb—for two simple, scandalous words: oral sex.

None of this, of course, could have been foreseen, as Virginia Clinton moved into her new home at 213 Scully Street, near Greenwood Cemetery, between Summer and Seventh, off Wheatley, on the other side of Hot Springs, in 1962. Her divorce had been finalized on May 15. With custody of her two boys, child support of $50 per month toward Roger Jr.'s upbringing, her favorite crystal chandelier, and her beloved 1960 Buick Le Sabre, Virginia was determined now to live an independent, modern life as a single mother again, but in her very own home.

To mark this New Family scenario, Billy—without telling his mother—

now went, the next month, to see the chancery judge at the Garland County Court with a view to changing his name.

Virginia, when the judge telephoned to say he had her underage son in his office, intent on petitioning to alter his surname, was flabbergasted—for the name Billy was proposing to take was that of the very man Virginia had just divorced!

I Was the Father

Billy Blythe could never quite explain his motives, even to himself.

What did the choice of name signify? And why had he not first informed his mother or discussed such an important matter with her? Sometimes in after years he would say, "I decided it was something I ought to do. I thought it would be a gesture of solidarity. And I thought it would be good for my brother, who was coming up." Other times he'd just shrug and dismiss the episode: "The name doesn't matter, it's the man."

Psychologically the significance seems all too clear, however. As he later said with pride, thanks to Roger Sr.'s departure, "I was the father." As William Jefferson Clinton—his new name legally recorded by the judge at Garland County Court once his mother gave her reluctant permission over the telephone—he would henceforth supplant his awful stepfather. He, not Roger Clinton, would be the man of the family: father to Roger Jr. and quasi husband to Jocasta, his mother. "I never regret changing my name," he'd say with pride.

However, if the fifteen-year-old hoped thereby to supplant his stepfather in his mother's eyes, his strategy didn't work. Oedipus did not become Rex.

Making a Mistake

Virginia inevitably caved in to Roger Clinton's emotional blackmail. Her firstborn had all the right credentials for male mastership of the household on Scully Street, but he could make no headway against Virginia's big heart or a relationship that went back to before he was born, when her father had first introduced her to "The Dude" from Hot Springs.

Virginia felt *compassion* for Roger—that was the trouble. Sitting in his car across Scully Street and begging Roger Jr. to fetch his mom, Roger Sr. looked a wreck. He'd lost thirty-five pounds and was, he claimed, bent on beating his addiction now, not her. He'd even started going to church, he said.

Whether Virginia truly believed Roger Sr.'s promises of reform is questionable—she was gullible, but not stupid—yet she could not, as a trained and dedicated nurse and a wife to Roger since 1950, take responsibility for his further slide toward ruin. He would simply not, she knew, be able to look after himself. Moreover, though her friends told her she was mad to remarry Roger, she went ahead. "Mother, you're making a big mistake," Bill warned, but Virginia's heart was too big. In August 1962 she remarried Roger, to Bill's chagrin and despite his protest that it would never work. It didn't—but had she not taken Roger back, he would have petered out, like one of his ailing cars. As it was, even with her patient nursing, within five years Roger would be dead.

"This Is Wrong!"

For William Jefferson Clinton, the return of the king was a tragedy. As he did with other disappointments, however, Bill accepted his mother's decision; indeed, in some ways it served to redouble his determination and efforts to succeed in his *own* career. Education would, he determined, become "the instrument of my liberation."

What would that liberation be, however, as the big, mop-haired youth turned sixteen on August 19, 1962?

Paul Root, Bill's advanced-section world history teacher at Hot Springs High School in 1962, recalled how "in those days we had ability grouping. We moved kids according to their tests. Some of my classes would be thirty to thirty-five people, whoever wanted to be there. But in Clinton's class there were eighteen people who were all headed for college and professional skills of some kind, so it was an easy class to deal with, to teach, they were all interested and worked hard. And I just found him to be an excellent student— he was always pleasant, but always prepared. And I've told this as a joke, it's really not true, but it shows how in essence it was. I've told that I flunked thirteen of those eighteen students—trying to make out a test he, Bill Clinton, couldn't make a hundred on!

"In fact," Root was quick to point out, "I didn't flunk them, they were all good students. But you know, a *bad* grade for Bill would be *ninety-eight!*

"So he was a top student. He just never forgot anything you said. And he always did his reading, and he was interested!"

A committed Baptist with a strong interest in choral church music, Root found himself so uncomfortable in the "sin city" of Hot Springs that he actually left the town after teaching Bill Clinton. "It's not like anything in Arkansas!" he explained. "When we were there, the population of Hot Springs was thirty-four thousand. Downtown there was wide-open gambling, there were nightspots where top entertainers would come in, and it was a little-bitty Las Vegas, of a sort, at that time. I was there three years, from '59 to '62. And one of the reasons my wife and I decided to go back to school in Fayetteville was: we weren't sure we wanted to raise our kids in Hot Springs! Some of the nicest, brightest kids I had in class, their parents were *gamblers,* you know—made a livin' *gamblin'!* Well, I'm just raised a Baptist, I'm just like other Baptists, you know: *'This is wrong!'*

"Those kids were good," Root was careful to emphasize of Bill Clinton and his classmates, "and they were strong, and they were nice. But they didn't see what was wrong was what their fathers were doing!"

Sweet Sixteen

While Paul Root decided to take his postgraduate degree in the less wicked city of Fayetteville, the main campus town of the University of Arkansas set in the picturesque Ozark Mountains in the northwest of the state, Bill Clinton seemed to have no intention of attending university in his home state.

In retrospect, Root saw that he'd made a mistake: that the things in Hot Springs that had concerned him, as a Southern Baptist raised in a small Arkansas community near Little Rock, were perhaps the very things that had opened Bill Clinton's mind to a wider world. "I don't think there's any doubt about that!" Root later remarked—recalling how, in terms of gambling and suchlike, Bill "floated above things that bothered me in Hot Springs. I think he had an open mind as early as fifteen or sixteen—and mine only started to come when I was in my thirties!"

In the meantime Bill shone at English, Latin, and math, as well as music. At six feet, two inches, he now towered above most of his classmates, especially the girls. Yet it was not simply his brains or his size that mattered in the minds of those who began to predict a great future for the prodigy so much as the easy way in which he meshed with people of every age and background, like a chameleon. It was not that he thereby surrendered his developing personality, rather that he was willing to apply an abnormally high intellect to the most ordinary of tasks and connect with the most ordinary of people. He looked after his six-year-old brother, Roger, for example, with an affectionate, relaxed sibling responsibility that surprised his contemporaries; lived on peanut butter and banana sandwiches that he made himself with relish (and speed); played and sang Elvis songs—indeed, creamed and brushed his hair and wore long sideburns to imitate Elvis. At sixteen he had obtained a driver's license and drove his neighbor, the Baptist pastor's daughter Caroline, to school in one of the Clinton convertibles. Yet he seemed to have no conceit, no snobbery, and none of the ethical righteousness that so often crippled the South by its bigotry, internecine malice, and narrow-mindedness. He liked people and loved company. Except when studying on his own late at night, he seemed to shun solitude, preferring to move in a crowd rather than be alone.

Such gregarious sociability ensured Bill, it was true, a larger audience among whom to shine, yet at a deeper level it betokened more: a flight from self. Even his closest friends sometimes found this odd: this deep-seated need to be accepted, liked, and kept company by people of all ages. At times he seemed almost manic in this regard. One of his contemporaries would later remark that Bill was "disgustingly responsible, always trying to impress his elders." When his mother took him to the racetrack, he left after one race, saying to her, "That was the dumbest thing I ever did"— whether from exasperation at the odds against winning or disgust at an activity so ritually denounced in his church services, Virginia was unclear.

Older folk, however, were almost invariably impressed by Bill's moral earnestness, his precocious wisdom, his wide reading for a teenager, and his retentive, almost photographic memory. He seemed able to turn his hand to almost anything except sports. Yet even there, despite his intelligence and personal ungainliness, he neither felt nor affected disdain for jocks but loved to join a basketball game or touch football with others. For a teenager he seemed remarkably at ease with himself; yet there was also a part of him, as his bosom pal David Leopoulos recalled, that was sometimes not present, not there—moments when his mind seemed to have wandered into some distant land or thought. "Bill has this thing," Leopoulos noted, "from the time we were eight years old to today: if we're together, and we're watching TV or something, he just sort of checks out. He's there, but his mind is somewhere else. I remember that quite a bit from when we were little kids. I would imagine he was playing back some of the awful things that were going on—but he never said a word!"

When Leopoulos learned, much later, what actually had been going on in the Clinton household, he was "devastated. I wrote him a letter 'cause he was on the campaign trail—and I said, 'Man, I wish I could have shared it with you!' "

Kay McClanahan, Kathy's sister, meanwhile recalled with amazement how, when Bill would come over to visit with her family at their lakeside house, the younger McClanahans water-skied, but Bill seemed happier talking politics with the older folks. Kathy, as a tomboy, assumed it was because Bill was so unathletic—indeed he'd say to his neighbor Carolyn, "a duck can waddle. I don't want to waddle." But Kay McClanahan recognized it was not simply an evasion of sports at which he did not excel that made him gravitate indoors or to the adult gatherings on the porch. He possessed a remarkable ability to get others to talk, by asking questions that brought people into a conversation, not that left them out—indeed Kay's parents were unusually smitten, forseeing a considerable future for the boy, many of whose school colleagues—like Warren Maus, a classmate—considered him bright, "but certainly not a person I felt bound for greatness."

Irritated, "I used to tease him," Kathy McClanahan recalled, about being "a politician in the womb," for he had an "overly pleasant" manner, wanting to be liked not just by his intimate friends but by everyone, especially adults. "Parents loved him," Kathy recalled, "and he was so complimentary. If your mother had shorts on that she'd worn for forty years, he'd say, 'Oh, I love your outfit' " something that made the tomboy in Kathy want to "slap him and say, 'Give it a rest.' "

But Bill Clinton couldn't. It was like an addiction: a manic anxiety to please everybody, to be in teachers' good books, parents' good books, adults' good books, his male friends' good books, his girlfriends' good books. Such an addiction could be irritating. Finally one friend screamed at Bill in despair, "Don't you ever do anything wrong? You're a teenager . . . you're supposed to do things wrong!"

"Daddy's Killing Dado!"

As time went by, Bill Clinton would do wrong: megawrong. In the meantime, however, he seemed to work night and day as a teenager to do right—against a home background that, after Roger Sr.'s return, occasionally veered close to homicide. There was, for example, the day his brother came running to fetch him from the neighbor's house, screaming "Bubba!

Bubba! Daddy's killing Dado!" He rushed home to find his stepfather in the laundry room, holding down his mother with a pair of scissors at her throat. "He bent me backwards over the washing machine, and he was practically lying on top of me," Virginia recalled.

Pulling little Roger behind him with one hand and his mother with the other, Bill faced down his stepfather, telling him he'd have to kill him first. Roger put down the scissors and unbuckled his belt to administer "southern punishment." Ignoring him, Bill shepherded his mother and brother into the living room, then turned back to confront Roger in the kitchen. "We could hear them shouting," Virginia recalled, but Bill was too big to be knocked down, too clever to intimidate, and too determined to give way. Before long she heard the door slam, and Roger vanished.

Somehow, in order to survive, Bill had to separate the strands of his life and dissociate himself from those that were too threatening or painful—"blocking out," as he himself termed it. That dissociation, that pulling away from an insistent, alcoholic scenario that—since his mother's decision to remarry Roger—Bill could clearly never change, then led to a further dissociation, whereby Bill increasingly lived in the moment, wholeheartedly and with all the brilliance of a talented, attractive, energetic teenager, yet at the same time not quite there, as his friend David Leopoulos noted.

Where the nonthere place was, only Bill knew: a heart of darkness he could not or would not share with anyone. He thus seemed to be, beyond his enthusiasms and engagement with people, always plotting, at a deeper level, his getaway, his ascension, so to speak: to a place of power where he would not have to—unless he chose to—defer to his alcoholic stepfather, to the bigotry of people of low intelligence and limited compassion, even to his adored mother, who had chosen to take back Roger Sr. in pity rather than listen to her son's warning that she was making a terrible mistake. Bill was, in other words, at once intimately bound up in his community—his home, his friends, his school, his church, his many extracurricular activities—yet also consumed with ambition to move on: to escape.

The launch pad for that escape would, as it turned out, be the American Legion's annual Boys State program.

Boys State

Joe Purvis, who hooked up with Bill at Camp Robinson in North Little Rock in the summer of 1963, remembered the moment well. Age sixteen,

Bill Clinton had been junior class president at Hot Springs High and had subsequently put his name forward for the annual training week in politics and government. "The Boys State is a program where the leaders or the people at various high schools will pick a number of boys who are finishing their junior year. You get sponsors, and certain boys are selected for leadership qualities, and they go to this summer school—it's essentially an extension of, an acted-out, civics class. You spend a week learning about the workings of government. You are divided into cities and counties and states. People run for office. You carry out elections. It's designed to foster knowledge about the American political system, the American governmental system, really, and get you involved in government. So that, theoretically, you'll have men that will know about government and be very involved in the system.

"When we were going there, it took place at Camp Robinson, which is a military installation—it was a World War II military army camp—and we used the barracks out there and would line up and march to three meals a day in a chow house and have communal showers and sleep in open barracks that you lived in for a week."

Bill Clinton was "podgy. He was podgy at Boys State," Purvis—who himself became seriously heavy in later years—recalled. But Bill was not content with Boys State: "He was running for Boys *Nation.*" Election to Boys Nation, held at the end of the session at Camp Robinson, would take the two winners to Washington, D.C., to participate in a week of mock political meetings, sightseeing, meetings with real senators—and a visit to the White House to meet the President of the United States!

Purvis, having voted for his Hope friend Mack McLarty for boy governor, promised Bill his vote for boy senator—an irony, given that Bill would later become governor of Arkansas, not a U.S. senator. But, as Purvis recognized in retrospect, Bill Clinton's decision to compete for senatorial rather than gubernatorial election was both tactical and strategic. He had no athletic prowess that would make him popular enough to win the gubernatorial top spot at the very start of the summer camp, for he would have to compete with the golden boy and top-flight athlete from Hope, Mack McLarty, whom he'd known since kindergarten days and who came from patrician white stock. McLarty was popular among the delegates and mixed wealth with ease. Strategically, moreover, Bill had his eyes set on senatorial election, which would take him to Washington, the nation's capital, for the first time in his life.

By dint of careful preparation and energetic, indeed tireless, lobbying—

"Hi, my name's Bill Clinton, I'm running for Boys Nation, I'd sure appreciate your vote"—Bill won his first significant election outside school at the end of the week. Mack McLarty, who had meanwhile won election as Boys State governor, was photographed standing proudly alongside the archsegregationist, Governor Orval Faubus, in the Boys State review parade, in an army jeep. Although it made the state's newspapers, this was not a picture that McLarty would be proud of in the years to come. By contrast, Bill Clinton's photograph would become historic—for several weeks later, in July 1963, Boys Nation senators Bill Clinton of Hot Springs and Larry Taunton of El Dorado, Arkansas, flew to Washington, D.C., Bill declaring to a reporter at the airport, "It's the biggest thrill and honor of my life. I hope I can do the tremendous job required of me as a representative of the state. I hope I can live up to the task."

Lunching with Senator Fulbright

In Washington Bill Clinton certainly did not live up to the task of representing his state—if representation meant supporting Governor Faubus's—indeed, the southern—line on segregation or Governor Faubus's hostility to federal programs.

Day after day, after being taken into Washington, D.C., by bus, the one hundred young senators drafted bills and then debated them. Paramount among the issues was civil rights, with Bill Clinton one of the three leading proponents of measures to improve the civil rights of blacks in America.

Clinton's stance surprised his colleagues. Though an Arkansas parents' action committee had finally forced a reluctant Faubus to reopen Little Rock's public schools a year after the Central High School drama, almost no desegregation had taken place in the state. As Paul Root recalled, desegregation in Hot Springs was a joke. "The school was desegregated—in theory!" he laughed in retrospect. "There were three black guys in the automobile mechanics program—about two miles away! So it was, technically, desegregated—but the students didn't know it! Most of the teachers didn't know it!"

Bill, however, knew it. "If you look at that—the issue of desegregation—objectively and start thinking about people who are being hurt, and start thinking about equality and justice, then it broadens your mind to all sorts of other things, it seems to me," Root reflected, having experienced his own epiphany in Fayetteville, when a black fellow graduate student had found it impossible to get lodging in the almost completely white town. As Root recalled, for his assigned outside reading in eleventh grade Bill had chosen George Orwell's *Animal Farm*—not to get higher or extra marks but simply because he was fascinated by Orwell's symbolic study of power and its corrosive effects. Moreover it wasn't, Root felt, that life in Hot Springs had caused Bill Clinton to become acutely aware of racial prejudice and bigotry, for it had not. Rather, it was that Hot Springs—however derided by bigots such as Johnson—had by its openness and diversity allowed Bill Clinton, with his questing, open mind, to learn to challenge the tenets of his contemporaries and elders and to be sensitive to the indignity imposed by segregation. Brought up to be polite and respectful, he was, as Virginia remarked, no rebel. In time, indeed, he would become despised by real rebels, who saw therein his lack of courage, of backbone, of moral fiber. "People say my number one weakness is that I'm conflict averse," Bill would later acknowledge their criticism. "I think part of that is I'm always trying to work things out," he admitted, "because that's the role I played for a long time"—putting an "end to the violence in my house," as he explained. It had been tough, but "It seems like every hill we climbed, he just got stronger," Virginia recalled—something Bill was proud of. "I think I did develop enormous skills in understanding human nature—the darker and brighter sides of human nature—because of all the things I've lived through, and that gives me skills at bringing people together."

In Washington, meanwhile, sixteen-year-old Bill Clinton argued his case against segregation: namely, that "racial discrimination is a cancerous disease and must be eliminated." It failed to win the crucial vote on public accommodations law, however, the majority feeling that only by a process of education—which might take several hundred years in a state like Arkansas—could the situation be improved for blacks. Meantime, an Alabama resolution calling for the constitutional primacy of states' rights—the basis of the Civil War of 1861–65—was passed 48–46! Revealingly, Clinton was told by one of the Alabama representatives that he "didn't need to be voting for these civil rights resolutions."

Perhaps not, as a southern Boys Nation senator. But as Bill Clinton he did—and when, at lunch in the magnificent surroundings of Congress, he sat down to eat with a real senator from Arkansas, the famed William J. Fulbright, his intelligence, knowledge, and political passion made a lasting impression on the chairman of the Senate Foreign Relations Committee, who had signed the Southern Manifesto but then deliberately absented himself from Arkansas, indeed from America, while the Little Rock school crisis exploded!

Both the senator and the boy senators were inspired by the meeting. Larry Taunton, the other boy senator, never managed to get a word in, but for Bill Clinton the lunch that day in the Senate Dining Room on Capitol Hill betokened the start of a relationship that would not only provide him with an important part-time job when he became a college student but help him win a prized international scholarship and catapult him onto the fast track in American politics.

In the life of a demiorphan born in humble circumstances in Hope, Arkansas, this alone would have comprised a major milestone. It was not all, however. Several days later, the hundred Boys Nation senators were ushered into the Rose Garden of the White House—there to meet President Kennedy himself.

In the Rose Garden

With his long legs and pudgy build, Bill Clinton was determined to get to the front, muscling his way in front of the others and listening with rapt attention as the President made a stirring address.

Kennedy had just returned from Berlin, where he had given his "*Ich bin ein Berliner*" speech, denouncing communism and promising that America would stand by the walled-in western part of the landlocked city deep inside East Germany, just as if it were defending America's own homeland. Nor was this merely a concession to nervous West Berliners. In the Rose Garden, again, Kennedy affirmed that, on behalf of the democracies, the United States "stands guard all the way from Berlin to Saigon"—a hardline approach that would, tragically, be tested all too soon in Vietnam.

The toughness of Kennedy's rhetoric, in the summer of 1963, was certainly beguiling: the notion of a world shield behind which freedom and democracy could flourish, especially in the heartland of America. This freedom was not designed, the President added, to license the freedom of white people to oppress American minorities, especially on the basis of skin color—and having heard the substance of the Boys Nation debate in preceding days, Kennedy complimented the Nationalists (the boy senators had been arbitrarily divided into Federalists and Nationalists) for their outright condemnation of racial prejudice as a social cancer, even if their resolution had been outvoted.

Bill Clinton beamed. The speech over, Kennedy was about to head into the White House when he changed his mind and turned back to shake hands with some of the boys. Breaking ranks, the hundred youngsters thronged around him. At the front, reaching out his big hand, sixteen-year-old Bill Clinton clasped that of the thirty-fifth President of the United States and thanked him.

The moment was, fortunately for Bill, captured by an American Legion photographer—and Boys Nation Senator Bill Clinton returned to Hot Springs, Arkansas, a foot taller—as though he'd undergone an epiphany.

With Jack Kennedy

"When he came back from Washington, holding this picture of himself with Jack Kennedy, and the expression on his face," Virginia recalled, "I knew right then that politics was the answer for him."

Virginia had "never seen him get so excited about something." Nor had Bill's guidance counselor, Edith Irons. "He came into my office one day and he was holding this manila folder with his arms crossed over it, just holding it with both his arms. He said, 'Mrs. Irons, I bet you can't guess what I've got.' " It was a picture, she recalled, "of him shaking hands with Jack Kennedy, and of course, that was the beginning of his senior year."

The principal, Johnnie-Mac Mackey, had refused to allow Bill to stand for student president, given his already burdensome array of extracurricular, especially musical, commitments; indeed, she even tried to stop him giving talks and small speeches at local clubs such as the Elks, the Heart Association, and the Optimists—where he was in increasing demand as the "darling" of parents and adults. She meant well, fearing that Bill's grades, and thus his choice of university, would be affected. It was no use, however. Not only did Bill win the Elks Leadership Award and continue to talk to any group that asked him, but, to the dismay of Mrs. Mackey and Mrs. Irons, he filled in but a single college application: to Georgetown University in Washington, D.C., for entry into the Edmund A. Walsh School of Foreign Service, founded in 1919 at the time of the establishment of the League of Nations.

Bill's neighbor Carolyn Yeldell later recalled Mrs. Irons's anxiety. "Suppose they don't take him?" Mrs. Irons asked Carolyn. "After all, it's a Catholic college."

Carolyn only shrugged, knowing that Bill's mind was made up and that he was filled with a sort of blinding faith in his own destiny now.

The Three Kings

Carolyn—who had attended Girls Nation and had also gone to Washington, D.C.—had worked with Bill Clinton for part of the summer at Clinton Buick Motors in the parts department, helping Roger Clinton, Sr., compile the company's annual inventory. There and at the Clinton house on Scully Street, behind her own home, she'd noted how withdrawn Roger had become. At home Roger Sr. merely sat in his chair and watched television; at work he remained at the back of the dealership, almost invisible. The Dude was now The Dud.

Bill, some six inches taller than his stepfather now, was polite to Roger Clinton, but it was obvious they had nothing in common—indeed, it was suddenly becoming clear that Hot Springs and the Clinton Buick agency were, after the excitement of the trip to Washington and the meeting with the President of the United States, too small for Bill Clinton, erstwhile orphan of Hope, to whose house by the railway tracks youngsters had not been permitted to go and play. Even the state university at Fayetteville seemed too local, too marginal, too irrelevant—which accounted for Bill's refusal even to apply there.

The high school's music director, Virgil Spurlin, was equally amazed at the way Bill now set his life focus on Washington. As a tenor saxophonist, he recalled, Bill was "good. In fact he was first chair for the entire state of Arkansas on tenor sax." Bill was a brilliant sight reader as well as improviser, and a tireless manager, too. As a result Spurlin had appointed Bill band major, in charge not only of the high school orchestra's rehearsal and performance arrangements but of the annual statewide band festival in April 1964, involving some 140 bands. This necessitated the planning not only of full orchestra performances but of solos, accompanied solos, ensembles, sight reading, and marching bands. Judges had to be lodged—at the Arlington Hotel—and some forty pianos rented. It was a tour de force, especially when set alongside Bill's own musical ability. He played in the school orchestra and in the high school dance band, the Starbusters. He also played in the Pep Band during basketball season and in a jazz trio, the Three Kings, who played in the auditorium during lunch hour, as well as at the Quapaw Community Center on Quapaw Avenue, which housed both the YMCA and YWCA in those days. It was at the "Y" that weekend dances for area high school kids took place, the Three Kings trio (nicknamed the Three Blind Mice because of the dark sunglasses they wore) advertised with the slogan "Swing pretty hard with some cool jazz."

Given his manifest musical and organizational talents, Bill Clinton could have won a music scholarship to any university of his choice in the United States—but this, Spurlin realized after the trip to Washington, Bill simply wasn't destined to do. "He might have gone the route of music," Spurlin lamented, "but since he met and talked with JFK personally, that had a great influence on what he turned out to be."

Bill's former history teacher Paul Root witnessed the same change in Bill's persona. Returning to Hot Springs in the early summer of 1964, he found a transformed student. "I went to his church to direct his choir for two or three weeks while the director was on vacation. And Bill came to church and saw me," Root recalled. "That night he came back again. When church was over, he came up and said, 'Let's go drink some coffee, I want to talk to you.'

"We talked for about an hour, in a coffee shop downtown, straight from his church. And I saw a new Bill Clinton, then, than the one I had known two years earlier, you know. He was talking about changing the world! He was talking about the things he had *done!*"

Root chuckled at the memory. The master-pupil relationship had reversed. "*I* was asking *him* questions, and *he* was answering—instead of the other way around! So I really got a new look at him then!"

Bill Clinton was determined, now, to be a politician.

Global Vision—For Girls

One of the joys of playing saxophone, Bill later reflected, was "the opportunity to create something that was beautiful, something that I could channel my sensitivity, my feelings into."

Though music had not proved to be the career path he wished to follow, it had certainly furnished an alternative, nonverbal, nonviolent world in which he could play without fear of confrontation or pain.

Bill's later friend from Fayetteville Jim Blair posited additional benefits of school music, however. "Looking at American culture, and this is particularly true of Arkansas, particularly where you have kids in grade school, there is a social pecking order," Blair later reflected. "All these struggles kids go through to find their own identities: they have to find groups that they can be comfortable in. And the kids who are not at the top of the social ladder at the grade school frequently become 'bandies'—they frequently join the band. The band becomes a group that they can identify with and be part of.

"Now, I've never sat down and talked with Bill about that—and I doubt if I could get the truth if I did!" Blair remarked with an engagingly conspiratorial, knowing smile. "But I've always suspected that in his early years he had some social problems at school and that he became a member of the band, consciously or not, to find a group that would accept him, and in which he could function comfortably. And it's particularly true of boys who aren't really good athletes." Though Bill "at times likes to think of himself as an athlete, he's not!" Blair insisted.

The Hot Springs High School band was "a group for the outcasts," Blair felt. The tenor saxophone, as an instrument, had thus become a social agent, he was sure, permitting Bill to connect with others—especially girls. "I think it's some of this that drove him into the band," Blair recounted. "He excelled at that. He came up here [Fayetteville] to what they call the All State Band gathering, which used to meet on the university campus, and he came to those band camps as an All State Band player."

Carolyn (Yeldell) Staley seconded Jim Blair's interpretation. Without athletic credentials in the traditional hunting-fishing-sports state of Arkansas, Bill had chosen music and an instrument that would provide a passkey for meeting girls. "He'd go to band camp in Fayetteville and there'd be this sort of 'be-still-my-beating-heart' if he saw a good-looking clarinetist," Carolyn recalled. He had "a girl in every band," she added. "He had the eye for girls everywhere. He had global vision even then."

A Bolder Kind of Model

For all her professional training as a nurse, her savoir faire in the real world, and her lust for life, Bill's mother found herself too shy to tell Bill "the facts of life," she later confessed—trusting like most parents that he would somehow find his way as a male through the modern sexual jungle on his own. Had she had daughters, Virginia reflected, she'd at least have warned them that, though sex could be divine, they had nevertheless to take precautions.

Clearly, from Virginia's point of view there were no religious or moral taboos on premarital intercourse—a fact that worried Carolyn's father, the preacher at the Second Baptist Church. Carolyn's mother was even more concerned; indeed, she had been horrified when hearing that Virginia had taken Carolyn with her to the hospital to witness the birth of a baby. "It was personal," Carolyn recalled of her mother's instinctive reaction. "It was *sex.*"

If sex, as a sweet and beautiful thing, didn't worry Virginia, other social issues did. Reflecting on his childhood, Leopoulos noted that Virginia "seemed strict to me, as a child. You knew there were rules. There was wrong and there was right, fair and unfair: and fair should take precedence over unfair.

"Now, Virginia, typically in the early part of the day she'd be at the hospital, but I remember her driving up in that Buick of hers, a convertible, driving up and parking, and we'd go running out the door to say hello. And she'd take her purse and she'd throw it on the kitchen counter and make herself a cup of drip coffee—I'll never forget—and we'd just start talking, usually about some issue she was upset about, or something, 'cause she saw a lot of people, who maybe didn't have health care or came into hospital too late to save 'em, because they couldn't pay their bills—so she'd start talking about that. Oh, yes, she was a *strong* person! And her working—it wasn't at all usual, back in the fifties! That was rare! She did a lot of things other women didn't do!"

Rendered irrelevant now to the family proceedings, Roger Sr. kept quiet and stayed in the background, save occasionally when he would become desperately drunk again and create an Arthur Miller–like scene, pulling off his belt—only to be told to belt up. Virginia would take little Roger to school before dawn, to avoid having to leave him alone while she worked in the hospital operating theater, but she made no stipulations to her elder son Bill, save that she liked him to call and tell her roughly when to expect him if he went out in the evening or was delayed getting home. Her marriage to Roger Sr. was over, she realized. She felt sorry for him, but she didn't love him any longer—and it showed.

Unashamedly loving makeup, loud clothes, bright costume jewelry, dancing, and glitzy entertainment, Virginia was an interesting role model for a seventeen-year-old son in Arkansas in the sixties. Family legend had it that, on his first visit to his mother's beloved establishment, the Vapors, on a night when Jack Teagarden was playing, Bill had asked, as soon as the music stopped, "Mother, can I go home now?" Such innocent embarrassment had given way, over the years, to social ease and an enjoyment of the world of entertainment, whether performing himself on his tenor saxophone or teenage cruising. In the context of Hot Springs as a gambling, horse-racing, vacation city with a profusion of impressive, elegant bathing houses, massage establishments, and nightclubs, sex was hardly a forbidden fruit, let alone a dirty one. To his mother's delight, Bill gravitated toward girls with the same aplomb. She liked what she called beauty queens—girls who wanted to look pretty—and Bill obliged handsomely.

A Dream Is Shattered

Another man who liked pretty women was Martin Luther King, Jr. Like President Kennedy, the Reverend King worked hard and played hard. Moreover, he saw Washington, D.C., as the nexus of power—and the agent of social change. His March on Washington at the end of August 1963 was the largest demonstration that had ever been staged in the capital, and it reflected a new era in American history: an era in which Washington, D.C., not New York, would dominate the front pages of the nation's newspapers. The march spoke, moreover, for a new era of African-American expectation and in phrases that would never be forgotten. Broadcast by CBS, ABC, and NBC, the March on Washington focused world attention on the capital—attention that would never leave the city. From across America famous actors and musicians came to support King's mission, especially the sort of stars who, only a decade before, would have been arraigned by Senator Joseph McCarthy and his Un-American Activities Committee. Lena Horne, Odetta Holmes, Sammy Davis, Jr., Josephine Baker, Mahalia Jackson, Sidney Poitier, James Baldwin, Jackie Robinson, Charlton Heston, and Harry Belafonte came forward onto the Washington Monument stage. There was Marlon Brando, too, holding a cattle prod, the symbol of white police supremacy in the South, as well as Joan Baez, Peter, Paul and Mary, even Bob Dylan.

"I still have a dream," Dr. King declared to rapturous applause. "It is a dream chiefly rooted in the American dream. I have a dream that one day this nation will rise up and live out the true meaning of its creed: 'We hold these truths to be self-evident, that all men are created equal.' "

It was Dr. King's address, given from the steps of the Lincoln Memorial before a crowd of 300,000 on the Mall, that mesmerized the march and its spectators, both in Washington and abroad: a speech that, like JFK's

1961 inaugural address, would go down in history—and Bill Clinton, would-be politician, would recall where he was when he first heard the speech and go on to memorize every word. "I remember where I was when Martin Luther King gave that 'I had a dream' speech; in 1963. I was home in Hot Springs, Ark., in a white reclining chair all by myself. I just wept like a baby all the way through it."

Back at school in Hot Springs that fall, armed with the photograph of his meeting with the President, Bill Clinton felt he was now part of a great movement, with a new civil rights bill being readied in Congress and President Kennedy signing a nuclear test ban treaty with the Soviet Union. Bill was determined to go to Georgetown University and still refused to put any alternative institution on his college application forms.

It was in this moment of pride and hope that news of a terrible event sped around the nation. In an annex of Hot Springs High School, Bill's advanced math class teacher, Mr. Cole, went to answer the phone. When he returned, he buried his head in his hands. "He was totally-ashen faced," Bill recalled. "I had never seen such a desolate look on a man's face."

It was November 22, 1963. President Kennedy had been assassinated in Dallas, Texas, only a couple of hundred miles away. The South, for so long resentful of easterners and "northern mendacity" in pressing for civil rights, had claimed its most prominent victim.

High School Graduation

Historians would later reveal the darker side of the Kennedy administration, particularly with respect to the FBI, the CIA, and the nefarious underpinnings of a huge democracy in its self-appointed struggle with communism. Biographers, in particular, would expose the seamier side of JFK's private life—his penchant for gangster's molls, pretty young campaign workers, secretaries, wives of colleagues, almost anything in skirts—but such revelations lay in the future, as in late November 1963 the nation grieved: the funeral orchestrated on the model of Abraham Lincoln's in almost balletic splendor by the young widow of the President in her charming black veil, dark stockings, and high heels. For another decade, thanks to Jackie's perfect performance and the nation's shock, JFK would be immortalized as the slain hero: the charming prince of Camelot.

Once Kennedy was lowered into his grave in Arlington, Virginia, however, the question arose: Was the liberalization of America over? A classroom colleague remembered looking at Bill Clinton's face as the news of Kennedy's assassination sank in: completely frozen, yet retaining its composure—as when his stepfather would get drunk. His eyes narrowed, and "you could feel the anger building up inside him," the classmate recalled.

For young Bill Clinton it was another turning point in his life, a moment when he was confronted with the most ominous warning of the cost of a political career in America: that all the pretty women and the idealistic excitement in guiding one's country toward a juster, more tolerant society— "making the world safe for diversity" in Kennedy's memorable words—might well lead to an assassin's bullet through the back and head, as it had done for so many Negroes in other American cities in previous months—and would eventually do for Robert F. Kennedy and the Reverend Martin Luther King, Jr.

To some, Bill Clinton would ostensibly lack courage, since he was never attracted by the military, sickened as a child by television film and newspaper photographs recording Orval Faubus's misuse of the National Guard amid "daily barrages of racial venom." Were politics to be his chosen career, he argued, courage of another, nonmilitary sort would be required: responding to ignorance and exclusionary prejudice "not with ugly words and hate, but with the dignity," as he later put it, instilled by "strong parents and strong faith." Was that option now extinguished?

The callous bombing and deaths of four young girls inside Birmingham's Sixteenth Street Baptist Church on September 9, 1963, two months before Kennedy's assassination, had already epitomized the struggle now confronting America. Die-hard white supremacists in the South would tolerate no change in the racial status quo. As a southern state, Arkansas was therefore facing a stark choice, just as it had a century before. It could go the same route as that of South American oligarchies, with police, secret police, and military forces supporting the agendas of the white power elite. Or it could become a nonviolent North American model of multiethnic tolerance of diversity and equality of opportunity.

It was this challenge that seemed increasingly to galvanize the seventeen-year-old student in Hot Springs. With Kennedy's assassination, politics in America was clearly taking on a new and frightening face: it had become a literal battleground with real bullets flying, not simply verbal and judicial arrows. Ignoring this and Mrs. Mackey's concern about the effect on his grades, Bill Clinton gave more, not fewer, talks and speeches to local organizations—yet the graduating senior still managed to win fourth place in the Class of '64, in terms of his grades. Mr. Spurlin could only shake his head—for Bill had won a raft of distinctions for his tenor saxophone playing and his leadership skills had promised a brilliant career in music directing, which would certainly ensure him safety from violence or an assassin's bullet.

The saxophone, however, would be put back into its case and become but a hobby. For his Hot Springs High School graduation on May 29, 1964, in the city's football stadium, six months after Kennedy's murder and on JFK's birthday, Bill Clinton prepared his first political "speech": the religious benediction. He still did not know whether he had been accepted by Georgetown University, but his mind was made up now, more than ever: it would be politics or nothing.

"Leave within us the youthful idealism and moralism which have made our people strong," the prayer ran. "Sicken us at the sight of apathy, ignorance and rejection so that our generation will remove complacency, poverty and prejudice from the hearts of free men."

As if to confound such idealistic hopes, however, the lowering heavens opened just as the graduation ceremonies began. In the subsequent downpour all the speeches were canceled and the 363 diplomas were quickly handed out before the students hurriedly dispersed. Bill's prayer was last on the program—and was never given.

CHAPTER EIGHT

GEORGETOWN YEARS

Letting Him In

Appearing for interview at Georgetown, Bill Clinton had intrigued the admissions panel. He was not a Catholic, but then, he was not applying for admission to the university's main campus, housing its School of Humanities, in which 96 percent of students had to be Catholic.

The School of Foreign Service, by contrast, was an almost separate arm of the university. A maximum of only 3 or 4 percent of students actually went into the U.S. Foreign Service, but by providing a distinguished undergraduate program in the social sciences—combining history, political science, and economics—the school had become, as one of its professors reflected, "one of the best preparations available for law school or graduate work." Through its mix of social sciences it provided "an understanding of this nexus as a basis for decision-making in active life."

The admissions panel had debated the merits and disadvantages of offering a place to the Baptist from Hot Springs, Arkansas. He seemed supersmart, a high achiever, and a born leader, to judge by the many activities he was running at high school and in the community. On the other hand, he lacked social status and the social or political or alumni connections that most successful students applying for entry at Georgetown boasted—connections that guaranteed that a student would "fit in."

Nevertheless, he radiated an unusually adult confidence in himself together with a blindingly intelligent curiosity about the world and about what he could learn. His application was not accepted, therefore, but it was not rejected, either.

In the end—at the insistent urging of Mrs. Mackey, Bill's principal in Hot Springs—Bill Clinton was belatedly offered a place, though when he arrived, proud and excited, at the end of the summer of 1964, his reception was chillier than he expected. Father Dineen, the dean of freshmen, wondered aloud whether the university might have made a mistake in admitting a Southern Baptist whose only "foreign" language was Latin. "Don't worry, Mother," Bill wrote to his mother afterward. "By the time I leave here they'll know why they let me in."

They would—though whether the good fathers would later regret it was another matter.

East Pampas

On his first day on East Campus, Bill Clinton made inquiries about running for student office. A few days later he was running for East Campus freshman *president*.

Running immediately for the top post was taking early-birdism to extremes, yet it worked. A clique of often idle students from eastern states and with predominantly Irish Catholic backgrounds had expected to sew up the proceedings in terms of an agreed-upon slate of candidates—the old-fashioned, Tammany Hall way. Aided by his new roommate, Tom Campbell, and a young JFK worshiper, Tommy Caplan—who had worked as a student intern in the White House before Kennedy's assassination—candidate Bill Clinton undertook a whirlwind southern-stump-style campaign of self-advertisement never seen before in the staid halls of Georgetown's East Campus. To his delight the campus included not only the Edmund A. Walsh School of Foreign Service but a school of languages, with many hundreds of female students, who were still (until 1970) denied entry to the all-male School of Humanities on the main campus. Campaigning in such a coed environment thus had a double reward—and within days he knew most of his fellow students by name as well as sight.

The "amiable farm boy," as he was condescendingly described by the college magazine, *The Courier*, had stolen a march on the rest of the class. He seemed indefatigable: jovial, well-meaning, idealistic, and self-confident. "Hi, my name is Bill Clinton. I'm standing for class president, and I'd sure appreciate your vote!" he'd say, his six-foot, three-inch bulk bursting into dormitory room after room until the entire East Campus knew him, his distinctive southern accent, his unashamedly modest Arkansas background, his energy, and his cause: his willingness to work hard for East Campus student representation within the university councils of power, as well as on local issues requiring reform.

Because he had no slate of colleagues, no raft of fellow Irish Catholic "pols," Bill's sincerity proved convincing to the majority—though it irked both Republicans and rivals no end. To those who liked his manner, he was a breath of fresh air; to his rivals and those who disliked him, he seemed too slick, too energetic, too anxious to please to be real—like a child who will trade anything to get into a game and be accepted. Now, however, he was trying to get into a game not merely to be included but expressly to run it.

For a just-turned-eighteen-year-old from the backwoods of Arkansas, this was pushing ambition to the point of arrogance, especially in a college larded with the sons (and a handful of daughters) of diplomats, senior military officers, judges, millionaires, and lawyers. "How could the only guy from Arkansas show up there and within a few months win an election like that?" a fellow student mused. That he did win—had by the end of October become the coveted East Campus freshman president of the Class of '68—was a triumph of will, a tribute to his youthful determination, and the third in a string of victories. Being elected senator at Boys Nation and meeting JFK was one thing; getting into the School of Foreign Service at Georgetown University a second; but winning the freshman student presidency out of nowhere was an even more extraordinary achievement. No known member of his family had ever even gone to a university. Now William Jefferson Clinton, né Blythe, was the head of his class at one of the elite schools of America, his career virtually guaranteed.

Bill Clinton was determined not to mess up. It was "a school with curfews and dress codes," as a Georgetown journalist later put it, "not yet affected by the student rebellions of the '60s." Though students could drink beer in Washington from age eighteen, Bill did not, preferring soda. Nor did he smoke. He even went to mass with Catholic students and to Episcopalian services with Protestants, figuring such worship to be not only a weekly Christian ceremony not far removed from his own Baptist background but a sign to others of his essential willingness to compromise, to muck in: to please.

It was the same in class.

The Goody-Goody

"Bill Clinton was not a normal 1960s undergraduate," his *American Spectator* nemesis and Georgetown graduate contemporary Emmett Tyrrell would later reflect. At an "epochal moment in American history" Bill was, Tyrrell claimed, "a student government goody-goody," in other words, "a sycophant. Generally of prosaic mind, the student government goody-goody rushes through four years of college, living a delusory life usually in frequent and unwholesome proximity to precisely those professors judged by serious scholars and discerning students to be decidedly flaky. Always, the student government goody-goody imagines himself cast in the role of a famous leader."

William Jefferson Clinton certainly drew unashamed inspiration and example from famous leaders. In a Western Civilization history class given by the eccentric Harvard-educated Carroll Quigley, Bill first learned of Napoleon's—and Churchill's—short nocturnal slumbers and frequent daytime catnaps: snatched twenty-minute sleeps that allowed one to rest and then produce the adrenaline required for nonstop work and leadership. Bill immediately adopted the technique—testing the patience of his roommate each time Bill's alarm clock roused him. He studied comparative religion in a class nicknamed "Buddha for Baptists." He "knew everybody," got mostly top grades, and ran the East Campus freshman Student Council effectively, adopting a largely centrist stance—despite, for example, his strong antisegregationist beliefs and his desire to support Georgetown faculty involved in Freedom Rides in the South. His home situation had made him a peacemaker from his earliest years. The challenge, as Bill saw it, was successful compromise between competing constituencies, not the railroading of his own views. In this sense Tyrrell was right: Bill Clinton was far from the student revolutionary, even protester, commonly equated with the sixties.

Bill's freshman grades certainly served to convince the skeptical Father Dineen he'd made a mistake in denying him a scholarship. The grant, helping to cover $2,450 of fees, was a godsend. The "goody-goody" had became not only East Campus freshman class president but a scholarship boy.

Intervention in Vietnam

Clinton spent the summer of 1965 working at Mount Pine Camp at Hot Springs, after which he returned to Georgetown for his sophomore year, putting himself forward for East Campus sophomore student president— and winning!

Bill's success, however, upset his critics still more, and in a way that would become a pattern throughout his life. "Bill, you've got your nose up their ass all the time!" one student complained of his familiarity with the campus faculty. Another student, Paul Moloy, the freshman treasurer, agreed, decrying Bill's "choirboy" determination to keep on the right side of the authorities, especially his lack of shyness in talking with the school's professors and teachers. Moloy considered that Bill was "flim-flamming you," using "90 percent bluff and 10 percent bluster." But others admired the way in which the big Arkansan constantly sought to defuse opposition and dissent by his efforts to empathize and see the perspective of his oppo- nent: "analogical," his young philosophy teacher, Otto Hentz, called him.

This was a talent that JFK had developed at the same age, as he strug- gled with his father's isolationism in the lead-up to World War II, and which JFK had used together with humor to charm his opponents. Now, however, times had changed. America, by 1965, was moving into a danger- ously interventionist mode, not isolationism, its aggressiveness tragically heightened by the legacy of JFK's own "pay any price" rhetoric in relation to fighting communism. A pinprick raid by North Vietnamese PT boats in the summer of 1964 had provided an excuse for the U.S. military, under its new commander in chief, Lyndon Johnson, to declare, in August 1964, vir- tual war in Southeast Asia—and Congress to vote in unanimous support of Johnson's direct military intervention in the struggle between North and South Vietnam. Such intervention had pleased Republicans, but had aroused deep concern among Democrats.

For all the rhetoric of anticommunism, few civilians in America really wished for a new war in the East. For those Democrats, especially, who es- poused nonviolence in the struggle for civil rights under the leadership of Dr. Martin Luther King, Jr., President Johnson's escalation of the United States' involvement in Southeast Asia was anathema—especially when such direct military intervention promised, thanks to the Communists' guerrilla tactics, to become a major land campaign, leading inextricably to American casualties and Vietnamese civilian injuries. "Let's hope there'll come a time when guns won't have to win our battles for us," Bill had written to his new girlfriend, Denise Hyland, from camp in Hot Springs; indeed, he had even considered the idea of learning Vietnamese at the Institute of Language and Linguistics at Georgetown, which Denise—an Irish-American Catholic from New Jersey—attended. "If I go to summer school next summer, I can take it in my junior year," he outlined his thinking. "Someone has to be there after—and during—the war to speak and help the people—probably not over one or two people in our embassy can converse fluently."

While many of Bill's close friends, especially those from the northeastern states, agreed with him on civil rights, there was no such agreement with his distaste for America's military operations in Vietnam. Georgetown University, in this respect, was as establishment-led as the military colleges of the nation, despite its Catholic priesthood—and poles apart from the more liberal campuses of the University of California at Berkeley and New York University. Roommate Tom Campbell, for example, wanted to go into naval flying—indeed, had persuaded Bill to join the ROTC air force program for a semester in their first term (the program was, however, axed)—while most of Bill's other buddies would enter, or entertain the idea of a stint in, the military in due course. It was a tribute to Bill's personality and political open-mindedness that he could keep such friendships intact while disagreeing on fundamental issues that affected the campus and the nation—indeed, would soon affect their own lives and careers.

Whether Bill Clinton would be able to maintain such an open-minded posture—defending Lyndon Johnson before Tom Campbell's father, a rabid Republican, for example, on a visit to Campbell's home, yet increasingly critical of Johnson himself for ordering military involvement in Vietnam—remained to be seen. U.S. bombers had been dropping napalm since early 1965 and by June that year American soldiers had abandoned the mask of military "advisers." Combat units were now in open battle with North Vietnamese Communist troops. As earlier in Korea, the military involvement was turning into a full-scale war.

A Doomed Campaign

In the event, Bill Clinton did not stay at Georgetown over the summer of 1966 to learn Vietnamese. Instead he headed home to Arkansas, where, with the help of his stepuncle Raymond, he had gotten a job as a volunteer aide on the gubernatorial nomination campaign of Judge Frank Holt, an Arkansas Supreme Court justice who had been selected as the Democratic "machine's" nominee to succeed the retiring Democratic governor, Orval Faubus—if he beat off other Democratic rivals for the Democratic nomination. Whoever won the primary would then face the Republican challenger, millionaire Winthrop Rockefeller.

In Arkansas, Bill found, there was little or no discussion of national or international issues—a lesson that caused him to recognize at first hand the limitations on a candidate seeking state rather than congressional or Senate office. By the same token, however, there was an undoubted fascination in participating in a gubernatorial contest that allowed him to visit almost every hamlet in the state and to see close up the state's racial prejudice, poverty, and educational backwardness repeated again and again in community after community. "I think the heat has burned G[eorgetown] U[niversity] out of my system," he acknowledged—but in writing this to his girlfriend, Denise Hyland, he was coy about the heat he was generating in the women he was meeting on the campaign trail. Offering to drive Mrs. Holt and her daughters Lyda and Melissa, he set off on the literal campaign trail. "I never took orders from three women before," he wrote to Denise—two (his grandma and his mother) having previously been his limit.

The Holts, chauffeured, shepherded, and protected by the hulking six-foot, three-inch nineteen-year-old, visited villages such as Altheimer, Wabbeseka, Ulm, McGehee, Lake Village, Arkansas City, Marmaduke, and Piggott. Most had just a village square and a street of buildings as old as the town. Schools for blacks were in shacks. "I would give anything if you could see all the tiny towns we've been through," Bill wrote Denise, saddened. It was like visiting the Third World—but with the towns of America's supposed First World still stuck in their racist ways. "Now we are campaigning in the heart of cotton country, south and east Arkansas," he related to Denise, "where Negroes are still niggers—and I couldn't believe my eyes when I saw restrooms and waiting rooms still marked in Colored and White. It made me so sick to my stomach."

For a young man born and raised in the state, this was saying something. In spite of the Democratic "machine's" backing and the six hotel rooms in the Marion Hotel in Little Rock, rented with money provided by Witt Stephens, the local party financier, Judge Holt managed to come in only second place on the first ballot—and seemed destined to do no better in the runoff. The fact was that Judge Holt was simply no match for "Justice Jim" Johnson, the man with the golden quip, who scorned Holt as a witless candidate "hand-picked by the big boys" and ridiculed him as a "pleasant vegetable."

For nineteen-year-old Bill Clinton, though, the campaign provided invaluable experience. It not only gave him the chance to master the geography of his home state but to learn speechwriting, campaign organization, debating—even television political program making and appearance on the TV screen. As much as Georgetown was providing an education in politics, economics, philosophy, and international relations, the doomed primary campaign of Judge Holt offered him a practical course in media communications—with lessons that would remain with Clinton for the rest of his life.

Little Black Sambos

Television came naturally to the former Hot Springs saxophonist; indeed, he found he had to coach others for the medium, such as his colleague Dick King, to whom he had to whisper his lines. The Georgetown undergraduate was even given the opportunity to make his first political speech on the stump—in his birthplace, downtown Hope, on July 7, 1966. There, in front of his beloved grandmother, relatives, family friends, and people who'd known him since he was a toddler, the nineteen-year-old openly challenged their racial prejudices.

Bill's grandmother had been wont to send him postcards of little black Sambos polishing watermelons; now she listened as her adored grandson pleaded for Holt as official Democratic Party nominee for governor: an honest man, Bill pleaded, a man of sincerity and principle, who believed in civil rights and could lead Arkansas into the future, not back into the past; a man who had a vision of the state as a place worthy of a new generation of Arkansans.

The heat of Arkansas might make Georgetown's liberal notions seem far-fetched, yet Bill was unabashed. One of the major ideas Bill had imbibed from his philosophy professor, Dr. Quigley—whom he later characterized as "a bit crazy" but also "a genius"—was Quigley's notion of "future preference": the notion that human beings have not only the will to propagate, in the same way as nonhuman species, but the desire to improve future life for their offspring, in a time beyond themselves. It was a notion that made its way into many of the speeches Bill drafted for Holt—and in the mouth of the young orator, it was certainly heartfelt.

Though Holt's daughters were impressed by Bill's precocious "ability to take feelings and emotions and match them to words," the people of Hope were not. He could keep William Faulkner, Ernest Hemingway, Evelyn Waugh, Edward Albee, and other twentieth-century writers and their fine English prose, they felt for the most part. The town would reconsider desegregation—and reject it. White citizens had nothing against "niggers," as such. Of some of them they were genuinely fond in a paternalistic way, especially their servants; they just didn't see them as fit to attend school with their children. And no white teenager with thick, long, curly hair from the house down by the railway tracks, who'd moved away to the sinful city of Hot Springs, was going to tell them differently.

This was Hope, Arkansas, in one of the most ornery areas of the entire United States—yet, for that very reason, one of the most challenging.

The Summer of '66

In this sense, at a moment in American history when the young *Peyton Place* star Mia Farrow—only a year older than Bill—married roué Frank Sinatra, age fifty, and set off on a honeymoon to England, land of the Beatles and the Rolling Stones, and American bombers pounded the demilitarized zone between North and South Vietnam and Buddhists in South Vietnam set themselves aflame, the summer of 1966 became the next great turning point in Bill Clinton's life.

On the campaign trail Bill had met and impressed the young David Pryor ("You're gonna hear a lot about him," Pryor told his wife), a liberal activist pursuing and winning the state's Fourth Congressional District seat. Logically, this was a path to Washington that Bill, too, might one day try to take—a path that Mrs. Holt's own father had taken, when he'd been congressman for the district around Hope.

With this in mind therefore, before returning to Georgetown, Bill decided to call in his IOU. Commiserating with the defeated judge following his defeat in the primary runoff, he asked a favor. He was now determined to get into politics, preferably in Congress. He had his eyes on a job as an intern on Capitol Hill—and though he had no political connections, with Holt's help Bill was sure he could get it.

Judge Holt, grateful for Bill's indefatigable summer service, duly called J. William Fulbright's administrative assistant in the senator's Washington office, Lee Williams. Impressed with Holt's recommendation and Bill Clinton's résumé, Williams offered the Georgetown student a choice: either a part-time job at $3,500 or a full-time post at $5,000 per annum. Clinton thought for barely a moment then parlayed both positions (and responsibilities) into one part-time job that would allow him to continue to study at Georgetown University, but with two part-time salaries!

On Fulbright's Staff

Bill loved his double job in Washington from day one.

"Someday, this is going to be my office," he confided to a colleague on Fulbright's staff. John F. Kennedy, after all, had been a U.S. senator representing the state of Massachusetts before becoming President of the United States in 1961. So had LBJ, in representing Texas, before election as Vice President and assumption of the presidency in 1963. If Bill still intended to fulfill his boyhood dream of one day becoming President of the United States—as his girlfriend, Denise, told all who would listen—then he would need to pave the way for such an ascent: a route that would be, he believed, via the halls of Congress.

Thus, three years after Kennedy's assassination, it was Senator Fulbright in Washington, D.C., former Rhodes Scholar and the man behind the Fulbright Scholarships for American students pursuing their studies in foreign countries, who became Bill Clinton's new hero and model as he sought to master the intricacies of senatorial conduct—an internship, however, that would lead to a bruising upset in his hitherto stellar student success at Georgetown University.

Student presidents traditionally "rested" from student representation in their third, or junior, year, to concentrate on their studies and internships. This Bill did, immersing himself both in the study of foreign relations at Georgetown and in Fulbright work on the Senate Foreign Relations Committee on Capitol Hill. He kept up with his classes and classwork, but, absorbed by his work on the Hill, he neglected his fellow students. When the election for all-important president of the Class of '68 came at the end of his junior year, he would find himself disastrously out of touch with student sentiment.

No Student Warrior

Bill Clinton's chief rival for senior year class president was a Republican, Terry Modglin, a working-class student from Saint Louis. Seizing on Bill's work for Senator Fulbright, Modglin cast Bill Clinton as Judge Holt had been cast by "Justice Jim" Johnson: as a "machine" man, a political insider, slick, already working on the Hill, and concerned with power and influence; not a genuine representative of the student body, devoted to student matters, like himself. It was the first but not the last time that Bill would be caricatured—a foretaste of what would later be called "negative advertising."

Unaware of what was coming and still buoyed by the honorable example of honest Frank Holt, Bill Clinton went down without fisticuffs, unwilling to destroy his opponent by stereotyping, let alone vilifying, him. His "basic instinct was to find, even with the most basic asshole, something good," one of his supporters complained. "We wanted him to get angry in that campaign, but he would not do it."

Why? Was there at heart a soft core that made Bill Clinton unable to play rough? JFK, his earlier idol, had been a warrior in sports, combat, and politics: charming on the outside, steely and determined on the inside. Bill Clinton, however, was no sportsman. Moreover, Bill was increasingly antiwar, as was the entire staff of Senator Fulbright's office. This in itself did not make him ineligible as senior class president, however. What did was his cautiousness and his long-term ambition, which made him unwilling to stand up and lead demonstrations on the issue of Vietnam—or, indeed, on any other issue—in an era of student protest.

In the fifties Bill's credentials for office would have been impeccable— for two years the student class president, member of the Alpha Phi Omega club, member of the university band, chairman of the Sports Week Contest, chairman of the Interdenominational Service Committee, and of this committee and that. He was editor of the first Georgetown University Student Directory, he was on the dean's list for academic performance, was proponent of mild, apolitical issues such as lower campus car-parking fees, cheaper cafeteria milk, and critiques by students of their courses. Indeed, he considered himself opposed to the "radical segment of the student body."

Here, then, was no student warrior in the likeness of Daniel Cohn-Bendit, say. In the spring of 1967, as no fewer than 2,500 women protested outside the Pentagon, demanding to confront "the generals who send our sons to die," and as the gentler, nonviolent flower power of the sixties turned more abrasive, challenging, and radical, it became worryingly clear even to his supporters that Bill Clinton of Arkansas had somehow missed the beat of his generation, indeed the young people's boat: had been perhaps too excited by his privileged internship in Fulbright's office, by meeting the President, Vice President, senators, and congressmen in person, and had become too awed by the corridors of power on the Hill, rather than sensing the mood, concerns, and ambivalences of the East Campus corridors of the powerless. Terry Modglin, by contrast, cleverly portrayed himself as the "Modge Rebellion" against Bill Clinton and a Student Council that too often "merely administers to its own existence"—especially, as Modglin sneered, in using the profit from fund-raising events for the "parties afterwards."

Bill Clinton, Beaten

Bill Clinton's posters pictured him under the heading "A Realistic Approach to Student Government": a peacemaker rather than a provocateur or protester.

As the day of the election approached, Bill's campaign helpers finally woke up to the fact that Modglin's criticisms and negative portrayals were attracting serious attention. Indeed, so anxious did Bill's team become that they even attempted some last-minute dirty tricks on Bill's behalf, including the heist of all Modglin's posters tacked up on the walls of East Campus.

It did no good, however. The writing had been, literally, on the wall, in Modglin's hand, and was now all too clear to read, as the election chalkboard for the East Campus class president of the Student Council of '68 registered the rocketing numbers. "About three-fourths of the way through the ballot counting in the Hall of Nations, it became evident who the winner was," recorded *The Hoya,* "as they began to shout 'Modglin, Modglin.' "

Some 717 votes were cast for Modglin, only 570 for freshman-and-sophomore student president Clinton. Bill Clinton had been beaten.

After Judge Holt's defeat the summer before, the failure left a bitter taste in Bill's mouth as he got up to make his own generous concession speech.

An Inner Reluctance

In some ways, defeat in the election for senior class president was the most personal rejection Bill Clinton had ever suffered, save perhaps his mother's

142 · BILL CLINTON

decision to ignore his warnings and remarry the alcoholic nonanonymous Roger Clinton, Sr. For such an intelligent young man, Bill's response, however, was profoundly superficial. "Instead of handbills under every door, I'll have to talk to everyone in person," he vowed. "I'll have to find out the people I thought would be with me," he added, "who voted for the other guy and go out and talk to those people."

Tragically, this would be Bill Clinton's response to all the hardships and obstacles that would face him in the years ahead: as if some deep-seated pride stood between him and the truth—the truth that he was not only out of touch with the concerns of the majority of his classmates but *out of touch with himself;* that he had projected, in the end, no clear, robust convictions that would give students the confidence that in voting for him, they would be represented by a president ready, willing, and able to buck the system, the faculty, and the establishment. "Realism" for sixties students, even in conservative Georgetown, was a euphemism for accepting the status quo. Convincing more students to vote for him by personal bluster was not the answer; learning to have the courage to articulate and stand by his convictions was.

Nevertheless, defeat at Georgetown was a landmark in Bill Clinton's life journey. Distracted by his work on the Hill, he had not done enough campaigning. Politics, retail politics, was not something that could be done via handbills, he belatedly recognized, unless one had a clear and popular message. Even then, it would, as JFK had found, entail unending personal campaigning, of making sure more voters met him, voiced their views to him, felt that he had listened, felt they knew the guy in person, and liked him. It was a message he would take deeply to heart—a lesson that would make him, in time, the greatest political campaigner of his generation: able, single-handedly, to thwart the tide of Republican Party presidential voting that would, with the advent of Ronald Reagan and his successor George Bush, increasingly grip white America. But it would not, sadly, force him to reexamine his own soul and his reluctance to stand up and be counted on controversial issues, lest he thereby court dislike or lose a vote.

CHAPTER NINE

TURNING TWENTY-ONE

Turning Twenty-One

Swallowing his pride, Bill Clinton concentrated, in his final year, on his studies as well as his job on Senator Fulbright's committee. He also moved into a house on Potomac Avenue with four of his classmates—all of whom would embrace the military at a time of escalating war in Vietnam.

For Bill, Vietnam was an issue even more divisive, if such were possible, than civil rights. In the matter of white supremacy and racism, he suffered no inner conflict. Despite the Arkansas environment in which he'd been brought up, he simply did not "have a prejudiced bone in his body," as one friend would remark, for it was as if his natural, human empathy as a semi-orphan from a socially reviled family was with those who suffered preju-dice, not those who inflicted it—and this natural sympathy was reinforced by his astonishing intelligence and curiosity about the world beyond Arkansas, even beyond Washington. He was blessed with a photographic memory and could recite texts from Shakespeare and, more significantly, major portions of Martin Luther King, Jr.'s "I have a dream" speech by heart—for it was his dream, too. But Vietnam was different.

Vietnam, tragically, split the nation, and it also split Bill's own con-science as an American. With each day's news of battles and bombings, of-fensives and attacks in Vietnam, Bill squirmed—his housemates taking the

attitude "My country, right or wrong" but his Fulbright committee colleagues in open combat with the President, Lyndon Baines Johnson.
"There was not a hawk on that staff," one member recalled. But with almost half a million American troops—"our boys"—in Vietnam and General William Westmoreland, the commander of the American forces in
Vietnam, calling for yet more, it was heartbreaking to have to speak
against one's own countrymen and thus aid, undeniably, the morale of the
Communist enemy. Moreover, with a national draft board operating as it
had done in World War II, it was becoming possible that, once his Georgetown student deferment came to an end, on graduation, Bill might himself
be called up.

Fulbright's approach was to use his office to question the very legality of
the U.S. military involvement in Vietnam, based on the Gulf of Tonkin incident in 1964, when Bill had started at Georgetown. Working on the Senate Foreign Relations Committee's investigation into the incident, Bill
discovered just how duplicitous was the military and how wrongful had
been Johnson's subsequent pressure on Congress to authorize what
amounted to the President's "blank check" in Vietnam, as Bill described it
in a letter to his girlfriend, Denise. The war, he told her, was now over-
shadowing, in fact retarding, the nation's commitment to desegregation
and civil rights—pursued by air force generals and "the good Americans
who want to bomb North Vietnam into the Stone Age."

Throughout the summer of 1967, Bill remained in Washington, work-
ing for Fulbright and preparing a twenty-eight-page paper on the Gulf of
Tonkin for a Georgetown class on U.S. Foreign Relations in the Far East.
His friend Tommy Caplan paid for a twenty-first-birthday bash for Bill at
JFK's old haunt in New York, the "21" Club, including a bottle of Dom
Perignon champagne for each guest as well as rooms at the Carlyle Hotel
(another old haunt of JFK)—but the celebration was out of kilter with the
times. Ronald Reagan, governor of California, was calling for the President to threaten the use of nuclear weapons in Vietnam; Stokely
Carmichael, former chairman of the Student Non-violent Coordinating
Committee, changed tack and, in a broadcast in Cuba, called for black revolution in America, saying there was now "no alternative, but to use aggressive armed violence in order to own the land, houses and stores inside
our communities, and to control the politics of those communities." To
Denise, Bill wrote wondering whether "our nation has any shared values"
anymore.

It was a moot point. As a future candidate for public office, Bill was, however, loath to be a firebrand, to stick his head out too far—not only because his natural bent was toward compromise and peaceful resolution of conflict but because he wished to maintain a clean slate, one that would allow him to campaign and garner votes irrespective of who eventually won the war in Vietnam or came out best in the struggle for civil rights—a struggle that was increasingly being taken to the streets in cities not only in the bigoted South but in the North and West, from Detroit to California, as "blacks"—the new, self-made label of former Negro leaders—asserted their claim to a share of American prosperity.

There was, however, one area of JFK's famous New Frontier where Bill was less circumspect and was proud to be a firebrand, fondly, though wrongly, believing it would not, in an age of new moral license, affect his political career. Thanks to his defeat for the Class of '68 presidency, Bill now felt doubly entitled to explore that frontier.

Nice Girls Do

Bill's romance with his fellow Georgetown student Denise Hyland, a slim, beautiful upper-middle-class girl from Upper Montclair, New Jersey, had given him an emotional and social anchor in a new eastern city. Tall, graceful, and beautiful, she represented Catholic respectability and loyalty, tirelessly helping him with his early student campaigns and his work as freshman and sophomore class president, as well as introducing him to her family during their class vacation. But with Bill's failure to win the class presidency in his senior year and his new intimacy with Senator Fulbright and his Foreign Relations staff—indeed, his growing friendships across Capitol Hill—he had less and less need of Denise or her upper-middle-class eastern seaboard world of respectability. He had arrived—liked and respected for his brains, hard work, and friendly personality.

Dumping his Catholic "steady" (though remaining lifelong friends with her), Bill belatedly eased himself into the "sexual revolution," letting his hair grow fashionably long, wearing sandals, and making out with girls "like a guy getting out of prison," as one friend described him. Another friend, Jim Moore, recalled Bill's sexual epiphany in his final year at Georgetown, having lost the class president election and having dropped Denise: he no longer needed to pretend to be pure, or behave like a Baptist choirboy. The "goody-goody" could finally relax and reap the benefits of the new sixties amorality: miniskirts, exotic eyelashes, and cutesy hairdos.

Catholic girls had traditionally been brought up to be virgins at marriage and to eschew sex that was not directly directed at procreation. The sixties, however, struck a sharp and penetrating nail in this Victorian coffin. Never before had youngsters represented such a massive part of society; never before had youngsters had so much money; never before, in America, had so many gone on to college. The Pill, introduced in 1960, had given women a chance to control their own fertility; the sixties had then legitimated premarital intercourse—Helen Gurley Brown, in *Sex and the Single Girl,* proclaiming in 1962 that "nice, single girls *do.*"

For Bill Clinton it was as if the pioneering protofeminism of his mother had finally been validated, as *Cosmopolitan* went on sale from the spring of 1965 and the liberating agendas of *Playboy* and *Cosmo* announced a cultural revolution, licensing men to salivate over large-breasted, long-legged "bunnies" (named in allusion to the phrase "fucking like bunnies") side by side with more serious articles, but without worrying about marriage and tedious human responsibilities, such as bringing up children. Indeed, *Cosmopolitan*'s editor, Helen Gurley Brown, encouraged girls themselves to smash the Victorian ideal of "one man per lifetime," declaring they needed marriage only as a later "insurance for the worst years of your life. During the best years you don't need a husband"—only a succession of males, who were "cheaper emotionally and more fun by the dozen."

Procreation and maternity were suddenly on the back burner—and men like Bill Clinton were licensed to reap, for a while, the unexpected but glorious harvest.

Sex and the Single Male

For Bill Clinton, hitherto the Georgetown University School of Foreign Service "goody-goody," women's lib now became men's lib: a feast, a cornucopia after he broke up with Denise Hyland. Traditionally, it had been the athletes on campus who scored best with girls, as JFK had found—a fact that had made JFK determined to excel in college football at Harvard despite his life-threatening ill health. The sixties, however, changed all this.

It was not only on college campuses that sexual attitudes were changing—"giving bearded nerds an equal chance," as one wit recalled—to Bill

Clinton's advantage as a nonathlete. It was also his good fortune that, in a time of rising skirts and loosening moral strictures, he was an intern on Capitol Hill—where power, always acknowledged to be an aphrodisiac, provided yet more passkeys to the bedrooms of the capital. Released from his "steady" relationship with Miss Hyland, Bill Clinton now dated the voluptuous Miss Arkansas and a succession of striking women. As Jim Moore put it, "He had met women on the Hill before but never followed up on the opportunities. Then he became a free agent, and young ladies figured it out, and it was, 'Holy shit, Bill Clinton is free and available and looking forward to having a good time!' "

Bill's Georgetown college friends—preparing for military service in short-clipped hair and for fifties-style marriages to "nice" middle-class girls—were somewhat stunned by the change. A colleague who had joined the elite Marine Corps recorded his amazement at Bill's transformation, seeing him in a local restaurant. Gone was the well-mannered, establishment-oriented former class president. In his place was a veritable hippie with long, shaggy hair, wearing sandals—and berating the President of the United States for involving America in a futile and bloody war in a geopolitical area of no strategic importance to the United States. They almost came to blows.

Il conformista had, at last, become a rebel—like his mother.

The Death of Roger Clinton

Virginia Clinton, however, could not help her son avoid the draft. By 1967–68 there were 10 million students at American colleges—a vast reservoir of young military manpower available, as in World War II, to be tapped for service in Vietnam under the draft system.

Understandably, in a war that had nothing of the nobility of America's stand against Nazism and Japanese conquest after Pearl Harbor, the majority of students had no desire to be drawn into such a conflict. Thus, as General Westmoreland appealed for more and more troops in Vietnam, an equally determined system of avoidance was perpetrated by middle-class parents to protect and preserve the lives of their sons—hippies or not—by finding ways out of their serving in combat. Al Gore, son of a U.S. senator, and George W. Bush, son of the U.S. ambassador to the United Nations, were just two of the many millions for whom were found "safe harbors," whether behind the front lines or at home.

Bill Clinton's parents were of no assistance in this respect, however. Roger Clinton, Sr., had finally died in the fall of 1967, of throat cancer. Despite his deep resentment, Bill had made his peace with Roger, driving several weekends to his stepfather's hospital in the 1963 white convertible Buick with red trim—supplied by Clinton Buick in Hot Springs—that Virginia had given him to use in Washington.

As he lay dying, the wasting, enfeebled alcoholic had seemed pathetic, his long reign of domestic southern terror almost unimaginable in retrospect. Bill had not spoken to his stepfather in any meaningful way for six years, he claimed, and virtually not at all following Virginia's divorce and remarriage. In one letter Bill had counseled Sunday worship to his stepfather as a means of beating the bottle rather than Virginia but had admitted—in his junior year—that he hadn't "been much help to you—never had the courage to come and talk about it." He'd assured Roger, nevertheless, that he did love him, as a stepson—adding that, although Roger had probably never "ever realized . . . how much we have all been hurt," the miracle was that he, Virginia, and Roger Jr., "still really have *not* turned against you." For Bill, the answer had been clear: "Don't be ashamed to admit your problem."

From a boy who had himself been so careful never to admit to anyone that his family had a problem, this was perhaps jejune, but in any case such exhortations were too late. It was not drinking that was killing Roger Clinton but cancer. Bill's letters of final reconciliation, in the fall of 1967, were moving in their sincerity, but they masked an uncomfortable truth: that neither his mother, Virginia, nor his little brother, Roger Jr., could even look at Roger Sr. in his last months of life. To help his mother, Bill flew home, and each night for several weeks he took Roger Jr. over to friends' houses to spare the child the sight of death. Virginia recalled their subsequent dismay at her husband's longevity. Roger Jr. was especially disappointed. "To have his father hanging on when it was obvious he was at death's doorstep seemed like one last act of terrorism," wrote Virginia, describing her little boy's feelings.

For Bill, however, the need to support and counsel his mother and his little brother was, after the failure to make class president, a welcome responsibility, as was the task that fell on him of sitting with his stepfather for two long weeks of the death vigil. He had not been born when his putative father had died; now, however much he might have despised the alcoholic, he had a father to say good-bye to and to bury: two rites of passage in familial maturity.

In English Tweed

With Roger Clinton's death in November 1967, a long chapter in Bill Clinton's life came to an end. The Dude, so long a cipher of his former self, was no more. Bill Clinton, senior at Georgetown University, was at last able to become the head of the Clinton household on Scully Street in Hot Springs. He would also, once he graduated, be able to enroll to take a postgraduate law degree at the University of Arkansas in Fayetteville, the cheapest and most popular graduate college for Arkansas students, and thereby secure Vietnam draft deferment—if the President didn't change the rules.

Whatever he might tell his family friends and relatives at the funeral, however, the truth was that Bill had no wish to return to Hot Springs, to Fayetteville, or to Arkansas. From the age of sixteen, he later confided, he'd been interested in the system of Rhodes Scholars, funded and named after Cecil Rhodes, the archimperialist who had made a fortune from the mining of African minerals. Bill was now secretly determined to go to Oxford University as a Rhodes Scholar—on a scholarship that would, he hoped, permit him to defer being drafted for two, even three years. However, "I want you to understand," he told his mother, to whom he'd confided his ambition, "my chances of getting this are literally one in a million."

In truth, his chances were a lot better than that. With his high grades at Georgetown and the support of Senator Fulbright, he had little difficulty in getting through the Arkansas selection board stage. It was the regional board of selection in New Orleans in December 1967, shortly after his stepfather's funeral, that posed a more formidable obstacle.

At Washington National Airport he was blessed with luck. Seeing a copy of *Time* magazine on the newsstand, he bought it—and found himself engrossed by an article about the world's first heart transplant, carried out by Dr. Christiaan Barnard in South Africa. During the Rhodes panel interview, he was asked, among other things, about the heart transplant—a subject of which he would otherwise have been completely ignorant, despite his mother's medical background. With the *Time* report imprinted on his memory, however, and his mother's years in anesthesia, he was able to speak with confidence and insight.

The Rhodes selection panel was duly impressed—though more, it transpired, by his pride in his home state, Arkansas, by his humble origins, and by his articulate and genuine determination to do something with his life.

Just as JFK had once found a self-deprecating yet vibrantly intelligent way of impressing his elders such as Arthur Krock of *The New York Times,* who first suggested that Jack Kennedy publish his senior-year thesis as a book, *Why England Slept,* so Bill Clinton had undoubtedly developed a manner that mixed high intelligence with youthful zest and lack of pretension. Whereas so many of the candidates betrayed their nerves and desire to impress, Bill had, in the end, decided to be himself: a gregarious, energetic, curious, smart young man, not well traveled but clearly destined for big things in life. In the view of the Rhodes panel, the six-foot, three-inch Arkansan, with his southern drawl, extraordinary intelligence, and *joie de vivre,* was head and shoulders above his regional rivals.

"Well, Mother," Bill began his telephone call to Virginia from Georgetown shortly after New Year 1968 (Virginia having stayed at home to hear his news, refusing to do any operations that day), "how do you think I'll look in English tweed?"

PART TWO
VIETNAM

Class stars Bill Clinton and Hillary Rodham

CHAPTER TEN

THE END
OF AN ERA

A Nation at War with Itself

The award of a Rhodes Scholarship to Oxford more than made up for Bill Clinton's failure to make class president of Georgetown's East Campus. A brilliant future now beckoned—if the war in Vietnam didn't ruin it. Only draft deferment, as a graduate student, now stood between him and military induction.

On June 28, 1967, however, Congress had given President Johnson power to cancel the draft deferments of *all* college students, both undergraduate and postgraduate, except those taking medical degrees. Eight months later, on February 16, 1968, the new ruling came into effect—despite a new Gallup Poll claiming that an alarming 49 percent of Americans felt the war in Vietnam to be "a mistake."

President Johnson, in his heart of hearts, felt so too. But how to rescue America from his fatal error in the Gulf of Tonkin? Negotiation was one way, carpet bombing another. In May 1968, the first peace talks between North Vietnam and the United States took place in Paris, France—in a country that had good reason, after its defeat at Dien Bien Phu, to sympathize with the United States' military difficulties in Vietnam, but that was also uniquely able to foresee its failure in the jungles and forests of Southeast Asia, for all the napalm and explosives American bombers might drop. The peace talks were, however, doomed—as seemed the case with Johnson's nobler War on Poverty and his White House attempts to right civil wrongs with economic action.

In his student house on Potomac Avenue, Bill Clinton debated the issues each night with his housemates. Words, so much a part of university education, were, however, increasingly giving way to violence in the cities of America, the Watts riots of 1965 setting a pattern for simmering urban summer violence in successive years, especially in Detroit in July 1967. Little beyond a presidentially directed commission seemed to change. Frustrated, Martin Luther King, Jr., had therefore begun preparing, in the early months of 1968, another March on Washington for the spring—a Poor People's March. Before it could take place, however, Dr. King was called upon to support a strike in Memphis by black garbage workers—and it was there, in the heart of the South, in April 1968, that he fell victim to an assassin's bullet outside the Lorraine Motel. Dr. King, on arrival at the hospital, was dead.

Rioting almost immediately broke out in the cities and black ghettos of the nation, more than two hundred years of political, social, and economic frustration spilling over and venting in arson, riot, looting, and threatened anarchy. Beginning in the South, mayhem spread north like a forest fire. In all, more than a hundred American cities were affected, including Baltimore, Harlem, Brooklyn, Newark, New Jersey, Boston, Detroit, and Chicago.

Washington, D.C., with its predominantly black population, was subjected to some of the worst excesses. A pall of smoke drifted ominously above the capital, echoing the destruction of South Vietnam. Troops were called out to protect the White House as fires burned across the center of the capital. Businesses were boarded up and closed down; the Red Cross was called in to distribute food to innocent victims.

Carolyn Yeldell, Bill Clinton's next-door neighbor from "sin city," Hot Springs, who was studying music at Ouachita Baptist College, had accepted Bill's invitation to stay with him for a few days over the college break. As her aircraft circled D.C., she looked out the window and saw an astonishing sight: a nation at war with itself.

Make Love, Not War

Change had characterized the 1960s in almost every field of human endeavor, but 1968 brought change to a climax. President Johnson, his popularity sagging in early primaries, had already announced, for the strangest of reasons, that he would not stand for reelection. Vice President Hubert Humphrey, Senator Eugene McCarthy, and Senator Robert F. Kennedy then found themselves fighting for the Democratic Party crown—while former Vice President Richard Nixon, the defeated 1960 candidate, toughed his way through the spring and summer's Republican contests.

Had the torch truly passed to a new generation, as JFK had foretold? Or was there a counterrevolution in train, with collision inevitable? Allen Ginsberg, lecturing at Georgetown University in March, had appealed for a pacifist, ecologically friendly society in America—perhaps a pluralistic family structure, a matriarchy, or maybe just a system of matriarchal descent. Communes would probably be better—"and they are experimenting with that sort of thing in the Haight-Ashbury right now," he explained.

Ginsberg's appeal for matriarchy in America, however, did not address the most urgent threat now facing American's student sons: the draft. From February 1968, they became liable to be co-opted into America's increasingly unpopular war, irrespective of academic status—thus making virtually every student in the United States a future combatant, a medical misfit, a conscientious objector, a draft avoider, or a fugitive. Demonstrations and draft-notice burnings increased—while, among blacks, the noble platitudes of civil rights led to increasing civil disorder, with revolutionary movements splitting into factions and groups with ever-wilder agendas, from the Black Panthers to the Weathermen.

In France the situation was similar, indeed potentially more anarchic, as the great student protest of May 1968 brought Paris, indeed the entire country, to a standstill. President Charles de Gaulle's authority was tested to the point of insurrection; the forces of the Left—socialist and Marxist—were ranged against the power of the Right. Revolution was in the air, the old order or *ancien régime* seemingly about to topple. Behind the Iron Curtain, meanwhile, the Prague Spring threatened the Soviet Communist stranglehold on Eastern Europe. Slogans in Paris epitomized the blind hope and naiveté of the confrontation, "Make love, not war" being the most popular.

Even before the great *grève* in France, however, an American youth-versus-age confrontation had come to a head in the wake of memorial services for Dr. Martin Luther King. Student frustration escalated into violence at Columbia University in New York, where military funding, cadet programs, and CIA recruitment had polarized the student community. The university president had banned all demonstrations and had taken disciplinary action against six students who had disobeyed his personal edict. The student leader Mark Rudd responded by writing openly to the president, announcing a confrontation through occupation of university buildings: "It may sound nihilistic to you, since it is the opening shot in a war of liberation. I'll use the words of LeRoi Jones, whom I am sure you don't like a whole lot: 'Up against the wall, mother fucker, this is a stickup.' " Students then took over Fairweather Hall, the graduate social science building, with four hundred of them cooking, singing, and making love together, "in public view, nobody cared, we were 'liberated': here was a single commune in which the adult hypocrisy did not apply any longer, where people shared and shared alike, where democracy decided everything, where people were free of adult values and codes," as one eyewitness recorded.

To imagine that the authorities would cave in to such naive, self-gratificatory behavior was, however, immature. In a demonstration of force not unlike that which would overwhelm Alexander Dubček's Prague Spring, more than a thousand baton-wielding policemen put an end to the student occupation on April 30, 1968. The much-vaunted New York student "revolution" was over.

Anarchy and Looting

In Georgetown, meanwhile, the university was under curfew for much of April, its campus protected from black rioters by the National Guard. Washington's was a different kind of revolution from that of Columbia University, one that threatened the multicultural dream of which Martin Luther King had spoken with such eloquence only a handful of years before.

Bill Clinton, having volunteered to drive Red Cross provisions into the burning city, took his Hot Springs neighbor Carolyn Yeldell with him. They were both frightened and exhilarated. Bill deliberately drove his Buick convertible down to Fourteenth Street, where, he predicted, the sight of such anarchy and looting—burned-out storefronts, broken glass everywhere—would be a sight Carolyn "would never forget."

She didn't. Violent confrontation rather than progress by negotiation had reached the very epicenter of America, its capital—and the outlook for peaceful democratic change, both that day and in the ensuing months of 1968, seemed bleak.

The ending of draft exemption for American postgraduate students raised the specter of press gangs followed by forced combat service in Vietnam, where the number of weekly casualties was mounting alarmingly in the aftermath of the Tet offensive. For a final law class, Bill Clinton even prepared a radical paper arguing that the principle of conscientious objection to war in general should be rephrased and extended to cover objection to specific immoral wars—a recipe for national impotence, he knew intellectually, yet an expression of his own intellectual conflict as he faced the prospect of military induction and the dashing of his hopes of going to Oxford.

The world, so long—outwardly at least—a place of hope and socioeconomic improvement, was suddenly topsy-turvy. And nowhere was this more so than in the realm of romantic relations, as the two Southern Baptists from Hot Springs spent the Easter break together.

Spring Break

Carolyn, whose romantic yearning for Bill had turned fervent the previous Christmas in Hot Springs, had arrived in Washington expecting an affair of the heart. Instead she'd gotten arson in the city and a strange, postbourgeois version of romance. Certainly, if Carolyn thought she was the new number one flame in Bill Clinton's heart or his exclusive *amor,* she soon found she was mistaken.

Carolyn was disgusted. Bill, it became clear, was a heel, so determined to enjoy a simultaneous romantic attachment with a fellow Georgetown senior sweetheart, Ann Markesun, that he didn't even cover his tracks. "I would be in the house [in Washington] and he was on the phone with Ann," Carolyn later recalled. Carolyn felt betrayed. Indeed, even Bill's housemates were "furious with Bill for not being honest," she remembered.

Honest or dishonest, Bill—the onetime Baptist—was clearly beginning to move away from his own fifties-style past. He was twenty-one and grew his hair so long that he would be referred to as "Jesus Christ" when walking down Scully Street, Hot Springs, his mother recalled. He no longer played the classical pieces he'd loved at Hot Springs High; instead he played the songs of black Motown and the Beatles and the protest ballads of Bob Dylan and Pete Seeger—not only on his gramophone but on his saxophone. He still worked in Senator Fulbright's office, which was rapidly becoming the center of national political dissent against the war in Vietnam. He might take food, blankets, and provisions to Red Cross centers in burned-out D.C. in good Christian style, but his leanings were, finally, adapting to the mores and politics of the new student era. And these now included sexual politics.

Polyamory

Like JFK, Bill Clinton was a born campaigner, for votes and for women's hearts: blessed with genuine human curiosity and relentless energy and focus on any individual with whom he connected.

To Bill, the affection of every woman counted, even that of initially hostile ones; indeed, such women challenged him more than pushovers, as if, in dueling with such individuals, he might best sharpen his skills—even, on occasion, win an unexpected conversion.

Hitting on attractive but initially reluctant women was therefore not so much a matter of male chauvinism, as it had been for JFK and was for LBJ. Rather, it was a challenge of more modern seductive skills requiring psychological, intellectual, physical, and emotional interplay, not simply power and sex appeal. Whereas JFK had bedded women in a seemingly endless need for phallic conquest as an affirmation of his sexual attractiveness and charm, Bill Clinton by contrast sought increasingly to charm and even bed women in order to assuage his curiosity: to *learn more about them,* their strengths, their weaknesses, their uniquenesses.

Mere conquest, as numbers or notches on a competition pistol, was therefore not Bill Clinton's purpose, as it had been to JFK at a similar age. Both students had imbibed distinctive religious moralities from birth: the one Roman Catholic, the other Southern Baptist. For both of them, therefore, there had been the heightened awareness, and temptation, of sin as a religious construct. Yet there the similarity ended. For JFK, the hunt for love, through seduction and fornication, was a pursuit that energized and electrified his entire personality: the Addison's patient, suffering terminal adrenal insufficiency, seeming literally to come alive and to glow in the presence, or potential presence, of attractive women whose physical subordination ("Wham, bam, thank you, ma'am") would offer temporary sexual relief and erotic fulfillment—usually followed by boredom and the need for renewed chase elsewhere as an affirmation of the elusive elixir, *life.*

For Bill Clinton, abounding in good health, however, boredom played a lesser role than curiosity. The fact was that Bill *kept* his girlfriends even after he'd bedded them; indeed, once he'd moved beyond the morally comforting but asphyxiating constrictions of Denise Hyland's Catholic heritage and overcome the Baptist doctrines on the evils of pre- and extra-marital sex, his preferred game at the age of twenty-one became and would remain for the rest of his life polyamory: the excitement of running several fillies in the same race.

Existential Highs

Outraged and disappointed, Carolyn Yeldell, dutiful Baptist minister's daughter, returned to Ouachita Baptist College. For her, as for almost all members of her sex, monogamy (at least serial monogamy) was the natural, biological, and socialized expectation, as well as a commandment of her religion. For Bill, as a male, it was clearly not. Having the pretty, musically gifted blonde from Hot Springs in one room of his house while whispering tendernesses on the telephone to the striking senior from Georgetown University in another was exhilarating: an affirmation of Bill's modern masculinity, his gregarious personality, his growing love talents.

Bill was certainly not alone. Albert Camus, the doyen of existentialism and one of his favorite novelists, had, on his final, fatal journey to Paris in 1960, composed letters to no fewer than three separate mistresses in the French capital, saying he was looking forward to seeing each of them and to making love. In the White House itself, in the early 1960s, President Kennedy had begun to enjoy this same existential high; indeed, he had also played a whole field of girlfriends, taking this proclivity to the very limits of presidential recklessness: not only continuing to make love with his wife and then with Judith Campbell, his go-between in dealings with the Mafia, but, in the final year of his presidency, inviting one of his favorite "society" mistresses, Mary Pinchot Meyers, to dinner with Jackie in the West Wing, caressing her thigh or rubbing ankles with her while Jackie summoned the soup.

Sudden death had brought the revels of both Camus and JFK to a tragic close, but there had been, for their relatives, a silver lining: the self-censorship of the serious press, which had declined to investigate or reveal their polyamorous escapades at the time.

For Bill Clinton, however, there would be no such cover-up.

The Death of RFK

Five days before the Georgetown degree ceremony, on June 5, 1968, another assassination struck America.

Bill Clinton and his four graduating Georgetown housemates at 4513 Potomac Avenue—Tom Campbell, Tommy Caplan, Kit Ashby, and Jim Moore—had argued all evening, some on behalf of Eugene McCarthy, some against, as they stayed up to watch the results of the California Democratic primary, which would show whether Senator Robert Kennedy had a real chance of becoming the party's candidate for the 1968 presidential election. Kennedy's late intercession and his belated opposition to the war in Vietnam—a war arising out of his brother's escalating involvement of American forces in Vietnam—seemed to some of the Georgetown students opportunistic rather than principled behavior; worse, it would split the Democratic Party, they predicted, while Republicans rallied behind Richard Nixon.

Bill Clinton disagreed. As a would-be politician, he felt a candidate should stand not so much for chosen policies as for a constituency. Bobby Kennedy had begun political life as a Joe McCarthy–ite anti-Communist but had later learned to hearken to a deeper American voice, especially that of the black minority. His privileged socioeconomic background might have screened him both from poverty and from blacks, but the sixties had stripped away the latter veil, as they had for so many Americans. John Kennedy had died a martyr's death; young people still mourned his idealism and in brother Bobby saw a second Kennedy coming. How could RFK ignore that growing constituency? How could he *not* seek to lead it? Some politicians made waves, like prophets of old; some rode the wave once it was rolling.

With Robert Kennedy's triumph certain, the boys had gone to bed. The next morning, however, they awoke to the news of his murder.

The mood at 4513 Potomac Avenue turned from elation to depression. Had Bobby been the first Kennedy to fall to an assassin's bullet, his death might still have led to a landslide Democratic victory in 1968, as had happened to LBJ in 1964. But as the second assassination—indeed, the third in the wake of Dr. Martin Luther King, Jr.'s murder that spring—it seemed like the closing of a door upon an era: the era of virile debate, free discussion, fresh ideas.

The Columbia University sit-in had ended in police brutality. In France, General de Gaulle had suppressed the May "disturbances" with police and military force. In Czechoslovakia too, the Prague Spring was heading toward catastrophe as Soviet troops prepared for war not against the West but against their own Communist brethren. Everywhere, lines were being drawn between Right and Left, power and protest, violence and nonviolence, old and young. Might was proving right. And each day, the Vietnam draft drew closer.

Leaving the Capital

As a young man averse to violence, given the traumas associated with his domestic upbringing, Bill Clinton was out of his depth in such an era. His heart sympathized with the tens of thousands of poor and discriminated-against blacks marching on Washington on June 25, 1968, without their great leader, yet his study of world history did not lead him to believe that the anarchy, arson, and looting he had seen in the city in April could possibly achieve anything other than the mobilization of the Right, which was now happening, King's successor, the Reverend Ralph Abernathy, arrested by the police as his March on Washington deteriorated into vandalism.

It was in this context that the senator's intern, who had once predicted he would occupy Fulbright's seat, decided to leave the capital after commemoration and spend his summer helping the senator's Arkansas campaign for party renomination, prior to leaving for England—if his draft deferment held.

The ceremonies at Georgetown University were, as they had been at the end of his high school years, abandoned due to heavy rain, and the students were told to expect their degrees in the mail. In Arkansas, however, the sun shone on The Graduate, returning in triumph. The president of Georgetown University, Father Campbell, had personally congratulated Bill. "I want you to know how proud I am of you," he'd written on hearing of the Rhodes Scholarship award—only the second ever given to a Georgetown University student and the first ever to a School of Foreign Service undergraduate—"and of your studies and activities at the University, which merited for you the singular honor of being selected for the Rhodes Scholarship. I know you realize what a personal tribute this is to you and how warmly we feel towards your achievements."

Bill Clinton was equally proud. Yet he was glad, too, to be able to leave his Georgetown years behind him and move on. As he put it to his housemate and rival for top grades at Georgetown, Jim Moore, when persuading him to come help Fulbright's reelection effort, the campaign trail in Arkansas would be "great. We'll drive around the most beautiful state on the planet and talk to judges during the day and date their daughters at night."

In the summer of 1968, with Anne Bancroft in the forefront of the public consciousness slipping off her silky stockings before the mesmerized young graduate in Dustin Hoffman's debut film, no young man in Moore's position would need much persuading.

CHAPTER ELEVEN

ON THE FULBRIGHT TRAIL

Big Fish, Small Pond

Daughters and their mothers, as Jim Moore found, took to big Bill Clinton; indeed, southern hospitality took on a whole a new meaning in the backward state where Bill had been shunned as a small child but was now treated like a prodigal son.

Such treatment was interesting, given Bill Clinton's childhood. Though he had been admired by his teachers at Georgetown University and his friends, there had remained always the fact that he was not, in the end, a patrician: was not well born or well connected in a way that would ease his path in the capital, socially or even in the hierarchical wheels of government. He had no money or class; indeed, he was still looked down upon by the snobs of Loyola as a "country boy," despite his bravura performance on "East Pampas."

Thus, as he thought about politics while preparing to do battle for his political mentor and boss, Senator Fulbright, Arkansas did not seem such a bad place to start a career—as his Washington friends, better born and better connected, were quick to see. Tom Campbell, who visited Bill again that summer in Arkansas, recognized Bill's ambition to become, ultimately, U.S. President. He did not mock it; "Why not?" he asked in retrospect. Yet it did not seem "a realistic possibility," Campbell recalled, owing to the finance necessary to mount a national campaign, indeed the need to attain national prominence before one could think of such an eventuality. There were other offices, however, to which the twenty-one-year-old could aspire, indeed for which Bill's Arkansas background would be a perfect base, Campbell reckoned—for instance, becoming one of the state's two senators, "like Senator Fulbright," if he chose. At all events it would be in his home state, Campbell felt, that Bill would be wise to first stake his claim and "make his future"—a state where, given his extraordinary talents, Bill would stand out as a major potential player even *without* money: a big fish in a small pond.

Another student friend, several years later, agreed. As this friend saw it, Bill's pride and comfortableness in Arkansas was a powerful asset. Arkansas was "a part of Bill Clinton in the way that baseball was a part of Joe DiMaggio," he claimed, without intentionally exaggerating.

However much others might mock the legendary land of hillbillies, lunkheads, and watermelon growers, Bill Clinton was and would remain genuinely proud of it. Moreover, Bill represented a change in culture, from patrician to populist, that was in tune with the times. He might not be a student revolutionary or even a Haight-Ashbury pothead: but he was, nevertheless, a child of the sixties—an era in which the old class distinctions, indeed distinctions in every field of Western society, were fast eroding. With his manifest multitasking talents, he might well go straight to the top.

The Fall of Class Barriers

The erosion of class barriers would be an aspect often ignored by political pundits and even cultural historians of the period, who tended to assess the 1960s in terms of the issues and values that divided the old and new generations. Allen Matusov, for example, would excoriate the "fashionable theories and permissive claptrap" that "set the scene for a society in which the old values of discipline and restraint were denigrated." Margaret Thatcher would, characteristically, be even more damning. "We are reaping," she liked to say, damning the moral legacy of the hippie generation, "what was sown in the sixties."

Doubtless this was so, but it overlooked the fact that Margaret Thatcher, a simple rural grocer's daughter, could go to Oxford University and become, thanks to the sixties, the first woman Prime Minister of the most class-conscious country in the West. Her ascent owed itself to a liberalization of social attitudes that permeated every stratum of Western society, as traditional distinctions—in both senses of the word—were questioned and often found wanting. As the cultural sociologist Pierre Bourdieu would show, taste had always served to keep the lower orders in line. Thanks to the sixties, however, the lower orders dared to scale the walls of the citadel and share in the business of power.

With working-class grandparents and a working single mother, Bill Clinton, coming of age in the 1960s, would thus be heir, as much as Mrs. Thatcher, to the social and political dismantling of old frontiers. And nowhere was this more vividly apparent to Bill Clinton than in the summer of 1968, traveling and campaigning with patrician Senator William J. Fulbright.

Traveling with the Pin-up Boy of Hanoi

Making twenty-one-year-old Bill Clinton his personal driver, Senator Fulbright attempted to move with the times. It would be his last primary victory, however. He had toed the white line in the South, not only signing the ignoble Southern Manifesto but voting against President Johnson's Civil Rights Act of 1964 and the Voting Rights Act of 1965. In this less-than-noble way, in a still bigoted southern state, Fulbright had held on to his Senate seat, allowing him to remain, as chairman of the Foreign Relations Committee, a world statesman—a quid pro quo wonderfully illustrated by a confrontation between the sixty-three-year-old senator and four hundred drunk supporters of his nemesis and main rival for Democratic nomination, the Arkansas jack-in-the-box "Justice Jim" Johnson, at the Poor Boy Duck Club in Lonoke County. Criticized for being unpatriotic in opposing America's war in Vietnam and labeled a "Communist" or "Pin-up boy of Hanoi" by the venomous-tongued Johnson, Fulbright told the four hundred hunters and farmers where to get off. They were experts on farming, he grunted. He promoted their agricultural interests in the Senate without question, even their views on segregation; he, however, was the expert on foreign relations; in that arena they should simply accept that he knew better.

Bill Clinton, turning twenty-two on August 19, was awed by Fulbright's campaigning courage, on the one hand, and acceptance of racial bigotry, on the the other. Puzzled, he felt that Fulbright did not necessarily need to pose as a leader of civil rights (Fulbright had, after all, been brought up in Fayetteville and had scarcely ever met a black person in his youth) or as a proponent of integration. But he did, in Bill's eyes, need to *engage* with such a cardinal issue of his times and encourage others in his home state to do the same—not simply run away from it.

The stage was thus set for confrontation, not only between Senator Fulbright's team against "Justice Jim" Johnson and his wife, Virginia (who was running for the Democratic nomination for governor), but between the senator and his young aide/driver.

Driving Fulbright Crazy

"Affable and obviously smart," one of Fulbright's aides later described Fulbright's chauffeur, "Clinton had won a Rhodes Scholarship and planned to go to England in the fall. His southern manners were spiced with just a bit of eastern brashness. Bill [Clinton] was quick to voice opposition to the war in Vietnam, but he seemed just as happy to talk about Arkansas folkways and personalities." By contrast, Senator Fulbright was "sardonic" and "no longer knew a lot of people in our state. 'All my friends are either dead or in nursing homes,' he told me."

The aide was Jim McDougal, head of Fulbright's office in the Federal Building in Little Rock. Wealth was both a boon and a problem for Fulbright, McDougal knew. The Fulbright family had owned not only the Fayetteville newspaper, *The Northwest Arkansas Times,* but a bank, a furniture factory, and controlling shares in a railroad connecting Fayetteville and the family's lumber mill in Madison County, next door—a financial empire of which Fulbright had become president at age nineteen, when his father had died. Funded in large part by his wealth, Fulbright had never had the common touch and by the late 1960s had lost touch with his constituents.

Bill Clinton, by contrast, had inherited nothing save an anonymous gift of high intelligence, an alcoholic stepfather counting Buick spare parts for his brother's dealership in Hot Springs, and a nurse-anesthetist mother. As such, if he himself were ever to succeed in politics, he would have to do what he'd done in his freshman and sophomore years at Georgetown University when canvassing for East Campus student president: go out and win support from the widest possible constituency of voters.

Bill recognized, however, that he could not pose as an old-style politician, espousing this issue but not that, according to the arbitrary, contradictory, and even eccentric logic of old-fashioned southern Democrats. That kind of politicianship belonged to a dying breed, he felt: a generation born, raised, and living their formative adult years in simplistic times with simplistic polarities; a binary world in which every issue had its positive or negative. Fulbright was against civil rights ("I never heard him utter a word in support of civil rights," McDougal recalled), but also anti–war in Vietnam—while the majority of Arkansas voters were pro–war in Vietnam but also against civil rights. "They hated the Viet Cong as much as they despised the civil rights workers who had been spreading leftist beliefs around the south," McDougal said.

What worried McDougal more, on the domestic front, was Bill Clinton's arrogance. "Fulbright expected the deference normally paid to senators. Convinced of his own brilliance, Clinton expressed opinions at variance with Fulbright's views. Neither yielded. They drove around jabbering at each other, and it drove Fulbright crazy."

Chauffeur Dismissed

The candidate and his driver admired each other's intellects across the forty-two years that separated their ages, but they were clearly poles apart in their notion of political responsibility, campaigning, and leadership: a contrast that would one day characterize the difference between old Democrats and the new Democrats of the baby-boom age.

So crazed did Fulbright become over the behavior and arrogance of his young driver, meanwhile, that the senator's campaign journey became a veritable nightmare. Not only was Bill a bad driver, but he was entirely ignorant of car mechanics. On their very first day on the road together, the car's floorboards began to fill with water. They called McDougal, who told them to open the car vents and release the moisture from the air-conditioning system they'd turned on—"two goddammed Rhodes scholars in one car," McDougal sneered, "and they couldn't figure out that they were making it rain."

Worse still, in Hot Springs, Bill Clinton got into an argument with the editor of his birthplace's newspaper, the *Hope Star*—jamming all access to the Arlington Hotel with the senator's car he'd driven into the driveway and causing the senator to be summoned from his room in person. Fearing that the newspaper editor, riled by his young aide's argumentativeness, would declare against Fulbright's reelection, Fulbright went "out of control. He couldn't bear any more. He couldn't bear another minute of it," McDougal recalled. Bill Clinton would simply not "shut up."

When the senator set off again the following Monday, he was at the wheel, alone. Bill Clinton, aide de camp and chauffeur, was sacked. The Rhodes Scholars were parting ways, literally as well as metaphorically.

Dangerous Liaisons

Fulbright's dismissal of his opinionated young driver did not help the senator on his road trip. In place after place the senator's "foul mood" did him in. "You're not leaving here until you answer some questions," a voter said, barring the senator's exit from a barbershop in Forrest City. "Fuck you," Fulbright responded, "I'm leaving." As McDougal recalled, Fulbright "lost Forrest City by an overwhelming margin in the primary. Hell, he lost every county he visited on that trek." Though he won the primary overall, the writing was on the wall.

Bill Clinton, meanwhile, went home in disgrace. He made a few speeches—especially against Alabama Governor George Wallace's candidacy for the presidential election, which could only further disgrace the South. Otherwise The Graduate concentrated in his final months in America on girls. In Hot Springs and Little Rock—where Bill shared an apartment with a couple he knew from his time with Judge Holt, the Frays—Bill dated a bevy of women: Sharon Ann Evans, the reigning Miss Arkansas and a staunch Republican, who came to see him in Hot Springs and took him, for the first time, into the governor's mansion in Little Rock, from which the first Republican governor since Reconstruction, Winthrop Rockefeller, had ousted Faubus after the latter's record six terms in office; Ann Markesun, the tall, handsome, blond, argumentative fellow graduate of Georgetown, who flew from Washington to see and fight with him; Carolyn Yeldell, his beautiful, blond, musical next-door neighbor in Hot Springs; and a host of women he'd gotten to know on the Fulbright campaign trail. Virginia was proud of him; indeed, his bedroom was kept as a sort of shrine to her trailblazing son. She had a picture of him playing cards on a band bus, where his likeness to the young Elvis Presley was extraordinary. She could legitimately become her son's groupie.

Virginia thus welcomed one buxom blonde after another into her Scully Street home, as did the Frays in Little Rock. It was up to the women to decide if such *liaisons dangereuses* were acceptable to them. Some, like the Arkansas beauty queen, were fatalistic. "I don't know if I thought of us as an item. If I did, it was fleeting," Sharon Evans later acknowledged. "There were so many other people in Bill's life," she allowed. "Maybe deep down I had a sense that I knew where his life was headed"—not only politically but in terms of his relentless promiscuity.

Poor Carolyn Yeldell, however, was less clear where Bill was heading. She had only just adjusted to the rivalry with Ann Markesun when she discovered that Sharon Evans was a serious player, too! "I walked out my back door and up the front walk to Bill's front door—and saw Bill and Sharon through the window. They were standing embraced in a major kiss near the table. It was that classic moment, right before I was going to ring the bell."

Transfixed, the voluptuous, talented daughter of the Baptist minister not only saw her dreams of becoming Mrs. Clinton turn to dust but in that moment finally had a psychic vision of Bill's polyamorous future. As she later put it, Bill wore "good on one shoulder, bad upon the other." The once charming boy from next door, happy to play Monopoly or Scrabble or race her to finish *The New York Times'* crossword puzzle or practice his saxophone to her piano accompaniment or sing simple ballads with her, was still the same charming, affectionate, loyal, and gregarious young man, devoted son and responsible, angelic older brother to Roger Jr. It was just that in the six years since he'd moved into the show house next door, he'd come of age. Insisting on studying in Washington, D.C., even when he failed to win a scholarship for his first year, he had expanded his personal world exponentially.

It was not only women, though, who felt hard done by. Men, too, could feel aggrieved. "Bill had the need and the facility to reach out to everyone," his Georgetown friend Tom Campbell explained later. "The rest of us were content to have our circle of friends and others we just 'knew.' " Bill, by contrast, "wanted to meet everyone, and he wanted everyone in the circle."

Bill's inclusiveness inevitably gave rise to jealousies. For those women who saw themselves in a special place in Bill's affections, especially, this promiscuity of friendship, this indiscrimination and blurring of frontiers, could be galling. Carolyn Yeldell felt hurt as well as deceived. "I needed honesty," she maintained. Though Bill had not been overtly dishonest, she couldn't help feeling betrayed, at least insofar as monodating was concerned. "He hadn't ever said to me, 'I'm going to start dating Sharon now, so you're not my girlfriend anymore,' " she acknowledged—but the effect of his inconstancy was almost worse. "He would sort of play the field," she said, overlooking the fact that upper-class and upper-middle-class women had practiced premarital polydating (known as "coming out" in higher English society) for centuries.

For Bill, by contrast, "playing the field" while not actually committing himself to any one relationship was the closest he could get to honesty. Not only did he not wish to confine his amorous intentions exclusively to one woman, but after his relationship with Denise Hyland came to an end he could not turn a former, current, or new friend away—and saw no reason why he should.

For Carolyn, who had attended Ouachita Baptist College in Arkadelphia, not far from Hot Springs, such an attitude, though it might be replicated across America among millions of male graduates and undergraduates—indeed might be institutionalized in any one of the five thousand young people's communes springing up across America in the sixties—was immoral and immodest. Her mother had been appalled over the notion of her witnessing a childbirth, an event in which Carolyn necessarily got to see another woman's private parts. Although her own attitude to nudity was not as close-minded, her character had inevitably been molded by her upbringing in the house of a Second Baptist Church minister and his wife. Neither as a minister's daughter, nor as a woman with the evolutionary agenda of her sex, could she condone polyamory. "I turned around," Carolyn recalled, "and went back home"—in more ways than one.

A Personal Agenda

"The woman I marry," Bill had already warned Carolyn emphatically, "is going to be very independent. She's going to work outside the house. She needs to have her own interests and her own life and not be wrapped up entirely in my life."

Such was Bill's personal agenda as, once again, he prepared to leave home, this time for his first trip abroad. His uncle Raymond Clinton, appreciating Bill's teenage decision to change his name to Clinton and proud of his stepnephew's Rhodes Scholarship, had managed to finagle things with the local Garland County Draft Board so that Bill could spend at least a year at Oxford before being inducted into the military (for which he had been classified as 1-A, fit for service in March that year). The chairman thus kindly agreed to "put Bill Clinton's draft notice in a drawer someplace and leave it for a while"—to give the boy "a chance."

Bill was over the moon. He still loved Arkansas, but he was not sorry to leave. His home state was as rich in contrasts and contradictions as ever—an aspect that was epitomized somehow in the latest family scandal. To the consternation of old buddies such as Gabe Crawford and the Clinton side of the family, less than a year after Roger's death, Virginia had fallen in love with her former hairdresser, Jeff Dwire, who'd been sent to prison for fraud and was suspected of being a gold digger. Ignoring the Clinton family concerns as she'd once ignored the Cassidy family's predictions of disaster if she married Roger Clinton, Virginia seemed hell-bent on marrying Dwire.

Oxford, England, in such circumstances, promised to be a blessed relief.

CHAPTER TWELVE

RHODES SCHOLAR

A Voyage to the Old World

Aboard the twenty-year-old steamship SS *United States,* smoke from its two funnels billowing behind the vessel like curling Arkansas twisters, the thirty-two Rhodes Scholars of 1968 began to visit with one another. As if campaigning for office, Bill Clinton was determined to get to know each one of them before the voyage's end at Southampton, when they would be bused to Oxford and dispersed to the various constituent colleges of the university to which they were assigned.

In New York, before sailing, Bill had been given an introduction to the writer Willie Morris, who came from Mississippi and who'd been a Rhodes Scholar a decade before. He and Morris, driving around New York, had discussed their southern roots; "against the glittering Manhattan back-drop we talked of how poor Arkansas and Mississippi were, and how much he loved and felt for his native ground," Morris later reminisced. "We spoke of history books and family, and dogs and cats, and the feel of be-longing in this country."

They also talked about "women and love. The youngster had grit," Morris—who found the young Arkansan "intelligent and inquisitive and warm"—reflected. On board the SS *United States* most of Bill's fellow Rhodes Scholars—men such as Frank Aller, Strobe Talbott, George Butte, Darryl Gless, and Rick Stearns (women scholars were ineligible by the terms of the Rhodes Trust, though there were a number of female Fulbright fellows and postgraduate students heading to Britain)—felt the same. It was almost impossible, in fact, to dislike the young man once you met and spoke to Bill in person—"down to earth," as Gless put it, "and altogether lacking in pretense."

The weather, however, quickly turned inclement, and most of the scholars retreated to their cabins. One whose hand Bill had not yet shaken was the diminutive Robert Reich from Westchester County, New York, a four-foot, ten-inch student with a brilliant mind and speech like a machine gun. Reich, a Dartmouth College graduate, had already been the subject of a *Time* magazine article pinpointing him as one of the most promising figures of the upcoming generation, along with a brilliant student friend of Reich, Hillary Rodham, at Wellesley College. "She and I were self-styled student 'reformers' then," Reich recalled of Hillary, "years before the radicals took over administration buildings and shut down the campuses. We marched for civil rights and demanded the admission of more black students to our schools."

Hearing that Reich was unwell and confined to his cabin, Bill went down. "The ocean is choppy," Reich later described the encounter. "I'm below-deck in a tiny cabin, head spinning and stomach churning. There's a knock at the door. I open it to find a tall, gangly, sweet-faced fellow holding a bowl of chicken soup in one hand and crackers in the other. 'Heard ya weren't feeling too well,' he drawls."

Reich took the soup and crackers with no intention of imbibing.

" 'Chicken soup will cure anything,' the young man insisted.

" 'But what's your name?' I ask.

" 'Bill Clinton, from *Arkansas*,' he answers, without my having asked where he's from. 'Like some company?' "

Reich was too sick to contemplate conversation—"if this goes on much longer, I'm going to puke all over him," he remembered feeling, as well as Bill's next remark: "This ocean is terrible. Where I come from we don't have anything like *this*."

In a matter of moments, big Bill Clinton had communicated a generous heart, a desire for conversation, and a distinct, even proud sense of his home state. His final words, in the doorway of Reich's cabin, were about the experience they were undergoing—not the rolling of the vessel but the singular privilege of setting forth to the Old World as Rhodes Scholars: "I never thought it would happen to me. Bet you never thought it would happen to you either."

Reich hadn't—but he was too ill to think about that. "I close the door and barely make it to the can," he recalled.

The Silliest Group of Americans

In time Reich would become one of Bill Clinton's intellectual gurus—to the fury of certain Republican critics, who saw in the group of American Rhodes Scholars the root of all later evil: the personification of all that was bad, rotten, and corrupt in the baby-boom generation. The founding editor of *The American Spectator,* R. Emmett Tyrrell, Jr., for example, excoriated the "Rhodies," as he called them. The "Rhodes Scholars who joined Clinton at Oxford constituted the silliest group of Americans to go abroad since the last world tour of Ringling Bros. and Barnum & Bailey Circus," Tyrrell mocked. "At Oxford they became even sillier, if arrogance can beget silliness—and surely these insufferable marplots have demonstrated that it can. Their arrogance was first acquired in America, where they were dubbed 'the brightest, most idealistic generation in America's history.' "

What incensed Tyrrell was that at Oxford, "amongst the Marxists and Marxists manqué," Clinton and his chums "were confirmed in the belief that intellectually and morally they towered above their countrymen"—a "delusion," as Tyrrell put it, that they were "superior in mind and spirit." As Rhodies, they "quickly came to believe that they comprised a momentous generation. More accurately," Tyrrell corrected their mistake, "what they comprised was only a subgroup of a generation."

For his part, Tyrrell suffered no such delusions of sixties grandeur. "My peers in that generation shared almost none of their conceits. As an undergraduate I avoided politics and student government," he boasted. Indeed, Tyrrell considered himself and his more ordinary colleagues "pretty much like earlier generations of Americans," that is to say, "normal, conservative, and protesters only of the protesters." In his view, "the Rhodies who shipped off to England gained an arrogance that set them even above their pompous pimply faced peers back home. They returned to America exalted even above the colonized, the feminists, the neurotics."

Oxford

Certainly, in being shipped, literally, to Oxford, Bill Clinton and his fellow scholars were journeying to the heart of English intellectual arrogance. Far from making them swelled heads, however, they would find themselves deeply appreciated by those British students who felt that Oxford, as the most elite of English universities, required a good dose of American salt.

Both Bill Clinton and Robert Reich were assigned to University College, on the High Street, at the center of town, Bill given a suite of spartan rooms in one of the older quadrangles, comprising a simple bedroom and study. The bathrooms were, traditionally, on another floor.

Far from feeling arrogant at this stage in his life, Bill Clinton was anxious about the extent of his draft deferral and awed by the sheer oldness of the place, a seat of learning since the thirteenth century. It had a reputation for religious thought, history, and politics, almost every Cabinet in the British government for the past hundred years having boasted a majority of Oxford men in it. Spread along the low banks of the Isis, the Thames, and the Cherwell, the city was both a museum of medieval, Renaissance, and neoclassical architecture and a great teaching university, its faculty offering lectures in different academic fields while its college fellows instructed undergraduates and graduates in one-on-one, or at most one-on-two, weekly tutorial classes: individual undergraduate tuition of the very highest order.

For Bill Clinton, who had shone in the competitive atmosphere of classroom instruction and discussion, this was a new concept in education. The sleepy lecture theaters, with professors reading from scripts written years before, and personal tutoring based on short weekly essay writing, seemed (as it did to most English students) a pleasant but outdated form of learning. Seminars were still virtually unknown.

However, the true virtue of an Oxford undergraduate education was in the collegiate system, where students from across Britain and its Commonwealth mixed with one another, eating together, joining societies, playing on sports teams from hockey to rowing, and gathering in favorite pubs. It was this interaction that was the real arena of competition, and, given his gregarious nature, his curiosity about people, his photographic memory and quick thought processing, Bill thrived. He was a Yank at Oxford—and proud of it.

On Borrowed Time

Although they were honor-course graduates of American universities, Rhodes Scholars were encouraged in their first year to take courses with second- and third-year Oxford undergraduates, who were still studying for their final B.A. examinations. In the second year, they could continue their chosen studies toward an M.A. or M.Lit., followed by a Ph.D., depending on how long the Rhodie stayed in England.

With the cloud of draft induction hanging over most Rhodes Scholars' heads, however, the prospect of a master's degree or doctorate was truly academic. Given the new ruling on graduate student deferment coming into effect, it was simply impossible for the thirty-two new Rhodies to plan their studies in advance unless they had been classified as unfit for military induction. Thanks to the efforts of his uncle Raymond, Bill Clinton had a one-year deferment by the Garland County board at most. There was no guarantee it would be honored, let alone be extended. Every day at Oxford was therefore on borrowed time.

For the Oxford faculty, there was nothing new in this. Vast numbers of British undergraduates and graduates had been drafted in World War I and again in World War II—dons such as Bill Williams, the Rhodes House warden himself, whose career as a budding historian in the late 1930s had been cut short by Hitler's invasion of Poland and the Low Countries. Williams had risen from second lieutenant in the North African desert to brigadier in six years, interpreting the incomparable Ultra decrypts from Bletchley Park (still a closely guarded historical secret in 1968) to help the Allies plan the D-Day invasion and the subsequent campaign to defeat the Nazis on the continent of Europe.

Vietnam, however, was a different kind of war, waged thousands of miles away, in junglelike terrain, against a mix of uniformed enemy and guerrillas, even civilians, working as the dreaded Vietcong. British experience of such wars, as in Malaya, had taught that the days of colonial rule were over and there was no ultimate alternative but to hand over power to the emerging leaders of such countries. It was a jungle war America could not win—and sacrificing the "best and brightest" for such an enterprise was foolhardy, bringing back memories, for British historians, of World War I and a conflict in which neither side would negotiate peace.

Peace, not war, was what Bill Clinton was interested in—indeed it was, increasingly, his rationale for going into politics. "I remember meeting Clinton and him telling me within forty-five minutes that he planned to go back to Arkansas to be governor or senator," recalled Rick Stearns, "and would like to be a national leader someday." But if Bill did not obey the inevitable, eventual draft instruction to report for military service, any hope of political success would be vitiated. Not even Winston Churchill, who had predicted the futility of the Battle of the Somme in 1916, in which 57,000 of his countrymen and fellow soldiers from the British Empire would become casualties on the first day of battle and 400,000 by the end—had dared to oppose his own government policy in public in time of war. To be sure, Rhodies such as Bob Reich and Strobe Talbott had already demonstrated publicly or gone on public record as seriously opposing the Vietnam War—as for example Talbott's petition, at the Yale commencement that summer, on behalf of 40 percent of the student class, refusing to "pledge ourselves to kill or be killed on behalf of a policy which offends our deepest sense of what is wise and right"—but neither Reich nor Talbott would ever be elected to public office.

Anguished over Vietnam and the looming draft, Bill was thus destined to spend his year at Oxford debating the issue, a recurring nightmare that would never go away.

A Great Appetite for Life

"I am happy if lonely," Bill meanwhile wrote to Denise a week after arrival. "And I'm convinced I was right to come even if I'm drafted out soon."

To his high school contemporary and Hot Springs neighbor Kathy McClanahan Bill was equally appreciative of his new surroundings. "The sun seldom shines till March, or so I'm told; however, there have been a few beautiful days, great for taking long walks through the centuries-old buildings," he reported. "I walk down wooded paths which then follow quiet rivers across the most lush green meadows you ever saw. It's a beautiful and serene place."

If Bill was lonely in Oxford, it was not a condition that lasted long. Cliff Jackson, a Fulbright scholar at St. John's College and also a native of Arkansas, was awed by the ancient university city. "Did I feel, being Americans, we were quite exotic in Oxford? No, not really," he recalled, "I didn't feel I was exotic, I thought Oxford was exotic! I'm from Arkansas! I'm a real Arkansan—so Oxford was certainly an experience for me!" It was not long, however, before the six-foot, three-inch history graduate received the almost proverbial knock on the door. It was Bill Clinton, who had been through his list of Rhodes Scholars and was now going through the Fulbright students. Asked if Bill enjoyed networking, Jackson laughed. "Bill, networking? Oh, absolutely! *Was he breathing?* Of course he was networking!" Jackson scoffed, adding with a disarming smile, "I mean, he invented networking before NBC!"

Contrary to Tyrrell's assumption, each scholar reacted to Oxford in his own way. Some American graduates found social life in Oxford stifling—"like being put in a crypt and awakened one hundred years before," as Tom Williamson, a lonely black student, recalled. Even the diminutive Bob Reich recalled a sense of living in "seventeenth-century and eighteenth-century ruins!"—and with colonial attitudes to match. The college porter, for example, referred to Reich as "the shortest freaking American I've ever seen in my life!" (Reich suffered from Fairbanks disease), but to Bill Clinton this only made the place quainter and more eccentric. He quickly made friends with the porter, despite the latter's fearsome reputation, and was adopted almost as an American mascot. "I read a lot, explore a lot, talk a lot to people from all over the world, try my hand at familiar and unfamiliar sports, take French lessons and an economic tutorial on the side and attend a few lectures a week," he wrote to Kathy. "The pace is much slower than I'm used to."

Such empathy and ability to inspire affection hardly bore out Emmett Tyrrell's later accusation of "Rhodie" arrogance. By contrast, British undergraduates, not subject to military induction and enjoying free tuition at Oxford, felt entitled not only to be vociferously critical of U.S. policy in Vietnam and the failure to redress discrimination against blacks in America but even to call for an Oxford Union debate to discuss the proposition that American democracy had failed! The motion, typically, was passed—by 266 votes to 233.

But if America was becoming unpopular in England, this hardly indicated to Bill the imminent demise of democracy in the United States; indeed, the very opposite seemed to him to be the case. The very fact that across American campuses there was so much ferment and opposition to the administration, compared with the slow, sleepy, even creepy student atmosphere of British universities, encouraged him to see in American democracy an enormous strength that more than made up for the United States' relative newness as a nation. The Beatles, Twiggy, and British pop fashion were altering the face of London, but in Oxford the old divisions of class, gender, and intellectual snobbery made for a conservative, staid environment that was desperately out of tune with the real world.

Too polite to openly criticize or mock his hosts, Bill joined the university basketball club and began to play for its B team at other universities around the United Kingdom. It was as if, in the unspecified months he'd be allowed before draft induction, he was determined to socialize, travel, and learn as much as he could. "I'm continuously on the move, save the unavoidable work in the library," he reported to Kathy McClanahan. "Trying to get to know town and country people," he described his agenda. "Always the character who wanted to do one more thing, go one more place, stay up one more hour, have one more drink," a contemporary at Oxford, Doug Paschal, put it. "He came across as somebody with a great appetite for life."

But if Bill Clinton had an appetite for life, he enjoyed an even greater appetite for girls.

Despoiler of Women

Bill Clinton's promiscuity had already begun at Georgetown: youthful profligacy fanned by the power aphrodisiac of the Capitol and the campaign trail in Arkansas and fueled by a baby-boom society in which the century-old edifice of Victorian sexual morality was finally crumbling.

Following in the great World War II wartime tradition of American troops stationed in Europe, Bill was now in England, "overfed, oversexed, and over here." The power aphrodisiac of politics might be excluded, given his "foreign" status, but Oxford basketball B team trips, even English college rugby, soon made up for it, he found.

Years before, a member of Harvard's football, swimming, and boxing teams, Jack Kennedy had found the same, boasting to a schoolfriend that he could "now get my tail as often and as free as I want." Labeled "Playboy" by his coaches, he described his college self as "Stouthearted Kennedy, despoiler of women"—though with the constant fear of getting one or more of the women pregnant. One of his teammates, for example, on a trip to Cape Cod in which he'd "got fucked 3 times," had afterward received, JFK had confided to his best friend, "a very sickening letter, letting [him know] how much she loved him etc + as he didn't use a safer he is very worried."

For women with access to the Pill or intrauterine devices, the threat of unwanted pregnancy was becoming a thing of the past, however; indeed, the virtues of premarital sex were increasingly being accepted, even by priests concerned with the contracting of stable, enduring marriages in modern Western conditions. Prior sexual experience and a chance to check out one's partner's sexual compatibility before tying the proverbial knot seemed a sensible modern way to proceed: a latter-twentieth-century version of bundling.

Bill Clinton, Despoiler of Englishwomen, thus had no pregnancy worries. Cliff Jackson, who played with Bill on the Oxford University basketball B team, clearly recalled his friend's savoir faire since leaving rural Arkansas. "Women weren't supposed to stay overnight in the rooms," Jackson recalled. "And yet I know during that period he had a woman living with him in his room at University College! She was Indian, from India, that is. I remember meeting her and his telling me about it."

As Bill himself was discovering, the new availability of prophylactics did not address, let alone redress, the age-old difference between male and female agendas. Consciously or unconsciously, women were still in search of a child-giving mate; men might be open to the advantages of a mate but were driven by evolutionary drives to spread their seed. Therein, he found, lay the modern rub.

A Modern Doll's House

Oxford in 1968 was an interesting social environment in which this new collision of agendas took place. In the ancient university town, with its rich assortment of traditions and architecture, some of the smartest girls in Britain were finally challenging the traditional male chauvinism of the university. Two kinds of male response to the challenge were now illustrated by fellow Rhodies Robert Reich and Bill Clinton.

Given his diminutive size, Reich could not compete in athletic games, so he joined the Dramatic Society. "Bill and I were settling into our rooms at different ends of the ancient courtyards of University College when I decided the best way to get to know any of these shy Brits was to audition for a student play and hope to land a part," Reich recalled. A young student, "beautiful like a fawn" (and at five feet five more than half a foot taller than Reich), also auditioned. "In that split second I fell for her," Reich later chronicled his love affair. "Neither of us got parts, and I realized the only chance I'd have to get to know her would be to direct a play *myself* and to cast *her* in it—which I promptly did."

The play was unexceptional, but the real-life story of Mr. and Mrs. Robert B. Reich was to be an old-fashioned drama, a sort of *Doll's House* with a happy ending, in which—whatever the male of the species' biological penchant—sexual freedom would prove no match for the security of trust and love and children, in a marriage of equals.

For Bill Clinton, however, such a whimsical, old-fashioned approach to romantic exclusivity held no allure. What Bill favored was not a Robert Reich–style, but a Wilhelm Reich–style drama. If and when he himself got married, Bill was certain, it would also be a marriage of equals, but an equality of convenience and independence—a seventeenth-century Restoration comedy revived in modern dress, rather than a nineteenth-century melodrama in which the partners run away from a frightening world into each other. Bill and Bob—the "certified dwarf" alongside the "big and lumpy and overweight" giant, resembling Laurel and Hardy as they crossed the college courtyards, engaged in titanic arguments, as Chris McCooey, one of Bill's English friends at University College, later described them—were thus poles apart: the one a thinker, dreamer, visionary, writer, and actor manqué, save in his own self-directed play; the other a born actor on the world's stage with an extraordinary empathy for people, a gregariousness bordering on the manic, and word-perfect recall.

Which play would attract the greater audience was yet to be seen.

Lacking Firm Convictions

Meanwhile, as the afternoon hours of November 5, 1968, ticked away in England, former Vice President Richard M. Nixon's assault on the presidency came nearer and nearer to triumph for the American Right as the Republican—defeated eight years earlier by JFK in the most tightly contested election in American history—picked up (along with Governor George Wallace, standing as an independent) the votes of Democrats unwilling to continue supporting a liberal Democratic Party devoted to civil rights.

American opinions at Oxford polarized. Some students, in despair, sought a single, coherent ideological truth, left or right, Marxist or Conservative—a well-worn path down which they might go in order to make their own mark on the world. Bill Clinton, however, was diffident: too intelligent to believe, after worshiping in Georgetown in a variety of Christian sects, that there was any one church that had a monopoly on God or any one party that had a monopoly on political truth or ideas. Though he had been East Campus student president twice at Georgetown, his name had never been connected with the Young Democrats there, and at Oxford he also steered well clear of any label. As his Republican friend Cliff Jackson reflected, "I never had any sense that he had an abiding, deeply entrenched conviction. On the contrary, my sense was that he did not." Joe Chyrty, who also played on the basketball team, agreed. Joe was passionately opposed to the Vietnam War and became a draft resister. "He and I had conversations about Bill Clinton," Jackson recalled. "And Joe was disturbed that Bill didn't have the courage of his convictions. Of his purported convictions."

In the ideological sense, Jackson was right. Where, though, had twentieth-century political "convictions"—if the word signified principled ideology from which one did not waver—led to? Nazism? Communism in the Spanish Civil War—and in the Soviet Union, which had then destroyed the Left in Spain? McCarthyite anticommunism? Maoism?

"Conviction" sounded good but raised serious questions about humanity in a supposedly civilized world, its certainties all too often accompanied by concentration camps, gulags, graves, incarceration, mental hospitalizations, and show trials—whether Moscow-style or McCarthy-style. Was there not a third, more secular, less ideological way, such as Jawaharlal Nehru had pursued in India, whereby the virtues of democracy—pluralism, diversity, compassion, nonviolence—could be advanced without antihumanist fundamentalism? Would such a centrist, nonpartisan approach necessarily mean lack of conviction? Surely conviction came from somewhere deeper than borrowed political or religious tracts; came from an inner certainty, an optimism about the improvability of human society, a willingness to employ whatever tools were effective, regardless of party or political allegiance, and took into account the realities of a situation, its past, its present, and its potential in order to effect Professor Quigley's "future preference."

Other contemporaries at Oxford, such as Tariq Ali and Christopher Hitchens, boasted clear slogans, saw simple enemies, and wore dark glasses in which everything looked either black or white. (Later, the lenses of such convinced students would be reversed.) Bill Clinton, however, could not see life or politics that way, even at twenty-two. That fall, his long paper on political pluralism in the USSR for his anti-Communist Polish politics tutor Zbigniew Pelczynski was considered, by the tutor, such a model teaching tool that he would keep it and use it with other students. As Pelczynski noted, the normal Oxford essay of five to ten pages did not suit Bill, for it demanded a driving view that shaped the argument of the author as an indication of an incisive mind, employing insightful reading to advance an argument; whereas Bill's forte had become, thanks to Georgetown and his work for Senator Fulbright's office, extended analysis: mastering complex material, synthesizing it, and doing justice to different interpretations. He would not be as dispassionate or distanced as a true academic scholar, yet by the same token he was not prepared to take a radical or ideological stand that did injustice to the complexity of a subject. In reviewing prospects for the Soviet Union and having read some thirty books in two weeks for his paper, Bill typically allowed for six alternative futures for the USSR, of which two—moving in the direction of either parliamentary democracy or collapse—were, he felt, the most likely. Yet he refused to pretend, as a twenty-two-year-old student of politics, that he had any profound grasp of Soviet life or its system and warned the reader that any conclusions must necessarily be "hypothetical." As he noted, "Certainty is precluded by the volatility of Soviet politics, fragmentary evidence, questionable evidence, questionable reliability and variety of plausible interpretations of available evidence"—adding a final caution, "this writer's very limited background."

It was, in its carefulness, leagues away from the Rhodie arrogance men such as Emmett Tyrrell would later impute; indeed, it was all too illustrative of Bill's besetting sin: verbosity and inability to make decisive judgments.

Mrs. Dwire

While other students went back to their books or their homes for Christmas, Bill Clinton had hoped to travel behind the very Iron Curtain he had studied and written about. At heart he wanted to *understand* better, not leap into easy certitudes. Whether it was a trait that would make him an effective leader or administrator, only time would tell. He was still, he recognized, only at the beginning of his political journey, but at least he had a clear idea of his goal at an age when few of his contemporaries even knew what they wanted to do with their lives.

Bill's biggest anxiety, as the fateful year of 1968 came to a close, however, remained the draft—a cloud that was darkened further by a new and menacing family storm gathering over his mother's personal circumstances. A few years before, he had changed his own name to be the same as hers. Now, in a phone call from Hot Springs, he learned from Jeff Dwire that his mother was about to become Mrs. Dwire, abandoning the Clinton name. Jeff asked Bill if, instead of traveling to Communist Eastern Europe, he would attend the wedding as a surprise for his mother—and, on Bill's affirmative reply, he sent him a ticket.

Hot Springs, when Bill reached it, was worthy of its name. Virginia, Bill found, was simply head over heels in love with Jeff; it was impossible not to be excited for her as she went down the isle at the Oaklawn Methodist Church, not far from her beloved racetrack.

But as Bill turned from his mother's future to his own, in the wake of Richard Nixon's triumph in the presidential election and the Oxford Union debate, he was increasingly uncertain where American democracy was heading.

The Demise of Sin City

Virginia Cassidy Blythe Clinton Dwire's third marriage outraged a number of the righteous burghers of Hot Springs, a town that, thanks to Governor Winthrop Rockefeller's new crackdown on illegal gambling, was busy being converted by the powers that be from a Las Vegas–style gambling town into a retirement city for pensioners, its errant soul and vitality ripped right out of it—and, sadly, out of Arkansas.

Virginia was furious with the new governor, but Rockefeller—the first Republican governor since Reconstruction—intrigued Bill Clinton. Bill had visited the governor's mansion in Little Rock with Sharon Evans in the summer. Now he found himself being *asked* to meet the governor, whose son was going to go to Oxford. A meeting was thus arranged for the day after Virginia's wedding, at the Rockefeller estate at Winrock, at the top of Petit Jean Mountain.

It was Winthrop Rockefeller's candidacy in 1966 that had persuaded Governor Faubus to retire after a record six terms. Rockefeller had thereafter trounced the "fanatical segregationist" Jim Johnson and as governor had spurred black voter registration, indeed had almost literally single-handedly faced up to Arkansas's civil rights responsibilities and other problems in the legislature, where he had the support of only 3 Republicans out of 135 seats. Rockefeller's courage and conviction, especially in pushing black voting rights and pressing for prison reform, tax increases, and the revival of a genuine two-party (instead of a corrupt Dixiecrat one-party) system, would raise him head and shoulders over any other Arkansas politician of his generation. But in the case of Hot Springs, his directive to smash the gambling edifice of the "sin city," once and for all, was, in Virginia Clinton's eyes, wholly disastrous. Arkansas archivist Tom Dillard acknowledged that Rockefeller's directive was the "most dramatic success" of his regime, with police raids conducted under the "glare of television lights" and a resultant reign of legality that would allow Hot Springs to cast off its criminal past and "enter a new era of prosperity based on tourism and industry." Virginia, however, as a resident of Hot Springs since 1950, was mortified. The new governor, as she put it, "finally put the kibosh" on illegal gambling, and the town reeled. Hot Springs would no longer compete with Las Vegas; indeed, its days of glory were over. In time it would become just a pretty, fabled retirement community, devoid of excitement.

The effect, in her view, was worse than that of a tornado. For almost two decades she had been living, working, gambling, and enjoying life in Hot Springs. Henceforth she would see fewer, not more, tourists, no industry, and more and more Harley-Davidsons—as well as hookers plying their grim trade on the sidewalks instead of inside civilized, clean establishments. And it was all Governor Rockefeller's fault, she later lamented.

While Las Vegas, Nevada, mushroomed from a small city less than twice the size of Hot Springs into the world's single most profitable and vibrant entertainment metropolis, with new hotels, museums, art galleries, theaters, restaurants, and spas, Hot Springs fell increasingly into disrepair and despair. Without illegal gambling income to help pay for the city to be cleaned and policed and its facilities to be maintained, the city became no longer a "place apart," a "state of thought," cosmopolitan and enriched by visitors of every background and faith, but a close-minded Bible Belt city much the same as other Arkansas towns. Central Avenue quickly deteriorated, its bathhouses closing down and topless bars offering sleazy business at complete variance with its once celebrated spa town venues. Prostitution flourished openly, as did drug dealing. Hell's Angels would ride into town for weekend bouts of raucous abandon. Indeed, Virginia blamed her son Roger Jr.'s gradual slide into drug trafficking and addiction on Rockefeller's supposedly noble act—the backdrop, as she saw it, against which her second son was forced to spend his teenage years.

All this, Bill granted, might be true, if colored by the passion of a mother who loved betting. But what interested him in visiting with the governor—who had just been reelected for a second term—was Rockefeller's politics: progressive politics in a backward state.

Arkansas as Key to the Future

Few young Democrats can have been as impressed by a Republican governor as was Bill Clinton at New Year's 1969. Following his visit to Rockefeller's farm, Bill thanked the governor in a charming note. As a result of Rockefeller's patient account of the issues and problems he was facing, Bill claimed to understand better "where we are in Arkansas and what we should be doing." Such knowledge humbled the Rhodes Scholar. "Now I have more sympathy for you," he confessed privately as a Democrat. "But I have envy too, because your hard won chair, for all its frustrations, is full of possibilities."

Watching Senator Fulbright tailor his coat to Arkansas cloth while pursuing a radical anti–Vietnam War agenda in Washington, Bill had been intrigued by "how you move into the new world and hold on to the power at the same time," as he had confided to Jim Moore in the summer of 1968. But reflecting on Fulbright and Rockefeller—both men born in a different era and both men coming from privileged and wealthy backgrounds—Bill wondered whether they sufficiently recognized the need to communicate with ordinary people and to feel the real pulse of their constituencies: constituencies in which voters wanted to feel courted, listened to; in which the issues could be debated, a dialogue established, and a sense of democratic *journey* be established as people were encouraged to embrace change, once they were drawn into the political process.

Hitherto, Bill had seen the offices of Senator Fulbright in Washington, D.C., as his goal—"Arkansas Senator J. William Fulbright was Bill's mentor and model—a man of principle who stood up against the war," as Reich remembered from his first discussions with Clinton at Oxford. But discussing with the Republican governor in Arkansas the issues of tax increase, penal reform, black voter registration, and commercial incentives for new industry in the state, Bill began to wonder if this moment in Arkansas history, at the tail end of the 1960s, was the turning point not only for the people of the former frontier state but for America too. Suppose the age-old division between Democrat and Republican were a red herring, a construct of the traditional mind? Suppose, regardless of political party, that the issues of modernizing a society with entrenched attitudes in a poor, traditional, backward state such as Arkansas were to prove the key to America's own future? And suppose that political process, once undertaken on the gubernatorial stage and successfully completed, could be transferred to the presidency? Had not the majority of American presidents reached the White House via the governor's mansions of the nation's constituent states?

The prospects were, indeed, exciting. There remained two problems, however: avoiding the draft—and, if he could, matrimony.

"He'll Never Be Faithful!"

Jack Kennedy, as a playboy congressman, had avoided the holy estate for as long as possible, until in his thirties it was forced upon him by his father after JFK had won a seat in the U.S. Senate. Until then (and often afterward) JFK had "played the field": a dance or ritual in which he had held out the lure of romance and possible marriage to tempt beautiful women into his arms and bed without committing himself. In this way, JFK—rich, spoiled, handsome, charismatic, highly intelligent, and ambitious—had cut a swath through the field of America's debutantes and eligible women, enjoying the game as he scored, literally, time after time, without being sent off or losing.

Bill Clinton had the same high intelligence and ambition as JFK, but not the rich father. Times, however, had changed to his advantage. The sixties had transformed the playing field: lower-middle-class boys from Liverpool could top the popular music charts on a global scale; a working-class son of Slovakian parents living in Pittsburgh could become the quintessential avant-garde artist of his age—shot but not killed the day before Robert Kennedy, after having altered his name to "Andy Warhol" and having become "one of the most sought-after guests on the social circuit."

Warhol, a homosexual, found it easy to avoid matrimony. For Bill Clinton, a heterosexual, it was far more difficult—the more so since his energy, drive, and ambition were the very qualities that, according to evolutionary theory, women most looked for in a potential spouse. It was therefore unsurprising that a procession of American women should wish to hitch their wagon to his star. Sharon Evans, for example, had infuriated Bill's mother, the new Mrs. Dwire, by actually suggesting in the hearing of a town gossip that she, Sharon, might become the new Mrs. Clinton just as Virginia surrendered that name. Meanwhile Carolyn Yeldell, daughter of the Second Baptist Church minister living next door, also entertained lingering illusions, despite the previous summer's experience. Carolyn and Bill were, after all, compatible: quick at crossword puzzle solving, both musically gifted, with a common determination to "make a difference" through their lives in the Kennedy political tradition.

Aware that Sharon had set her cap for Bill, Carolyn used the opportunity of Bill's visit home from Oxford to ask, when alone with him at a reception on Lake Hamilton for the newly married Dwires, whether he was "really interested in Sharon"—meaning marriage.

Bill did not respond, and though Carolyn's heart leaped at the notion that Bill might still be "available," she was also troubled. As she had known the previous summer, when watching him passionately kiss another woman, so now in 1969 she recognized another truth: that Bill had changed still more. He had grown up, was no longer simply the fun-loving, playful, loyal, responsible boy next door. He was all of those things still. But like the biblical Adam, it was abundantly clear that Bill had been tempted by Eve and had eaten of the apple. His innocence was over—and in the real world of manhood, he was fated, she recognized, to wander, unable to say no to sexual temptation. *It would always be so,* she realized. As she got down on her knees to pray that night, she asked God whether it was right to even think of marrying such a man.

The answer was unmistakable; indeed, it was like a clash of cymbals. Marriage to Bill was not only wrong but potentially disastrous. "No!" sounded the celestial instruments. "He'll never be faithful!"

The Full Catastrophe

Bill Clinton, as a young man of the sixties, saw it all very differently. Fidelity for him was old-fashioned: an out-of-date concept; a surrender, in terms of the gender wars, to a feminine agenda; imprisonment for life; a denial of a man's inherent masculinity in order to placate women's desire for security, domesticity, and children. Looking at his mother, he saw he'd made a mistake in initially assuming Jeff Dwire to be a gold digger and therefore unworthy of his mother. For the very reason that Dwire *was* a gold digger, the marriage might work—as a trade-off between Jeff's need for financial support and Virginia's need to be in love and for companionship, fun, and respect.

Marrying Sharon Evans, Bill recognized, would get him nowhere—and the same held true for marriage to Carolyn Yeldell, however much he loved her as a friend. He had no wish to be tied down by a house, kids, "the full catastrophe" as Zorba the Greek had so memorably put it. Old-fashioned marriage in the modern world, with its unrealistic, romantic expectation of lifelong fidelity, was a very questionable institution.

The advantage of returning to Oxford, Bill realized more and more, was that it enabled him to sidestep that whole arena, allowing him to sow his wild oats without shame or embarrassment; to travel, learn, meet people, mature.

If, that was, he could continue to avoid the draft.

One of the Healthiest Men in the World

"Time to get back to my other newer life," Bill wrote from Hot Springs to his former *amor* Denise Hyland on New Year's Day 1969. By the end of the first week he was, moreover, confident that he could "finish the year now" in England, if the Garland County Draft Board held off inducting him until the end of the academic year, in June 1969.

Whether it would now depended on pressure that could still be exerted in Arkansas. At a medical examination at a U.S. air base in England, Bill was passed "1-A" ("one of the healthiest men in the western world," he boasted ruefully to Denise in Jack Kennedy fashion, in spite of his numerous allergies). But would the draft board in Arkansas accept the English system of annual year-long university study programs, or would it confuse the three-term components of an English university year with the two independent semesters common to American universities, ending in May? If so, he might not be allowed to complete the third English trimester—a prospect that weighed heavily not only on him at University College but on almost all his American male contemporaries at Oxford save those, like Robert Reich, who were too small or medically unfit.

The parallel with World War I became more and more marked at Oxford, whose college honor rolls recorded the names of students tragically slaughtered in the long butchery on the western front and other theaters— a war that had brought a Pyrrhic victory for the Allies in November 1918 but a profounder defeat within that victory: a sense of a criminal waste of human life. Indeed, the victory had disappointed the victors to the point where the United States had withdrawn from the League of Nations and become deeply isolationist, while the people of Britain and France had become profoundly defeatist, unwilling to risk such sacrifice of life for their country ever again.

In the summer of 1969, word of terrible massacres of civilians in Vietnam by American troops would filter out of the war zone in Southeast Asia, confirming humanists' worst fears. For the moment, though, American students who had been called up attempted to put a brave face on their impending induction. It seemed sad they would not be able to claim the second year of their Oxford scholarships, but one had either to accept such a prospect or refuse to serve. Brigadier Bill Williams, the Rhodes House warden who had risked his own life as a young officer in the western desert in 1941 and 1942, asked pointedly if they could ever look at themselves in the mirror if they didn't, but for students like Bill Clinton, aspiring to political careers in America, there would be other faces to confront: voters'. Refusal to do one's patriotic duty would damn one as a draft resister—a criminal offense—and end any hope of future political service, leading to arrest and imprisonment if the resister ever returned to the United States.

Though his close friend, the sinologist Frank Aller, would decide to take that path, it was not one that Bill dared contemplate.

Don Giovanni

The only other possibility of avoiding service in Vietnam was a third way: doing some form of alternative service. All across America students were seeking legal exemptions. Since neither the Peace Corps nor VISTA was usually classed as a legal alternative to military service, this left only the finding of a "safe billet" as a way out: by joining a university reserve officer training corps, with a minimum of two years' service as a commissioned officer thereafter, preferably in the National Guard, whose forces were for the most part kept in America.

Almost all of Bill Clinton's contemporaries had already chosen this solution or an alternative one that would keep the individual out of the firing line. Had Bill not won his Rhodes Scholarship, and had he gone instead to the University of Arkansas Law School after Georgetown, this was, indeed, the course he would have adopted. His mistake, ironically, was to have won a Rhodes Scholarship to Oxford—where, despite the many U.S. air bases and military installations in England, there was no American ROTC program!

To make matters worse, if Clinton were once drafted by the Garland County board in absentia, alternative ROTC solutions in America would be considered inoperative, as they would constitute clear avoidance or dodging of the draft.

For Bill, so ambitious to serve in politics, the problem of having to do his duty in an unjust war thus became the greatest trial of his early life. Millions of his contemporaries would rely on their influential fathers to keep them out of combat. But with only an impecunious new stepfather, former owner of a beauty salon and ex-felon, to help him, Bill's prospects of combat evasion looked bleak. Without his Rhodes Scholarship he did not have a penny. Nor did his mother, Virginia, beyond her salary check. Thanks to her remarriage "only" a year after Roger Clinton's death, the Clintons of Hot Springs had pulled away from Virginia, and Raymond Clinton had more or less left the picture to keep the family peace. Bill no longer worked for Fulbright's office, and though he had sent a congratulatory telegram to the senator on his successful reelection in November, their falling-out the previous summer meant there was little prospect of assistance from that direction.

For Bill the issue thus became a recurrent nightmare, and his habitual self-confidence began to show cracks. In Arkansas he'd seen his Georgetown girlfriend Ann Markesun again, and they'd argued vehemently. When she came over to Europe in April and the two attempted to travel together, the plan quickly came to grief. "She was very attractive and fiery, and they were always fighting," Bill's Rhodie friend Rick Stearns, a veteran of Eugene McCarthy's presidential campaign and Bill's travel mate, remembered. From Munich, "in the shadow of the Alps with beautiful light snow falling," as Bill reported to his old girlfriend Denise (without mentioning Miss Markesun), he traveled to Vienna and watched Mozart's *Don Giovanni*. It seemed all too appropriate.

It was in the capital of the former Austro-Hungarian Empire, however, that the American Don Juan's relationship with Ann Markesun came to a bitter end. Like Carolyn Yeldell, Ann wanted fidelity. Bill could neither provide nor promise it, as a fully grown man. Just as he knew he was constitutionally incapable of killing Vietnamese people in an unjust war, so, at twenty-two, he refused to pretend he was willing to contemplate a life of sexual faithfulness.

Paying for the Sixties

Having parted company with Ann in Austria, Bill traveled to Bamberg, in West Germany, to meet up with Rudiger Lowe, a German student he'd once met and helped at Georgetown. Together they visited the infamous East German border, a strip of cleared and plowed land running from Austria to the Baltic. Bill stepped into the no-man's-land to have his picture taken, brushing off Rudi's warning that he could be shot with the words "They wouldn't shoot an American." The guards, he was certain, were more interested in watching for their own citizens, not foreign intruders.

Lowe was less certain. The watchtowers of the Iron Curtain dividing the two Germanies seemed a palpable symbol of internal political oppression and self-hate. In this context America appeared, by contrast, a bastion of freedom and tolerance, for all its current troubles—and Bill Clinton a brave and intellectually open-minded democrat.

Back in England, Ann Markesun's doomed visit was followed by one by Sharon Evans, who flew over early in April 1969. Bill squired her around the country, including to London, where they watched the great anti–Vietnam War demonstration in Trafalgar Square beneath Nelson's column— from the safety of the National Gallery's raised portico. Bill tried to maintain his optimism and composure, yet remained racked inside. "Times are getting tough," he reported to Denise. He was sitting on the proverbial fence, and the discomfort was often excruciating.

For all his glamour seeking, his womanizing, and his restlessness, the young JFK had managed to get himself into the U.S. Navy even before America's entry into World War II, despite being patently unfit for military service—and to become a war hero in the Pacific thereafter. Equally ironically, it was this self-same John F. Kennedy who, as President of the United States, had later stepped up the country's military involvement in South Vietnam—leading inexorably into war.

Nixon, during his 1968 campaign, had promised a swift, negotiated conclusion. But like Johnson, the new President would not, as commander in chief, bite the humiliating bullet for another four years, until his own reelection chances hung in the balance. By then another thirty thousand American lives would have been lost and several hundred thousand American casualties sustained—all in the name of pride: of refusing to admit to the enemy, to the world, and above all to oneself that it had all been a mistake, an unwinnable war, in the wrong region, however right the cause.

For Bill Clinton, Vietnam was always a tragic conflict, and for him it was a deeply personal one. More than any other event in his young life, it would make him, as will be seen, into both a liar and a cheat: a basically good son, educated by Baptists and Catholics, blessed with an extraordinary intelligence and a questing mind, a young man with genuine idealism, encouraged by the examples of JFK, LBJ, and sixties liberal Democrats to create a Great Society, yet whose ethical center, his soul, would now be warped and contaminated by America's terrible mistake.

CHAPTER THIRTEEN

AVOIDING THE DRAFT

Goodbye to All That

In 1928, the young English poet Robert Ranke Graves, embroiled in a tumultuous *ménage à quatre* with his wife, his American mistress, and an Irish poet, decided to have done with his past and to start life afresh with his lover, who had thrown herself out of an upstairs window in Hammersmith, west London. Written while Laura Riding recuperated from her back injuries, *Goodbye to All That,* the precocious autobiography of the thirty-three-year-old Graves, not only made him a fortune but permitted him to run away to Majorca with Laura, the source of his White Goddess muse and his abiding inspiration. Even his scandalous accounts of his family and the sufferings of the troops in World War I were forgiven as being the result of shell shock or war trauma.

Goodbye to All That certainly offered an extraordinary account of Graves's intensely homoerotic life at an English boarding school, his surrendering a place at Oxford University in 1914 in order to enlist in the Welsh Fusiliers, and his enduring the horrors of World War I trench warfare thereafter, fighting against an enemy from whose people he himself was partially descended. Yet at the core of the book was the failure of the Allied governments to make peace—and the growing despair of the combatants, who were treated as cannon fodder in a war of artillery attrition.

Graves had served alongside the legendary poet Siegfried Sassoon, a homosexual who won the Military Cross for extraordinary feats of valor while in treasonable pamphlets he opposed continuation of the war—leading to Sassoon's court-martial, his hospitalization in a mental asylum for officers, and his quasi-suicidal resolve to return to action in order to look after "his" men.

Vietnam, too, was a war being continued to the point of human butchery, in which napalm was being used in place of mustard gas. Would Bill Clinton become a Robert Graves or a Siegfried Sassoon? At Oxford he was torn between conflicting options. On the one hand, he knew that he, like JFK, *had* to serve in order to succeed in American politics—at least, he had to be *seen* as someone willing to serve his country. On the other, he objected to the war. But he was unwilling to voice that objection, as Sassoon had done, from inside the military—at least, the combat military—lest in the process he be court-martialed or, as had happened to JFK's older brother Joe, killed.

It was in that conundrum that, at the end of April 1969, Bill Clinton, Rhodes Scholar and former model student, received the letter informing him of his draft induction—and went to pieces.

The Farewell Party

Paul Parish, a Rhodie friend, recalled Bill Clinton's confession, the next day, that he'd tried to get ahold of him. Paul had been in bed with his girlfriend, however, and hadn't answered the insistent knocking—leaving Bill bereft and in despair. According to Bill's own account, he'd "put his head in his hands, and cried."

For the first time in his life Bill had literally no idea what to do. Telephoning his mother and his new stepfather, he begged them to help. Since the new and final term of the academic year had already begun (the draft letter had been sent by sea mail), they were able to get the board to grant a three-month extension, but only until his return to Arkansas in the summer.

Frantically, Bill then called and wrote his friends to see if it would be possible, however belatedly, to get into a National Guard or graduate-level ROTC program, whether at the University of Arkansas Law School or any other—though any such recourse would be dependent on the approval of the State Selective Service System director in Little Rock, appointed by the

Republican governor, Winthrop Rockefeller. To that end Bill wrote to his friend and fellow American student at Oxford Cliff Jackson, who had already returned to Little Rock, and begged his help also. Meanwhile, in an extended three-day party at University College, he bade farewell to his English and other friends with an Arkansas-style hog-roast barbecue in the medieval courtyard, the party spilling up onto the college roof and down onto a punt on the Cherwell.

Bill had become perhaps the most popular Yank of his year at Oxford. He had "this room at Univ that was easily accessible," his friend Sara Maitland recalled, "and the college porter adored him. All was waived for Bill at Univ. It was just, 'Oh, yes, go on in!' It was all sort of looking the other way. Bill was to have all the rules broken. It was dead impressive."

Hundreds of people attended the farewell party. Not even the longest party most people at Oxford could remember, however, could distract from the simple truth: Bill Clinton, one of the most intelligent Rhodes Scholars of the '68 class and certainly the most promising political careerist, was going to war. Would he be a hero, in the tradition of Teddy Roosevelt and John F. Kennedy? Would he be killed—like Teddy Roosevelt's son Kermit—captured, or wounded in the service of his country?

His English friends gave him, as a gift, a deerstalker hat and jungle stick. But the joke fell flat. Bill Clinton simply did not want to go.

Prince Hal

Was it simply that Bill lacked courage, that virtue so extolled by Senator John F. Kennedy in his 1955 Pulitzer prize–winning book on the subject?

Every day Bill felt different, as he wrestled with his conscience. Sara Maitland took him to Heathrow with her boyfriend, Paul Parish. Bill was "just a mess," she recalled. "We had this tearful departure at the airport. It had all become an enormous sort of emotional drama." At least Bill had "decided to go" rather than ruin his career by resisting the draft, like his Rhodie colleague Frank Aller. "Was it the right thing to do? The wrong thing to do?" he asked himself and others. "It was all very stressful, going back to Arkansas," Sara remembered.

It was; indeed, it was leading inexorably to the deciding moment of Bill's early life. "My friends just don't understand my need to serve," he'd insisted to Sharon Evans, for they were all aware of the subversive side of his character: a wayward, humorous, rambunctious daring that was the counterpoint to his more serious, hardworking, toadying self. In befriending the Falstaffian college porter, Bill had played Prince Hal, flouting the college rules with zest and humor. If Bill could just liberate that daring, courageous, princely side of his personality on his return to the United States and induction into the military in the footsteps of his hero JFK, who knew? He might, in embarking on his own journey to Agincourt, win medals and become, like Churchill and JFK before him, a hero and young man of world political prominence.

But this was not to be.

Getting the Draft Notice Killed

Bill's "need to serve," at least in combat, did not survive the transatlantic flight. No sooner had he arrived in New York than he set about pulling the necessary levers to get his draft induction rescinded so that he could fulfill his military obligations in either the National Guard, the army reserve, or ROTC.

How this could be effected, given the ban on switching to such programs after the issuance of a second, official SSS Form 252 notice of induction, appeared at first an insurmountable problem. He was in luck, however— for in an office in Little Rock, working for the head of the Republican Party in Arkansas, was Cliff Jackson, whom he had befriended at Oxford.

Arriving in Little Rock, Bill told Jackson he was quite prepared to serve his country—but not in Vietnam. If Jackson could only help him find a way to get his draft notice killed, he assured his friend, he would happily undertake military training as an officer—and on this understanding, Cliff Jackson agreed to help him.

Whether Jackson could do so in time seemed doubtful. Though he got Bill an interview with Colonel Willard A. Hawkins, the head of the Arkansas Selective Service Board, a new date to report—July 28—had been issued by the Garland County Draft Board, and according to Colonel Hawkins there was no alternative Arkansas National Guard slot or ROTC place available. On July 8, with less than three weeks to go before basic military training, Bill wrote to Denise to tell her the sad news: "I'm going to be drafted. There isn't much else to say. I am not happy, but neither was anyone else who was called before me, I guess."

Bill would not give up, however. He tried medical examinations for entry into both the air force's and the navy's officer candidate programs but failed both—the one for eyesight, the other for hearing. On July 10, with only eighteen days to go, he saw Cliff Jackson again at the Republican Party offices in Little Rock. "He is feverishly trying to find a way to avoid entering the army as a drafted private," Jackson wrote to his girlfriend in England the next day. All avenues, however, "seem closed to him. The Army Reserve and National Guard units are seemingly full completely, and there is a law prohibiting a draftee from enlisting in those anyway. The director of the state selective service is willing to ignore this law, but there are simply no vacancies."

Awed by Bill's extraordinary talent in meeting and getting along with people, Jackson sympathized with his friend's dilemma. He did, however, have a possible solution up his sleeve—if Bill would agree to take a law degree in Fayetteville. "I have also arranged for Bill to be admitted to U[niversity] of A[rkansas] law school at Fayetteville," Jackson related to his girlfriend, "where there is a ROTC unit which is affiliated to the law school. But Bill is too late to enter this year's class unit and would have to wait until next April. Possibly Colonel Holmes, the commander, will grant Bill a special ROTC 'deferment' which would commit him to the program next April, but the draft board would have to approve such an arrangement. . . . I feel sorry for him in this predicament—it could easily [since Jackson had been granted a medical deferment] have been me!"

Too Good to Be True

Thanks to Cliff Jackson, the hastily arranged scheme actually seemed to work. Fulbright's chief assistant in his Little Rock office agreed to call Colonel Eugene Holmes, while Jackson got the head of the selective service board to agree to the 1-D deferment of the draft. Governor Rockefeller's aides then piled further pressure, at Jackson's urging, on Colonel Holmes's office. With so much weight—both Republican and Democrat—behind the effort, Colonel Holmes gave in, after interviewing Bill personally.

At almost the eleventh hour, Bill Clinton had been granted his wish. His draft induction was killed on the contractual understanding that he fulfill his stated intent to go to the UA Law School from September 1969 and to serve in its army ROTC from the following spring, becoming a commissioned officer in three years' time. He would thus be saved from serving in Vietnam.

"On the 17th, eleven days before my induction date," Bill wrote to Denise in excitement and intense relief, "I was admitted to a two-year, two-summer ROTC program at the University of Arkansas for graduates and junior college transfers. I will have a two-year obligation just as if I've been drafted, but I'll go in as an officer three years from now." He was over the moon. "It's all too good to be true, I think."

No Intention of Serving His Country

But almost immediately after he lined up his safe billet, Bill began to have second thoughts. Both his conscience and his political ambition pricked him. Ought he just go to Vietnam and get it over with? "There is still the doubt that maybe I should have said to hell with it, done this thing and been free," he confided to Denise, afraid that the University of Arkansas Law School was an academic backwater. To another girlfriend, Tamara Kennerley, he explained on August 15 that the notion "of not being in the Army now and going to Arkansas law school is almost more than I can handle—just having a hard time adjusting to it." To yet another friend, a Rhodie who had introduced him to some interesting friends on a trip to Washington, Bill referred to himself as "a sick man" and remarked that Arkansas was "barren" of such stimulating people.

Few, however, could really understand Bill's renewed torment, considering that he had legitimately avoided the draft. Did he really now feel he should go to Vietnam? Or was the University of Arkansas, after the spires of Oxford, a fate worse than the Vietnamese jungle? If the latter, did he think, as an ambitious and brilliant young "politico," that the Fayetteville law school's reputation was insufficiently high or its three-year course too long for a Young Man in a Hurry, as one author later titled his biography? Even Cliff Jackson, who did take his law degree at Fayetteville, later confided that the UA school was "not a particularly good one, no. If truth be told, no, it's really not. I think it was beneath him, quite frankly. I mean, as a student he would not have gotten the education as a lawyer that he received at Yale."

Bill had, however, made his commitment and was spared at least service in Vietnam. To Jackson's consternation, however, almost from the moment he received his 1-D deferment, Bill began scheming not to go to the University of Arkansas at all but to go back to England if he could! He duly invited Cliff Jackson to his birthday party in Hot Springs on August 19, but Jackson wouldn't attend, as he later recalled, "because his actions had offended me to the point that I declined. I mean, I'm kinda not the type to go, have a confrontation, and say, 'Bill, you promised me, you promised everybody—'"

This "wiggling" seemed to Jackson far, far worse than Bill's unwillingness to serve in an unjust war. "I went on the hook for him, by lining up the head of selective service, through my boss—they were good friends—[and] by calling Rockefeller aides who were good friends of mine, who then got the governor's office involved in getting that draft notice killed. And to every one of those people, I said what Bill Clinton said to me: 'I want to serve my country. I will go into the ROTC, the army reserve, whatever—I just don't want to go as a draftee. But if you will just kill this draft notice, I will serve my country.' Now, that was an honorable way to avoid the draft, in my mind," Jackson recalled. "I mean, according to my principles. He said the same thing to Colonel Hawkins, the head of Selective Service. He said the same thing to Colonel Holmes and to ROTC up in Fayetteville. He said the same thing to Dean Barnhart at the law school—because law school admissions were already closed! Strings had to be pulled to open an admission slot to get him in so he would be eligible for the ROTC. Strings had to be pulled because ROTC slots were filled and an exception made so he wouldn't even have to participate the whole first semester. I mean, everybody in the Republican Party, at my instance—and I know he was using [Senator] Fulbright on the Democratic side and others, Lee Williams, for example, who was Fulbright's chief of staff—I mean, *everybody's* going to bat for this guy! And yet, within two weeks, after what we did, Bill Clinton had started to 'wiggle' out of his commitment! And you know, that defined him then, in my mind, and defines him today."

A Quagmire of His Own Choosing

For himself, Bill was aware he was digging himself into what he called "a quagmire" of his own choosing—though he could not see the proverbial forest for the trees. "Nothing could be worse than this torment," he lamented to Rick Stearns in Washington as he sought to avoid having to go to the UA Law School. "It seemed really strange going back to Fayetteville," he confided to Denise, "like going back to my boyhood"—a time when there had been simple, inalienable rules about behavior, dress, and righteousness. He'd had his hair cut and "will not be run out of the hometown on appearance," at least, he joked, assuring his Catholic friend that he would in the meantime have a month in which to "get involved with some interesting and fairly forthright activities of the local blacks and kids of both races."

The question of whether to go to the University of Arkansas Law School, a second-tier institution, or just go to Vietnam and have done with it drove him almost insane. "My mind is every day more confused than it was before; and countless hours doing nothing save waiting for the phone to ring are driving me out of my head," he complained. By having gotten his draft order killed, he felt he had demeaned himself in the eyes of Arkansas folks whose sons were in the military—"most of them in Vietnam." Attempting to explain his "anguish," he acknowledged that he was "running away from something maybe for the first time in my life."

The sense that he was making a wrong choice was debilitating. "I know one of the worst side effects of this whole thing is the way it's ravaged my own image of myself, taken my mind off the higher things, restricted my ability to become involved in good causes or with other people—I honestly feel so screwed up tight that I am incapable I think, of giving myself, of really loving. I told you I was losing my mind," he told Stearns. He found himself unable to work with the black kids of Hot Springs, as he'd intended, and did nothing to prepare for law school in Fayetteville. He wanted to hear from Stearns. Above all, "I want so much to tell you we're going back to England."

This was the crux.

Cliff Jackson was appalled.

Becoming a Fugitive

"I knew it by July 26, I think—within two weeks of the time that we did what we did. How did I know? Because I had discussions with him," Cliff Jackson recalled. "And he told me what he was going to do—that he was not going to Fayetteville! The draft notice had been killed, and he was going back to Oxford. Despite his commitment."

As far as Jackson recalled, Bill Clinton had no intention of returning to UA and signing on with the ROTC once the promised officer's slot became available. "No. And I just didn't see how anybody would do that. I mean, you know, what happened was unprecedented—I mean, a draft notice, once issued, is simply not killed, it's not revoked, it's not recalled! Only two people in the country have the authority to do that—the head of Selective Service in Washington, and the head of Selective Service in Arkansas. And they don't do that! Well, it would be extremely rare that that happened. And it happened only because of Bill's commitment to serve in the ROTC and enroll in the law school."

Oxford, however, with its ancient colleges, meadows, and English girls, offered a sanctuary. As Bill's old housemate from Georgetown Kit Ashby recalled, Bill's "basic desire was to be able to go back" to England. Abjuring his conscience and his promises, Bill now simply ran away, in his own words, for the first time in his life.

He was no longer the proud son of Arkansas, the first student from Georgetown's School of Foreign Service to win a Rhodes Scholarship, the brilliant, genial Baptist boy who'd held his alcoholic family together and protected his mother and younger brother through their domestic trials, the believer in civil rights who seemed to have no prejudiced bone in his body. He was going to be a fugitive.

Slipping Back to Oxford

Cliff Jackson was not the only one to be disappointed in Bill Clinton. Colonel Holmes's drill sergeant was equally disgusted. "A lot of people in the unit were kind of mad about it, angry that he didn't show up. We did not know where he was," Sergeant Howard recalled. "We didn't normally have people promise to do something and not do it."

Leaving a vague message for Colonel Holmes that he would be going to Oxford "for a few months" that fall but promising to keep in touch and to enroll at the University of Arkansas Law School as soon as he returned at Christmas to take up his promised ROTC slot in the spring, Bill set off from Arkansas in October 1969 with Rick Stearns—bound for an Oxford that did not expect him back!

The official journal of the Rhodes Association in the United States did not list Bill Clinton for the 1969–70 academic year. Even his tutor Zbigniew Pelczynski thought that Bill had "left and been drafted"—and lamented the "extraordinary and tragic" situation whereby Bill returned, incognito, attending neither lectures nor tutorials. "I might have been able to help him in a difficult time," Pelczynski later berated himself. "I have a feeling he felt his future was so uncertain, his Oxford life was so hanging on a thread, that he simply stopped attending tutorials regularly."

It was in this unfortunate way that Bill Clinton absconded from the University of Arkansas's Law School and its ROTC program, failing the very people who had done so much to help him get out of Vietnam duty: traveling to England with guilt as his baggage and failing even to see his tutor.

In a Funk

Virginia had watched her son all summer with the eyes of a concerned parent. "I didn't really know the agony that he was going through," she admitted later in an interview. "I just knew he played a lot of basketball in the driveway. He shot baskets hour after hour. Shooting off the frustration." In her autobiography, however, she preferred not to mention the episode at all.

Some of Bill's friends, though, felt ill used. "Bill has succeeded," Cliff Jackson reported for example to his girlfriend in England, "in wiggling his way back to Oxford"—leaving Jackson and a host of other implicated individuals feeling embarrassed and distressed.

In the years ahead, this would be an all-too-common kind of experience for those who knew Clinton. Meanwhile, for Clinton himself, the flight to Oxford was the worst of all possible worlds. He had avoided combat service. He had failed to enroll in the UA Law School—the precondition to being granted the special voidance of his formal draft induction. And he had knowingly misled the very colonels who had granted him the draft deferment so that he could enter ROTC the following spring, when a place would become available. At Oxford, whether in shame or in a funk, he simply collected his Rhodes Scholarship funds, then disappeared, ducking out of his B.Phil. program and using the university's famously lax educational system to avoid studying or appearing at tutorials, as well as fulfilling examination and dissertation requirements.

The once idealistic, gregarious, ambitious "politico" had done the very thing he feared—had run away and was alone. Hoping not to be recognized, he grew his hair long once again, even adding a big orange beard, like Vincent van Gogh's. He began to smoke and to doss down or bunk in wherever there was a free floor.

In this, the final year of the sixties, Bill Clinton finally became a real child of the era, a hippie among hippies: demonstrating, taking drugs, playing protest music, fornicating. For those who'd admired the innocent, idealistic, optimistic Rhodes Scholar of the year before, it was not a pretty sight.

A Criminal Legacy

Strangely for Bill Clinton, his second, "incognito" year in Oxford would ultimately become one of the most important of his life. The "goody-goody" student, as his nemesis Emmett Tyrrell would term him, found himself free for the first time in his life to find his *own* way. That self might be tormented, thanks to Vietnam—but then, Vietnam was tormenting Bill's entire generation.

In reneging on his promise to Colonel Holmes and the UA Law School staff, Bill Clinton was committing his first perjury, so to speak, after a life of being good—leading to a lifetime of perjuries. But those who behaved more morally over Vietnam, did they necessarily emerge with a better conscience? Bob Kerrey, for example, would become a decorated naval officer in Vietnam, a commando Seal (in a Sea-Air-Land unit) trained to move in behind enemy lines, and was awarded the Bronze Star (and later Medal of Honor); however, he was also suspected of indiscriminately killing at least thirteen unarmed Vietnamese women and children—possibly more—on the night of February 25, 1969, while Clinton was at Oxford. Like Clinton, Kerrey would later succeed in becoming governor of his state. Like Clinton, he would become promiscuous, enjoying, as a divorcé, a well-publicized affair with the actress Debra Winger. He would support gay rights, win a Senate seat, and compete against Bill Clinton for the Democratic Party nomination to become President of the United States. Then, in the spring of 2001, having given up his Senate seat and become president of New School University, *The New York Times* would reveal his terrible Vietnam secret: that he was, in reality, a war criminal.

At the end of the day, neither man could draw comfort from his Vietnam service or lack thereof; indeed, very, very few Americans of the baby-boom generation would be able to do so. Like World War I for Europeans, the Vietnam War would destroy the self-respect of an entire generation of Americans—and Bill Clinton was, in this respect, no different from anyone else.

As an inheritance from the previous generation, Vietnam was a poisoned chalice, a criminal legacy that turned a whole generation of Americans from sixties idealists into liars.

"We thought we were going there to fight for the American people," Bob Kerrey later complained. "We come back, we find the American people didn't want us to do it. And ever since that time we've been poked, prodded, bent, spindled, mutilated, and I don't like it."

Bill Clinton didn't, either. The previous generation had faked the pass, handing the baby boomers a bum rap: forcing them—heroes and anti-heroes alike—to learn to deceive in order to survive, while the previous generation stood in judgment upon them as liars.

For example, "Justice Jim" Johnson, Judge Holt's gubernatorial opponent in 1966, was at pains to point out, in later years, how much he saw Bill Clinton not only as a product of Hot Springs as a sinful city but as a product of his age. In his southern drawl he'd say, "I liked Bill Clinton, and he has always been ver' courteous to me"—but both Bill and his baby-boom generation were difficult for such critics to excuse. Like others—such as the Little Rock newspaper columnist and editor Paul Greenberg, who coined the phrase "Slick Willie" for Bill Clinton—Johnson would come to see the Hot Springs prodigy as a quintessential "child of the sixties": a time, Johnson later remarked with visceral distaste, of "Vietnam pro-testers, Communists—and homo-*sexuals.*" ("Mama, get me another coffee, will ya?" Johnson would add, wiping his parched lips with the upper edge of a gnarled but still beautiful, Dürer-like hand.) Johnson was a die-hard, unrepentant segregationist of the old school who saw no need to apologize, prevaricate, or lie about his own beliefs, however racist or bigoted. He was proud of his white supremacy: proud to be antiblack, anti-Communist, and antigay and to peddle other right-wing views.

For such archcritics of sixties "children," Bill Clinton would become, over time, the great whipping boy of his generation: a prize example of sixties cultural effluence. "Clinton, the out-of-control dope-and-sex fiend, was their scapegoat," the historian Eli Zaretsky would write. Men like Greenberg and Johnson had passed the torch of an older generation to a new generation of Americans, who, in the earlier generation's eyes, had dropped it. Its flame, however, was Vietnam.

The simple fact was this: If both Bill Clinton and Bob Kerrey became deceitful liars, it would be in part because, tragically, the presixties generation had forced them to become so—a tab that, in their self-righteousness, neither the Greenbergs nor the Johnsons would ever pick up.

CHAPTER FOURTEEN

THE
FUGITIVE

Switching Tactics

For a month Bill Clinton slept on an illegal rollaway bed in the room of his friend Rick Stearns and wore an old Royal Air Force greatcoat to keep warm—and stay unrecognized. He helped Stearns organize the English anti–Vietnam War teach-in and sympathy demonstration outside the U.S. Embassy in London, in line with the 250,000 people who would demonstrate in Washington, D.C.—a demonstration planned to take place in the fall, on October 15, 1969. Then, as the days went by, somewhere between the beginning of October and the fifteenth, he decided to switch tactics in terms of his own draft status.

Three years in the UA Law School ROTC and another two years in uniform as an officer now seemed a heavy price to pay for avoiding the draft, if there was an alternative—and, thanks to President Nixon, there was a new one. If the President introduced—as he had promised in September—his new lottery system, would it not be better to chance that than commit to four or more years of part-time military training?

By switching from ROTC service to the lottery, Bill would, even if he proved unlucky in the lottery, be spared induction for at least another academic year—i.e., until the summer of 1970—since the President had also introduced new rules guaranteeing that all graduate students enrolled in university classes could complete their current academic year before being subjected to the draft. Either way, with Nixon reducing troop numbers in Vietnam and a giant new pool of eighteen-year-olds becoming eligible for the draft lottery, Bill's chances of being inducted for service in Vietnam would lessen appreciably. Calling his stepfather, Bill thus asked for his 1-D ROTC deferment to be switched back to a 1-A classification—in other words, to heck with Colonel Holmes and the ROTC at Fayetteville.

A Palpable Change

The decision, instead of nagging Bill Clinton's conscience, seemed to free him. Instead of going back to Arkansas at the end of the Christmas term, as he'd promised Colonel Holmes, and belatedly enrolling at the University of Arkansas Law School in the second semester, he would take off the entire academic year and ignore the ROTC, chancing his luck with the lottery—as long as it was approved and passed into law by Congress. This seemed almost certain now, for Nixon, desperate to placate his student critics and their middle-class parents, had threatened to introduce the lottery by executive order if Congress dragged its feet or opposed him.

Helping Stearns organize the London teach-in and demonstration, Bill now seemed a different personality. Afterward he would thank Stearns for "taking me in and making the time bearable and then happy when I was so low down." The change was palpable. Steve Engstrom, an Arkansas student on junior year abroad, met Bill at a Vietnam protest–planning meeting at Oxford. As a student politician, Engstrom was amazed he hadn't even heard of Bill before then. Told that he was about to meet a future governor of his state, Engstrom laughed aloud. But when he saw how Bill handled the "intense" meeting—listening to the views of participants and speaking in a calm voice of moderation—he was "amazed." "You're right," he told his companion, "the guy probably will be governor some day."

Bill might be a bearded hippie, but under the unkempt locks he had recovered his composure and knew what he wanted—if his plan worked.

An Absolute Slum

Simultaneously with the demonstration at the U.S. Embassy—at which Bill Clinton acted as a marshal, helping to guide and control the five hundred–strong miniprotest—Bill moved into a house on Leckford Road in

North Oxford, where his Rhodie friend Strobe Talbott, a Russian and Chinese scholar, lived with Frank Aller, who had decided to resist the draft and stay in England.

For £3 per week the bearded boy from Arkansas was given his own room. The house was "an absolute slum," Sara Maitland later remarked, "a mess." The floor was never cleaned, and no repairs were ever done. Visitors and girlfriends moved in and out, sleeping wherever there was space or a bed. "It was rather hippieish," Sara acknowledged. "You never knew who was going to sleep quite where. All the mattresses were on the floor and there were books everywhere."

"Oxford at the end of the 1960s was a place where soft drugs were commonplace and LSD was widely available," recalled another Oxford English contemporary, Martin Walker. With pot, hash, and sometimes a little mescaline being smoked, Maitland recalled, the situation was archetypal sixties: a commune, cheap, domestically anarchic, and intensely human.

Bill Clinton, the little boy who'd been to church and Sunday school on his own since age three, Bible in hand, was finally slumming with the rest—even hitchhiking to Wales one weekend, vainly searching for the poet Dylan Thomas's boathouse home on the river Taff, near Cardiff, while reading American, English, and European novelists and waiting, if not for Godot, then for the new draft lottery, set for the end of November, after Thanksgiving.

Germaine Greer's Phone Number

Many of Bill Clinton's postgraduate colleagues and contemporaries had a live-in girlfriend or "steady." Bill was different. Like his martyred mentor JFK—who had also spent time in England, in the run-up to World War II—Bill Clinton seemed to collect girls like postage stamps. Both men were narcissists, needy of loving attention, but they were predators also, needing the daily excitement of the chase: the thrill of a sighting, the challenge of stalking, approaching, cornering a chosen prey, of confrontation—and, if lucky, of the sweet surrender of his quarry.

"Make love, not war!" was thus a slogan of the times that Bill Clinton did his best, in the fall of 1969, to live up to, with woman after woman. When his friend Rick Stearns asked what he was doing wrong that the object of his latest infatuation was so uninfatuated, Bill offered a simple explanation of why he, Bill, "was successful with girls and I was not," Stearns related. "He said, 'Have you ever thought about listening to someone else? If you let them do the talking, they'll be far more interested in you. To have someone listening to you is flattering.' "

This was not a tactic JFK had used; but then, the times were no longer those in which John F. Kennedy, son of a multimillionaire, had reaped his womanly harvest. Betty Friedan's *The Feminine Mystique* had opened the floodgates of a new feminism, producing women who were no longer the faithful listeners of society but wanted to speak their own minds. Bill Clinton was sensitive and astute enough to recognize this. Possessed of high intelligence, high ambition, and high testosterone, "their brains alternately in their heads and their dicks," both the young JFK and the young Bill Clinton were youths who loved to graze and hunt in the lush meadows alongside female herds. But whereas JFK, restless and unable to form the same sort of lasting love relationships he had with men, kept his women at emotional arm's length, Bill longed to have the same quality of intellectual attachment to women as to men. Just as he sucked men's minds on every topic from political philosophy to literature, so he sucked women's minds, too. English social snobs found him dowdy—"plumpish and ill-kempt— not a ladies' man," as one Englishwoman sniffed with contempt—but such ladies were thinking of their engagement pictures in *Country Life,* in the manner of would-be Brahmins. By contrast, the more feisty, independent, and intelligent women were often drawn by his sheer size, energy, goodwill, curiosity, and unusual comfort with women—as with blacks and all minorities. Unlike Reich, who had been rejected for military service and was intent upon taking his single English prey back home and marrying her, Bill was clearly not interested in marriage, thus permitting him to propose intimate friendship: impure but simple.

For Englishwomen weighed down by the pressure of their parents' hopes that they find a suitable husband, such a temporary American partner was often a relief. Compared with male English students, who mostly came from elite boarding school backgrounds in which their relationships—both social and sexual—had been exclusively with fellow males, Bill was rampantly and unashamedly heterosexual. Homosexuality was simply not his thing. "Bill liked female company," his friend Sara Maitland recalled. Unlike the typical English male undergraduate, epitomized in Evelyn Waugh's *Brideshead Revisited,* he was simply not excited by the homoerotic atmosphere of the university; indeed, he "found the boys' world that was Oxford more difficult than men who had come from public [i.e., private English] schools," Sara observed. The result was that he warmed to women, both for their company and for the interplay of gender. "We became such good friends," Maitland recalled. "It wasn't," she emphasized, "just S-E-X."

To those Englishwomen open to physical intimacy, however, it did include s-e-x. For example, Bill took Maitland to a lecture on women in literature by the archfeminist Germaine Greer, an Australian academic then writing her chef d'oeuvre, *The Female Eunuch.* "I'd never heard of her and, as far as I know, the only thing Bill had heard was that she was more than six foot tall, had great legs, and was going to talk about sex," Maitland remembered. "Her gist was that middle-class men were terrible at sex and intelligent women would only do it with lorry [truck] drivers."

Bill was appalled at the notion that, *pace* D. H. Lawrence's *Lady Chatterley's Lover* (publication of which had finally been permitted by the British courts in 1960), only working-class men in England could get it up with a woman. When none of the middle-class, homosocial males—or females—dared to pose a question at the end of Ms. Greer's deliberately provocative peroration, Bill rose to his feet. He was wearing an outrageously pink poplin suit.

"In case you ever decide to give bourgeois men another chance," he asked, "can I give you my phone number?"

A New Man

Though Greer emphatically declined Bill Clinton's offer, many women did not. And if Bill was not as "well endowed" as some of Greer's truck drivers, he more than made up for this by his enjoyment of the mutuality of sex.

Sara Maitland, nicknamed "Lady Sara" because of her "posh" background—she came from a wealthy landowning family in Scotland—was and remained impressed. In many ways Bill represented a new kind of man: clearly and unashamedly ambitious, yet without pretension or conceit, wonderfully optimistic for the most part, a young man who brought people out, rather than intimidating them. D. H. Lawrence's character the gamekeeper Mellors had been surly, almost humorless, a misogynist after marital separation, and so profoundly determined to bring down Lady Chatterley from her elitist English throne that he deliberately sodomized her as part of his lovemaking. By contrast, Bill's engaging quality was the way he tempered his brashness with humor, his ego with genuine attentiveness, his ambition with empathy. He was "very cuddly" and "quite easily the most gregarious human being" she'd ever known, recalled his part-time lover Katherine Vereker, daughter of a professor of philosophy. Bill wanted to know about life, literature, religion, politics, human relationships. And he listened. Maitland's housemate, Mandy Merck, for example, admitted to Bill, in telling him of her latest *maladie d'amour,* that she was a lesbian—the first time she'd ever admitted it to a man. Bill responded, Merck recalled, by telling her—in the wake of the repeal two years previously of the draconian English law on homosexuality, under which Oscar Wilde had been ruined, imprisoned, and broken—that he was a strong supporter of the movement to establish gay rights, both in America and in Britain.

In the words of another of Bill's girlfriends, Tamara Eccles-Williams, Bill was usually penniless, "but he was a very easygoing and a very caring person." Another English girlfriend said the same: "He was a softie. He wasn't afraid of expressing his feelings." When "Lady" Sara suffered a nervous breakdown, Bill visited her in the local mental hospital every single day, just as he had visited Strobe Talbott in hospital the previous year when Talbott had fallen ill. A friend in need was a friend indeed—and Bill was willing to prove it.

To women in England, then, Bill was a refreshingly new kind of man: vital, loyal in terms of friendship if not in sexual fidelity, unashamed about his sexuality, superintelligent, and utterly without pretension—a far cry from most Oxford English wimps and poseurs, whether aesthetes or Marxists.

In the trials to come later in his life, Bill would need feminist, gay, and lesbian support. The fact was that no matter how much he would try to defang Republicans' opposition with his charm, charisma, flexibility of mind, compassion, compromise, and entreaty, his very brilliance and his habit of sliding out of positions and promises—his combination of sexiness and sorcery—were bound to elicit envy, jealousy, malice, even malevolence.

It was, Bill would find in an increasingly Republican America, simply the way of the world: a world that, as sociobiologists were beginning to realize, represented man's struggle for survival not only against other species but against challenges within his own: the Red Queen syndrome, in which human beings have to keep running in order to stay in the same place, their survival maintained only by constantly battling with mutating internal predators.

The Lottery

Sexual competition as part of a complex evolutionary system was a subject gradually being explored in the anthropology, sociology, and science departments of Oxford, Cambridge, and a slew of other British and American universities. Almost all aspects of gender difference were now being reexamined in a search to disentangle the mysteries of evolution. Men needed to find ways to seduce multiple females to maximize their own genetic offspring; women needed sperm to procreate but also needed to keep males sexually amused and attentive while their mutual offspring matured. What was common was what lay behind this dance: the critical importance of sexual attraction, copulation, and reproduction as a biological means of warding off the predations of pathogens in the never-ending struggle for survival of the species.

Bill's unconscious contribution to this natural process would be his pioneering skill in the area of modern seduction—while avoiding, if possible, reproductive hobbling through fidelity to one female or nullification of his genetic endowment through early death.

The latter factor remained a constant and looming threat for young Americans facing the draft. Finally, on December 1, 1969, the first draft lottery since World War II was held in Washington, D.C. From that day, new draftees would be called up in the order in which their birthdays were picked in the lottery—each day of the year marked inside a blue capsule in a glass goldfish bowl.

Outside the offices of *The New York Times* and newsstands selling American newspapers around the world young men lined up, waiting anxiously to know their fate. Of the 365 capsules in the bowl that night, Bill Clinton's birthday was picked close to last: 311th. With some 850,000 eligible males to choose from and Nixon attempting to wind down the war in Vietnam, Bill was, effectively, home free. His ploy had worked: there was zero chance he would be drafted.

Naturally he was overjoyed. His running away had involved deceit—but then, Oxford researchers were concluding that deception was at the very core of modern biological, anthropological, and sociobiological understanding, the power to deceive increasing an individual's chances of survival in a competitive world.

To foist such deception on fellow members of his species, however, man had first to deceive himself. Certainly, in his own mind, Bill convinced himself he'd acted honorably. From a scheme to avoid combat service in Vietnam by ROTC enrollment he had decided—without informing his ROTC commander—to switch back to submission to the draft and to chance his luck. Luck had dictated that his lottery number be called at the end of the draw, not the beginning, thus taking the outcome out of his hands.

Had he left the matter there, the episode might possibly have been forgiven and forgotten—a lucky break for the boy from Hot Springs, a town famed for gambling. But Bill Clinton would not have been Bill Clinton, Baptist child of the sixties, had he let it rest. Instead, he felt impelled to write at length to Colonel Eugene Holmes to vindicate his behavior, salve his conscience, have his name expunged from the upcoming ROTC program at Fayetteville—and vent some of his spleen: the anger he felt at the way an older generation had forced a younger generation into mass deceit.

Letter of a Lifetime

Bill's letter, written the very day after receiving the results of the draft lottery, would stand for an entire generation of baby boomers who felt betrayed by their parents.

"Dear Colonel Holmes," the letter began. After apologizing for not having carried out his promise to write before then, Bill explained that no day had passed without his thinking on the matter and what he should say. He was now taking this opportunity to thank Colonel Holmes not only for "saving me from the draft" that year "but for being so kind and decent to me last summer, when I was as low as I have ever been." He acknowledged that the agreement they'd made had been "struck in good faith" and claimed he'd been willing to take the ROTC route in avoiding the draft because of his "high regard for you personally."

Whether the colonel would have had a similar regard for the Rhodes Scholar had he known Bill's true "political beliefs and activities," though, Bill doubted—and now that he was virtually certain of legally escaping being drafted, thanks to the lottery, he intended to tell the colonel about those beliefs and actions. He began by recounting his role on Senator Fulbright's Foreign Relations Committee, by the end of which he had "opposed and despised" the war in Vietnam "with a depth of feeling I had reserved solely for racism in America," and he explained how he'd participated in the national organization of the Vietnam War Moratorium, both in America and in London.

"I have written and spoken and marched against the war," Bill claimed—a boast that, like the "depth" of his feeling on Vietnam, somewhat exaggerated his public contribution. The truth was, Bill was not by nature a street protester; he was too smart to be comfortable with slogans, too uncomfortable with violence to be an inciter, and too concerned about blotting his future political copybook by attracting the attention of the police or security services; thus he'd been much happier as a *marshal* of marchers, outside the U.S. Embassy, than as a speaker or marcher himself.

Yet, however much he chose to dramatize his anti–Vietnam War role in retrospect, Bill Clinton was trying to say something on behalf of his age group, of those young Americans forcibly made to serve in a dishonorable war. On November 30, only days before he wrote his letter, details of the My Lai massacre had begun to emerge: 567 unarmed civilians murdered in fifteen minutes by a single American platoon under the command of a young American army lieutenant, William Calley. The London *Times* quoted an army private as saying, "They had them in a group standing over a ditch, just like a Nazi-type thing." It had taken more than a year and a half to track down the story, but its publication had finally provided the world with proof of the human degradation to which America was sinking in Vietnam. For Bill, the news was appalling. "No government rooted in limited, parliamentary democracy should have the power to make its citizens fight and kill and die in a war they may oppose, a war which even possibly may be wrong, a war which, in any case, does not involve immediately the peace and freedom of the nation," he opined. "The draft was justified in World War II because the life of the people collectively was at stake," he pointed out. "Individuals had to fight, if the nation was to survive, for the lives of their countrymen and their way of life. Vietnam," he now declared, "is no such case."

Bill then alluded to several of his friends at Oxford who were conscientious objectors (COs); even one of his roommates who "is a draft resister who is possibly under indictment and may never be able to go home again. He is one of the bravest, best men I know. His country needs men like him more than they [*sic*] know. That he is considered a criminal," Bill remarked, "is an obscenity."

In his own case, Bill had, he explained, confronted the "most difficult" decision of his life, in choosing whether to be a resister, to take another path of draft avoidance, or to submit to the draft. In the end, however, he had decided "to accept the draft in spite of my beliefs for one reason," he confessed: "to maintain my political viability within the system. For years I have worked to prepare myself for a political life characterized by both practical political ability and concern for rapid social progress. It is a life I still feel compelled to try to lead. I do not think our system of government is by definition corrupt," he pointed out in an effort to show he was no revolutionary, "however dangerous and inadequate it has been in recent years."

In explaining why he had first thought to avail himself of Colonel Holmes's help, Bill blamed the "prospect of fighting a war I had been fighting against, and that is why I contacted you. ROTC was the one way left in which I could possibly, but not positively, avoid both Vietnam and resistance"—in other words, the battlefield and jail.

ROTC, Bill acknowledged, had thus determined his decision to go to UA Law School rather than the other way around; indeed, he would rather have spent "a year out perhaps to teach in a small college or work on some community action project," he claimed, "and in the process to decide whether to attend law school or graduate school and how to begin putting what I have learned to use." Signing the "ROTC letter of intent," which in turn had gotten him his 1-D draft deferment and out of service in Vietnam, however, had brought him no peace of mind; indeed, "the anguish and loss of my self regard and self confidence really set in," he confessed. "I hardly slept for weeks and kept going by eating compulsively and reading until exhaustion brought sleep."

In that anguished state of mind he'd written a letter to tell Colonel Holmes he would like to be drafted immediately, to put himself out of his moral misery, "because I had no interest in the ROTC program in itself and all I seemed to have done was to protect myself from physical harm." He hadn't posted the letter, though, "because I didn't see, in the end, how my going in the army and maybe going to Vietnam would achieve anything except a feeling that I had punished myself and gotten what I had deserved. So I came back to England to try to make something of this second year of my Rhodes scholarship."

Some of this was true; some of it was false or misrepresentational. Where the true line lay between his own life agenda and his conscience, not even Bill really knew, which was the reason he had succumbed to such anguish. Essentially, however, his account was genuine. He hadn't wished to be dragooned into attending the UA Law School without proper forethought and had run away from it. To be sure, there was little evidence that he was trying "to make something" of his second Rhodes year at Oxford beyond reading Dylan Thomas's poetry, growing a beard, helping organize anti–Vietnam War demonstrations, and making love on mattresses on the Leckford Road floor. Yet in writing as he did, Bill knew he was doing far more than offering an excuse for his failure to honor his written commitment to join Colonel Holmes's ROTC program. "I began to think I had deceived you, not by lies—there were none—but by failing to tell you all the things I'm writing now," he confessed; and "all the things" related not simply to Bill's own, personal case but to his whole generation. "I am writing too in the hope that my telling this one story will help you understand more clearly how so many fine people have come to find themselves still loving their country but loathing the military, to which you and other good men have devoted years, lifetimes, of the best service you could give. To many of us, it is no longer clear what is service and what is disservice"—a disastrous state of affairs for the world's number one democracy.

Speaking for a Generation

Bill's letter to Colonel Holmes would become historic, since it—or its strange disappearance and stranger reappearance—would later be used to try to stop him from becoming President of the United States. It certainly exaggerated Bill's anti–Vietnam War "activities" and gave a woolly version of something that was, in essence, quite simple: his deliberate decision not to honor a written undertaking in return for being saved from the draft at a critical moment in July 1968.

The letter was thus less than truthful. Yet, in a larger sense, the letter was, as David Maraniss, the biographer of Bill Clinton's early years, neatly put it, "the best known essay of Bill Clinton's life," for it stood, with all its exaggerations and elisions, for all the millions of young Americans who wrestled with their conscience over an unjust war. Barbara Hausam, who worked for the University of Arkansas ROTC, recalled how "powerful" an impact its receipt in Fayetteville made. It was, she later confessed, an "extraordinary letter" that made a "lasting impression" upon her and upon her colleagues, a letter that was "almost like rhetoric" and that she would never forget.

The fact was that almost half of all ROTC officers would later, in surveys, admit they had joined the ROTC to avoid service in Vietnam. Later statistics showed that almost 16 million young American baby boomers (out of 26.8 million of draft age) had avoided military service—with millions more avoiding it by entering the ROTC and other maneuvers. Bill Clinton might not, in his letter, have told the whole truth or expressed it most concisely ("Forgive the length of this letter," he concluded his letter, apologizing), but he had at least attempted to voice the moral torment of his entire generation, saddled with having to go to Vietnam to fight an unnecessary war involving unpardonable murder and crimes against humanity. In this respect, Bill's was a most noble letter on the part of a twenty-three-year-old—and it was recognized in Fayetteville as such.

The sad fact remained, however, that however articulately Bill had recorded his opposition to the war in Vietnam, he had failed to fulfill his sworn and written promise to Colonel Holmes. Had he done so, he might well have become a more trustworthy, honorable individual and have learned the difficult art of command: of issuing clear orders, delegating authority, and standing by his word as an officer and a gentleman.

Instead, posting a different kind of letter a few days after his missive to Colonel Holmes, Bill Clinton set his sights on a new platform for his ascent to the presidency: an application not to the law school of the University of Arkansas but to that of an Ivy League institution: Yale.

CHAPTER FIFTEEN

THE END
OF THE
SIXTIES

A Peek Behind the Iron Curtain

Yale Law School was only too pleased to take Bill Clinton; indeed, it gave him a scholarship: his third. Bill's final six months at Oxford were therefore really coasting. An English B.Phil. degree was irrelevant to his career, and the D.Phil., or doctorate, which he was recommended by his tutor to complete, would have taken at least another year and required a 100,000-word dissertation. It would have given him international university teaching credentials in politics; but Bill was more than ever certain he didn't wish to research and teach politics, like Robert Reich, but to practice it.

In the circumstances Bill did what he was now in a position to do, despite his relative poverty: he stayed in Europe rather than returning to America over New Year's 1970 and used the money he had left to travel, still determined, as he had been the year before, to peek behind the much-vaunted Iron Curtain, about which his roommate Strobe Talbott was an expert.

Talbott was, in fact, secretly translating Khrushchev's memoirs at 43 Leckford Road. Had the KGB known of Talbott's work, Bill might well have been refused a visa by the Russian Embassy in London. Certainly H. Ross Perot, sitting in Copenhagen aboard a Boeing 707 loaded with Red Cross provisions for American POWs in North Vietnam, was denied a Russian visa at this time. Had Perot been permitted to fly, though, the two men, who would face off for the presidency of the United States twenty-two years later, would almost certainly have met in Moscow. Instead, however, it would be a fellow scourge of the Vietnam War, Senator Eugene McCarthy, whom Bill met in the Russian capital on January 6, 1970.

American Everyman

The trip to the Soviet Union, via Norway and Sweden, and the return via Prague and Germany, was memorable, similar to one that Bill Clinton's hero JFK had made at a similar age, the son of the U.S. ambassador to Britain touring Russia, Prague, and Germany—Hitler's Third Reich—just prior to the German invasion of Poland and the outbreak of World War II.

John Kennedy, however, had traveled as a millionaire's son and been treated like American royalty, given his father's wealth and ambassadorial status; Bill Clinton, by contrast, had hardly a bean to his name and, even when visiting the son of the deputy American ambassador to Finland, was palmed off onto the YMCA at night.

Ginger-bearded and hippie-looking, with bushy, curly dark brown hair, Bill was unfazed. It was here that he was most like JFK, yet most unlike him: a young man pulsating with intelligence, optimism, ambition, and gregariousness, always preferring being in company to being alone—yet a child of the sixties, not the thirties, without social snobbery or conceit and with an almost chameleonlike ability to change his exterior to match his surroundings. He was comfortable with blacks; indeed, he spent most of his time in Moscow with a black student, "Nicki" Alexis, who was studying at the university there. But he consorted with plumbers and politicians just as readily. Freed from the nightmare of the draft, he was once again American Everyman, still only twenty-three, with a fund of knowledge that went way beyond his years and an innocent curiosity that was almost bewitching in its intensity, as though he had a head and a heart that were at once sincere and fathomless.

A Week in Prague

After Russia, Bill Clinton stayed in Prague for a week with the parents of Jan Kopold, a Czech graduate he'd befriended in Oxford. The Kopolds treated him like a son.

In the Prague Spring, eighteen months before, the iron fist of the Soviet Union had been reasserted. Jan's parents were anxious, as Czechs, that Jan remain in England until the situation improved. The arrival of Bill, who brought messages of love from their son, was therefore emotional; it was as if, symbolically, he was bringing a hope of peaceful coexistence between West and East: of democracy engaging constructively with communism.

Tirelessly the young American toured the city and saw its treasures. Moreover, with Professor Kopold, his wife, their daughter, and Jan's grandmother—a former Communist revolutionary—Bill talked "politics, politics." The Kopolds had been through the political gamut: prewar independence; through World War II under the Nazis; through the short postwar period of Social Democratic rule; then through the Stalinist clampdown; and finally, in the aftermath of Dubček's reforms, through Soviet and Warsaw Pact military occupation. For Bill Clinton this was a seminar far more revealing and more human than the "anarcho-Marxist" environment of late-1960s Oxford—and he was enthralled.

A Congenital Apple-Polisher

Years later, Bill's trip would be used by the American President, George Herbert Walker Bush, to cast aspersion on his motives in going behind the Iron Curtain. R. Emmett Tyrrell, Jr., *The American Spectator*'s founding editor, afterward ridiculed such a smear. It was not, Tyrrell pointed out, that there was any serious question about Bill Clinton's patriotism, despite the speculation of idle right-wingers during the 1992 presidential campaign that Bill was somehow on the Soviet payroll or a fellow traveler. On the contrary, Tyrrell accepted that the young graduate student was broke, sponged off friends' parents all across Europe, and was genuinely interested in what was taking place socially, politically, economically, and culturally, behind the Iron Curtain. What Tyrrell excoriated, however, was the innocent liberal idealism: Bill's idealistic belief in "progress" instead of a hard-line, McCarthyite response to the "evil empire."

Revolutionary Czech socialists, like the Kopold grandmother, had worked for and welcomed the benighted nightmare of Soviet communism; they had gotten what they deserved, Tyrrell felt, and Clinton's opposition to the Vietnam War was sacrilegious—"our soldiers [Tyrrell himself not among them] were facing death in Vietnam" while protesters screamed words of support to the North Vietnamese, he scolded—adding that Bill's attempt to find common ground with the socialist Kopolds was "a convergence of political nitwits."

For Tyrrell, who had deliberately and deceitfully visited the Kopolds twenty years later by writing to them and pretending to be a sixties liberal, the process was clear: in the sixties Bill Clinton had been subverted by an Oxford professoriate who were "Socialists" with a capital S. "Faced with the ubiquity of left-wing thought among the university faculty," Tyrrell wrote, "it is not surprising that this congenital apple-polisher would become a sentimental acolyte of Progress." Clinton's belief in social and economic improvement was, Tyrrell admitted, "alluring"—but, he mocked, was "a trait he shares with the patrons of the gaming tables."

To such a right-wing cynic, Bill Clinton at twenty-three was simply a reflection of the "sentimental Left. Such was his network of acquaintances that even behind the Iron Curtain he found himself in the company of the sentimental advocates of utopia." The Kopolds might have had "admirable intentions," Tyrrell allowed after meeting them, but they had no appreciation of history, even though history had "landed them in Communist jails. Experience meant nothing to them."

Walking with Mrs. Kopold's mother to see the twelfth-century Stahov Monastery housing the Czech Memorial of National Literature, Bill had confided to the old lady his intention of going into American politics. "I can see them now," Tyrrell mused, "two defiant idealists sweeping down St. Wenceslaus Square, the secret police discreetly shadowing them." Bill's "enthusiasm and charm," he could see, "had sozzled them, as it would later sozzle America's true believers."

Far from seeing in Bill Clinton's stance the open mind of a twenty-three-year-old student at a time of hardening political attitudes in America, Tyrrell saw only naiveté and delusion. "The irrefutable fact is that while at Oxford Clinton was deeply involved with the counterculture," Tyrrell admonished, however much Bill had later covered his sixties traces in his "campaign propaganda."

Tyrrell's agenda—he had embarked on a book about Bill Clinton that would expose and ridicule the liberals of the baby-boom generation—was unambiguous. That it involved duping the Kopolds (whose son, Jan, was tragically killed falling from a rooftop in Turkey a few months after Bill Clinton's visit) into inviting him into their home did not disturb Tyrrell's righteous conscience—for subterfuge and lies were thought to be permissible, as President Nixon would soon demonstrate, provided they promoted conservative aims.

What Tyrrell and other right-wing stalwarts could never quite recognize, let alone accept, was that in the field of subterfuge and necessary lies, Bill Clinton, a Democrat, would prove a better performer than even the Republican President.

Franco's Spain

Back in Oxford, Bill sent off thank-you letters to all his kind hosts across Europe. For a moment he even contemplated a last-minute attempt to take his B.Phil. exams without having done the necessary work. Warned by his tutor (possibly wrongly, since he was a natural examinee) that he would not succeed, however, he withdrew his name and, once the brief summer term at Oxford was over, set off without an Oxford degree on his last European journey for several years, this time to Spain.

The trip proved as instructive as the one to the Soviet Union and Eastern Europe. He boned up on George Orwell's *Homage to Catalonia* (in which Orwell for the first time exposed the sad truth about Stalinist communism, namely that the Soviets, using the NKVD, were much more interested in destroying fellow socialists and potential freethinking Communists than fighting General Franco), as well as reading Hugh Thomas's *The Spanish Civil War,* but he was equally interested in seeing the result of decades of right-wing conservatism backed by the Catholic Church.

This was not a journey the rabidly right-wing Emmett Tyrrell chose to make, in Clinton's footsteps, two decades later, for the truth was that Franco's archconservative Spain had been as awful and as stifling as the Soviet system Bill Clinton had encountered in Moscow and Prague: stultifyingly male chauvinist, repressive, cynical, and at the same time politically fundamentalist, with no tolerance for divergence or diversity. Tyrrell would have been ashamed. Bill Clinton was merely fascinated—his conviction strengthened that there must be a middle course to be steered between liberal idealism and conservatism.

Time to Return

In a matter of months Bill Clinton had now seen the two sides of the Western political spectrum in Europe at first hand. Collecting his few possessions—saxophone, books, and an armful of clothes—Bill thus bade a brief farewell to his Rhodic and other colleagues and flew gratefully home to the land of the free. America's was by no means a perfect society, but in comparison with the alternative regimes he'd seen in operation, it was vibrant, huge, diverse, and economically in a league of its own. The notions of Soviet bloc productivity so airily spawned by the John Kenneth Galbraith/Paul Samuelson clique of economic philosophers were simply theoretical. Such men, pompous and easily flattered, lived in academic glass palaces; they had not the remotest idea of reality on the ground.

Where, though, was America heading as the sixties came to a close? Despite his domestic travails Bill Clinton had begun the 1960s full of hope. Now, as the decade came to an end, these hopes were tainted by the Vietnam disaster, an imbroglio that the older generation had imposed on his generation as the ultimate sin of the fathers.

No other generation in American history had been saddled with such a moral dilemma, in which normal patriotism and the male initiation rituals associated with military service could find no morally acceptable outlet. No other generation had been so racked, and none would emerge so scarred. Lying and cheating of necessity, its members had made their pacts with the Devil, either serving in an unjust, inhumane civil conflict abroad or avoiding combat—but none would survive untouched.

The fact was that the fabled sixties were now over. The Beatles had split up in April of that year while President Nixon sent American combat units into Cambodia and the Weathermen continued their slew of bombings in New York. Worst of all, following California Governor Ronald Reagan's declaration that he would welcome a bloodbath if it were provoked by nonviolent student demonstrations, four unarmed protesting male and female students were massacred on the campus of Kent State University in Ohio by the National Guard.

A new era, the 1970s, was clearly beginning, a decade in which new battle lines were being drawn. In New York, thousands of homosexuals were protesting against antigay discrimination. Women were demanding abortion rights. Henry Kissinger was spreading lies about Daniel Ellsberg in an effort to stop the publication of the Pentagon Papers ("Ellsberg, according to Henry, had weird sexual habits, used drugs, and enjoyed helicopter flights in which he would take potshots at the Vietnamese below," H. R. Haldeman later wrote). Senator Edward Kennedy had destroyed his chances of a future bid for the presidency by inadvertently drowning a campaign worker in his car at Chappaquidick, on Martha's Vineyard, and then failing to report the fatal accident to police for a full nine hours. Kennedy was later charged with leaving the scene of an accident after causing personal injury.

Truthfulness, in other words, was becoming a relative word, whoever used it—whether on the left or right.

CHAPTER SIXTEEN

ATONEMENT

International Relations Expert Manqué

Would Bill Clinton have done better to stay a third year, even a fourth, at Oxford and take his Ph.D. in politics before attending an American law school? In the world of American politics, an Oxford doctorate in political science would certainly have made him an unusual and esteemed figure—an expert on international relations in the manner, say, of Dr. Kissinger. Examining a chosen political dissertation subject in great depth, and writing a major thesis in his own right and under his own name, would have given Bill Clinton's later Cold War political consensus rhetoric more torque, especially after his outstanding paper on Soviet communism for his tutor, Zbigniew Pelczynski, and his subsequent trip behind the Iron Curtain to Moscow and Prague. John F. Kennedy, after all, had used his pre-war European experiences to inform his Harvard dissertation—which had become a national best-seller in 1940 under the title *Why England Slept*.

Had Dr. Clinton then gone on to enter politics, as JFK had done, and win a Senate seat—perhaps even Senator Fulbright's seat on the Senate Foreign Relations Committee—he might have become, in an era of Reaganist-Thatcherite "evil empire" simplicities, a political force for East-West understanding and development, on behalf of a younger generation of Americans. He clearly had the brains, the political interest, and the capacity for sustained work, whether at college or in politics. Moreover, it was from the Senate that JFK had launched his own assault on the presidency, beginning with his failed bid for the Democratic vice presidential nomination in 1956.

It was not to be, however.

The Next Stage in Life

The fact was that at a critical moment in his personal development, the Vietnam fiasco had destroyed Bill Clinton's self-confidence, even, for a while, his very sense of mission in life. Thanks to the lottery, the draft nightmare was now over—but in its aftermath a Ph.D. thesis at Oxford was not Bill Clinton's way of dealing with the next stage in his life. Those colleagues who did attempt to follow such a course did not, thanks to Vietnam, necessarily fare better. Frank Aller, Bill's housemate, for example, remained at Oxford, but his subsequent death would illustrate in the most tragic way the ethical dilemma that an immoral war had posed for the baby-boom generation.

What course, what way would now be best, Clinton wondered? In the medieval campus city, thronged with students and pubs, Bill had learned to drink alcohol (in moderation, owing to his allergies), smoke pot and hash (likewise in moderation, owing to his allergies), grow his hair long in shaggy brown locks, and to shag—far from the strictures and watching, judging eyes of people "back home." The yellowing, uncleaned linoleum floor of the Leckford Road lodging house, with mattresses on the bedroom floors, was all very well, but it was a "squalor of exile" that only half appealed to the Southern Baptist in Bill Clinton at a time when his morale as well as morals was lowest. As his self-confidence had returned, he had felt increasingly impelled to return to the United States and throw himself into political activities—activities that would somehow absolve him from the deceit that had spared him from service in Vietnam, indeed in the military. To atone.

Project Pursestrings

Too ashamed to show his face in Arkansas after reneging on the agreement with Colonel Holmes, Bill Clinton stayed in Washington, D.C. There, in the shadow of his alma mater, he shaved off his beard, had his hair cut, and, before enrolling at Yale Law School in New Haven, Connecticut, took a central role in a bipartisan anti–Vietnam War program: Project Purse-strings. After a two-year absence, he was back in the political fray—and loving it.

Project Pursestrings, with its well-funded headquarters on Washington's K Street, was designed to pressure Congress into withdrawing funding for the war in Southeast Asia. It not only proved to be a useful experience but also opened the way to another political campaign, for Bill's work in Washington so impressed Tony Podesta, a Eugene McCarthy campaign veteran and fellow activist on Project Pursestrings, that Podesta then recommended Bill to a would-be senator for the state of Connecticut. This was Professor Joe Duffey, a thirty-eight-year-old university ethics teacher and civil rights activist who had, in August 1970, won the Connecticut Democratic primary as candidate for the U.S. Senate.

Dr. Duffey took Bill onto his Connecticut campaign staff—and, because Clinton would be attending Yale Law School that fall, the twenty-four-year-old graduate (he had celebrated his birthday on August 19, the day of Duffey's successful primary election) was given the job of running Duffey's senatorial campaign in the New Haven/Yale University congressional area district.

The Friendly Giant

Those who had anticipated that the smiling, heavily built young southerner, with his distinctive Arkansas accent, would turn people off in the working-class areas of New Haven and surrounding towns were soon disabused of any such notion.

"Oh, my God!" the district coordinator had sighed when she first heard Bill's introductory drawl on the telephone, but when Bill Clinton appeared alongside Chuca Meyer, one of the Smith College advance team showing him around in her Volkswagen beetle, the registered nurse was instantly won over. Here was a friendly giant of a boy, his mother a nurse and his grandmother before her, too; a boy with a big smile, a bear hug, and an almost evangelical love of life. His energy and intelligence were formidable: you never needed to tell him anything twice, and his memory for names and faces was phenomenal. He would snatch a Churchillian forty winks on her sofa in the living room, then rise refreshed and ready for more battle. In the rough-and-tumble of electioneering, which many politicians hated, young Bill Clinton came into his own, helping prepare political positions on major issues—local, national, international—by seeking to make them important and palatable to the broadest possible spectrum of electors.

For Bill himself, the Duffey campaign cast aside all thoughts of academic law school work. It was the first time he had been actively involved in a political campaign since Senator Fulbright had sacked him in 1968. He was inspired—so much so, in fact, that a number of participants thought he would have made a better candidate than the candidate himself!

The End of Democratic Liberalism

Other people took positions that squared with their ideals, prejudices, and consciences. Bill Clinton seemed more concerned to listen to the mood of the time and the concerns of the voters, and to tailor the candidate's positions accordingly. Duffey, an ethics professor, was amazed by the multitude of political stances he was required to take—"more positions," he quipped, "than the Kama Sutra."

To Bill Clinton, the art of politics was the art of campaigning, of dialogue with real people. His chameleon nature was here a manifest advantage; in many ways he was the personification of the best of the sixties. He came from working-class grandparents and had a working mother; he believed in equality of opportunity and the inclusion of society's marginalized and dispossessed. As the stepchild of an abusive, alcoholic parent, he also believed in personal empowerment: liberation from psychological, social, and material oppression. His admiration of his mother, and his desire to make her proud, was the very cornerstone of his existence—something that made him comfortable with women of all ages and backgrounds and a natural supporter of feminism. His strange upbringing in Hope, with neighbors not allowed to play over at his house because of his grandmother and mother's social status, gave him an acute awareness of elitism, of social exclusion, of injustice toward the poorer, weaker, less privileged members of society—indeed, caused him to believe in a society that would be more tolerant, more just, more inclusive, more compassionate, more caring: society as community.

Tirelessly, Bill Clinton and his young New Haven staff campaigned for Professor Duffey, but it became clear, as the weeks went by, that two things would prevent a Duffey victory at the polls: the growing shift toward white Republican candidates and the spoiler candidacy of the former Democratic senator Tom Dodd, who, censured by the Senate for financial irregularities, was determined to wreak vengeance on his party by running as an independent. Thus the Democrats, in a move that somehow symbolized the fracturing and internecine squabbles that would haunt the party for the next twenty years, were defeated by a former Democrat. The Republican candidate, Lowell Weicker, was delighted—and won the seat.

Here was an arresting lesson to any serious student of politics; indeed, Bill Clinton's own bid to win election to the presidency in 1992 would owe much to that earlier story of a divided party in Connecticut that allowed the opposition candidate to sail through the middle.

Beginning his belated studies at Yale Law School, Bill Clinton meanwhile reflected on the official Democratic candidate's performance. Chuca Meyer had been convinced that there would be a miracle, as if in answer to their collective idealistic prayer for the candidate. Bill's friend Tony Podesta had been more sanguine, however. "No one there thought Duffey could win," he later commented.

While conceding the justice of Podesta's appraisal, Bill nevertheless saw a deeper trend. The promise of the early 1960s was disintegrating. The Heroic Period of the Movement, or its Bronze Age, as sixties radical Carl Oglesby called it, was over. Indeed, in retrospect, it was amazing that it had proved so powerful for so long.

Tom Hayden, author of the famous Port Huron student manifesto, later wondered where "this messianic sense, this belief in being right, this confidence that we could speak for a generation, came from. But the time was ripe, vibrating with potential." By 1970, however, the time was no longer ripe—as the "apple-polisher" of Arkansas was beginning to realize. The Vietnam War, prosecuted by Democrats, had poisoned the well of liberalism. "We had nothing left to say," Oglesby later admitted—hating the way he and fellow coat-and-tie radicals left the field to "Nixon and the militarists," yet unwilling himself to follow the downward path of the Weatherman manifesto. Retiring to a commune in Vermont, Oglesby confessed that he could offer no viable "alternative."

Could Bill Clinton? Richard Nixon's election as President in 1968 had been no mere aberration. Lowell Weicker, the Republican, took almost 42 percent of the vote in Connecticut, and in voting for former senator Dodd, rather than the official anti–Vietnam War pro–civil rights activist Democratic choice, Professor Duffey, a further 25 percent of the electorate had eschewed sixties idealism. Such predominantly working-class, "hard-hat" voters, as they were known at the time, would become easy pickings for both Nixon and Ronald Reagan in the years ahead.

The truth was, the long day of Democratic liberalism, so nobly launched under FDR, was nearing its end. Even Duffey could see what was happening. Picturing the political struggle as a simple appeal to the consciences and votes of either the rich or the poor/pro-poor was no longer good enough. As Duffey noted after his defeat, "somewhere between affluence and grinding poverty stand the majority of American families, living on the margins of social and economic insecurity. The new politics has not spoken to the needs and interests of those Americans." These middle classes—especially the lower-income middle classes—increasingly felt like "victims of decisions in which they have no voice."

For Bill Clinton, this failure was the truly disturbing lesson as he went "back to school" at Yale.

A Pact with the Devil

Turncoats such as the writers Peter Collier and David Horowitz, and rabid Republicans such as Emmett Tyrrell, later sneered at the "lost boys and girls of the Sixties who never grew up," scoffing at the "amorality and self-righteousness" of the era. Tyrrell in particular mocked the "Coat and Tie Radicals," who were "colossal megalomaniacs. More specifically, they were stupendous narcissists, often solipsists, who, despite all the bosh about their idealism, were coolly amoral in their ambitions and in their goatish pursuits. . . . So closely have they identified with all the good causes they have espoused that at some point in their development they assumed that they themselves *were* good causes."

Tyrrell had a point. Sixties "Coat and Tie Radicals" certainly espoused grand causes while failing to live up to their high ideals in their personal lives—a truth that would become more and more evident in subsequent years. Republicans, however, were no better behaved, no less "goatish" in their behavior, no less likely to abuse power. Certainly Bill Clinton, following in JFK's footsteps, was aware at a young age of Lord Acton's dictum about the corruptive effect of power; even at age twenty-two he had worried about it, telling his lesbian friend Mandy Merck while at Oxford, "Politics gives guys so much power and such big egos they tend to behave badly towards women. And I hope I never get into that."

These were famous last words. The "apple-polisher" from Arkansas, as a child of the sixties, might still want to *do* good as well as *be* good; but was this really possible in a postmodern world? What *was* good? The Vietnam War had corrupted the nation's belief in its own goodness as a democracy; meanwhile, the new movement of "cultural relativism"—the notion that rules and conventions in art and in human society are merely constructs designed to favor elites—saw one man's good as another's evil. In such an era, people of intelligence—congregating in universities—gave way to a collective soul-searching, epitomized in the plague of post-structuralism that swept the academies, subjecting every notion or premise to "deconstruction." This, in turn, further exasperated conservatives and moralists who espoused simplicities.

On this cultural cross Bill Clinton would later be crucified, in the Gay Nineties: but for the moment, at the end of the sixties, he was simply one of many millions of young American men who had made a pact with the Devil, like Dr. Faustus. In return for not serving in Vietnam, or even in the ROTC, he had sold his soul. Now he wished to make up for that: to rededicate his life to the service of others as a politician.

First, however, he wanted a law degree: an opportunity to find out how the American system of government, industry, commerce, and society was legally construed and constructed; how it actually worked at a legal level; and thus how he, as a future politician, could best work it and improve it. He was inquisitive and intellectually acquisitive—almost, his colleagues described, like a sponge.

This sponge would absorb not only the law lessons of Yale but one of its top female students.

CHAPTER SEVENTEEN

BILL AND HILLARY

Law School

Bill Clinton's classmates, when he finally appeared at Yale Law School in fall of 1970, had no idea who he was. Pretty Nancy Bekavac recalled a curly-haired, bearded guy who came up to her and "asked if he could borrow my notes." Nancy was skeptical. "I said, 'Who are you?'" The young man's response was puzzling. "Well, I'm in your class."

Suspecting a put-on, Nancy told him he couldn't be, that class had begun in September. It was now November.

"Well, I've been real busy running Joe Duffey's campaign for Senate," the student insisted, "but I'm here now." He needed her notes. When she suggested he use those of Robert Reich, he was dismissive. Reich had no gift for synthesis, he remarked. "He writes too much." Amazed, Nancy asked if the student knew Reich—whereupon he told her about Oxford and their Rhodes Scholarships. "I was pretty charmed by this discussion," Nancy recalled. She agreed to loan the young man her notes but wanted to take out some pages first. "Love letters?" he asked impertinently. Blushing, she told him they were poems.

"Well, I'll read them."

"No, you won't."

They were on a roll. Far from feeling offended when she learned he had asked around to find out who took good notes, she was flattered. Asked when she had first figured out Bill Clinton would be a politician, Nancy claimed it was "in the first five minutes." In fact, "I probably figured in the first day he could be president," she added. "It's like meeting Wilt Chamberlain. You meet Wilt Chamberlain, you think, 'Gee, this guy could be a great basketball player.' You meet Bill Clinton, you think, 'This guy could be president of the United States.' I mean, I never met anyone else like that and I've met a lot of people."

Nancy's colleague Robert Reich was certainly "smart" and "talkative" and had a "beautiful kind of printing handwriting." He too was clearly going to go places. "There were all these sort of sharp guys who looked like they were going to wreck the world," Nancy recalled, "but I knew damn well they probably couldn't get someone to open a door for them."

She was right. Men like Reich would never win even a primary election, whereas Bill Clinton exuded intelligence, wit, energy—and compassion. Within weeks he was almost an icon, learning and remembering the names of every soul he met, from colleagues to the canteen staff and secretaries. Girls went gaga over him, this young champion of civil rights, of anti–Vietnam War, of minorities, who loved poetry, had absorbed the dark, garish majesty of El Greco in the Prado in Madrid, and had sought vainly to find Dylan Thomas's boathouse in Wales. As Nancy Bekavac described him, Bill was "Mr. Aura": a young man who had already worked for Senator Fulbright, had helped on gubernatorial and senatorial campaigns in Arkansas, had helped organize a protest march in London, had held a Rhodes Scholarship, had traveled through Europe and the Soviet Union. Yet at the same time, he played the saxophone beautifully, loved popular music, and read the most eclectic cross section of books. "He liked country music. He loved Joe Cocker. He liked real rock and roll. He liked jazz. He loved gospel music," Nancy recorded. "I got really sick and he brought me Janis Joplin's *Pearl* which is I think her best album. He adored *Nashville* by Robert Altman. He loved that film." He also loved the tormented saint of Postimpressionism, Vincent van Gogh, whose works were being shown in an exhibition at the Brooklyn Museum in New York. "We went there together," Nancy recalled, treasuring the memory, "and we saw 'Cornfield with Crows' which is a pretty shattering picture. Just an incredibly moving picture"—hand in hand.

Through his fellow Rhodie Doug Eakley, Bill had arranged to live with three other students, one of them black, in a rented house on Fort Trumbull Beach in Milford, Connecticut, about fifteen minutes' drive from the Yale campus in the old purple Gremlin convertible he'd bought. He wore his English air force officer's woolen greatcoat, relied on Nancy's notes, and cast a spell on the female tribe of the law school.

Bill's Arkansas friend Jim Blair recalled his impression that Bill "went through law school, which is a terrible ordeal for a lot of people, without breaking a sweat." Bill's black housemate, Bill Coleman, personally witnessed the truth of this. "He did not," Coleman recalled with amusement, "spend lots of time trying to master Marbury v. Madison." Rather, Bill wished to know everyone: socially, educationally, and on occasion carnally. Moreover, what Bill remembered about people, Nancy recalled of their conversations, was not their achievements or pedigree but sentimental, even emotional things—as if he had an uncommon ability not only to relate to people of different backgrounds but to get them to relate to him what mattered in their lives.

This ability to relate to real people on an intimate level was an extraordinary skill—the more amazing because, as his roommates in Georgetown had noted, he was not interested in drawing the wagons around a chosen clique or gang of friends. Instead, he moved around New Haven like a combine harvester, reaping, threshing, and baling new "friends" on a seemingly endless mission.

Perhaps, a girlfriend of Cliff Jackson had once posited, Bill needed "to overcome fears of rejection and insecurity" by such ceaseless extrovert proselytizing. If so, the insecurity went way back into his early childhood and was now sublimated into an unusual openness of heart.

Meeting His Match

"Bill was cool," Oliver Franklin, a black student at Balliol College, later recalled of their time at Oxford. "He was easy around black folks, like a lot of southern boys. None of that tensed up nervousness you met in the Ivy Leaguers."

Now Bill was himself at an Ivy League university—as a minority student. Being one of the few southerners at Yale, with a distinctive drawl, set him apart in an otherwise predominantly East Coast community. Instead of feeling irked by this, Bill relished it. To the consternation of the black students, who, from the start of the term, had established their own "black table" in the school cafeteria, Bill plonked himself down with them. "Man, don't you know whose table this is?" Bill Coleman—himself one of only 10 black students in an intake of 125—recalled their first reaction. "By simply being himself," Coleman reflected, however, Bill Clinton "dissolved the un-

spoken taboo and became a regular and welcome member of the table."
Bill even broke the unwritten and unspoken taboo against dating a black
student, trysting with a graduate who later became a psychiatrist. But then,
as Nancy found, Bill dated many women, of all ethnic and social backgrounds. "You're reading my favorite book!" was his favorite pickup line—
and almost invariably it was, or at least a book he knew well, Nancy
recalled. Women keeled over like ninepins. His talent for "fitting them all
into one semester" was truly phenomenal.

Bill's whirlwind "minority" performance at Yale, however, was destined to
come to a quick end. Some weeks after his satellite reentry from the New
Haven political orbit, he sat near a second-year law student who had become
a legend at the law school. Among the intake of females the previous year, she
was already a star: the associate editor of the *Yale Review*, a girl who'd caused
a sensation by her commencement address at Wellesley when she'd dared to
openly attack the distinguished black Republican senator for Massachusetts,
Edward Brooke, a woman who had since become a prominent activist in campus protest meetings. By all accounts she was in a steady, long-term relationship with a Georgetown graduate whom Bill had known distantly, David
Rupert. Bill's seduction antennae began immediately to vibrate.

Just after Christmas 1970, the Wellesley graduate—one of forty women
in her class—found herself being followed out of the lecture she'd attended
by a "tall guy with his mop of ginger hair sticking out over six feet of navy
blue wool," walking so closely behind her he could smell her hair.

The tall guy, however, did not make a move on the girl—yet. Instead, he
watched her from a distance. Until one day, in the law library, the girl grew
irritated by his cowardice and accosted him directly: "Look, if you're going
to keep staring at me, then I'm going to keep looking back, and I think we
ought to know each other's names."

The tall young man, so he later claimed, could not at that moment remember his own.

He had met his match.

Rodham and Rupert

Republican Hillary Rodham was not quite as smart as Democrat Bill Clinton (she was hopeless at piano and advanced math), but she had a formi-
dably focused intellect, a ruthless ability to pare away the irrelevant and
less relevant and cut to the core issue. In a conventional woman this was a
most unattractive trait, since it negated traditional society's ideal of mater-

nal love: soft, cuddling, assuaging. Hillary Diane Rodham was, however, a new breed of woman—one who generally got what she wanted.

Unlike Bill Clinton, Hillary had, for example, succeeded in becoming senior class president at her women's college. Her "steady," an intern for a Republican congressman when they'd met in Washington, had been bewitched by her outward toughness and the allure of a less bridled inner self. A Georgetown graduate, class of 1969, David Rupert was an American Irish Catholic and devastatingly handsome: an earnest, dedicated young man who'd also avoided the draft, in his case by claiming conscientious objector status. They'd begun their romance with "pulsing hormones," Rupert later explained, leading over the years to an open-ended sort of affair in which "ours was a primary relationship but not an exclusive one," the feisty little associate editor from Yale being known to "shack up" with him in a cabin in Vermont but, with his agreement, to be "available" for relationships in New Haven.

Despite being a Catholic, Rupert had used a condom and for a while had managed to stay the romantic course with Hillary, but his own uncertainty over Vietnam and his rejection of the corrupting dangers of a high-profile career in Washington had made him less and less ideal as mate to an ambitious woman, despite his good looks. Like Bill, Hillary had spent her childhood carrying other people's burdens and solving their problems, the goody-two-shoes of her somewhat sterile, emotionally repressive family, so reminiscent of the Clutters in Truman Capote's *In Cold Blood*. With David becoming a conscientious objector, however, working for VISTA in Alabama and then Head Start in Vermont, their life paths had begun to diverge. "I never stated a burning desire to be President of the United States," David later sighed. "I believe that was a need for her in a partner."

This, however, was said in retrospect, decades after the three-year-long, sexually open romance had petered out. Whether it was true was debatable. Rupert was interested in grassroots activism after his experience of the "fucked-up" world of Washington, as he saw it. As Hillary saw it, David was withdrawing from the arena and challenges of the real world, haunted, like his whole generation, by the specter of Vietnam.

Hillary, by contrast, was emerging from her Republican upbringing in Chicago, her starry-eyed support for archconservative Senator Barry Goldwater, her presidency of the Young Republican Club at Wellesley, and her more intellectually and politically challenging college years. She had a social mission. David had watched this transformation with concern. "You're not a Republican. That's a bunch of crap," he'd scorned her one day in Washington, way back when they had first met. "You're either a conservative Democrat or a Rockefeller Republican."

David had been right—and inevitably Hillary's liberal Rockefeller Republicanism took her at Yale into a very different camp from the one in which David was interested. Like Emmett Tyrrell, David was excoriating about sixties liberals. She was, he claimed, "wasting" her time consorting with "those schnooks" at Yale Law School. "They're off the wall!" he complained. "Their values, their behaviors."

"I'm trying to understand them," Hillary said, defending her growing familiarity with hippielike activists, protesters, subversives—and Democrats.

The Ultimate Rescue Operation

In truth, Hillary was making much more than an effort of "understanding" as she actively tested the waters of civil rights, the anti–Vietnam War movement, and feminism, as well as activism on behalf of children's rights at Yale Law School.

In the spring of 1970, toward the end of her first academic year at the school, Hillary had already become involved in the Black Panthers' cause. Whereas Bill Clinton had marshaled five hundred well-mannered student protesters in London, Hillary had helped marshal 15,000 Yalies on the university green in support of the Black Panthers, watched by gas-masked police, armed units of the 82nd Airborne and 2nd Marines, and National Guardsmen waiting for a second Kent State fiasco. As an unelected but prominent spokesman for law school students, Hillary had negotiated with the university administration, achieving high marks for her cool handling of the hotheads in a volatile situation (the Yale Law Library had been torched). She also achieved high marks for her class work. She was, her professors recognized, going to go to the very top—and a conscientious objector working for Head Start in Vermont, however "ruthlessly handsome" and however good in bed, was not going to be a great support. Their lives were spinning in opposite directions, and the sudden appearance of Bill Clinton on the scene—big, friendly, like a Saint Bernard dog—was the ultimate romantic rescue operation.

A Meeting of Ambitions

The beach house Bill Clinton showed his new friend was full of "junk everywhere and rattan furniture." Was it nicely painted and papered?

Nancy Bekavac was brutally honest. "Guys don't decorate," she explained. "I mean, Bill decorate? No."

There were the house, the ocean, a cat, and four men—some with their significant others, some with less significant others.

Bill was keyed up, indeed on tenterhooks, warning his housemates to raise the tone of their conversation when the visitor came. He'd dated girls of every size and description and had had tremendous fun, but he'd almost always been, in intellect as in size, somewhat above them. "Listen, don't bother with her," he'd once advised a friend in England who'd expressed interest in a beautiful girl Bill knew. "I have had one date with her," he'd said, shaking his head, "and when you scratch the surface, you'll hit rock bottom." He loved intimacy, especially games with groups of people casually petting and fooling around, and he loved foreplay. Mandy Merck, for example, remembered how one evening, in Oxford, they'd played strip poker. On crossing the border from Finland into Russia, Bill had been ordered, he told his companions, "to strip down to the bare skin" on account of the Soviet authorities' concern with drug smuggling, but now he was being asked to strip as part of the entertainment. "Five of us were in the game," Mandy remembered, aware even then that "whoever didn't win the game could be staying the night."

Such parties had for centuries graced the drawing rooms and boudoirs of country homes among Europe's upper classes. What was different was that the licentious mores of the rich were now being enjoyed by the middle classes, indeed the masses, in the sixties and seventies.

As the daughter of a midwestern Republican, owner of a drapery business, Hillary Rodham was not by upbringing comfortable with such group activities, especially the skinny-dipping parties that were popular at Yale at the time; indeed, she much preferred to act as "den mother" to her women friends and colleagues. Known since high school as "Sister Frigidaire," she was certainly not "date bait," as the phrase went. Thus she wasn't Bill's usual style of companion. Nor was he hers. But that was part of the lure.

Snobbery, New England Style

Those who'd watched Hillary Rodham's ascent as a "Rockefeller Republican" at Yale Law School since 1969 saw her as a rising champion, a female heavyweight for all her diminutive frame. By contrast, they saw Bill, despite his hulking frame, as a Democratic lightweight and therefore dismissed rumors of a budding relationship.

They were making a big mistake, one that would cost Republicans the presidency in due course. At Yale the problem was, ironically, worse than at Oxford: snobbery. At Oxford, Americans had enjoyed an exotic standing that entitled the more confident among them to insider status, coming as they did from a fabled land of plenty. At Yale Law School, however, southerners were still outsiders, not very different from Faulkner's suicidal character Quentin Compson at Harvard: distinctly unexotic. Southerners were, in fact, in a greater minority than blacks or women; indeed, when Bill first met Hillary, according to one account, he was in the process of being asked to join the board of *The Yale Law Journal,* not because of his talent, legal ability, or political views but simply because of his unusual background. "They were trying to get Southerners, they wanted geographical balance on the Law Review," Bill himself recalled. "I just didn't much want to do it."

At Oxford, at least in his first, triumphant year, Bill had been a star; now he found he was merely being trawled for his minority status. As one of Hillary's more egregious biographers, David Brock, recorded, Bill "was regarded by his classmates not as a future president but as a glad-handing hillbilly in floodwater pants." There were "forty or fifty guys" at Yale who seemed better presidential material than Bill Clinton, Brock quoted Hillary's classmate Richard Grande as saying. The associate editor of *The Yale Law Journal,* Jerome Hafter, put the matter more bluntly. From as far back as high school, he said, Hillary was "probably considered to be marked for success. He [Bill Clinton] could have ended up selling insurance in Hot Springs."

"They hated him at Yale," Nancy Bekavac, daughter of an undertaker, once confided. "I've just never really understood it."

But the reason was clear—and Bekavac, the daughter of a local undertaker, knew it.

Icing the Cake

The snobbery of New England proved, ironically, more English than that of Old England. Bill Clinton not only came from a humble background but lacked New England reticence, "was too ready to brag about the brilliant political future that awaited him in Arkansas, bad form on a campus where it was assumed that everyone had the potential to become a leader," as one contemporary Yalie recalled. Michael Medved, another fellow student, agreed: "It was considered rather bad form to talk about it."

"Bad form" had been the bugaboo of Virginia Cassidy's life in Hope:

the twisted barb on the electrified wire erected around southern snobs. Here, however, it was being used by northerners to exclude southerners—something that caused Hillary, as one who had a natural sympathy for the underdog, to feel sorry for Bill. Snobbery (in others) vexed her. When paying a visit to the Harvard Law School campus in Cambridge, Massachusetts, while at Wellesley, she'd unwisely explained her dilemma—whether to go to Harvard or Yale Law School—to a prominent member of the admission faculty. "This tall, rather imposing professor," she later recalled, "looked down at me and said, 'Well, first of all, we don't have close competitors. Secondly, we don't need any more women.' "

Hillary had been dumbfounded. "That's what made my decision . . . that fellow's comments iced the cake."

A Man of the People

In choosing Yale, Hillary had intended to turn away from the notion of a greenhouse for corporate lawyers and instead learn law as a branch of politics and social work. As a schoolgirl she'd been taken by her inspirational young Methodist minister, Don Jones, to hear and meet Martin Luther King, Jr., a sort of counterpart to Bill Clinton's meeting with President Kennedy.

Gradually the feisty Republican rhetoric of Barry Goldwater had paled, at Wellesley, beside the need for compassion and contribution. Her views had swung further and further to the left of her party. She'd met Marian Wright Edelman—the first black woman admitted to the Mississippi Bar—and become involved in developing the legal rights of children in America. Though her intellect might entitle her to a future in corporate America, her Republican heart was elsewhere. She was, she later declared, "a mind conservative"—but "I'm a heart liberal," she added, recalling how in her student years at Yale she'd edited Yale's "alternative" law journal, the *Yale Review of Law and Social Action,* which had run in its first issue a call for a "Jamestown '70" in the manner of the first English colony of 1607. "Experimentation with drugs, sex, individual life-styles or radical rhetoric is an insufficient alternative" to the ills of modern American life, the article claimed. "Total experimentation is necessary. New ideas and values must be taken out of heads and transformed into reality"—even to the point of mass takeover of one of the American states by young folk: "What we advocate is the migration of large numbers of people to a single state for the express purpose of effecting the peaceful political takeover of that state through the elective process . . . where alienated or "deviant" members of society can go to live by their new ideas, providing a living laboratory of social experiment through radical federalism."

Publishing such radical solutions was a long way from the suburban Chicago environment in which Hillary had been raised. In accepting Bill Clinton's invitation to the Fort Trumbull Beach house, therefore, the young Republican had already proved she could look beyond New England snobbery, both social and intellectual. She was into alternative ideas.

To Hillary's surprise, however, the new kid on the block, or oceanfront, was no campus activist or student intellectual. He'd said no to *The Yale Law Journal,* just as he'd cut most of his classes. He was, Hillary recognized, already miles ahead of his peers, even the policy wonks such as Robert Reich. He literally towered above them, yet without disdain or condescension, holding nothing back and refusing to hide behind the usual New England veil of superiority, based upon breeding and arrogance. There was nothing arrogant about Bill: he was, quite literally, a man of the people, but blessed, she realized as she got to know him better, with an extraordinary mind, capable of stepping out of the normal parameters and limitations of conventional thought and approach. The fact that he seemed to be reading a mystery, a novel, a work of social description, and a law textbook all at the same time summed it up. He was looked down upon, even sneered at, by many of her colleagues: yet the gentle giant seemed to her to have more humanity, intellect, and talent in his little finger than whole hordes of Yalies who, having successfully avoided the draft, were intent upon their legal careers.

Hillary thus began to fall in love with the misfit, the stray—his bloodline even more mysterious than she could possibly know, indeed, more than Bill himself could know. Embracing the furry southern animal, her remaining Republicanism finally went out the window. In the warmth of his embrace she promised herself she would take him under her wing and make the WASP world bow down before him.

"Holding Our Breath"

Bill Clinton, for his part, basked in the manifest admiration felt by a Republican midwestern Ivy star. Behind her deliberately outsize goggle glasses, moreover, her face was quite pretty, with pert lips, striking blue eyes, and a firm, slightly pointed nose, full of purpose. He found himself deferring to her in such WASP surroundings. "I loved being with her," he later confessed, "but," he added, "I had very ambivalent feelings about getting *involved* with her."

Involved meant romantically—and romantically, for women, usually meant wedding bells. Since his liberation from the draft Bill felt he knew again where he was going, politically. As a lover, he did too. But as a possible mate he still had little idea.

Hillary, by contrast, knew exactly what she wanted in a partner—and in Bill Clinton, she saw it.

"They were both very strong personalities," one of Hillary's Wellesley and Yale Law School classmates, Kris Rogers, recalled. "They were ambitious—they both had aspirations to make a mark on the world. And what is often the case with those types of couples is that they either work wonderfully or fail miserably; there's no in-between. And so we were all kind of holding our breath, wondering if it was going to work or not."

Lady Macbeth

Hitherto Bill had dated great lookers—the sort of women, as his mother observed approvingly, who win beauty pageants. But the female scion of a WASP suburb of Chicago—a cold and forbidding city where Virginia had once intended to live with Bill Blythe?

Richard Grande was pitilessly dismissive, claiming that Hillary belonged to the "look-like-shit school of feminism," with Gloria Steinem–style spectacles, no makeup, and no attention paid to her appearance. Bill, however, seemed unconcerned about her looks. He himself belonged to the "look-like-shit school of masculinity"—at least in terms of New England dress codes, with his "wild shrub of hair and high-water pants revealing impossibly hickish shoes."

More significant was the vibration between two powerful, intellectual egos. Right from the start, the two "politicos" were challenging each other: in terms of their social backgrounds, political views, lifestyles, academic abilities, and genders. Other intelligent women, from Denise Hyland to Ann Markesun, had challenged Bill, but never in such an alarming way. It was as if Lady Macbeth had set her cap for him and there was no escape. What Hillary wanted, she tended to get.

Actually, what Hillary wanted more than anything was an equally ambitious partner. To be sure, a part of her still wanted to fulfill her girlhood dream of becoming a "senator's wife in Washington," as she'd once listed in her aspirations; but the older she grew and the more she achieved in her own right, the more she wanted a less wifely, more equal opportunity to shine. Her father had treated her like an academic robot, and she had complied, frightened of failing his relentless expectations. Her mother, a stay-at-home mom, had hardly counted in Hugh Rodham's driven world of social ambition, his Cadillac parked ostentatiously in the Park Ridge drive. "Don't forget, her father walked on her," her college friend Nancy "Peach" Pietrefesa memorably recalled, referring to Hillary's real self. In its tyranny, such paternal control was sexually threatening—so much so that she had never dared let her father know she was sleeping with David Rupert, whom she had introduced merely as her "boyfriend." Privately, however, Hillary had controlled Rupert, however much he sought to evade her clutches in their open relationship. "She didn't like not to have the upper hand with men," Pietrefesa added—as if, in keeping the upper hand, Hillary could avoid being jilted.

Would she, though, have the upper hand with big Bill Clinton, the genial extrovert from Hot Springs, the Rhodes Scholar with a thrice-married mother and a stepfather who ran a hair salon?

From the start, the question of power hovered over and between them. "I was afraid of *us,*" Bill confessed frankly later, thinking of Shakespeare's dark Scottish fiction. He'd told his housemate Donald Pogue that he had two ambitions: "one was run for president and the other was write a great novel." But what if the great novel wasn't a tale he would write but a saga he would *live:* a Steinbeckian story of a boy from rural poverty in darkest white supremacist Arkansas with an unknown father; a supposed father dead before the boy is born; an alcoholic, abusive stepfather for seventeen years, from the age of five; a feisty, determined protofeminist mother; a boy who by talent and determination wins a scholarship to Oxford, then to Yale Law—where he meets a woman with an ice-cold brain and, beneath the off-putting gogglelike glasses, a pretty face and petite figure: a little princess? Was this *his* Jackie, his passport to the White House?

It seemed improbable. And yet . . .

Romance

Thus the romance between William Jefferson Clinton and Hillary Diane Rodham gathered pace in the early summer of 1971. For her part, Hillary, like thousands of women yet to know Bill, carnally and otherwise, not only believed in her man but believed what he said. He was the American Everyman, as representative as any of the modern American psyche and able to talk his way out of any situation, any obstacle to success, as when on one of their first dates he took her to visit the college art gallery, found it closed—and persuaded the caretaker to let them in!

Almost from the start Hillary felt inspired, not only to accompany Bill on the next stage of his life journey but to help shape it, guide him, be proud of him, adopt him, while using him to further her own goals.

Did Jackie Kennedy love her husband? people would later ask. "What makes you think I am in love with Jack?" Jackie had demanded when, at her wedding in 1953, a naval friend of Jack's had asked when exactly she'd fallen in love with the bachelor senator. Jackie's response—flashed as she deliberately stopped dancing—was in part a refusal to be bullied into a role of doting, doltish young bride; but in part, too, it had been an unconscious self-preparation: a self-toughening for the years of sexual betrayal that lay ahead and to which she would have to come to terms in marrying such a womanizer, so like her own father. (She immediately smashed the camera of a reporter who snapped Jack kissing an old girlfriend at the wedding party.)

Did Hillary Rodham love Bill Clinton? He was certainly not like her father, who was fearsome: an English immigrant, a humorless midwestern Methodist despot from a dry town who'd worked in the coal mines during the Depression and had pulled himself up in society by his own will, late education, and sheer, relentless hard work. The only time Hugh Rodham took his daughter from the suburbs into town as a child was, she recalled, to see the bums: "what became of people who, as he saw it, lacked the self-discipline and motivation to keep their lives on track," as she later described it. Hugh Rodham was as cold and miserable as a Dickens character; indeed, love as the spirit of joy seemed a foreign word in the Rodham family during Hillary's upbringing.

What drew Hillary to Bill, then, was his very promiscuity with love: his very refusal to count out his love beads or be miserly in love. Compared with the cautious New England approach to money and affection, his was a generous, giving spirit. That he did not date her exclusively and saw, perhaps even had relationships with, other women only increased the challenge. Instinctively, she could sense his need for her: of the hard, ambitious intellect within her little body. He had sometimes introduced women in

England to his friends with "This is the girl I'm going to marry!" but they had always been flash-in-the-pan enthusiasms that had revealed his adventurous, questing nature, not his deeper, almost frighteningly powerful and ambitious intellect. Within the big, furry animal-like head with its big chin and slightly bulbous nose, behind the bright blue eyes, was a mind that would never rest content with a beauty queen bimbo or a shy, pretty wallflower, however devoted to him, nor with a mediocrity. He needed a tough, no-nonsense partner who could say "fuck" and could call a spade a spade. He needed *her*—whether he recognized it or not.

Hillary's Pink Slip

The summer of 1971 found Hillary in California, where she'd found herself another internship, this time working for a left-wing law practice, Treuhaft, Walker and Burnstein, in Oakland, across the bay from San Francisco.

Treuhaft and Burnstein were defending the notorious Black Panthers, who had broken into the California state capitol in Sacramento armed with guns (albeit empty) to protest the treatment of blacks. The Panther case never came to trial—"we pleaded it and got everything knocked down to minor charges," Malcolm Burnstein recalled—but though she worked industriously and accompanied Burnstein to the "pokey," or county jail, to meet some of his other clients, Hillary was oddly discomfited by such legal work, involving the violence of a man's world.

In this context Hillary was described by a contemporary as "washed out and very small, like the dormouse from *Alice in Wonderland*"—a dormouse, it had to be said, who seemed much more comfortable protecting the rights of children in New Haven.

By contrast, Bill Clinton, when he joined Hillary at Oakland, seemed wonderfully big and unfazed by violence, even though he did not like it. He visited with some of his old Rhodie housemates from the Leckford Road era—Strobe Talbott and his fiancée, Brooke Shearer, who was now at Stanford—and seemed quite unawed by the law firm or the San Francisco Bay area. Hillary proudly introduced her new boyfriend to her boss.

Burnstein had assumed that Bill, as a former Rhodes Scholar and smart young Yale Law School student, would be inundated with offers to work for big law firms after Yale. " 'No,' " replied the twenty-four-year-old. " 'I'm goin' back to Arkansas, and I'm going to be governor.' Period," Burnstein emphasized in retrospect. "He didn't say he was going to *try* to be governor. Or that it was something he *hoped* to do. He was going to *be* governor."

For Hillary, who'd never been to Arkansas, this was fighting talk. She'd never really been to the South, other than to Washington, D.C., and knew little of the Bible Belt, American Christian fundamentalism, or the depths of white supremacism—racism in the North being more a class problem than a color one. At any rate, Bill's big, easy nature, his pride in his home state, and her less-than-inspiring experience in Oakland convinced Hillary that she was truly in love with Bill—indeed, ready to make a momentous decision: to put an end to her open relationship with David Rupert. Meanwhile, she and Bill showed up at Brooke Shearer's house and went with the gang to a Joan Baez concert at Stanford, at which the famous folksinger sang, among other songs, "The Night They Drove Old Dixie Down."

With trepidation she then called David Rupert, and they met. She had been unfaithful, she admitted. So had he, he said. Without tears or recrimination she nevertheless handed him the proverbial pink slip—though Rupert preferred to see it less as a jilting, more as the end of an affair.

Then, gathering her things, Hillary went back to New Haven, moved into an apartment with Bill Clinton—and began to live in sin.

CHAPTER EIGHTEEN

LIVING
IN SIN

A Changing Morality

As a result of the famous trial of Linda LeClair in 1968, cohabitation had become a cause célèbre; indeed, Beth Bailey, a cultural historian, later considered the LeClair case to be a "symbol of change" in the sixties, a red rag to the conservatives' bull.

Linda LeClair, a student at Barnard College in New York, had "shacked up" with her boyfriend, Peter, in an off-campus apartment until arraigned before Barnard's judiciary council. Once the matter became public knowledge, the university president's office had received more than two hundred telephone calls, calling for the most part for LeClair's expulsion. More than a hundred letters also demanded her departure. Before long there had been editorials "in newspapers, large and small, throughout the country. Some of the letters were vehement in their condemnation of LeClair and the college. Francis Beamen of Needham, Massachusetts, suggested that Barnard should be renamed 'BARNYARD'; Charles Orsinger wrote (on good quality letterhead), 'If you let Linda stay in college I can finally prove to my wife with a front page news story about that bunch of glorified whores going to eastern colleges.' An unsigned letter began: 'SUBJECT: Barnard College—and the kow-tow female "students" who practice prostitution, PUBLICLY.' "

Quoting more parents' outraged correspondence, especially the criticism that the young couple were "openly flaunting their disregard of moral codes," indeed "openly flaunting rules of civilized society," Beth Bailey reflected that the "letter writers were correct." The "public-private question *was* the issue in this case," she emphasized. Some, perhaps most, parents were "willing to allow for some 'discreet' sex among the unmarried young"—but none was yet willing to accept that Linda should claim the *right* to determine her own private life.

As Professor Bailey saw it, this notion pitted Linda and Peter publicly against society: "an issue of individual rights versus institutional authority," as exercised by Barnard College's Judiciary Committee. It was, Bailey considered, "a moment in which the morality of an era changed."

Whether the morality of the era really did, however, was a moot question—as Bill and Hillary would learn, two decades later.

Cresting the Second Wave

To contemporary (and later) moralists, cohabitation outside marriage was a mortal sin. The liberalizing rhetoric that attached to the subject would become grist to the moralists' mill, moreover. John Sinclair of the rock group MC5, for example, had declared in March 1968 that "rock and roll, dope, and fucking in the streets" were the "three essential human activities of the greatest importance to all persons." "Our position," Sinclair announced in the Detroit *Sun,* "is that all people must be free to fuck freely, whenever and wherever they want to, or not to fuck if they don't wanna— in bed, on the floor, in the chair, on the street, in the parks and fields . . . fuck whoever wants to fuck you and everybody else do the same. America's silly sexual 'mores' are the end-product of thousands of years of deprivation and sickness, of marriage and companionship based in the ridiculous misconception that one person can 'belong' to another person, that 'love' is something to do with being 'hurt,' sacrificing, holding out, 'teardrops on your pillow,' and all that shit."

This was an extreme position. What was more prevalent in America was a growing concern among young people to find—whether in friendship, cohabitation, or marriage—a companionate relationship in which the cultural and gender differences between the sexes might be neutralized to empower women and create more equitable partnerships. It was for this reason that cohabitation, in the 1970s, became an increasingly popular lifestyle among students. Whether or not parents were privy to the choices being made by their offspring, the young people themselves were unrepentant, renegotiating not only their traditional gender roles in the new era of feminism, but intimacy itself.

A new University of Kansas survey on coed housing, conducted in 1969 and used as the basis of student proposals in December 1970, found, for example, that students were attempting "to formulate and articulate a new standard that looked to a model of 'togetherness' undreamed of and likely undesired by their parents." *Life* magazine, which featured Hillary Rodham as one of three outstanding student commencement speakers in the spring of 1969, had investigated campus sexuality in a major article the year before and had concluded that for most students, intercourse was less *Playboy* and more *Peanuts*—a still innocent place in their maturation where "sex is not so much pleasure as a warm puppy." While this was perhaps wishful journalistic thinking, there was a serious truth to be revealed, articulated by the California girl who told the reporter, "Besides being my lover, Bob is my best friend in the world." A cohabiting male student emphasized, "We are not sleeping together, we are living together."

Professor Bailey called such students—the majority, by far—"modest revolutionaries," and she was right. It was not only intercourse that was in mutation in the late sixties, as feminists called for more and better orgasms—with a new acknowledgment of the primacy of the clitoris, in defiance of Freud's view that clitoral orgasm was adolescent—but the very nature of male-female relations in modern secular democracy. "Living in sin" would, in fact, become one of the most enduring legacies of the sixties. Between 1960 and 1970 the number of cohabitating couples in the United States had shown only a modest increase, to approximately half a million couples—but over the next decade, in the wake of the LeClair trial, the figures trebled, Bill Clinton and Hillary Rodham among them.

An American Suicide

Bill Clinton had no sisters, unfortunately, whereas Hillary had two brothers. Despite his warm relationship with his mother, did Bill really have the patience, on a 24/7 basis, to put up with a woman's emotional needs, let alone her whims? In agreeing to "shack up" with Hillary at 21 Edgewood Avenue, then, twenty-five-year-old Bill Clinton was finally cresting what came to be known as "the second wave" of feminism—a tide that would take him way beyond his own mother's pioneering effort to achieve independence as a nurse-anesthetist in Arkansas, to a place in the very bowels of a new war, utterly distinct from the *Boys' Own* war in Vietnam: the war between the sexes. Yet the question for Bill Clinton was: For all his manifest talents as a potential politician and his skills of listening and seduction, did he actually have what it took to live with a modern woman in a new companionate relationship? How important was fidelity to Hillary? Could he be faithful—he, whose evolutionary drive to be promiscuous and whose need for constant, widespread female affirmation were so powerful?

In undertaking the sinful step of cohabitation, Bill was supported by his friends Brooke Shearer and Strobe Talbott. After all, cohabiting was what Brooke and Strobe had done in Leckford Road and were now doing at Stanford, where Brooke was doing postgraduate work. Together with Frank Aller, who was also back from England, they'd had a great reunion of the Leckford Road group. Shearer was studying, Talbott was finishing his work on the Khrushchev memoirs, and Frank Aller, who had resisted the draft at Oxford, had recently returned to the United States, been arrested, and undergone psychiatric examination. He'd been declared 1-Y at his physical, been mercifully forgiven, and was seeking work as a journalist on the *Los Angeles Times* after penning a novel about a Vietnam draft resister: himself.

It would be the last time Bill would see Aller, however—for hardly had the Yale Law School whiz kids set up shop in the small student apartment on Edgewood Avenue, New Haven, a short walk from the school, than news came that Aller had blown out his brains.

Bill was shocked. He had written a conscientious objector testimonial for his friend and fellow Rhodie Paul Parish, and felt the same respect for Frank Aller, the thin, ascetic, red-bearded scholar and draft resister who seemed such a cross between Haight-Ashbury hippie and Asian mystic. Aller's moral questioning had made him a hero to his Oxford friends, and his decision to resist the draft had become a cause célèbre; but once Aller had been released from custody in Spokane, Washington, his moral battle—*Aller v. The Draft*—was over, and he seemed to lose his will to live. Resisting participation in an immoral war in Southeast Asia, an area of the world he so admired, had become the supreme ethical challenge of his life. But once Talbott, Clinton, Parish, Reich, and all the other Rhodies had evaded, dodged, or legitimately gotten around service in Vietnam, Aller had been left footloose and in exile in Europe, resisting a draft everyone else had bypassed. They wanted, he realized, to *forget* the war: to move on. Finding his manuscript no longer of any significance, the moralist had returned to face the music in America—and had found none. Becoming a lowly journalist on the *Los Angeles Times* had seemed a comedown from the high, self-martyring plane on which he'd so long battled with his conscience. He'd therefore put a bullet through his head.

Aller's suicide left Bill sick to his stomach. As de facto, card-indexed "class secretary" of his generation, he proceeded to inform Aller's friends and contemporaries, telling them there was no reason for such a tragedy. In truth, however, he was racked to his core, since by implication it questioned the validity of all their post–Vietnam War life aims.

The cohabitation with Hillary that had seemed so adventurous, indeed noble—two star graduates pooling their resources to form a political A Team—thus suddenly palled on September 14, 1971.

In Love

There is no evidence that Bill Clinton stopped seeing or having intercourse with other women in the fall of 1971; indeed, several Yalies would afterward boast, truthfully or not, of the sex they enjoyed with Bill at this time. But whereas he'd never before had to answer for his sexual actions save to himself and his God, his situation had now changed. For the first time in his life he had to face up to the reality of a live-in partner in the little one-bedroom apartment: a feisty little woman who seemed to think the world of him, indeed was almost besotted with him. Michael Medved later recalled how Hillary had taken him aside one day, whispering, "Look at this. I'm in love, I am happy and I have got this great guy who is going to change the whole world."

If Hillary was swept off her feet, Bill remained hesitant. Was he good enough to be a quasi spouse, let alone good enough for her in the bedroom? Bill wondered as they watched their experiment in cohabitation unfold. "You know, I'm really worried about falling in love with you, because you're a great person, you could have a great life," he later recalled warning her. "If you wanted to run for public office, you could be elected, but I've got to go home. It's just who I am."

Bill's Arkansas background and his personal political agenda were only one part of his nervousness, however. He worried, too, about whether he was really up to the image she'd formed of him, however flattering. He was indisciplined, he knew, and had not even completed a postgraduate degree at Oxford or written a single published article in his life. In that sense, however, Hillary promised, he felt, to complement his personality: to be a sort of iron corset, stiffening his backbone intellectually, lending the decisiveness of her own intellect to his more encompassing, empathetic mind. Others thought so too. "Bill and Hillary really were a good match," Bill's housemate Don Pogue said. "She was more Midwestern, schooled in straight, analytical thinking. He noticed subtle differences."

A Wellesley classmate of Hillary, Ellen Brantley, put the difference between the two tentative lovebirds better: "She is very articulate, very good at *communicating* her intelligence. I don't think she is smarter than Bill," Ellen added—it was simply that Hillary had a more Republican-style clarity of perception and conviction. "If they were in the same class, she would attend all the classes, read all the assignments, outline her notes, study hard for the exam. Bill would stop by some of the classes, read some of the assignments while also reading other, related things, and then write an exam that brought in some ideas that had been introduced in class, some outside—linking them in an original way. They'd both get an A." In other words, Bill was the more open-minded, creative, imaginative thinker, Hillary the more conventional and focused. "She is much more of a traditional kind of lawyer's mind—quick, you know, a little brittle," one of their professors, Guido Calabresi, reflected. "Bill is much more a kind of all-encompassing intelligence, with a great deal of originality." To Calabresi, Hillary was "more of a cold shower," compared to the "hot bath" of Bill Clinton's intelligence. Together, however, they made a potentially formidable team—if they could manage to stay together.

A Hostile Period

A paper Bill wrote for a class discussion on pluralism that fall was memorable to his colleagues, for in it the normally upbeat, optimistic liberal Democrat in Bill Clinton seemed overwhelmed by the magnitude of forces ranged against change—principally the power of corporations. "It was a tough time for him, an angry, hostile period of his life," one classmate recalled.

Politics still obsessed and absorbed Bill Clinton, however, coloring everything he said or did, even the papers he wrote for his law school classes and exams. He later told his Arkansas friend Jim Blair how, in his corporation law class, he had gotten an A in his final exam without attending any of the lectures. "He said his professor called him," Blair related, "and wanted to know, since he'd missed most of the class, how he'd managed to do that. And Bill said, 'Well, I don't know much about corporate law, but I know a lot about politics. And it seemed to me that in most of these questions that political solutions applied. So I just answered 'em like I thought how they oughtta be solved!' "

Cliff Jackson, the Republican friend who'd helped him evade the draft, was treated to a deeply confessional letter from Bill that November. Jackson had graduated from the University of Arkansas Law School at Fayetteville but was interested in obtaining a White House fellowship as another step up the rungs of the political ladder. "Can't say I look forward to it as much as you do," Bill responded, with reference to a law job after graduation, "but I am trying at least to learn the stuff this year, and perhaps I'll figure out something to do with it that I can really care about."

The Vietnam imbroglio, with Aller's suicide as its coda, had left him angry with himself, as well as cynical. "You know as well as I do," he reminded Jackson in relation to winning a White House fellowship, "that past a certain point there is no such thing as non-partisan, objective selection process. Discretion and diplomacy aren't demanded so much by propriety, as by the necessity not to get caught.

"I don't mind writing to Fulbright for you, if you'll tell me what you want me to ask him to do for you," he assured Jackson. It would, he was aware, be a quid pro quo for Jackson's help in saving him from the draft, "but you ought to know," he pointed out, that Fulbright "won't give your politics a second thought. It would look good for Arkansas if you got the thing." It was as simple as that. Moreover, Bill had no illusions about Fulbright's views as a Democrat. The senator's "politics are probably closer to yours than to mine," Bill pointed out. "He was here last year and wanted to ask only why I wouldn't cut my hair." Even Congressman David Pryor was "in the favor-doing business now, as you know," and could be approached, despite being a Democrat.

As for the fellowships themselves, however, "the best story I know on them is that virtually the only non-conservative who ever got one was a quasi-radical woman who wound up in the White House sleeping with LBJ, who made her wear a peace symbol around the waist whenever they made love. You may go far, Cliff," he commented. "I doubt you will ever go that far!"

From Antioch to the White House

How far would Bill go, himself, though? It was, as Bill put it, "a long way from Antioch to the White House." Or, in another letter to Jackson, "The White House is a long way from Whittier and the Perdernales"—roots of Nixon and LBJ. It might not be "a bad thing to make the leap," he allowed, but he warned Jackson not to look back. "Just remember," he wrote, "it's far more important what you're doing now than how far you've come."

Both boys had risen from humble circumstances in Arkansas— Jackson's even humbler than Bill's. But getting to, and through, law school did not, of itself, guarantee success in politics or in life. Bill had read with fascination in Strobe Talbott's manuscript translation of Nikita Khrushchev's memoirs that "Khrushchev couldn't read until he was 24"—but Khrushchev had been called to take part in the heroic defense of Russia against the German armies, so "those facts leave a lot unsaid," he cautioned Jackson. "If you can still aspire," he concluded in Kiplingesque encouragement, "go on; I am having a lot of trouble getting my hunger back up, and someday I may be spent and bitter that I let the world pass me by."

Disturbing Undercurrents

Surprised by Bill's dispirited tone, even disengagement, Jackson wrote back immediately to thank him for his help but also to question the "disturbing undercurrents" in Bill's letter. Did such cynicism imply that Bill was no longer considering a political career?

Bill's response was revealing. His cynical remarks "were not meant to sway you from your course, or to express disapproval at the kind of things you seem destined to do," Bill explained. "You cannot turn from what you must do—it would be a kind of suicide. But," he added, acknowledging how steep and corrupting the ladder to the political stars would be for a young man without wealth or social status, "you must try not to kill a part of yourself doing them either."

Certainly Bill's advice seemed as much aimed at himself as at Jackson. Moreover, it was not just Aller's suicide and the legacy of Vietnam that was tormenting Bill. Life with Hillary was undoubtedly the most "disturbing undercurrent" at the time.

Hillary Rodham was *already* a star, one who was rising all the faster because the seventies, quite clearly, were set to become the decade of women.

Her decision to cohabit with Bill—indeed, her latest decision to delay her own graduation by a year so that they could graduate together—was deeply flattering, but it implied, indeed *demanded,* an equivalent commitment from Bill. Gone was the unpainted, messy, homey anarchy of his four-man beach house the year before. He was in a "relationship," a quasi marriage—which was tough. Cohabitation entailed myriad decisions that were, themselves, political in a domestic context, from who got to drive the car to matters of cooking and fidelity, if the partnership was to survive. It necessitated, for a Democrat from Hope and Hot Springs, an adjustment to Hillary's Chicago-Republican approach to politics, indeed to law and to work. She would, for example, give Bill short shrift when he waffled, whereas other women, lacking Bill's intellect, had found themselves uncertain whether to criticize him when he became loquacious. "You could never view his performance in a totally positive way," Nancy Bekavac mused in retrospect. "You wondered, is it real? There were moments that were so genuine that there was no doubt about it," she allowed. But there were also "moments when you wondered—is this posture?" Hillary did not wonder. "Come off it, Bill!" she'd interject harshly when she found him unconvincing. Or, when irritated by his long-windedness: "Get to the point, will you, Bill!"

It was, in embryo, a vibrantly modern relationship, in a modern world, involving two equally strong ambitions operating in the same three fields of power: the home, the law, and politics.

Seeing Past the Surface Charm

Despite the celebrated romantic elopements and cohabitations of history, few such partnerships had ever endured in the long run, given the historical pressures of patriarchy and the divergent biological agendas of the sexes. For this reason, however, the experiment in cohabitation was one of the most radical efforts Bill Clinton undertook at the end of the "long sixties."

Not having taken time out between Wellesley and Yale Law, Hillary Rodham was already a year ahead of Bill Clinton, though a year younger than he. For the first time in his life, despite his two years at Oxford and his travels through Europe and behind the Iron Curtain, Bill found himself intimidated by a woman, by the intensity of her intellectual concentration, her feminism, and by her exclusive focus on him. Hitherto Bill had woven intricate webs of romance, deceit, and betrayal in his encounters with the opposite sex: encouraging, tantalizing, and seducing with a veritable fire-work display of charm. Like Queen Victoria, Hillary would not be amused by such antics. "Hillary is not easily charmed," a fellow Yalie reflected. "I don't believe she was charmed by Bill."

Inasmuch as Hillary looked beyond the surface glamour of Bill Clinton, this was true. What Hillary saw in him was his *potential*—and for her, noth-ing less than his best would do. Other Yalies, like the snobs of Oxford, had pictured him as a glad-handing "ersatz" man, a "pretender" compared with her more northern, cold-climate Puritan ethic, which resonated so well with the ivy-clad Gothic of the Yale Law School building. Hillary, however, knew in her heart of hearts that it was she who was, in terms of her life story, the real pretender: the Republican who had supported Barry Goldwater in door-to-door campaigning during his fight against Lyndon Johnson's vision of a Great Society; the woman who had been elected pres-ident of the Young Republican Club at Wellesley—and who had later changed her mind. It was she, Hillary recognized, who was the real turn-coat, though overawing her onlookers by her sharp intellect and relentless, somewhat humorless seriousness. No one dared contradict the little woman—the reason, she often said later, she so took to Bill. He wasn't, she recalled, "afraid of me."

Intellectually, this was so. But socially, romantically, emotionally? Squiring Hillary to art exhibitions and movies while they dated, Bill had wanted to show the activist and star student that he was not simply a bum-bling Arkansas hillbilly but a highly educated young "politico" with an ap-petite for art, literature, travel, history, music, and people that would mesmerize her—and did. "He's more complex than I thought," Hillary had said, defending her romance when her snootier friends first questioned her, having seen her suddenly bopping around New Haven and environs in Bill's purple Gremlin.

"She saw past the surface charm," a colleague at Yale commented; saw "someone who deeply wanted to make a difference and cared about the less fortunate." That caring element was genuine—more *rootedly* genuine, Hillary recognized, than the charitable, even guilty conscience inspired by her own rather sheltered Republican, upper-middle-class, Cadillac-driven upbringing in Park Ridge, Chicago.

The question was, though: Could such an embodiment of genuine po-litical caring travel beyond the confines of Bill's hillbilly state of Arkansas? Could it be harnessed? Would Bill Clinton, so gregarious and easy with people, knuckle down and focus on the issues that would shape the future and that needed political leadership? At times he seemed almost messianic in the largeness of his vision, mission, and understanding; at others, though, he seemed to lose it, for whatever reason—distracted or bored, or perhaps just unable to rise to the occasion: her occasion.

In the spring, they had seemed to be "basking in each other's admiration, taking pride in their mutual possession," but as the fall of 1971 turned to winter and the dawn of 1972, it was Hillary's possession and expectation that sometimes daunted, even oppressed Bill. No longer was he simply the brilliant young man from backwoods Arkansas, gifted as musically as he was academically, blessed with a photographic memory and an extraordinary ability for multitasking. He was now Hillary's partner: the man whom she had designated as being capable of changing the world.

For a young man who'd spent his life bringing prizes home to his beloved mother, this was a momentous change—though Virginia, like Hillary's parents unaware of the cohabiting arrangements in New Haven, had no idea what was coming.

CHAPTER NINETEEN

ON THE
TEXAS *TITANIC*

Appearance in Court

As the end of Bill Clinton's second year at Yale approached in the spring of 1972, there came the great annual test of student lawyers' skills: the Barristers Union Moot Court prize trial.

As two of the top students of their respective years, Bill Clinton and Hillary Rodham were chosen by their colleagues to form the prosecution team for the trial, to be held at Yale on April 29, 1972. They had both pursued not only their studies but outside legal experience in New Haven— Hillary working for children's rights at the New Haven Hospital, drafting guidelines for the treatment of abused children, Bill earning extra money by assisting an attorney in New Haven as well as teaching law to police officers at the local community college. Now, finally, they would appear in court for the first time together, as a professional couple, and Hillary was especially determined to do well. Diligently she prepared the moot court case, involving police brutality, with Bill designated as the courtroom lawyer. Before a live jury chosen from New Haven residents, it was thus Bill who presented the prosecution case, backed by Hillary.

To their chagrin, they lost.

A Bad Day

"I just had a bad day," Bill blamed himself afterward. In an attempt at wit, he also blamed the jury's decision on its members' dislike of Hillary's "bright orange outfit."

In truth, he was angry and depressed by their defeat. Fighting a case they'd been given that was riddled with holes, they might well have won, had they not been up against several of the sharpest legal minds of their generation. This was Yale—and in a strangely symbolic way, the defeat pointed up the difficulties that would face them if, in an increasingly Republican era, they sought to make their careers in the East. Hillbilly Arkansas, to Bill at least, suddenly seemed a much less fiercely competitive environment in which to make his name, if he did go into the law.

Nancy Bekavac did not think he would—at least for more than a brief while. "It would make as much sense for him to be a practicing lawyer as for a greyhound to carry in the snow," she later remarked. "He wasn't bred for it. He wasn't made for it."

The question, then, was where and how Bill would start his career—and how many more defeats he would have to suffer before he made his mark.

George McGovern's would be the next.

The Cicero of the Cabdriver

While visiting with Strobe Talbott in California the previous year, Bill Clinton had discussed Senator George McGovern's looming campaign for the Democratic Party's 1972 presidential nomination. McGovern's campaign had since ignited—and Bill was determined to become a participant.

George McGovern had been the first to attack American involvement in the Vietnam conflict on the Senate floor, as far back as 1963—and the steady toll of American casualties thereafter had sickened him. On September 1, 1970, he had famously risen to his feet and, before a packed house, had declared, "This chamber reeks of blood!"

McGovern blamed himself and his elderly colleagues. He and his fellow senators had permitted the carnage—"young men without legs, or arms, or genitals, or faces, or hopes"—as well as tens of thousands of American soldiers returned from Southeast Asia in body bags. "It does not take any courage at all for a Congressman, or a Senator, or a President to wrap himself in the flag and say we are staying in Vietnam," McGovern had admon-

260 · BILL CLINTON

ished his colleagues, "because it is not our blood that is being shed." Every senator, he reminded them, "in this Chamber is partly responsible for sending 50,000 young Americans to an early grave."

Ranged against McGovern was Hubert Humphrey, Lyndon Johnson's former Vice President, but a somewhat spent force by 1972. McGovern's main opponent for the Democratic presidential nomination was therefore Governor George Wallace, the southern racist known as "the Cicero of the cabdriver."

While McGovern had achieved national prominence by his stand against the war in Vietnam, Wallace had done so by his stand against civil rights. He had deliberately defied a court order to desegregate the University of Alabama and had headed the national white revolt against busing (which had been approved by the Supreme Court) in 1971. By early summer 1972, Wallace was on a roll. McGovern lost badly to him in the South and in Florida, but in the North, in Wisconsin and Massachusetts, McGovern topped the polls. The race for the Democratic nomination was thus becoming a reflection of a new civil war: a fight between North and South that would tear the Democratic Party apart, dividing it into racist and antiracist camps—tragically turning the focus away from the issue of Vietnam.

On May 15, 1971, however, Governor Wallace was shot while campaigning in Maryland.

President Nixon, seeing immediately how the Democratic rift could be exacerbated, suggested that pro-McGovern literature should be planted in the shooter's apartment and rumors be spread that he was a "leftie"—a retired CIA agent, E. Howard Hunt, being swiftly dispatched to Maryland by air to get into the shooter's apartment.

Hunt arrived too late, however, as the FBI had already seized the home. Nixon's orders proved unnecessary, though; the Democrats themselves would do all that was required to self-destruct.

A Punk Kid

Certain that he could beat Wallace in the November election and intent upon splitting the Democratic Party, President Nixon decided Wallace must be given every assistance in recovering from his gunshot wounds. The President therefore not only visited his potential rival in person in hospital but arranged for the crippled Wallace to be flown from hospital to the Democratic Party's national convention in Miami Beach in an aircraft specially provided by the President—a Republican!

Governor Wallace was thus ennobled and became a national martyr—a sort of white counterpoint to Martin Luther King, Jr., but still alive. Not only did Hubert Humphrey now suggest taking Wallace as his Vice President, if nominated; even Jimmy Carter, acting for Senator McGovern, sounded out the possibility of Wallace's running as vice presidential nominee to McGovern, if McGovern won.

The Democratic Party's unholy compromise in the summer of 1972, bonding anti-imperialism to anti–civil rights, was in retrospect doomed to fail. Yet those who attempted to broker it were not being cynical; they were merely making a last-ditch attempt to stanch the flow of blood from their crucial Democratic constituency—the Dixiecrats of the South—to the Republican Party: ironically, the very party that, under Lincoln, had opposed slavery!

Rick Stearns, Bill Clinton's Rhodie colleague, had by now been appointed Senator McGovern's campaign research officer, and with his backing, Bill was appointed to marshal support for McGovern at the Democratic National Convention. Once the Yale semester was over, Bill therefore returned to Arkansas and was soon racing across his home state, trying to tie Democratic state party delegates to the McGovern ticket on behalf of the liberal senator.

Flying to Miami Beach to participate in the Democratic convention in July 1972, Bill was then treated to an acid aperitif, in terms of what beckoned. Sitting beside him on the plane to Florida he found "Justice Jim" Johnson, the "hellfire and brimstone reactionary," who was working for Democratic Congressman Wilbur Mills, chairman of the all-powerful House Ways and Means Committee and "favorite son" of Arkansas. Both Mills and Johnson were dedicated to stopping McGovern, while Bill was dedicated to getting McGovern nominated. "I looked at him as a punk kid then," Johnson sneered after Clinton himself became President of the United States, "and I look at him as a punk kid now."

The bitter wrangling in Miami—where Wallace was finally defeated, while Humphrey and his vice presidential nominee, Edmund Muskie, withdrew—was, however, only the prelude to an even more grueling combat between McGovern and President Nixon, the nominated Republican candidate.

262 · BILL CLINTON

Unfit to Govern

Senator George McGovern held deep convictions, but he had neither charisma nor an appreciation of the power of modern media. Inexplicably, he had given little thought to the choice of a running mate, having assumed (without first checking) that Senator Edward Kennedy, as a fellow liberal, would accept the role, since Kennedy's own presidential aspirations had been dealt a mortal blow by the Chappaquiddick incident three years before. With an alcoholic wife and suffering from a compulsive sex-and-alcohol addiction himself, however, Kennedy proved unwilling to accept the offer, knowing the right-wing press would tear into him and his family, still recovering from two assassinations and the death of his passenger, Mary Jo Kopechne. Kennedy thus said no.

McGovern, however, had no alternative candidate in mind—and, with only hours to go before the Miami convention broke up, decided to choose Senator Tom Eagleton of Missouri, whom he barely knew.

If the Democratic convention delegates were willing to endorse the choice of a virtual cipher, however, the press was not. Within minutes of the news, as Kennedy had predicted, members of the Fourth Estate were busy screening the would-be Vice President—who would become President if, as in the case of JFK, the president was shot or was forced to resign. Soon Eagleton was "exposed" by the newshounds, not only as a heavy drinker in the past—a story he was able to dismiss—but as a former mental hospital patient, who had been treated for depression by electroshock—a story he could not refute. McGovern nobly but unwisely stood by him. Inevitably, though, as the polls reported a disastrous drop in public support, McGovern felt forced to compel the unwilling Eagleton to withdraw.

The unholy mess would be a salutary lesson to Bill Clinton. Three weeks after the party convention and nomination of candidates, the Democrats had no vice presidential nominee—a disastrous start to McGovern's campaign. A further week later, on August 1, 1972, Senator Kennedy's brother-in-law Sargent Shriver, first director of the Peace Corps, was nominated—but the damage was done. Kennedy, who was at loggerheads with Shriver, withdrew his support, and McGovern, in the eyes of many older folks, looked unable, with or without the Mc, to govern.

Among younger party stalwarts the Democratic cock-up did not, however, diminish their political ardor, now that the Wallace dragon had been slain. Along with his fellow southerner Taylor Branch, Bill Clinton, six foot three and looking even younger than his twenty-five years, had been appointed Texas campaign "co-coordinator" by Senator McGovern. The appointments were not universally welcomed. "One of them looks ten," an Austin organizer complained to Gary Hart, the national campaign manager, "and the other twelve!"

On the Titanic

On September 8, 1972, there was a second disaster when Senator McGovern's new campaign director, Gordon Weil, resigned, unable to stand the way McGovern overrode normal lines of communication and command, as well as his tendency to "say what he thought his listener of the moment wanted to hear even if it ran counter to what he had told some other staff member," as Weil complained. "He would bend the facts to demonstrate how, in his own mind, there was no contradiction. Some might call this lying."

George Will, the columnist, certainly thought so. "McGovern cannot tell, any more, when he is lying," Will wrote publicly. Analyzing this, Weil—who had served since 1971 as McGovern's speechwriter and press secretary—attributed it in part to McGovern's tendency to interpret what people told him as "not so much what he wanted them to say, as what they would want to say if they shared his outlook." It was a penetrating, if nuanced, insight.

In Austin, Texas, however, Bill Clinton did not in the main deal with McGovern, who came to the state several times, gave speeches, and conferred with the ailing former president, Lyndon Johnson, in Johnson's home state. Instead, Bill's job was to look after myriad squabbling Democratic officials, volunteers, and campaign workers. As the veteran campaign chronicler Theodore White wrote, the problem was to "deradicalize McGovern" in the eyes of potential Democratic voters in a state that was Democratic only in name—a state where "liberal" was a dirty word, and the "ethic of the money men" ruled.

The challenge proved to be beyond McGovern's young team's ability. Bill Clinton was at once typical and yet atypical of these innocents. To some he seemed, turning twenty-six, a born campaign "pol," sitting at a desk with his feet up, working the lines and chomping on an unlit cigar. To others, however, he seemed but a rank amateur, an outsider working for a candidate who, as LBJ's crony Horace Busby reported, was heading for a colossal defeat in November. "I felt," McGovern's pollster quipped memorably, "like the recreation director on the *Titanic*."

A Huge Amount of Sexual Energy

Hillary, having obtained a summer job working on voter registration for the Democratic Party in Texas and spending the weekends with her partner, watched Bill's metamorphosis from stellar Yale law student into southern chauvinist with some concern.

In Texas, feminism was virtually unknown and certainly absent from politics as practiced in the Lone Star State. Hillary's biographer Gail Sheehy blamed Gary Hart, McGovern's campaign manager, for setting an appalling example of male chauvinism. Having left his wife and two children behind in Colorado, Hart allegedly played Don Juan, seducing political science majors at college campuses while getting them to join the campaign, yet leaving them "weeping as Hart passed their desk without so much as a hello" on Monday mornings.

Sheehy's admonition missed, however, the cultural point. Sexual congress, for male politicos, had gone with the campaign territory since JFK's charismatic, transformative campaigns and would now always do so, as much as cheerleaders were inseparable from American football. Contrary to earlier times, moreover, it was a mutually welcome arrangement. "At the beginning of Bill Clinton's political career," his Arkansas friend Jim Blair later explained, "most of the people around him were—you know, this was the sexual revolution—these were the children of free love! Nobody ever thought about it—they didn't think it mattered."

Blair had first gotten to know Clinton in Miami. "Where I got acquainted with him was: I was a delegate to the 1972 Democratic Convention in Miami, Florida, that nominated maybe the most decent guy ever to be nominated for President of the United States—which ensured he had no chance of being elected—and that was George McGovern. And Bill Clinton was a kind of multistate organizer for McGovern after McGovern's campaign was launched. Arkansas was part of his territory. Texas was his main focus, but he would come through here [Fayetteville] on behalf of the McGovern forces." The level of youthful excitement had, Blair felt, to be seen and felt to be believed. "I've been on political campaigns—there's a *huge* amount of sexual energy!" he confided. "At one time in my life I had a mistress, big blond girl who used to work in all Bill's political campaigns, and she kinda got older and more in charge; she used to call all the young girls together—I remember one time, she called us up and said, 'And *nobody* gets their cookies until the arrangements for this and this are done'—and they knew *exactly* what she was talking about."

Blair nodded his leonine head, shifting his big frame in his chair. "Yeah, a lot of screwing goes on in political campaigns!"

Not Saying No

The Texas capital, Austin, in the summer of '72, was even more open than Fayetteville. There was marijuana smoking at late-night parties, even outdoors at Scholz's beer garden. "Stories of who slept with whom among Texas Democrats have been a source of titillation for as long as I can remember: sex was always part of the game," one campaign aide, Bebe Champ, recalled. "All the women thought Bill was absolutely adorable and precious, I saw his attraction, the groupies around him, but he didn't seem to take it very seriously."

Bill didn't—but he didn't say no, either, to a girl in his bed, if it could be wangled while Hillary was absent on her voter registration drive. In this respect Bill was the opposite of die-hard male chauvinists such as Don O'Brien, an old Kennedy operative who followed the Kennedy line in gamic politics. "Not a day went by with this man," one of the women staffers, Betsey Wright, recalled, "when I tried to talk to him about some of the political factors we had to consider, that he didn't ask me about my hormones or when was the last time I had been laid."

Bill was different. Politics came before coitus. And between them came human interaction, or intelligent foreplay. After intercourse, however, there was no expectation of fidelity, indeed, fidelity was simply not a concept Bill Clinton could understand, any more than JFK had done. Girls liked him, generally, and he liked them—especially pretty or well-endowed women.

The fact was, Bill had cohabited with Hillary for a whole year. After that somewhat challenging trial, he felt he needed more feminine, less intellectual attention—and the women on the campaign gave it freely. Hillary's weekly apparitions therefore not only intruded on his trysts, they threatened them.

The Ethical and Pure Force

At least once that summer, colleagues later related, the "power couple" seemed on the verge of splitting up—Bill attempting, at various moments, to "run [Hillary] off," as Betsey Wright memorably recalled him admitting, "but she just wouldn't go."

Defensive and often lacking in humor in company she did not know well, low on human warmth with strangers, and relentlessly businesslike, Hillary charmed no one at the campaign headquarters on West Sixth Street, where she sometimes sat at a desk next to Bill's, wearing jeans or brown corduroy pants and large, square spectacles, armed always with a yellow notepad. "*Nobody* had met anyone like Hillary before," recalled Betsey Wright.

At the West Sixth Street campaign headquarters, Betsey, however, was one of those who *did* like Hillary, indeed relished her no-nonsense, non-sexual business style. If this offended the traditional transactional nature of campaign politics, it seemed to Betsey a small price to pay for the emergence of women as "the ethical and pure force that American politics needed."

Bill, by contrast, was brilliant, hardworking, a natural politician—but ethically impure.

The Key to Hillary Rodham

Betsey Wright had "been working in Texas and on campaigns for years and years, mostly in the liberal-labor minority factions of the party," when young Bill Clinton hired her. "He heard about me. And I was summoned by some of the party elders to come and sit down with him. And you know, I thought he was interesting," she recalled, "but I don't think I had any clue he was as smart as he was. As far as I was concerned he was another college kid from the East who thought they could take over Texas, or something! I liked him and Taylor Branch, being the other guy who came. I liked them enormously—enjoyed them. We did an awful lot of things, Hillary and Taylor, Bill and I, together. But I never thought they knew as much about Texas as they thought they did!"

Despite Bill's ignorance about Texas, Betsey was impressed by his people skills. "Bill gets into people and understands people so quickly, and better than Hillary. Hillary's job—she was working for the National Democratic Committee, working on voter registration—was more defined, I guess. I was amazed that people could be enrolled in law school and yet spend the semester in Texas working on a campaign—I mean, I'd never heard of doing that before. And then they just went back and read and did the exams!"

Politically, though, Betsey was "far more intrigued by Hillary" at the time, "mainly because I was learning how to wield my own feminism in the early days of that movement, and she clearly was someone I found a lot in common with, as a politician. And I knew that that wouldn't happen if she married Bill Clinton—because Arkansas can't have it, a woman politician!" she stated, mockingly, casting her mind back thirty years to the McGovern campaign. "I guess," she reflected, "I just didn't believe she really would come to Arkansas and give up all of her other places of possibility and potential"—something about which, in the aftermath of Texas, Hillary herself was uncertain.

A Depressing Period

Once smitten, the only daughter of the Chicago draper had opened herself up to Bill Clinton emotionally and sexually. Thereafter she found it almost impossible to relate to other men in the same easy, trusting way. She could be a good listener, a good friend to certain men whom she respected—such as Taylor Branch, whose marriage had recently come apart—but she could never give herself, her entrusting emotional and sexual self, however much she might, on occasion, threaten in anger to do so. Bill thus became not only her only lover but her talisman. He could be tough and would need to be if he were to survive in the piranha-infested waters of American politics, but he could be wonderfully soft as well, and she loved that aspect of him: his compassion and sensitivity to her as a woman, behind her Joan of Arc mask.

How to limit Bill's compassionate sensitivity, though, to her alone? Women threw themselves at him, she saw, and to turn them away was simply not in his nature as a human being, a narcissist, and a man. She and Bill had many rows; indeed, at the end of the summer she returned to Yale while he remained in Austin to help run McGovern's campaign right up to the November election, even though it would mean his missing all his classes at Yale till then.

For Hillary it was a depressing period—and not only because McGovern's chances of winning the presidency seemed to slip lower with each day. In the grip of true love she'd chosen not to graduate in 1972 but to take a fourth year in order to graduate with Bill. Now, returning alone to New Haven, she was uncertain whether they would remain an item—and what she would do with her life.

"Someday I'm Gonna Be Governor"

McGovern's seemingly inevitable defeat at the polls on November 8, 1972, signaled the true death knell of the "long sixties" in America. The old southern Dixiecrat alliance with FDR liberalism had finally died. The largest number of Americans in history voted in the election, and Nixon won by the greatest margin ever recorded—47 million to 29 million. Though Democrats held on to their majority in the two houses of Congress, the shift was clear. White Republican politics—at least, at a presidential level—was now here for good. After a decade of improvements in civil rights, America was turning against blacks and to "the most brutal reality of domestic politics—which is that white people fear black people all across the country," as Teddy White, historian of the 1972 presidential campaign, put it.

Bill Clinton thus returned to Yale saddened and defeated, more than ever aware that a career in politics was what he wanted but that it would entail a struggle against a fast-ebbing Democratic tide. Increasingly, though, he had in mind a different kind of politics than the one Senator McGovern and others espoused: a politics where the candidate did not simply represent sectional interests in the manner of a labor leader but in which the politician created a network of friends, colleagues, and allies from the ground up while also seeking to find answers to political problems that were less ideological and more practical.

In such circumstances one could not bring back Democratic electors by ideological appeals: one could only hope to appeal to voters on a personality level, a level that transcended policy issues. Here Bill Clinton would score his highest marks, as a politico who listened carefully and sought compromises that both sides could live with. As one campaign coworker in Austin put it, "every time a war broke out among ethnic groups, they would have certain demands and Bill would mediate between them all." Thus the big Arkansan saw himself increasingly as a peace broker between conflicting party interests rather than as an ideologue: a mediator rather than a standard-bearer.

In a Mexican restaurant in Houston, Bill had confided his new gameplan to the legendary liberal Democrat organizer Billie Carr, a generation older than himself. "As soon as I get out of school," he told her, "I'm moving back to Arkansas. I love Arkansas. I'm going back there to live. I'm gonna run for office there. And someday I'm gonna be governor. And then one day I'll be callin' ya, Billie, and tellin' ya I'm running for president and I need your help."

Christmas with the Rodhams

Back in New Haven after the 1972 election, Bill and Hillary, cohabitees and lovers, made peace. Bill might sleep with other women, as in Texas, Hillary tacitly accepted, but Hillary, as both personality and presence, was to be treated and respected as a partner in a league of her own, a sort of *maîtresse en titre*. With Nixon's landslide Republican victory (in Texas he won almost 70 percent of the votes in a staunchly Democratic state), it was clear that Bill would have greater need of her than ever. She was not only a former Republican who could help him understand the mood of Republicans; she was, literally, his better half: had made him believe in his serious self, while he had unlocked her steely heart. She would provide the intellectual-political solidity, he would provide the flexibility and facility with people that could, potentially, take them to the top.

From notes taken by fellow students, Bill now crammed for the semester-end exams—then plucked up his courage and accepted Hillary's invitation to spend Christmas 1972 at the Rodham home in Chicago.

Hillary had just published her first major law article, "Children Under the Law," in the *Harvard Educational Review*—a pioneering argument for children's rights on the basis of their status as "child citizens" and based upon her observations of child development at the Yale Child Study Center. All eyes at Park Ridge, however, were on her new beau: Bill Clinton.

"He came back with her one Christmas," Hillary's mother, Dorothy Rodham, later recalled casually. "I don't think her father was too impressed."

Hugh Rodham, self-made millionaire and martinet, was certainly a formidable obstacle to any suitor for his daughter's hand. For Hugh Rodham no man was good enough—especially if he came from darkest Arkansas. "We always had this picture of the barefoot, hillbilly type," his wife confessed: the type of overgrown Ozark clodhopper.

Dorothy Rodham was, however, fair-minded. "I thought he was interesting," she reflected. "He was sincere and had traveled a lot. I remember asking him what he was going to do after Yale, and without blinking he said: 'I'm going to go back to Arkansas—to help the state.' I thought, Gee, that's great for him. Least he knew what he wanted."

Hugh and Dorothy were, in fact, both relieved. A career in Arkansas, they were certain, was *not* where their daughter was heading.

PART THREE

A CAREER
IN ARKANSAS

Arkansas's youngest-ever ex-governor, 1980

CHAPTER TWENTY

LAW
PROFESSOR

A Letter to the University of Arkansas Law School

Al Witte, chairman of the faculty appointment panel at the University of Arkansas Law School at Fayetteville in 1973, remembered with a wry chuckle the lead-up to Bill Clinton's career in Arkansas. It was the spring of that year when the dean of the school showed him a letter from Burke Marshall, former deputy attorney general of the United States in charge of civil rights under President Kennedy, recommending one of his top students at Yale Law School for a teaching appointment in Fayetteville.

The name Bill Clinton "meant nothing to me—I'd never heard it before," Witte recalled. If there had been any hard feelings over Bill's undertaking to attend the law school and his broken Vietnam pledge in 1969, the intervening four years, during which Bill had kept an exceptionally low profile whenever in Arkansas, had effaced any traces. In the wake of Nixon's new peace agreement with the North Vietnamese, signed in Paris in January 1973, the Vietnam War was effectively over for Americans. The POWs came home. Draft resisters abroad were offered no amnesty or pardon (the "few hundred that deserted this country, the draft-dodgers, are never going to get amnesty when boys like yours died. Never," Nixon had warned in Ohio. "They are going to have to pay a penalty for what they did"), but the many millions of draft avoiders at home were excused. The nation breathed a collective sigh of relief.

Vietnam had been a bitter, expensive misfortune in American foreign policy, enacted by Democrats and pursued by Republicans—but ended, it had to be said, by a Republican president, who had almost literally bombed North Vietnam back to the negotiating table. A Republican president, however, who, it was also becoming clear in the spring of 1973, was suspected of having been involved in breaking into the Democratic Party's headquarters in the Watergate complex in Washington, D.C., and the subsequent cover-up. As Congress began investigating accusations of dirty tricks and unconstitutional behavior, the prospect arose that, despite Nixon's landslide victory over McGovern, Republican congressional representatives might be vulnerable in the 1974 elections.

Burke Marshall's letter of recommendation, meanwhile, "was very enthusiastic," Witte remembered. It was received before Bill Clinton's own letter asking if the UA Law School had a vacancy for a teaching professor, which arrived about a week later.

"Now, there were several things about the letter that were, let's say, curious," Witte went on. "One was that he [Clinton] had not yet graduated from law school! And to hire someone for a faculty, who did not even have a law degree yet, would be unprecedented, to my knowledge!"

Witte shook his head. "But on the other side, we'd rarely gotten applications from Rhodes Scholars, and he had taught constitutional law at a law school in New Haven, which I think was called New Haven University, or something to that effect. So he already had law school teaching experience in a subject we were looking for someone to teach! And that was also something unique!

"Well, in his letter he said he was coming to Fayetteville anyway, so would it be all right if he were interviewed for the job? I thought, Since he's paying his own way, why not? Especially given Burke Marshall's recommendation."

Poor Witte, already in his fifties, was, as he later realized, "light-years" behind the twenty-six-year-old. "I kind of assumed that no one else around here knew him, but, as it turned out, the people who were interested in politics, who were with Senator Fulbright and so on, knew all about him. And I was just out of that loop—as I always have been."

For Bill Clinton, graduate student at Yale, this was a godsend. He had only to charm the head of the faculty appointment committee when he visited Fayetteville and he would be assured a job as a teaching professor on graduation. Not because he wanted to teach law, to be sure, but because he had another agenda in mind.

The Whitest of Lies

"So my memory is, I arranged to meet him on a Sunday in May at the Fayetteville Country Club," Professor Witte later recalled. "I brought with me my two sons, who were then ten and eleven, and over the Sunday noontime meal we visited with him and set up whatever interview process he would go through while he was in Fayetteville. I had no idea what he looked like, other than what little came through that correspondence.

"My first impression, was, he was very tall. He seemed to be—he was wearing his high school graduation suit, which he had outgrown by two or three inches, because the pants cuffs were what they used to call 'high water'—indicating that there were about four inches of sock visible at the bottom of the cuffs! He had this blue suit on, and he had this remarkable personal charm, I guess charisma is an unavoidable word. And I would say that from meeting him as a total stranger, fifteen minutes later I wanted to hire him! I didn't need more convincing than that. And my two sons wanted to hang out with him—they were also charmed!

"I don't remember any strong opposition to hiring him. I think there may have been some grumbling about his lack of a degree, but the other factors seemed to be so strong, including his personality, his obvious brilliance."

Bill Clinton was offered the job by a unanimous vote. One member of the faculty, charged with taking Bill around the campus, had asked him point-blank if he had any political intentions "Bill, are you coming to Arkansas to teach with us," the member of the appointment committee challenged him, "or is this just a stepping-stone?"

Bill looked at him innocently—and was forced to dissemble. "I have no plans at this time to run for public office," he responded.

Legally—since he had formulated no actual plan by then—it was the whitest of lies.

Number One Agenda

"I've thought a lot about Bill's long-term agenda," Professor Witte later mused. "It became clear eventually, even to me. But I think I was one of the last ones to realize this. In other words, I was oblivious or obtuse or whatever: that his number one agenda was to be a politician! That he had moved to this corner of the state because he thought that the local Republican congressman incumbent was vulnerable—as it turned out, for the one and only time in his life. I would guess he had decided that before he moved here! That he was going to enter that race. . . . In any event, I am positive he had it all mapped out well before he wrote me that letter about a job."

Witte was right; indeed, it is a testament to Bill Clinton's brilliant, calculating mind that he so plotted his rise to political prominence in Arkansas that he was able to move from graduate school to the presidency of the United States in just twenty years. Others, like JFK, had made it in less time—but JFK had had a millionaire father to plot and guide his trajectory. Bill had a hair salon owner.

He did, however, have a live-in girlfriend who would make history as a quasi copresident, or "two for the price of one," as some supporters later dubbed them; Lord and Lady Macbeth, as their detractors saw them.

It would take them several decades, but possibly no president of the United States has ever worked so hard, or charted his life course so carefully, from the beginning, to reach the sanctuary of the White House as the young man from Hope and Hot Springs did. That the coveted position, the presidential sanctuary, would self-destruct in his hands, he could not know in advance. It was as if he was increasingly driven, from his time at Yale, by something even he could not control. Its common, generic name was "ambition." The whip for this drive, however, was Hillary Rodham.

Up to Here with Beauty Queens

Hillary Rodham would never forget her meeting with Virginia in the spring of 1973, when Bill was interviewed for the UA Law School and took his bar exams, which would permit him to practice law in the state—exams that Hillary also took "just in case"—i.e., in case they decided to move to Arkansas together.

If the reception the Rodham family had given Bill Clinton in Chicago had been chilly, the reception given by the Clintons to Hillary in Hot Springs was chillier—in fact, it was glacial.

Virginia had already met Hillary once in New Haven, on East Coast soil, but only as a student colleague of her elder son, without knowing the couple was living in sin. Hillary's appearance in Hot Springs, on Bill's arm, was "electrifying," Virginia recalled. "Electrocuting" might have been a more appropriate description. Hitherto Bill had brought home numerous girls, and been keen to impress them in JFK-like manner—even borrowing the family lawyer's motorboat on Lake Hamilton and speeding off into the sunset with them.

Bill's new companion did not look the speedboating type. Virginia recalled her surprise at the sight of Hillary's Coke-bottle glasses, absence of makeup, greasy hair, awful clothes—and sandals. She looked, in short, positively ugly.

Hillary Rodham, for her part, was equally appalled by Bill's mother. With her signature white streak in her thick, coiffed hair, her clown-painted eyebrows, and her heavy tan-colored makeup, she was all too ready, for a very private Chicagoan, to "love ya and hug ya."

Thinking back, Virginia blamed herself: "A mahogany brown woman with hot pink lipstick and a skunk stripe in her hair" and beside her, a teenage son who wanted to leave school and become a professional rock musician. Later, she would understand how shocked Hillary had been—in darkest Arkansas with her boyfriend's parents hoping she'd take the next plane out.

Bill was furious. Indeed, "the minute Hillary went to her bedroom to unpack her bag, Bill shot us a withering look," Virginia wrote, reconstructing the scene. " 'Come here, you two,' he said, and you could tell he meant *right now*. It was like he was the father and we were two bad children."

In the family kitchen Bill Clinton, age twenty-six, read his mother and his brother the riot act: "Look, I want you to know that I've had it up to *here* with beauty queens. I have to have somebody I can talk with. Do you understand that?"

For both Virginia and fifteen-year-old Roger, all this was too difficult to understand at the time. Looking back, however, Virginia could see that the times had already changed—that the sixties era of James Bond and his lovely bimbos was over. The issue was, in any case, "bigger than Hillary and me," as she put it. Her elder son, of whom she had always been so proud, was not necessarily going to marry a beauty queen or even a southerner. His education had taken him beyond the cultural confines of Arkansas, and though his heart remained with Mama and he planned to come back to work in the state, his *mind* had moved on; a brilliant mind that might require a brilliant mind as its counterpart, however poor Hillary's dress sense, her attention to makeup, or her personal hygiene (she perspired heavily and used no deodorant).

In the Scully Street kitchen, therefore, Virginia said yes, "we absolutely understood what he was saying about having had it with beauty queens, about needing someone to talk with. We understood it intellectually, at least; emotionally we had a long, long road ahead of us."

The same, in truth, could have been said for Bill Clinton.

The Worst Part of the Country

Behind every great man, Churchill said, there is a great woman. Without Hillary Diane Rodham, would the stepson of an alcoholic spare parts manager and then a beauty salon owner ever have made it to the White House? Without Hillary, how would his life have fared?

That Bill Clinton, né Blythe, was talented, there was no question. That he wanted to succeed in politics, there was equally no doubt. But how, without money or influence, coming from a hillbilly southern state smaller in population than many American cities, to reach the White House? "Talk about being clueless!" Bill's friend and chair of the Democratic Party in Fayetteville, Ann Henry, later exclaimed, scoffing at her own naiveté. "I mean, I helped all kinds of people in campaigns later on, but I would never have dreamed—I mean, I was brought up with the idea that there is *no way* anybody from Arkansas could ever be elected President! I mean, the whole system is banked against a guy from a little old tiny state that doesn't have more than whatever, four electoral votes, for Pete's sake! But I honestly think now that what he had in his heart was: he would be President."

How, though? Beyond the chain of hillbilly hills, Delta poverty, and the lack of personal or family wealth, was there something missing in his character, thanks in part to his difficult childhood? Ever the outsider who wanted to be liked and accepted, was there some lack of inner fiber that made him welcomed by all, even by the black table at Yale, yet afraid to commit himself *definitively* to people, issues, even to his word, thus dooming his chances of making it to the very top? And if so, did he, in falling in love with Hillary Rodham, recognize what is sometimes called, in social introductions, "my better half"? A half that *was* morally courageous, brave, relentlessly committed—a half that would stick with the program, his program. A half that would ensure his talents were not wasted and lead him through the dark hours when things would go wrong or seem hopeless.

Intellectually and morally, Bill might have need of the personal backbone of a feisty little Chicagoan, he acknowledged in his saner moments.

There were other moments, too, though: moments dictated by his background, his upbringing, his gender, his biology. Could he ever commit to one woman emotionally, socially, politically, sexually? And could that woman be Hillary Diane Rodham? Would she ever fit into the world of southern chauvinism, of southern belles and beauty queens?

One of Bill's girlfriends, Dolly Kyle Browning, for example, later described her first view of Hillary in a privately printed novel. It was far from flattering, describing a "dowdy-looking woman" who steps up beside a Clinton-like character. "Kelly [the heroine] realized that she was of their generation, not middle-aged as her first glance had indicated. . . . She was wearing a misshapen brown dress that must have been intended to hide her lumpy body. The garment was long, but stopped too soon to hide her fat ankles and thick calves which, to Kelly's amazement, were covered with black hair. Thick brown sandals did nothing to conceal her wide feet, and the hair on her toes."

The heinous portrait did not stop there. The frog's eyes "bulged out of focus behind coke-bottle thick lenses in dark, heavy frames." The protruding orbs were capped by a "dark, thick eyebrow which crossed from one side of her forehead to the other." Adding injury to insult in this image, there was "a definite odor of perspiration and greasy hair."

Even nonrivals, however, such as Bill's friends Paul Fray, and his wife, Mary Lee Fray, in whose apartment in Little Rock Bill had lived rent-free while campaigning for Senator Fulbright, felt insulted when, on arrival, Hillary would at first not even get out of the car to meet them. Hillary was naturally exhausted after the long journey, but to the Frays it was as if she were too arrogant, too superior, to descend to the level of ordinary people in a poor and backward state.

Whatever impact Hillary made on Arkansans, however, was reciprocated. After Chicago, the East Coast, Washington, Wellesley, and Yale, Arkansas seemed to her truly the back of beyond: a Third World state. If Bill was to run for president one day, he must earn his spurs—but why, oh why, had he been born in such a backwater? "I mean," Bobby Roberts, one of his later aides when he was governor would admit, "we're the worst part of the country. If you look at murder rates, poverty rates, lack of education. . . . You pick it, you know, we're bottom of the pile."

For Hillary, the once romantic idyll of partnership with a brilliant, genial giant who made her laugh and was even more intelligent and talented than herself, who radiated fun and contrasted so wonderfully against the dour snobs of New England, palled greatly in the reality of Arkansas. Here was a backward, cultureless former frontier society in which she could never be at home or belong.

In the mail, once back in New Haven, Bill duly received the University of Arkansas job offer. For several tormented days the "power couple" mulled it over.

Professor William J. Clinton

Hillary Rodham had no wish to relocate to Arkansas. "I was very unsure about where I wanted to be," she later confessed. "I certainly was not ready to move completely to Arkansas yet, because I just didn't know whether that would be a decision that Bill would stick to. I really didn't know what to expect."

What she hoped was that Bill, were he to "stick to" his agenda and hers, could win election to a congressional, even a Senate, seat that would take him to Washington, D.C., where she, Hillary, could fulfill her childhood ambition to be a senator's wife: but a modern wife with her own career there, perhaps working with her own hero, Marian Wright Edelman, on children's issues.

To Bill's surprise, local "pols" in Arkansas did not think the idea of young Bill Clinton entering the race for U.S. Senate at all ridiculous. Bill had Georgetown, Oxford, and Yale Law School to his credit; Senator Fulbright was considered to be out of touch with affairs in the state and vulnerable, whereas Bill had youth on his side.

Running against his old employer, hero, and mentor was not something Bill was prepared to do, however, even as Macbeth. Whereas a congressional seat . . . He had talked the matter over with his friend Paul Fray, who was now chief of staff to the lieutenant governor, whose election campaign he'd run in 1971. Fray had told him he thought John Paul Hammerschmidt, the Republican congressman for Bill's home constituency, the Third Congressional District of Arkansas—an area that covered almost the entire western portion of the state, from the Missouri line down to Texarkana on the border with Texas, including Bill's hometowns of Hope and Hot Springs—might become vulnerable in 1974, if the impending investigations into Watergate malfeasance in Washington continued.

On May 22, 1973, five days after the U.S. Senate opened hearings on the

Watergate conspiracy, Bill thus decided to wait no longer. He accepted the University of Arkansas Law School offer of employment—his first-ever full-time job. From the summer of 1973, he would be Professor William J. Clinton of the University of Arkansas.

The future of Lady Macbeth, however, was far less clear.

CHAPTER TWENTY-ONE

CAMPAIGN FOR CONGRESS

The Road to Elkins

It did not take Bill Clinton long to settle into Fayetteville. New Haven had had the ocean, but Fayetteville was a university campus town set in some of the most scenic surroundings of the South. "There's a beautiful small cabin-style house out here," Professor Witte explained, "that he rented. It was his first bachelor's abode. And I recall the highlight of our first collegial friendship was right here. Twenty-eight years ago, this was considered far out of town! It was built as a country abode for a local banker and his wife. The banker died fairly young, and so when Clinton moved here the widow was ready to rent it to him—and I had the privilege of having a future president cook a steak, toss a salad, and bake a potato for a dinner for my wife and I! There it is," he said, pointing to the ranch-style bungalow tucked back a hundred yards from Highway 16 East. " 'The Road to Elkins' as folks around here call it!"

Witte considered himself "a sort of minor champion" of the young law professor, having hired him as a teacher. Twice Bill's age, however, and a senior member of the faculty, Witte did not socialize with Bill. "There would be stories that on Friday afternoons the younger members of the faculty would gather in the backyard of Dick Richardson's house and play volleyball or badmin', drink beer and have a good time." Witte heard about the gatherings but did not participate. "At any rate, I did have good collegial contact with Clinton from the beginning," he recalled, "and I wasn't really aware, until he really started gearing up for the congressional race, that he had this strong interest in politics!"

Witte blamed himself—"As I say, I was kinda dumb." But he was not the only member of the faculty to be unaware of Bill's ambitions. Milt Copeland, a law professor, for example, later shared an office with Hillary when she moved to Fayetteville and admitted, "I didn't even know they were dating." It was a confession that, in Ann Henry's eyes, typified the un-wordliness of legal academia. "I think many lawyers live in the legal world, so to speak, or law world," Ann Henry—who had graduated from UA Law School in 1971—reflected. For herself, she had never been under any illusions. Already in August 1973, before giving his very first class at UA Law School, Bill Clinton had come "for a party at my house," Ann—whose husband was an ophthalmologist and member of the state legislature—later recounted. "And all of the guests were political. His hair was curly and kind of unkempt, but he knew *everybody,*" she remembered with surprise. Where he didn't, he soon did. Diane Kincaid, a young political science professor, was there, with her boyfriend, Jim Blair, a lawyer and "politico" who served as general counsel for Tyson Foods, the state's biggest and most rapidly expanding poultry business, and who was Senator Fulbright's reelection campaign manager. Bill was completely at home. "You don't show up in a political thing if you're not interested in getting involved somehow. He started networking then," Ann Henry commented, "and never stopped!"

Drumming Up Financial Support

Since Bill proved a brilliant and popular teacher among students, the notion of a faculty member pursuing a political career on the side was not necessarily disturbing to his teaching colleagues, but it did leave his status unclear. "He did not get leave of absence, though he asked for it!" Witte recalled. "It's a sort of bureaucracy-type of decision that drives people crazy: that is, that the university had no policy *against* running for office, and they also did not have a policy granting a leave of absence in order *to* run for office—even though Clinton requested one." Contemporary and later criticism on this score Witte felt to be unfair, since "this was a world he didn't create. But, yes, he was criticized by students who felt that he wasn't spending the time on his classes and getting ready for his lecturing and whatever, as he should have done, because he was out on the campaign trail."

Before the constitutional law professor announced his candidacy or hit the trail, however, he had to drum up some money. "I kept hearing a little anecdote here and there about Clinton and his developing contacts for fund-raising and support in this area—going to the wealthy Democratic classes in northwest Arkansas," Witte recalled, "to drum up financial support."

Here was the raw nub of modern American electoral democracy: the quest for money. It was, however, a two-way process, since money followed candidates—either because wealthy people wished to feel they could then pull political strings when required or because commercial and professional firms wanted political leverage via their congressional representative in Washington for the furtherance of their business. Neither of these pressures was necessarily inimical to democratic ethics since capitalism is dependent upon economic and social dynamics—so long as the broad electorate was satisfied by their candidate's representation in the legislature.

Bill Clinton was certainly happy with the arrangement—which was very much "the southern way." It was said, for instance, of LBJ that when he was Senate majority leader, he turned away a delegation of cotton goods manufacturers who had left more than $125,000 in dollar bills on his office desk. LBJ's simple message—"Not enough!"—said it all. With this approach, Bill was more than comfortable, the more so because, unlike LBJ, who had bought a big ranch and lived grandly after a childhood of poverty, Bill had no personal interest in money or wealth. "Money has never been his object," Ann Henry remarked. "He never set about trying to make it—I mean, it was just policy and enacting it and raising campaign funding."

"There's not a bitch alive in this country that can raise money like he can," Paul Fray put the matter less prosaically. "Nobody can." Another campaign worker agreed. "He can raise money like nobody's business. He could go into poverty-stricken areas of Arkansas and come back with more campaign checks than anybody I've ever seen in my life. He would literally go door to door, coffeeshop to coffeeshop."

Other men might yearn for flashy cars, homes, or exotic travel possibilities; Bill seemed as comfortable in the YMCA as in the Ritz; in the porter's lodge at University College, Oxford, as in the master's lodge. His uncle Raymond sold cars. His mother anesthetized patients, rich and poor. In asking for money—which he would become famous for—he had no shame or embarrassment, since it was not, nor would ever be, for himself. It would fund his campaigns, his staff, his cavalcade—not furnish Macbeth's wardrobe.

Impeaching the President

Though she had delayed her own law degree by a year to graduate with Bill, Hillary had not accompanied Bill to Arkansas, nor was she a party to his fund-raising efforts in Fayetteville. Parting company in New Haven, Hillary had, instead, traveled north to Cambridge, Massachusetts, in the shadow of Harvard—whose law school she had earlier turned down—to work for Marian Wright Edelman's nonprofit Children's Defense Fund. In January 1974, however, she received a call from Burke Marshall asking if she would be willing to serve on the Senate Judiciary Committee's Watergate investigation staff in Washington. Professor Marshall had already asked Bill Clinton, in Arkansas, who had said no—but had recommended Hillary.

Thus, while in Fayetteville, Arkansas, twenty-seven-year-old Bill Clinton announced, on February 24, 1974, his intention to run for Congress, Hillary Rodham announced to friends in Cambridge that she would be joining the Watergate investigation—and by the spring of 1974 she was living in the nation's capital with Sarah Ehrman, a former colleague on the McGovern campaign, researching the constitutional history of impeachment. To this end she also began transcribing President Nixon's taped conversations and dictations in the White House.

For a young woman so private and emotionally defensive, there was something ironic, indeed uncomfortable, about a project that required her to eavesdrop on the President's most secret, personal, and unguarded thoughts. It was, she later confided, "surreal, unbelievable," sitting each day "locked in this soundproof room with these big headphones on, listening to a tape. It was Nixon taping himself while he listened to his tapes, inventing rationales for what he said." If she had ethical qualms, she declined to share them with her coworkers, however. "I worked with her day and night for nine months," her colleague on the Watergate committee Terry Guzman recalled, "and I still would not say that I knew her. Just very closemouthed about everything."

Hillary was nevertheless transfixed by the White House tapes and by the

President's clearly personal involvement in the plot to break into the Democratic National Committee's office in the Watergate building, then to cover up such transgressions. In this murky world of "plumbers," the truly medieval character of politics at the top was revealed to the twenty-six-year-old law school graduate, and she blanched. But she did not shy away. Shakespeare had gotten it right: in the web of the court, at the center of political power and influence, there was intrigue everywhere, with plots and subplots spun behind a facade of propriety and executive privilege. Though Hillary's boss, John Doar, recruited only supposedly "objective" lawyers who had no preconceived views of the President's guilt or innocence, Nixon was too tainted by Vietnam to be viewed as innocent, even by the daughter of a Republican Cadillac owner in Chicago. Though Hillary had endless compassion for children, with whom she was able to identify easily, she seemed to lack all magnanimity toward adults, especially men. She thus became determined to help impeach the President.

Two Simple Facts

For Bill Clinton the situation was more complex. President Nixon had prolonged, in fact escalated, the war in Vietnam. But he had had American national prestige to uphold, and he had, after all, in the end brought the war—Kennedy's war and LBJ's war—to a conclusion for American forces. He had also reversed American policy toward Communist China. Even his social agenda, despite the Republican shift to the white Right, was in many ways closer to that of Arkansas Governor Winthrop Rockefeller than that of Democratic Governor Faubus. Moreover, in thinking of raiding Democratic National Committee headquarters for information, had Nixon contemplated anything different from most "pols"—however few politicians actually dared to carry out such intelligence-gathering strategems? Intelligence about your enemy was the cardinal precept of modern war, Brigadier Bill Williams had made clear to Bill and other students at Rhodes House, Oxford—indeed, that very year the incredible story of "Ultra," the Allied cracking of the German High Command's most secret codes in World War II, was finally and for the first time revealed—intelligence without which the Allies might never have beaten the Nazis. Moreover, deception had made the Allied D-Day landings the largest, yet most successful, amphibious landing in military history. Deception and its concomitant, covering up, were an almost elemental rule of politics, as Bill had remarked in his letter to Cliff Jackson: the need to avoid being caught! In a preelection interview Bill had claimed that "If I run and am elected there will be at least one less congressman to support Nixon's vetoes, applaud his impoundments of federal funds and think that all the illegalities that have been revealed in the last year are unimportant, which is the record of the incumbent [John Paul Hammerschmidt]"—but even with Hillary's confidential reports on the President's tapes Clinton had no real notion of how fantastical Nixon's intentions in the Oval Office had been. That the President had seriously proposed and threatened to use nuclear bombs in Vietnam would not be publicly revealed until decades later. In the meantime, hounding the President of the United States, at a time when he was attempting to manage the fortunes of the nation in the wider, global world, seemed cruel and nationally degrading.

Bill's natural sympathy, then, lay with the beleaguered President—who was, after all, a peacemaker in the same mold that Bill Clinton would himself adopt. (President Nixon's tombstone, twenty years later, would bear the simple words "The greatest honor history can bestow is the title of peacemaker.") Nixon had been the first President, in office, ever to visit Moscow, initiating historic arms agreements with Soviet General Secretary Leonid Brezhnev in 1972.

Ranged against this there were two simple facts, however.

The President, it began to be clear, *had* been caught in the matter of the illegal Watergate break-in conspiracy—as the tapes confirmed. Second, the more revelatory the investigation into Watergate and the disclosures of political, indeed criminal, impropriety, the more Bill Clinton's own campaign against the Republican incumbent in Arkansas's Third Congressional District would prosper. From this point of view Hillary's investigation should *under no circumstances* be prematurely concluded, however cruel, lest this give the Republicans time to recover in time for the November midterm elections—thereby taking the pressure off Congressman John Paul Hammerschmidt. This was, however, to run ahead of his own story, Bill recognized. First he had to win the Democratic nomination—*without* a Republican scapegoat.

The Barn Burner

"Actually, what tends to get overlooked, when you get into the finer points of the period, is that he had to get the nomination," Professor Witte recalled. "And there were other bright young Democrats who also realized Hammerschmidt might be vulnerable. And so Clinton had to run two very tough races to get the nomination—much more draining than might be assumed."

As a prodigal son, recently returned, Bill initially lacked sufficient local know-how or even adult experience of life to look like a serious contender—but "from the time he hit the ground he was doing nothing but networking," Ann Henry recalled, "and on weekends he was out going in the district having people take him around to meet people, even before he announced he was going to run." Here was a young man with inexhaustible energy. By dint of indefatigable personal campaigning he exemplified "retail politics": the willingness to get to know and solicit the vote and financial contribution of every constituent in the congressional district. In the primary in May 1974, he duly beat out the governor's man, David Stewart, but did not do quite well enough to avoid a runoff in June. With term teaching over, he threw himself into a second primary battle— and was rewarded this time by victory, trouncing the state senator for nearby Fort Smith, Gene Rainwater. In November 1974, Professor William J. Clinton would be the official Democratic Party candidate for Congress, facing the incumbent, Congressman John Paul Hammerschmidt.

Hammerschmidt would be a tough opponent to bring down. The Republican had already served four terms, "and he made a decision which served him very well," Ann Henry noted, "that he would serve Republicans *and* Democrats." In a predominantly conservative, white corner of the state, "Hammerschmidt was really a constituency service kind of guy— very buttoned-down, very low-key, very unassuming-looking. He had some money, was a businessman, he had served in World War II—he had all of that stuff."

Ought Clinton to have kept his powder dry to help his mentor, Senator William Fulbright, who was facing a tough primary fight against the young governor, Dale Bumpers? "Some felt that Clinton was dodging the major face-off between two major politicians by running his own hopeless race," recalled Jim Blair, who would have welcomed Clinton's help on Fulbright's "ill-fated campaign, but the fact is, what impressed everybody was, it turned out to be not all that hopeless!"

Blair was not the only one to be surprised. Hammerschmidt had at first appeared unbeatable. "Then, when Clinton comes along with his bushy, kind of curly, unkempt hair," Ann Henry recalled, the outcome had suddenly become unpredictable. Bill, on the stump, came across as a "barn burner," a young politician "who got people really excited. When you give a barn-burner speech, by the time you finish it, they're ready to burn the barn if that's what you're telling them to do! So he could really get out there and speak, and he had tons of young people involved in the campaign."

It was these young people who now worried Hillary Rodham.

A Spying Mission

Bill's fund-raising efforts would become legendary—not because they were different from those of other candidates but because they encompassed every level and were more successful, being conducted on a vast scale, from mailings to personally negotiated deals. As Bill's later aide Bobby Roberts reflected, "He doesn't mind asking for money. He just doesn't mind asking you for money. A lot of politicians hate that. You hear them bitching all the time about it. Not him. He didn't think anything about it." Bill didn't mind the source, either. Thanks to Jim Blair, the heir to the local Tyson poultry agribusiness, Don Tyson, became an early sponsor—as well as pretty well every high school and university friend and colleague from the past, to each of whom Bill would write personally.

Behind this successful fund-raising front, however, there were, Hillary suspected, organizational, ethical, and even women problems. Since the McGovern campaign had suffered an imbalance of young idealists compared with older folks, Hillary, who was tied up day and night in the effort to impeach the President, asked if her father, Hugh Rodham, and her brother Tony might assist in the campaign in Arkansas. Bill reluctantly agreed. Paul Fray, his chief of staff, was indignant: "It was her little spying mission."

What Hugh Rodham found was a moral cesspool, from his midwestern, sexually repressed perspective. It was not that Bill Clinton was a villain, a predator of the old order. It was the opposite: the candidate was a magnet for young campaign volunteers and incapable of sexual restraint once propositioned by a female. In this sense Bill was simply *too* talented, *too* appealing. In five minutes he could charm even the most skeptical voter; equally, he seemed to charm all too many birds off their trees. A Yale Law buddy watched in astonishment as "all of a sudden, all those women appeared. For the first time in his life he could have all the pussy he wanted."

Thus, whereas the environment of John Doar's Senate Judiciary Committee impeachment staff in Washington, D.C., resembled a monastery—

its thirty-six lawyer-monks and three lawyer-nuns wholly devoted to their work, twelve hours a day, seven days a week, without any hint of sin ("The most extraordinary thing is how little sex there was," Bob Sack recalled)— Bill Clinton's campaign in Arkansas literally reeked of sex; indeed, for many unpaid young volunteers the excitement of human interaction and possible intercourse was the very fuel on which the campaign was run. JFK had made such sexual excitement his pioneering contribution to modern American politics, a contribution that had brought hundreds of thousands of young people into the modern political arena, whether as participants or audiences, in a hands-on democratic experience not dissimilar from Woodstock. As a wannabe politician and a saxophone player of consider-able talent, Bill Clinton was merely continuing this trend. Senator Ful-bright had once warned Bill not to model himself on JFK in the sexual respect—"Bill, if you're going to idolize the womanizing side of Jack Kennedy, you're gonna end up turning out that way yourself"—but Ful-bright was on a downward slope while Bill Clinton was on a continuing sixties roll—in an era of hardening Republican-versus-Democrat attitudes.

Nixon's impeachment served to draw the battle lines between the two parties, as Bill—apprised each night on the telephone by Hillary—had hoped it would. Tirelessly Hillary's Star Chamber worked to find reasons to bring down the sitting President of the nation, in an atmosphere of dra-conian secrecy ("Don't keep a diary. Don't talk to anybody. Just do your work" were Doar's orders to his staff), with documents kept in locked safes and nothing entrusted to computer or other electronic forms. It was war between armies—a war that month by month, week by week, hour by hour drove the President toward a mental breakdown in office. Indeed, by July 1974, it is said, the military became so profoundly worried by the mental health of the president that Nixon's special codes briefcase for nuclear hos-tilities was exchanged for an empty one and the chiefs of staff agreed not to act on any presidential order Nixon gave as commander in chief, unless by unanimous agreement of the chiefs.

Hillary Rodham, as John Doar's right-hand woman, was at the very epi-center of this relentless pursuit of the President: Nixon's words on the infa-mous White House tapes laboriously transcribed and retranscribed in order to expose Nixon's "high crimes and misdemeanors." "It was an unbelievable experience. I got to hear all the tapes, all the other evidence." Simultane-ously, however, she was eavesdropping on another sinner: using her father and younger brother to watch and report on the behavior and misde-meanors of the official Democratic congressional candidate in Fayetteville.

Two Vulnerabilities

Hillary Rodham had many talents. Her most serious deficiency, however, was perhaps her lack of imagination. She loved Bill Clinton but could not see that the hounding of the U.S. President to impeachment and trial for a political misdemeanor—the attempted theft of rival political and personal documents—would inevitably result, given the two-party binary culture of America, in Republican revenge one day.

Dimly, however, Hillary Rodham was aware how treacherous were the piranha-infested waters of high-profile democracy and that Bill must be careful to give no hostage to future fortune. For the larger part of his life Bill had been a model student, a star performer, but in two key respects, she knew, he was vulnerable: Vietnam and women.

These two Achilles heels would remain constant for the next twenty years and more. Her response to the danger was, first, to ensure removal of the evidence of Bill's Vietnam misdemeanor; second, to keep her father and brother in Fayetteville on Bill's case, as spies and guardians of the candidate's personal morality. And third, to help her lover use Nixon's impending impeachment—about which she had unique knowledge—as a stick to beat Congressman Hammerschmidt.

Day after day, night after night, Hillary would thus call from Washington to help direct the young Arkansas candidate's campaign, which, in the relentless national focus on President Nixon's misdoings as a Republican, was really catching fire—but could at any moment be dampened or extinguished by the wrong revelation concerning young Bill Clinton.

Ironically, the man who could produce such a revelation was none other than Cliff Jackson, Bill's friend from Oxford who had helped save him from the draft. Would Jackson "rat" on his friend? An emissary was quickly sent to see Colonel Eugene Holmes, and Bill's letter from Oxford, on behalf of his generation, was secretly removed from the ROTC files at the university, to be destroyed. Meanwhile every effort was made to keep Cliff Jackson sweet.

Consumed with Bill

Later, much later, Cliff Jackson would be excoriated for running what seemed a personal vendetta against Bill Clinton, but in 1974 Jackson held Clinton's political future in his hands and declined to use his power to embarrass his Democratic friend. "I mean, people have posited the stupidest reasons for the [later] opposition—yet it overlooks the fact that I did help him [avoid the draft] and that I remained silent about it," Jackson pointed out. "I was research director to the Republican headquarters when Bill ran against John Paul Hammerschmidt for Congress. I didn't tell John Paul what Clinton had done to avoid the draft—John Paul was a World War II veteran, he could have used that!" Jackson laughed. "And I didn't squeak."

Loyalty between friends precluded the use of such private information. Clinton's private life in the Ozarks worried Jackson, though. "I always thought he would be President, because he and I had a lot of discussions about it. I knew that was his ambition, and I knew he was capable, and I knew he was on his way." Yet it was a way that seemed strewn with obstacles; moreover, one where Clinton's recklessness betrayed a disturbing lack of principle, at least in Jackson's eyes.

"In 1974, I guess it was, when Bill was running for Congress against John Paul Hammerschmidt, my law office turned over the phones one night to his campaign, to a telephone bank. I was up there working as a young lawyer," Jackson related, "and a young lady introduced herself to me—she was running the operation—as Bill Clinton's fiancée! I was somewhat astounded, because I'd been through Fayetteville not many months before and met Hillary, and knew that Hillary was his fiancée! Yet she went on and on about how she was—how he would call her every night after he was on the campaign trail, this and that, and so on . . ."

Jackson had known of Bill's predilection for pretty women since Oxford—and of their predilection for Bill. Nevertheless, there was something different now that disturbed him—and would disturb him twenty years later, when Monica Lewinsky became a source of national debate. "Now, how did that strike me?" Jackson asked, thinking of 1974 and the young volunteer. "You know, I—I mean, I've been accused in the media of being a moralist. My background is Assemblies of God; it is evangelical; it is fundamentalist in many respects. However, I went to a Presbyterian liberal college, I have a great strain of liberal Presbyterianism in me. And I am not judgmental, in the narrow-minded sense. I am perceptive—and I differentiate. And how did that strike me?"

Jackson—a distinguished trial lawyer—turned over his question once more, then explained. "I don't condemn people for making mistakes," he began. "I mean, all of us do! No one is without sin. No one is without fault. No one is without character flaws.

"Okay. But how I perceived that situation: it wasn't the fact that he was . . ." Jackson shook his head. "I mean, the guy wasn't married," he acknowledged. "It wasn't the fact that he was involved with the woman and he was engaged to Hillary—I mean, that was one level. It wasn't even that he may have had, or was having, sex with her while he was engaged to Hillary—I mean, that's one more level. The one that offended me, however, in that situation is that . . ." Jackson paused, again, anxious not to be misunderstood. "Let me just slow down. He had apparently caused her—if someone had caused, or maybe she did it on her own, let me be generous—but *she was in love with the man!* For what purpose? For sex? Yes—but not just for sex! For helping him, because she was working her heart out to do her best for his political election, as a volunteer. And that offended me.

"Did I feel he was exploiting her? I did, I did! Because she was not his type!" Jackson emphasized. "She was somewhat chubby, if I recall—fairly nice face, but just not his body type. I mean, she was the daughter of a somewhat powerful politician in Arkansas, and she liked politics, and she was *utterly and totally consumed with him!*"

Nor was Bill Clinton's exploitative charisma confined to women. "I mean, this is just one example that happened to involve a female, an example that happened to involve sex. But he does this with men, too! He seduces men—and when I say seduce, I mean the minds, the commitments, the emotions—yes, the affections. He demands a kind of loyalty, complete, consummate loyalty, while giving *nothing* in return!"

For Jackson, the encounter with the chubby young lady on the phone bank was thus, in retrospect, a first glimpse into Bill's "Monica complex"—the encouragement of hopes in both men and women that he could never fulfill and the weaving of friendships that—"as George Stephanopoulos and Robert Reich would find out," as Jackson sighed—would inevitably founder. "*I* found out a long time ago!" Jackson reflected on his own learning curve in relation to Bill Clinton. "I mean, that was the conclusion I drew from the whole draft thing!"

Running Around with Other Girls

For Bill to be promiscuous while campaigning on behalf of other candidates was one thing. Now, however, he was the candidate himself—and his promiscuity seemed to proliferate, not ameliorate. JFK had been his model; but to take such risks while campaigning against a family man, church leader, respected veteran of World War II, and congressman admired and honored for his service to the district seemed utterly reckless.

Betsey Wright later recalled being asked by Bill Clinton to "come down" to Arkansas to help. "It was clear he was running around with other girls, too," not just Hillary. "It was silly, because, hell—you can't come in for a couple of weekends and be any real help," Betsey later reflected, "so I've never really considered it working on the campaign. He had this little house/cabin place out in the country and that's where I stayed. I stayed there, and I said, 'Bill, you cannot, as a single guy running for Congress, be having women stay in the same house!'" She shook her head with exasperation. "He just doesn't think that way! But that's where I stayed."

Looking back, Wright could see the advantage of Bill's tactical approach to the problem: that by affecting casual indifference, even ignorance, his intimacy with women might be seen as innocent, a naive unawareness of how other people might see such relationships. "He was always fairly oblivious," Betsey recalled, "to possible scandal. And he claimed a lot of obliviousness that was . . . I mean, that became his cover, I discovered, in his other relationships too."

In the meantime Betsey was astounded at Bill's waywardness. "He was careless. That's the way I would put it: careless. Given the moral strictures." Very soon there seemed to be a different Clinton fiancée in every town. His affair with one of the Fayetteville student volunteers, Marla Crider, who later became known as "the college girl," was, in particular, common knowledge—indeed, impossible to sweep under the electoral carpet, Hillary's father reported. There were inevitable jealousies, especially among the "fiancées." "Rumors were flying about drugs, sex, and violence in the Clinton camp," Gail Sheehy chronicled—leading former Governor Faubus, still a stalwart of the Democratic Party in Arkansas, to vow that "unless Bill Clinton cleaned up his campaign, no one in it was going to D.C. and drag down the reputation of his state."

Paul Fray, Bill's campaign manager, remembered vainly attempting to reason with Marla, as Fray later explained to Sheehy. "'Look,' I told her from day one"—after the student had asked if "Bill is dead serious about me"—"that ain't going to fly, darlin'. You got to understand Bill Clinton—he's going to have a woman, a different woman, every damned day. Don't get yourself caught up in that little stratagem." Marla, however, only became more infatuated. "She still wouldn't back off," as Fray recalled.

Only Hillary's stern presence, Hugh Rodham felt, could bring the candidate back to his senses—and get the pretty "college girl" out of campaign headquarters.

Hillary's Goal

Hillary, hearing from her father, was nothing if not decisive.

Once the transcript of the tape of Nixon talking to H. R. Haldeman and John Ehrlichman—the tape that would finally tip the scale against Nixon and force him to resign as President of the United States of America, the first to do so in American history—was leaked, Hillary began packing her bags to move to Fayetteville to take personal direction of Bill's congressional campaign. Moreover, to make quite sure that Bill zipped up his pants, and to test whether a renewed and possibly more permanent partnership would work in the context of backward Arkansas, Hillary accepted the offer of a teaching post in the University of Arkansas Law School from the fall of 1974, alongside Professor Clinton.

The faculty had already been aware that Hillary was Bill's girlfriend. Indeed, Hillary, visiting Bill during the annual school jaunt to New Orleans in 1974, had agreed to interview with Bill's colleagues on the hiring committee. According to Professor Witte, the chairman of the appointment panel, there was some surprise but also great delight when Hillary Rodham now accepted the university's lowly offer. She was clearly supertalented: the brilliant Wellesley and Yale graduate who had worked with Marian Wright Edelman and had been tapped for John Doar's staff in Washington.

In truth Hillary hoped her new job, beginning in the fall, would be short-lived. If Bill won the congressional seat in November 1974, she would immediately surrender the law school appointment at the end of her first semester's teaching and move back to Washington in January 1975. "That was Hillary's damn goal from day one—to get back to D.C.," Paul Fray later reflected with disdain. "She didn't give a fuck about staying down here. Clinton and I talked about that one day. He told me, 'We've got to win this race. I want to get *her* back up there to Washington.' "

But if Bill didn't make it—well, then Hillary would help him develop Plan B.

Bound to Fail

Certainly Hillary made no bones about her ultimate agenda for Bill. Marla Crider had already seen, in Bill's bedroom, a letter from Hillary, written while Hillary was still in Washington, that reminded him of "the goals we've set for ourselves. You keep trying to stray away from the plan we've put together," Marla remembered the warning. "I still do not understand why you do the things you do to hurt me," Hillary had complained. Bill, on their last encounter, had left her "in tears and not knowing what our relationship was all about. I know all your little girls are around there," she'd mocked him, adding that "you will outgrow this. They will not be with you when you need them. They are not the ones who can help you achieve your goals." As for his infatuation with Marla, the "college student," "this too shall pass. Let me remind you, it always does."

Marla, reading the openly displayed letter, was crestfallen—unable to compete with a twenty-seven-year-old who, once she arrived in Fayetteville, treated her like a whore: telling the college girl, for example, to go fetch the candidate's missing socks for a new trip and afterward thanking her for finding them in Bill's overnight bag with the words "Thanks—somehow I knew you'd know that."

Eventually, after an "anonymous" caller tipped off her mother, Marla, whose uncle was a judge, gave in and withdrew from the campaign. Bill, who'd never hidden the fact that he was deeply involved with Hillary but had denied he was engaged, now assured Marla, in a parting note, that "You just don't know how much you mean to me." But to how many girls did he say the same thing? In a legendary fit of indignation Hillary had torn to bits a list she found of Bill's "special friends"—but shredding the telephone numbers of Bill's favorite floozies did not thereby reduce, for Bill, the challenge of illicit fun. Each liaison was a feather in his cap as an egoist—but, in his Hillary's eyes, each was also a potential embarrassment in his ascent to the White House.

Taking the reins of the campaign that summer, Hillary became more and more the candidate's manager, in part because she set her sights so much higher than his other helpers did. To all who would listen, inside and outside the campaign headquarters, she would boast of Bill's prowess in politics, and his goal. "You know, Tom Bell," she'd bragged to one of her colleagues in Washington, D.C., when in a good mood, "Bill Clinton is going to be president of the United States someday!" So serious was she in saying so that few mocked her.

Meanwhile, his own brilliance as a political operator told Bill Clinton what Hillary Rodham, with her blinkered focus, could not see: that her strategy of beating Hammerschmidt over the Watergate head would fail if Nixon prematurely removed *his* head from the block—in other words, if Nixon was driven into resigning months *before* the upcoming midterm elections. If the President did, Clinton agonized, it would give the Republicans ample time to recover.

Nixon Resigns

On June 27, 1974, President Nixon had visited Secretary Brezhnev for a third U.S.-USSR summit, after signing an accord with Egyptian President Anwar Sadat committing Egypt to help in the search for peace between Israelis and Palestinians. Hardly had the President returned to America, however, than he learned he would have to hand over his remaining tape-recorded diary or private confessional; and by a 27–11 vote, the Senate Judiciary Committee, on John Doar's legal advice, voted for impeachment proceedings to begin, accusing the President of obstructing justice.

Then, as later, Hillary would class Nixon as an "evil" President, but at least Nixon, in the end, had the courage to spare the country the indignity of an impeachment trial and do the honorable thing. A week later, in highly emotive televised farewell language in the Oval Office, surrounded by his family, the President brought America's legal and ethical torment to a close. He had already denied being "a crook." Now, on August 9, 1974, he reluctantly resigned: "I have never been a quitter. To leave office before my term is completed," he bewailed, speaking from his heart, "is opposed to every instinct in my body." Watching, transfixed, in the home of some friends in Mountain Home, Arkansas, Bill Clinton thought of Richard II and the plays of Shakespeare he'd seen in Stratford-upon-Avon, Oxford, and London. To the journalists who called for his reaction, he said soothing words about the future of America and the prospects for his campaign. In his heart of hearts, however, he knew the inescapable truth.

There were still three long months before the electorate would go to the polling booths. Thanks to Nixon's decision to resign and hand over the reins of office to a modest, respected Vice President, Gerald R. Ford, Bill Clinton had in all likelihood lost his bid to go to the capital as a U.S. congressman. Hillary's successful effort to smash the President, he lamented to his host, Mike Lee, "is going to cost me the race."

Not Stuffing the Ballot Box

Nixon's resignation did cost Bill Clinton the election—though by dint of indefatigable personal campaigning throughout the hills, valleys, hamlets, towns, and plains of the Third Congressional District alongside his teaching schedule in Fayetteville, Professor Bill Clinton came within a tantalizing 2 percent of snatching John Paul Hammerschmidt's crown.

So close was the November 1974 race, that at least one campaign adviser, Steve Smith—a young, wide-eyed Fayetteville liberal—had even begun to plan his accommodation in Washington, D.C. Bill, however, had feared the worst since August 9 and knew there was now only one way to win, beyond busting his gut in getting out and meeting the voters: by stuffing the ballot box.

In Arkansas, as in Illinois, Texas, and elsewhere, this was not unusual, but, as if to knock a second nail in Bill's political coffin, Hillary—who had impressed both fellow faculty and her students by her teaching abilities—vetoed the arrangement that Bill and Paul Fray had made in Fort Smith, the largest town in the Third District, the most vital, and the most Republican. "She nixed it," Paul Fray recalled angrily. "She got adamant. She said to Bill, 'No! You don't want to be a party to this!' I said, 'Look, you want to win or you want to lose?' She said, 'Well, I don't want to win this way. If we can't earn it, we can't go.' "

There was, however, one further alternative: ensuring that Hammerschmidt's supporters didn't stuff the ballot box. Accordingly, Bill, Hillary, Paul Fray, Ron Addington, and a U.S. attorney did actually travel to Fort Smith and monitor, late on election night, the ballot-counting operation in the local courthouse. But if there was any skullduggery, they were too late or unable to identify it. At any rate, Fort Smith returned John Paul Hammerschmidt by an overwhelming tally, tipping the congressional district's evenly balanced scales in favor of the incumbent. Congressman Hammerschmidt was duly pronounced the winner, and Bill and Hillary returned to the Fayetteville campus chastened—and broke.

From Fayetteville, over the holiday period, they flew to California, to stay with "Peach" Pietrefesa, a Yale girlfriend of Hillary's. Bill was in a state. "He was literally on our floor, in Berkeley, for ten days," Peach recalled, "lying there moaning and groaning and counting the noses of everybody who didn't vote for him. He spent hours on the phone sharing vile stories about his opponent, talking about how the Republicans had stolen the election."

The shame of defeat, for a young man who'd won so many of his battles since childhood, was galling, irrespective of the fact that few had expected him to win such a fight. It may have been "lost from the start," Betsey Wright recalled, "but he didn't believe that, no! I think losing was a blow.

He had not really lost anything before—this was his first big defeat in life. And it was a great race, everybody was excited about it!"

The change of air did Bill good. And once he returned from California to the University of Arkansas Law School, he realized he was quite the local hero.

CHAPTER TWENTY-TWO

THE
WEDDING

Blocked Paths

The narrowness of Hammerschmidt's win in the Third Congressional District made twenty-seven-year-old Professor Bill Clinton a man to be reckoned with. "He didn't win, but he did so much better than anybody thought he could do," his friend Jim Blair recalled, "that he kind of created his instant base." The force, clearly, was with him.

In other circumstances, this would have boded well. Unfortunately, in Arkansas there were two other major players working in the Democratic Party, both of them honest, upstanding middle-aged men with formidable political skills. The first was the outgoing governor, Dale Bumpers, age forty-nine, who had successfully ousted the legendary Senator William Fulbright from his long-held Senate seat. The second was the new governor of Arkansas, David Pryor, age forty, who had failed to oust Senator John McClellan from the other Senate seat in 1972 but, after teaching at the University of Arkansas in Fayetteville, had won the Democratic nomination and then the race to the governor's mansion—from which post he hoped to renew his bid for the Senate soon.

For young Bill Clinton, the presence of these two older yet still youthful Arkansan politicians threatened to skewer his plans to reach the presidency via the Senate. Al Witte recalled the situation well. Dale Bumpers had made a tremendous governor in succession to Winthrop Rockefeller, transforming the management of the state bureaucracy and, by his handling of the state legislature, succeeding in raising significant taxation for education and other measures—a record he would improve upon still further in the Senate. Bill Clinton liked and admired Bumpers, which made a challenge between them even more unthinkable. "Bumpers and Clinton are like soul brothers," Witte explained. Meanwhile, "David Pryor was a bright young, solid, middle-of-the-road politician. I doubted if Bill could have defeated Pryor, even though Bill's much more brilliant. Pryor's more native Arkansan." Pryor was also dedicated to causes; indeed, he had even posed as an orderly in an old people's rest home to prove how badly homes for the elderly were being run. "He's just a solid human being, who'd have been real tough to beat," Witte reflected.

Ironically, then, Bill Clinton's senatorial path to the presidency was blocked by two men of the utmost integrity, conviction, and political skill. If Bill Clinton, with his extraordinary mind and his interest in international relations, wanted to exercise his talents in the capital, it would have to be by appointment to a post in a Democratic administration, Witte believed.

Witte was, as ever, way off Bill Clinton's track. "I didn't know they were talking about President way back then!" he said, recalling the naiveté with which he'd joined Bill and Hillary for a dinner to discuss Bill's political prospects several years later when Jimmy Carter became President. "What job should he take?" Witte remembered the discussion. "I said, head of the CIA!"

This was not received well. Indeed, Hillary thought the response downright "frivolous" even though George H. W. Bush would ascend to the presidency by that route. But Hillary, blinkered and ambitious for her man, wanted Bill to become President by the direct, conventional electoral ladder, with no time-consuming deviations to learn other skills—and on that steep ladder, every potential step was measured in terms of whether it helped or hindered "the agenda."

With Bumpers and Pryor blocking Bill Clinton's path to the Senate and his own resistance to the idea of running a government agency or department, Professor Witte could later see the problem for Hillary. "I think there was frustration at the fact that his route to the presidency . . . he had no options *but* be governor of this state that historically enjoys a reputation as a backward, hillbilly place." For Hillary this would, he recognized, mean a long Arkansas trial. "It has a history as a butt of jokes—the popular entertainer Bob Burns had a home-made 'bazooka' [a musical instrument], and he typified the image of Arkansas as a land of hillbillies; and Mark Twain's *Huckleberry Finn* has a chapter when Huck visits Helena, you remember: a violent, vicious, criminal place. So the picture of Arkansas goes back to America's greatest writer—and that's a long time ago! The state has always had that image, and I can see where . . . You want to be President, and your only choice is to be governor of the state: you've got your work cut out for you!"

For someone as brilliant as Bill Clinton, governorship of Arkansas thus seemed to Hillary almost a sentence. Whether it would be a life sentence or a term sentence with early remission or parole—parole in which he could take a shot at becoming President of the United States—was yet to be seen. First, however, there was the question of "the couple."

Hillary or Nobody

John F. Kennedy is widely believed to have entered, in a moment of abandon or recklessness, into a brief marriage following World War II—a marriage that was immediately ended and eradicated from the record by JFK's father, Joseph P. Kennedy. Continued bachelorhood, however, was equally unacceptable to the "founding father" in terms of his playboy son's chances of winning the presidency. In the early fall of 1953, in a grand wedding in Rhode Island horse country, Senator Jack Kennedy had therefore wedded Jacqueline Bouvier. Seven years later he was President of the United States.

Bill Clinton's story would be less fabled, yet equally historic. Bill had known, soon after he began dating Hillary Rodham, that she was the perfect partner for him if he seriously intended to get to the top in national politics. "Mother," he'd told Virginia when she'd questioned his choice of such a potential partner, "pray that it's Hillary. Because I'll tell you this: for me: it's Hillary or it's nobody." To Marla Crider, the "college girl," he'd admitted he was deeply in love with Hillary. His hesitation was that, if he yoked her to his ox, her budding career would be stifled at birth, "and I don't know if she can fit in here. That's important to me, and I just don't know if she can do it."

Hillary Rodham, in Bill's eyes, might not have natural or even cosmetically improved beauty, but she did have brains and she did have what, for the boy born by the railroad tracks in backwater Hope, Arkansas, was class: not high class, but solid middle class. When he was with "birds," Bill might croon; when he was with Hillary, he scrapped with an intellectual equal who gave him no slack but expected the best of him and his extraordinary mind. "She challenges me, every moment of every day, intellectually," he explained to Marla. "She makes me a better person. She gets me started, kicks my butt, and makes me do the things I've got to do." Was Bill truly in love, then, or enchained? His answer was revealing: "Well, maybe my problem is I've had those [romantic] feelings too often."

If the relationship lacked what Marla thought of as romance, however, this did not mean it was merely cerebral. Once, for example, while Hillary was still in Washington working for the Judiciary Committee, she had turned the tables on Bill. Citing her father and brother's reports of Bill's infidelities—since she still saw herself and Bill as an item, despite their geographical separation—Hillary had threatened to have sex with a colleague in D.C. Bill was genuinely appalled. That she could land any job she wished in America as a brilliant and strident Yale Law School graduate, he had no doubt; that she might sleep with and become emotionally attached to another man stunned him. Paul Fray actually overheard a conversation in which Hillary informed Bill she'd carried out her threat—had "gone out with some guy in Washington and slept with him, on and on and on. Billy broke down and told her, 'Well, damn you, why are you doing me this way?' He was really torn up about it."

Thus the push-me-pull-you relationship had coughed and spluttered through the year of their post-Yale separation. As Betsey Wright recalled, Bill had for a long time been unsure whether "he would really marry Hillary." In Betsey's view, it was Hillary who had "finally just pushed him to the wall—that the relationship had to move to some other status: a marriage or off. Because she had to make plans also. And I mean, she couldn't just live with him in Arkansas—that was just out of the question if he were to be running for office." Hillary had thus moved into the lodgings of another professor and his family near the campus.

After the excitement and disappointment of Bill's failed bid for Congress in November 1974, however, the question now arose: Would Candidate Bill have done better had he been married—thus quashing certain rumors concerning his promiscuous private life? And if so, would Hillary have been a wife of whom the Arkansas electorate approved?

"You're Going to Marry Me"

On both sides there was uncertainty. Bill had seen all too clearly that Hillary, starting her teaching assignments at the law school in Fayetteville in September as he crisscrossed the state while attempting simultaneously to teach his courses, was a fish out of water in Arkansas. On the East Coast, in the upper Midwest, or even in California, she would have every prospect of distinction in the field of law, whether teaching, practicing, or working for a public agency. In the opinion of her best friends, she was crazy to follow her soft heart instead of obeying the dictates of her hard head.

To Bill's relief such friends failed—not only in dissuading Hillary but in understanding her life agenda. In following Bill Clinton to Fayetteville, Hillary had not intended to start devoting her life simply to supporting Bill Clinton; rather, she saw their relationship as a prospective partnership: a partnership that could take *them,* not simply Bill, to Washington and perhaps ultimately to the White House. It was for this reason that Hillary did not think to pluck her eyebrows, wear makeup, or even use deodorant—prompting Virginia's famous sigh: "I would grind my teeth and wish I could sit Hillary on the edge of my tub and give her some makeup lessons." But Hillary would never be able to compete with Miss Arkansas, given her own stout calves and poor eyesight—so why bother? Better to concentrate on what she brought into their partnership, not what others promised. Bill was charismatic, brilliant, lovable; she was only brilliant. However, she was strong-willed, feisty, and determined—indeed, as strong-willed as Bill's mother, Virginia. That was, in the end, the key, as even Virginia, belatedly, came to see. Carolyn Staley, Bill's former neighbor in Hot Springs, put the matter all too bluntly. "Look," she stated, "Hillary's tough as nails. Bill has always deferred to women to fight his battles."

The point was, Bill *needed* a strong partner: a woman he could look down upon sexually but up to intellectually; a woman he could respect and whose expectations of him he could strive to live up to. Conversely, Hillary worried that without direction or a director Bill would self-destruct. After all, Bill's dear friend Frank Aller had committed suicide when the rationale of his great ethical protest over Vietnam had become redundant. It was important, Hillary felt, that Bill should have someone by his side who would steer him in the direction of future Good Works—works that seemed to them both, as sixties idealists, to be the raison d'être of a worthwhile, worthy life. Without her, would not Bill, so fickle and inquisitive, be sidetracked, waylaid, perhaps mortally wounded?

Hillary's instinct was profoundly correct. Indeed, it is inconceivable that Bill Clinton, for all his brilliance, could have undertaken and survived the grueling ascent from the backwoods of Arkansas to the presidency in Washington without a partner of such firmness and faith: truly Lady Macbeth. But in the context of 1970s feminism, and given the nature of Hugh Rodham's only daughter, it would not be a conventional marriage—indeed it would be most *un*conventional: something that came to a head in the summer of 1975, two years after Bill had begun teaching and politicking. Driving Hillary to see the little dark redbrick home he'd secretly purchased in Fayetteville, on California Avenue, he told her, "You're going to marry me."

Testing Hillary's Resolve

Hillary pondered Bill's "proposal"—or version thereof—for several months. "Making the decision to get married took time for me," she related afterward. "I just could not bring myself to take the leap marriage requires. I never doubted my love for him, but," she added, "I couldn't envision what my life would be like in a place where I had no family or friends."

Had Hillary had another job at the time, either in Washington or at another university, she might have declined. But she had, in a sense, already made her bed when agreeing to teach in Arkansas and felt increasingly that she would have to lie in it. She did not earn as much as Bill as a professor—$18,000 per year against his $26,000—but she supplemented her salary from a federal program she helped run, so that they were more or less equal earners. She had never met anyone like Bill and perhaps never would. As Carolyn Staley and other women knew, Bill was constitutionally incapable of fidelity—but what real men were? The very males who, in Arkansas's Bible Belt, were most censorious of Bill's loose morals were themselves for the most part sinners—such as former Governor Faubus, who ranted about morality but had had numerous extramarital affairs himself, indeed was guilty, like so many Arkansans, of wife battery. At least Bill was a gentle giant—too intelligent to beat his women, and also too submissive, as a boy wonder or "Wonder Boy," as he was now called in political circles, to beat the members of his harem as sexual dominator. As his assistant in the congressional campaign Ron Addington recalled, Bill loved to sit "in the middle of a circle of girls at his headquarters, pointing from one breathless volunteer to the next and dictating letters for them to type."

Addington, a Vietnam vet, was frankly envious, recognizing that the nonvet had perceived a major shift in modern sexuality and the sexual dynamic, at least among the baby-boom generation. Although Bill flirted incessantly, he wanted to *be* seduced; indeed, once he made the initial play, he ran backward with the ball, hoping to be tackled. Even Marla, who'd attached herself to him, limpetlike, during the congressional campaign, had seemed unable to comprehend the game Bill was playing with Hillary, one that did not seem to her "a normal, healthy relationship, in my opinion." That Bill wanted Hillary as a wife-mother and was, at a psychological level, testing Hillary's resolve by almost openly consorting with pretty, feminine rivals, was at that time a puzzle to the twenty-one-year-old college girl. Even after Marla was banished from the palace, Bill was not done. Instead he had stepped up the pace and excitement of the game with Hillary, deliberately arranging for the wife of his campaign manager, Mary Lee, to employ Marla as a nanny so that Hillary, when entering their house, might bump into her, Mary Lee recalled!

As a rehearsal for modern marriage after the first, reasonably successful trial in cohabitation in New Haven, this was the ultimate test in a five-year saga of battles royal: battles in which Hillary had cussed, fought, and argued—had even thrown insults in the manner to which, as a child, Bill had become accustomed, indeed addicted. Having engineered such violent expressions of her affection, Bill had always managed to calm her down by sweet talk—followed by sweet surrender. No other man in her life offered her such a deal—and as events would turn out, their long premarital trial would prepare the couple for probably the longest-lasting, most intense political marriage of the century.

Eleanor's Example

Hillary might be blinkered, unimaginative, and shortsighted, but she certainly approached the possibility of marriage with her eyes wide open. "She is quick and gets right to the point. She doesn't meander," a Little Rock lawyer later described. "There is no wasted emotion." In this case, however, Hillary wanted to get it right. Before finally deciding, she asked others for their opinion.

Ann Henry, a Democratic Party stalwart in Fayetteville, responded with cautionary words. When Hillary told her that FDR's spouse, Eleanor, would be her role model, Ann was doubtful. "But, Hillary," she cautioned, having just finished reading Joseph Lash's biography of Eleanor, "that wasn't until after she didn't care about the marriage anymore. That's when she was able to go and do all those things—she did not open up until *after* she discovered the affair." For Hillary, it would be different, going into a marriage. "I said when she, Hillary, didn't care about the marriage anymore, *then* she could go do what she wanted to."

Hillary wasn't going to wait that long, however. Her marriage *would* include sex, she was adamant—her own, with Bill, while tolerating Bill's "relations" with others, if it had to be so. It wasn't an ideal setup from the point of view of a proud woman, but it was frank, and it was pioneering, not only in Arkansas, but in modern, companionate America. She would not expect Bill to be sexually faithful in their partnership, but she would expect him to observe reasonable discretion—to avoid rubbing her face in his sinful escapades and to put her wishes first: indeed to treat her as the queen and "the others" as lesser mortals, mere courtiers and mistresses. Marla, for example, would never forget one particular encounter, when Hillary had unexpectedly flown down from Washington and, after the Democratic primary celebration, had sneaked up behind Marla and taken her glass to taste the drink, remarking, " 'Hmm, wine, I'll have to get some of that.' It was her way of letting me know—like a cat—marking its territory. . . . And Hillary just had this kind of half smirk on her face and strolled on off."

The cat was now making up her mind. On the basis of her understanding with Bill, she was eventually convinced—or convinced herself—that they could make it to the very top, in the fashion of the French, as America's first modern "power couple."

She therefore said yes.

Impromptu Wedding

Getting married, however, would be a political, not social, event.

To the consternation of all in Fayetteville, almost no attention was paid to the logistics, mechanics, protocols, or niceties of the town's wedding royal. The couple had determined, as if to mock conventional expectations, that the ceremony was to be held in Bill's new house on October 11, 1975, not in a church. The house itself was a trash heap—"mess everywhere," Virginia recalled, without even lampshades to cover the naked bulbs, so that when Virginia and her party arrived, they took one look and moved to the local Holiday Inn. Paint pots and brushes lay around everywhere. When Hillary's mother, Dorothy, arrived and asked to see the bridal gown, Hillary looked blank. A quick trip to the local Dillard's department store furnished her with an off-the-peg Jessica McClintock Victorian retro gown with lace and a high waist. No plans had been made for a honeymoon. In the end Hugh Rodham offered to take Hillary's mother and brothers, Hillary, and Bill to Acapulco, Mexico, where—ever the businessman—he'd found a cheap group rate.

"Whoever heard of a bride doing that?" Ann Henry shook her head. But that was not all. In conversation with Hillary's mother, who had been on a prenuptial visit, Ann had casually suggested using her big old house, which was often the venue for political parties thanks to a two-acre yard, for the reception afterward. "I said, you know, we could have the reception there." Hillary grasped the opportunity, which would relieve her of the burden of organizing the event. Then, since Hillary's mother had returned to Chicago and Hillary had no understanding of what was involved or indeed interest in the mechanics, "it was just left to me to do the whole thing! I didn't think of it as any big deal," Ann recalled generously. "To me it was just a matter of having another party." At the baker's shop, "they wanted to know, did I want a bride and groom on top? And I said no, I didn't think so!"

Ann was right. Whereas only a handful of family members had attended the wedding in the groom's house on California (performed by Vic Nixon, the assistant pastor of the Methodist Church, which Hillary had never attended, and with nineteen-year-old Roger Clinton, Jr., as best man to his older brother), an unexpected number turned up for the reception. Ann Henry was not certain how so many invitations had gone out. "Lots of people from the law school were there. And then all the people, including friends, who had helped in the campaign—I don't know how they got there! I mean, I didn't send out invitations, let's put it that way. I would be willing to bet it was word of mouth, calling and saying, 'We're going to get married, but the reception is going to be at a certain time at the Henrys' house.' And people came."

No one in Arkansas had seen anything like it, in terms of its impromptu informality. No one offered to pay the Henrys even for the wedding cake Ann had ordered. But when Hillary announced that she was going to keep her maiden name, rather than change it to Clinton, everyone who knew anything about politics in Arkansas shook his or her head.

Paul Fray, Bill's campaign manager—who had clashed with Hillary to the point almost of fisticuffs in the congressional campaign the year before—put the matter bluntly. "Hillary Rodham," he predicted to Bill, "will be your Waterloo."

Hillary's Name

Bill Clinton and Hillary Rodham's agenda went directly to the heart of modern marriage in a traditional, male-dominated, patriarchal society. Ann Henry had warned Hillary that there was still a vast gap between the ideals of feminism and reality. "I might want to push something," Ann later remembered cautioning, "but I don't want to hurt my husband's career, so I mean, I might pull back."

Hillary rejected such advice. Indeed, her response mirrored her response when she was asked if she was having a lesbian affair with her friend from Yale Peach Pietrefesa: "Fuck this shit." It was no one's goddamned business, she felt, but her own. And it was in this spirit that she adamantly refused to change her name.

In one sense Hillary's attitude was pioneering. But in American politics, in Arkansas, and after Watergate? The very tapes she'd pored over in the Nixon impeachment process meant that henceforth nothing, in politics, would now be sacrosanct, sacred, or off limits—that even a sitting president's innermost thoughts privately confided to his own tape recorder for his later memoirs would be grist to the political mill. What Hillary had helped do to another human being, a politician, would, as in some Greek drama, inevitably be done unto her. After the Nixon resignation, the gloves were off in electoral combat, the media now licensed, as it were, to invade a politician's most guarded privacy. No prisoners would be taken in this new competitive rat race, moreover. What had been started as a move by *The Washington Post* on behalf of the Fourth Estate, and taken up by Congress and its judicial arm, would inexorably become the juicy meat of increasingly rivalrous media as newspapers and broadcasters sought increased sales, increased readership, and higher advertising ratings—their investigative impulses spilling into riotous carnival, propelled by scandal.

The prospect was hardly edifying. Nevertheless, it belonged to a larger cultural change that was taking place in the seventies—and that, far more than in the case of Richard Nixon, was eerily presaged in the life of Bill Clinton, married man, law professor, and would-be politician.

CHAPTER TWENTY-THREE

STRIKE TWO

The New Narcissist

In his book *The Culture of Narcissism,* begun in the mid-1970s, Christopher Lasch painfully described a national trend toward trivialization: the dumbing-down of America.

The old cultural order based on distinction and quality was, thanks to the sixties, finally reaching its appointed end, and Lasch, like many of his generation, deplored the Götterdämmerung. With distaste he delineated the historical culture of America giving way to "the psychological man of our times. The new narcissist is haunted not by guilt but by anxiety," he remarked penetratingly. "He seeks not to inflict his own certainties on others but to find a meaning in life." Seeing through the mythologies of the past, and understanding the dynamics of history and the pluralities of religions, he is both liberated and rootless. "Superficially relaxed and tolerant, he finds little use for dogmas of racial and ethnic purity but at the same time forfeits the security of group loyalties and regards everyone as a rival for the favors conferred by the paternalistic state. His sexual attitudes are permissive rather than puritanical, even though his emancipation from the ancient taboos brings him no sexual peace. Fiercely competitive in his demand for approval and acclaim," he "extols cooperation while harboring deeply antisocial impulses. He praises respect for rules and regulations in the secret belief that they do not apply to himself. Acquisitive in the sense that his cravings have no limits, he does not accumulate goods and provisions against the future, in the manner of the acquisitive individualist of the nineteenth-century political economy, but demands immediate gratification and lives in a state of restless, perpetually unsatisfied desire."

No better portrait of Professor Bill Clinton could have been painted in 1975, as he examined his future.

The Way Is Blocked

Bill Clinton's advantage in a small, backward state was his education. This raised him head and shoulders over most rivals in the state, even at age twenty-nine, but it also meant that, with only nine top positions—governor, lieutenant governor, attorney general, the state's two U.S. Senate seats and the four in the U.S. House of Representatives—and a stranglehold held on such positions by the Democratic Party, there was very little room in which to jockey for position as the youngest and least experienced contender. Dale Bumpers had been a popular governor and had made an immediate mark as a U.S. senator in Washington. "Bumpers, you know, is astute, really smart—a good guy," Ann Henry, the Democratic Party chairperson, recalled. "And then Pryor was a fabulously popular governor—an enormously popular person who has great guts" and who, if he won the next senatorial contest, looked set for a life in the capital as the state's second U.S. senator also. For the next twenty years, in fact, these two Democrats would duly block younger contestants to the U.S. Senate—including Bill Clinton.

Despite his closely run race against John Paul Hammerschmidt, Bill Clinton accepted that the moment of opportunity had passed—that he would not beat the popular Republican congressman in the Third District in a rerun in 1976. In many ways, therefore, Bill Clinton's political career in Arkansas was circumscribed from, and by, the start. In the years to follow he would constantly consider alternative options, but they remained always, in the end, theoretical. To reach the White House, you had, de rigueur, to have been a governor or a senator, usually after service in the House—or be a five-star general. Since military distinction was never going to be Bill Clinton's destiny, and since Dale Bumpers and David Pryor were going to tie up the two U.S. Senate seats from Arkansas for another generation, this left only the governorship—which was not currently vacant.

The only clear post Bill Clinton would be able to run for in 1976, after his wedding to Hillary, therefore turned out to be attorney general of Arkansas. At Ann Henry's wedding celebration party he had met the incumbent: Harvard-educated Jim Guy Tucker, who was thinking of giving up the post to run for Congress in the Second Congressional District, which included Little Rock. For Bill Clinton—who had secured an extra teaching appointment at the University of Arkansas Law School campus in Little Rock to teach criminal justice and build up a presence in the capital—Tucker's run would mean another congressional seat *hors de combat,* yet by the same token it would also mean a vacant attorney general's office—an office that could, in turn, become a stepping-stone to the governor's mansion, assuming that Governor Pryor, the widely respected incumbent, chose to contest Senator John McClellan's seat in the U.S. Senate again in 1978.

Becoming attorney general would mean, however, taking a huge step down in salary—to a paltry $6,000 a year as against his current $26,000 as a law professor. There was nothing else to be done, however, if he were to pursue politics in Arkansas at the top. Via the attorney generalship, then, the governorship of Arkansas would have to be Bill Clinton's fate if he wished to become President of the United States.

Buoyed by Hillary Rodham's faith in him, he decided he did.

Moving to Little Rock

In January 1976, Bill Clinton formally requested leave of absence from the University of Arkansas, and his candidacy in the Democratic primary for attorney general of Arkansas was officially announced on March 16. Very little opposition was offered within the Democratic Party; indeed, Clinton won the primary by a more than 30 percent margin, so that no runoff was required. As there was no Republican candidate, this meant that in the election in November 1976 Bill would walk through unopposed. By the summer of 1976, Bill Clinton was already, therefore, a shoo-in as attorney general.

Assured of political office, Bill surrendered his professorship in Fayetteville, as did Hillary. The couple sold the house on California Avenue and immediately after New Year's 1977 moved to a house they purchased for $33,000 on L Street in Little Rock (population: 183,000). They had no children yet and were used to camping and decamping; indeed, for Hillary it would have been hard to say where her home or even home state was. In terms of mobility this was a boon, but it was negative in terms of loyalty. "Hillary regarded Arkansas as a place to go and then leave," one of Bill's subsequent campaign strategists once complained. Meanwhile, since Bill's new salary would be so low—a charity job—Hillary therefore accepted that she would have to be the breadwinner. She applied for an attorney's job at the prestigious Rose Law Firm, starting salary $15,000. Mercifully, she got it. Even so, they would be earning, together, less than half what they had as law professors in Fayetteville.

But if all went well, both jobs—attorney general and a lowly lawyer's desk at the Rose Law Firm—would lead to bigger things.

Building Up a War Chest

Though he claimed to have "a background in each and every one of the areas needed to be Attorney General—law enforcement, anti-trust suits, consumer protection, and dealing with county officials," Bill had little intrinsic interest in being attorney general, let alone remaining attorney general for long. He began to give countless speeches, shake countless hands, and raise uncounted funds for the Big Campaign: his "war chest." He already had Don Tyson, the chicken magnate from northwest Arkansas, behind his candidacy. Next was Sam Walton, founder of the Wal-Mart retail chain—destined to become the wealthiest man in the United States—and third was Witt Stephens, cofounder with his brother Jackson of the nation's largest brokerage firm outside Wall Street.

But it was not the only chest the new attorney general was out to secure. His marital understanding with Hillary, he felt, licensed him to solicit not only votes and campaign funding but women. And prominent among those whose mammary charms he sought was, ironically, a Republican: a broadcaster and nightclub chanteuse, the former president of Young Arkansans for Rockefeller: Gennifer Flowers.

Geannie

The genie was twenty-seven when she emerged from Bill Clinton's oil lamp, soon after she interviewed the tall, genial young attorney general for KARK-TV, the local Little Rock television station. At five feet, two inches, the diminutive Miss Flowers was more than a foot shorter than Bill Clinton: a brunette and child-prodigy singer with a string of early records to her earlier name, Gean Flowers. Always known as "Geannie," the genie had, like Bill, changed her own name as a young teenager. Later, blessed with a magnificent head of dark, lush hair, blue eyes, and major-league breasts, she had been spotted in a television commercial by the president of KARK-TV and awarded a reporter and feature journalist's job in Little Rock.

If Bill Clinton had doted on his mother, Gennifer had doted on her father. Gene Flowers had loved his only daughter unconditionally, she later claimed. He was a handsome, Clark Gable–style self-made millionaire from a poor background who had become a flyer in World War II. By the time he'd died in 1973, he owned a string of airfields in Arkansas and the South. He would fly anywhere and dare anything. He was also, as Gennifer acknowledged, a prize rake—indeed, after endless "womanizing" on his part, Geannie's mother had divorced him in a bitter and prolonged lawsuit, though she later wept uncontrollably at his funeral.

As in the case of Bill's mother, Gennifer Flowers had grown up to become a feisty, outrageous young woman: a woman who, like Virginia, felt no shame in later years recording her life story without dissimulation. *Leading with My Heart* would be Virginia's devastatingly honest 1994 account of four marriages and two sons, one of whom became President of the United States, the other a drug dealer; *Passion and Betrayal* would be Gennifer's brazenly candid account, a year later, of being Bill Clinton's longtime mistress and confidante—and of her erasure from the President's record.

Meanwhile, however, getting off a plane in the summer of 1977 at Little Rock airport with Senator Dale Bumpers after a trip to Washington, Attorney General Bill Clinton had smiled a "lazy, sexy smile" at the KARK reporter and had appreciatively asked in his Arkansas drawl, "*Where* did they get *you?*"

Very Married

The paucity of female journalists, as opposed to secretaries, in the television news world was all too real, however sexist the attorney general's remark. In part the reason was that existing male journalists were so chauvinistic, the men hitting on the women all the time. It was as though, in men's eyes, the women were only there for their figures, not their fact-finding abilities. Consequently, for Gennifer—who was sensationally pretty—it became a battlefield, made all the worse as there was another female, the black singer and reporter Deborah Mathis, who seemed happy to talk sex without inhibition or concern about the consequences. Only the president of the station seemed utterly professional—the only man who "didn't try to get into my pants."

If Gennifer thought that she'd be able to get Bill Clinton to further her own ambitions as a journalist without paying a price, however, she was profoundly mistaken. She had managed to keep the men of KARK out of her more intimate apparel by the fall of 1977—but not Bill Clinton, the attorney general. He would stare at Gennifer, when she was reporting for her station, and "other people began to notice." One day, outside his office, he blurted: "I really can't take this anymore. I need to see you"—and made her give him her phone number. "I knew he was married and I shouldn't have given my number to him," she berated herself later. At the time, however, she felt powerless. "He was a very sexy man, and I couldn't help myself from being interested."

Thereafter Bill began to phone Geannie, "and we'd talk about everything under the sun. In every call, he'd suggest coming over to my place. He kept asking when we could get together."

Finally, after two weeks, Gennifer gave in, and Bill appeared on the doorstep of her apartment. Inside he proved to be a perfect gentleman—so perfect his first visit could only have been the work of a master seducer, in the manner of Giacomo Casanova, often considered the most notorious lover the Western world has ever known. "We held hands and talked for hours," but when Gennifer said it was time for him to leave, he made no protest. Reflecting on the seduction later, Gennifer realized Bill had "consciously manipulated" her that first date. As she put it, "He is an expert with women. He played me like a violin that night."

A rising star in his party, the young attorney general had been scrupulously polite, a wonderful listener, empathetic, humorous, and just occasionally touching his fingers to her hand or thigh, sending "little sparks of electricity through me." By leaving with only a gentle peck on the cheek, he'd allowed Gennifer to feel she was in charge of her own destiny—knowing that, like any Southern Baptist, she rigidly separated virtue from sin: a dichotomy which only made her the more susceptible to transgression when teased or tempted by a "master of his game."

Bill's game was seduction. Miss Flowers was well aware of the pluses and minuses. Bill Clinton was, as she put it, "a public figure and a power-ful man in Arkansas. He was also very married."

Casanova Moves

Gennifer Flowers, ironically, had herself been mortified by her parents' di-vorce when she was in her teens, feeling it was quite wrong for her father to have broken his marriage vows. Yet she was clearly about to help Bill break his—at least in terms of adultery. "We both knew we were ready to make love," she recalled—indeed, she turned down the lights and turned on the music. As she confessed later, she could hardly wait.

The sexual anticipation, or anticipation of intimacy, was almost un-bearable. This time, she hardly had a moment to shut the door before they were embracing. "He was such a good kisser—he has a real pretty mouth," Gennifer conceded later. "Everything about this man excited me: his brains, his charm, and his incredible sexuality."

To her surprise, when Gennifer undressed the attorney general she found that he was "not particularly well endowed"—indeed, was down-right small for a man of his size. But there was scarcely time to take this in, for "his desire to please was astounding," she recalled. "He was determined to satisfy me, and boy, did he! At times I thought my head would explode with the pleasure."

To his credit, oral intercourse, for Bill, was not simply a matter of being served but of serving a woman—and being rewarded for doing so. "This man made me want to give back what he was giving," Gennifer recalled, "and what he was giving was sensational."

In this respect, Bill Clinton was, indeed, a New Man, in a different mold from the legendary Giacomo Casanova. Casanova had impressed women by his understanding of the often powerless female's erotic need, in an eighteenth-century context, to be flattered as well as dominated, whereas Bill Clinton understood that in a new era for women, as feminism swept the nation, flattery plus sexual subservience rather than dominance might be a tactic that would prove irresistible. As his affair with Gennifer deep-ened, his approach became increasingly submissive: the giant subordinat-ing himself to the former teenage beauty queen, the saxophonist playing homage to the singer. "His stamina amazed me. We made love over and over that night," Gennifer recalled of their four-hour tryst, "and he never seemed to run out of energy." Her bed was "built for a king"—a four-poster canopy "draped with luxurious fabrics and buried in soft, sensuous pillows" and she had her king to grace it.

This psychosexual dynamic would fuel their twelve-year affair: the king, so powerful, so universally admired in public, coming secretly to his morganatic queen, pleasuring and being pleasured by her.

Getting Caught

For Bill to stay overnight at her apartment was "out of the question," Gennifer knew, for the attorney general "had a wife to go home to." In such a traditional society this meant that lying, deception, and discretion would be necessary if the adulterous couple wished to continue their dangerous liaison. But would this really be necessary in 1975 in an America where, thanks to the sixties, the whole notion of sexual fidelity seemed outdated, not only thanks to the Pill and prophylactics but to a questioning of fidelity itself, especially by women who considered they had for centuries been sold, in marriage, into sexual slavery? Marital rape, indeed, became a new offense in many states.

It was not so in Arkansas. Nor was it so in the field of politics, where hypocrisy ruled undisturbed by changing American culture. Deceit was, as in times past, a sine qua non of both private and public life—deceit practiced according to both a male and a female agenda. They were not the same.

For Gennifer Flowers, an affair with the young attorney general promised excitement and possible advancement in her journalistic profession, through Bill's contacts and beckoning career path. In a society in which divorce, at least, had become more accepted, a possible marriage to Bill would make this advancement the more fulfilling, as well as allowing her to fulfill her biological destiny as a woman. Inevitably the Geannie of Bill's lamp began to weave dreams of nuptials and infants—if Bill could only cast off his current wife.

Hillary Rodham, however, had no wish to be cast off. Nor, in truth, did Bill's agenda require that she should be. The move from Fayetteville and Bill's shoo-in election as attorney general had offered the first stepping-stone in the "power couple's" ascent to the governor's mansion—and later, hopefully, the White House. How could divorce and remarriage to a five-foot-two Arkansas KARK reporter possibly advance *that* agenda? Others had and would continue to mock Bill's presidential ambitions—but neither

Hillary nor Bill thought the White House an impossible goal. As such, it underscored their relationship—a relationship that, if it lacked sexual excitement, was in many ways more intellectually bracing and rewarding than any Bill had thought possible as a teenager. His agenda, in pursuing his Geannie, was therefore limited to sex, and sex with a sort of dream starlet: a diminutive Marilyn Monroe, curvaceous and teasing, full of fun and yet vulnerable, too.

Yet if Bill's agenda was subsidiary to his marital partnership with Hillary, why, in terms of his career, did he exhibit such recklessness? It astonished even Gennifer. Attending nightclubs such as the Pinnacle Lounge in the Excelsior Hotel, where she still sang, late in the evening after work, Bill was "casual about his behavior," she recalled, "and never seemed to care that we could get caught." Miraculously, they weren't. Instead, they were caught out in a potentially much more serious way, as Bill's mother had been in 1945.

Thanks to Bill's carelessness, Gennifer became pregnant.

The Unborn Child

Bill had assured Gennifer "he didn't think he could have children since he and Hillary had been married almost two years," Gennifer afterward related, "and she hadn't gotten pregnant."

For a Rhodes Scholar, this merited an F. Indeed it had now got him a G—in fact, a PG: Pregnant Gennifer.

Gennifer, significantly less intelligent but endowed with a more beautiful voice and a deeply affectionate nature, was stunned by her gravid state yet hopeful that the news, in December 1977, might be a catalyst. After all, "he'd talk about leaving Hillary for me, and I wanted so much for that to happen, but that was my heart talking. My head told me he'd never leave. He was too ambitious to risk his political career with a divorce." Hillary was smart and ambitious for him: With her backing, he could achieve his goal; without her, he might not. For him Gennifer was and would remain a mistress.

Having a mistress, in patriarchal Arkansas as in the South generally, had always been deemed socially acceptable behavior. Governor Faubus, for example, had had a number of mistresses and had been elected governor five times. In the good-ole-boy South, despite its strict rules of hierarchy, family, and southern etiquette, eccentricity in both men and women had always been prized and often written about by authors from William Faulkner to Tennessee Williams. Keeping a mistress was barely eccentric—but it was, like other eccentricities, generally tolerated only as long as it conformed to the expectations of a male chauvinist huntin'/fishin', white electorate. The archracist governor of Alabama, George Wallace, for example, would keep on winning big in elections well into the 1980s, despite divorcing his wife, Cornelia, amid much scandal in 1978 and marrying a thirty-two-year-old former singer, Lisa Turner, three years later.

Would Bill Clinton, then, have survived politically, indeed have profited from divorce and remarriage to a singer, as Wallace did? Wallace's example, however, was misleading. By the time he was shot and incapacitated, the southern Caesar had already become a national name with a hard-core, blue-collar constituency wedded to his views on race; moreover, Wallace had by then made money and could support a new as well as an old wife, despite being in a wheelchair, paralyzed from the waist down. By contrast, young Bill Clinton was virtually penniless: a sexually active, strapping wannabe; a predator; moreover, a figure who was potentially subversive in southern electors' eyes since he'd failed to serve in the military, was no athlete, did not fish or hunt—and was too liberal and clever for his own good. Getting a TV reporter/nightclub singer pregnant could thus easily become a high-profile sex scandal in which Attorney General Bill Clinton might be portrayed as a seditious new antisouthern hero, pulling and impregnating chicks with new, "modern," eastern seaboard/California techniques (brains, genuine interest in women, love of mutual foreplay and oral gratification) rather than the traditional subordination of the second sex, even wife battery (which was almost never punished in Arkansas). Making a baby with Gennifer would certainly delay his political agenda, if not destroy it.

Preemptive action, divorcing his wife and marrying such a woman, would equally not play well in traditional, antifeminist Arkansas. Virginia, Bill's mother, seemed to wage a lifetime battle against the snobberies and patriarchal rules of the male-dominated southern society, especially in the medical profession. Gennifer Flowers would, if she became Mrs. Clinton, fare no better—indeed, with her questionable credentials as a local television reporter and nightclub singer, Gennifer might fare worse than Virginia had done.

To her credit, Gennifer Flowers recognized the impossibility of marriage—unless it was something that the attorney general, in the manner of

King Edward VIII's abdication and marriage to Mrs. Wallace Simpson, was determined to do. In Bill Clinton's case this would have required intent to make her not only pregnant but the new Mrs. Clinton and thereby abandon his kingly ambitions outside the bedroom.

Abdication had led to permanent exile for ex–King Edward and his bride. With that example in mind, Bill was not minded to pursue marriage, despite Gennifer's pregnancy. The question then arose: What should they do about the unborn child?

Strike Two

If Bill Clinton, the once "pure" little boy who had proudly attended Baptist church school with a Bible under his arm and an increasingly encyclopedic knowledge of the ancient texts, was perplexed by the stark reality that suddenly faced him as attorney general of Arkansas—a state in which abortion was still illegal unless parturition posed a life-threatening danger to the mother—he did not show it. Domestically he had known strife on a scale that would tip his brother into drugs and criminality but that had toughened Bill's heart and head. More than most of his contemporaries, he had learned to opt out of reality when it became intolerable—an extraordinary ability in one so endowed with natural empathy.

It was this ability that now led Bill Clinton to the next, inexorable moral decision that would define his life as an adult. He had been forced, like the majority of his own generation of baby boomers, to find a way of avoiding being drafted but, in doing so, had reneged on his freely given commitment to undergo military training in the ROTC at the University of Arkansas: strike one. Now, almost ten years later, the former law professor who had once spent weeks discussing with his class in Fayetteville the pros and cons of *Roe v. Wade* and the legal right of a woman to determine the life or death of her unborn child, was forced, as the state's top law enforcement official in Arkansas, to decide the fate of his own first child.

He paid for Gennifer to abort their child. Strike two.

CHAPTER TWENTY-FOUR

ATTORNEY GENERAL

Ahead of Their Time

Gennifer Flowers had hoped—as so many of Bill Clinton's conquests would hope—that the Arkansas prodigy would become completely enamored of her, divorce his wife, and marry her. She did not understand that divorce and remarriage were simply not on the cards for Promiscuous Bill, child of the sixties—indeed, that keeping a tolerant Hillary as his spouse would provide Bill with his best, sometimes his *only,* weapon in maintaining his promiscuous lifestyle.

The fact was that consciously or unconsciously, Bill had trained Hillary for the job. Again and again he'd attempted to shrug Hillary off, yet she'd clung to her vision of the partnership they could construct, and the difference they could make in modern American politics. For good or ill she'd passed every test of her ability to cope with his libertine ways, as well as her stamina and faith in his abilities. By her loyalty she had proved to him that she loved him intellectually, emotionally, and physically—his big, bearish body, his humor, and his intelligence.

Conversely, in acknowledging that it was "Hillary or nothing," Bill had proposed marriage to keep and to hold Hillary in his personal stable, knowing in advance that it would be a major undertaking, given his proclivities. More even than the Machiavellian art of politics, it would require prodigious artistic and manipulative skills to manage both a modern wife and a traditional harem, with, from time to time, grave problems, even crises, to confront and overcome. Gennifer's abortion had been but one of those.

Paradoxically, Gennifer's pregnancy had only confirmed Bill's love for Hillary. As the weeks and months had gone by since his wedding in the strangely private little ceremony in his house on California Avenue with its bare bulbs, pails of paint, and unfinished decor, Bill had found himself more and more moved by Hillary's willingness to compromise her deeply monogamous sexual principles; by her readiness to share his fortunes— and, with others, his body. Thus he'd compromised in his turn, accepting that she was not, and perhaps never would be, interested in erotic lingerie, makeup, or the exciting sex he craved—especially polyamorous sex—but had a steel intellect and a plodding, relentless focus that helped to center and stabilize his wayward imagination.

The tragedy was that this modern Western marriage, a companionate marriage of loving equals and convenience, was—in politics at least—way ahead of its American time.

Bill Clinton's Conundrum

Bill's baby-boomer lifetime had seen the final casting off of the inhibitions of the Puritans who'd founded the country: a licensing of sexual promiscuity in the sixties and seventies that was almost biblical in its reenactment of Sodom and Gomorrah and a cultural development that would reach its apogee in New York's swinger club Plato's Retreat in the 1980s.

Such a development, however, furnished no effective replacement model for marriage as the best basis for healthy and successful reproduction in America. In societies such as South America or southern Europe, there was still a venerable tradition of quasi-arranged marriages involving, for a man, respect for his spouse as mother of his children but social acceptance on her part of his extramarital lovers, concubines, mistresses, and harlots. Men, it was accepted, were simply "like that." American feminism, however, while promoting a healthier equality of the sexes in the United States, had rendered that South American/European style of marriage an impossibility. Feminists in particular deplored and rejected patriarchal libertinism, however much it might still be part of man's ancient, evolutionary makeup. Nonfeminist women, emboldened by changing attitudes toward equality between the sexes, also failed to take account of men's genetically determined promiscuity. Thus, paradoxically, in the wake of feminism modern American marriage became—with the help of Hollywood and American "pap" television—*more,* not less, romantically idealistic and un-realistic. It was thus the misfortune of the Marla Criders and Gennifer Flowerses to collide with a man as seductive as Bill Clinton during this transitional era.

The resurgence of Hollywood-fanned romantic ideals proved for the most part to be a disaster, at least in terms of the durability of marriages, and there can be little doubt that, had Bill Clinton married young Marla Crider or Gennifer Flowers, or any of the starry-eyed maidens who fell in love with him, the unions would not have lasted. Modern, companionate, romantically inspired "closed" marriages, in which the male evolutionary urge to be promiscuous was not recognized, simply left no room for man's still genetically coded agenda; indeed, the concept of the "blank slate"—a blank slate on which men were supposed to write a new kind of monoga-mous fidelity—entailed a new and terrible naiveté on the part of women: a naiveté in which male promiscuity, once it was "discovered," was taken as betrayal, resulting in rocketing divorce rates. The American answer was re-marriage: serial remarriage—the triumph of hope over nature.

Although some sociologists saw the phenomenon of such wishful re-marriages as the mark of a major step toward the twenty-first century and perhaps a new stage in cultural and sexual evolution—a stage in which men would be forced to tame their promiscuous desires on pain of being slung out of hearth and home—the cost of serial divorce and remarriage, in terms of its impact on America's children, proved catastrophic.

To his credit, since he actually loved Hillary Rodham, and was all too aware from his own childhood of the price of divorce, Bill Clinton would not give in to the new national fashion for serial remarriage. Hillary, more-over, stood by him in this resolve. But, unable to conform to an American standard that, in politics especially, licensed infidelity—once uncovered—only on condition of serial remarriage, Bill Clinton insisted upon conduct-ing, in secret, a European-style marriage, the reality of which would necessarily have to be kept from public view, lest it destroy his chances of contributing to modern American society as a politician.

Here, in essence, was Bill Clinton's conundrum, as it had been when seeking to avoid service in Vietnam along with so many millions of his con-temporaries.

It would be upon this sad, domestic rack that, like Oscar Wilde at the close of the nineteenth century, Bill Clinton would become the most celebrated victim of public attitudes toward sexual behavior in the twentieth century.

Attorney General

"From humans' earliest days on Earth, several million years ago," Joann Ellison Rodgers would acknowledge at the start of the third millennium, "the pattern has been 'monogamy with clandestine adultery' by both males and females." Such philandering, from an evolutionary perspective, "increases the chances that new combinations of genes will be passed on to new generations and keep dangerous, recessive genes at a statistical disadvantage in the survival-conservation game." Evolutionary biologist Dr. Olivia Judson agreed. The following year she wrote frankly: "True monogamy is rare. So rare that it is one of the most deviant behaviors in biology," speculating that "once we know more about the genetics of human behavior we will find not only that different men have different proclivities for monogamy, but that a given proclivity goes along with a set of other traits"—such as the size of a man's testicles. One morality, in such circumstances, did not fit all.

Such scientific wisdom, however, lay far in the future as Bill Clinton assumed the office of Arkansas attorney general. He had no intention of being or becoming a sexual pioneer, but was merely responding to his natural drives as a male in a society of loosening sexual mores and behavior. Moreover, if Bill Clinton was vigorous on the extramarital front, he was even more so as state attorney general. Attorney Burl Rotenberry, who served as one of the six heads of department on the twenty-five-man team under Clinton, was immediately impressed by Bill's personality: "energetic, enthusiastic, youthful, attractive, ambitious," as he later described him; "a comer—somebody who aspired to go someplace!"

Joe Purvis, Bill's childhood friend from Hope, was also working in the attorney general's office the day Bill Clinton arrived—in his case in the criminal division. "I remember going into the interview to decide whether or not I would stay. And just kinda looking at each other and smilin' and grinnin', because we knew each other, and he just said, 'You want to stay on?' And I said, 'Sure!' "

Purvis felt Bill was "a great administrator as attorney general. He picked some young, very bright people—bright and energetic. We would have staff meetings among the leaders and deputies, about twice a month. He wanted to know what was goin' on—he was a supremely quick study. If there was something goin' on, he would understand it—would listen to what you had to say in terms of what to do but would make up his own mind. He would then pretty much leave you alone to run your department. I mean, I thought it was great. My department would largely run itself—the criminal end of it."

Rotenberry had also served under Bill's predecessor, Jim Guy Tucker, who was, like Bill, "going places" and had taken the congressional seat of the state's most distinguished congressman, Wilbur Mills. (Mills, who had risen from the tiny town of Kensett to one of the most powerful jobs in the nation as chairman of the House Ways and Means Committee in Washington, had "shot himself in the foot" by getting "involved with a dancer and stripper in Boston," the Argentine bombshell "Fannie Foxe," thus handing the congressional seat on a plate to his successor, Jim Guy Tucker.)

A Harvard graduate and experienced lawyer who had been in private practice in the real world, Jim Guy Tucker as attorney general had "tended to keep sharp reins on his staff. He wanted to know daily what people were doing, and where they were going with their cases, and what were the issues. He had the knowledge and the ability—Jim Guy Tucker was a helluva damn good lawyer," Rotenberry felt, "and he knew how to lawyer."

Bill Clinton didn't. "I don't mean this in a derogatory way, but Bill Clinton never was a lawyer. He didn't do the mechanical work, and I don't think he was real curious about how to do it! It's not something he wanted—he didn't *want* to know how you went and took a deposition in a civil case. It didn't turn him on to be able to stand up in a crowded courtroom before a jury and to cross-examine the opposition's star witness and break him down—I mean, these were not things that seemed to really motivate him. So he didn't micromanage. He delegated."

Instead of delegating via his six heads of department, however, Bill did something almost unique in the annals of the attorney general's office. His miserly salary had been increased to $13,000, but this was still half what he had earned as a law professor in Fayetteville. He therefore felt morally entitled to commit less than half his time to overseeing the office and instead to bring into the department, on payroll, a young chief of staff who had been with him since his abortive bid for John Paul Hammerschmidt's congressional seat: Stephen A. Smith.

Rotenberry, for one, liked this delegation of authority, since it permitted him to take more responsibility for the work and agenda of his own division, which dealt with utilities and corporations. "I mean, after all, I was ten years older, I'd had a lot of experience and I didn't really need him to be directing how I handled my work. He wanted to know—we conferenced every couple of weeks—what cases were going on, what cases had booby traps in them. He was no different from the other attorney generals in this respect. You could give him advice. He analyzed it, and he'd let you know if he thought you were on the right track and all." But the bottom line was that good work meant good political credentials for higher office: "He wanted the work of the attorney general's office, its staff, under his watch, to look and be good—on a high level. He could focus on both aspects: where he was next going politically and the fact that his staff put out a good work product."

Where exactly Bill was going politically and when were moot questions, though—questions that the young Steve Smith was there to help him determine. "I would say that's unusual," Rotenberry reflected on the chief-of-staff innovation, for Steve was "not a lawyer"! He was, however, a politician manqué: "the youngest man ever elected to the Arkansas legislature, when he was about nineteen years old. He's also very astute as a politician—a political wannabe, but smart enough to realize he's not as electable as others. Steve loved politics and wanted to be a participant in politics, and Bill Clinton did too. Bill was electable—he was attractive and articulate." Smith wasn't—but could work for one who was. Thus Smith didn't get involved in any of the actual legal work of the A.G.'s office in Little Rock; "He was there because he was helping Bill to prepare for higher political office: guiding, advising, and counseling Clinton on a long political journey that began there, in the state attorney general's office in 1977."

On this long political journey, however, Smith would be one of the first casualties.

The Gladiator

"Historically, the state attorney general's office has been a stepping-stone to higher political office," Rotenberry pointed out. "Specifically: the governor's office, or a United States senator or a U.S. representative. To say that Clinton saw it as a stepping-stone is not saying anything more uncomplimentary about him than you could say of about a hundred years' worth of politicians in the state of Arkansas! State attorney general's office was a very low-paying office. It's not the type of office someone wanted to wind up in for a long time."

The handsome Jim Guy Tucker had given the post four years of service; Bill Clinton was prepared to give it only two—much of which was spent calculating and preparing his next step, as Rotenberry witnessed. "In the entire two years he served in the office," Rotenberry recalled, "a significant part of his energies, his thinking, and his time was devoted to what he was going to run for next."

In this respect, Bill was in a league of his own. "He had an enormous capacity for work," Rotenberry later reflected. "I am trying to stay away from the word 'driven,' but when he has an elective goal as a target, his capacity for work is something I have always been envious of, and others should be, too: I mean, he's just phenomenal! He can work eighteen, twenty hours a day, seven days a week, and he can do it with energy and enthusiasm, when he's after something. And his energy level and his enthusiasm is at its maximum when he's *seeking* office."

JFK had been the same as a young politician—with the same criticism being made of his subsequent performance. "This is probably uncomplimentary," Rotenberry remarked, "but I would tell this to him also: I think he runs for office better than he conducts the office after he has attained it! It's almost like: it's a boredom! It just doesn't turn him on as much to actually manage the office as when he's seeking it! He loves the challenge, the debate, the discussion, meeting people, the matching wits with opponents. He's a *gladiator*! He has, I guess, part God-given and part acquired charm. He is, one on one, one of the most charming individuals that I've ever known. And I'll throw this in: I've said for years, ever since I got to know him pretty good and considered him a friend, he's one of the two most intelligent human beings that I've ever known! I'm a person who makes a distinction between intelligence and judgment. He doesn't have particularly good judgment in his personal life."

Speaking as one of many millions who believed in, or lived by, the modern American system of serial divorce and remarriage, the divorcé Rotenberry found Bill's penchant for promiscuity *within* marriage a matter not only of morality but of imprudence. "He has made mistakes in judgment," Rotenberry commented coyly but with quiet emphasis. "We all know that—we've seen those mistakes in judgment that he's made! But as far as pure intelligence goes, the ability to understand, comprehend, to learn and to retain information and to analyze situations—there's only one other person in my life who was on his level."

Bill's lack of personal judgment—his driven promiscuity—was, however, never openly paraded in front of others, in Rotenberry's recollection. Indeed, in much the same way as in JFK's career, such hubris as would develop came only later, as more power inspired more excitement in more women. For the moment, in the attorney general's office, an old-fashioned Arkansas decorum reigned. Rotenberry had a "vague recollection that there was the best-looking mid-twenties-year-old coming in and out of the attorney general's office"—Gennifer Flowers—but "he wasn't flaunting it, in my presence at least." As an older, more experienced lawyer, on whom Bill Clinton necessarily leaned in the management of a top-class office, Rotenberry was not privy to Clinton's most private desires. "He may have been a little inhibited, in my presence, of revealing too much," Rotenberry reflected. "That's a gut feeling, looking back. If he was that active in extramarital affairs, girlfriends, from the stories that came out during his presidency—well, there were a lot of us who thought we knew him pretty well in the attorney general's days, and we didn't know about those things!"

Bill Clinton's ability to segment the different parts of his life—his capacity for compartmentalization—was the more awesome as Rotenberry reflected on his old boss. But if Bill had proved effective in the "stepping-stone" office of attorney general, where relatively little political fallout could be expected from decisions that were made, things would be quite different in his next position. There his failings of character and judgment would not simply prove disappointing but would result in the electorate throwing him out after only two years.

Eyes on the Prize

Should he go for the governorship of Arkansas? Bill wondered. Or should he compete for the state's second seat in the U.S. Senate, Senator John McClellan having died of a heart attack in 1977?

The gladiator needed advice. He was therefore particularly receptive to the sales pitch of a young New York political strategist, Dick Morris. "I had never before met a candidate my own age with sideburns and hair as long as mine and with an attitude towards the Vietnam War that was the same as mine," Morris noted with satisfaction. "What wasn't the same," he added, "were our bodies. His six feet, two inches—compared to my five feet, six inches."

The glaring physical disproportion was almost as great as that of Bill and the diminutive Robert Reich. The same ambition that had animated his conversations with Reich as a Rhodes Scholar, however, now beat the more insistently in the thirty-year-old politician's heart—as everyone around him knew. "Eventually Washington was where Clinton wanted to go," Ernie Dumas, the editorial writer for the *Arkansas Gazette,* recalled the situation in the mid-seventies. "That was where he really wanted to be. He and Jim Guy Tucker, his predecessor as attorney general, they both have their sights on the White House. And Tucker's a couple of years ahead of Bill, he wins the congressional seat from here in '76."

Jim Guy Tucker was both brainy and good-looking. "With his liquid blue eyes, perfectly dimpled chin, and a chiseled jaw that Superman would have envied Jim Guy Tucker was so handsome it hurt to look at him," Jim McDougal's wife, Susan, would later swoon. Would the former attorney general and the current attorney general *both* go into battle for the deceased senator McClellan's seat in Washington? To do so would mean sparring with the outgoing governor of Arkansas, David Pryor. "Bumpers has already gone to the Senate, and nobody's going to beat Bumpers as long as he wants to stay in office—he'd beaten Fulbright and is enormously popular and nobody even *thinks* about beatin' Bumpers! So this"—the competition for the only remaining Senate seat—"is a chance of a lifetime!" Dumas recollected. "Pryor was convinced Clinton was going to run. They were getting ready to run against Bill Clinton."

Such a battle with Tucker and Pryor made Bill's blood run faster. "Do you think Pryor can win?" he asked Morris nervously.

Competition

Bill Clinton didn't, in the end, challenge Governor Pryor and Congressman Tucker for the open Senate seat. Those who could later not understand why, unlike Richard Nixon, Bill Clinton would not resign before being impeached as President simply did not understand Clinton or the constant humiliations and insecurities he had suffered as the stepchild of an abusive alcoholic. Like a chameleon he had learned to find acceptance in almost any circle, able to converse and share with people of all ages, backgrounds, ethnicities, educations, professions. But in wanting to be liked and accepted, he had an almost pathological fear of the opposite of acceptance: rejection. And losing an election fight against Governor Pryor would mean rejection—for a second time.

Would he lose, though? In a two-way race, Morris concluded after polling a cross section of the Arkansas electorate, Bill Clinton might have a real chance of winning, but in a three-way, even a four-way, race, his chances were slim. As Dumas recalled, "Clinton was really torn—and he almost ran for the Senate." Discretion proved the better part of valor, though. "Bill decided," Dumas recounted. "Too risky!"

Reluctantly, the young attorney general turned his attention back to the governor's mansion, which David Pryor would be vacating.

A Pretty High Negative

In contrast to a Senate race, election to the soon-to-be-vacant governorship promised to be almost indecently easy for Bill Clinton, despite his age. Playing for safety, he decided to exercise that option. To raise money and promote his name, he and Hillary had already begun to speak at as many as twelve engagements per day, rising at six in the morning and crashing late at night. By the time he officially announced his candidacy at the Old State House in Little Rock on March 5, 1978, therefore, they had already raised a campaign war chest of half a million dollars—far more than all their opponents combined. They'd built up a paid staff of fifteen, plus thousands of volunteers, a rented plane, a mobile telephone in the car, a new pollster in Dick Morris, and media consultants to boot.

"Heretofore in Arkansas we didn't know anything about hiring campaign consultants. You'd get a local advertising agency and a couple of local outfits did polling—but Clinton goes off and gets this Dick Morris, of Morris and Dressler, and gets him to craft a campaign," recalled Ernie Dumas, impressed.

Not all were won over, however, as Dumas also recalled: "He's always had a pretty high negative in Arkansas—all the years Clinton ran for office he'd always have a pretty high negative." In part this was, Dumas considered, inevitable, given Bill's fabled journey beyond the frontiers of Arkansas, indeed of America. "Part of the source of the dislike of Bill Clinton is, he goes off to Georgetown and to Yale and to Oxford and puts on airs—he goes out and gets this elegant education. Now, he never came back and flaunted it. He didn't do that, didn't act like 'I am superior, I've got this great education' " in the manner of other Rhodes Scholars. "Nevertheless, it was always part of his résumé. And there was kinda resentment. As Arkansans we have this terrible inferiority complex. It's awful—we've always felt, the whole world thinks we are inferior. You go back through our history—H. L. Mencken used to write these things, even though he'd never been to Arkansas—he'd talk about hillbillies, he'd write about Arkansas as one of the dark places of the earth: the jungles of Arkansas—the image of Arkansas, barefoot. . . . And here this guy goes off and gets this fantastic education and so on.

"Now, there's an element of Arkansas that's very proud of this guy, and that's part of Clinton's appeal: pride. People are very proud of him. He's well spoken—same thing with Dale Bumpers."

Bumpers, however, had been a young marine in World War II and was a graduate of the University of Arkansas at Fayetteville and Northwestern University Law School. This was—as it would be throughout Bill Clinton's professional life—the crunch: education versus life experience. Senator Bumpers had run his parents' hardware store after their tragic death in a plane crash and had managed a 350-acre Angus cattle ranch, as well as being a pillar of the local community as a devoted Methodist, choirmaster, Sunday school teacher, and courtroom lawyer who virtually never lost a case. Clinton, by contrast, had simply been to Georgetown, then Oxford and Yale, before returning like the Prodigal Son. Worse still, for many Arkansans, was the fact that he'd brought back with him a northerner: a feminist who wore dykey clothes, did not wash off her perspiration or look after her hair, and used no makeup! Worst of all, she refused to take Clinton's name as his wife.

Hillary: No Nonsense, No Frills

The fact was, with Hillary working in the Rose Law Firm in Little Rock, where she was soon promoted to partner, the attorney general and his wife were not only a "power couple" but a highly professional couple: something that was bound to raise hackles in an antifeminist southern state such as Arkansas.

Inevitably, then, rivals for the governorship now launched into Hillary, not Bill—excoriating her for conflicts of interest, such as her provision of legal advice on behalf of the Rose Law Firm to a company owned by the Stephens family, which in turn owned the Arkansas Oklahoma Gas Company, with which the state was in litigation.

Hillary had seen no connection. Indeed, she had blamed the press, which, she claimed, had been nonaccountable since Nixon's downfall. "One of our problems is trying to control a press that is far out of line because of Watergate," she'd declared at a Rotary Club function, ignoring the fact that she had herself helped to unleash this tiger: a tiger she was now finding it difficult to ride. She seemed unable to comprehend why the more successful she and Bill were at such a young age, the more they would be bound to incite envy and suspicion, particularly in view of the campaign finance they were attracting. Bill had won backing not only from labor unions, teachers, and commercial companies but from one of the state's wealthiest individuals, Witt Stephens. His Democratic Party competitors felt increasingly awed by the young Clinton juggernaut and aggrieved at the disparity in funding. "Is it for sale?" one rival had asked of the governorship of Arkansas at a rally. "No, it's not for sale!"

It was, however, as could be seen by any spectator watching Bill fill his electoral campaign chest with the largest amount of funding ever raised for a gubernatorial bid. Inevitably, seeking financial sponsors for his candidacy on such a scale would, critics argued, make him a pawn of major corporations. Conversely, thanks to his humble Hope background and his deeply empathetic personality—eternally seeking to please—representatives of minorities and labor unionists saw him as *their* pawn. Thus arose a contradiction that would dog Bill Clinton throughout his political career: that to some he appeared an archcapitalist puppet—a "pied piper in a pretty suit with a pretty flute," as one rival put it—and to others an archliberal.

Hostility toward Hillary was, however, the most painful part. If people only knew how "old-fashioned" Hillary was "in every conceivable way," Bill complained in an interview, they would not look at her so critically. "She's just a hardworking, no-nonsense, no-frills, intelligent girl who has done well, who doesn't see any sense to extramarital sex, who doesn't care much for drink, who's witty and sharp but without being a stick in the mud," he explained. "She's just great."

Clearing the Road to the White House

Despite a strong undercurrent of resentment, especially toward Candidate Clinton's wife, Bill Clinton sailed through the Democratic primaries in the spring of 1978. The *Arkansas Gazette* had backed his candidacy in glowing terms—"He has extraordinary credentials, an unusual intellect and a dazzling personality to bring to bear upon the problems and opportunities that will confront the next governor"—and his clear victory not only obviated the need for a runoff but guaranteed election as governor in November, since no Republican of note would contest the mansion. To Bill's concern, however, outgoing Governor Pryor found himself struggling for his political life against Congressman Tucker and Congressman Thornton in *his* primary, necessitating a runoff for the senatorial nomination.

Would Pryor be beaten by Tucker, the "Superman," Bill Clinton wondered—and if so, would Senator Tucker go on to a brilliant career as senator on the Hill, ending perhaps in the White House? "David's too nice, and Tucker can clean his clock," Bill confided to Morris. "That's my problem. In the long run, Tucker's competition for me. We're both young, smart guys."

This was, perhaps, the most Machiavellian moment in the young Rhodes Scholar's life. Fearing Tucker as a *future* rival, Bill decided he must fell him *now* rather than have to compete with him later. Instead of preparing himself for his imminent leadership role as governor of Arkansas, aged only thirty-one, Bill thus threw himself in the summer of 1978 into the annihilation of his potential future rival, offering Governor Pryor not only the services of his political strategist, Dick Morris, but his own.

The Destruction of Jim Guy Tucker

"It is one of the reasons Jim Guy Tucker hates Bill Clinton," Dumas confided years later. "Tucker felt Clinton meddled in the Senate race."

Clinton and Morris certainly did. As Morris later revealed, "Clinton and I went to work as a consulting team, designing hard-hitting ads for Pryor"—including, in both Morris's and Dumas's recollections, deliberately "negative" ads that made a mockery of Tucker's message that the state needed leadership and toughness. Smearing Tucker as an absentee congressman, missing roll calls in Washington, D.C., where he was supposed to be promoting Arkansas voters' concerns, Clinton and Morris trashed his candidacy.

The negative ads proved lethal, and in the runoff between Pryor and Tucker, the governor triumphed—though the first lady, Mrs. Pryor, disgusted by Morris, would never permit him to enter the governor's mansion. Bill Clinton, however, would. Indeed, he was awed by the effectiveness of Morris's "secret weapon." "Pryor's comeback earned me Bill Clinton's respect," Morris boasted.

It did. With Morris's help Bill Clinton had learned, in fighting another man's battle, the politics of personal destruction that he would later so decry but that would serve him well in electoral combat, especially with Republicans priding themselves on the use of such electoral tactics. Intrigued and entranced by the business, however, the young attorney general had spent too much of his limited time on political spinning and on destroying someone else's opponent, not preparing himself, in mind as well as policy, for the huge task of state leadership that lay ahead of him.

Sadly, this failure to ponder, introspect, and develop his own leadership skills would prove electorally fatal over the subsequent two years—just as it would fourteen years later.

Clouds on the Horizon

Hillary was no frills. Bill, by contrast, was full of frills and relished them in others. His curiosity about people and about life made him a natural gypsy. Moreover, like the majority of full-blooded male members of his baby-boom generation, he saw enormous excitement in extramarital sex, now that it was more socially acceptable and, as he saw it, entirely consensual.

Such youthful dynamism and testosterone raised a question, though: Who was Bill Clinton, the likely next governor of Arkansas? His stellar education had certainly not made him a snob, his friends pointed out. He loved popular musicians such as the Commodores, and popular tunes such as "I'm Easy" and "Three Times a Lady"; he could watch football, basketball, and baseball with the best of sports enthusiasts; he could talk about Shakespeare with English professors, and about constitutional and criminal law with judges, fellow law professors, and attorneys. But who, at the end of the day, was Bill Clinton, aside from his political ambition? Where did his own self reside within the brilliant, charismatic chameleon? Was there a point where his endlessly elastic personality stopped and a hardcore, real-life Bill Clinton began: a Bill who was Bill and could be relied upon not to compromise or bend any further? Or was Bill Clinton an optical illusion like the proverbial rainbow—a function of light refraction?

Was *this,* then, the supreme importance of Hillary Rodham in Bill Clinton's young life: that however much she might be resented by antifeminists in traditional Arkansas, Bill Clinton had wrapped himself around a woman who was not only almost as smart as himself, but who *still possessed a soul*— a soul he himself, wallowing in the flow of the sixties and seventies, had sold?

As victory over his three rivals in the May 1978 primary campaign propelled him toward the governor's mansion, Bill's political prospects looked excellent. On the other hand, there were darker clouds on the horizon: clouds that if resentment turned to cruelty and the press turned to rainmaking—which after Watergate they were wont to do—might result in a nasty downpour.

Diamonds and Denim

The fact was that for every voter who saw in the photographs of Bill and Hillary Clinton the picture of a young, committed, virtuous couple, there was another voter who bristled. Envy at the "upstarts" began to grow, especially when it was revealed Bill had published *ten thousand* copies of his self-preening "Attorney General's Report" at public expense. It was Georgetown all over again—indulging in self-congratulation and making exaggerated claims for his work on behalf of electors.

Impossible to dislike in person, Bill was aware that if he could but shake the hand of every voter in the state, he would have no opposition. But he couldn't. Nor could he or Hillary hope that opponents would simply roll over and watch the "power couple" walk over them, as if casting youthful intellectual and political diamonds before swine.

Thus, although Bill triumphed in the election in November 1978 to become the state's youngest-ever elected governor at the age of thirty-two, winning 65 percent of the votes cast, it was a victory tinged with ill omen. A retired air force colonel living in Fayetteville had taken umbrage at Bill's 1969 draft evasion—and, with a Republican stalwart beside him, had announced before the press in Little Rock that Bill had reneged on his contractual agreement to serve in the University of Arkansas ROTC program, a program that had saved him from the draft. Though Bill's self-incriminating letter to Colonel Holmes had "disappeared," a version of it might resurface anytime. The accusations of conflict of interest in terms of Hillary's work for the Rose Law Firm—conflicts that would become even more exacerbated once Bill Clinton took over as governor, not simply attorney general—increased. Bill's hugely successful fund-raising efforts had skated within the law—but often on the thinnest of ice. As Jim McDougal, Bill's former political colleague, later recalled, in order to avoid the $1,500 limit on individual contributions, he and his wife had, for example, funneled $9,000 to Bill's campaign via a barely legal series of six $1,500 con-

tributions from the different businesses he and Susan McDougal owned—
a stratagem that was repeated time and again by other colleagues and supporters. Moreover, beyond the draft avoidance issue, the conflict inherent
in Hillary's law work, and the matter of campaign finances, there was the
matter of women: Bill's women. At least one of them had become pregnant and had had an abortion. Another, Juanita Broaddrick, a nursing
home executive, would later claim that, during a Nursing Home Association conference in Little Rock in 1978, the attorney general had forced her,
in her bedroom at the Camelot Hotel, to have nonconsensual sex—rape.
By then the statute of limitations had run out on a possible criminal or
civil lawsuit, but, according to author Jeffrey Toobin, Clinton did confide
that sex had taken place. Clinton "suggested to one friend that he had slept
with Broaddrick, but that it had been 'a consensual deal' "—both of them
cheating on their spouses. Juanita's version was that their sexual encounter
was not consensual, indeed that Bill Clinton not only knew he'd gone too
far, but had subsequently apologized to her—and that Hillary not only
knew about her husband's extramarital needs, but that "she always covered
up for him." Could all this be kept from the press in the long run?

The result was a sort of mixed blessing: a victorious aura of youthful
idealism and hope tinged with a certain arrogance that presaged, in the
"Diamonds and Denim"–themed inaugural gala on January 9, 1979, an
American fall.

CHAPTER TWENTY-FIVE

YOUNGEST-EVER GOVERNOR OF ARKANSAS

The Boy Scout

"My theories seemed to work," Dick Morris, one of the pioneers of negative advertising, later boasted. But when Morris tried to advise the governor-to-be on his legislative program, warning Clinton not to impose new taxes, Clinton dropped his pilot. "When he fired me," Morris recalled painfully, it was with words that smacked of insecurity: "You do as well or better than I do what I do best," Bill announced: "politics. And that is an assault on my vanity."

This fear of sharing, let alone ceding, the limelight would dog Clinton to the end of his political days. Reflecting in the late 1990s, the diminutive New York strategist saw Bill Clinton as a strange amalgam of "the Boy Scout and the politician." Thanks to Morris, the politician in Bill Clinton had learned to use a secret weapon—negative advertising—purchased from a store in Manhattan, with which he could now cut down any Arkansas rival who dared campaign against him but that embarrassed the "goody-goody" in him. Firing Morris once he'd done his job, the Boy Scout governor would lead Arkansas into a new era of prosperity and change—without the need for secret weapons.

The governor's mansion was certainly a dream abode for a thirty-two-year-old semiorphan raised by the railroad tracks in Hope. Built in Georgian Colonial style during the governorship of Sidney McMath in the early 1950s—using traditional red bricks from the former Arkansas School for the Blind, which had stood at 1800 Center Street—it was fronted by high, imposing white portico pillars. Inside, however, it was delightfully homey. In the marble-floored foyer one looked up a sweeping, curved staircase to the governor's private quarters, but to left and right of the foyer were the small living and dining rooms. Antiques abounded, from Samuel Morse's painting of the first governor, James Miller, to the 1770 grandfather clock. Beyond the living room was a study room, lined with green-painted shelves on which Bill Clinton would display his growing antiquarian collection of Arkansas history, and a bust of President Theodore Roosevelt. It was here, rather than at the capitol, that Governor Bill Clinton would hold court with his first lady—or in the literal kitchen cabinet, next to the dining room and pantry, which gave onto a private dining area overlooking the tree-sheltered grounds of the estate.

With virtually no idea of how, in the real world of legislative negotiation and political leadership, he would achieve his Boy Scout vision, Bill had already begun to assemble his formal cabinet before entering the mansion. "Clinton's Cabinet May Represent First Sweeping Change Since 1971," the *Arkansas Gazette* had trumpeted in a headline on December 18, 1978, and a few weeks later, after his inauguration, Howell Raines of *The New York Times* noted that among "New South governors" Bill Clinton and his neighboring governor, Lamar Alexander in Tennessee, were motivated by "public embarrassment at being held up to national ridicule" for their states' poor highways, poor public schools, and poor public services—including prisons. "Clinton, a former Rhodes scholar, has equally lofty ambitions for the school system in Arkansas, which ranks 49th among the states in per capita expenditure for education. He has recommended $1,200 annual raises for teachers for the next two years. And, in one of the few tax-and-spend proposals to surface anywhere in the region this year, Clinton is seeking a one-cent-per-gallon gasoline tax and an increase in vehicle fees to raise $45 million annually for highway improvements that Clinton sees as essential to economic growth."

Far from directing his new cabinet through Steve Smith as his chief of staff, however, Bill decided to divide and rule by having *three* young men like himself as his deputies, who became known as the Bearded Troika or "triumvirate": Steve Smith, Rudy Moore, and John Danner—the last of whom was married to Nancy "Peach" Pietrefesa and came from California. All three would become bitterly resented in Arkansas in subsequent months, even vilified by the *Arkansas Democrat* in the newspaper's editorials and cartoons. Moreover, all three would have to be ditched when the governor's new vessel ran aground, took on water, and eventually sank—taking its master, Captain William Jefferson Clinton, down with it.

Boy Scout Squared

Even Ernie Dumas, a political writer on the more liberal, stately *Arkansas Gazette,* was unsparing in his recollection of Clinton's first term as governor. Like many political observers, Dumas was admiring of the energy, youth, and idealism Bill Clinton brought to the governor's office—but scathing about the way the young governor sought to administer the state.

As an electoral campaigner Bill had proved himself *sans pareil*—inventing an almost "carnal" relationship with voters, as the journalist Joe Klein later put it. "When he first gets elected governor," Dumas recalled, "he was so *physical* about everything, and with everybody: great hugs and kisses, even with reporters—so hands-on! And you saw that with black people: just bear hugs, and so perfectly natural."

Jim McDougal had been made economic development liaison officer in the Clinton administration; his wife, Susan, later remarked of Clinton that she had "never known another human being who needed to be told all the time how great he is." Betsey Wright, his later chief of staff, seconded this—though she came to see it in terms of a two-way relationship. The public needed a user-friendly leader and spokesman; Bill Clinton needed a public. "There's a terrible insecurity there! It's huge!" Betsey remarked. "And that in some ways defines Bill Clinton, counter to his intellect which is the other way that defines Bill Clinton!" Nor did Betsey see Bill Clinton's familiarity and comfortableness with black people as intrinsically different from his familiarity with others. He needed them all. "He adores people! And he wants people *to love him*! And the bigger the diversity, the happier he is!"

"Clinton has also led the way in pushing beyond tokenism in the appointment to cabinet-level jobs of women and blacks," the *New York Times* reporter noted. Indeed, Clinton seemed almost gung ho. "If you want to do things and to change people's lives," he told Raines, "run for governor. That's where the power is."

If so, the youngest governor in the country did not know how to use it wisely. Operating in the governor's office in the northeast corner of the capitol in Little Rock, all Bill's failings came tumbling out. His best friend, Jim Blair, would be married by Bill—"I discovered a clause in the state constitution which says the governor for the time being shall have the power to perform a marriage," Blair recalled, so that he and Diane Kincaid, politics professor at the University of Arkansas, were able to get remarried in Ann Henry's home in Fayetteville, with the governor acting not only as best man but as presiding official of the nuptial. But even Blair was derisive of Bill's performance as governor of the state. Bill's progressive liberal program bore no relation to the conservative realities and obstacles of Arkansas business, politics, or the state legislature; indeed, it was as if the governor's office had been hijacked by a group of teenage liberals. "Things were changing," Blair acknowledged of the late seventies, "but he tried to change 'em too fast! And he brought in young guys, who were very bright, but they wore beards, they had long hair—I mean, all the things that drove the older generation in Arkansas up the tree! And Arkansas's population is probably more weighted towards the elderly than any other state."

The Clinton agenda, and the inexperience of the staff Bill chose to carry it out, would be tragically repeated fourteen years later. In the meantime his first administration unfolded as if in a children's play. Arkansas had the third-fastest-growing retiree population in the country, yet Bill Clinton "was in an Eagle Scout mode (Boy Scout squared)," Dick Morris remarked sarcastically. "He probably felt like an Olympic pole vaulter who had just soared twenty feet through the air with the aid of a fiberglass pole," the strategist added, remembering how he himself had been discarded almost immediately after the election, in favor of the Bearded Troika. "I was the pole, useful for making it over the bar but expendable once it had been cleared."

Without Morris as strategist or a single-minded, single chief of staff— a figure who might become too much a power behind the throne— Governor Clinton now ran headlong into the legislative fray with his program of measures to be introduced and passed in his first term. As Diane Kincaid Blair later recorded, Clinton called for "small business development and international marketing over traditional smokestack-chasing activities"; he wished for teachers to take the National Teacher's Examination, as well as for students to undergo regular testing and new programs for gifted children to be instituted. He wanted an Energy Department to regulate utilities, a Natural and Scenic Rivers Commission to be established, as well as a State Land Bank. Rural health development was to be improved by a new office, a new state perinatal intensive care nursery was to be provided, better in-home service for the elderly was to be promoted, and a Washington, D.C., office was to be set up to ensure that Arkansas got its fair share of federal funding—all in his first two-year stint, during an economic recession!

For Diane, as a political scientist, this was "one of the most productive legislative sessions in the state's history," but to her husband and many others—especially those who had marveled at the way Dale Bumpers had introduced reform after reform and raised taxes to pay for them without a bleat from the legislature or the public—it looked foolhardy. Even Diane admitted that "Clinton's bright young aides were better at policy innovation than personal outreach, a serious mistake in the homegrown style of Arkansas politics." She blamed the Bearded Troika for infuriating "many of the state's most powerful interests including utilities, timber, trucking, poultry, construction, and medicine."

This was quite an assemblage to confront, in one go. Whether it was the fault of the Bearded Troika or of Bill Clinton's own failings as a leader, however, was a moot point. Bill Clinton would learn legendary skills at political finessing over the years, but they would never include truthfulness or responsibility for his own actions. As his longtime chief of staff, Betsey Wright, would later sigh, he was in some ways like a child who could never admit having made a mistake or having done something wrong—it was always someone else's fault. In Wright's view, it was a trait Bill got from his mother, whom Betsey grew to love but who clearly "had an extraordinary ability to not be at fault, and to conveniently forget things—two of Bill's greatest attributes. I mean, there were times when I was just *amazed* that they could both be so dipsy that way." Jim Blair agreed. "I mean, it's hard for me to play armchair psychologist," he reflected as one of Bill's best friends, "but there is an unwillingness at times for him to accept responsibility for his own actions."

In the case of Bill Clinton's first term as governor of Arkansas, however, it was ultimately no one else's fault but Bill's. It was he who had discarded Morris and had sought to rule via his Bearded Troika—yet who declined to take the blame when the legislature, public, commerce, utilities, and press balked at being railroaded into change. In this they mirrored the time, as poor President Jimmy Carter, elected two years earlier, in 1976, had also found. At a meeting at Camp David in September 1979, young

Governor Clinton had urged the President to "plunge himself into trying to implement an energy policy and talk to the people and get them to support that policy. I told him very frankly," Clinton told reporters at Little Rock Airport, that "his administration was too withdrawn, too stiff, too stilted, too involved in day-to-day administration. And I said he ought to throw away his notes to his speeches and quit watching his teleprompter and talk frankly to the people like he talked to the governors and others at the meeting."

Would that it had been so simple! America, balking at the magnitude of changes required in order to modernize, was moving backward rather than be egged into the kind of multiethnic, multicultural modern liberal democracy that Bill Clinton vaguely stood for. The fallout from President Nixon's impeachment had temporarily interrupted the nation's shift to the right, but President Jimmy Carter's "stilted" naiveté was bringing submerged conservatives back to the surface, where they torpedoed the former submarine commander's well-intentioned ship of state unmercifully, eventually sinking the Democratic vessel in a single term. And with it, thanks to Bill's close connection with the commander in chief, would go down Bill Clinton's proud command of the state of Arkansas.

Carter's Coattails

From the start of Jimmy Carter's campaign for the presidency in 1976 Bill and Hillary Clinton had tied themselves to Carter's coattails. Hillary had campaigned for Carter in Indiana, while Bill—benefiting from Carter's close funding ties with the Stephens family in Arkansas and on Wall Street—had supported Carter as his election manager in Arkansas. Both had been duly rewarded. Hillary had been offered an important position in Washington (a job she had declined, though she accepted an appointment to the board of the Legal Services Corporation, as its youngest member, at the end of 1977 and the chairmanship in 1978), while Bill had become an adviser to the President on federal appointments in Arkansas and a frequent visitor to the White House.

Such cozy familiarity with the U.S. President and First Lady by the young governor and first lady of Arkansas had soon encountered problems, however. America, in a sort of backlash against national humiliation in Vietnam, once again began to take up Nixon's white conservative banner. President Carter was increasingly denounced as liberal, pro-black, and a pacifist. His extraordinary efforts on behalf of international peacemaking and peacekeeping—epitomized in the historic Israeli-Egyptian peace accord and Salt II missile agreement with the Soviet Union in 1979—were downplayed, even derided by those who felt America was going "soft" on communism and anti-American extremism abroad. The Ayatollah Khomeini, having caused the downfall of the secular shah of Iran, rode a new wave of popular Islamic fundamentalism that branded the United States as corrupt, capitalist, and ungodly. In November 1979, Iranian militants and revolutionaries seized the U.S. Embassy in Tehran, imprisoning its staff as hostages in defiance of all international rules of diplomatic immunity. Meanwhile in Afghanistan, the Russian military began to take over the country in what appeared to be an expansion of Soviet power. Carter's responses—authorizing a doomed rescue mission to bring out American hostages in Tehran and punishing the Soviet Union by pulling the United States out of the Olympic Games—seemed inadequate to Americans humiliated by Vietnam and hungering for a tougher, more muscular military approach to world problems. Even Governor Bill Clinton began to lose faith in his president. Receiving an honorary doctorate at his alma mater in the spring of 1980, he called for a "restoration of trust in America's pronouncements on foreign policy. If we could adjust our rhetoric," he claimed, " 'we could do better' in relation to Western allies who seem to have lost a degree of trust in American leadership." He was not, he hastened to add, firing "a wholesale or broadside attack" on Mr. Carter's foreign policy initiatives, but he believed the United States must be prepared to back up rhetoric in foreign affairs with action.

The same criticism, ironically, would be made of Bill Clinton's presidency, two decades later—indeed, in numerous ways the Carter era would presage the nineties *fin de siècle* and the start of the new millennium. World terrorism was on the increase: the Italian Red Brigades assassinated ex–Prime Minister Aldo Moro, while in Ireland the IRA bombed the yacht of Lord Mountbatten and his family. Wars of insurgency and counterinsurgency spread across Africa like infections. President Carter's responses seemed always well meaning and ethically sound but lame—his sympathy for the Panamanians leading him, like the British decision to vacate Hong Kong, to promise the surrender of the Panama Canal to the Panamanian government in 1999. "Save our canal—Give Carter to Panama" was a typical placard paraded by American protesters in April 1978. His warnings about spiraling energy costs and the need for conservation sounded a

344 · BILL CLINTON

schoolmarmish tone, while his solution—higher fuel taxes, proposed in March 1980—struck fury into the hearts of a nation of gas-guzzlers.

Carter's problem was that, in a period of high inflation, escalating interest and mortgage rates, the decline of traditional industries in the Rust Belt, and economic uncertainty, the American economy looked top-heavy, as well as unsavvy in terms of government.

Resorting to raising taxes in order to address outstanding and emerging social, environmental, and other problems had become the traditional Democratic approach since FDR. Now however, with California's Proposition 13 having started a West Coast tax revolt in 1978 and Governor Ronald Reagan having declared in 1979 his intention to run for the Republican presidential crown, the renewed antitax Republican revolution of the Right was approaching.

Margaret Thatcher, leader of Britain's Conservative Party, had been elected Prime Minister in May 1979, having declared her abhorrence of the laxities of the sixties. Ten months later, in February 1980, Ronald Reagan won a landslide victory in the New Hampshire Republican primary.

In 1980, the writing was on the political wall—and Bill Clinton, basking in the perks and excitement of power for the first time in his life, seemed alive to what was happening nationally, indeed internationally, but oblivious to what was happening in his own state of Arkansas.

Inviting Electoral Challenge

Jimmy Carter's days were now numbered—as were Bill Clinton's as governor of Arkansas. The two men were similar in many ways. Southerners, both had risen from humble backgrounds, both had embarrassing brothers—President Carter having repeatedly to apologize for his brother Billy's public remarks, alcoholic behavior, and poor judgment while Bill Clinton's brother, Roger, was flunking college and already making his descent into narcotics addiction.

As if to mirror the growing failure of the Democratic Party to fix upon a modern vision of leadership that would rise to the American occasion, the very friendship between the U.S. President and the governor of Arkansas was also coming to an end.

Carter's stand on humanitarian issues, such as Vietnamese refugees, had always been noble and in the best traditions of American charity. It was in that spirit and to find favor among Cuban exiles in Florida and elsewhere that when Peru refused to accept the growing number of Cubans wishing to leave Fidel Castro's Communist Cuba (a small number had stormed the Peruvian Embassy in Havana), President Carter agreed to take 3,500 in the spring of 1980. He ended up with almost 120,000—many of them convicts and patients simply turned out of Cuban prisons and mental hospitals. "At last! Now we will not have to lock our doors!" people were heard to sigh with relief in Havana. But in western Arkansas, around Fort Chaffee's Relocation Center, people bolted them the more tightly.

Governor Clinton, age thirty-three and a political friend and ally of the President, duly accepted the first refugees on condition that no more would be sent to Arkansas. Carter ignored Clinton and sent more by air. When hundreds of the detainees began to riot over bad conditions in the summer heat and broke out of the fort, a wave of revulsion and fear swept through the Ozarks and Ouachitas. The result in Arkansas—when taken with the growing national and local objection to raising taxes—was, for Bill Clinton's political career, to invite real electoral challenge to his governorship. And if that challenge did not emerge within his own party, it would come from a Republican.

The man whom fate chose for the role was an experienced, business-oriented and businesslike individual, who had headed the Arkansas Industrial Development Commission for several years: the Fellowship Bible Church's Frank White.

Representing the Libertine Generation

Watching Bill Clinton's rise to political stardom, Frank White—thirteen years older than Bill Clinton, a graduate of the New Mexico Military Institute, Texas A&M University, and the U.S. Naval Academy, and a pilot in the U.S. Air Force for five years, retiring in the rank of captain—was skeptical of the young governor's approach to leadership in Arkansas. White had made a successful postmilitary career in banking, had divorced his first wife and had chosen for his second spouse a deeply devout, indeed fundamentalist, Christian, Gay Daniels, also divorced, who like him had also worked on the Campus Crusade for Christ. Switching from the Baptist to the First Methodist Church and then cofounding the Fellowship Bible Church with forty other couples, White reflected the escalating fundamentalism to be observed in almost every contemporary religion—the search to return to core values in an era reeling from cultural and economic change at the end of the seventies.

Bill Clinton, as a product of the Southern Baptist Church, watched the growing schism in his church with alarm, since it mirrored a yawning divide between Democrats and Republicans. Among Baptists the clash was between progressives who felt that the text of the Holy Bible was neither infallible nor fair—indeed, was marred by ancient racist, chauvinist, and antifeminist ideologies not in the true spirit of Christian doctrine—on the one hand, and supporters of the Inerrancy Party in the Southern Baptist movement, on the other: men and women who believed the Bible was to be taken as literal, nonsymbolic, nonfigurative truth. By 1979 the "bittersweet arrangement" between the Moderate Party and the Inerrancy Party was becoming "increasingly bitter," religious historian Joe E. Barnhart chronicled in his subsequent account of the Southern Baptist Holy War dividing its fourteen million members—"a million and a half more than all the Jews throughout the world," as Barnhart pointed out, and with "billions of dollars at stake."

Judeo-Christian Western society certainly seemed on the cusp of tremendous changes in the wake of the sixties and seventies—changes that Bill Clinton, thanks to his advanced education, grasped intellectually perhaps better than any other leading presence in the Democratic Party. As he would declare in his National Convention speech on behalf of the Democratic governors in 1980, Americans—Republicans and Democrats alike—were faced by an economic system that was clearly "breaking down. We have seen high inflation, high unemployment, large government deficits, the loss of our competitive edge. In response to these developments, a dangerous and growing number are opting out of our system," he observed. "Another dangerous and growing number are opting for special interest and single interest group politics"—an understandable but nevertheless disturbing failure to respect the larger importance of community, country, and global needs, and one that "threatens to take every last drop of blood out of our political system."

There was, however, an enormous gap between analysis and effectiveness. Bill Clinton's social, political, and economic perception did him credit. But in eschewing old or simplistic remedies he was inevitably hobbled by his own sixties relativism, which infuriated older absolutists. As his longtime aide Bobby Roberts commented, looking back at the late seventies, "The middle ground of people simply felt this country's in a great state of flux, and not necessarily for the better all the time. A lot of people just saw him as a sort of symbol of that problem."

Ernie Dumas agreed—though he wondered whether there was not a racial element in the malicious envy that the "Wonder Boy" quickly attracted as governor. "There's the race thing," he reflected. "You can go across the state, and people are rabid here, in talk shows especially—people foam at the mouth about Bill Clinton! He's incarnate evil to such people. If he were killed, they would think it a wonderful thing!" To them, Bill Clinton represented the worst evils of "modern society, I guess! In a way he kinda represents this libertine generation—what's happened to us, screwing around and smokin' dope and doin' all those kinda things—lying, cheatin', and not going to church and prayin'."

Frank White, by contrast, went to his Inerrancy church regularly—and there felt empowered by the gust of regressionary change. Bill Clinton, Frank White later considered, "would have been well served" to stay in the attorney general's office "and season a little bit. But he turned right round and ran for Governor," an office in which he immediately "deemed himself invincible. He just thought he could change the world. That he just couldn't do any wrong. And o' course everybody—all the media were in adoration of him, because he was the rising star of the Democratic Party. So he did what he did—he just alienated the people who put him where he was! They couldn't go to see him without having to go through his staff." The staff was not up to it—indeed, quickly became infamous. "He hired three guys who were symbolic of his age and who brought to the office the values that he brought. They were deemed politically as the Bearded Wonders at that time. They all had beards—and they were all going to change the world.

"Did they have political experience? None! Zero! And they were very abrasive to legislators, very abrasive to elected officials across the state: talked down to them, like 'You don't know what ya talkin' about!' And so no Democrat would run against him, because they didn't think they could beat 'im."

White thought he could. But not as a Democrat.

"Way Immature"

"I just thought he was way immature!" Frank White later said of Clinton. "Some of the actions he had taken, the way he treated people—every month or two there was some documentation about some temper tantrum that he'd had, throwing stuff in the office. I mean, they would get out! And he was just real abrupt with people. You have to understand the culture of the legislature. You know, a senator out there, or a member of the House, they're elected officials also, and these county judges—it doesn't matter how much education they have, or whether they have any! In their county they're tryin' to serve the people. And so there was this attitude that kind of permeated his administration, that looked down on these people. These people would go to his office—maybe they'd be looking for disaster aid, or maybe they needed help on highways, or maybe the health center wasn't up to what it needed to be—and the reception they got wasn't up to what it needed to be: the reception they got at the governor's office just turned 'em off!"

Even the wife of Clinton's economic development liaison recalled that "many of the young reformists in the governor's office didn't even try to disguise their contempt for state officials"—an arrogance that became, increasingly, laced with testosterone. "Discussions on budget compromises tended to run a poor second to discussions on who was sleeping with who, and more important, who could possibly be slept with. This was the late seventies, the giddy peak of the sexual revolution . . . these young people possessed the aphrodisiac of power—and their boss, who set the tone for the office, certainly made no secret of his own sexual appetites."

As a Democrat, Frank White ought logically to have challenged Clinton in the Democratic primary in the spring of 1980. He didn't. Instead, he switched parties. "I had never voted Republican, had never been to a Republican meeting!" White later explained. As chairman of the Arkansas Industrial Development Commission, though, he'd traveled the entire state and was known by "shakers and movers, and industrial development people. But I was an unknown political figure—I mean, I just never had been involved, other than giving some money to a friend that ran, sometimes. Never been involved in politics. But when nobody filed against Bill Clinton in the Democratic primary, except this guy who was kind of a joke, a turkey farmer from south Arkansas, his name was Monroe Schwarzlose—an old country boy, uneducated but a good guy, had served in the military, wore overalls, campaigned in the south, raised five thousand dollars . . ." White raised his hands, not needing to finish his sentence. He'd had, he felt, no option.

Beating the incumbent governor as a Democrat seemed a tall order in the first months of 1980. "Well, I decided I couldn't beat him in ninety days—that's how long the Democratic primary is, ninety days from filing deadline to the vote, the Democratic primary is ninety days. So that meant

I had to go from one percent name recognition to be able to beat him in ninety days! That's tough!

"Now, I took the position that if I had six *months* to travel across the state and tell people what I think Clinton is doing wrong, and what we'd need to be doing in Arkansas, then they'd elect me."

It was the impossibility of achieving sufficiently high name recognition as a Democrat that thus changed Frank White from a sure-to-fail Ninety-Day Disaster into a Six-Month Wonder Republican. Almost nobody gave White a chance "in hell." Of some ninety friends and colleagues he called to ask if he stood any chance of winning, in a state that had elected a Republican governor but once since Reconstruction, only three thought he had. White nevertheless filed—as a Republican.

Thereafter, everything went White's way—and against Bill Clinton's.

The Picture on the Wall

To pay for his new Arkansas highway program, Governor Clinton had made what Frank White saw as a most misguided decision. Feeling that an extra sales tax would be regressive as it would hit poorer people the hardest, Clinton had worked to get the owners of big commercial trucks to pay most of the tax hike for highway improvement, but their operators had lobbied legislators, and the compromise—a tax on private vehicles according to weight—penalized owners of old-fashioned, heavy American cars and pickups. In a state that either elected a new governor or reelected the incumbent governor every two years, raising private license fees was a divisive and dangerous decision.

"He raised the license fees," White recounted, "and he raised the title transfer fees in the state. He made Arkansas the most expensive in the nation to transfer the title on your car! And on the license fees, the impact of that was that in every county you'd have to go to the courthouse or the revenue, to change your license. Okay. Everybody has to do that—because back then we had annual license renewal: you had to renew your tags every year. Well, nobody knew what had been passed in the legislature, they really didn't feel the impact of that till it happened. But then, when people started going out in the country to register your pickup and your boat trailer to take your boat fishin'—to register those two things went up from $35 to $100! And all what broke loose out there! As I would travel across the state, I'd go in these revenue offices and these people would tell me that

they had had the most abusive language ever received in their office! They'd
say, 'I can't believe he did what he did!' And when these people would really get upset about it, the revenue people would say, 'Well, you need to call
him!'—and they'd point to the Governor's picture on the wall!"

Worst of all for Bill Clinton, the Arkansas licensing system made the
problem a constantly recurring one. "You come up to your birthday, or
whenever it was you bought your vehicle or license the first time, and it was
a constant rotation—the further we went towards November," White recalled, "the more people had to renew their licenses. And I mean, they were
just *livid*!

"The legislators *told* him not to do it! They said, put a sales tax on it!
Nobody knows what a sales tax is! It's hidden in the price of gasoline, in
the decal. 'Of this dollar twenty-seven of gasoline, eighteen cents goes to
the state of Arkansas'—that's what's on it. And gasoline prices vary from
one pump to the next one down the street, so they really don't know about
it. But boy, when you do it with your license fee, *everybody* knows about it!
'Cause they'd go back and say, 'Well, I paid twenty-eight dollars last year,
and it's gonna be forty-eight dollars this year—what's he *doin'?*' And hey: it
all came to one person!

"Hey, it was an explosive issue! But there again, it was a case where you
couldn't tell him anything! See, he was smarter than anybody else! There
was this arrogance about him. And his wife! He got so much heat across
the state . . ."

Dick Morris had warned Clinton not to go down this path and been dismissed for his pains. The legislature, which was in any case a part-time
body, meeting only once every two years for two months, washed its hands
of the issue. "When people started raising hell about it, the legislators said,
'You need to call the governor, 'cause he's the one that made the decision!' " It was true "they [the legislators] passed it," White conceded, "but
because this is the way *he* wanted it, so they gave it to him."

There was another negative working against the incumbent governor,
however: Cubans.

Every Kind of Criminal

"Car taxes was a big issue," Frank White enumerated. "And Cubans."

Young Governor Clinton's failure to stem the tide of Cubans arriving at
Fort Chaffee, in the western part of Arkansas, and the resultant rioting,

was a particularly sore point among citizens of a small, rural, somewhat xenophobic state. "See, Jimmy Carter told us, after the first batch, we weren't going to get any more. And a lot of people didn't like him sending 'em in the first place," White explained. "We had taken the boat people from Vietnam, I mean, it had been a very positive experience, many stayed on after they got to Chaffee, went into business, some of our finest restaurants in Fort Smith are owned by them—but this was different. Castro had just let everybody leave—he put all the perverts, all the people who had mental illnesses, every kind of criminal that he had in his prisons, he unloaded 'em! I mean, it wasn't voluntary, *he sent 'em*! And all of a sudden *we* had 'em! And it was a real problem trying to deal with 'em."

By June 1980, dozens had been shot and injured, both inside and outside Fort Chaffee. "They rioted—and what infuriated people was, Carter said we weren't goin' to get more—Jimmy Carter told us that. Well, he turned round and sent two big C5As, two big aircraft, with hundreds more at midnight one night. All the last ones—and he sent them to Chaffee! After telling everybody that we weren't going to get any more! All of 'em to us! Well, boy, when the sun came up, and people realized what he'd done, Jimmy Carter was mud!"

Bill Clinton was, too. Indeed, the incident marked the start of a historic shift of Democratic votes to the Republican Party both in the country and in Arkansas. And White would be the beneficiary.

Chelsea Morning

"Like I said, I'd spoken a lot, so I'm a pretty good speaker," White explained. "Okay, I could hold my own with him out there. So it wasn't a case of some bumblin' guy that had never been there. When I talked to him, I *knew* what I was talkin' about!"

Clinton, buoyed by the birth of his first—and only legitimate—child on February 27, 1980, named after Joni Mitchell's famous song "Chelsea Morning," was as indifferent to the threat from White as to the impact of the child's birth on his favorite mistress, Gennifer Flowers. After her abortion Gennifer had moved to Dallas, though in some ways this made the affair easier to manage, out of state. For Gennifer the news that her lover's wife was expecting, however, was "devastating." She could not but reflect on the baby she'd conceived with him, indeed the thought was like a knife through her heart. How could he be so innocently joyful over the birth of

Hillary's baby, but not hers? She tried to feel good about it, since it made him feel so proud, but inside she admitted to pangs of resentment that he should be so excited about having a baby by a woman he found it "so easy to cheat on."

If the proverbial penny did not drop in terms of man's urbiological drive to "cheat," it certainly dropped regarding possible marriage, however. Any notion that he would ever leave Hillary and forge a life with the singing genie went up in smoke that day.

Her day for revenge would come, however, with almost Greek *moira*. Meanwhile, Bill had intended to attend the natural childbirth, but complications had necessitated—as in his own birth—a cesarean, or C-section, delivery. The tiny infant would perhaps never be a beauty, but in Bill's eyes she was. Indeed, in Diane Blair's view, Bill went about the parental bonding business "like he'd invented fatherhood."

Did the birth of a daughter, Chelsea, take Bill's eye yet further off the electoral ball? "I think they knew they were in trouble and hoped that they could still pull it out," Betsey Wright recalled of her telephone conversations with Bill from Washington, D.C., where she was working. Most of the time Bill talked about "governor's stuff," and the "rest of the time we were into Chelsea being born and all *that* stuff!" There were no debates, Frank White recalled. "No, he didn't even give me the time of day—just tried to ignore me for a while." When Monroe Schwarzlose, the country turkey farmer who had come in fifth in the 1978 primary, polled more than 30 percent in the Democratic primary in late May 1980, the warning was simply not heeded. In the Republican camp, however, it was—and it gave White a shot in the arm. "When the Cuban crisis came, he couldn't ignore me anymore. All of a sudden I started comin' up in the polls. See, they didn't give me a chance to win, they thought, that's a joke. They said, there's no way I could win. But all of a sudden I got out there, and I began to come up in the polls. That's when he got scared. Yeah, he began to get kinda frantic!"

The Number One Issue

The *Arkansas Democrat,* the second biggest circulation newspaper in the state at that time, had lampooned Clinton's youthful administration from the very start. John Robert Starr, the paper's prime columnist, was particularly virulent. To add to Clinton's woes, the newspaper used the feminism of the governor's wife as a further stick to beat the governor.

Poor Hillary Rodham had defied the advice of her best friends in moving to Arkansas, instead of forging her own political career in the East. Whether in response or in love, Bill had proposed, and after considerable reflection, Hillary had accepted his offer of marriage. Yet Hillary had refused to take his name: proud to become the real breadwinner in the family, at the Rose Law Firm, as well as of other positions she took and decisions she made. She had served, for example, as chair of the Legal Services Corporation in Washington, D.C.—though was now being evicted by a Senate committee that felt the scheme was wasteful and her chairmanship too strident. More controversial still, she had decided to play the stock market—indeed, had made $100,000 profit in a highly controversial investment the year before. Urged on by their friend Jim Blair, Hillary had played the cattle futures market in Chicago, where she'd grown up, but the trades made on her behalf were later the subject of intense scrutiny for their extraordinarily—some say impossibly—high rates of return: an initial "investment" of only $1,000 had permitted her to trade, as governor's wife, without the usual full stake being requested or margin being called when, in subsequent trades, she guessed wrong. Profit and loss were apportioned by the broker, who passed on losses exclusively to his less fortunate clients—who later sued. As if this were not enough, Hillary had urged Bill to go along with a fifty-fifty partnership in Jim McDougal's latest real estate development overlooking the White River—a scheme that went disastrously wrong when bank interest in Arkansas reached 20 percent and the parcels of land did not sell.

Hillary herself had been uncomfortable about her trading and investment adventures "and the level of testosterone in the air" at the capitol (as Susan McDougal recorded). When Bill's old lesbian friend from Oxford days, Mandy Merck, came to visit them in Little Rock, Hillary astonished those present by declaring there must be "more to life than this greasy pole, this rat race. I'm thinking about getting back into religion."

Married to a politician with an improved salary ($30,000) but no interest in earning money on the side, Hillary could be forgiven for trying to bolster the family finances—especially if, as transpired, the governorship proved a short-term employment. Moreover, though Mandy Merck professed to be astonished by Hillary's remark about turning to God, her remark reflected the growing anxieties gnawing at American voters—anxieties heightened by nervousness about the health of the nation's economy and future job market.

"I remember feeling sorry for her," Susan McDougal later recalled. "She just seemed so gawky, and had trouble relating to people." Hillary had brains but not "warmth, and as a result she had very few friends in Arkansas." Unwilling to pay attention to her appearance, "she'd already begun to attract the kind of criticism and vitriol that would follow her all the way through the White House and into the Senate," Susan reflected. In her awkward, shy, private, often irritatingly self-righteous posture, Hillary had seemed completely unaware of how she was viewed by voters or even her husband's friends. When Carolyn Staley, for example, composed a special song to commemorate the birth of Chelsea with the words "We may not be worthy, but we'll try to be wise," the musically illiterate Hillary went up to Carolyn and denied that she, Hillary, was unworthy. "That's a nice song, Carolyn," she said with the trace of a sneer. "But who's not worthy? You and your tape recorder?"

Such lack of humility—even ingratitude—played badly in a part of the South where folk music, whether ballads or blues, ran through the lives of most people as powerfully as the Mississippi. "You know what the number one issue was on the exit polls, why they voted against him?" Frank White would later ask rhetorically. "*His wife didn't have his name!* And that was what we heard more than any other issue out there. When he was attorney general, people didn't realize it. When he got to be governor—hey, all of a sudden they were making jokes about whether Chelsea was going to be Chelsea Rodham or Chelsea Clinton! That really ran against the grain of the conservative element of Arkansas, the traditional families, if you would. In some parts of the world, New York, perhaps California, for a wife not to have her husband's name, that was fine, but boy! The South wasn't ready for that! Not an elected official . . . number one issue!

"They just rubbed people the wrong way! They didn't like it. They thought, the governor's wife ought to have his name!"

Along with the three Cs—Cubans, car tags, and the missing name of Hillary Clinton—there was a B, too, which would prove decisive in the November 1980 election. White recalled the element with glee—for it, too, reflected the old South.

Hauling the Black Vote

"The culture of Arkansas is, if you want the black vote," White later explained, "you have to haul it! You pay the preachers, and they load 'em up in the car, or put 'em in a schoolbus and carry 'em to the polls. And they tell 'em how to vote! And that's still done today," White claimed in 2001, "like it was twenty years ago!"

The system not only was expensive for a candidate but required considerable advance organization. "The only way you can get that is to go in and pay the preacher in advance and let them organize it. It's called 'drivin'-around money.' You give 'em some money and say, 'Look, you put 'em together and bring 'em to the polls, and show 'em how to vote.' And they do that! And in the Delta and the southeastern part of the state, you know, that's the culture, and that's the way you get the vote out! Now, there's nothing I could [as a Republican] do about that. But Bill Clinton—he didn't think I could beat him, *so he didn't haul 'em in!* He didn't put the money over there! And by the time he realized that I had him in trouble, it was too late to get it organized! You gotta do it two months out! You can't just go over there tomorrow and say, 'Hey, we're gonna do it next week!'

"So he didn't do it! The congressman in the Fourth District was a guy named Bill Alexander, and he didn't have a big race, and there wasn't a Senate race that year, so they had no reason to haul for the Democratic party—and Bill, he just didn't feel like I could beat him. So he didn't make the provision to do that! Which, some people say, it cost a quarter of a million dollars. I don't know, I've never hauled 'em, but hey! They take a bag o' money. All cash!

"So he didn't haul the black vote! And all of a sudden, over there in counties where he should have beaten me seventy-thirty, he beat me fifty-five-forty-five! And as we came towards Arkansas River valley, going up to northwest Arkansas, I started blowin' him out!"

A quintessential handshaker, Bill had belatedly become aware of the magnitude of the problem in the summer. "Rudy, they're killing me out there! They hate my guts," he told one of his three chiefs of staff after giving several speeches in the Texarkana area. In the days running up to the election the situation became yet worse, with even the members of his own extended family and relatives turning against him on the issue. His aunt Floris Tatom, for example, who worked in a courthouse near Hope, warned him in no uncertain terms about the car license fiasco and recommended he recall the legislature to repeal the act. As Frank White recalled, Clinton "panicked. He—one of the last things that he did—the story is told that he called John Miller (he was Speaker of the House at the time), he called John Miller and offered to have a special session to repeal the increase in the license fee!"

It was too late, however. Meanwhile, aware there was considerable ill feeling toward his triumvirate of young chiefs of staff and that their sixties beards had become especially resented, Clinton made the decision, according to Ernie Dumas, to demand that the Bearded Troika shave off their beards! "The conservative *Arkansas Democrat* was just hammering him, every day, in the newspaper's editorials and cartoons—assailing these hippie-looking characters who were running the government!" Dumas recounted. "So finally they were summoned out to the governor's mansion one Sunday morning."

Typically, Governor Bill Clinton was too timid to speak to Smith, Moore, and Danner directly. "Bill couldn't tell 'em—but Hillary called 'em out there," Dumas related. "And Hillary said, 'We want you to cut your beards. Shave your beards off!' And Steve [Smith] said, 'Okay, I'm going back.' And all of a sudden, one Monday morning, they showed up clean-shaven!"

But if Bill Clinton thought he could save his cascading polls by such a cosmetic measure, he was mistaken. One by one, he was forced to dispose of the formerly "bearded liberals" themselves.

For Bill Clinton, who had never served in the military and had no stomach for the most painful task of all—dismissing members of one's own staff—this was once again, like the edict on beards, too much for him to undertake himself. Steve Smith had known Bill Clinton intimately since the McGovern campaign, when they had both attended the Democratic National Convention. "Steve and Bill became the closest friends, for five or six years, from the time Bill was a teacher at the University of Arkansas, then when Clinton ran for Congress, and finally as attorney general," Dumas recalled. "Steve said, 'He was the closest friend I had in the world.' And now, today, Steve is not fond of Bill Clinton: they had a falling-out in the fall of 1980, before Bill lost the race." As head of Clinton's team investigating the desecration of Arkansas's remaining forests through clear-cutting, Smith had drawn the ire of some of the most influential businessmen in (and out of) the state. "We probably did too much head-bashing in the first term," Smith acknowledged afterward. "Part of it was that people like me on the staff were sort of smart-ass, and angered a lot of people. We were after every dragon in the land. I used language like 'corporate criminal,' which did not really endear the governor to the timber companies."

It did not. Fearful of alienating big corporations and wealthy businessmen in Arkansas, Clinton decided to fell his colleague rather than stop the felling of timber. "The falling-out was over the timber thing," Dumas recalled, "and Clinton decided he had to cut Steve loose, that he was disposable." Again, however, Clinton could not face the business—or the consequences. "And so Steve left, without even a parting good-bye from Clinton. Steve was pretty bitter about it, because, as he said, 'Bill was the closest friend I had in the world.' " They'd smoked pot together and planned so much that seemed noble and good, from improvements in education to improving the environment. " 'And all of a sudden,' Steve said, 'I was not part of his life at all. I never heard from him again.' "

Marks of Despair

Almost from the beginning of his governorship Bill had been on the defensive in public over the label "liberal"—synonymous in conservative circles of Arkansas with being "a commie." As the public disquiet mounted in the late, roasting summer of 1980, Frank White had heard from his own sources that there was an increasing atmosphere of panic in the governor's mansion. The second member of the triumvirate, accordingly, was thrown to the wolves.

"Basically, all the people that were with him the first time, they were all pushed aside," Dumas recalled. "John Danner was one of the 'three bearded liberals.' Bill and Hillary had met them someplace—they were not Arkies. And Danner was obviously a very bright guy, and so was his wife. But they were clearly not Arkies, and they didn't have much in common with people here. John came on the staff as part of the Bearded Troika, as they called them. And the cartoonists loved to lampoon 'em. But Danner didn't have a way about him. Everybody on the staff hated him, and his wife, Nancy, had some other job in the governor's office. And the two of them just pissed everybody off. And so, finally, there was a petition by the staff, apparently—people were going to walk out unless something was done about Nancy. Particularly Nancy, but both of 'em. So something had to be done about it."

Since Nancy (nicknamed "Peach") had been a bosom pal of Hillary since Yale, Hillary did not volunteer this time. Rudy Moore, the third of the triumvirate, told Dumas "he was called to the governor's mansion. And Bill and Hillary were there. And Rudy told Bill and Hillary about how everybody's upset, it's true everybody on the staff is upset about Nancy and John. And so Bill says, 'Yeah, yeah. I'm afraid they'll have to go. Rudy, eh, will you take care of that?' "

Moore was apparently stunned. "They were their dearest friends!" Moore afterward confided to Dumas, unable to credit the Clintons' casualness and cowardice, for, as Dumas recalled Moore telling him, "they had brought 'em in from California or someplace! And neither of 'em, Bill or Hillary, could face 'em!"

Moore, incredulous, nevertheless carried out the deed. "So Rudy had to go tell Danner and Pietrefesa 'You're out!' " Dumas shook his head compassionately, recalling Moore's account of the dismissal. " 'I don't know that Bill or Hillary ever said good-bye to 'em—they were just *gone*! And I had to take care of it! That was a terrible thing for me to do. I've never seen or heard from those two people since!' "

Though the manner of such firings smacked of arrogance, it was, as Dumas pointed out, the very opposite: a mark of Clinton's *weakness* in execution, not his ruthlessness. "Bill Clinton can't do it, he can't face 'em!" Dumas shook his head in exasperation at such failure of firm yet caring leadership. "Because he knows, and Hillary would know, that if he faced 'em, Bill would wind up saying, 'Oh, stay on board!' He *couldn't* do it! He *wouldn't* do it!"

To Dumas such a weak-kneed performance was, at one and the same time, pathetic and yet, for all that, "a desperately human trait!"

Rudy Moore, too, as executioner, would in turn be executed—but it was already too late. The election was sliding out of control, and such last-minute efforts, like the notion of calling an emergency session of the legislature to repeal the car tag taxes, were marks of despair.

A Creature of His Time

While Clinton's belated firings were a response to rumblings among his staff and stinging criticism in the press, the young governor's actions—blaming the very people he himself had appointed and failing to stand by programs, such as forestry conservation, that he himself had initiated—left a sour taste among his supporters. They left an even sourer taste among those who felt he should display character, one way or the other. Such people saw him, at the end of his two-year term of office, as vacillating, weak, juvenile, and too anxious for compromise to be an effective leader. "Here's a poser for Clinton fans," wrote journalist Paul Greenberg in the weekly *Arkansas Times,* in a piece entitled "Godzilla Versus the Hollow Man": "What political principle, aside from the vast importance to the nation of his own political destiny, runs consistently through Bill Clinton's career?

Take your time," Greenberg added; "it may require some to answer that one." Behind Clinton's self-portrait as "a good guy," Greenberg concluded, "there's nothing there."

But was it all a matter of character? Was not Bill's fumbling path between progress and tradition, idealism and realism, ambition and conscience a mark of his generation, tormented by a war foisted upon it by a previous generation of leaders and unable to set its dreams into the context of reality? Bill's own longtime aide when he was governor, Bobby Roberts, could see that, in retrospect, Bill mirrored his age: "Oh, absolutely. I mean, he's like all of us: he's a creature of his time!"

As a creature of politics, moreover, Roberts knew and accepted that Clinton would have to make concessions in order to get and stay elected: "I mean, it is a process of compromise, and there's nothing wrong with that— except in his case, because you have such high expectations of him, some people, I think, some of his supporters are let down by that."

They were: the picture of the country's youngest-serving governor, panic-stricken at the rising prospect of being beaten, dismissing his staff while being unable to face them in person, man to man or man to woman, creating a lasting sense of disappointment, if not bitterness.

Big, jolly-faced Frank White, by contrast, was filled with joy, watching the young politician, who was "too big for his boots," floundering.

When did White first realize he had a real chance of beating Bill Clinton? "About six days before the election!" White said later with a chuckle. When asked how he had known, White smiled like a Cheshire cat, his hands folded across his extensive stomach. "I had some big Democratic money in Arkansas that called me," he recalled with pleasure, "—said they wanted to help *me*!"

White shook his head at the recollection and laughed. If *Democratic* funders were now deserting the sinking ship, White realized, he was home free. "That told me they were looking at the polls! And they knew I was gonna beat him! And they decided they wanted to get on board!"

The end was cruelly simple. " 'Hey,' they said, 'what d'you need to do a good radio ad, and television?' "

Buy the Ads

Frank White, his heart pumping with excitement, told his prospective backers what he needed.

"I said, '$70,000 would help,' " White recalled. "I only had $250,000 in the

360 · BILL CLINTON

election, in the whole thing"—against a reputed $500,000 in Clinton's campaign war chest before he even began running for reelection. "I said, $70,000 would be dynamite. They said, '*Buy the ads!* You'll have it tomorrow!' "

Thus, funded by Democrats from his own party, a series of Republican ads hit the "Boy Wonder," pillorying his performance. They came like left hooks and brought the young governor to his knees.

In desperation, like a boxer unable to rise on his own, Bill asked Hillary to call Dick Morris, his previous trainer. It took time for Hillary to track Morris down in Florida and fly him to Arkansas. It was too late, however—and the special weapon Bill had reserved for such a crisis, namely Morris's negative advertising, failed to find a target to shoot at. "Well, hey! What could he say negative about me?" White grinned, shrugging his broad shoulders twenty years later. "I didn't have any record! I only had the Arkansas Economic Development Commission, where I'd done a good job."

Wearing his new Republican colors, Frank White had found his Democratic target with unerring accuracy. "I hit him hard on car tax—hard," White acknowledged, unashamed. "I had an ad that ran like a slot machine—just kinda rolled up how much the car tax was goin' up. And every time I'd run that ad on television, for about a week out there, he'd have dropped about five more points!"

Bill Is Indisposed

Still, Bill Clinton prayed for a miracle in the fall of 1980: that on polling day, electors would forgive and favor the incumbent.

For a brief moment, Bill's prayers seemed to have been answered. Given the high proportion of blacks living in or around Little Rock and the Delta, the early exit interviews "showed him beatin' me pretty good," White recalled. "I think I got fifteen percent of the black vote in the state, so on those exit polls they showed me losin'. And the two major [television] networks declared him the winner—in the first thirty minutes!"

It was a short-lived reprieve. "At ten o'clock they all put me back in the race," White remembered with satisfaction. "And we could see it comin'. When they called me and told me that in Benton County, the biggest in northwest Arkansas, I'd beaten him seventy-thirty, I knew I was gonna beat 'im. And I ate him *alive* in west Arkansas. He could see it comin'—he knew it was comin'."

Bill could—and was mortified. Just as he had failed to find the courage to speak personally to his staff members when firing them, so now also he could not find the courage even to call White and congratulate him. As White later recalled with another toss of his white-haired, leonine head, "He *never* conceded to me! Never! Never called me! His *wife* did! She said, 'Bill's indisposed right now and can't speak to you, and I'm calling to congratulate you.' "

It was an ignominious end to the youngest-ever elected governor of Arkansas and the youngest serving governor in America. The meteor had flamed—and gone out.

CHAPTER TWENTY-SIX

RECOVERY

Bursting into Tears

According to the young baby-sitter who arrived at the governor's mansion on the night of the November 1980 election, the governor was lying writhing on the floor of the front hall, kicking, screaming, and bawling like a baby.

Bill felt rejected; indeed, in a matter of weeks he would be *e*jected from the mansion. From youngest elected governor in the United States, he had become the youngest ever overthrown, after only two years in office. When he pulled himself together enough to address his staff and election workers, he burst into tears once again.

"My recollection of that," Jim Blair recounted, "was that they had a bunch of tents set up in the backyard of the mansion. And a bunch of us were down there"—invited both to be thanked for their support in the campaign and to celebrate the reelection of the governor. "When the [bad] news came in," Blair recalled, "he was really very upset, in tears. He had known that he had got behind, he had thought he had pulled it back—or wanted to feel he had pulled it back."

For some, the sight was pathetic: a child rather than a man. The famous Arkansas cartoonist George Fisher—who had marched with Patton's Third U.S. Army—had portrayed Bill throughout his governorship as an

oversized, curly-haired baby in his carriage. That picture now seemed uncannily appropriate.

Into the governor's mansion would be moving an older, divorced man
with children, but one who had seen the light in the literal scripture—indeed, was determined to pass a law requiring state teachers to teach once
more the biblical version of Genesis alongside Darwin's theory of evolution; a successor who believed in cutting taxes rather than promoting new
educational, social, and environmental programs. In this, Frank White
would be a carbon copy of the new Republican President taking over the
White House from Jimmy Carter—for Governor Ronald Reagan, also a
divorced man, had triumphed on a platform of reduced taxation, the
teaching of creationism, antiabortion measures, and a return to "traditional values." The countercounterrevolution had triumphed.

Most of Bill Clinton's friends, including Jim Blair, now counseled a
switch away from politics, while he was still only thirty-four years old. The
mood of the country had palpably changed, they pointed out; the New
Deal heritage of Democratic liberalism, in which people of wealth, privilege, and education had felt concern for the less advantaged, was clearly
over. The wealthy and the well-off now wanted more for their bucks—at
least, not to have to pay so many bucks in punitive taxation in order to help
others. Patriotism was trotted out to mask such self-centeredness, the new
President surfing the "Proposition 13" tax-revolt wave with extraordinary
skill for a seventy-year-old. As Reagan's assistant chief of staff, Michael
Deaver, unashamedly described the 1984 election, "We kept apple pie and
the flag going the whole time."

Control of the Senate passed to the Republicans for the first time in
twenty-six years. The New Right was jubilant, especially at Reagan's determination to stop the trashing of America's long and disastrous involvement in Vietnam but instead to paint it with retrospective pride as the
country's noble if doomed struggle to free Vietnam of dreaded communism—at whatever cost to Americans or others. Frustrated, President
Nixon, in his tape-recorded conversations with his national security adviser, Henry Kissinger, had actually proposed using nuclear weapons on
the North Vietnamese, regardless of civilian casualties—"You're so goddamned concerned about the civilians and I don't give a damn. I don't
care," Nixon had sneered in 1972   while Ronald Reagan, in seeking the
governorship of California, had proposed to "level Vietnam, pave it, paint
stripes on it and make a parking lot of it." Now, under Reagan's eloquent,

patriotic leadership, the New Right was legitimized not as gung ho nuclear madmen but as a combination of rugged American individualists and family wealth builders in the old pioneer tradition.

Instead of Vietnam it was government that was now trashed by Reagan. Fifty years after Roosevelt's New Deal, the federal bureaucracy was no longer seen as providing solutions to America's myriad social and economic problems. As Reagan had been fond of repeating during his campaign, government was the problem, as were liberal ideals. For the average American citizen, Reagan had added, "The message is clear—liberalism is no longer the answer, it is the problem."

Bill Clinton was understandably depressed. "You need to go out and make some money! You know, do something out in the real economic world," Jim Blair told him.

But if Democrat Bill Clinton left government after a mere two years as Arkansas governor, what would he do? Teach law again? He had never wished to be a law professor; it paid little and had always been but a stepping-stone into Arkansas and then national politics: to the U.S. Congress, the Senate—and ultimately the White House.

Teach political science, as Governor Michael Dukakis would later do in Massachusetts after his defeat? But Bill had studied politics at Georgetown and Oxford to be a *player,* not an observer.

Go into business? Though he was interested in economics as an aspect—a crucial aspect—of political science, Bill had no interest in money itself, or *for* himself. "I mean, he's never cared about money," Blair reflected with a mix of admiration and disdain. "And if he had some, he'd be just apt to give it away. I mean, money's never been a problem"—though it could be when he allowed others to act on his behalf. By letting his aide Jim McDougal persuade Hillary and himself to invest in the Whitewater property development in the Ozarks, he had unthinkingly put himself in harm's way. McDougal had previously involved both Senator Fulbright and Congressman Jim Guy Tucker in his real estate schemes, and Clinton had no reason to question his ability. Neither he nor Hillary had ever visited the site or was interested in it other than as a speculative venture promoted by their friends—a friendship that, however, had cooled considerably as Hillary fell out with Jim, Whitewater lost money, and Bill was kicked out by the voters of the state. A long, four-hour drive from Little Rock, Whitewater had simply not been a success: the high level of inflation that had marred Jimmy Carter's term of office as President (rocketing from 8 to 20 percent) had destroyed any chance of the investment paying off. Instead of the failed McDougal Whitewater speculation simply ending there, in 1980, however, it would become subsumed in Reagan's catastrophic savings and loan disaster, as the new administration demanded complete deregulation and the lifting of restrictions on the federal savings and loans and the Department of Housing and Urban Development—thus licensing the cash-starved McDougal virtually to print money via a small bank he bought, and an S and L he then started.

Reagan's ideological belief in unrestricted and deregulated capitalism was designed to free up the stalled engine of the vast American economy. In due course it did precisely that. On the way, however, it facilitated corruption and loose accounting, encouraging Jim McDougal and thousands of speculators across America to use Franklin Roosevelt's Depression-era government guarantee of ordinary people's funds, backed by the U.S. government, to indulge in swindling on a vast scale—resulting, in the state of Arkansas, in a series of scandals collectively known by the name of one of its more trivial failures, Whitewater: a scandal in which, although loan deregulation was the love child of Republicans, only Democrats would be prosecuted!

In the meantime, however, former governor Bill Clinton—who had even less knowledge than federal bank and loan examiners about McDougal's endlessly rolling collateral loans to keep the little Whitewater investment from bankruptcy—was clearly not cut out for the joys or vicissitudes of business, whatever well-meaning friends such as Jim Blair might urge.

A Leaf out of Churchill's Book

Defeat is hard for any human being to bear.

Conscientiously William Jefferson Clinton tried to bone up on stories of great statesmen who had suffered reverses—such as Winston Churchill, who, resigning in 1931, had left the British government and repaired to his country estate (bought for him by political admirers) in Chartwell, Kent, not far from London. There he could concentrate upon authorship, while constructing an English walled garden around his proverbial castle.

What had Churchill achieved politically by such retreat, though? In order to curry favor with Britain's right-wing conservatives and financiers who might assist him back into power, he had become an embarrassingly racist, flag-waving British imperialist, making it his life's task to frustrate the British Labour government's move to grant colored India independence (or dominion status) alongside white Canada, Australia, and New Zealand. The political development of India had thereby deliberately been set back almost two decades, leading to its tragic and ultimately bloody partition into Pakistan and India.

It was not an example Bill Clinton was minded to follow.

Nor, indeed, did Bill Clinton have Churchill's laurels to fall back upon, laurels that even at that stage of Churchill's life, a decade before World War II, had crowned a long career stretching from the life of a swashbuckling young subaltern on India's northwest frontier with Afghanistan through battle in the Sudan and the Boer War in South Africa to ministerial rank under Lord Asquith as First Lord of the Admiralty and, after Allied defeat in the Dardanelles, command of an infantry battalion in World War I, ministership of munitions, responsibility for Britain's colonies, and chancellorship of the Exchequer . . .

By contrast, Bill Clinton had never worn military uniform—only the uniform of a high school band player. Instead of the military training that might have made a man of him, he'd suffered what amounted to a nervous breakdown over the Vietnam draft, running away from his obligations to old England and reneging on his commitment to serve in the ROTC. Thereafter he had learned and then briefly taught constitutional law; then had served as attorney general of Arkansas for a mere two years and as governor of one of America's smallest states for a single two-year term. If this was food for the great American novel he had once thought of writing, it would, Bill knew, have few readers.

But if not his own life, what about the life of the party—the Democratic Party? There was much to be questioned and said about the failure of the modern Democratic Party, in its post-Roosevelt, post-Johnson phase. Somehow, despite the noblest of intentions, it had clearly failed to find public support as Reagan Republicanism and the New Right were clearly doing—and Bill's own failure at the polls in Arkansas, a traditionally Democratic state, was proof of this. Taking a leaf out of Churchill's book, could not Bill pen a critique of that larger American political development? Even a much-needed political history of Arkansas and its men and women of distinction might well have done Bill Clinton a host of good in terms of literary name recognition. Senator John F. Kennedy's book *Profiles in Courage* had, after all, won the Pulitzer Prize for biography in 1957. Such a work would have redounded to the credit of Bill Clinton's political image, statewide and across the South—even nationally. It would also have been therapeutic, given the hurt and rejection he was feeling. Political analysis and biographical writing, in other words, might have done the thirty-four-year-old a power of good.

Unfortunately Bill Clinton lacked then—as he would later—the focus or will to concentrate on such a historical-political project: too shamed by his rejection at the public's hands and too angry that he had "screwed up" despite his superior education. He felt he had been "whacked between the eyes" by the voters, as he put it, and could simply not stand back and see his own downfall, like Jimmy Carter's, as part of a national swing toward the New Right, with implications that needed perhaps to be addressed by the now trailing Democratic Party of Franklin D. Roosevelt, Harry Truman, John F. Kennedy, and Lyndon Baines Johnson, author of the Great Society—whose great policy was, in terms of minorities, now a shambles.

Instead Bill Clinton wrung his hands, asking everyone he met what he had done wrong to deserve such a fate and what he should do now. At no point did he really look inward and address the vacuousness in his soul and the deep, indeed tragic, inconsistencies in his style of leadership.

Commutations

Had Bill Clinton's hand-wringing been all, it would have been enough. However, in the waning days of his defeated governorship, he tempted yet more fate by granting a series of pardons that brought yet more scorn down upon his tearful head—as would happen in an almost identical manner two decades later!

"The thing I remember," recalled Jim Blair, "but nobody else seems to, is that in the campaign of 1980 they were saying 'Cubans and car tags.' But I am remembering *commutations*, Cubans, and car tags—I'm remembering triple C here! I remember the commutations, in the light of his later pardons."

Blair was right, as Betsey Wright, who would be brought in to mastermind Bill's return to office, had cause to know. "I mean, the biggest problems that we had in his comeback campaign in '82 were all of the pardons and clemencies that he gave as he left office in '80–'81, when he was defeated! I mean, it was *so* bad that he had even given commutations to first-degree murderers that nobody was recommending—and one of them had gone out and killed again!"

Betsey was at a loss to understand why Clinton had done such a thing, other than that he was riven with shame at his failure in the public eye and wished in some strange way to atone in a symbolic manner. "I don't know why he commuted them," Betsey sighed, "because all of his staff was arguing against that too!" To be sure, "he knew that Governor Rockefeller had commuted an awful lot of sentences and pardons and things—but, my God! The whole justice system and prison system had been so *different* when Rockefeller came in."

Now, in the aftermath of defeat, the departing governor was a mess—and for a while ran away. "Mr. Clinton has been vacationing in Mexico since his defeat by Republican Governor-elect Frank D. White," the Associated Press reported. For a moment, fuming on a Mexican beach, he seemed tempted by the possibility of an alternative political job—chairing the national Democratic Party in Washington or even fronting one of the large liberal interest groups, People for the American Way, even relocating to California and working for Governor Jerry Brown as his chief of staff in Sacramento. Unsure, the vanquished governor, on his return to America, flew backward and forward to Washington and the West Coast.

In California, however, Bill Clinton saw only how brilliantly the former B-movie actor, President-elect Ronald Reagan, was beginning to bewitch the nation from his ranch, using a blend of simplistic rhetoric and a homespun style.

Like Clinton, the sixty-nine-year-old Ronald Reagan had been brought up the son of an alcoholic father. Tall and good-looking for a man of his age, Reagan was completely at home in front of the camera. He'd managed to parlay his failure to serve overseas in World War II, as well as his divorce (from starlet Jane Wyman) and remarriage (to a small-time actress, Nancy Davis, who promptly gave up her career), into a moral crusade to clean up the excesses of the sixties and restore America to a mythic past, dominated by 1950s-style anticommunism and family values. Democrats and intellectuals were aghast, but, commenting on the "amiable dunce" (as Congressman Tip O'Neill was heard to call the new President), Bill Moyers remarked, "We didn't elect this guy because he knows how many barrels of oil are in Alaska. We elected him because we want to feel good."

Reagan's presidential performance was mesmerizing in its political effectiveness. In the weeks, months, indeed virtually the decade after his election as President, his personal popularity would override the worst scandals of Republican and Republican-sponsored greed in the twentieth century, as the American national debt soared from $900 billion to $2.7 trillion and the cost of the savings and loan and HUD scandals milked taxpayers of $500 billion. Reagan, with his endless fictions, use of popular myths, vague memory, and remoteness behind the amiable facade, would survive unscathed—untainted even by the Iran-Contra scandal despite the testimony of all concerned that the President had known of, indeed had authorized, the sale of arms for hostages and the use of the financial proceeds for right-wing guerrillas in Nicaragua, in clear defiance of Congress. Far from being impeached, the wartime noncombatant would be hailed as an authentic American hero who had steered America out of its post–Vietnam War "malaise" and, via his relentless military buildup, had bankrupted the Soviet Union's "evil empire," which could simply no longer compete with America on the world stage. The Hollywood actor had won not only his spurs but his people's hearts.

Against such a formidable Republican foe, able to bring together and to lead religious fundamentalists, racists, and selfish capitalists, what chance did old-fashioned Democrats have, attempting to hold together a more and more fractured coalition of minorities and minority interests that traded on altruistic liberal notions sanctified under FDR: notions of social conscience and care for the underprivileged? "We will mine more, drill more, cut more timber," prophesied Reagan's brash new interior secretary, James Watt—and the words had a symbolic, openly callous, selfish ring to them, as "deregulation" and military buildup became the mantra of the ideological Right.

War and American military preparedness for war had always been the bugbear of the Democrats. After President Eisenhower ended the Korean War, JFK's brief attempt to hit the Republicans from the right by leading the Democratic Party into an ever-tougher military stance even than that of Vice President Richard Nixon had secured the White House—just—for the Democrats in 1960. But it had also led, the following year, to the Bay of Pigs disaster, a world-threatening military standoff over missiles in Cuba, and then, more tragically, to war in Vietnam—an albatross the Democratic Party would never wholly escape.

Bill Clinton certainly possessed the intellect to analyze such historical and cultural trends, as his old Rhodie-and-Yale friend Robert Reich now did in a series of books and manifestos. For psychological reasons, however, Bill Clinton lacked the relentless intellectual focus required to pen such work. Nor did he feel confidence in his ability to provide answers—es-

370 · BILL CLINTON

pecially answers that might later be used against him by adversaries. Thus the youngest-ever governor of Arkansas, and the youngest serving governor in the United States, left office without taking up his pen.

What would he do? The Clintons hurriedly bought, for $112,000, an empty 1910 yellow-and-white wooden clapboard house on Midland Avenue, in a nice white middle-class area of Little Rock called Pulaski Heights, where Chelsea, as she grew older, could go to school. Yet even there, on the deep wraparound porch, Bill seemed unable to sit back and contemplate either the currents of world history or the different possibilities he might pursue, in terms of a job, before possibly making a comeback. Ronald Reagan, after all, had stood aside from political office for *years* after his retirement as governor of California and his failure to beat Vice President Ford for the Republican nomination for the presidency in 1976. But then, Reagan was not a defeated governor of his home state. Bill Clinton was. And it rankled.

"A Sick Butt"

"After he lost the election," Jim Blair reflected, Bill Clinton "didn't want to take all that responsibility for it! He wanted to blame it on Jimmy Carter, and the Cubans down here."

Clinton's agonizing search for culprits for his defeat and uncertainty over his own personal future upset many of his outgoing staff, who found themselves without even the prospect of a job in the growing recession. "You sonofabitch!" one of his aides snapped after one typical Clinton lament. "You've got every offer. You can do all these things. What are *we* gonna do? What am *I* gonna do? You've got everything in the world!"

It was true. Bill Clinton had a wife earning—now—a big salary at the Rose Law Firm, having been made a partner and having pocketed a veritable fortune in 1979 on her ultimately notorious cattle trades as first lady. Bill Clinton would hardly be a pauper.

But defeat still festered—and the only way to erase that hurt, Bill felt in his heart of hearts, was to externalize: to blame circumstances and others. And to run for something, again, in Arkansas.

"I said, 'Bill, it's too early,' " Blair recalled pleading with his friend, '*don't do it!*'

"He looked me straight in the eyes, and he said, 'There's nothing else I want to do.'

"I thought, Man! You're a sick butt!"

"Bill! Get over It!"

In the final weeks before having to surrender the imposing, absurdly small, yet at the same time delightfully intimate three-bedroom governor's mansion to Governor Frank White, Bill Clinton telephoned his old colleague from the McGovern campaign in Texas, Betsey Wright.

"He called me a week after he was defeated in '80 and said, 'Can you come and see if anything can be salvaged?' " Betsey recalled. "And that's when I came—at the end of '80, a few days after he had been defeated.

"It was a blow to both of them. And he was in such a state of what I called self-punishment—for *months* after I got here! Going around asking people to tell him how he screwed up. He would then—not to that person, but to the next—he would be rationalizing around that. I mean, he had the most masochistic ability to get up every day and go find somebody else to tell him how he screwed up! And I thought after a point it was sort of repetitive, that he didn't need to keep doing it. But he didn't stop. And Hillary would say, 'Bill! Get over it!' "

Hillary could at least go to work. Bill, however, though he took an office within a Little Rock law firm, *was* work—Hillary's and Betsey's. Both listened to Bill's self-flagellation with womanly patience but diminishing sympathy. "I listened to this guy ask people, 'Tell me what I did wrong!' and I listened to people's theories about what came out. And it was 'the Bearded Troika,' and it was 'Hillary's name,' and it was 'You got too big for your britches,' and it was 'Cubans and car tags' and all of that stuff," Betsey recalled. "But in reality—in terms of an image of him governing—the problem was that *he did too many things!* He and the young staff assumed that they could fix everything at once—when it would take two or three terms! And we found out that no one could say anything concrete, name any good, that Bill had done as governor. They could name bad things, but they were just parroting Frank White's ads from '80; they knew Bill had done *something* good, they just didn't know what it was!"

Here was an unusual challenge—and Betsey's first job thus became archiving the records of what Governor Clinton *had* done. "I was just stunned at how primitive the campaign records were," Betsey recalled. "But of course, why would they need to be very sophisticated, when he was just the golden boy who was going to win everything? So I was into developing software programs and computerizing it, trying to get familiar with all the names and what the political lay of the land was."

There was no question in her mind but that Bill would return to politics—it was merely a matter of when and in what capacity. Former senator Fulbright had cautioned against taking the chairmanship of the Democratic Party National Committee, as it would have necessitated moving to Washington, away from Arkansas, for a minimum of four years. If he wished to return ever to elective office, Fulbright advised, Bill should stay at home. "We always knew that he would run again. We didn't know it would be for the '82 election," however, Betsey recounted. For that determination they would await the results of regular polling. Meanwhile, Betsey "stayed in the basement of the governor's mansion, and then when they bought their house on Midland, I stayed there with them." Until finally, having fetched her things from Washington, Betsey got her own place in Little Rock.

Betsey was smart, hardworking, relentlessly focused. She would become Bill Clinton's amah and his vizier: his Joseph on the path back to power. If he could pull himself together.

Depression

Far from trying to find a more profound relationship with Hillary based on mutual respect, Bill seemed to have lost all self-respect. Neighbors called them "Bill's dark years." They would see Hillary, but rarely Bill, who "stayed up late into the night in his first-floor room that had been converted to a study," making telephone calls. Wallowing in self-pity, he sought to drown his humiliation and despair in more and more womanizing. He complained to Gennifer Flowers, for example, of Hillary's somewhat frigid personality. He called her the Sarge or Hilla the Hun. "I thought I was giving him something he wasn't getting at home," Gennifer recalled—especially once he introduced her to "things I'd never done before, like oral sex. We made love all over the apartment, not just in the bedroom—on the floor, in the kitchen, on the couch—even in the shower." When Gennifer warned him she'd heard rumors that Hillary was a lesbian, Bill merely laughed, snidely remarking, "Honey, she's probably eaten more pussy than I have," According to what Bill told Gennifer, Hillary was all business, with no interest in bedtime frolics. She wasn't willing to try new things, and insisted on no other position than missionary. It was, he claimed, deeply disappointing—so clearly a duty rather than a pleasure—and Gennifer wanted to believe him. According to the best and most painstaking biographer of Bill's early years, David Maraniss, not only did rumors of this affair with Gennifer and others abound, but Bill was even heard to chant, as he played with his one-year-old daughter, "I want a div-or-or-or-orce!"

Divorce, however, was no solution. Nor was the office in the kindly Little Rock law firm, Wright, Lindsey and Jennings, which gave him a modest income similar to that which he'd earned in the governor's mansion ($33,000). Bill was expected, indeed employed, to bring in new clients after his precocious years in the attorney general's and governor's offices. But Bill was clearly not interested in law itself. He had never tried a case nor even filed a suit—and he was not about to start. He missed having a free car and driver, free food, household servants, a staff catering to his whims, his charm, his *amour propre* . . . and amours. At Wright, Lindsey and Jennings he even had to do his own photocopying. The firm did not bear his name. He felt a nobody in it.

It was in this situation that Dick Morris was summoned to Little Rock by a worried Hillary yet again.

The height-impaired New York strategist found the former governor whining about having to live in the little yellow frame house on Midland Avenue and having do his own laundry after two years in the governor's mansion. "I found him in this state of confusion when I returned," Morris recalled with near contempt. "I saw that it would be futile to talk him out of his depression." Bill was simply floundering in helplessness, while "pretending to practice law for the Wright firm," as his attorney friend Jim Blair caustically put it.

The saddest part, to Morris, was that Bill Clinton seemed incapable of drawing any personal lessons from his defeat. He saw only that he had "screwed up" in his reelection campaign—not that he needed to mature as a human being and as a leader of men and women if he wished to go back into government.

Thus, from this second electoral defeat Bill Clinton seemed to learn nothing personal or spiritual, save that his script should next time be better written and that he and his staff needed to work harder to win back and hang on to his crown. The real issues—learning to become a leader through self-discipline, decisiveness, determination, depth, and self-critical honesty—were simply either ignored or overlooked. Winning back became all, with no compromise or sacrifice too big to further his avenging agenda.

When Morris, working with Betsey Wright and having polled voters, found that the deposed governor was widely considered by Arkansans to have been too big for his britches and that the election upset had been their way of showing their resentment, Bill refused at first to agree to Morris's idea that he should go before electors and apologize. "But Clinton didn't want to apologize," Morris recalled—for the former governor could see nothing he had done wrong. "How was I going to improve roads," Bill retorted, "without getting the money from someplace?"

"Wake up! People believed it was wrong!" Hillary was heard screaming one morning as Bill, cowering and with his head in his hands, walked outside their house. "Can't you see that?"

Achilles Heel

Bill never would accept he was wrong or apologize for his own behavior or actions. Accepting blame was, as his friend Jim Blair reflected, beyond him—as, when he was a child, he had been loath to admit to his stepfather he'd done wrong, knowing he would be paddled. The lack of a real father, Blair felt, had been a crucial missing link in his makeup. "There's not a father there. His mother is a very domineering woman. She praises him and extols him and thinks he's the most wonderful thing in the world. But if he has done something she disapproves of, he's not going to take the blame for it! He's—I think it goes back to his relationship with Virginia," Blair speculated. The relationship explained, for Blair, his "unwillingness at any time to accept responsibility for his own actions—as when he got beat for governor."

The inability to address or realize the truth about himself—that he had proved a disappointing administrator and needed to learn new lessons in self-discipline and leadership, starting in his own life—was potentially debilitating. "This guy has evolved zero," Hillary's exiled bosom pal, Peach Pietrefesa, later reflected with some bitterness. "Einstein's definition of insanity," she mused, thinking of Bill as a prime example, "is doing the same thing over and over again and expecting a different result."

Had it been anybody else, Bill Clinton's political career might indeed have run into the proverbial sand—one of many thousands of wanna-be politicians who dreamed of high position but lacked, in the end, the moral fiber necessary to stay the course. But in Bill Clinton's case a wonderful native instinct had caused the beaten politician to turn to those few people on earth who could, in fact, restore him to his throne. With their patient, focused help and guidance William Jefferson Clinton would find himself rescued from historical oblivion not by his own inner spiritual maturation but by several extraordinary characters beyond his fractured ego who believed in him and in his promise: Betsey Wright and Dick Morris. And Hillary Rodham: his breadwinning, loyal wife and mother to Chelsea, their beloved daughter.

The New Triumvirate

Two of Bill's three top aides as Governor—John Danner and Steve Smith—had already been thrown to the wolves; the third, the tireless Rudy Moore, would soon be cast away. The aides had, it was true, upset a number of influential people. Certainly John Robert Starr, the influential *Arkansas Democrat* editor and political columnist, blamed Clinton's Bearded Troika for his defeat. "Had Clinton been a student of history instead of the law," Starr tartly noted in retrospect, "he would not have tried to divide his power three ways. Triumvirates did not work in Rome. This one did not work in Arkansas."

This sounded clever on paper. But the parallel was wrong, as Ronald Reagan now brilliantly demonstrated. Using the triumvirate of James Baker III, Edwin Meese III, and Michael Deaver as his chiefs of staff, President Reagan, former Hollywood actor and Screen Actors Guild president, managed to co-opt a Democratic Congress in Washington and run the ship of American state with amazing dexterity, despite recession, inflation, and even a dramatic air traffic controllers' strike. Leadership, Reagan understood, was really the ability to decide upon priorities and, under a mantle of unwavering decision-making at the top, choose effective people to ensure those decisions were carried out.

Each member of Bill's *new* triumvirate—Betsey, Dick, and Hillary— was hyperintelligent. Each was capable of relentless focus on what needed to be done to succeed. Yet none of them possessed Bill's charismatic ability to inspire mass affection. Thus they all looked to "the Wonder Boy," knowing he had a talent for communication, empathy, and the generation of affinity. With his photographic memory, enormous intelligence, and range of knowledge from popular music to literature and history, he could make it to the very top—whereas none of them, individually, could do so. Thus it was that even though Betsey Wright disliked Dick Morris and though Hillary Rodham was nervous about entrusting Bill's career to another woman, they all, collectively, believed in The Candidate.

Only one of Bill's first triumvirate survived his governorship—to be cast off shortly thereafter. Only one member of the new triumvirate would survive the renewed journey with Bill. Who that person would be, in the next years, remained to be seen.

Meanwhile, "As we watched Clinton speak," Morris recalled a speech Bill made a year after his defeat, "I said to Hillary, 'He could be president.'"

"We have to get him elected governor first," was Hillary's calm response.

CHAPTER TWENTY-SEVEN

THE COMEBACK

Spinning the Hero

Buoyed by the faith of others and gradually developing a Reagan-like ability to construct a personal mythology that appealed to people's goodwill and would allow him to ride the inevitable waves and storms he would encounter ("I am an orphan Democrat from Hope, Arkansas; my Granpappy ran a store which catered to black people as well as white; I was raised a Southern Baptist, and to know right from wrong. I have traveled and have worked hard at my studies. I play the saxophone. I mean well. I believe in education and in progress . . ."), Bill Clinton went about his resurrection as governor of Arkansas in 1981—aided and abetted by Betsey Wright, Dick Morris, his own wife, Hillary, as well as an extended family of relatives and friends who "developed" what Bill's old neighbor, Carolyn Staley, called "a spin to their lives to make Bill the conquering hero."

Arkansas history did not favor comebacks. Only two other governors of the state had been booted from office after one term; neither of them had been able to fight their way back to the governor's mansion—indeed, no former governor had *ever* been reelected after losing his crown.

Undeterred, in a corner outside Bill Clinton's downtown law office in Little Rock, Betsey set about putting the ten thousand card indexes of

Clinton financial contributors, staff, volunteers, journalists, and well-wishers onto computer. She also arranged a schedule of talks and meetings for Clinton across the state—anxious, always, that Bill stay within telephone contact and not get himself "into trouble." According to Bobby Roberts—who took leave of absence from his studies to be Bill's personal driver in his own ten-year-old Oldsmobile—Betsey was successful. "As God is my witness," Roberts recalled, "the whole time I traveled with him, I never saw him do anything other than be flirtatious."

If so, Bill was learning to be more discreet, for his amorous exploits were well known to other aides. Ten years older than Bill, Betsey Wright had few illusions. Nor did she blame Bill entirely, for it was most often the women who came on to Bill, rather than the other way around. "The frustrations I went through in the eight years of being his chief of staff" Wright recalled as being an almost perpetual trial, forced as she was to watch "the groupie girls hanging around and fawning all over him."

Politics in 1980s America, it had to be said, was as contradictory as sexual politics. In the wake of the feminist movement, women, or the majority of women, now wanted greater equality in employment as well as in the home. Hillary Rodham was already ahead of this curve—indeed, in her case Hillary was earning almost twice as much as Bill at the Rose Law Firm and from her directorships and investments. Yet if feminism discouraged male chauvinism, it did little to rein back those women who enjoyed flirting, tempting, and taunting men—especially iconic, rich, or powerful men—and who now felt more licensed to do so than in earlier times. The way young women fawned over Bill was, increasingly, akin to the pubescent infatuations of schoolgirls for pop stars, while mature women also fluttered their eyes appealingly. It was perhaps inevitable that Bill Clinton would take advantage of such a cornucopia; indeed, it would have taken a man of much greater self-control and character than Bill Clinton to fight off the swooning attention he aroused. Like a pop star, Bill did not bother—indeed, he went out of his way, like his own earlier idol, JFK, to elicit it. "You got to go back to Aisle Thirty and look!" he'd rush to tell the *Arkansas Gazette* reporter John Brummett while visiting a branch of Wal-Mart, the Arkansas company for which Hillary's law firm acted, "—she's a knockout." At night, having asked for the young lady's phone number, he'd call and make verbal love to her: enjoying the chase and the promise of, possibly, oral love, his favorite. "Bill was always very careless, out of an unbelievable naiveté," Wright reflected on his philogyny. "He has a defective shit detector about personal relationships."

Wright was not worried on Hillary Rodham's account. Not only was the Clinton-Rodham marriage a political partnership that Bill would be crazy to dissolve, but it had a deeper, more interesting chemistry than many outsiders could fathom. Hillary was still emotionally buttoned up; she went forth each day like a lady knight in armor, unwilling to show the least chink, softness, or weakness. She had had no compunctions about leaving baby Chelsea with a nanny while flying to a regional Bar Association meeting in Memphis, as her former friend Peach Pietrefesa had observed, for Hillary Rodham was a feminist lawyer working a man's world and would accept no one's pity or even sympathy. The "gray area" where a woman's determination to succeed in her career intersects with mothering was simply white, according to Peach. "Hillary denied any concerns whatsoever on that front. Raising the gray area, I discovered, was horrifically threatening to her. She denied having any ambivalence. She'd say, 'I am absolutely sure, and I don't even want to discuss this.' "

Such no-nonsense, black-and-white certainty was a blessing for Bill, who was perpetually and by nature unsure about everything. "It was awful watching him so-called govern," Pietrefesa commented. "He never committed himself to anything. His word couldn't be counted on."

Hillary's could. She wanted to be crystal clear; he wanted to look at every angle, every configuration, every perspective before deciding on his view—and then would change it, at the next encounter, to a different opinion. This made him infuriating as an executive but made the two of them— Hillary and Bill—a formidable couple, like twins, devoted to each other's accomplishments. Thus Bill remained genuinely proud and respectful of Hillary—whom he considered the "smartest woman I've ever known"— while Hillary remained doggedly certain Bill could eventually become President of the United States, if he were reelected governor. To achieve this end, they would use Dick Morris's despised but effective secret weapon, negative advertising; indeed, they would do more, they decided. Bill began going to church—the Immanuel Baptist Church of Little Rock, where many of the city's top business leaders, socially prominent residents, and lawyers worshiped—but also a church where Bill would be seen by Arkansas voters on television every Sunday, singing behind the minister, W. O. Vaught, in the choir. Hillary and Chelsea remained firmly established on the rolls of the First Methodist Church, on the other side of town. Meanwhile new polls were conducted that showed Governor White becoming less than unanimously popular—and therefore vulnerable to a Clinton comeback already in 1982.

"There was always an assumption that, if it was feasible for him to run in '82, that I would run the campaign," Betsey recalled. "And if that wasn't feasible, we'd just figure just how far down the line . . . I mean, I always knew he would run again, we just didn't know it would be that soon. But it became so clear from the polling that we did in September–October [1981] that Frank White did not win that [1980] election: that Bill Clinton lost it."

With the "Scopes II" trial in December 1981, it now became Governor Frank White's turn to lose.

Scopes II

Act 590 had been passed by the Arkansas legislature and signed into law by Governor White as one of his first contributions to Arkansas educational development: a bill requiring that all Arkansas public schools should teach "creationist science," or Bible-dictated anti-Darwinism, giving it equal time alongside the teaching of evolutionary biology.

Once again, like Governor Faubus's use of the National Guard to stop black children going to white public school in 1957, the episode would make the state of Arkansas look bigoted and regressive. A U.S. Supreme Court ruling had in 1968 made the enforced teaching of creationism—the literal interpretation of the Bible's Old Testament, that God created the earth, including animals and man, in six days—definitively unconstitutional on First Amendment grounds. Governor White's personal Bible group, as well as other fundamentalist congregations in Arkansas, however, had persuaded the state legislature to defy the U.S. Supreme Court— and, like Faubus before him, White had decided to approve their new law rather than warn the people of Arkansas of the federal consequences. As under Faubus, these had come quickly, in federal court in Little Rock— where Bill Clinton's successor as attorney general was forced, on behalf of the governor, to argue the Arkansas case *for* creationism!

Named "Scopes II" after the infamous 1925 Dayton, Tennessee, case, the trial brought six of the world's foremost natural scientists and professors of the philosophy of science and theology, to Little Rock. Since expert testimony had been disallowed by the judge in Scopes I, it put real scientists on the witness stand in a public trial for the first time in the twentieth century, testifying on behalf of the American Civil Liberties Union. As *The Arkansas Traveler* quipped, "The Creation-Science act did, however, in White's favor, bring more scholars to the state than his teacher's salaries could have. The problem is, most of these scholars spoke against Frank White and his act."

Professor Stephen Jay Gould, doyen of evolutionary science in America, later recalled the occasion well—indeed, he saw the trial as something essentially and distinctively American, as much as "apple pie and Uncle Sam." It was also, he recorded, a landmark in the cultural evolution of the United States in the twentieth century. As he later described it, Governor White's "movement to impose creationism upon the public school science curricula" reflected "distinctively American contrasts" or oppositions—including "North versus South, urban versus rural, rich versus poor, local or state control versus federal standards." Beginning with the Pilgrims at Plymouth, Gould pointed out, Protestantism in America had "diversified into a rich range of sects, spanning the full gamut of conceivable forms of worship and belief"—some unfortunately more virulently fundamentalist than others. Thus "a few groups—mostly Southern, rural, and poor" had "dug in against all 'modernism' with a literalist reading not subject to change, or even argument: 'Gimme that old-time religion. It was good enough for grandpa, and it's good enough for me.' "

To the year he died, Professor Gould would never forget the second-grade Arkansas teacher who, asked to testify how he currently taught the age of the planet Earth to his students, explained he did so by stretching a string across the classroom and placing the children at appropriate points along it to mark the origin of life, the death of the dinosaurs, and lastly the human beginnings next to the wall at the string's end. In cross-examination, the assistant attorney general had then asked a question he later regretted: "What would you do under the equal-time law if you had to present the alternative view that the earth is only ten thousand years old?" The teacher replied tersely, "I guess I'd have to get a short string." An anti-Darwinist scholar brought over from the Indian subcontinent to counter the evolutionists, when asked "What do you think of the idea that earth is only ten thousand years old?" responded tartly, "Worse nonsense."

The trial was, for Governor Frank White (who claimed he hadn't read the bill carefully before signing it into Arkansas law), a disaster. Bill Clinton had been portrayed by the *Arkansas Gazette*'s cartoonist, George Fisher, as a baby in a carriage. Governor White was now drawn by Fisher in an even more belittling pose: as a prehuman ape with a half-eaten banana in his hand!

The trial, which ended with the state's defeat in court, was another black mark in its long history of backwardness—only this time a backwardness deliberately foisted upon small children. It was, as *The Arkansas Traveler* afterward commented, "a fiasco to say the least." Professor Gould left Little Rock relieved, feeling he'd performed a useful, indeed important task in protecting the next American generation from the willful ignorance of religious zealots. On the plane, going to the bathroom, however, he was stopped by a man who, he recalled, "said in a local accent, 'Mr. Gould, I wanna thank you for comin' on down here and heppin' us out with this little problem.' 'Glad to do it,' I replied, 'but what's your particular interest in the case? Are you a scientist?' He chuckled and denied the suggestion. 'Are you a businessman?' I continued. 'Oh no,' he finally replied, 'I used to be the governor.' "

Mea Culpa

Sitting in coach class on the flight out of Little Rock, Bill Clinton had reason to be grateful. His successor had made a royal blunder. If Bill played his cards right, he would soon have back his free vehicle with a state trooper as driver and be able to travel in first class.

With that agenda in mind, one new card Bill intended to play was Hillary.

"I had so much admiration for her abilities," Betsey Wright later recalled. "I had so much appreciation for the Devil's advocate role that she played with Bill. And he was always stronger after this. More sure of what he believed in or how he wanted to say it. So I really wanted her involved more than she would ever be involved. She did have to go make a living."

For a start, it was agreed that Hillary should go harass Governor Frank White wherever he was speaking, once the campaign began—knowing that, as a southern gentleman, he would find it difficult to respond to a woman opponent.

But first Morris—who had wrecked Governor Mike Dukakis's chances of reelection in Massachusetts by running a negative campaign for his Republican opponent, Ed King—resurrected his brilliant and—for Morris—novel idea. Former governor Bill Clinton should, he insisted, go down on bended knee and in a series of TV commercials apologize to the electorate for having imposed the car taxes and granted unwarranted clemencies and commutations. Not only would voters—in a Protestant state where forgiveness is a biblical injunction—forgive him, Morris reckoned, but the former governor's admission that he'd made bad mistakes would inure him to subsequent attack by opponents—whether rival Democrats or Governor White himself—in the November election.

Betsey Wright was all for the TV spots—"what I call the *mea culpa* ads, saying that it was mistaken, he'd never do it again, before he ever announced that he was gonna run."

Bill, however, refused—prefiguring a far more traumatic refusal fifteen years later.

Clintonspeak

As Morris recalled of 1981, "Clinton didn't want to apologize. 'It's not me; it's not my style.' "

It never would be—for Bill, by virtue of his tough childhood, could never see *himself* at fault. Hillary, becoming more and more the corporate lawyer, sided with Bill, however, on the grounds that her husband would look weak if he said he was sorry—and thus make a bad image worse.

Fortunately, Bill's high intelligence and perceptiveness forced him to face up to the fact that only drastic measures would overcome a public impression of young hubris and incompetence. In the end he therefore accepted Morris's idea of making a television commercial, several weeks prior to his public declaration that he'd run again, in order to prepare or 'soften' the market." He said he was still resolutely opposed to saying the word "sorry," however. "I'll do it your way except for the apology," he told Morris.

Morris shrugged, wondering what would happen. In Tony Schwarz's special studio in New York, Bill Clinton duly filmed the advertisement—inventing his own version of an apology. As he put it, "Many of you have told me you were proud of some of the things I did as governor. But," the former governor acknowledged, "you also think I made some big mistakes"—especially over car taxes. "When I became governor, we had serious problems with our streets and roads, and I did support those increases to try to solve the problem," he reminded viewers, instancing his "car license and title transfer fee" hikes. "But it was," he went on, "a mistake because so many of you were hurt by it. . . . And I'm really sorry for that. When I was a boy growing up my daddy never had to whip me twice for the same thing. And now I hope you'll give me another chance to serve as governor because our state has many problems and opportunities that demand strong leadership."

Morris admitted, afterward, to being "amazed." "The line about his daddy was folksy and descriptive," he commented admiringly. "Clinton has a genius for saying powerful things in homey language. I could never have scripted such lines. . . . 'This guy could be president,' I distinctly remember thinking."

Clinton's version was masterly. Like JFK's broadcast after the Bay of Pigs catastrophe in 1961, it indicated a willingness to acknowledge his error. In the promise not to do it again, and the reference to the need for strong leadership, he looked, indeed, presidential—as JFK had done twenty years before.

There, however, the similarity ended. JFK *did* believe the Bay of Pigs was a cock-up: that he'd been sold a bill of goods by the CIA and the military. Nevertheless, JFK was willing, as President, to take the blame for not having nixed the plan—the prelude to an extraordinary display of *real* leadership: national and international, over civil rights, the Cuban Missile Crisis, Berlin, nuclear disarmament . . .

Bill Clinton, by contrast, did *not* genuinely take responsibility for his own error of judgment. He believed that his ambitious political program and his tax hikes had been right—but that electors had *seen* the tax increases as wrong, something he could mend by not doing the same thing again. He seemed unable to recognize the failures of his own poor leadership skills, that he had *not* shown "strong leadership" as governor. He'd made his Bearded Troika take the rap for his own rushed, overambitious agenda and poor management skills, involving endless changes of tack, broken personal assurances, and, ultimately, "bunker mentality," as Jim McDougal's wife, Susan, called it. In matters of personnel he was, as his head of the criminal division in the attorney general's department noted, a disaster. "Personnel management was his worst area—as a personnel manager he was awful!" Burl Rotenberry recalled. "And the reason he was awful was because he delayed making personnel decisions. Basically he delayed making appointments and hiring people because he [felt he] had to assess the political fallout. Now, all politicians are like this. But he would leave people hanging and twisting slowly in the wind for too long. Personnel was his absolutely worst area. He wanted to reward his friends! He wanted to reward people who had helped his career! And sometimes he would almost seem paralyzed with indecision in making appointments."

Bill would also make rash decisions without consulting others—as if fearful of their reaction, knowing the decisions were questionable yet impelled for opaque reasons to make them nevertheless. The sentences of a large number of prisoners he'd commuted had included *twelve* lifers imprisoned for first-degree murder and rape. "Bill, you're out of your mind! You can't do this, you just can't do this," Hillary had protested vainly. As Hillary's biographer Gail Sheehy pointed out, Bill would later claim he had "never released a single first-degree murderer from prison. I did not do that." Technically he had not—but, as he well knew, he'd made it possible for them to be subsequently released on parole by commuting their sentences, which amounted to the same thing. It was, as the term would become known, classic "Clintonspeak."

Far from being able to show the "strong leadership" that he claimed was demanded by the state of Arkansas, indeed by the nation, Bill Clinton had proven completely unwilling to look at his own administrative style and to address his failings as a leader and chief executive. Indeed, he was unable to see such personal faults, only other people's sufferings or reactions over some of his policies and their enactment. The tragedy, as both his friend Jim Blair and his aide Bobby Roberts noted, was therefore that Bill, thrown out of office, never really dared go into the wilderness for forty days and address his own personal approach to management; he merely became determined to find a way of avoiding mistakes and covering up the ones that were made, while blaming others—who then became expendable in the quest for reinstatement and political advance toward the White House: "the Cause." As Max Brantley, later editor of the *Arkansas Times,* once observed, Clinton's ambition increasingly overrode colleagues and subordinates: "If someone turns out to have flaws, they [the Clintons] just jettison them. They don't look back." Peach Pietrefesa, Hillary's once closest friend, seconded this aspect of the Clintons' ascent, noting that Hillary Rodham was not only coeval but co-evil: "She thinks everyone needs to understand that she's about such important business, other people are expendable. There is no traction in their lives with other human beings."

At the end of the day politics is, however, about winning—and Bill had lost. In an Arkansas political history in which no cast-out governor had ever reclaimed the mansion, both Bill and Hillary accepted that new ruthlessness would be required: an absolute determination to win this time. To do so, they could take no prisoners.

In Reagan's Footsteps

Paradoxically, it was Republican President Ronald Reagan who provided the paradigm for Bill Clinton's comeback. The second-rank actor was becoming known as "The Great Communicator"—though, as he pointed out with some humility, he was not communicating his own ideas, simply those of others that resonated with his time.

As his biographer Michael Schaller remarked, Reagan had certainly developed an extraordinary ability to elide his own past into "the ideals and the mythology of American culture." Reagan had first made a name for himself by faux-narrating, or dramatizing, on radio the stories of baseball games that came in via ticker tape to his station at Des Moines. His capacity for fictionalizing not only baseball games but his personal history grew over the years until he pictured himself having served in action in World War II, even having personally liberated Nazi concentration camps.

Happiest on a horse in the pose of an eternal cowboy, Reagan personified a new and yet older kind of Camelot, one that elicited the admiration of all who, in modern suburbia, yearned for the rugged *simplicitas* of the Wild West; people who dreamed, after the cruel revelations of American conduct in Vietnam, that it could be rewon.

While Reagan would continue to ride serenely over, and away from, his manifold fictions and mistakes in the years ahead, protected by people's respect for his venerable age, so Bill Clinton would attempt, in his own way, to do the same—but trading on public forgiveness and sympathy for his young age.

When asked what kind of a governor of California he would make, Reagan had earlier quipped, "I don't know. I've never played a governor"—an ability to cast himself in his own fable that would enable "the Gipper," as he was known, to become the most popular chief executive of late-twentieth-century American times—second only to FDR, in fact, in the twentieth century. But for Bill Clinton, attempting to elide his own Horatio Alger story with the ideals and mythology of American culture, the task would prove immeasurably more difficult. No lapses of memory or other signs of senior citizenship would excuse the young Arkansan and former Rhodes Scholar. Indeed, the reverse would be true, as will be seen.

As Reagan's assistant chief of staff, Michael Deaver, remarked, Ronald Reagan "enjoyed the most generous treatment by the press of any president in the post-war era."

Bill Clinton, by any reckoning, would enjoy the least charitable.

Hillary's Makeover

Watching Bill fall apart after his defeat, Hillary Rodham had belatedly accepted that she herself must adopt a new persona if Bill was to succeed in Arkansas. She must downplay her independence as a partner in the Rose Law Firm, not boast of it. Instead, she must project an image of the committed spouse across Arkansas. That commitment entailed, however, altering her image.

"Hillary is beautiful," Ann Henry later declared. "She has great bones. She has great hair—but she didn't really comb her hair that much because her appearance has never been her interest."

Now, suddenly, it became of great interest. *It mattered.* With almost deadly earnestness Hillary began to dress fashionably; to have her hair cut, dyed, and styled, and to wear—to the delight of Bill's mother, Virginia—makeup. She also decided to use contact lenses instead of her goggle spectacles. But the biggest transformation of all was in nomenclature. Hillary Rodham, proud and confirmed feminist, decided henceforth to use the name Hillary Clinton. Mrs. Clinton, as she let herself now be known, would, if her husband demanded a rematch, stand by her man.

Rocky Balboa

"A Fighter. A Lover. A Legend. The Greatest Challenge . . ." the film ads ran.

There was one other figure in America in the early eighties who, successful in his field, had been seen to become complacent; who had lost his title fight, suffered depression, and been nursed back to victory by his trainer. His name was Rocky: Rocky Balboa . . .

In May 1982, Sylvester Stallone launched his latest boxing movie, *Rocky III,* as writer, director, and lead actor—the same month as Bill Clinton's entry in the primary fight for the Democratic nomination for Arkansas governor.

As moviegoers welcomed the story of Rocky's revival struggle, so the electorate of Arkansas seemed to warm to the idea of a Clinton comeback fight. The young ex-governor's arrogance and complacency had been punished, and although there had been alarm at 816 Midland Avenue when Morris's television advertisement produced an immediate 10 percent drop in Clinton's public rating, Morris had held fast to his strategy. "I feared I had killed Clinton's career. I thought the ad would work, but now he seemed dead because he had listened to me. I flew to Arkansas like a prisoner about to receive his sentence," Morris recalled. To a panic-stricken Hillary he explained that apologizing was like inoculation for smallpox. "You get a little sick," he assured her, "but you don't get the disease when you are exposed to it for real."

The team held its collective breath. To get into the ring to fight the Republican turncoat who'd beaten him for governor, Bill must first secure the Democratic nomination. The contest, as Betsey Wright related, was certainly no pushover. "The primary was tougher than we thought it was gonna be," she admitted later, "because we ended up with Jim Guy Tucker and Joe Purcell."

Fighting his predecessor as attorney general—a politician whose fight for the state's second Senate seat he had destroyed—promised, from the start, to be a battle royal for Bill Clinton. From positive advertising, stressing his regret, Bill now switched to the secret weapon with which he'd earlier destroyed Tucker's fight against David Pryor: negative advertising.

This time Tucker had learned his lesson, however, and had fashioned his own counterweapon: negative advertising.

Amazingly, Tucker's weapon didn't work.

Panzer Commander

Bill Clinton's electoral skin seemed armored with a special plastic coating, for Tucker's many barbs and accusations simply ricocheted. The former congressman "attacked him on car-tag fees, crime, taxes, schools, and anything else he could think of," Morris recorded, "but none of it worked. It all just bounced off. Why?" the strategist asked rhetorically. The answer to him was clear: Bill had "apologized."

Others were impressed, too. Cartoonist George Fisher, watching with fascination, upgraded Bill Clinton's baby carriage to a panzer. Meanwhile, like President Reagan, Bill revised and improved his storyline. His quasi apology had exonerated him from all criticism. He could simply say, when tackled, that he had made his statement of repentance. The cherub-faced chorister of Immanuel Baptist Church was, he intimated, now a reformed character—and was certain he could help Arkansas, if Arkansas would allow him the privilege of leading the state into a new age where better, not worse, education would be vital. The plethora of programs he'd pushed in his first term would be whittled down, in the public eye, to just two: education and economics. "So out of that thing"—the failure to spotlight a platform of issues for which he could be identified and judged by the public—"a governing style grew that was focused, PR, on one issue," Betsey Wright explained. "So it was education, and then it was economic development. And the vow that he made was that never again would people be unable to name something good he had done."

Meanwhile, as Jim McDougal recalled, having prophesied a "good and hot campaign," Clinton slung enough mud Tucker's way that the ex-congressman became virtually unrecognizable. "His voice bristling with scorn, Clinton described Tucker as a tool of the 'special interests' and a dilettante with a lousy attendance record when he was in Congress," McDougal recounted. As a consequence, "Jim Guy's bid failed miserably. He still couldn't connect with common folks. He didn't even make it a two-man race. After winning only 23 percent of the primary vote, Jim Guy was left out of the runoff."

Tucker would never forgive Clinton. Joe Purcell, another former attorney general and lieutenant governor, now almost sixty years of age, faced Clinton in the second round, two weeks later, but was easily felled (54 to 46 percent of the vote), leaving former governor Bill Clinton to face the current governor, Frank White, in the November 1982 election.

Betsey Wright was disappointed that Tucker's opposition had crumbled so easily. "We had geared everything to running against Jim Guy—but we pulverized him far worse than we thought we had, and running against Joe Purcell was like running against a warm bowl of Pavlova," she sighed. "It was tough. Once we finished that, though, I knew we would beat Frank White, because there was no intensity of warmth for Frank White" among voters. "And because we had done an incredible job of rehabilitating Bill," she congratulated herself and her team in retrospect.

She had every reason to. In less than two years she had, with Dick Morris and a new army of campaign coworkers, lifted the lifeless ex-governor back onto his feet and put him back in the ring.

"We want Frank! We want Frank!" a crowd now chanted outside a downtown building in Little Rock. "We want Frank, so we can kick his butt!"

McDougal as Cuckold

Simultaneously Jim McDougal, who had been Bill Clinton's liaison with the state senate (and, together with Bill's former aide Steve Smith, the lead partner with the Clintons in the Whitewater real estate investment) had also won *his* Democratic primary. In his case it was the Democratic nomination for the congressional seat in the Third Congressional District, to face the widely respected Republican incumbent John Paul Hammerschmidt, the man who had beaten Bill Clinton eight years before, in 1974.

McDougal now found himself having to share with Bill Clinton the political platform at rallies in western Arkansas. For McDougal—an ex-alcoholic who suffered manic depression and would be indicted for financial impropriety, dying in prison—it was torture to have to stand on the same platform as Bill, for he was certain, after overhearing certain telephone conversations, that his wife was sleeping with Bill. How, McDougal wondered, could such an adulterer stand beside him on the stump and show no "hint of guilt"?

Wearing proverbial horns, Jim McDougal was in a quandary, "unprepared to hail the man who had been running around with my wife," as he later put it sarcastically, "as a great American."

This potpourri was certainly *pourri,* yet it was also, in its way, all too representative of the contradictions and anomalies of modern American, indeed Western, society in the 1980s. (In her own account of her life Susan McDougal did not allude to the alleged affair with Bill Clinton, but she acknowledged "flirting with half the Arkansas legislature" and having had a passionate affair with one of her husband's bank officers, Pat Harris, once McDougal ceased to have sex with her.)

Meanwhile, Bill Clinton campaigned with an energy and intensity no one could match. Though he would allow himself to be forced back into an antitax, less openly liberal position (he had promised voters he would be "more restrained, more conservative and more cautious" if elected a second time), Bill Clinton could not, however, be made into a fifties man, with all the sexual repressions, shame, and denials of that homophobic era. Though he seethed with envy, jealousy, and desire for revenge, Jim McDougal (whose own promiscuity with coeds was well known) could do nothing but acquiesce to what he saw as his wife's right to sexual gratification in the modern world—even with, he suspected, Bill Clinton. In his speeches, therefore, McDougal swallowed his male pride and, wearing his horns, depicted former Governor Bill Clinton to their audiences in northwest Arkansas "as the ideal candidate to restore Democratic principles and common sense to the governor's office."

Postmodernism in America

The fact was, whatever the New Right might urge, the clock could not be turned back, whether toward creationism or sexual abstinence. Along with the great political protest movements of the 1960s against racial segregation and the war in Vietnam had come more relaxed political and social views about sex and sexual orientation. In fact, virtually all the traditional tenets and approaches of Western social hierarchy and thinking had come under fire as a new youth culture—ironically, led by older gurus from Herbert Marcuse to Jean-Paul Sartre—had attacked establishment notions and sought a revolutionary framework for understanding the changing world. Academic Marxism had led to "structuralism," which had led to "poststructuralism" and, in literary criticism, to "deconstruction"—a process of turning received ideas on their head that in turn would lead to a broad, catchall term: "postmodernism."

Under the rubric "postmodernism" almost any combination of traditional and nontraditional approaches to art was now deemed acceptable—if not to Mrs. Thatcher and President Reagan, then to the new critics and purveyors of Western culture. And in this development, with his big, unathletic frame, his awesome intelligence and intellect, his love of the saxophone, his wide reading, curiosity about ordinary people, unpunctuality, respect for elders, penchant for fatty, unhealthy food, occasional temper tantrums, photographic memory, comfortableness with black people, liberal idealism, sentimentality, genuine interest in as well as love of women, Bill Clinton was the quintessential Postmodern Man—and a natural hero to young people. If he appeared on the same platform as a colleague who suspected him of cheating with his wife and the colleague was prepared to live with that—rather than challenge him to a duel, as in Arkansas's early days—then American politics, for all the claims of Reaganism, was surely also becoming postmodern.

It was not, however, as Bill Clinton would find out to his immortal cost.

Not only would politics, as we shall see, become the last arena in which fifties attitudes—or sexual McCarthyism, as Alan Dershowitz would call it—would survive, but McDougal, suffering from bipolar disorder, would become Bill Clinton's Judas.

Ambushing Frank White

For the moment, however, Bill Clinton was protected by the traditional propriety of American political warfare. Not even Governor White, who heard the proliferating stories of Clinton's womanizing, would fight sex-dirty, however harsh the political punching in terms of negative advertising and counteradvertising.

Governor Frank White had, he later explained, hoped to serve two terms in the mansion, and with this in mind had managed to raise a formidable half-million-dollar war chest to make his reelection feasible, even in such a Democratic Party–dominated state. But former governor Bill Clinton, he quickly found, had raised still more, especially after beating out Jim Guy Tucker and Joe Purcell for the Democratic Party spot.

The Clinton team had not simply raised more money. This time it was determined to overlook nothing in its campaign tactics—including "hauling out" the black vote. In this slugfest, while avoiding any mention or accusation of sexual misbehavior, the two candidates would spend some $3 million, the largest amount ever expended on a gubernatorial campaign in Arkansas history.

White had won the governor's mansion as an outsider, able and willing to excoriate the incumbent on his record. Now, however, the shoe was on the other foot, with White forced to defend his own gubernatorial performance—including the fiasco of his law on the teaching of creationism.

An even more formidable problem White had to contend with, however, was the contender's wife. Not only had she changed her name to Hillary Clinton and started to wear makeup, natty clothes, and contact lenses, but she had also taken indefinite leave of absence from the Rose Law Firm— and was out campaigning on Bill's behalf. Inevitably, Governor White was forced to cross swords with the feisty former first lady—a confrontation he would never forget.

"She ambushed me," White recalled, remembering how Hillary came to heckle him at a civics club meeting in North Little Rock. "You couldn't win," he sighed. "She was a woman, and this was the South. You'd look like a bully."

Hillary's outspoken feminism, especially her refusal to change her name, had contributed mightily to her husband's fall in 1980. Now her very feistiness was contributing to his resurrection, as she manipulated old southern manners to tie White's patriarchal hands behind his back and "eviscerate him," as Bill's old colleague Paul Fray put it. It was Hillary, not Bill, who "beat Frank White when Clinton ran against him in '82," Fray emphasized. "She gets up there on that stump and she could kick the dog shit out of you. Frank is still reeling from it, I don't mind telling you."

Co-Candidate

As the summer of 1982 wore on, polls began to show Bill Clinton's chances of reelection rising. He had at last, in Betsey Wright, a campaign manager with balls, so to speak—but then, as observers noted, this was only part of Bill Clinton's transformation. The other was Hillary, who not only was morphed in terms of makeup, hair, clothes, and name but became Bill's consort in a way she'd never been before.

For Bill Clinton, the effect would be significant. Ronald Reagan had his Nancy, complete with astrologer; he even had a brilliant female speechwriter, Peggy Noonan; but, while such women might feed the aging president and feed his lines, they did not presume to be co-candidate or even chief of staff. By contrast, cartoonists in Arkansas, adding Clinton's press secretary, Joan Roberts, to the lineup of Betsey Wright and Hillary Clinton, now depicted the three women as the three Valkyries, maidens bearing Bill Clinton from the political battlefield into Valhalla, there to minister to him—and restore him to warrior-ready status.

Hillary, however, was more than a Valkyrie. Putting aside her law firm work, she was now a warrior herself—and she struck terror into her opponents. Conservative opinion had been shocked, first time around, that Hillary Rodham was not a traditional southern wife, resenting the fact that she was following her own, independent career path. Now, however, Hillary had paid her dues to southern conservatives by changing her name—and had allied her path to that of her husband, the former governor. Frank White's wife, by contrast, had found the business of being first lady, after being the wife of a businessman, horrible. "My little wife was just in culture shock when I put her in a political race," White later conceded. "That's just not her, it's just not our style." Hillary, by contrast, seemed to come to life—not only cosmetically revamped but appealing directly to women and young voters by campaigning herself. Very soon she began to evoke memories of FDR's wife, Eleanor: passionate in her support for causes she believed in and not caring to mind her tongue.

It was not only the Republican governor who was bewildered, indeed awed, by this apparition. Voters also found it increasingly difficult, even though they still felt sore at Bill for having raised car taxes, to resist a new combination of husband and wife that reversed all known precedents in the state. "Justice Jim" Johnson, it was true, had campaigned with his wife, Virginia, both of them seeking high political offices, but both had failed, and both had retreated into their racist corner. Here, by contrast, was a highly educated and intelligent woman, a mother and top attorney, fighting alongside her husband *as a teammate*—but with Hillary the more aggressive of the pair!

This, in 1982, was the truly revolutionary movement—not planned or strategized, yet devastating in its effectiveness. Years before, in Moot Court at Yale, Bill and Hillary had failed to win the annual mock trial proceedings before a live jury. This time, however, the times had caught up with them or they with the times—even in darkest Arkansas. Big Bill Clinton's personality, so devastatingly caricatured as babyish, childish, unfocused, obsessed with winning friends rather than offering effective leadership, was now balanced by a tandem effort in which his distinctly feminine personality—his affectionate response to people and to human relationships—was matched by Hillary's more masculine persona: a tough, no-nonsense, emotionally sterile, morally clear personality. As psychologist Carol Gilligan showed in a seminal work published that year, new research suggested "that women impose a distinctive construction on moral problems, seeing moral dilemmas in terms of conflicting responsibilities"—a lens that often made women's approach to moral questions seem flabby or relativistic compared with typical male responses. From this perspective, Bill Clinton's sensibility was broad and feminine, in line with the majority of Gilligan's female respondents', Hillary's as cold and analytical as that of Gilligan's male students.

Thus it was not that anyone, in the whole state of Arkansas, actually *liked* Hillary or saw in her cosmetic transformation the true taming of a shrew. Her leopardess could not change its spots, for she had a brittle, arrogant, ruthlessly self-righteous approach to issues as to people—an "all-business" attitude ("You're either useful or extraneous to her," people felt after meeting her), which, in a southern environment where business was an almost exclusively male preserve, was not only subversive but not even in tune with southern manners. It was, however, distinctive, even eccentric, in the South. And for all that the good-ole-boy patriarchal society of the South was deeply, irremediably conservative, often racist, and all too often opposed to change or improvement; it *was* a culture that appreciated eccentricity.

Hillary's metamorphosis could not therefore be likened to that of Jackie Kennedy, who deliberately changed her voice in the 1950s to a whisper and concealed her size ten shoes and heavy eyebrows in a calculated "Barbie doll" image, in order to be seen to be more submissive—and seductive. Rather, Hillary adopted the technique of British Prime Minister Margaret Thatcher. Revising her attitude to her name, her hair, her spectacles, her makeup, and her clothes, she now went out each day to disarm men—then punch right through their defenses. Men might not *like* her, but they would, if she removed their excuses for instinctive chauvinism, *respect* her. Women would, too, when they were not discomfited by her feisty, subversive example. Thus, to the extent that Hillary won a new political esteem in the state, it went a surprisingly long way toward counterbalancing the disrespect people felt for her overly affectionate but unfocused and inconstant husband.

Without the electorate, political commentators, or even political historians becoming aware of the change, then, the Clintons became a *pair,* allowing almost every voter to find good in one or the other. The concept of co-candidacy was born: "Vote for one—get two!"

Seducing Starr

The politics of seduction had always existed, whether in dictatorships or in democratic polities. What was different in America in the late twentieth century was that such politics coincided with modern advertising and marketing, using television as the primary form of mass communication.

Franklin D. Roosevelt's fireside chats—radio broadcasts that concealed his paraplegia—had been eagerly listened to by tens of millions of citizens. Then, on black-and-white television screens, John F. Kennedy had seduced a nation—indeed, foreign nations too—with a new form of appeal, namely youth, wit, and handsomeness allied to great intelligence, visible compassion, and a non-WASP, Catholic background. Pursuing a different political agenda, Ronald Reagan, an ex–Hollywood actor, then invented a new meaning for the "body politic," taking his politics of body language to new heights on color television, where it was no longer important what the President said but how he said it. "Haven't you people figured out yet," a White House staffer scoffed at a CBS news correspondent who thought he'd produced a feature criticizing President Reagan for attending the Special Olympics while urging Congress to cut federal aid programs to the handicapped, "that the picture always overrides what you say?"

Not having worked in Hollywood and lacking the advantage of public respect for Reagan's age, Bill Clinton was nonetheless acutely aware of Reagan's example, especially in terms of media manipulation. He therefore decided—to the chagrin of Ernie Dumas, the *Arkansas Gazette* editorial writer—to ignore the *Arkansas Gazette* and concentrate all his efforts of charm and persuasion upon the *Arkansas Democrat,* which—in an increasingly cutthroat circulation war with the *Gazette*—had vilified him during his first term as governor, especially in the columns of John Robert Starr. To Dumas's astonishment, and the surprise of almost everyone in Arkansas who knew them, not only did Bill Clinton suddenly begin to court their most hated and hateful adversary, John Robert Starr, but so did Hillary too!

"His first term, he got hammered by the *Arkansas Democrat,*" Dumas recalled. "I always thought it didn't make much difference, but Clinton would talk about it afterwards. He'd say that that was what defeated him—the *Democrat*! You'd see him at these parties, and it's all he wanted to talk about: the *Democrat* hammering him so unfairly and vilifying everyone in his administration, making fun of 'em. I said, 'Governor, they didn't have anything to do with it! They don't have any circulation! The only place they circulate is here in Little Rock—and you got 70 percent of the vote here! You got defeated in the *countryside,* down in south Arkansas and out in the rural countryside in east and south Arkansas, where they'd voted heavily for you. They voted against you because of the car tax—the biggest part of it. They felt betrayed. Plus a lot of other stuff—Hillary not taking your name—they hadn't realized that when they voted the first time.' "

Bill and Hillary's seduction of the *Arkansas Democrat*'s editor appalled the gentle, intelligent Dumas. "When Clinton decided to run again, they felt they had to do something about the *Democrat,*" he recounted sadly.

"Clinton felt like he couldn't stand being hammered that way, 'cause he was so thin-skinned. He said he didn't think he could even ask people to serve in his administration because everyone who worked for him was just vilified, and so he had to find some way to neutralize the *Democrat*. I remember Betsey [Wright] talking to me once; she called and we talked about it, that Clinton was thinking of running again. And my recollection is, she said Hillary had kind of figured it: the archenemy was John Robert Starr, who was the managing editor of the *Arkansas Democrat*. He was a crazy, a lunatic, who was running the paper over there. And he had turned on Clinton. Although he did not write the editorials—the editorial page was just a bunch of crusty old right-wingers that didn't know how to write an editorial page anyway. But he directed the news staff and wrote a seven-day-a-week column, three hundred sixty-five days a year—and three quarters of them were attacks on Clinton. So all of his stuff, and the headline writers, the cartoonists, the graphic artists—everything in the paper, all the reporters—it was all 'Get Clinton!' "

With Max Brantley, the city editor of the *Gazette*, Dumas frequented a certain downtown restaurant. "Bill Clinton used to go to the Country Club to eat, but we saw Hillary quite frequently downtown—and *she'd be with John Robert Starr*! I mean, she *had* to hate him—he was such a pompous, arrogant, unlikable person—*nobody* liked him! Just *insufferable* person! Even his own *staff* despised him! Nobody liked to be around him. Well, we'd see Hillary and John Robert Starr over in the corner. And of course she would kinda roll her eyes! We'd always make it a point to walk by and let Hillary know we saw them! That was quite frequent.

"So Hillary was part of that effort to co-opt John Robert Starr—and they considered it worked! They were obsessed with John Robert Starr! I began to see this little thing in Starr's column, every so often: 'Well, Bill Clinton called me—he liked a column I wrote about so-and-so.' Or 'I ran into Bill at lunch and he stopped by the table, and he liked this or that.' You'd begin to see it appear more and more often in Starr's columns: these conversations with Clinton! *And with Hillary!* And then," Dumas recalled with a despairing chuckle, "Starr goes in and has heart surgery. *And Clinton goes to see him in the hospital!* Even Hillary goes in to see him! And of course Starr writes about this in his columns—he can't help it, he's the biggest name-dropper!—that Hugh Rodham, Hillary's father, said he was his '*favorite* columnist'!

"So you begin to see: Clinton's a different kind of person in Starr's eyes.

He's changed! His defeat has humanized Bill Clinton! He's no longer this arrogant son of a bitch that he was.

"By the time Clinton runs again, Starr is his big champion! And the *Democrat*," Dumas marveled, "just turns around."

The Better Half

The Clintons were now playing doubles in a singles tournament, one standing at the net, the other at the baseline, so that no single opponent stood a chance.

Those who thought Hillary Rodham had changed her name merely for convenience, moreover, were quickly disproved as Hillary moved into top political gear. No longer was she simply an independent lawyer married to an Arkansas politician: she was Hillary Clinton, the literal "better half" of the candidate.

That Governor White refused to debate in public with Clinton, the Rhodes Scholar, was one thing; the fact that he refused to debate Hillary, as well, spoke volumes. "If Frank's smart enough not to speak at the same time as Hillary, he might not be smart enough to be governor," Bill was quoted saying. Hillary's response was far more emasculating. "Frank White would probably try to avoid being in the same room as Chelsea," Hillary declared, referring to her two-year-old daughter. "Chelsea could debate him and win."

This was intellectual contempt of the worst Yankee kind, particularly in view of White's outstanding military and business record, compared to Bill Clinton's lack of either. But White was not combating Bill—he was being savaged by Hillary, and the remark hit home. With her iron, inflexible purpose and the relentless backing and supervision of Betsey Wright in the background, the Candidate and his Co-candidate were, in 1982, becoming an unbeatable couple—as even Governor Frank White, despite his swelling war chest and negative television ads, recognized.

A Black Man in the Pews

No one in Arkansas politics had ever seen anything like it: a man-and-woman team in which the man was feminine and the woman was masculine!

Defeat, however, had made the candidate hungry. "He knew that if he lost, it was the end for him in elected politics," one of Bill's organizers reflected. Betsey Wright's new computer system, having digested the data from myriad card index files, churned out hordes of letters to thank, beg, cajole, congratulate, and remind people of Bill's candidacy. A fortune was spent on television advertising—and to Morris's delight, the same phenomenon as when fighting Bill's rival Democrat, Jim Guy Tucker, was found: Governor White's negative ads bounced off, while Clinton's—denouncing White's softness with utility companies, failure to deal with rising unemployment, his support of creationist "science" and other issues—struck home. "We felt like we were behind bulletproof glass watching somebody aim at us and pull the trigger," Morris recalled, "and watch the bullets splatter harmlessly." Not even White's put-down—that Bill Clinton had never "run anything in his life except an antiwar demonstration"—seemed to resonate with voters once Hillary, a woman of iron, stood beside him.

Centrist Democrats helped Bill raise more and more funding as his campaign gathered steam and momentum. Volunteers abounded—and brought more in their wake. Reagan's personal popularity remained undented, but that of the Republicans was taking a beating, thanks to rising joblessness and interest rates, adding more fuel to Clinton's fire. Complacency had permitted Bill to take the black vote for granted in 1980; now, however, nothing would be taken for granted, and with three black organizers on board—Rodney Slater, Bob Nash, and Carol Willis—Bill sought and "hauled" the black vote as no other candidate in Arkansas history had ever done. "We worked twenty-four hours a day, Saturday and Sunday," Willis recounted. "If there was an event involved black people, we were there. And we would get Clinton there."

Slater would never forget the "difficult campaign" of 1982. In the Delta, in Forrest City, eastern Arkansas, Slater recalled how he'd gone with the candidate to a meeting of local African-American leaders in a barbecue restaurant. Someone suggested that Bill had had his chance to be governor and that "blacks in that community should look at some other candidates." A "deafening quiet fell over the room," Slater recounted. It was then that the mayor of a small town called Haines stood up.

"My little old town is a poor town," Slater recalled the peroration. "Few people even think about my town. And clearly, very few people who are governor, or attorney general, ever come to my town," Mayor John Lee Wilson had acknowledged. "But when Bill Clinton was governor, I invited him to my town. We had sewage running in the streets and couldn't get any help to fix that problem until Bill Clinton came here and walked the street with us. Now he may not win this election, but I'm going to stand with him because he stood with me and he stood with my people, and he gave me hope. And he may go down, but if he goes down I'm going to go down with him."

As Slater recalled, it was for him the "most powerful" endorsement "of the whole campaign"—indeed, of Bill Clinton's whole career in politics, then or later. "John Lee then sat down and Clinton got the group's support," Slater added. "And as it turned out their endorsement was not about political calculation. It was not about maneuvering. It was not about positioning. It was about where someone had been for them," he pointed out, "and where they were going to be for that person in his time of need."

Reflecting on the episode years later, Slater felt the meeting was "a defining moment of Clinton's relationship with black America and black America's relationship with him. [Mayor] John Lee Wilson was speaking for a lot of black folks," he summarized, "who knew Bill Clinton—or who would come to know him."

In truth there was, of course, endless maneuvering and positioning—such as with the Tyson-dominated poultry lobby, which wanted a raising of the truck weight limit despite the further damage this would do to Arkansas's grossly underfunded highways. But in terms of Bill Clinton's popular, campaigning appeal, there could be no doubt that the candidate was, in 1982, on a roll. After his months of self-pity and quasi breakdown, "pretending to be a lawyer," as his friend Jim Blair sniffed, he was reconnecting with ordinary people: not as the arrogant, overeducated, "too-big-for-his-britches" incumbent of 1980, but as the underdog—a position that endeared him to blacks in particular. As Joseph Lowery, a Georgia civil rights activist, later recalled, Bill was a saxophone player, a fact that singled him out from any other white politician—indeed, in Lowery's eyes, caused many a white man to hate Clinton as a traitor to his race. "See, if he had played the violin or the oboe, white folks would not have been disturbed. But a saxophone is about as black an instrument as you can get. It even surpasses the piano," Lowery remarked. Moreover, Clinton could preach. "I preached in Little Rock when he was governor. He and I became friends because he loved preaching. He can preach, but he also knows how to go to a black church and just melt into the woodwork. He becomes an invisible white man. He becomes a black man in the pews."

What had Governor White done for blacks, Bill Clinton asked black audiences? White had, it was true, brought back Orval Faubus from "exile" in Texas and appointed him to a high state position, Bill reminded audience after audience in his campaign: a move that was especially painful to African Americans. In a Clinton administration this would never happen again, Bill promised.

There was no stopping him now.

Today Is Easter

On November 2, 1982, the people of Arkansas went to the polls. Governor White's numbers, for a Republican in a traditionally Democratic state, were still extraordinary—357,496 votes cast in his favor. However, as Frank realized once the returns began coming in, it was not going to be enough.

Outside the campaign headquarters on Seventh Street in downtown Little Rock, an army of supporters and well-wishers had gathered as, inside, Betsey Wright, running the tally board, called out the winning counties and margins. Eventually, as the tide of victory became irreversible, Bill's sense of euphoria broke out and he ran into the street and into the arms of the crowd, hugging everyone he could see.

Bill Clinton's eventual 431,855 votes proved more than decisive. They were a landslide. Bill won fifty-six of the seventy-five Arkansas counties, including thirty-two that White had seized in 1980. The third-ever governor deposed after a single term had become the only defeated governor ever to regain his crown.

"I think for the rest of my life I will look back on this election with a mixture of disbelief that it happened," Bill confessed a few weeks later at a meeting of teachers—the Arkansas Education Association, which had endorsed him—"and with a profound sense of humility and gratitude for people like you who worked their hearts out and went the extra mile to do something no rational person ever thought could be done."

Such gratitude would not stop Governor Bill Clinton from taking on the teachers' union in almost hand-to-hand combat in the months and years thereafter, indeed, making the union the scapegoat in a test not only of his gubernatorial authority but his ability to become President of the United States. However, it did denote the change in Bill Clinton. As Betsey Wright later claimed, his staff had done an incredible job of rehabilitating him. "And it became clear," she added, "the different way he would have to behave, to operate, as Governor, than he had before."

Betsey was not only Wright but right. No one would ever say, thereafter, that Bill Clinton was arrogant or too big for his britches. He had truly learned not only his political lesson but the practical lessons of campaign defeat: never to let charges go unanswered, never to be seen or portrayed as out of touch, never to be seen as too soft on crime or too complacent to seek and haul the black vote—which, as it had been for Republican Governor Winthrop Rockefeller, was critical to his electoral chances in an era of white flight and the shifting of traditional white voters in the South to the Republican camp.

On January 11, 1983, five weeks later, Bill Clinton's second inauguration took place at the state capitol—a "veritable lovefest" as one journalist recalled. Mothers even brought their children, as if aware that this was a historic occasion like no other in Arkansas history. Or, as one irritated legislator was moved to remark, "Today is Easter. He has risen."

PART FOUR

BORN-AGAIN GOVERNOR

Born-again Governor Bill Clinton, 1983

CHAPTER TWENTY-EIGHT

ON THE
A TEAM

In the Pot Together

Bill Clinton's record in his first term of office as governor of Arkansas had not even been mixed: it had been deeply disappointing, inviting a "sea of troubles," in Shakespeare's words, that had led to shipwreck.

Bill Clinton, given up for drowned, had nonetheless been rescued and, moving out of 316 Midland Avenue and into the familiar rooms of the governor's mansion in Little Rock for a second time on January 11, 1983, restored to grace. "In Arkansas," the *Arkansas Gazette* had welcomed Clinton's return, "we do not recall a governor before Clinton having come back to the office after leaving it." But what had really happened?

Writers and commentators later made much of Bill Clinton's resultant political reconstruction: that, in essence, having had the liberal stuffing knocked out of him, he climbed back onto the remains of his wrecked vessel and, hoisting a limp sail, set off again, becoming cautious to the point of impotence, a conciliator and a compromiser, not a leader, bending neither to the winds of change nor the march of reactionary forces but to both, while attempting to ride both incoming and outgoing tides.

Such a view would have merit since, in the real electoral world, no politician can be an island. But the most important change was the least noticed: that Hillary became, as Gail Sheehy famously put it, Bill's *doppelgänger*—

indeed, more than that. Without Hillary's inclusion, to use an alternative analogy, the Bill Clinton Group, with its lead singer and office trio, had failed in 1978–80. By contrast, the Hill-and-Bill Group triumphed in 1982—and would continue to do so as long as the duo stayed together, with backing from Betsey Wright as director of music and extra marketing help from Dick Morris.

This was not how things had been intended to go; indeed, Hillary herself could scarcely understand what had happened. Dazed by the success of Bill's comeback, she could hardly credit it herself. In the week after Bill's second inauguration, she spoke of the disastrous period following his first: "This might sound naïve now," she admitted, "but I really felt being a public official was a job like any other. He would do his job and I would do mine, and we would have our private life." She confessed that, looking back, the reality of a political marriage "really did come as a surprise to me." She had expected to develop her own career while giving Bill advice and moral support when requested—even, on occasion, when not requested! But she had not expected to be a player in his band. "A person who marries a doctor," she said, using her own simile, "isn't expected to stand by his side as he performs surgery."

There is no evidence that Hillary was being disingenuous. She was often lawyerly in concealing the truth or sidestepping it, but she was not given to lying. Her enormous respect for Bill's political talents—his ability to use his high intelligence to communicate with people of different backgrounds in the service of Democratic causes—had permitted her to take a backseat, offering advice as and when needed in the manner of a thousand political wives. But Bill's defeat had changed the rules.

Bill's life—his political life—was now in the hands of Hillary. Or rather, they were in the pot together. Setting education as her number one agenda, Hillary would become Joan of Arc, with Bill as Dauphin.

The A Team

The combination of Bill Clinton as governor and Mrs. Clinton as cogovernor proved surprisingly effective—and unique. Churchill had acknowledged the importance of strong women in support of great men, in order that they might fulfill their destinies—but Clemmie Churchill had never shared a speaking platform with her husband, nor would Winston have permitted her to do so. In Argentina, Eva Perón had, until her early death, mitigated the darker aspects of her husband's dictatorship, and in the

United States, Eleanor Roosevelt had won both wide respect and opprobrium for her crusading work among the disadvantaged. But Bill and Hillary Clinton, as they became after Hillary's change of name, represented a wholly new deal in American politics. For the first time in Arkansas history, an up-and-coming political leader had been felled, only to right himself with the aid of his feminist consort—thereby inventing a new electoral and political *combination* that would be unique in twentieth-century democracy.

In the Arkansas public's eye Hillary's somewhat humorless, all-business approach to issues contrasted with Bill's charismatic but endlessly veering, unstable, well-meaning, but often contradictory personality and behavior. He was a superlative campaigner and no mean politician, but he had proved, in his first term as governor, to be a disastrously poor and endlessly prevaricating *leader*. Hillary, by contrast, was a born administrator—"quiet and bureaucratic," as Susan McDougal described her—but a poor politician. It was this accidental combination, not the Faustian bargain that Hillary's friend Peach Pietrefesa read into the scenario, that would take the A Team from 1982 to the presidency ten years later—for together they would be unbeatable.

If, of course, they stayed together.

Change Is in the Air

With national recession and a projected state revenue shortfall of $30 million, Governor Clinton's second administration was clearly going to have its work cut out for it. Nevertheless, beyond the difficult business of axing programs, people, and agencies, with Betsey Wright's help the Clintons concentrated their positive energies on education—"I mean, it's not that we ignored other issues, but we didn't *talk* about them," as Betsey explained the governor's new strategy.

Education was an area that interested both Clintons—Bill the more broadly educated and traveled and the more musical, Hillary the more deeply involved in children's rights and advocacy since attending Yale. The standards of public education in Arkansas were, in many respects, a disgrace, the field having been forever tainted by Faubus and the segregationist catastrophe of Central High School. It was a minefield that could make or break—indeed, make and *then* break—a politician's career, as Faubus had discovered. However it was, in 1983, a field that promised a better economic future for the state, if the state's children emerged better informed and more capable of adapting to the modern world. As the *Arkansas Gazette* had noted, in declaring for Clinton during the election, Clinton's "finest achievements," in his first term, had been in education: "His budget provided the largest increase in teacher salaries in history, extended comprehensive health insurance to all school employees, funded education for the handicapped for the first time and began the first educational program for gifted children." Unfortunately, his Washington, D.C., office had proved "fruitless" in getting greater federal funding, and his "study of the clear-cutting practices of the timber giants" had borne "no result except the implacable opposition of the timber giants"—who had promptly supported Governor White. The newspaper, in backing Clinton, had taken the view that "most people are not satisfied with the status quo in Arkansas, and, accordingly, the *Gazette* recommends the election of Bill Clinton in the faith that he has the imagination and energy, and the determination, to do something about it."

Bill did. Change, he was certain, was in the air. Recession could lead either to revolution—unlikely in America—or to retooling, indeed economic reconstruction. Traditional industries were now decaying and rusting away as global competition exposed the weaknesses of American manufacturing and design. Championing educational change, which could help America's children adjust and advance toward a postindustrial economy, thus promised to be a noble cause, at once genuine and enhancing the Clintons' reputation, not only in the state arena but—if the Clintons got it right—in a national spotlight.

Bill Clinton's inaugural address in Little Rock, on January 11, 1983, thus put education first. "Over the long run," the incoming governor declared, mindful of the further disgrace to Arkansas resulting from his predecessor's "Scopes II" act and federal court trial, "education is the key to our economic revival and our perennial quest for prosperity. We must dedicate more of our limited resources to paying teachers better; expanding educational opportunities in poor and small districts; improving and diversifying vocational and high technology programs; and perhaps more important, strengthening basic education. Without competence in basic skills our people cannot move on to more advanced achievement."

In the months and years that followed, education would remain first on the Clinton gubernatorial agenda. In their wildest dreams, however, neither Bill nor Hillary could have foreseen the way the teachers of Arkansas—whose union had contributed to Bill's reelection—would play straight into their hands, permitting the governor and his wife to come across not as overeducated Yalies in a proud southern state but as two local parents committed to see that their daughter, like anyone else's daughter in Arkansas, indeed in America, would have a fair chance of learning the skills she'd need in the modern, postindustrial world. In Britain, the Conservative prime minister, Mrs. Thatcher, would make her iron reputation by smashing striking coal miners and steelworkers; in the United States, Republican President Reagan had already done the same by destroying the air traffic controllers' strike in 1981. Ironically, Bill and Hillary Clinton, nominally Democrats, would establish the same reputation for union smashing—thanks to the Arkansas Education Association's steadfast refusal to agree to teacher testing.

More than any other issue, it would be the contest the Clintons would have with Arkansas educators that would, in time, make Bill Clinton President of the United States. His proposal, advanced in his first governorship, was simple: that not only students but *teachers too* should be examined. Amid the many other initiatives that had been promoted at that time, teacher testing had been ignored as rhetoric by the teachers' union. With education now on the front burner, in 1983, the issue became positively incendiary—an insult to adult instructors, worthy in the nineteenth century of a duel.

An Arkansas Duel

The great Arkansas fight that now took place was not with pistols. Instead, with the authority of the state legislature, in 1983 Governor Clinton appointed his wife to head up a fifteen-person Arkansas Education Standards Committee to draft new standards for Arkansas's public schools. With that, the two sides faced off.

Hillary was certainly not interested in taking prisoners. She immediately insisted that the committee hold hearings in all seventy-five counties of the state—in other words, that the committee's work itself should become educational, as well as visible to taxpayers and voters. As more and more parents voiced their dissatisfaction with the state of public education in Arkansas—where almost every principal was a former athletics coach and classroom education took second place to sports—Hillary declared what would soon become war. She did not, as chairperson, mince her words. A national report simultaneously lambasted the "rising tide of mediocrity" in American schools, empowering Hillary to address civic clubs and school graduation ceremonies, as well as doing radio and television interviews.

"Folks either loved or hated the first lady," the Arkansas journalist Philip Martin would later describe her campaign—for, in effect, this is what it became. She didn't mind whom she offended as she called for better pay for teachers and more classroom equipment such as computers, as well as parental involvement and support for teachers in instilling discipline and motivation for learning. Moreover, she insisted on an end to in-schooltime athletics. Each of these demands raised concerns among teachers from administrative, financial, and sociological standpoints. But what really stuck in teachers' gullets was teacher and administrator testing.

If teachers were outraged at the suggestion that they were neither good nor qualified enough to instruct children in the modern world, Hillary's colleagues on the committee were awed by her clarity in diagnosing the public school problem, her boldness in setting out the cure, and her resolve to administer the medicine. "She visited one school where teachers would slam their doors as she went down the hall," C. C. Chaffin, a much-admired female science teacher, recounted. "That must have hurt her to the bone. But outwardly she was stoic."

She was. Hillary wrote her own preface to the final committee report in the fall of 1983 and stood for two hours presenting it personally at a special legislative session (separate from the meager biennial two-month sitting of the state's lawmakers that had taken place earlier in 1983) called to address the issue. There, before the legislative committees of the Arkansas House and Senate, she outlined her controversial proposals, including the need to raise taxes in order to offer teachers more pay—but only in return for teacher testing. Improving state education, Governor Clinton was quoted as saying, was "more important to me than anything I have ever done in politics," but few believed the governor had the guts to push through the necessary measures to improve it. Hillary did. Standing in the white marble corridor, the governor listened through a crack in the doors as his "little lady" faced the legislature, described the moribund situation in Arkansas's schools, and gave her committee's recommendations.

"I think we elected the wrong Clinton," one legislator, applauding Hillary, was heard to say.

A Herculean Task

It was now no longer a duel, but, as the leader of the Arkansas teachers' union, Grainger Ledbetter, bluntly put it, was "war": Hillary's war. Moreover, it was war fought in a new medium, namely on television, where Bill Clinton's hoarse but human voice and easy manner could captivate and seduce. As Jim McDougal's wife recognized, Bill Clinton was "brilliant." But perhaps his greatest brilliance, in comparison with other men of near-genius intellect, was his brilliance in concealing it. He was, with his baby face, with chubby cheeks and a happy, aw-shucks grin, a chameleon, "always able to make people feel he was just like them," she recalled. "He was incredibly ambitious, and aspired to the national spotlight early on—yet he came across as the kind of guy you'd meet any day of the week, any place in Arkansas."

The special session addressing Arkansas education lasted three weeks—which Governor Clinton likened to the wait for his daughter, Chelsea, to appear in the outside world. Both were successful births, and after hearing that the legislature had finally voted to back his reform proposals, Bill was profoundly relieved. "I feel," he remarked once the two houses—with some senatorial amendments—passed the education bill, "like we can deal with the remaining issues in an expeditious manner."

These were famous last words, however. Before the session ended, the teachers' union—the Arkansas Education Association—had proclaimed its implacable opposition. Teachers would take the legislators' money, they announced, but would refuse to take the tests of their basic competency.

The AEA was making a disastrous mistake. Fidel Castro's released Cuban convicts had exposed Bill Clinton's greatest weaknesses as an Arkansas leader who had avoided military service and training. By contrast, the Arkansas teachers' challenge to his authority as governor was perfectly suited not only to the political skills of the still young chief executive, aged thirty-seven, but to his core beliefs as a self-made man who had risen to a professorship in his twenties, then to the attorney generalship and the governorship, all thanks to his education.

Bill Clinton had learned his lesson, too. In order to face down the union, he would need the backing of the press and media in putting across his and Hillary's mission—and the reasons for it.

To win that media backing, Bill and Hillary were now willing to go to any lengths, as Ernie Dumas recalled. "From 1982, when he gets back into office, all the way until about 1989, when Starr feel he's not getting the right amount of attention," Dumas recounted, Bill Clinton ensured that the *Arkansas Democrat* became and remained his "biggest cheerleader." The task was almost Herculean, Dumas added. Joan Roberts, Clinton's press secretary, "told me that her job was that 'I have to talk to John Robert Starr *every day*! That's my job description: I have to talk to John Robert Starr *every day*! Because frequently Bill can't. I talk to him Saturdays, *I talk to him Sundays*! I sometimes spend two *hours* on the phone!'

"She told me, one night, over at Bobby Roberts' house, she'd had over a bottle of wine, 'I spend my *life,* I think sometimes, talking to John Robert Starr—that's my first job of the day: I've got to talk to him *every day*!' "

"*And it worked!*" Dumas conceded. "It kept them off his back for five or six years."

A Net Advantage

While John Robert Starr and the *Arkansas Democrat* were neutralized and then won over, NBC television's coverage of the struggle between Governor Clinton and the teachers of Arkansas helped catapult young Governor Bill Clinton into the national limelight.

Education was not the only fight Bill Clinton chose. Transportation and utility rates were also made into do-or-die issues that would, as Betsey Wright strategized, enable voters to identify and define their governor. Thus Clinton propelled the legislature into raising extra truck usage fees to pay for the damage caused by authorizing bigger loads (from 73,000 to 80,000 pounds) on Arkansas's deteriorating highways; meanwhile, the governor insisted upon elected rather than appointed representatives on the state commission overseeing utility rates.

As Ernie Dumas commented at the time, the governor's new game plan—concentrating on selected issues and going into battle for them— made good political sense, indeed far better sense than those people who predicted another defeat for the ambitious governor could discern. By the spring of 1984, as the next gubernatorial campaign beckoned, the Arkansas governor "has three groups of unalterable foes," Dumas commented in the *Arkansas Gazette,* "—the truckers, utilities, and teachers— but in each instance," he judged, "the fights have proved to be a net advantage for him."

Dumas was right. President Ronald Reagan had made the politics of the wealthy palatable to the nation by his handsome, elderly charm—behind which his team of right-wing economists and militarists was toughing out Republican issues (tax cuts, defense increases, antiwelfare and antiabortion measures) with Congress. As Reagan found in Washington, such measures did not necessarily succeed in the halls of either the House of

Representatives or the Senate, or indeed at the election box—but whether they did or not, his own presidential standing as a man with a firm agenda remained remarkably secure.

The proof of this was in the voting. In November 1984, Republicans lost significantly in both the House and Senate, but President Reagan himself was reelected by a landslide majority. Against Democrat Walter Mondale and vice presidential nominee Geraldine Ferraro, Reagan won an incredible forty-nine states—a victory that would deeply impress Bill Clinton. The lesson was simple and yet subtle: if he were to emulate Reagan's success, it would be *unnecessary* to try to seize the reins of his party, riven and hamstrung as it was by internal dissension as America underwent its painful postindustrial transformation. Rather, what was necessary was to create a mythological image of the crusading yet compassionate young leader, a mantra with which the electorate could identify. It would be the "vision thing."

By choosing education and economics as the centerpieces of his comeback identity, indeed, making it what Hillary called a "crusade," Bill Clinton had created the platform for an eventual Democratic presidential comeback—if he could stay in the Arkansas saddle.

The Grandest Intentions

Electorally the new Bill-and-Hill combination confounded opponents and would-be opponents. Those who found him slick and phony found her blunt, sassy, and genuine. Those who felt that Bill's morals were too lax found Hillary sensible and blessedly old-fashioned in her insistence on traditional standards of behavior. "I know I sound preachy," Hillary had apologized in the fall of 1983, as her Education Reform Report was readied, "but I believe in this." Speaking before the statewide television cameras, she had "the mien of a tent evangelist," journalist Philip Martin wrote. In the land of all-male biblical tongues, this was no mean, let alone mien, achievement. "Discipline holds no mystery," she declared with the conviction of a school principal speaking to her staff. "When it is firm, clearly understood, fairly administered and perceived to be so," she went on, "it works." She paused. When discipline wasn't administered, she cautioned, "it doesn't."

Such words might have issued from a Reagan Republican—as, perhaps, Hillary was, deep down. She spoke of how the Vietnam War and its aftermath had shaken "our entire social foundation. People have lost a lot of confidence in themselves and in their institutions, whether it be government or churches or public schools."

Bill Clinton, for his part, personified a more traditional Democratic Party line in which compassion for the poor, the underprivileged, the neglected, and the needy was paraded alongside an uncommon appreciation of the patterns and direction of modernity. Their approaches were, in this sense, like day and night. For Hillary, everything and everyone outside the governor's mansion, save for certain chosen acolytes, was potentially hostile. "I watched Hillary turn the world into Us versus Them," her former bosom pal Nancy Pietrefesa related. "That's how she looks at the world," Peach mourned, shaking her head over the concomitant notion that Hillary and Bill were, in Hillary's self-righteous myth, "good people with the grandest intentions who keep getting screwed."

In Hillary's case this was, at a literal level, only occasionally true. In Bill's case, as the 1984 election loomed, it was almost addictively so.

The Babes

Peach Pietrefesa, working in the governor's office from 1979 to 1980, as well as observing since Yale Bill's tactics of seduction at close quarters, was not unimpressed by his savoir faire. "He had two levels of women: smart peers who he could tell were having trouble with their spouses," she described the big Arkansan's tactical antennae, "and of course the babes."

Betsey Wright, Bill's director of staff, felt his feelings for his "smart peers" were serious. "They were intellects—those were the people he really cared about! The women who were his good friends and that I think he had the most serious relationships with *weren't* beautiful. But they were very smart."

By contrast, "the ones that were just to meet some psychological need—but he didn't really love them at all—were beauties," Betsey recalled, "raving beauties." They had "long, long hair . . . were what we call 'Rodeo Queens'! And they weren't smart. They weren't anybody he was ever going to care deeply about. Now, *they* may have thought differently, but, I mean, they weren't anybody he was going to have a real relationship with!"

Max Brantley, whose daughter went to school with Chelsea, was of like mind. Such women "have misinterpreted seven or eight boffs," Brantley remarked with the characteristically cavalier attitude of his gender, adding: "if they thought he cared about them, it's sad."

What was sadder was Governor Clinton's assumption that starstruck ladies would understand they were merely food for the giant's inexhaustible appetite. He worked harder and more intensely than any politician who had ever occupied the governor's office, took home little pay, and was not interested in money. The perks he was entitled to were women—of whom there were, he later confided, several hundred. A star student of "the female condition," Bill's timing and angle of approach were uncannily good. "He knows human nature so well, he knows how to lay that little 'test' on a woman," Peach recalled. Successful testing of the product bred intimacy—but intimacy, unfortunately, bred swifter contempt. "Handfuls of women had their feelings hurt," Peach recalled. "Clinton would come on to them and then be distracted or interrupted. When he came back he'd look at the same woman like he didn't know who she was. He'd already forgotten their exchange!"

There were longer-lasting liaisons, however, where Bill *did* remember the names of his paramours. Gennifer Flowers, in moving away from Little Rock after Hillary's pregnancy, had found it hard to make a clean break from the "Wonder Boy." Nevertheless, she did make a "mental shift" and began dating other men. She no longer looked to Bill to be her exclusive man. She knew and accepted that "we had no future together" and thus looked to "what I needed"—which was, she elucidated, "fun."

Working in Dallas, Gennifer had nevertheless entertained Bill while he made his out-of-state forays. She also made trips back to Little Rock for a regular or irregular "Bill fix." Then, after Bill's reelection in 1983, as Hillary Clinton toured the state to determine the educational fate of Arkansas's children, Gennifer moved back to the state capital permanently. Bill suggested she take an apartment in the Quapaw Towers, not far from the governor's mansion, across from General MacArthur's birthplace, on the corner of Ferry and Seventh Streets. They had not seen each other for almost six months while she sang nightly at a family entertainment theater. Unaware how many dishes there were on Bill's table, Gennifer claimed Bill was as famished as she was—recalling that their reunion in her four-poster bed was as passionate as the first time they had gotten together in the altogether.

A Bout of Crying

As the governor and his returning mistress lay together, however, Gennifer could not help but ask herself how Bill Clinton made peace with his conscience. She herself had struggled with the facts: that he was married to someone else, had a child whom he loved by that someone else, and that they were therefore doomed like spies to keep their assignations secret. Did he, she pondered, undergo the same wrestling with his moral self that she did? Fearing she might break the spell of their trysts and add to the pain of what she understood to be Bill's joyless marriage to Hillary, Gennifer did not ask aloud—knowing that, given his compassionate as well as passionate nature, it was natural he should not want to cause Hillary unnecessary pain, when she was doing so much to advance his political agenda in the state.

Nevertheless, soon afterward, Gennifer got a sort of answer. One night Bill came over and they had just embarked on their lovecraft when Bill leaped overboard, and having reached the safety of the bedroom wall, began weeping hysterically! Gennifer was stunned—and concerned. She begged him, but he wouldn't divulge the reason for his anguish.

What was going on? Thinking back on the scene, years later, Gennifer wondered if Bill had suffered a sudden attack of shame or remorse. Had he, she wondered, made an extreme effort to be good—and finding he could not, had he been mortified by his own lack of self-control? That he was still deeply fond of her, as his partner in extramarital relations, Gennifer had no doubt—but surely he had experienced sometimes a poisoned dart of guilt?

Whatever the explanation, however, the crisis quickly blew over, like a summer cloud, and a few minutes later, Gennifer recalled, Bill swam back to his love-raft, "ready and eager for oral sex."

Oral Sex

Gennifer might be wrong about Bill's breakdown, but she was certainly right about his love of intimate physical pleasure. Oral sex was, Gennifer claimed in her autobiography in 1996—a year before Bill's special penchant became an international sensation—Clinton's panacea.

Betsey Wright, awed by Bill's brain and political skills in the chamber of deputies but equally aware how self-absorbed and insecure he was as a person, simply refused to believe that Bill was as good a lover as the "Wonder Boy" prided himself on being. "Of course, all these women were lying about relationships and what a grand lover he was—the man is far too narcissistic to be a great lover!" Betsey snorted. "I mean, that's *my* opinion!" Susan McDougal suspected the same, in terms of Bill's infidelity. As she recounted, "it always struck me that it likely had nothing to do with sex and everything to do with approval"—a suspicion that made her question his performance in bed. "Whenever I heard about Bill having an affair with someone, I always speculated that the sex probably lasted for five minutes and the discussion about how good he was at sex lasted for thirty," she recalled. "If Bill is not being praised in sufficient quantity, then he practically begs people for it." His need for approval was almost pathological. "Hillary gave him everything he needed in a wife: intelligence, ambition, character, and, I believe, a great deal of love. But the one thing she did not give Bill, at least when I was around, was the constant approval that he craved."

Betsey Wright found this craving at once infuriating and yet deeply human. Bill's narcissistic need had "*nothing* to do with sex," she also emphasized. "It has to do with this inferiority complex that he's carried his entire life: his great need to be accepted." Oral acceptance was the simplest, cheapest, least dangerous sex in terms of pregnancy and even sexual disease—the equivalent of "cottaging" among gays. It stemmed, she believed, from the same "need" he had for public approbation—driven, as she put it, by the underlying "fear that he wasn't good enough to be accepted. I think he's spent his entire life being scared that he was white trash." He even "smelled kind of earthy, like a farmer who never could wash the aroma of soil out of his skin," Susan McDougal recalled.

The Pasha

Like many narcissists, Bill Clinton wanted to do better. In *The Culture of Narcissism,* published during Clinton's first term as governor, Christopher Lasch had lamented the corruption of public education in America, where the "concept of industrial discipline deteriorated to the point where intellectual and even manual training became incidental." To combat this decline, Lasch recommended the educational lash—as did Hillary.

Bill was receptive to such a militant response, in education, in the home, and in the boudoir; indeed, he rather liked the lash. He certainly seemed to welcome it from Hillary, who was on his case much of the brief time they spent together. "If I didn't kick his ass every morning, he'd never amount to anything," Hillary would often complain, and it was true, as it was probably true of the majority of America's adolescents who were in danger of failing. As Hillary's biographer Gail Sheehy put it, after Bill's reelection Hillary had become the veritable Arkansas "regent," exercising "the ruling

power in Bill Clinton's kingdom much as a European regent does when a
sovereign is too young, absent, or disabled to rule." Diane Kincaid Blair,
Hillary's best friend at the University of Arkansas in Fayetteville, worried
lest Bill remain "locked in adolescence."

Certainly Bill behaved like many a young European monarch or Middle
Eastern pasha. He worked long hours, addicted to politics, which he understood in range, depth, and detail in a way that Hillary would never do.
Even his Republican counterpart, former Governor Frank White, would
pay tribute to Bill Clinton's knowledge and political skills—"best I've ever
seen," White conceded, and much improved thanks to "that shelac'n I give
him." In the fullness of time White came to see that "He's an incredible
politician—I mean, he knows how to motivate people, and he's still ver',
very popular in the African-American community. You have to understand, he developed an expertise that hadn't been seen on the political
scene as effective as . . ." White searched for a parallel. Failing to find one,
he described the skills with which Bill Clinton had bounced back to the
governor's mansion. Bill was "as good as I've ever seen on a fifteen-second
sound bite! He had a vocabulary where, when they asked him a question
about something that may be very complex, in fifteen seconds, looking at
the camera, without having any prior knowledge of the question, he could
answer to where that guy who is sitting in the bar in Dumas, Arkansas, or
doin' the dishes in the kitchen in Pine Bluffs, she'd say, 'That's *right*! *That's
how I feel about that*!' And so I would put him in the level with Ronald Reagan as a communicator. They were two incredible communicators! They
knew how to talk to people! And people related to 'em!"

Betsey Wright, though as a feminist she might recoil at White's old-
fashioned sexism, agreed. Indeed, seeing Bill Clinton's interaction with
people at even closer quarters than White, Betsey remained amazed at how
transparently genuine it was. "I have never met another human being," she
would later say of Bill, "who genuinely loves people, of incredible diversity,
the way Bill does." Later, after the frustrations, scandals, and the veritable
legal tornado that would blow as a result of her work for Bill Clinton, she
would declare solemnly that she would "*never* work for an individual, in
politics or anything else again, as long as I live!" Yet even so, Betsey recognized how unique Bill Clinton was as a political animal in the zoological
garden of American politics. "I will spend the rest of my life learning from
the empathy that he could have with people," she confessed, shaking her
head wearily. "He *always* had the ability to understand where they were

coming from! And therefore, even if it were a piece of legislation, and the legislature could be creating a huge obstacle for him, a problem over something he *really* cared about, he would say, 'What you've got to understand is that Joe Smith came from here and there, and that's the way he saw it, and if you can't see it from his perspective, then you're not appreciating what his [political] role is. So for us to get him, you know, we would have to come at him from *this* angle'—and I've never known anybody who could do that about just *anybody,* on *any* position. He wasn't angry at them for the difference, he understood where they were coming from!"

Bobby Roberts, his gubernatorial aide, was equally amazed by Clinton's grasp of the science of state government: "I was always struck by how much he knew about government and how much he would absorb from talking to people!" Yet Clinton's knowledge base, for a politician still so young, had a deeper source. "He probably understood how state government worked as well as anybody I knew, and that was not from experience in it: that was from reading about it. He's a voracious reader," Roberts remarked.

Reading was, as in JFK's case, an addiction as powerful as sex. Betsey Wright saw it, in fact, as a carryover from childhood—a habit that had become, in his earliest years, Clinton's escape route into another, less threatening world than that of his alcoholic home, yet one that later "opened so many worlds when he was governor. It is truly one of the things that distinguishes him from most active politicians, that he *never stops reading*! Most politicians don't have the time for it and furthermore convince themselves that they pretty much know what they have to know. And he never knew enough! He never read enough! He always had three or four books going—*always*! From trash to economic treatises! And he also would think nothing of sitting up all night watching old movies and then coming back with the metaphors for what was going on in the Capitol that day! Out of that movie! He was *constantly* jumping perspectives of time."

Jim Blair, Bill's friend near Fayetteville, felt that, coming from very modest Arkansas backgrounds, and becoming enormously successful in their respective professions through sheer brain and willpower, the two of them were remarkably alike—indeed, they even looked alike, both almost six foot four—and blessed with endless curiosity about the world around them. "I think Hillary thought Bill and I were very much alike," Blair recalled—a reason why, perhaps, "I understand him better than most people." Even Blair, however, was awed by Bill's "encyclopedic interest. He runs on multiple tracks—that's one of the few things he could do better than I could! I have seen him carrying on an important conversation while he was carrying on a telephone conversation with me, and while he was working on a *New York Times* crossword puzzle—all these things at the same time. In fact, I've been on the phone to him when I heard a little hesitancy in his voice and I've said, 'Look, if you're working the crossword puzzle, I'm going to hang up!' 'No, no, I'm not'—but I know damned well he was! But he just has this ferocious energy and ability to multitask."

Inevitably, however, such multitasking went beyond the *NYT* crossword puzzle. Side by side with the business of statecraft, at which Bill excelled like no other in the land, there was the business of play. To more than seven thousand educators and parents in Arkansas, Mrs. Hillary Clinton had, in advancing her education reforms, hammered home the message that "When you play, you should play hard. And when you work, you should work hard. But you shouldn't confuse the two."

Bill didn't. He not only worked hard but played hard—much too hard for a married man.

The Importance of Sex

In the aftermath of his scandals Bill Clinton would later deplore the assumption that a man's private or play life had anything to do with his public performance. White trash or not, in the conveniently located Quapaw Towers he was able to sublimate his political anxieties. As Gennifer recalled, he freely indulged in his favorite elixir, involving the same mouth organ as in his undiscriminating food consumption: greedily savoring, nibbling, feasting. Therein lay not only the cradle of his stunted sexual psyche but the essence, the core craving of his personal life: a need that transcended morality and offered a crucial antidote to his relentless focus, as governor, on other people's problems. As an energetic, ambitious politician he felt that, like his hero JFK, he understood the prime importance of play—as, unfortunately for him, Hillary didn't.

Hillary's notion of marriage included intimate companionship, tenderness, and sexual connection, even the release of tension through sexual intercourse. She wore a delectable Victorian-nouveau gown (Chantilly lace over charmeuse silk) for her second inauguration as first lady, and though she certainly did not simply lie back and think of her country, as English daughters had been urged to do at the peak of Victorian arranged marriages (in which marital sex in well-bred families was seen to be a distasteful but reproductive necessity), she was not really *entertained* by sex. As a narcissist Bill, by contrast, *craved* sexual entertainment.

A pasha in a traditional Middle Eastern context would not have required his wife, or wife number one, to participate in wild or promiscuous sex—a potentate has a harem for that very purpose. Having experienced some of the same difficulties in "letting go" while married to JFK and even in her years as a young widow, Jackie Kennedy had later found herself intrigued by the subject of extramarital entertainment, indeed had commissioned and personally edited while working at Doubleday an entire, beautifully illustrated book on harems. Older than Hillary by a generation, Jackie Kennedy was aware that feminism might be bringing women untold new equalities but that the eternal battle between the sexes would continue—indeed, in a modern Western context, could only get fiercer and more bloody before it got better.

Hillary knew this, too, but took a more proactive view: that men, like children, could be *trained* to do better.

Jackie Onassis's passivity, to be sure, had stemmed from her own childhood. She had never made any attempt to change either her first or her second husband's predatory sexual behavior, for she was quite used to such roguishness, having seen it throughout her childhood in "Black Jack," her beloved, alcoholic, and philandering father, Jack Bouvier. When Jackie had found a pair of panties under her pillow in the White House, she'd thus famously simply handed them to the President, saying they were not hers—they were the wrong size. Taking visitors around the West Wing another day, she'd stunned them by opening the door to one office and introducing the visitors to "two of my husband's mistresses": "Fiddle" and "Faddle." In other words, Jackie Kennedy had accepted JFK's promiscuity as part and parcel of the husband she'd loved—something that could, and would, never be changed in his lifetime.

Hillary, however, was too fierce an activist in her feminism to be interested in harems. Unlike Jackie, she thought nature could be shamed and tamed, or at least kept within certain boundaries until such time as evolutionary pressures changed men's biologies. Unfortunately, she was unable to discuss the matter with Bill. As her friend Nancy Pietrefesa put it, Hillary was "in denial," not because she was unaware that Bill was, like most active men of his time, a base philanderer, but because she did not *want* to know and have to accept such a reality. Her own father, Hugh Rodham, was the opposite of Black Jack Bouvier: a sexually repressed tyrant with an unfortunate Richard III–like limp and a dire chip on his shoulder. Hillary had learned to please him, as an only daughter, not by Jackie-like femininity or the adoption of a whispery voice and the mute acceptance of a woman's subordinate place in a man's world, but by the opposite: doing a man's job better than any man in a man's world. "She was so deadly earnest about everything," Susan McDougal recalled; "whenever someone disagreed with her, she would eagerly engage them in debate, convinced she could persuade them of her point of view by the sheer force of her convictions." In the context of Arkansas, as a traditional, highly conservative, good-ole-boy state, this was bound to play badly. "Hillary made it clear to me that she felt superior to the people she met in Arkansas," Susan recounted—a contempt for the people Bill of necessity consorted with as governor of a poor and backward state that had contributed mightily to the general perception of northern hubris that had attached to Bill's first governorship. Now, however, as leader of the movement to reform Arkansas's own public education system, she had discovered a mission: a crusade, in which her intellectual and social snobbery might be seen as part of her intrinsic intellectual nobility, indeed even as democratic. She was not, after all, addressing herself to the rich or well-off, who could afford private education for their children, but to the ordinary parents of Arkansas—especially, but not exclusively, women.

Thus, Hillary was metamorphosing, like Hans Christian Andersen's ugly duckling, into a feminist star: a star Bill Clinton admired more and more deeply, just as JFK had come to respect and admire his wife's savoir faire, in fact, almost *savoir seduire*. Yet the transformation, the makeover of Hillary Rodham into a beautiful white swan, was not accompanied by any deeper sexual maturity. Getting her to wash her hair more often and use makeup had required her husband's electoral defeat. Necessity had been the mother of her cosmetic virtue, but neither that remodeling nor her name change had altered the fact that, driven by her father's expectations and with a mother equally difficult to please emotionally, she simply did not possess an erotic pheromone in her body—and to his credit, *Bill had never required that of her.* What he'd wanted, he had gotten: an outstanding intellectual companion; a not unpretty face behind the gogglelike spectacles; and a fierce loyalty to him and to his political potential that could help take him to the top, even, in the right circumstances, to the presidency of the United States. "Of course, Hillary provided him with so many more dimensions of relationship in his life than most marriages do," Betsey Wright—a passionate admirer of Hillary from the day she first met her—later claimed. Hillary had even—to Bill's surprise, since he believed one or both of them were infertile—given him a child, a daughter whom Bill loved sometimes to the point of obsession, Chelsea, who so tickled his self-centered fancy and made him the proudest of fathers.

Bill's respect for Hillary's mind, and for her willingness to bear and bring up his child, translated—as Jackie Kennedy's had done for JFK, over the years—into a deep and genuine tenderness for his spouse and adoration of their beloved offspring. Such intimacy of mind and heart was intense—"intellectual, political, parenting, sexual, the whole gamut," as Betsey Wright described it. Indeed, the union went far deeper than most people suspected. Close friends called them "soul mates," acknowledging that Bill and Hillary confided fully "in nobody else, not even family, only in each other," Gail Sheehy recorded. Yet the business of sex—of Bill's need for it with multiple partners, like his hero JFK—went largely unaddressed. Insofar as she knew of it, Hillary tolerated it; but where Jackie had seen in it the same, almost reassuring traits of her own much-loved father, for Hillary it was and would remain a foreign field, one that she implicitly forbade even her closest friends and colleagues to apprise her of.

Thus Bill Clinton continued to work hard and to connect with the first lady in his life, but also to play hard with second, third, fourth, and further ladies in his life. In bursting into tears during sex with Gennifer Flowers, Bill had not been squirming with torment over his adultery, as Gennifer naïvely assumed. This time there had been something else that was troubling him.

CHAPTER TWENTY-NINE

A BAD
APPLE

A Call About Roger

One afternoon Governor Bill Clinton's mother—Mrs. Dick Kelley since 1982, Jim Dwire having passed away—received a phone call from Steve Engstrom, her former attorney.

It was early August 1984: the eponymous year of George Orwell's famous vision of a totalitarian industrial future. That totalitarian nightmare had not come to pass, but in the personal lives of the Clinton family another, deeply sickening nightmare did take place.

Virginia, despite the warnings of her new husband, had recently sued the doctors of Ouachita Hospital in Hot Springs for $5 million compensation, incensed that they had forced her, as she saw it, to surrender her position as senior anesthetist in favor of a male, Dr. Robert Humphreys. Against a fully trained physician she had had no chance, however—indeed, it was the hospital's concern over escalating insurance costs resulting from lawsuits that had forced it to use more qualified staff. After a cruel deposition hearing in which she was ranged against a panel of male doctors and attorneys in a scene that reminded her of *High Noon,* Virginia had been forced to drop her lawsuit; indeed, she was lucky to get away with paying her own costs in the failed action. But if Mrs. Kelley thought attorney Engstrom was calling about her lawsuit against the hospital doctors, she was heart-stoppingly mistaken. Earning more than three times her governor son Bill's salary until she was forced out of anesthetics, Virginia had mothered, indeed smothered, her second son, Roger, with love, attention, patience, tolerance, gifts, and money—more and more money. Her reward, sadly, would be in Heaven. On Earth she received, after her failed lawsuit, the second great jolting of 1984.

"You mean you don't know?" the lawyer asked, incredulous that the governor had not already called her.

Father Figure

Bill Clinton, Virginia's elder son, had kept the news not only from his mistress Gennifer Flowers but from his own adored mother.

It was a sorry tale. Bill's brother, Roger—who had dropped out of college and, at twenty-nine, finally given up on his studies—had become not only a drug addict, but a cocaine peddler too.

The slit canvas roof that Roger's mother had seen the year before on the top of his Mustang convertible—which Virginia had purchased for him—was not the mark of an idle thief, she now learned. Roger had been carrying $8,000 of illegal cocaine in the car, and it had been stolen. Living then in fear for his life, even threats against the lives of his mother and brother, Roger had got his brother, Bill, to loan him the $8,000 via a millionaire Little Rock bond dealer, the nefarious Dan Lasater. Lasater, at Bill's request, had then found Roger a job on his 1,000-acre horse ranch outside Ocala, Florida, to help him recover from his addiction, keep him out of trouble—and keep him out of Arkansas.

Shipping Roger out of state—"I was told we were stashing him for some politician Mr. Lasater was working," one senior employee later recalled did no good. A twenty-nine-year-old nebbish, not big enough to protect himself, Roger Clinton had been given credit not only by New York cocaine suppliers but by the Medellín, Colombia, cartel itself on the strength of his gubernatorial connection. But if being the brother of a U.S. governor had opened doors to drug dealing and eased credit concerns, by the same token Roger had become too big for the authorities to miss. By the summer of 1984, as he returned to Hot Springs to face federal prosecutors, not even the governor of Arkansas could save Roger from himself. Nor did Bill try. His aide Bobby Roberts later recalled Bill's reaction. The "bad-apple brother" aspect of Bill Clinton's life was "an issue that nobody's looked at very carefully," Roberts later reflected. "I mean, there are ten years' difference in their ages. And Bill in a way was sort of a father figure for him—a father figure for a bad son.

"I mean, this is a guy who was everything Bill Clinton wasn't. The only thing Roger was, was in a shallow way sort of charming. I mean, I'd enjoy shooting pool with him or somethin'. But he's everything that most people who came from the background Bill came from would be. He doesn't finish college, he gets into trouble—I mean, all the things you think would happen to a boy being raised by a single parent, is Roger.

"Now, when I worked for Clinton, I also dealt with the state police. And Roger became involved in some drug stuff. I was the person who had to go tell Clinton about this—and it was not one of the things I particularly liked to do."

As historian Roger Morris pieced together the story, using FBI and other interviews as well as police documents, it was not Roberts but state police director Tommy Goodwin who had the unpleasant task of formally informing the governor—but, claimed Morris, given the number of "dissidents" in police ranks, it was considered politic to make sure the first lady was told, too, lest the governor try to get the impending indictment "swept under the rug" in election year.

Bobby Roberts remembered the story differently. "I mean, essentially what happened," Roberts explained, "is the colonel of the State Police, who was a friend of mine, came in and said, 'Shut the door! We've got a problem here. We've got Roger on a drug deal, and what we want to do with him is use him as an informant. This is what we're going to do.' He didn't ask me about it. He said, 'This is what we're going to do. But I don't want the Governor to read that in the paper. What will we do?'"

For the governor the news was clearly going to be devastating—and Roberts therefore went to fetch Hillary before informing the governor. "You've got to go with me, because I don't want to, you know . . ." Roberts explained, his words cut off by Hillary's instant response: "This is a family deal, and I'm the one that needs to tell him!"

The first lady and senior gubernatorial aide thus informed the governor. Clinton was "really in anguish over it, obviously, as any brother would be," Roberts recalled. "But he was in anguish over it almost as a parent. And felt terribly guilty about it. He told me, and I can't quote the words exactly, but the gist of the conversation was that Roger would have done all right if he [Bill] had had time to spend with him. That Roger's failure was his failure."

It was as well that, in such anguishing circumstances, Hillary was brought in from the start. In campaigning for better education in the state and more home "discipline," Hillary had asked "only that each of us decide that the time for excuses is over." That time had come, as Bill himself realized, listening to what the charges, based on videotaped DEA evidence, would be. Roger Jr. was out of control, just as Roger Sr. had been throughout their childhoods. Roger Sr. had never faced up to his problem—and had made the lives of those around him a misery for almost two decades before his own cruel death. If Roger was not careful, the same would happen to him, too—and to those around him.

The matter was urgent, for Roger's problem, the governor was told, threatened to be fatal. Roger was—as his therapist would soon testify in open court—snorting cocaine *sixteen* times a day, consuming four grams of the substance by nightfall: an amount approaching "a lethal dose." Yet to watch his own brother go to court, and very probably to prison, would destroy their mother, Bill knew, while leaving Bill himself racked with guilt that he hadn't been able, as governor and half brother, to stop or to save him.

Time and again Bill had helped Roger. He had gotten him appointed him to the Arkansas Juvenile Delinquency Board, until Roger was dismissed for nonappearance, and had even, according to some accounts, agreed to grant several gubernatorial favors. But in doing so Bill had merely delayed his brother's demise: a demise that in an election year threatened, were he not careful, could become his own, too.

A Marvelous Bit of Courage

Though he might weep uncontrollably, Governor Clinton's heartache was not unique in American politics at that time. There were other, much more prominent cases of fraternal failure, beginning with former president Jimmy Carter's ne'er-do-well brother, Billy.

Perhaps the worst case of all was in Massachusetts, however. There, the Boston Irish politician and leader of the Massachusetts House, Billy Bulger, also had a "bad apple" brother: the notorious and cynically nicknamed "Whitey." James J. Bulger's Irish-American mafia sins were black as tar; he was wanted in Massachusetts for multiple murders, prostitution racketeering, sexual abuse of young girls, white slave trading, and drug trafficking. Neither as a politician nor as a brother had Billy Bulger ever lifted a finger either to counsel "Whitey" to surrender to the authorities or

to help the FBI, the police, or other authorities to track or arrest his sibling—indeed, he had never needed to as a mere state legislator. "Whitey"
thus disappeared and was never caught.

Unlike Bulger, however, Governor Bill Clinton was chief executive of
his own state and the head of its law enforcement agencies. Though he
might seek solace between Gennifer Flower's tender limbs in Quapaw Towers, Bill knew that Hillary, alerted by Bobby Roberts, was right about
Roger. As she had counseled, he would have to do the most terrible thing
in the world: turn his brother in.

No one liked the business; indeed, many of Bill's male friends and colleagues afterward felt he had done wrong. "Why did he let his own brother
go to the penitentiary over a pissy-assed drug deal?" Bill's old Arkansas
buddy, Paul Fray, asked rhetorically. "Just to make himself look good," Fray
answered his own question. The sheriff's office and even the prosecutor
wavered—"They leaned till they cracked," a journalist later quipped. Hillary,
however, remained adamant, for, like Betsey Wright, she knew how damag-
ing a cover-up of Roger would be for Bill's future political prospects. As one
state policeman put it cynically, "We knew she'd tell him to feed ole Roger to
the feds for the sake of his career, and that's what he ended up doing."

Such was the way it looked to those who were unaware of the true extent
of Roger's cocaine addiction and trafficking. Having seen the evidence,
however, Bill was mortified—for not only was Roger approaching a level of
fatal consumption, but his addiction and trafficking had created a trail of
narcotics corruption that led way beyond Roger to a host of Arkansas figures and their children. It simply could not be covered up. "It was a very sad
situation," Roberts recalled. "But it was also again one of those cases where
I saw Bill at his best, in that he's the governor, he could have intervened in
some way with that and perhaps done something to help Roger out. And he
didn't. I mean, he said, 'Treat him like they would any other informant and
just let me know so that I can tell my mother before this gets in the paper.'
Which I thought was a marvelous bit of courage on a personal level."

Roger Is Charged

"That's what's so maddening about it," Bobby Roberts sighed years later
when recalling the eventual indictment that was brought to the governor's
office at the capitol on August 2, 1984—for Bill's courage in refusing to interfere with the due process of law did not, unhappily, extend to telling his

mother Virginia the awful news. "He could do something like that, and then he could turn round and . . ." Roberts's voice died away.

Be such a coward? Bill was certainly afraid of his mother's angry tears—and there would be more than tears over Roger, he knew. Roger was Virginia's pet, her adored Benjamin, a child who could do no wrong in her eyes, as Betsey Wright recalled. However badly Roger behaved, however bad the trouble he would get into, his mother "was always defending Roger to Bill," Betsey sighed.

Fearing his mother's reaction, Bill had therefore done nothing, leaving his mother to hear the news from Roger's lawyer. "I'm just calling to tell you how sorry I am about Roger," Engstrom had begun, unaware that Virginia had "no idea what in the world he was talking about."

"There was a deafening pause," Virginia herself recalled, followed by the attorney's consoling words: "Well, I've never been so sorry to call anybody in my life. I just assumed you knew. Roger is going to be charged."

Virginia went into a state of shock; indeed, in recalling that she had felt like dying, she meant it literally: that she would never survive the knowledge. Her sister-in-law Nancy Kelley later told her, "Never once had I seen you devastated until that day."

Betsey Wright was almost as mortified when Virginia then called the governor's office at the capitol. The governor had promised faithfully to call his mother—to spare her the agony of hearing this from anyone else. And he had not called. "It *hurt* her," Betsey recounted. "It hurt her very badly. I mean, a lot of times I saw that things which made me so mad about him, and were so hurtful to me, she was going through *also*!"

Both Betsey and Virginia were nonplussed by Bill's emotional cowardice. Yet there was a method in it, psychologically. In his heart of hearts Bill knew that, while he himself might be his mother's pinup, her idol, it was "little" Roger who was his mother's true love—and that, if he called her before the lawyer did, she would beg him, as governor, for a stay of legal action. This way, however cowardly on his part, she *had* to accept, as he did, the process of law. It was a fait accompli.

The Key to a New America

Two weeks later, in federal court, Roger Clinton, Jr., was released on bail until a hearing set to take place on November 9—*after* the 1984 gubernatorial election. Governor William Jefferson Clinton's career would be spared.

Roger's, however, would not.

For Hillary, single-minded in her pursuit of greater educational excellence, there was no question that Bill was doing the right thing: making the tough decision she was urging parents to do on her campaign trail throughout the state with regard to the education and future of children in Arkansas and the nation. Hillary had spoken of a "breakdown in shared social values" that had been going on in America "among all of our institutions for the last twenty years": a cumulative degeneration that had affected, indeed infected, the public schools. This had been marked by a "pulling away of support for the schools by the parents of the students whom the schools are trying to teach." Parents, like legislators, held the key to a new America.

For Bill, however, discipline was one thing, compassion another. His tears, in Gennifer's apartment in the Quapaw Towers, were for real. When his first stepfather had died, he'd wept for the man he'd hated and who had so wasted his self-preening, self-indulgent life. By contrast, Bill hadn't squandered his high intelligence, his talents, his promise, or the help and instruction that his elders had given him—yet had been forced to watch his own younger brother, his half brother, go to seed: filled with impossible dreams of success in the field of pop music yet bereft of the necessary musical talent or self-knowledge to know that he was not equipped to succeed. It was a terrible sight.

Yet for all his compassion, Bill had mixed emotions, too, if he were honest. In his own mind, at least, he'd never been consciously jealous of Roger Jr., though he might well have been, given the way baby Roger had intruded into his own hitherto exclusive world as Virginia's only son. Instead, Bill had cared for him conscientiously—indeed, in the eyes not only of Roger Jr., but of all witnesses, Bill had looked after his younger brother selflessly, like a parent. Often, in fact, better than a parent.

But in this sibling relationship, perhaps the very closest relationship in Bill Clinton's life, there were things going on that Hillary didn't know and that "Bubba"—as Roger Jr. still called Bill—didn't want her to know.

Things called wild sex.

Distraction and Debauchery

Only a psychologist would have been able to unravel the complicated tie between Bill Clinton and his half brother Roger—and in the wake of

Roger's arraignment, family counseling was indeed recommended both by the lawyers and by the court. By all accounts, however, the counseling did not lead to any profound change in "Bubba's" own life or personality. Instead it was Hillary who took over the meetings with the psychologist and the family discussions thereafter, infuriating both Virginia and Bill by her distanced, self-righteous dissection of Roger's addictive behavior. As Roger Morris wrote, "According to friends who heard contemporaneous accounts from Virginia, her daughter-in-law raised unexamined questions of denial and irresponsibility and other topics that sent the mother away in tearful fury and the thirty-eight-year-old governor into yet another round of distraction and debauchery."

Documented testimony confirms the debauchery. With his brother Roger, Bill Clinton enjoyed—and would continue to enjoy right up until Roger's imprisonment—episodes of extreme sexual dissipation, accompanied by drugs, that threatened, if they became publicly known, to land not only the governor's brother but the governor himself in jail. Who, then, was the addict? Was not he, Governor Bill Clinton, consumed by, and a consumer of, politics almost as a narcotic—a narcotic without which, he'd found after his electoral defeat in 1980, he could not live? Such self-tormenting questions led Bill inexorably to his other addiction, besides politics, as in the life of his hero John F. Kennedy: illicit sex.

"I think we're all addicted to something," Bill confided to his friend Carolyn Yeldell Staley at this time. "Some people are addicted to drugs. Some to power. Some to food." He shook his big head. "Some to sex. We're all addicted to something."

Cross-Addiction

Food addiction is still a controversial area of psychology and therapeutic practice, Bill Clinton becoming famous, among U.S. presidents, for his love of junk food, craving McDonald's hamburgers even after attending a state banquet. Like most addictions, however, food addiction is, as one writer aptly summarized, not only a craving for nourishment but "an illusory shortcut that leads to physical dysfunction. It delays the inner work that needs to be done, but does not remove the need to do it."

For Bill, such compulsive, escapist cravings often bordered on the reckless, but for the most part they did not spill beyond his ability to do his job, enjoy other forms of entertainment, or take care of his health. Side by side with his need for hamburgers and fatty southern food, for example, he attempted to exercise regularly. However, it was this very balancing of food and exercise that led him, literally, to his other addiction. Jogging downtown and through the Quapaw Quarter, grabbing a doughnut at the Community Bakery or a coffee at McDonald's on Broadway Street, visiting with the customers, then shuffling around the neighborhood of the governor's mansion, past General MacArthur's birthplace and the big old mansions of Little Rock's late-Victorian era, he might be seen by athletes and marathon trainees to be a big, overweight, sloppy mass of pink perspiring gubernatorial flesh that was unsightly yet strangely human in its unaffectedness, its lack of snobbery. But the warm, friendly governor, though he might press the flesh of potential voters on his jolly way, had his heart set on another kind of flesh to press.

According to Gennifer Flowers, Bill would "pop in" while jogging past her apartment block, to shoot not the breeze but his wad. To her there was nothing intrinsically perverse in this arrangement; it was just, unfortunately, adulterous, as it had always been. In a side door giving onto a side street, she would wedge a newspaper so that he could enter that way and not be seen at the front entrance. Now that he was governor again, however, he had to have a security detail with him or close by. "While he and I were in bed making love, his driver would be waiting for him downstairs!" Gennifer recalled. As she explained, in the quiet provincial city, in a leafy area to the south of the stores and offices of downtown Little Rock, it was all too easy to arrange such trysts. "He would jog just over a mile to my place, spend half an hour or so making love to me, then have his driver drop him off a block or two from the mansion. Then he would show up at home properly out of breath."

In some societies this would have been par for the patriarchal male course; in Little Rock in 1984, it was playing with fire. The city was admittedly small, but for that very reason people gossiped, and the chances of discovery were high. After working in FM and AM radio, Gennifer had landed a job she really loved, singing at an exclusive downtown restaurant, the Capitol Club, at the top of the Worthen Building, one of the tallest in the city. It was there, during a political fund-raiser for the 1984 election, that she met Hillary face-to-face for the first time.

Gennifer was stunned. The First Lady looked far more attractive than when she'd first caught sight of her. Several years had passed. Hillary's hair was transformed, as were the clothes she now wore as a successful lawyer. Hillary stared at her rival with such intensity Gennifer was certain she knew—indeed Gennifer was concerned Hillary might actually strike her, which is what she herself would have done. Indeed such was Gennifer's identification with her arch-rival that she recalled actually hoping Hillary, even if she did not pop her one on the nose, would at least pick Bill up and take him away, out of Gennifer's life. That way, her own mortification at being so attached to Bill but having to make do with the position of concubine would have been resolved, however painfully. Yet when Hillary made to do this very thing—to remove Bill from the scene—the eternal competitive streak that resides in every passionate woman flared up.

Instead, Hillary turned to Bill, and in a deliberately symbolic gesture, drew him down and planted a kiss upon his cheek—asking him to go with her to the bar and get a drink. As Gennifer later recalled, this was like holding a red rag to a bull. "You son of a bitch, you'd better not desert me!" her eyes blazed.

Bill got the message, as Gennifer painted the scene in retrospect. "He looked at Hillary, smiled, and said, 'I'll be over there later. You go ahead.' It was a showdown, and I had won—at least that round."

Orgies at Vantage Point

Revealing the "anguish in his soul" a decade later to another lover, Bill confessed to having always lived "a secret existence, a life filled with lies and subterfuge. As a little child he had lied to his parents, and even though he was a smart kid and knew the consequences of his actions, he had maintained that hidden life, safe in the knowledge that no one knew about it, knew the true Bill Clinton. After he married in 1975, when he was twenty-nine, his secret life continued. The number of his affairs multiplied and Clinton became increasingly appalled at himself, at his capacity not only for deceiving others but also for self-deception."

Some of this deception involved Roger Jr.—indeed, it was his sexual shenanigans with Roger that spoke of a deepening corruption at this time in his life: a Nero-like search for sexual excitement and novelty he could no longer bridle and that would eventually mark him down in the history books not as one of the greatest economic stewards in the history of the United States, as was his due, but as the most privately flawed of American presidents—even though, in comparison with JFK and LBJ, this was actually not the case! For this, despite the politically motivated cohorts of self-righteous and often hypocritical Republicans baying for his blood, Bill Clinton would, in the eyes of both his former chief of staff Betsey Wright and his bosom pal Jim Blair, have no one to blame but himself.

For the moment, however, Bill Clinton was in a 1984 that not even George Orwell—fascinated by politics but deeply sexually inhibited—had dared depict in his eponymous novel. As the months went by and the campaign for gubernatorial reelection moved into higher and higher gear, Bill kept going to check out his brother, Roger, at the Vantage Point apartment complex in Little Rock, where, waiting for his trial date, for two months Roger was a "nonpaying guest." Instead of acting like the good parent he had become to Roger, however, the governor—whether in guilt or lust, or both—reportedly joined in Roger's almost continuous orgies in the corporate suite, next to the office of Jane Parks, the manager of the complex. There, separated only by a thin partition wall, Roger held his clown's court, playing acid rock on his "ghetto blaster" and getting high from the moment he woke.

The scene was almost surreal. Brought in the governor's official car, Bill Clinton would allegedly appear from time to time in the afternoons and party with Roger. "This is really good shit!" Bill was heard to exclaim by Mrs. Parks, the Vantage Point manager, and her assistant, referring to the marijuana the Clinton brothers smoked. They also snorted cocaine together. "Sometimes the two brothers were alone," Mrs. Parks later told British author Ambrose Evans-Pritchard. "Sometimes young women were invited to join, and the little party was consummated with raucous orgasms. The bed was pressed up against the partition wall, just a few feet from the desk of Mrs. Parks. On two occasions she heard the governor copulating on the bed. Bill had his girlfriends in there." Jane Parks's assistant corroborated the account: "You could hear them through the walls. They looked to me very young girls, probably 17, 18 years old."

JFK had gloried in risk taking, yet this deliberate descent into the bowels of his brother's addiction seemed almost suicidal for Bill. What, the family psychologist might well have asked, was *really* going on?

Sadly, it seems, the psychologist didn't ask—and neither Bill nor Roger ever told.

Survival, Not Reform

Later, Virginia paid tribute to the family counselor in Little Rock, Karen Ballard. She wrote to thank Karen from the bottom of her heart for helping her son Roger, "because he didn't want to admit that he was addicted."

Nor did Bill. What Bill could not say in front of his mother was that he, too, was dependent, but on sex, for which Roger's drugs were merely a lure. Roger, however, was still unmarried, a failed musician and college dropout. Bill Clinton was a married man, a father, and governor of the state of Arkansas, seeking reelection: an election in which the Bill-and-Hillary Clinton team had become what promised to be the most effective marital political partnership in American history.

Ironically, it was this very political potential that made confession the more difficult, Bill too ashamed to confide his sexual addiction to Hillary. Here Hillary's stuckupness was a real obstacle, for had he done so, Bill might possibly have begun to come to terms with a part of his character that was perpetually on the edge of running out of control. Even Susan McDougal had noticed Bill's tendency to shirk confrontation if it might provoke Hillary's famed "screaming fits"—a response Bill Clinton would not "confront if he didn't absolutely have to." Fearing Hillary's wrath, Bill chose not to—afraid, in part, that Hillary would never understand, indeed might lose faith in him. "He cowered a bit when she laid down the law," John Brummett, the political reporter of the *Arkansas Gazette,* once recalled—a response that ensured survival, not reform.

The Death of a Child

In the November 1984 gubernatorial election, Bill Clinton was triumphantly reelected for a third two-year term, winning by a 63-to-37 percent margin against the Republican nominee, a Jonesboro contractor named Woody Freeman. It was a landslide.

Victory, however, was tinged with tears. Bill was compelled to watch, a few days later, as his younger brother pleaded guilty and was painted in court as the sole addict of the Clinton family on November 9, 1984. Other suspects had been interrogated. Once they'd begun to tell "authorities about cocaine deals being cut in the home of an assistant U.S. attorney in Little Rock" and other criminal acts, Roger had realised he would never get away with a plea of innocence. He had therefore changed his plea to guilty.

The judge accepted his confession of guilt and ordered him to be brought before the court two months later, after the inauguration in January 1985, for sentencing.

The maximum number of years in jail, newspapers speculated, would be fifteen. The newly reelected governor, the first lady, and the addict's mother and new stepfather, Dick Kelley, accompanied Roger Jr. with heavy hearts and no little foreboding from Virginia's house on Lake Hamilton to the Federal Building in Hot Springs. There Roger Clinton, Jr., who had complied with investigators and given evidence against many of his drug contacts, colleagues, and customers ("I guess I'm going to do Roger's time for him," Sam Anderson, Jr., would remark), was duly handcuffed and sentenced to two years' imprisonment at Fort Worth, with three further years suspended.

"We watched till they drove Roger away," Virginia remembered. Facing reporters, the governor accepted the judge's sentence on his brother "with respect. Now it is the duty of my family and I to do what we can to help Roger free himself from his drug dependency," the governor stated. "I feel more deeply committed than ever before to do everything I can to fight illegal drugs in our state, and I hope that in the future my efforts can spare some other families from the personal tragedy and pain this drug use has brought to my family."

Virginia listened, then she and her husband went home in silence. As she recalled afterward, it was as if she had "experienced the death of a child."

Emotional Breakdown

In actuality Roger would serve only a year in prison. Although he would always lead a somewhat wild and wooly life, without a real profession but with his brother's protection, he would nevertheless stay more or less out of trouble once released.

Prison had, as Bill Clinton had reasoned with himself, worked. For Bill himself, however, Roger's arrest and trial became strike three in his moral struggle insofar as truth and honesty were concerned. He'd failed to stand by his contract with Colonel Holmes to avoid induction and service in Vietnam. He'd failed to confront the truth about his own failure of leadership in his first gubernatorial term, externalizing the problem rather than introspecting. Now, once again, he had failed, in his counseling sessions and in his relationship with Hillary, to confront the truth about his own sexual addiction, while sacrificing his brother to the authorities for drug dependency and dealing.

Once again depression struck. Biographers Charles Allen and Jonathan Portis—the first a Little Rock teacher, the second an editor on the *Arkansas Gazette*—chronicled another emotional breakdown in the governor in 1985, after Roger Clinton's sentencing. "He hit a low in his mood swing and became self-destructive," they wrote—a view seconded by the *Arkansas Democrat* reporter and writer Meredith Oakley, who recalled that, with the Arkansas legislature assembling for its biennial sitting in the spring of 1985, Governor Clinton seemed distracted and unfocused. It was, Oakley recorded, "clear that Clinton did not have a firm grip on his office or the legislature for the first several months of his third term."

Bill Clinton was adrift, and despite the constant shoring up by Hillary, his co-candidate wife, and Betsey Wright, his loyal director of staff, he was in danger of collapse.

Survivor Guilt

"Many times if she wasn't in a meeting I would call her and give her my account of what was agreed upon," Betsey Wright recalled how she attempted to keep Hillary involved in the sometimes wayward performance of Bill Clinton, the governor. "I mean, I knew Bill would, too," Betsey chuckled, "but it might be slightly different!" She paused. "Their partnership," she added with complete sincerity, "embraced everything—in both their lives."

Almost. Yet in essence Betsey was right: that while Bill, so brilliant and mercurial, might undergo endless changes of mood and notion, Hillary was rocklike, relentless in her faith in what they could achieve.

While Hillary continued her struggle to reform Arkansas public education—a war that would go on for several more years as the teachers' union attempted to pocket increased salaries but contested teacher testing all the way to the Supreme Court—Bill's good-ole-boy chief of staff and phenomenal fund-raiser, Maurice Smith, and Betsey Wright—who had been falsely promised Maurice's job—attempted to keep Bill afloat at the capitol. Betsey had staked her professional life on making Bill Clinton an effective governor, not only in action but also in the mind of the public, and was therefore infuriated by Clinton's weaknesses. "Part of the role I played," she later acknowledged, "was organizing details which he couldn't be bothered with, so he could be the thinker—and in that sense, [it was] a kind of symbiotic working relationship." Yet Betsey could not simply stand aside and watch such a hugely talented individual, with such distinctive political skills, commit political hara-kiri. Her job therefore became that of Saint Peter guarding the morality gates to the capitol, in view of Bill's addictive proclivities—a self-appointed role in which she was constantly at odds with some of the governor's state troopers, who pimped for him in their cruisers. "Part of the role I gave myself, which I believed that he needed, was his Disciplinarian, Nag, Confronter of Behavior," Betsey recalled, shaking her head. "Challenging his every mood."

The good moods permitted Clinton to envision a brighter economic future for Arkansas, based on better access to education. In these he was indefatigable—inspirational, caring, knowledgeable, and dedicated to improvement. The bad moods took Bill into ever more debauchery. For Betsey it was often a thankless task. "I do know there were a couple of times when Hillary would say, 'Betsey—*he's an adult. Let him hang by his own mistakes. You know, this isn't your responsibility*!' I mean," Betsey sighed, "she was *right*! And I shouldn't have stayed as long as I did, working for someone for whom I was essentially a disciplinarian and a nanny!"

The governor, however, was hurting. He knew that, whatever he might say, Roger would inevitably feel Bill hadn't done enough, as governor, to save his own brother from jail—a sentence that made Roger ineligible, in return, to vote for his brother for the rest of his life. Given his own behavior, moreover, Bill could not help feeling survivor guilt—a guilt that was almost daily triggered owing to the gubernatorial pronouncements he had to make on the subject of parental responsibilities and drug addiction. "See, I didn't have a father growing up, and he was like a father to me, growing up, all my life, so that's why we've always been close," Roger had been recorded by a federal-state narcotics task force as saying. "There isn't anything in the world he wouldn't do for me."

Bill could only wring his hands in despair.

The Bedroom of America

Politics has always been a matter of power and influence. In a country as wealthy and capitalistically successful as America, however, electoral politics were now becoming, in ever-increasing degree, a battle between mon-eybags: contenders, rivals, and opponents all slugging at one another with expensive negative ads, commercials, mailings, and special tactics such as vote hauling. This was hardly Governor Bill Clinton's fault, nor could he hope to survive in the cutthroat U.S. political world unless he not only played the game but played it better than anyone else, either Democrats or Republicans. Guilt, however, clawed at his soul—not only over the busi-ness of Roger Jr.'s prison sentence, but because, alongside the business of sexual gratification in a celebrity-led world where political power was an aphrodisiac for susceptible women, the business of funding corruption now began to reach megalevels.

"Almost a quarter of Maurice Smith's big contributors to Bill Clinton represented major lobbies in the state," historian Roger Morris wrote in de-spair over the "culture of complicity" and corruption this betokened for both main political parties in Arkansas—and Morris was right. One of Bill Clinton's most generous sponsors, for example, Danny Ray Lasater, was not simply trafficking in cocaine, which ruined countless lives through ad-diction; he was also said to be running amok as a broker in Little Rock's virtually unregulated bond market—a financial mayhem in which the later Whitewater scandal would be but a tiny bubble.

Corruption, in other words, was becoming endemic to the American system of business and governance, and Bill Clinton could not change that, any more than he seemed able to change his sexual behavior or Hillary seemed able to. Even Gennifer Flowers, so traditional in her atti-tudes, was amazed by Hillary's tolerance, especially when one night Gen-nifer deliberately sent Bill home with lipstick on his collar. Afterward she could not imagine what had come over her, but acknowledged she did it purposefully. "Our lovemaking was always passionate," she recalled. In fact, he told her "this was the best sex he'd ever had. I wanted to believe that. He'd say he wished he could be with me always, and I believed that, too. I wanted him to spend the night with me, to watch him sleep, but he al-ways said he couldn't."

When Hillary saw the lipstick, she naturally asked how it had gotten there. "You know women are always hugging me," Bill brushed off her in-quisition, as Bill reported to Gennifer. Even Gennifer was amazed. "Bill treated our relationship as if he were bulletproof," she later reflected. Had it been her in Hillary's high heels, she would, she claimed, "have pinned him to the wall."

That Hillary did not do so, Gennifer speculated, was because the Governor and First Lady must have had an agreement. "I knew she knew what was going on," Gennifer claimed, but at the same time she didn't want to know. Bill told her, for example, that "after he hung up from talking with me one night, she walked into the room and asked 'How's Gennifer?' Bill had responded, cool as a cucumber: 'Just fine.' And that, Gennifer recalled Bill's story of the incident, "was the end of it."

Complicity seemed to have reached not only the bedrock, but the very bedroom of America.

Holding Off

Within Reagan's deregulated, free-for-all, unbridled capitalistic economy, as in American culture generally, the old rules were no longer being observed—at least not by power players such as arbitrageur and insider trader Ivan Boesky, junk bond trader Michael Milken, and others. It remained, however, to be seen how this newer, more rampant capitalism would play out in American electoral combat.

Despite President Reagan's personal popularity, Republicans had lost significantly in the 1984 elections—and would do so again in 1986, as the tensions between New Right and New Left, haves and have-nots, intensified. And in that melting pot of change, the press became the litmus paper on which the contradictions and changing face of modern America could be read. In the wake of Watergate the press would later be blamed for falling standards and for reveling in "scandal and sensational coverage," as communications historian Marvin Kalb noted, but such reveling was, in part, a reaction to the reduced standards of political and ethical behavior among leaders from President Nixon downward. A series of crises had, ever since Kennedy's assassination in 1963, resulted in "sour popular attitudes" toward politicians and government. "Reporters came to assume that officials lied routinely," said Kalb—prompting Nixon "to tell the American people that he was not 'a crook,' " since the public, in large measure, felt that he was one! As respect for politicians went down, admiration for journalists, as true representatives of the people, went up. After centuries of being admitted through the tradesman's entrance, they were now becoming celebrities themselves—especially those who presented and helped the public digest the daily news. In such circumstances, the journalist was not simply the public's anonymous messenger, acting on behalf of the Fourth Estate, but an increasingly powerful celebrity harbinger, empowered to ask questions that had never been posed in a previous, more "gentlemanly" age. Lurching from crutch to crotch, Bill Clinton was still able to drown his periodic sorrows in oral, cottaging-like promiscuity (one state trooper would later testify to having procured more than a hundred willing sirens for Governor Clinton in the two-year period from 1985 to 1987)—but this could go without press comment only as long as opponents, rivals, and the press declined to play up the governor's infidelity. Would they?

No previous governor in the twentieth century, even the notorious and adulterous Orval Faubus—who, having run short of the funding that had always maintained his lavish lifestyle, was now enviously waiting in the wings, in his seventies, for a chance to challenge Clinton for the governorship and renew his access to easy cash—had ever been exposed for philandering by the press. But *would* the press continue to hold off, given Bill's almost suicidally "reckless" womanizing, as Gennifer Flowers termed it?

"This Womanizing Thing"

To a large extent Bill Clinton owed his survival to Betsey Wright. "She works eighteen hours a day!" Ernie Dumas later commented, recalling the way Betsey had paced, growled, and even snapped on behalf of her master. "Everything Bill does, she examines! She runs his life, and then Hillary runs the rest of it! Between the two of them, there's not a moment. And I think Betsey always considered one of her roles is to keep him outta bed with women! She'd make arrangements, if Bill was going to Jonesboro—there was supposed to be some woman up there that he goes to see—she tells the troopers to be sure to keep him in their sights, 'Don't let him stray—get him back here!' On the telephone—everything!

"I doubt if she'll talk about it," Dumas added regretfully.

Distressed at the manner in which her hiding of Bill's skeletons had effaced her own positive role in devising, developing, and directing public policy for six long years in the Arkansas governor's office, Betsey *did* later speak—and forthrightly. "I mean, we were just *constantly* fighting this womanizing thing!" she recalled with exasperation. Tirelessly she had labored to ensure that the governor's idealism, his programs, and his intellectual leadership were acknowledged across the state—positives that far outweighed his rumored peccadilloes. That her labors were not in vain was reflected in Bill's fortunes at the ballot box. Frank White, who was considering a fresh battle for the governorship, came to respect the governor in his second and third administrations. "He did some good things!" White would acknowledge. "And I think in his heart probably means well. But his personal life? Hey, it got him into trouble when he was governor, and it got him into trouble when he was president! I mean, the word was gettin' out there—people were *talking* about it! It was common knowledge that he and Gennifer Flowers were having an affair for *years,* in Arkansas. *Wherever they went*—I mean, it's not a onetime deal. And Hillary knew it! But that's their lifestyle. And for whatever reason, she decided she was going to hang in there with him, and he was doing it anyway!"

Hillary's forbearance, and the widespread admiration she had engendered by her campaign to improve public education and funding, thus also countered potential revelations. "Your dominant newspaper was the *Gazette,*" Frank White explained, "really the only statewide circulation newspaper. Very much pro-Clinton. Protected him—otherwise it would have been out big time! Was I aware of it when I was running? Uh-uh. But I didn't use it. It's a hard subject to use! I mean: hey, it's not a subject that I felt had any role in a debate in a political campaign. You know, if he was runnin' around on his wife, and she knew it, and she wanted to stay in there with him, that's *her* business!"

Afraid of Hillary, White thus left Clinton's private life well alone. Moreover, thanks to Betsey Wright, the "runnin' around" on Hillary was kept to a minimum, and for the moment Bill was able to get away with it without scandal. While Roger Clinton served out his term in a federal penitentiary, Governor Bill Clinton served out his in the handsome governor's mansion with its beautiful tree-shaded grounds—even a plot where the family pets could be buried. The governor began to receive national accolades for his—and Hillary's—work on educational improvement in Arkansas. After an extended period of rampant inflation and unemployment, the economic situation in America had improved—and under Clinton's guidance the Arkansas economy did too. After a bitter struggle to get Clinton to fulfill his promise, chief of staff Maurice Smith was rewarded and made a trustee of the University of Arkansas, while Betsey Wright was finally and formally promoted to replace him. The governor's popularity soared, while Hillary's clash with the teachers' union gave the couple a dual authority. *National Review* might mock several years later, in a front cover-caption to a picture of Bill Clinton, "Stop—Or My Wife Will Shoot!," but the combination of Bill and Hillary was easier to deride than to beat, as the seemingly invincible Republican President would find.

Meanwhile, this time working as governor and first lady rather than as campaigners, the Clintons continued their historic partnership, leading to the inevitable question: Were they eyeing the White House?

Dissimulation

Since Arkansas had achieved statehood in 1836, its governors had been elected to serve two-year terms of office. In the fall of 1984, however, legislators had tentatively suggested changing the two-year term to four years, subject to voters' ratification—the new rule to begin with the gubernatorial candidate elected in November 1986, in line with other states. If it were passed into law and ratified by the electorate, and if Bill Clinton were reelected, he would become the first governor in Arkansas history to be given a four-year term—providing an ideal launch pad for a Clinton mission to the White House, halfway through, in 1988. As governor of Arkansas, Clinton would be fighting from a position of incumbent gubernatorial strength, not the political sidelines. If he lost the presidential nomination race or even the presidential election itself, he would still achieve national name recognition and still remain governor of Arkansas. Such a political moon shot would, however, risk the wrath of those Arkansas voters who wanted a stay-at-home governor for the full four-year term they had ratified—indeed, might well lead to an irritated Arkansas electorate failing to reelect him governor at the end of the new term, in 1990.

It was in this double bind, then, that Bill Clinton was once again forced to dissimulate once inaugurated in 1985. His "indecisiveness and lack of candor," as the Arkansas journalist Meredith Oakley noted, were "by now taken for granted," so that when, in June 1985, Clinton told an Atlanta newspaper that it would be "fun" to run for president and then, the following month, announced he would run for reelection as governor in 1986 for the new four-year term, which he vowed he would serve out fully, his audience listened with interest and respect for his lawyerly circumlocution. His words were carefully chosen. "I cannot ask you to stay the course if I am willing to spend the rest of this term as governor running for some other office instead of trying to push Arkansas forward," he declared in Clintonspeak. "To put it simply," he maintained, "I want to stay home to finish the job."

Journalists shook their heads. No one believed this half promise, least of all the governor himself, who soon departed for Idaho to attend the National Governors Association Conference. There he was elected vice chairman and set about mediating between Democratic and Republican state agendas—on a national platform.

All agreed that Governor Bill Clinton was brilliant—that he had a remarkable ability to absorb conflicting views and find a synthesis that was acceptable and could work. Despite his oversized brain, he had an easy, southern manner, as well as an extraordinary conversational range, trading dirty jokes with sexists and statistics with idealists. The chameleon in him was here a boon, however much it might infuriate Arkansas lawmakers. He seemed to possess indefatigable energy, requiring only four to six hours' sleep a night. With his intellectual curiosity and photographic memory— especially for people and faces—he came across as a polymath: the "Education Governor" who had a vision for America's future in an increasingly technologically competitive age. If it was difficult to know what principles he would truly die for, this was seen by many as a strength at a time when fundamentalisms—left, right, and religious—seemed only to breed terrorism or armed radicalism around the world, downing airliners and spawning assassinations.

As the next gubernatorial election approached and President Reagan's second term of office reached its midpoint, moreover, the Republican administration seemed to be running into increasing problems and scandals, leaving many people wondering whether the righteous were not also the damned. Reagan's personal popularity might have been undimmed, but his original White House chiefs of staff had disbanded their triumvirate and had left office—Michael Deaver going into public relations and being convicted of lying to Congress, while Edwin Meese, Reagan's attorney general, was the subject of two investigations by the United States Office of the Independent Counsel.

In this context "Slick Willie" (as Clinton was now labeled by his most ardent Arkansas skeptic, the journalist Paul Greenberg), while not being a paragon of virtue, could be considered no more flawed than the next man, whether Democrat or Republican.

Sex Appeal

There was one further political dimension, however, that was not under-stood either by political colleagues or by rivals, let alone the press—indeed, not even by Hillary, whose co-candidacy made Bill so unbeatable in Arkansas. That was sex appeal.

JFK, fluttering in and around Hollywood from the time he was a teenager, had correctly identified SA as a crucial ingredient in modern po-litical fortunes—a truth that "Daddy" Ronald Reagan, too old for sex but with a younger and attractive consort, had parlayed in the new television age into the most successful presidential performance since FDR.

The fact was, people no longer voted with their feet alone, but with their *eyes* too; and although he might not be as handsome as JFK or the Gipper, big Bill Clinton had a friendly grin, abundant hair, a solid chin, and blue, intelligent, humorous eyes. He spoke in a high tenor voice that always sounded hoarse; but when he came into a room or appeared on camera, he had a presence that marked him out as a visionary and a chieftain—even if he might lack the traditional skill associated with executive leadership, the ability to make decisions and stand by them. For that he relied on Betsey Wright and his wife, Hillary.

Thus it was that Bill Clinton came to be whispered of as a possible fu-ture presidential contender, several years before the 1988 retirement of Ronald Reagan. But first, as Hillary had cautioned Dick Morris in 1982, he had once again to get reelected governor.

The New Prohibition

The 1986 Arkansas primary and election campaigns for four-year gover-norship of the state of Arkansas would be described by journalist Mered-ith Oakley as "the most negative campaign in the state's history."

In a series of slugfests that reminded Arkansas historians of the early nineteenth century, the contestants traded blows like gladiators in the col-iseum. Former governor Frank White, having stood aside in 1984, was now aiming to reclaim the mansion for the Republican Party but was first chal-lenged by a Democratic crossover, Tommy Robinson, the ex–Pulaski County sheriff, in the Republican primary, while a batch of rivals, includ-ing former governor Orval Faubus, archsegregationist, contested the De-mocratic primary against Bill Clinton.

Vast sums had to be raised and expended on television and radio ads, with armies of handlers researching the opposition first within the candidate's own party, then in the other. With the very first teacher testing having taken place the year before, and more than *two thousand* teachers having failed it, passions in Arkansas ran high. Once again Hillary hit the stump, invading even the press conferences of Bill's opponents to counter wild accusations as each candidate looked for the vital chink in his rival's armor or Achilles heel.

This was a far cry from the Boston tea parties given by Rose Kennedy for her son Jack—though the money spent and the organization required were similarly inimical to democracy, if that term was taken to mean government by the people. Once White had disposed of the loudmouth sheriff and Clinton had put paid to the old segregationist, Orval Faubus, White set upon Clinton as the pawn of financial sponsors such as Dan Lasater— an accusation that, given Hillary's involvement (on behalf of the Rose Law Firm) in whittling down the federal government's claim for $2.7 million against Lasater to a mere $300,000, created considerable anxiety at the mansion lest White discover the truth. The former governor didn't, and in the televised debate between the two men, the verbal brawl resembled a kids' playground fight more than a serious discussion of issues.

In this new era of no-holds-barred, hand-to-hand combat between campaign millionaires, however, the contours and weaponry of the late-twentieth-century American political battlefield were emerging—with cameras as artillery, microphones as machine guns, and money as the potassium nitrate. Rocky was turning into Rambo, and the electorate judged the quality of the acting, sometimes reduced to tears of laughter.

Had this been all, it would have been enough. But it was not all. Negative advertising had transformed political electioneering into a modern equivalent of nineteenth-century stump-and-poster politicking, using new media; but there was, in comparison with the early nineteenth century, a late-nineteenth-century twist reminiscent of the plays of Oscar Wilde: the threat of scandal relating to the private lives of the combatants.

The new ethical minefield now covered the entire battlefield with tripwires and the most sensitive trigger devices, to the point where there was virtually no escape. By helping hound Nixon to his doom, Hillary had unwittingly encouraged this development; the press, like judicial committees, now licensed to snoop into every corner of a candidate's life, private as well as public, and hold the candidate to a kind of petit-bourgeois ransom.

By virtue of his age, President Reagan had been spared the need to cross such a minefield, but America was clearly in the grip of one of its periodic bouts of puritanism, just as it had been in 1920, when Prohibition had ended the legal manufacture and sale of alcohol in the United States.

That proscription had lasted thirteen years, until repealed under the presidency of Franklin D. Roosevelt. The new prohibition, requiring political candidates to have led sexually blameless private lives, would last just as long—with President William Jefferson Clinton its star victim and hero.

CHAPTER THIRTY

HEART OF DARKNESS

A Fourth Inning

The November 1986 election results told it all. Former governor Frank White carried a mere seven of the seventy-five Arkansas counties. By a landslide majority—439,882 votes to White's 248,427—Governor Bill Clinton, having been made chairman of the National Governors Association and chairman of the Education Commission of the States, was elected to a fourth gubernatorial term, this time for four years in consequence of a ballot item approving the legislators' amendment to the state constitution.

"He beat me pretty good," Frank White acknowledged manfully. But Bill Clinton had done far more than that. With a fourth win as governor of Arkansas, he would be able to run for presidential nomination in 1988 as a sitting governor, indeed the "Education Governor," if he chose.

If, that was, he could "keep his dick in his pants," as Hillary indelicately put it.

The Slaves Have Been Freed

How Bill Clinton had survived his reelection battles in Arkansas without falling foul of Sexual Prohibition, policed by the press, preachers, and the public, was, in retrospect, miraculous.

Meredith Oakley, writing in the *Arkansas Democrat* in October 1986, had complained that the campaign "has seen two men who have held the governor's office toss everything at one another that isn't tied down"—but she ignored White's gentlemanly reluctance to throw sexual taunts. Instead, as a woman journalist, Oakley had been incensed by White's attempt to blacken Hillary Clinton, the Democratic candidate's wife. White had successfully done so in 1980, when Hillary held to her own name and a haughty status, but now, in the wake of Hillary's unrelenting Joan of Arc performance on behalf of public education in Arkansas, White's barbs—accusing Hillary of conflict of interest through her Rose Law Firm work for the state, for example—failed to connect with a population that had begun to embrace feminism. "Someone needs to tell our former governor," Oakley snarled, "that the slaves have been freed, women have been given the right to vote and the wives of politicians, just like the wives of mere mortals, are entitled to pursue interests outside the home."

At a public meeting where both White and Hillary spoke, Hillary had been given more applause than the ex-governor. It had been a salient moment.

The victorious, youthful governor might be unpopular with failing schoolteachers and good-ole-boy legislators, but in the same way that Ronald Reagan played an important role in restoring American public morale after Vietnam, so Bill Clinton was perceived as having played a significant role, along with Governors Bumpers and Pryor, in raising the morale of Arkansans and the image of the state throughout the nation after Central High. The majority of voters were plainly proud of him—and of Hillary. "By election day, in fact," the two *Arkansas Democrat* writers Rex Nelson and Philip Martin recalled, "many Arkansans were saying they had voted for Bill because it was like getting two for one."

Far more than former governors Bumpers and Pryor, Bill Clinton had appealed to black and minority voters. However irresolute some of his legislative proposals as governor, he had appointed more black people to his staff than any previous incumbent, while incomes in the state had steadily risen and new industries had been attracted. Appearances by the governor on national television had raised the profile of the state, despite its tiny population (2.29 million). He had fulfilled his promise not to raise taxes without a popular mandate—why, then, rock the boat by voting him out?

With Bill Clinton's landslide success in November 1986 it was understandable that with the approaching mandatory retirement of the aging

President, political commentators, policy wonks, and gamblers began casting their eyes across the nation for a Democratic challenger to face Reagan's probable successor, Vice President George Bush. Bush's opponent in the vice presidential stakes in 1984, Geraldine Ferraro, had not proved a success for Democrats. The official Democratic nominees would therefore still have to be men—and white men at that.

In Big Bill Clinton, however, American voters would, it was argued, be getting a white man *and* his white woman: a smart, energetic, committed, young, and attractive couple weighed down with awards for their work over the previous ten years.

Rivals such as Senator Gary Hart, who had masterminded the failed McGovern campaign, and Mike Dukakis, who had built a fine reputation as a modernizing governor in Massachusetts, might have more individual name recognition among liberal Democrats, as well as hailing from more populous states, but Hillary's background was Chicago-Massachusetts-Connecticut, while Bill's was mainly the South—a North-South combination that had won the presidency for JFK with LBJ and for LBJ with Minnesota's Senator Hubert Humphrey. As a southern candidate, Governor Jimmy Carter had once again shown the advantages of conjoining the northern and southern wings of the party in a post–civil rights era. At the very least, a vice presidential offer to Bill Clinton might ensue in 1988, if Bill—like Lyndon Johnson in the Democratic primaries against JFK, or George Bush against Ronald Reagan—could mount a sufficient threat to the eventual winner of the nomination to be worth being taken under the nominee's wing, thus uniting the various factions of the party. In this vice presidential scenario, with Hillary alongside Bill, the Democratic Party would then boast not two but three candidates on its 1988 ticket.

Hillary was all for a try. Early in 1987, even before the first biennial Arkansas session of the newly elected legislature convened, Bill Clinton had thus begun to confide to colleagues that he would run for the Democratic nomination if all went well. He'd been running all his life, he reminded his friends—for college class president, for U.S. Congress, for attorney general, and for governor. Running for president would be, as he termed it, "fun": a step up, an opportunity to pitch his ideas and his appeal to a larger national audience. He had barely turned forty and was at the height of his powers.

These powers included sex appeal—especially when contrasted to alternative candidates. In this respect, Bill Clinton was in the same boat as Senator Gary Hart from Colorado, a front-runner Democratic contender for the 1988 nomination: both good-looking politicians with pasts—pasts that might, in America's new age of prudery, be used against them.

Hart Is Toast

Betsey Wright, the Arkansas governor's chief of staff, wasn't keen on a presidential run. "I think his adult life was an oxymoron," she later reflected. "He came from a very modest background, and went to highfalutin schools. He didn't come from a family that was particularly bright, but he was brilliant and made terrific grades. And I mean, he felt: there's gotta be a way to have it all! But the moment comes when you really do have to choose . . . !"

Was it hubris, then, for Bill Clinton to think he could make it to the White House while continuing to lead a private life of sexual addiction and self-gratification?

Betsey Wright thought it was—for Betsey saw as clear as day what Bill Clinton was reluctant to acknowledge: that times had changed, *but not enough;* indeed, that there was now a white conservative moral backlash to which Hillary was attuned, but which could vitiate any higher ambitions for Bill, unless he reined in his proclivities.

Bill Clinton was certainly not alone in having, at forty, a young man's powerful sexual libido—older men were often more, just as, or nearly as, lustful, as Edward Kennedy and other senators (Senator Robert Packwood, one notable example) demonstrated. But Kennedy, after all, had lost his opportunity to run for president because of Chappaquiddick and the potential revelation of his addictions, while other hopefuls had had to forfeit the possibility for the same or similar reasons. To hope, in a burgeoning era of American media inquisition, to combine high office and sexual freedom, as in the old patriarchal days, was therefore to court disaster.

In April 1987, Governor Clinton was nonetheless invited to Manchester, New Hampshire, there to speak to the State Democratic Committee's quarterly meeting. Traditionally, this was the preselection process for possible future nomination, for it would be in New Hampshire the following year that Democratic hopefuls would line up to be evaluated by voters in the state primary. Senator David Pryor, Bill's predecessor as Arkansas governor, now openly supported a Clinton run for president, and by the end of the month Bill finally acknowledged in public what journalists had begun to bruit: that he was eyeing the Democratic presidential nomination. "Oh, yes, I'd very much like to do it," he agreed on record—though he declined, for the moment at least, to resign as governor of Arkansas to make such a run.

This was just as well. If he and Gary Hart thought that the press would continue to permit polyamorists such as John F. Kennedy and Lyndon Johnson to enter the White House without invoking a public lynching, they had another think coming. Reagan's presidency had finally legitimized the notion of divorce and serial marriage as the officially sanctioned American way of enjoying more than one sexual partner during one's lifetime, within American presidential politics. But it did not yet legitimize polyamorous sex within marriage.

The following month, in May 1987, a tip-off alerted *The Miami Herald* to Senator Gary Hart's latest, in-your-face adultery. In his arrogance or generosity Hart had offered a Miami constituent, Donna Rice, the chance, when visiting Washington, D.C., to "sleep with the next president of the United States." Donna had slept with him—but, thanks to the vigilance of the *Herald,* had thereby ensured that Senator Hart would *not* be the next president.

A Damned Saint

Senator Hart's abject return to his wife and his shamed withdrawal from the Democratic field of potential presidential candidates left the 1988 nomination race wide open.

Should Bill Clinton run? Following Senator Pryor's support, the state's other popular and respected senator, Dale Bumpers, announced that he would not consider entering the race himself. The Arkansas runway was therefore cleared for a Clinton takeoff—if Clinton could avoid hitting the same parked plane as Hart had.

Bill made no effort. "Governor, you're gonna make Gary Hart look like a damned saint," one state trooper remarked, amazed at the governor's inability to curb his sexual appetite. "Yeah," Bill had responded. "I do, don't I?"

Like Hart, Bill was now on a collision course with American public morality, at least in the field of politics, in an age of moral confusion. Few had labored under the illusion that Hart was a senator of complete probity in his private life; he was, after all, following an old senatorial tradition established by his forefathers that had continued to the current day; moreover, the tryst with Ms. Rice had been consensual. Yet in an age of intensifying media scrutiny, a presidential hopeful who challenged the press to document suspicions of his philandering but could not then either control his lust or avoid getting caught in giving rein to it, was somehow unlikely to survive the grueling selection process. American voters did not necessarily want perfect rectitude in their presidents—Jimmy Carter's growing unpopularity when President, despite his complete probity, had been proof of that—but they did want candidates who could, in the battle between President and the press, come out on top. President Reagan had shown *that* it could be done and *how* it could be done; Senator Hart had shown how it should *not* be done.

Having Sex Day and Night

Governor Clinton's relationship with Gennifer Flowers, had it been publicly known then, as it later became, would have revealed the problem. Far from ending in reform and a chaste presidential candidate, willing to sacrifice sexual gratification for the chance to run for the nation's highest office, the affair, after years of playful fun, was now moving into its third and most disturbing mode.

The Quapaw Towers couple had given each other nicknames—"Pookie" and "Baby"—as well as nicknames for their private parts—"Precious" and "Willard." On the phone, if others were present, Bill would ask after "the girls," meaning Gennifer's breasts, while she would ask after "the boys," his testicles. He bought her exotic lingerie, and they'd begun to play games of fantasy and S&M. Living with a relentlessly masculine wife who was holding down a traditional man's job in a man's corporate legal world, Bill fantasized about being a submissive woman. Gennifer made him up with eyeliner, eye shadow, mascara, and blusher for his cheeks. "He was absolutely fascinated by how different he looked with makeup on," Gennifer recalled—unaware perhaps of Bill's profound identification with his mother, Virginia.

With her voluptuous bosom and her fountain of hair, little Gennifer Flowers tantalized Bill Clinton, invoking an Oedipal identification that spilled into fantasy and desire at a more and more intense level. He became "even more inventive in his sexual games," Gennifer recalled—games that resulted in his-and-her orgasms "beyond anything we'd ever experienced together."

This was light-years beyond the "Wham, Bam, Thank-you-ma'am" sex of Clinton's hero, President John F. Kennedy. Kennedy's famous torch had clearly passed to a new generation, and mutual sexual pleasure was—until AIDS reminded the wider world of the dangers of unprotected intimacy—the golden inheritance. As Gennifer acknowledged, they were both children of the sixties and seventies, and had both harvested the fruits of that extraordinary era. To Bill, for instance, oral sex was a perfectly normal part of lovemaking—though when he ejaculated in Gennifer's mouth the first time, she recalled her shock—which Bill was sensitive enough to recognize. When he asked if she was okay, she explained she hadn't actually intended to indulge in such an exchange of fluids until she was wed—and even then might have qualms. "He kind of smiled and held me close."

Clearly, Gennifer belonged to the baby-boom generation in certain respects, though not in others. Ten years later, in the wake of the Hugh Grant and Monica Lewinsky scandals, the business of oral sex would become a subject of national, indeed international debate; for the moment Bill and Gen kept it under their proverbial hats—Bill also urging Gennifer to allow him to take the role of sub, if she wouldn't let him be dom. She agreed to "spank him during sex play, and he got a big thrill out of it," as he did when she agreed to tie him up and tease him "until he was almost out of his mind with excitement"—even using a "dildo-shaped vibrator on him. It was exciting to see him getting so aroused, and I couldn't wait to untie him so he could use it on me."

Such sex games took them both to the edge of ecstasy, but they worried Gennifer, too. Behind the nightclub-singing, provocative facade she was as Republican as Hillary, and as old-fashioned, for all the game playing. It was as if Bill's addictive, fantasy-filled world were taking her way beyond her core cultural values. In love with him still after almost ten years, she had agreed to accompany him on that journey into sexual outer space, indeed found the trip mind-boggling in its intensity as they explored the matrix of sexual "normality"—but inside, Gennifer was never really comfortable with the extraterrestrial rather than extramarital experience. It was to her as if the sex was taking over, leaving the more charming interplay of their personalities and affection for each other far behind. She had once dreamed of marrying him, indeed had carried his child until he had paid for it to be aborted. Now she felt locked into a fantasy role in which, for example, they would have repeated phone sex—but it was sex where he, tense, overworked, and overexcited at the end of the line, would masturbate to orgasm, while she would only fake it. Knowing that she could stimulate him to emission by telephonic transmission was all very well, she remembered of her disappointment, but it left an empty space beside her where her man should be, touching her and being touched. In the end, after inventing reasons why she wasn't able to indulge him, she confessed—and phone sex came to an end.

Sex didn't, however—indeed it grew more, not less, thrilling. "Even though we'd known each other for years, the physical excitement was still there," she later recalled, remembering the time she performed at the governor's mansion, and Bill begged her to have sex with him in the downstairs bathroom. "Hi, I followed you," he admitted. Let's go in here"—pointing to the men's bathroom. Spooked by an icy glare cast by Hillary, who had "frozen" her out when she sang, and pretended not to see her on the path during the intermission, Gennifer told Bill he was "crazy" to take such risks, with that "wicked grin on his face." It was not only his recklessness that worried Gennifer, however, but a kind of metamorphosis in their relationship. In the smorgasbord of their dangerous liaison, sex had always been a delicacy, prized for its rarity. Now, it seemed, it was becoming something akin to a drug, prized for its mind-altering properties, to the exclusion of anything else. Her thoughts kept reverting to the high they'd had on their previous encounter, and how they might improve on it sexually at the next. Yet she knew, at the same time, that this was not what she really wanted in life—that she was doing it for the man she loved but that, in the end, his version of love was either very different from hers or reserved for others. Was he, she occasionally asked herself—since he refused to use a condom—seeing other women, apart from his wife? If so, how could he possibly find the time?

Like those who were later astonished by the way JFK and LBJ had intermingled their sexual shenanigans with such vibrant and responsible public lives, Gennifer found it difficult to imagine, afterward, how Bill had managed to hold down a high-powered, full-time job as well as fantasizing about, and consorting with, the numbers of women that he was later alleged to have been seeing. If it was true, she reflected the year before the Monica Lewinsky scandal, then Bill Clinton was worthy of a decoration not only for gallantry, but for multitasking, for how, she reasoned, could he possibly have had time for his duties as governor, as husband to Hillary, devoted parent to his daughter Chelsea, lover to his mistress Gennifer—and a host of other ladies?

Sex at an Ever-Higher Intensity

Thus, at the very moment when the prospect of a presidential run became thinkable, the question arose in the spring of 1987: Were Bill and Geannie, Pookie and Baby, becoming sex-obsessed—and would this lead to Bill's political ruin? Gennifer clearly thought so in retrospect; believing she and

Bill were not only in the grip of natural sexual desire, but now addicted to it, as if to a powerful medication or compound. The more addicted the two of them became, she noted, the more they literally hungered for sex at an ever higher "intensity."

Intensity now vied with quantity, with both Gennifer and Hillary un-aware of the extent of Bill's womanizing. Waving his gubernatorial wand, he was able and willing to seduce any number of willing young women from the "groupies" who, as in the entertainment industry, seemed happy to trade sexual favors for the chance to say they had tasted power.

In this sense, Bill Clinton's intense, perpetual-motion curiosity might be seen as hewed from the same block as his love of books, popular music, movies, and politics. He confided to Gennifer that he wanted her to partic-ipate in a threesome, as she recalled—a scene reminiscent of his hero JFK, who had also proposed a threesome, in his case to an outraged Judith Campbell. Like Judith, Gennifer balked, wanting to be the king's para-mour yet unwilling to share that position with rivals and especially unwill-ing to dilute the loving quality of their sexual intercourse by introducing an outsider, something she saw as degrading.

While Gennifer might be naive in assuming Bill Clinton was in love with her in the same way that she was in love with him, she was certainly right to become anxious about where all this fantasy and acting out was leading. Despite the widely acknowledged brilliance of his intellect, Bill Clinton seemed increasingly driven by his sexual desires and almost too drunk with the aphrodisiac that is power to care about consequences, let alone mean-ing. It was as if the roller coaster that was his "Wonder Boy" life, with the presidency of the entire United States looming as a real possibility, was taking him over, taking him—like so many drug-deranged pop and enter-tainment stars of the era—inexorably toward self-destruction.

The White House, Not the Cathouse

Sensing the dangerous spiral they were ascending or descending, Gennifer was alarmed. Hillary was, too. Hillary's financial involvement with Susan and Jim McDougal—or rather, her unfortunate refusal to rid herself of her Whitewater shares when Jim, embarrassed at the deepening debts in-curred by his wheeling and dealing, offered to relieve the governor and his wife of any potentially negative repercussions by assuming their shares as debts rather than investments—had turned sour. "Jim promised that Whitewater was going to pay for Chelsea's education," Hillary had snapped when refusing to stomach the $13,500 loss the surrender of her shares would have entailed.

Hillary's determination to hang on to her worthless Whitewater shares was, in contrast to her decision to get out of cattle futures after making $100,000, an almost fatal decision. It reflected, however, Hillary's growing lack of trust in Bill as either a faithful husband or provider. Like every mother, Hillary was determined that, whatever the future held—whether their marriage endured or ended in divorce or Bill lost his job—she would be in a position to put Chelsea through college.

Meanwhile, the prospect of Bill's making an early entrance into the race for Democratic presidential nomination energized Hillary—for here was another project in which she could work alongside Bill, one that promised, in such a political marriage, to keep them close. Bill's attention, she instinctively presumed, would be firmly focused on the White House, not the cathouse. Though she did not take leave of absence from the Rose Law Firm, she kept her legal work to a minimum and in April helped her parents buy a condominium in Little Rock, so that they would be able to watch over Chelsea while she traveled with Bill to the out-of-state venues, such as Massachusetts, California, Wisconsin, Montana, Indiana, and Tennessee, that would help determine his candidacy potential as he sought greater national name recognition. It would also guard against Hart-like indiscretions.

What Hillary did not appreciate—as Jackie Kennedy had failed to appreciate until years later, in retrospect—was that Bill was mired in sexual roaming at a much deeper, more adolescent level than she had credited. During family therapy after Roger's drug bust, the therapist had maintained that different human beings are born at different ages. Bill had confessed that his own age was, and remained, sixteen, whereas Hillary's was forty—but Hillary had missed Bill's warning. She had always felt uncomfortable about delving too deeply into her inner fears and anxieties, lest the process disable her in her manic determination to prove herself a quasi male—indeed better than a man—to her father.

For Hillary, as a child of a midwestern Methodist, the journey from Wellesley women's college to Yale Law School and partnership in a major law firm, motherhood, and wife of one of the fifty governors of America—indeed, the chairman of the National Governors Association—was to fulfill both her own and her father's dreams, as she proudly relocated Hugh Rodham in Little Rock. But although this agenda worked well for her professionally, parentally, and in filial terms, it felt to Bill like an increasing millstone. For all the cherishing love of their mother, his brother Roger had failed to grow up and had gone down. Bill would be next. And Hillary had no idea what was going on.

The Key to Success in Arkansas

Crisscrossing the country, between January and July 1987, Governor Bill Clinton made thirty-four trips to twenty different states. *The New York Times* was declaring him a definite candidate for the Democratic Party nomination. "Personally, I think he would be a terrific President," Hillary was quoted saying in an interview, "but that's because I think he has a lot of the personal qualities we need in our leaders."

In Arkansas, however, there were many skeptics. The *Arkansas Gazette,* so long a supporter of Bill's candidacies, now cautioned that he was still not ready for the sort of major international responsibilities that the presidency would entail, or even the daily struggle with Congress. He had an infuriating but immutable tardiness problem and a tendency to call for new standards while not knowing how to pay for them, at least out of current taxation. "Two chronic complaints legislators had about Clinton were that he could not be trusted to keep his word and that he was never prepared for legislative sessions," the *Arkansas Democrat*'s Meredith Oakley recorded, while the *Arkansas Gazette*'s John Brummett was even more scathing. By first promising journalists, before the 1987 spring session of the Arkansas legislature, that he would not permit any legislated interference with public access to state information—such as severance taxes, motor fuel taxes, and excise taxes—and then reneging on that undertaking, Clinton had earned the undying hostility of the press. As the regional director of the Society of Professional Journalists' Freedom of Information Committee complained, "I wonder how many times it takes betrayal by the governor for the press to get the message that he's anti–open government."

Even Betsey Wright, his chief of staff, was unenthusiastic about a presidential run. Since 1982, Bill had improved beyond belief in his political focus and tenacity, as well as his tactical ability. He had "learned his lessons the hard way, but he learned them. We made decisions, very tough decisions, about what we were going to do on education, and how we had to package them with people and the legislature in order to achieve them. He wavered on some positions," she allowed, "but they weren't ones of his initiative, usually—they were positions that he was helping somebody else with. But I've never know any politician who didn't!"

Betsey had, in other words, kept Clinton on task. "The key to his success in Arkansas, I think, is Betsey Wright," Bill's aide Bobby Roberts later considered. "She brought him back, I think, from oblivion. She was not only his political adviser, but she became his chief of staff, and I think most of the productive years of his government were when she was there—because she would hold him accountable. I mean, she didn't let him make any independent decisions if she could help it. And really, governors and presidents shouldn't, I mean they shouldn't. You need to know what they're doing. And she really held him accountable, and I think made him a much better governor."

Even Betsey Wright, however, could not make Bill into a more robust and mature individual, for his need to be liked and approved of was literally insatiable. His empathy with ordinary people rivaled that of Lyndon Johnson, whose tough childhood "doing nigger work" in the cotton fields and years teaching the children of poor Mexican laborers in Texas while at college had given him an indelible sympathy for the plight of the disadvantaged. "Compassion," however, "was not the only powerful force in his life," LBJ's biographer Robert Caro cautioned, for Johnson's "feverish, frantic intensity was fueled also by ambition"—an ambition, however, that was very, very different from that of Bill Clinton, his fellow southerner and later successor as president. Johnson became, in remarkably short time, the U.S. Senate's most ruthless, feared, and unprincipled leader. He voted in 1949 against the Fair Employment Practices Commission and anti-poll-tax legislation, and *for* segregation in the army. "He either cast votes on the side of the South or helped plan and implement its maneuvers against civil rights not only in 1949 but in 1950 and 1951 and '52 and '53 and '54 and '55," Caro reminded readers as he chronicled LBJ's relentless support of racial prejudice and discrimination in America. "His rise was financed and planned by men so bigoted that to talk to them when their guard was down was to encounter a racism of almost stunning viciousness." Virtually in their pay, LBJ as senator not only attempted in 1956 to overturn legislation banning segregation in National Reserve units but smashed a civil rights bill, "crushing it by a greater margin than ever before." As Caro concluded, "His empathy and tenderness for people oppressed simply because their skin was dark, strong though it was, had not been stronger than his ambition." It was an ambition characterized by "generic cruelty"—a sickening need to disarm, humiliate, and mentally torture anyone who stepped in his way, from senators to servants. "Let me tell you one thing, nigger," he once told his chauffeur. "As long as you are black, and you're gonna be black till the day you die, no one's gonna call you by your goddamn name. So no matter what you are called, nigger, just let it roll off your back like water, and you'll make it. Just pretend you're a goddamn piece of furniture." He never would call the chauffeur, Robert Parker, by his name. "I hated *that* Lyndon Johnson," Parker later recalled—while acknowledging that it was the very fear of Johnson's power and his coruscating tongue that caused southern bigots to fall into line when Johnson, as President of the United States, turned turncoat and introduced his own, historic civil rights bill to Congress in 1964.

Bill Clinton, however, lacked such toughness—a toughness he relied upon Betsey Wright and Hillary to provide. In Arkansas it had worked. But in control of the nation and command of its armed forces?

The *Arkansas Gazette* was dubious. It came to the considered conclusion that "Bill Clinton is not ready to be president of the United States" despite his "strong potential," John Brummett wondering "whether this man is equipped to deal with, as an example, the Soviets on questions having to do with the very security of the world."

"Slick Willie"

Paul Greenberg, editorial page editor of the *Pine Bluff Commercial,* was similarly skeptical of a presidential run by the man he had dubbed "Slick Willie" (after a local restaurant). Greenberg, the son of an immigrant pharmacist, found Clinton's inability to take responsibility for his own actions and decisions, such as releasing from overcrowded state prisons convicts who then committed murder, and then failing to pick up the tab—deeply disturbing.

With his old-fashioned notion of truth and honesty, Greenberg had watched carefully the manner and expediency of Bill Clinton's political comeback after 1982. A real man, a real human being, would have looked inside his soul, or even to his Maker, at the moment of defeat, in order to examine what he or she believed in; what was significant and insignificant; what he or she would die for—and not die for. Clinton had not. In Greenberg's view Bill Clinton had simply struck a Faustian bargain to win back political power—the young, promising idealist thereby surrendering whatever soul was left in him. Clinton's eyeing of the presidency was no longer the simple, even natural, touching ambition of an American born in relative poverty at the end of World War II. Clinton was no Lincoln, the house on Hervey Street, Hope, no log cabin. Clinton's performance as governor, though superficially populist, betrayed an inner vacuum, a lack of inner principle that frightened Greenberg in its weakness and spiritual emptiness. There was no Bill Clinton anymore; there was only "Bill Clinton," a registered trademark. And behind his possible candidacy a growing army of "supporters"—financiers, kingmakers, lobbyists, lawyers, and volunteers, assembling in Little Rock to crown the contender as soon as he made the expected announcement that he would run.

It was, in Greenberg's eyes, lamentable.

A 1950s Person

"I am basically a 1950s person," Greenberg explained in 2001. "Buttoned-down—in many ways an 1850s person!" he added jokingly yet unashamedly. "And Clinton—we're separated by this huge decade difference, akin to a generation.

"I don't like him," Greenberg stated candidly, "so I guess it would be correct to say that he offends me. I don't feel offended, as you would if someone came along and slapped you in the face or anything. I'm much more bored than offended—but that's because I've been following him forever and ever, and he'll drive you crazy. In fact he used to fascinate me. Early on I'd look for 'Clinton clauses' in his speeches, and little policy deviations, and how clever he was, and how he would get the better of his opposition. I used to follow Fulbright's speeches in the same way. And I was still interested, at that point. But after a while it becomes such a routine. You've seen him use the same lines again and again. You've seen him use the same techniques again and again. Mostly it gets boring. And you lose that edge of outrage. So it just elevates into a kind of disdain.

"He offends me in that general term, not personally—I don't have anything against him personally, for gosh sakes, he never hurt me. I mean a few shouting matches, but journalists and politicians don't take those things seriously. He offends me because I am a child of the fifties and he's a child of the sixties! And he never struck me as a serious politician or as a serious person. That is, as someone with a principle that he would adhere to, even if it meant the destruction of his political career or his administration or whatever. There's nothing he would stick by at any cost. So if you grow up in the 1950s and you study the great heroes and you have this romantic view—you know, Churchillian view and all that, and you believe, you think you believe that stuff, and you hope you never have to sacrifice anything for it yourself, but you never know. . . . Then someone comes along who, in your judgment, doesn't care a fig about principle: that offends you!

"Oh, yes, he had this sort of superficial empathy. But if he actually has to sell somebody down the river, out they go! I mean, he's just so self-absorbed! There's no deeper principle there! So that essential vacuum is what offends me. Because it sort of mocks what the rest of us, who actually believe this stuff, you know—and some of us still do!—we sort of write editorials in defense of these ideas, you know, and are willing to take certain—I mean, how risky can it be to be an American in the twenty-first century?—but measured risks. He takes political risks. He's a power politician, best I've ever observed. But, you know, it's like a tennis player takes risks. He doesn't step off the court, actually, and say, no, I'm going to let the Haitians come into this country, or yes, we're going to have a policy in Eastern Europe that'll actually do something, and do something *now*! It's all ad hoc, when it comes right down to it."

Exactly what made Bill Clinton so opportunistic rather than moral became, to Greenberg, lost in the sands of time and personal psychology. What Greenberg witnessed, though, as an Arkansas journalist-observer, was that Clinton merely "changed his tactics"—not his character—after losing the governorship in 1980. "He became much more adept. He no longer took the advice of his radical friends. But I think he always felt he could manipulate people—he just decided to rely on different advisers. And get closer to a more profound substratum of political opinion instead of just floating along with Steve Smith and other advisers who offended public opinion. I don't think," Greenberg reflected, "there's a change of principle." Instead, what changed was Clinton's political professionalism or realism. "He became much more sensitive to power structures. But I think basically he was always upwardly mobile."

The Bitch Goddess Success

Bobby Roberts, Bill Clinton's longtime gubernatorial aide, also considered that Clinton's lack of honesty was, given the "Wonder Boy's" manifest and manifold political talents, unfortunate. "I think he does face a moral dilemma that we all face," Roberts brooded in 2001, "and that is: Is your sort of truth and your honor going to come before your ambition? And I think in Bill Clinton's case in almost every call it never does. Almost in every call, his ambition is going to overwhelm his basic decency. And that's the sort of tragedy of him to me. I mean, I think he is an inherently decent guy, but his ambitions are such that they almost always overwhelm that."

LBJ had had the same problem but had had the toughness, in the end, to make his dream of a more decent society, a great society, become law in America. He was "the greatest champion Americans of color had in the White House during the twentieth century," as his biographer Robert Caro would justly claim, "the lawmaker for the poor and the downtrodden and the oppressed, the restorer of at least a measure of dignity to those who so desperately needed it, the redeemer of the promises made to them by America"; a president who, "above all Presidents save Abraham Lincoln, codified compassion."

Such a Christ-like portrait conveniently overlooked LBJ's war in Vietnam, the least compassionate of America's transgressions in the twentieth century. Yet the image of Bill Clinton as an ambitious baby boomer with no underlying moral convictions seemed a far worse transgression to men like Greenberg. In Bill Clinton, Greenberg saw the misfortune of a hollow man, lacking in moral courage. As such, Clinton was unlike the individuals whom Greenberg admired: men who "took the risk of not prospering at all," who "spoke out directly."

"In Arkansas in the 1960s we had Winthrop Rockefeller as our governor!" Greenberg recalled with pride. "*He* didn't care! *He* said all these things about integration!" Governor McMath—youngest elected governor, in 1948, since the Civil War, the son of a Hot Springs barber and a veteran of Guadalcanal, winner of the Silver Star, and major general in the Marine Corps—had also taken the high ground of racial tolerance—"he was *very* outspoken," Greenberg recalled. "Now, none of them became President of the United States, if that's what you mean by success." Even the *Arkansas Gazette,* which had defied Faubus's attempts to stop integration, eventually folded, whereas "Bill Clinton *survived*! He became President of the United States! Would you rather have that kind of success? Or would you rather have the *Arkansas Gazette*'s, and Winthrop Rockefeller's, kind of nonsurvival? I mean, that's a rhetorical question to me. I would much rather have the *Gazette* and Rockefeller—I mean, *they made a difference*! In a way that Clinton has, it seems to me, just marked time! So he's very successful himself, politically, I guess—but it seems an empty success to me. In terms of 'the bitch goddess success,' yes, Bill Clinton has succeeded! But God save me from that kind of success! I would much rather have the kind of failure—if it was failure—I don't even think of it as failure. . . . I think of the *Gazette* as very great, very successful; I think Rockefeller was a success story. Every time I see Sid McMath, I smile: I think, *there are still men of honor in the world!* So it does depend on how you look at the world. The *Gazette* is a byword—and Winthrop Rockefeller was the best governor we had in the last half century! Sid McMath is still alive and a man of honor! Now, *that* . . ."

In the background, journalists sat in front of computer screens; messengers delivered packets and documents as in the editor's office of the newspaper that had forced the *Gazette* to close; ironically, Greenberg's voice trailed away.

"As for the nature of your question—whether there was any alternative in Clinton's case, if he wished to succeed—that would be Bill Clinton's justification: 'How else could one prosper? How else could one survive?' And one could only respond, as a child of the 1950s, and with that kind of code of honor, to say, '*You don't want that kind of success!* You want an entirely different kind of success! You don't want to be concerned whether you succeed, you want. . . . If you have to be defeated, like Brooks Hays, if you have to lose an election, that's much better, in the long term!' I mean," the veteran journalist added, "long after you're dead.

"So that's the difference between us—and that's why, I think, someone like me, some hopeless relic, would think that Bill Clinton is not a serious person, by which I mean, someone who says, 'Well, long after I'm dead I will—I may get my brains beat out—but *I stood for this particular principle.* And I did not desert it! I didn't try to rationalize anything by 'Clinton clauses,' 'I didn't lie under oath'—you know, all those things. . . .

"Yes, the question of testifying, and testifying falsely," Greenberg mused, cocking his head to one side and wincing. "You remember the play *A Man for All Seasons*? It's a very antique play, the whole notion of . . ." Greenberg's very countenance began to light up at the memory. "In his preface, Robert Bolt says, 'By God, I am nervous about this play, because the people who will see this won't understand what in the world *possessed* this man! Why would a man put his head on the block rather than put his hand on the Bible and say a few meaningless words and go on?' And in the late twentieth century *a playwright has to write a preface to translate this idea to us!*

"So when you write your biography, you're going to have to say, 'I interviewed various critics of Bill Clinton. And you, the reader, must understand these people come from a different historical period: the 1950s! They have this idea that perjury is *serious*! I know you're not going to believe this, but they *actually* think that if you're called on to say something that will hurt your political career, embarrass you, it's better to say it than to lie about it under oath! And it's a completely unrealistic, mystical concept that derives from these ancient codes. And they think of *themselves* as serious people and *other* people as not serious! Naturally, *we* know that they're not the serious people, *we* are the serious, because *we* are going to succeed; *we* are going to be elected President.' " Greenberg smiled at his own mimicry—wistfully, sadly. " '*We're* going to enjoy,' " he continued his imitation, " 'the good things in life!' "

No One Better

All too intimately aware of the weaknesses in Bill Clinton's character, even Betsey Wright, for all her loyalty to Governor Clinton, had to allow that there was "something interesting there," for Bill Clinton's inability to say no was notorious—and was a perennial issue. "Where it drove me craziest," Betsey recalled, "was that he would sit there in his office" with supplicants, lobbyists, legislators "listening to them making a case, and be very understanding and very empathetic, and they would leave thinking that of course they'd won him over! And it was an *unending* story—I mean, it happened *over* and *over* again"—with the inevitable result that "when he didn't change his position just because he understood theirs, they felt he had betrayed them! He had, they felt, essentially promised his support for their position—which he didn't! I mean, I sat in on those meetings! I listened to it! I knew the difference he was making in his head. They didn't. They interpreted it as very supportive. It wasn't. It was empathetic. And that got him in trouble constantly."

In Betsey's view, the inability to openly nix or say no derived from Bill's childhood "insecurity." His bingeing—whether in terms of food or sex—was a part of a desperate need to be accepted, liked, approved—and rewarded. Psychologically needy, he wanted to "have it all" and therefore hated to have to choose—because to choose would mean *to surrender something on the table of life.* "And he's never been good at that," Betsey pointed out. LBJ had been cruelly tough with people; Clinton was almost cruelly weak, incapable of saying simply no.

"His dealing with tough interpersonal relationships is something that he's a disaster at!" Betsey reflected in later years, when it was all over bar the historical shouting. "A disaster at it!

"*I* did those things for him," Betsey confided reluctantly with a sigh. Nevertheless, there was the simplest of all facts, which Clinton bashers and haters so often overlooked in an imperfect world: that the alternative candidates to Bill Clinton were almost invariably worse. It was an undeniable fact that, whatever Greenberg might later say about "Slick Willie," he had often endorsed Bill Clinton for governor: not because he trusted him but because there was, at the time, no one better.

Making a Decision Soon

With newspapers and journals beginning to presume Clinton a candidate for president, the excitement in Little Rock became palpable by the summer of 1987. Bill Clinton, so long the "Wonder Boy" from Hope, Arkansas, was going to toss his hat into the presidential ring!

Hillary bubbled with excitement. She even telephoned her old colleague on the Nixon impeachment committee Bernie Nussbaum, whom she hadn't seen for years. It was the first week of July 1987. "Don't commit yourself to a presidential candidate," she begged him, "until I have a chance to talk to you"—and she flew to New York to tell him the great news! She was, Nussbaum later recalled, blooming with pride, talking of Chelsea and the future. When Nussbaum—who had always been skeptical not only about Bill Clinton but about the possibility of an Arkansan reaching the White House—questioned whether it was not too early, that at forty-two Bill Clinton was "kinda young to be president," Hillary brushed away his skepticism. Kennedy had run at forty-three—which was the age Bill would be the following year, when the election would be held. "He's going to make a decision soon," she proudly informed Nussbaum.

Bill, meanwhile, assembled Steve Cohen, an old Yalie friend, together with Sandy Berger and John Holum, both veterans of the McGovern and Hart campaigns, for a foreign policy briefing in Washington. He talked through the political mechanics and strategy with Dick Morris. Back in Little Rock, Clinton's staff began making preparations for Bill's announcement on July 15, which would be held—since state law prohibited use of the capitol—at the Excelsior Hotel, where Bill had so often entertained women. Letters had gone out to myriad friends and supporters. Ray

Stother, a Democratic consultant, came into town, with a series of advisers slated to follow him as the bandwagon began to swell.

Dick Morris, with his finger so intuitively on the pulse of voters' concerns, was both exuberant and nervous. He developed with Bill a notion, a slogan for the future, after Reagan: a "new partnership" between government and people that would address the continuing, indeed proliferating social problems within America. "We can't continue to ignore people's problems as President Reagan's administration has. They don't go away," their draft announcement ran. Having said this, though, one had to be honest. The old panaceas, such as government welfare, were clearly not working. Government couldn't just "pass out aid and hand out checks as we did in the New Deal and the New Frontier and the Great Society because when the money is spent, the problems remain, unsolved and festering. Instead we need a new partnership where government helps people if they are willing to help themselves, where government renders aid but demands standards and performance and commitment to self-help in return."

Hillary's new Republican-style approach was stamped all over the document, which Morris kept for posterity. In promoting her public education campaign in Arkansas Hillary had acknowledged the problems that teenagers faced in modern society, society that was "bombarding kids with sexual messages—on television, in music, everywhere they turn." Neither parents nor churches were doing enough, Hillary felt, to help teenagers say no to sex. "Adults are not fulfilling their responsibility to talk to young people," she'd declared, "about the future, about how they should view their lives, about self-discipline and other values they should have." She'd confessed that she, a baby boomer and child of the sixties, didn't know quite how parents and churches had "got off the track," but moral instruction seemed to have gone right out the window. "Adults don't feel comfortable telling their children not to do things, or they don't know how to communicate that message effectively. I'm trying to," she'd boasted.

If so, she had forgotten to include her own "sixteen-year-old": William Jefferson Clinton.

The Nature of the Game Today

"It's not birth control," Hillary had memorably emphasized in her speeches, to parental applause, "but self-control."

Poor Bill, however, had never been able to master birth control, let alone self-control, and it seemed too late now to do so—as he himself was painfully aware. "We've all done things," he'd told the *Gazette* journalist Max Brantley, in order to warn him of inevitable revelations, if he did run, "that we'd be embarrassed about if they ever came out in public, but it's the nature of the game today, that you never can be sure you won't have to answer for them."

The two men were watching Chelsea's softball game at the time, and the game seemed precisely that: softball. In their own political hardball arena—politicians-versus-the-media—the rules were different, and the governor was, however gingerly, sounding out his potential Judas. Yet the governor was not referring to drug revelations, as the innocent Brantley thought at the time; he was referring to the self-appointed, schizophrenic role of the press as sexual or marital morality police in modern society. For Bill, with his enormous intelligence and imagination, it seemed all too hypocritical that a press, which was increasingly devoted to making copy and money out of sexual titillation, should at the same time pretend to be surprised by extramarital sex—behavior that was, after all, increasingly prevalent for people born after 1945, according to all sex survey statistics.

Together with Dick Morris, Bill Clinton rehearsed the issue in the cold light of Senator Gary Hart's recent self-immolation. Morris could see Bill's "tremendous terror of the race," as it he put it, "because of the personal scandals that were visited upon candidates who ran," as Morris told the biographer of Clinton's early years, David Maraniss. "His experience watching candidates be destroyed by those scandals or impaired by them chilled him," Morris explained, "and led him to a feeling that this was a terribly inhospitable environment upon which to tread."

It was certainly ground upon which previous presidents had trodden without need to fear. JFK had been fully aware of the file kept on him by the head of the FBI, J. Edgar Hoover—but had known, equally, that Hoover would never dare leak it lest he lose his prized job, which allowed him to live a protected, privileged life as a closet homosexual addicted to horse racing. Even with the press Kennedy had known he would never be exposed. "Do you want Nixon as your president?" he had asked, as presidential candidate in 1960, openly challenging reporters who taxed him, privately, on his dangerously promiscuous lifestyle, then encouraging them to take advantage of the "personal services" of his cabin crew aboard his plane, *The Caroline*—named after his only daughter! Even academics such as Arthur Schlesinger, Jr., were—according to Schlesinger's first wife—offered seductive inducements to abandon Adlai Stevenson and join the lifestyle of the New Frontier, without fear of press intrusion.

Like Kennedy in 1960, Governor Bill Clinton a quarter of a century later also had a daughter, whom he adored and for whom, he felt at times, he lived. The times, however, had changed since the Kennedys, a thought he'd tried gingerly to rehearse with Brantley, wary of giving the journalist any specifics. The press neither would nor could be seduced any longer by a president, he was aware. The middle-class appetite for scandal and, increasingly, sexual revelation now made it simply too tempting for the press to play to the crowd baying below Pilate's gubernatorial palace, rather than rely on a quid pro quo with the White House. Revelation and moral outrage were simply too lucrative, for journalists as for journals. Whatever "moral" exemplars journalists of Paul Greenberg's generation might hold up as men of dignity and principle, the press itself was caught up in its own struggle for survival, with standards slipping, indeed cascading downward. Competition between and inside newspapers was such that, should a journalist choose not to pursue a lead, a rival journalist surely would.

The result was a form of licensed press mayhem—and, in terms of political coverage, the literal crippling of potential candidates in the name of a morality to which the majority of the public, and all but a few 1950s journalists, did not themselves subscribe!

Senator Gary Hart's withdrawal, meanwhile, left the Democratic Party without an electable candidate to offer in place of Ronald Reagan, the "Great Communicator," as he neared the end of his second term—leaving Dick Morris, as he later recounted, with "a dismal array of traditional Democrats as potential clients." Morris became so unimpressed by the Democratic lineup, in fact, that "in frustration" he would turn to the Republican Party, working for Vice President George Bush's campaign manager: the nefarious Lee Atwater.

Bill Clinton, however, could not and would not change party. Faced with the massive Republican artillery being brought up to the front line for the impending battle, he trembled with anticipation. He had become, over time, the most brilliant political strategist of his generation in the Democratic Party, instinctively pursuing a more centrist path, in tune with the electorate. As the hours ticked away before he had to declare his decision, he wondered, if he announced his candidacy, whether he could possibly make it—or whether, like Senator Hart, he would be destroyed by the press.

PART FIVE

TO BE,
OR NOT TO BE

ARKANSAS DEMOCRAT GAZETTE

Saying no to a presidential run, 1987

CHAPTER THIRTY-ONE

THE MEETING THAT NEVER HAPPENED

"A Terrible Conversation"

Ann Henry, in whose home Clinton had celebrated his wedding, later confided her own version of the dramatic moment in which the blue-eyed Arkansas "Wonder Boy" of the Democratic Party moved up to the national starting post.

"I have never told this," Ann began cautiously, setting the scene. "My children were brought up knowing Bill Clinton. I mean, they were brought up with him staying at our house. My daughter Kathy was in school. I guess she was about to graduate from college. The presidential candidacy was all the big discussion. Betsey Wright was still working for Bill. "And then my daughter called."

Ann bit her lip, recalling the telephone ringing and her daughter's voice when Ann picked up. "She was so angry, and so *upset*!" Ann recounted. "She'd been to dinner at a friend's house—one of my friend's houses, who was then Bill's big supporter—and there was a woman there *talking about her affair with Bill Clinton*! And Kathy called me and demanded to know.

" 'Oh, people talk,' I'm trying to say. 'All these stories—' And she says, '*No!* You have to *listen* to what I'm saying!' She was furious. She was very, very upset."

Though Ann calmed her child down, she was troubled. As a mother, as chair of the local Democratic Party in northwest Arkansas, and as a long-time supporter of the "Wonder Boy" from Hot Springs and Hope, she worried how such a story, if revealed in the press, would affect them all. Moreover, if a local woman was boasting openly of her affair with the governor, what more revelations might tumble out in the run-up to a presidential primary—and how much grief and heartache would ensue for those who were Bill and Hillary's supporters in Arkansas and elsewhere? "I called Diane [Blair], and I told her I had gotten off the phone after this terrible conversation. I said, 'I can't support him. Because if this is out, and it's going on, it's rampant: it will be everywhere!' I said, 'I just can't support him.' I said, 'Chelsea is eight years old, and this is going to devastate her—I mean, he *cares* about his daughter!' "

Bill Clinton's love for Chelsea, in the eyes of those who despised him, was the most redeeming feature of his unsavory character. Diane Blair, aware of Ann's almost hysterical concern, said, "I think you need to call Bill Clinton and convey that message."

Diane Blair, clearly, was unwilling to be the messenger. "Diane would never confront him with anything like that," Betsey Wright recalled.

Encouraged to do so herself, Ann called the mansion, "and I was told Hillary was there. I was asked if I wanted to talk to her. I said, '*No!* I need to talk to *him!*' I was not going to be put in the position of telling *her,* for God's sake, what I'd heard! I'm not stupid! I'm not going to do that! I said, 'I'm leaving town, and I'm heading to Houston [Texas] to a meeting, but I think it's important that we talk.' "

"Well," Ann continued, "he got the word."

To his shame and chagrin Bill did—but not from Ann.

Bad-News Messenger

"I was the bad-news messenger, yes," Betsey Wright later confirmed.

To ensure that Bill could not slide out of the truth-telling session, moreover, Betsey insisted a third person be present. "The point of my sitting down with him, with this other friend," Betsey related, "was to try to make him face reality instead of kidding himself about it."

Bill Clinton was finally being called to account by his chief of staff—a woman. And before a witness.

Ten years later the whole world would be witness as President Clinton wrestled with the truth and the impact it would have on his career, the nation, and the world. This time he had only Betsey Wright and her colleague present. "What Bill thought he was getting away with for a number of years," Betsey recalled candidly, "caught up with him."

Alerted to the impending scandal, Betsey had decided to have it out with the governor by presenting him with a list of supposed mistresses and demanding he tell her the unvarnished truth: Had he had sex with them? Who were they? *And were they likely to talk?*

The Meeting That Never Happened

Bill Clinton would later not only deny the sexual liaisons but that the meeting with Betsey had ever taken place. During the defense of President Clinton in the Paula Jones case, Clinton's lawyer had later shown Betsey Wright a number of documents, among them Maraniss's page proofs of his 1995 biography, *First in His Class,* with its account of Betsey's personal inquisition of Governor Clinton and his affairs in July 1987. "He pulled out this Xerox of that page or pages from the Maraniss book," Betsey recalled, "and they had Bill Clinton's margin notes on them, in his handwriting! And Bill's handwriting says, 'This never happened! I don't know why she makes such things up!'

"It just knocked me for a loop again!" Betsey recalled the moment—her breath literally taken from her by Bill's deceitfulness with his own lawyer David Kendall in a matter concerning Bill's most loyal former chief of staff!

Betsey was not, nor ever would be, a liar. Yet the most extraordinary part of Bill Clinton's loss of recall was that it came from a man with a photographic memory. Was Clinton later vaporizing unpalatable facts in some strange means of psychological survival, or had deceit taken on a Yale Law School cleverness that was positively Machiavellian, indeed Mephistophelean? Cornered by some of the most ruthless Republican lawyers in American history, had Bill Clinton once again slipped the net they had thrown over him? A most careful journalist, Maraniss had gotten the story of Bill's secret trial, held in camera before Betsey Wright and her companion, almost exactly right. Betsey *had* confronted her boss, with profound consequences for his political career and her own—but Maraniss had made a small mistake when quoting Wright. "The way Maraniss wrote it made it sound like I had gone with a written list. I didn't—I named names out of my head. It was that kind of a thing. [Later] I kept being subpoenaed for this list that didn't exist. I mean"—Betsey laughed—"I didn't write things like that *down*!"

Seeing Maraniss's slight error, had the lawyer in Bill Clinton seized on the incorrect detail, permitting him to claim to the investigating lawyers that the meeting had never happened *in the exact way that Maraniss described*? Yet happened it had—and Betsey had a witness.

Betsey shook her head sadly. "He has made this session nonexistent. And he was very angry about it, [the story as depicted] in Maraniss's book," later berating Betsey for having dared reveal such a thing. "And I said to him, 'Well, I offer no excuses. It's the sort of thing I don't believe in, talking about you [to journalists and biographers]. I was in terrible shape at the time. Thank goodness I never told him [Maraniss] there was someone else there!' And he said, '*Someone else there?* The meeting never happened! Who could have been there? The meeting *never* happened!' And I told him. I reminded him who else was there. And he said, 'I don't remember that!' "

If Bill didn't remember, it was because he didn't wish to. Not only had he wanted to avoid having to tell the truth to Republican attorneys seeking to destroy him as President of the United States, but he had found the very memory excruciating. Asked whether his memoirs, purportedly to be written in the evening of his life after he left the White House, would cast any light on this and other events, Betsey Wright was contemptuous. "I have no interest in him or that book!" she scoffed. "His ability to forget things and rationalize things and compartmentalize things will make it absolutely *useless*! Any book he writes is useless! I'm not interested in his book!"

Bill Clinton would, Betsey was certain, airbrush her name and contribution from his career, when penning his memoirs, to "minimize the importance of what I did for him"—just as he had cast Betsey out of his political life once she became identified with the secret knowledge of his own personal failings. "I had to be completely erased! This man whose mind never forgets the most incredible facts can forget stuff like that, that's too painful!" she exclaimed with emotion.

For Betsey had done the thing that, in the summer of 1987, no one else in Bill's gubernatorial entourage, not even his wife, Hillary, had dared to do: she had told him, after hearing his confession, that he couldn't run.

CHAPTER THIRTY-TWO

SAYING NO

Carnal Revelations

If the personal interrogation was excruciating for Governor Clinton, the replies were devastating to his chief of staff, who'd given her professional life to his cause. It was not, Betsey Wright later reflected, that the list put paid to a carefully planned Clinton agenda. "I don't think he ever plotted out a plan," Betsey reflected. "I think that his whole life he was reaching for the highest star he could grab. And to the degree that he had aspirations for the presidency, it was just that it was the highest star to grab. Just like going to Georgetown, just like going to Yale, just like being a Rhodes Scholar—those were the highest stars to grab, at those points in his life. I mean, no one was more closely involved with his political thinking than Hillary and I, and until 1987 we never had a conversation about running for the presidency.

"Now, *other* people brought it up all the time—'Ah, he could be president!'—but it was not anything weighing on his mind," she claimed. That said, "It was clear to all of us that he didn't think he would stop at being governor, and he would run for the U.S. Senate if it became open, or whatever but he was not sitting around plotting to become President of the United States! God knows, he wouldn't have done some of the things that he did," she felt, "had that been the case!"

Was Betsey right? Only Bill and Hillary could tell the depths of their own hearts—and ambitions. The irony was, with Senator Hart's withdrawal from the race, the time suddenly seemed so *opportune* for a Clinton run—not opportunistic but opportune. "There was such a natural progression, from the way he did things with the National Governors Association and the Education Commission of the States, the Democratic Leadership Council—it all fell into place serendipitously," Betsey allowed. All save one thing.

For Betsey Wright it had seemed obvious that, however appealing, this sudden presidential opportunity would have to be rejected. If Senator Hart's bid had failed over one peccadillo, how could Bill hope to escape the inevitable national press dragnet? It was disappointing. Yet only when Betsey argued his case did she realize how attached to the idea, indeed how tantalized Bill was by the opportunity and how he strained to be allowed to attempt the climb—at whatever cost to himself, his family, his staff, and his supporters.

Betsey's self-appointed task was to bring the would-be mountaineer back to earth. "We talked about it," Betsey recalled. "We talked about some of the women who had enough to claim something—I mean, where there was enough reality, truth to it."

Betsey would never forget Bill's naive, almost childlike certainty that he could get away with it, as they went through "the list" one by one.

"He said, 'But *she'll* never say anything!' "

"I said, 'You don't *know* that, Bill! First of all, you're telling me you don't where she is, so you don't know how desperate she is for money. Or whatever! You have *no* control over whether she would say something. *None!*' "

Saying No

At the end of Betsey's inquisition, after she had laid out the likely scenario—a press and media hunt that, like that for Senator Hart, would expose both Hillary and little Chelsea to the most hurtful shame and innuendo—Governor Bill Clinton had hung down his head, Betsey recalled, and "said he couldn't run."

The decision was deeply painful for Bill. Why must he surrender the ambition of a lifetime when he was no different from other full-blooded men? "I saw a lot of people that I thought were hypocrites in the very religious atmosphere that I grew up in," Bill later recalled, "saying one thing and doing another." *They* had never been called on their hypocrisy, he reasoned—a hypocrisy that had been part and parcel of that earlier generation's culture. Times and attitudes had, moreover, changed in the sixties—there had been "a loosening of the traditional bonds," as he put it, "that at least publicly bound private behavior." In almost every walk of life, adultery was now implicitly if not explicitly condoned. Other politicians, Bill Clinton knew, were just as promiscuous as he was, sometimes more so. The state legislature, for example, was replete with philanderers, Bible Belt or no. The capitol in Little Rock, even Ann Henry knew and accepted, wasn't actually full of *good* "ole boys," as people said, but *bad* ole boys—and girls. "I've been around politics enough to know that," Ann sighed in retrospect. "When [my husband] Morris was in the [state] Senate we knew a lot of people, people we'd known all our lives. I watched *every one* of our friends engage in affairs with women that were on their staff, or were provided by lobbyists. I saw the Senate, and I saw all of it. And one by one, I saw these people that I really admired succumb—just saw the whole sexual thing taking place. It's a real disillusion, in a way."

Why, then, did he have to say no to his presidential aspirations, Bill wondered, just because he would not say no to extramarital sex—sex that was oftentimes the result of women's desires, not his? Ann Henry certainly blamed such women as much as she did the weak governor. "It's the women who flock around Bill Clinton because they get their own boost, they build up their own self-esteem by being with someone who has power, you know—the 'power freaks.' And he *is* an attractive man. I have never been personally attracted at all, I'm just saying that apparently a lot of people really find him attractive."

This was indeed the conundrum, since—in the same way as with JFK—the very attractiveness and charisma that made Bill Clinton so electable in a modern democracy also made him, in the eyes of many women, so beddable.

The press, however, had learned that sex sold newspapers and, increasingly, television. What was tacitly accepted as par for the Arkansas course at a local level would, by contrast, be grist for the mill with regard to presidential candidacy—the hunt for a candidate's peccadilloes boosting media sales, yet bringing shame and embarrassment upon everyone connected with Bill Clinton. The lid would be off.

It was, in its way, an extraordinary glimpse into America's destiny.

The Reason Why

Bill Clinton had told Betsey he couldn't run. *But did he mean it?* All his life he had deferred to strong women. Typically, he'd told Betsey what she wanted to hear.

The next day, as ever more friends and colleagues came into Little Rock to offer their help and support, Wright had watched, anxiously, to see if the governor would keep his word.

The city filled with well-wishers, unaware what Bill had promised Betsey. Instead of telling them outright, he began to waver, aware not only of the magnitude of what he was surrendering—his cherished childhood dream, the White House—but also of their inevitable disappointment and the shattered hopes it would especially signify for Hillary, his still uninformed wife, once she learned not only that he wouldn't be a candidate for the presidency but why.

Withdrawal

Constitutionally incapable of decisiveness, Bill Clinton procrastinated, hoping for a miracle—that some angel of mercy would come and relieve him of this burden, offering him a way out. But there was no miracle.

With "tears welling in his eyes, and his voice thick with passion," as *Arkansas Democrat* journalist Meredith Oakley later recalled, Governor Bill Clinton finally addressed the 450 assembled journalists and supporters who gathered in the Excelsior Hotel on July 15, 1987. Was he running—or not? His office had announced his forthcoming decision, in a brief statement to the press the previous afternoon, followed by a draft of the speech he was expected to make. Though the *Arkansas Gazette* led with the story in its next edition, no journalist had quite believed it—indeed, halfway through his speech it *still* appeared that the governor might say yes, as the very features of his face seemed to twist and contort.

Eventually, having laid out the scenario of what he'd thought he could achieve were he to run, Governor Clinton made in public the irrevocable decision. It was the moment, finally, of truth. He was, he now confirmed in person, withdrawing from possible presidential candidacy in order to put his wife and child first. "I hope I will have another opportunity to seek the presidency when I can do it and be faithful to my family," Bill explained to the assembled press and supporters—adding the further constituencies of Arkansas and "my sense of what is right."

The word "faithful" was lost, drowned out in the gasps and tears over his decision, not only those shed by the candidate's wife and choked down by the candidate himself but those shed by his supporters, who felt let down. The national press had been advised not to come, but local people had. "Oh, it was a real emotional event," the journalist Max Brantley told Hillary's biographer Gail Sheehy. "Everybody was crying. I thought it was one of his great moments. And he was believable—at that moment, anyway. I remember being deeply moved at his consideration for Chelsea. Looking back on it later, I thought what a fool I'd been."

Commentators, biographers, and historians assumed that Bill had made up his mind only on the eve of his intended announcement—that, when reminded by Carl Wagner, a former McGovern campaign worker, of the importance of maintaining his beautiful relationship with Chelsea and protecting her from the grueling demands of a normal presidential run, Bill had caved in. Jim Blair, for example, told the *Arkansas Gazette* he'd talked with the governor on Sunday night, before the announcement, and was "convinced no decision" had at that time been made. One source maintained that as of 8 A.M. on Tuesday, July 14, "they were getting ready to go" for the presidential nomination. "It makes no sense," the informant lamented.

The sight of his sleeping child had certainly reminded Bill Clinton of what Betsey had foretold would happen if he dared run. Any contrition over his adultery (and Betsey's list encompassed only a fraction of the women with whom he'd actually had sex) was nominal, but he accepted that such behavior was disrespectful to a companionate wife who believed in monogamy and would hurt little Chelsea if it came out in the press and on television. Kids in the playground would kid Chelsea unmercifully; indeed, Bill could predict the joy with which the press would fall over itself in "exposing" yet another American philanderer, even though the majority of male journalists were guilty of the selfsame behavior—and a number of women journalists, too. This he knew, for he himself had sex with several of them! Their hypocrisy was galling, but then, *they were not elected officials.* He was. And the price of high office in the modern world was public scrutiny, indeed public prurience. Knowing this, during the previous, most vicious gubernatorial campaign, he and Hillary had, in fact, already prepared little Chelsea for the sort of cruel accusations people would make.

In almost funereal type, alongside a picture taken earlier in the month of the dark-suited governor pondering a text on his lap, the *Arkansas Gazette* headlined its front page on July 15, 1987, "Clinton says the word:

No." This time the newspaper's prediction had been right. In front of his many friends and supporters, the governor did indeed voice the magic, tragic word: No.

Amid tears and lamentations, the governor embraced his weeping wife and stepped down from the podium.

"Bernie," Hillary announced in a phone call to her old boss Bernie Nussbaum in New York, "you're released. He's decided not to run."

Nussbaum, who had been skeptical from the start, accepted the decision without demur, indeed with relief. "But I sensed that she wanted him to go," Nussbaum added, "despite whatever Betsey had told him."

Hamlet, however, had decided he could not be.

PART SIX

THE TEMPER OF THE TIMES

The nineties, beckoning

CHAPTER THIRTY-THREE

TELEVANGELIST PREVIEW

The Temper of the Times

Explaining his decision not to be a candidate for the Democratic Party's presidential nomination, Governor Bill Clinton had told reporters, "When it came time for me to step up to the bat, deep down inside, my head said, 'Go,' and my heart said, 'It isn't right for you now.' "

This was probably the reverse of what actually happened. In the political game there were few men who could match Bill Clinton's mind or his tactical perceptiveness. It was his heart that had urged him on—his head that had reined him back. In the weeks afterward Bill attempted further to describe the changing temper and tide of the times that caused him to make his decision. "In the '70s," he reflected, "there were a lot of people doing basically whatever they wanted to do in their personal lives. What [President] Reagan reflected [in the '80s] with all these family values and apple pie stuff was a deeper yearning that was in almost all Americans to try to get more grounded and have more discipline and order and integrity—not goody-two-shoes integrity, but wholeness in their lives." Side by side with that yearning, however, had gone a more negative, more punitive mood in which those lacking in "wholeness" were to be pilloried and destroyed—which increasingly worried him.

"I think something scared him out of it," the governor's trusted male aide Bobby Roberts later mused in his sunlit office overlooking the Arkansas River and downtown Little Rock. "The allegations have always been 'a sexual scare,'" Roberts acknowledged. Then he paused. In the grand white stone library building capped with the names of literary titans, the director of the state's Central Arkansas Library system balked at such a simplistic explanation of a landmark moment, indeed turning point, in his former boss's life. "*I don't know that that's true,*" Roberts remarked.

Roberts tilted his balding head a little as he looked down, toyed with a pen, then thoughtfully turned his gaze beyond his picture window again.

"I think he maybe just got cold feet. I mean," he added, "he got scared in the sense that *he just didn't feel it was the time for him to run.*"

Praise the Lord

Was it? If not, why not?

Television, and the fate of certain prominent television evangelists—televangelists—offered a clue.

Every Sunday William Jefferson Clinton, the governor, would be driven to Little Rock's Immanuel Baptist Church, where, as second tenor in the big church choir, he would sing lustily, his plump face beaming on television screens in tens of thousands of Arkansan homes: the governor who had seen the light and gloried in the Christian Lord. "It's a very important part of my life," Bill commented. He was not dissimulating. His Southern Baptist faith had been indelibly imprinted on his psyche in childhood, while its cultural influence was still equally powerful. With his strong belief in redemption, hope, and charity, the governor came across as a preacher manqué in a state that welcomed preachers; indeed, his next-but-one successor would be an ordained Baptist minister. "I think I feel more comfortable speaking in the rhythms of my faith in my speeches," Bill explained—at least "when I'm at home in the South."

What was taking place in the South in 1987 was, however, not always redeeming; indeed, it gave an interesting window onto America's destiny, both positive and negative. With their simplified, endlessly repeatable stories and biblical lessons of sin and salvation the Reverends Billy Graham, Jimmy Swaggart, Oral Roberts, Jerry Falwell, Pat Robertson, James Robison, and a host of American evangelical preachers had for decades been using commercial satellite and cable television to spread the gospel—their ministries flourishing to the point where even potential presidents had come to fear temporal denunciation by the evangelists, and sought their endorsement when running for office.

Not all preached fire and brimstone, however. Jim and Tammy Faye Bakker, leaders of the Praise the Lord Ministry (PTL), had in recent years achieved prime ratings on the American evangelical screen. Even President Ronald Reagan had been unsparing in his praise for the semiliterate, naive, but telegenic young Pentecostalist couple. In May 1984—the President's reelection year—"the Gipper" had sent Bakker a special letter, extolling the way in which, over the years, "you have been a strong and courageous voice in support of family-oriented issues, and have been very effective in helping us get this important message to the American people. I particularly want to express my deep appreciation to you, Tammy and the PTL partners for all your work in support of the School Prayer Amendment."

Republican approval had certainly helped Bakker to achieve his dream: the construction of a "Christian Disneyland" center that would include not only rides and entertainment but a shopping mall, cafeteria, conference center, and counseling facilities for struggling couples. To this end Bakker had announced a Lifetime Partnership Plan to get a thousand American couples to contribute at least $1,000 each in return for three free nights in his Heritage USA Hotel every year of their lives—a hotel that was, with a further hotel envisaged alongside, the center of his evangelical vision. The public response was stunning. "By the end of the 'Family Fun' telethon" in April 1987, for example, "PTL had issued more than $73 million in partnerships in the Tower Hotel and more than $64 million in the Heritage Grand," the Pulitzer Prize–winning chronicler of Bakker's rise and fall, Charles E. Shepard, reported. "All told," he noted, "the lifetime partnerships had generated $166.6 million."

With the presidential seal of approval, the Bakkers had seemed invincible, paying themselves $1.9 million in salaries and bonuses alone in 1986 and a further $640,000 in the first three months of 1987. "Nancy and I wish you the best for continued success with your ministry," President Reagan had added to his congratulatory letter, "and may God bless all of you."

The Bakkers certainly felt they were being blessed. Building on the "Prosperity Gospel" of the faith healer A. A. Allen, they had invented a new doctrine: the "Gospel of Health and Wealth," as it was called. "But my God shall supply all your need," the Bakkers quoted Philippians 4:19, "according to his riches in glory by Jesus Christ"—a passage that, they insisted, merited literal interpretation. The title of Jim Bakker's 1983 publication, *You Can Make It,* said it all.

Rumors of a Sexual Nature

Nervous about the votes that the ambitious evangelist Pat Robertson—who had burning aspirations to become the next Republican president of the United States—might win in the upcoming 1988 nomination race, George Bush's campaign aide Doug Weed had sought to arrange a personal meeting between Bush and Robertson's nemesis, Jim Bakker.

"It is extremely important to PTL and the Kingdom of God that you have a good relationship with the president of the United States, and there is a very real possibility that George Bush could be that man," Weed had written to the Reverend Bakker as far back as March 1985. "I sure would love for the vice president to get down to Heritage Village, stay in the hotel, and see how much bigger the evangelical movement is," he added. Though Vice President Bush did not make it, his press secretary and another political confidant did, flown first-class to PTL headquarters on May 14, 1985, where each was given $5,000, as well as bracelets for their wives. One of them, Pete Teeley, would be kept on a $5,000—later $10,000—per month PTL retainer.

So much loose money seemed disturbing for a Christian nonprofit organization enjoying tax-exempt status with the IRS, but it was well spent if presidential support for the Christian ministry on TV was to be retained. In an attempted sweetheart deal, the White House had pressed the IRS, the Federal Communications Commission, and the Justice Department *not* to investigate the growing claims of fraud and tax evasion by the televangelists.

Not even the White House could tame America's post-Watergate investigative press, however, as the Reagan "honeymoon" approached its end. By the spring of 1987, as Bill Clinton had readied himself, as he thought, to join the presidential race, Jim Bakker's number had come up. Bakker's wife had had relationships with other men, and so, it was widely rumored, had Jim—who was believed to be bisexual. These allegedly involved mutual homosexual masturbation—vices denounced from their pulpits—and more. Much more. However, these were still but rumors. It was the specific allegation that, in concert with one of his associates, Jim Bakker had enticed to Florida and then repeatedly raped an attractive twenty-one-year-old Full Gospel Tabernacle church secretary in 1980, seven years before, that proved the final straw that would now break Bakker's—and the PTL's—back.

The Matter of Jessica Hahn

The Jessica Hahn scandal, as it became known, would be a precursor of an even more historic scandal in the tapestry of American late-twentieth-century history: that of Paula Jones. "Why don't you hire somebody?" the twenty-one-year-old Jessica Hahn, who professed to be a virgin, said she pleaded in 1980 as the Reverend Bakker of the Assemblies of God Church and President of the PTL organization undressed her in Room 538 of the Sheraton Sand Key Resort, Clearwater Beach, all the while telling Jessica that his wife, Tammy, was unfaithful and he needed to "know I am still a man."

"You can't trust anybody," Bakker had explained his reluctance to use—as other preachers did—a prostitute. That was why, he said, he'd specifi-cally asked his colleague the Reverend John Wesley Fletcher to find him a trustworthy young virgin—adding that he trusted Jessica, since he under-stood she'd baby-sat for Fletcher for several years, she was known to Fletcher's family, and she worked for a faith healer, the Reverend Eugene Profeta, who had appeared on Bakker's television show. She was also loyal to the church, contributing $15 a month to the PTL ministry. Bakker had clearly done his homework. "You're not someone who is going to try and hurt me like the others," he continued naively—without specifying who "the others" might be. "You're here to help me," he asserted as he caressed Jessica's shapely young body, "and by helping me you're going to help a lot of people."

In sworn testimony Jessica later related how he had stripped her of her remaining clothes "and didn't stop for what seemed like an hour and a half. He did just about everything he could do to a woman . . . and he wouldn't stop. I told him I didn't want to be pregnant. He said, 'Oh, I've had an op-eration.' Once wasn't enough. He had to keep finding new things to do. I just couldn't stand him. I just wanted to pull out his hair"—especially when he demanded that she perform oral sex on him.

Afterward, Hahn said, Bakker had brushed his tele-famous hair before the mirror, brazenly using Jessica's brush. Then, restored to masculinity, he had slipped back into his signature white terry cotton swimsuit and had gone down to the swimming pool with the words "I'll see ya." When Jessica had demanded to know how he could have done such things to her, he'd laughed and had assured her, "You'll appreciate it later."

Helping the Shepherd

Alone, Jessica Hahn had been in a state of shock. When Bakker's aide, the Reverend John Fletcher, reappeared, she'd remonstrated with him also. He had clearly arranged to fly her down from New York deliberately in order to offer her as a sexual sacrifice to his boss, she accused him. Fletcher had seemed unabashed—indeed, Hahn later quoted him as using words that would become famous: "Jim is a shepherd, and when you help the shepherd you help the sheep." Thereupon, Hahn said, he had pulled her to the floor and, vowing she would rate his performance above that of the Reverend Bakker's, he'd ignored her remonstrations and raped her himself. When it was over, he'd also told her he had to rush. "I've got to get ready for the show. I've got to preach tonight."

On the PTL Club televangelist program with Jim Bakker that night, Fletcher had apparently been full of himself. "You had a good rest today," he'd remarked cynically on camera to Bakker. To which Bakker had replied, "Yeah, I need more rest like that. The Lord really ministered to us today. We need more ministry like that." The next day Hahn had been given $129 for her airfare home from Tampa.

Male hubris of this magnitude would, in the new America, backfire. Indeed for his "indiscretion" the Reverend Bakker—or rather, the viewers who funded his Praise the Lord empire—would pay dearly: $265,000 in "hush money" alone, much of which went to Hahn's lawyer. (It was, however, a mere drop in the ocean of money being donated to PTL and other televangelists at the time, which totaled more than $1.6 billion a year, it is calculated.)

How virginal Jessica Hahn really was would forever be disputed—she later acknowledged a six-year affair with her married preacher, the Reverend Eugene Profeta, but one that had begun only, she claimed, after the incident in Room 538; moreover, with the money she obtained from Bakker she paid for cosmetic surgery on her face and posed nude for *Playboy* magazine for a rumored $1 million.

Meanwhile, sued and pursued by the IRS, the FCC, the FBI, Jessica Hahn's lawyers, the press, and jealous other preachers—most notably his rival, the Reverend Jimmy Swaggart—Jim Bakker had decided he'd had enough. His wife was in rehab for pharmaceutical drug addiction; his nerves were frayed to the point of breakdown. An exit strategy was required. He therefore resigned from the presidency both of the PTL Ministry and Heritage USA and asked the Reverend Jerry Falwell—a fellow Baptist fundamentalist—to temporarily take over the PTL Ministry while Jim and Tammy put their rocky marriage back together. When Falwell asked what the terms would be for a permanent handover, the Bakkers had proposed a "lifetime" deal that would keep Jim and Tammy secure for the rest of their lives.

Pigs at the Trough

A sort of apocalyptic craziness certainly seemed to overtake the televangelist movement in America at this time. The Reverend Oral Roberts, pioneer of "feel-good" rather than "feel-bad" evangelism, had, for example, caused a sensation by threatening on television that if, by March 31, 1987, he did not receive $8 million for a pet project, God would "call him home." Thanks to a magnificent donation by a wealthy gambler, Roberts had got the money, but five weeks later, on May 6, 1987, the Assemblies of God formally defrocked the Reverend Jim Bakker, a married priest, for having relations with Jessica Hahn, a priest's secretary.

The televangelist scandals were, however, only catching fire. Jim Bakker was blessed with a wife whose telegenic appeal was as great as his. As author Ann Rowe Seaman recorded, "Television news ratings were astronomical whenever any aspect of the Bakker story was covered, largely because of Tammy Faye. Tammy's grotesque makeup, garish Nashville-style outfits, heaps of tasteless jewelry, low-cut necklines, wigs, breast implants, onscreen airing of marital problems, and confessed enslavement to a 'shopping demon' " made irresistible viewing "for a nation still wedded to the image of a preacher's wife as someone with decent hemlines and sensible shoes."

Aware of such audience fascination, ABC television's *Nightline* aired a program entitled "Billion Dollar Pie" on May 12, 1987. It was broadcast from a huge, plush church in Memphis, with host Ted Koppel and his preacher guests on a wide stage, backed by seven rows of gospel singers and seated before an audience of thousands. As social anthropologist Susan Harding later described, it represented a "pastiche of the religious and the secular, news and entertainment, postmodern electronics and a premodern God."

A generation before, the South had reverberated with the cadres of whites and blacks in contest over civil rights. Now, in a supposedly more rational age, Ted Koppel had hoped to represent the "voice of modernity for millions of Americans" by subjecting the growing battle between rival television evangelicals to rational analysis: to settle once and for all "what this has got to do with."

Koppel thought it had to do with money; indeed, he described his preacher guests to their faces as "pigs at the trough" of modern mammon, each competing for a slice of the vast annual televangelist donor pie. "I conclude from this," he declared sententiously, "that what's going on here is a battle royale in the business world. This has got nothing to do with saving souls. This has got nothing to do with evangelical Christianity. What this has got to do with," he cautioned to audience applause, "is a huge billion-dollar pie."

Koppel then gave his own theory: that in the cutthroat business of televangelism "one way of elbowing the other hogs away from the trough is this business of sexual infidelity."

Koppel was right: competitive sex scandaling had become a combat strategy for televangelists in America—a strategy eagerly abetted by the voyeurish proclivities and search for higher ratings and advertising income of the very press that Koppel represented! But if Koppel hoped by his accusations to shame the preachers, he was way out of his depth. Before an audience of more than 20 million viewers, the assembled preachers weighed into one another—and also into Koppel.

The sight of squabbling preachers, mixed with the whiff and whoof of sexual scandal, made for compelling viewing. Koppel's program was soon followed, beginning on May 26, by a three-night blockbuster *Nightline* series. In the first of these Jerry Falwell, the fundamentalist Baptist whom Jim Bakker had begged to take over the PTL Ministry, was accused of having taken over the organization under false pretenses. The following night Jim and Tammy Faye Bakker were interviewed live for the first time since the scandals had erupted. It was becoming, as Professor Harding dubbed it, "pure spectacle," with the Bakkers openly confessing sins yet speaking of love and forgiveness, so that Falwell, in fear lest the supremely telegenic Bakkers try to resume control of the PTL Ministry, was driven to destroy them. Before cameras at a special press conference Falwell was televised waving the handwritten note in which the Bakkers had suggested a $300,000-per-year lifetime salary for Jim, plus $100,000 a year for Tammy, rights to all their books and records (plus all remaining inventory) to be retained by the authors, a secretary, maid and telephone service for a year, the Tega Cay rectory with furniture, two automobiles, guards, security—and legal fees paid for litigation with the IRS. As Falwell announced, "I don't see any repentance there." Instead, having also given viewers his latest, shocking version of what he said Bakker and Fletcher—and even a mysterious "third man"—had done unto the young church worker seven years before, Falwell perceived only "the self-centeredness. I see the avarice that brought them down."

Cruelly but effectively, Falwell had scuppered all chance of a Bakker comeback. PTL was his.

Refusing to Be Shamed

Night after night, watched by an estimated 23 million Americans, the televangelist scandals of 1987 became a veritable national "soap opera," as Koppel called it—a term with which Jim and Tammy Bakker, the prime stars and victims, reluctantly agreed.

Falwell's snarling denunciation of the Bakkers' greed, however, was not quite enough to consign them to oblivion. As Professor Harding noted, "After every barrage of charges leveled at the Bakkers, they were still standing when the smoke cleared, smiling and chatting about God's love and forgiveness. They refused to be shamed into oblivion, escaped narrative grips and talked back, irrepressibly, from their own point of view."

This, alongside the public fascination with all things sexual, was a significant marker of change in an increasingly postmodern era. Punitive, even vindictive rivalry now characterized the television "market" for God. Shame, however, had become, thanks partly to television entertainment, a relative word.

Torn Apart

Poor Jim Bakker had seen the light of feel-good televangelism but not the dark that came with it: the jealousy he would engender and the righteous greed of other "pigs at the trough," pigs who would use whatever weapon came to hand in promoting their own success. The Bakkers' naiveté in the competitive, media-mediated world would be their downfall. Confessing publicly to numerous sins, Jim, as a well-meaning, flawed, but generous soul who believed in the power of love and compassion, had hoped for a pardon, as well as either his PTL Ministry back if he managed to put his marriage together again, or, if he could not resume control of the PTL Ministry, a lifetime pension. Instead, in the cutthroat, internecine business of high-stakes televangelism he was torn apart by his fellow preachers.

The Jessica Hahn business was merely skirmishing. Arraigned for fraud—however innocently engendered—Jim Bakker was poorly defended in court and ultimately sentenced to jail for forty-five years (he served six before his release) as a warning to others. To Bakker's further chagrin, his PTL Ministry was driven by Falwell into bankruptcy. Heritage USA was closed. Once behind bars, to add a final insult to his injury, Bakker would be divorced by Tammy.

It was by turns comic and tragic: a "soap opera" consuming the very stars it had created. What was crucial to note, however, was that the Reverend Jim Bakker had done himself no favors by resigning his chairmanship of the PTL Ministry he had created and relying solely on the Christian charity of others. A decade before, in the 1970s, President Richard Nixon had resigned before inevitable impeachment and been pardoned by his successor, but the style of the 1980s was increasingly uncharitable, more savage, less forgiving—a lesson that was not lost on the telegenic would-be President from Hope, Arkansas: Governor William Jefferson Clinton.

CHAPTER THIRTY-FOUR

THE FACE OF AMERICA'S FUTURE

The Face of America's Future

Ted Koppel had attempted to put the televangelist genie back into its bottle by ending his *Nightline* series in a small church in the Virginia mountains, where he asked an old priest to give the last religious word on a subject worthy only of ridicule. It quickly became clear that Koppel had failed.

What Koppel hadn't recognized was that the struggle between Falwell's "Moral Majority" and the Bakkers' "prosperity theology," as well as the concerns and fascination of the public with such issues, *was the face of America's future.* As Professor Harding analyzed it, Falwell and his allies stood for "production, hard work, restraint, sacrifice, delayed gratification, steady growth, contained crises, hierarchy, male dominance, sexual repression, obedience to Godly others, the word, narrative structure and authority, fixed identity, place, authenticity, depth and centeredness." The Bakkers and their associates, by contrast, had picked up on Oral Roberts's 1950s Pentecostalist doctrines: the notion of God as a "good God" who wanted his flock to enjoy comfort and rewards, not perpetual suffering and guilt. A momentous cultural battle was taking place, which disgrace and imprisonment of targeted individuals could not end. Although the Bakkers' conduct might be financially, even theologically, lax, their *appeal* across the South and Southwest and in California was unmistakable and met a burgeoning need among ordinary people in the late eighties for emotional outreach and for theater: televisual theater, even Theater of the Absurd.

The Nineties: Beckoning

Looking at the amazing sight of charismatic preachers denouncing and warring with one another on the television screen, as well as the outlandish makeup of a preacher's wife who reminded him acutely of his own mother, Bill Clinton was looking, in 1987, at a version of his own fate—and America's. The Bakkers, in particular, espoused an evangelical goodwill Christianity, tolerant, forgiving, and empathetic, that was surprisingly close to Clinton's own. Governor Clinton was confident that the majority of voters "believe in redemption," he maintained in an interview; indeed, he became certain the average American voter wanted "somebody who knows what it's like to feel pain and loss and defeat and disappointment in yourself, and to overcome that." As he put it, "those of us who come out of a religious tradition are far more comfortable talking about that than maybe others are."

The Bakkers certainly were. In fact, they never stopped talking of such things. For all their tacky tastes, they ministered, in particular, to those who were "hurting" or felt "hurt" in the modern world; they felt their pain and offered a bubbling, affectionate message of compassion. They were not excluding; they believed in inclusion—the inclusion of homosexuals, lesbians, and all who put "God's love," as illustrated through the life of His son Jesus, above hate and cruelty.

The sincerity of the Bakkers' vision was never in question, nor was their popularity. Their 2,300-acre theme park, Heritage USA, had attracted the third highest number of visitors per annum in America, after Disneyland: 6 *million* people in 1986 alone! As his Heritage USA promotional book explained, Jim Bakker wanted to "carry the spirit of the campmeeting movement into the 21st century," and it did. Overnight Heritage USA became "a kind of postmodern Pentecostal mecca," as Professor Harding noted, an "ensemble of replicas, relics, facades, imitations, simulations, props and sets drawn from Biblical Jerusalem, the Old West, small-town America, Hollywood, modern suburbs and tourist resorts. Nothing was simply itself; everything was palpably a production, a reproduction, or a performance."

There was even the actual dismantled and reerected boyhood home of evangelist Billy Graham and a supposed "exact replica" of the room where Christ ate the Last Supper with his disciples, as well as a Bayreuthian reproduction "ancient amphitheater" where the Passion Play was performed several nights a week.

Yes, it might be tacky—truly, madly, deeply so—but viewing it and its cultural context Professor Harding could see what Koppel, as a journalist, simply could not: that in their "baroque confusion" the "Holy Wars" of the late 1980s presented "an irrepressible sense of events-out-of-control, of confusion, disorder, and a constant instability of genres, borders, roles, rules." It had been, in its way, the cultural New Frontier of the nineties: beckoning.

Preposterous Categorical Hodgepodges

As an easterner, Ted Koppel could not see that the struggle between postmodernity and right-wing religious fundamentalism was not going to be resolved by the financial or religious victory of either one. Rather, the two would meld in postmodern chaos: "the opening up of a new world composed of preposterous categorical hodgepodges and antic crisscrossings of social boundaries," as Susan Harding put it. The very tackiness of the Bakkers appealed, as the professor put it, to "somewhat lower class factions than Falwell's movement," but it was a constituency celebrating, in a new era of American affluence, "consumption, play, excess, indulgence, immediate gratification, wild swings of growth and crisis, anti-hierarchy, feminization, polymorphous sexuality, the godly powers of ordinary men and women, visual images, spectacle and narrative fragmentation, disposable identities, movement, artifice, surfaces, and decenteredness."

Such an academic mouthful might itself have attracted ridicule, had it not been so true. Looking back, Harding felt that the evangelical telescandals, coming on top of Irangate, the Gary Hart affair, Ivan Boesky, and the gathering bubble and collapse of Wall Street (which took place in October 1987), as well as "a whole host of lesser televangelists, hungry, waiting for the titans to fall," had somehow changed America—or at least marked a profound cultural shift. Watching the soap opera, viewers could not avoid "the unshakeable sense that we, the audiences, were inside the telescandal too—that it had caught us up, variously, and put us down somewhere else."

It had. Where, exactly, it had put down postmodern Americans and where Governor Bill Clinton would fit into that scenario—whether he could somehow harness it to his own ambitions or would fare any better than the defrocked, humiliated, and ultimately imprisoned Bakker—was yet to be seen. But for the moment polymath Bill Clinton did not dare find out.

CHAPTER THIRTY-FIVE

THE SPECTER
OF DIVORCE

Victoria's Secret

According to a Texan friend from the McGovern campaign days, Bill Clinton fantasized at this time about "a statute of limitations on infidelity—whether you get any credit for getting it back together."

If so, "getting it back together" with Hillary in 1987, on behalf of their beloved daughter—the very reason Bill had given for his withdrawal from possible presidential candidacy—proved short-lived.

The new four-year term the Clintons had thought would give Bill an opportunity to stop perpetually campaigning and be with his family—"When we got the four-year term we were looking forward to something like normal life," Hillary claimed—had proved counterproductive. Hillary, going back to the Rose Law Firm, had worked harder and for more financial reward—but less home benefit. The Arkansas state legislature, fearing that the new, extended term of office would make the governor less accountable and more regal, gave Bill no quarter. The old Arkansas insistence on a balanced budget meant that any new programs would have to be funded from new taxation—in an era when, thanks to the Reagan revolution, the middle classes no longer wished to pay more than minimum taxes, while the poor had nothing to pay and the rich found endless loopholes to avoid paying at all. It was a dim prospect for a progressive governor.

Bill Clinton was, however, no longer progressive; indeed, in some respects he was no longer even interested in being governor. "See, he thought it was all over," Betsey Wright recalled Bill Clinton's descent into the underworld in the second half of 1987, after his withdrawal from the presidential stakes. "He was so disinterested in being governor after that. I mean, it was pulling teeth to get him to pay attention to things on his desk, the decisions that had to be made. He felt like his life was over, that his last chance to ever run for president, the first and last chance to run, had gone! And he was disengaged. And things just went from bad to worse."

"That was his worst legislative session," Betsey remembered painfully. "We had put issues [such as a new ethics in politics bill] on the ballot that offended the legislature, and they were—*the old guard was going to get him back for it!* It was his least productive legislative session, and he was disinterested! I mean, it was my hardest time with him, after the decision not to run for president—I think that he felt his life was close to being over."

Bill Clinton was certainly pained by having to surrender his ambition: "It hurt so bad," he himself confided, "to walk away from it."

Illicit sex became, as it had always been, Bill Clinton's escape from the unbearable heaviness, not lightness, of being. The former Miss America Elizabeth Ward Gracen later admitted to having "had sex with Bill Clinton," and she was not alone in her confession. Dolly Kyle Browning, Gennifer Flowers, and numerous others did the same. Rumors of an affair with Beth Coulson, a lawyer Clinton appointed to a state judgeship in 1987, circulated, as well as about one with Deborah Mathis, the black former co-journalist of Gennifer Flowers's on local television. As Hillary's biographer Joyce Milton wrote, Bill seemed to go into his "midlife crisis" with almost suicidal intent, politically speaking, carrying on "at least five simultaneous affairs" by the late 1980s, quite apart from one-night encounters.

This was multitasking on the part of a married man that evinced extraordinary social skill, on a par with John F. Kennedy in his senatorial and presidential heyday—but professionally suicidal in a new era of unfettered tabloid "kiss-and-tell-all" journalism that was spilling into mainstream newspapers.

Bill seemed not to care. Like Jim Bakker, his own brand of political evangelism had brought him extraordinary funding and perks, including colleagues, staff, and troopers who were willing—as John Wesley Fletcher had done for Jim Bakker—to pimp for him and perhaps even occasionally benefit from it themselves. For two of his mistresses—one living in the

Heights, the other in the Sherwood district—"Clinton assigned one trooper to each woman, charging him with handling phone calls and purchasing and delivering the occasional gift," Joyce Milton recorded. Often, she added, it was "lingerie from Victoria's Secret."

An Economy of Empty Air

From Potiphar's wife to Catherine the Great, and from King David to Chairman Mao Zedong, one of the perks of political power or influence has always been sexual; indeed, when reviewing the British monarchy's weakness for illicit sex *The New York Times* would suggest a deepening of the "view among some Britons that marital misbehavior is embedded in the monarchal genes." In the less monarchal United States in the late 1980s, however, as the divorced-and-remarried President Ronald Reagan's term of office came to an end, Americans seemed as confused and divided as Bill Clinton.

President Reagan himself seemed unaffected, in both senses of the word. His unremitting popularity had always owed itself in large measure to the way, as a former Hollywood actor, he appeared to operate, even float in a sphere, beyond the mess of ordinary American life. The President's success in freeing American hostages in Iran had been tarnished by his approval of congressionally unauthorized aid to right-wing guerrillas in Nicaragua. His efforts to reduce tax and deregulate the American economy had produced junk bonds, arbitrageurs, and a savings and loan scandal that were stimulating the economy and rocking—indeed bankrupting—the nation.

The fact was, behind the simplistic Republican rhetoric, a complex postindustrial economic change was taking place. And as that painful process proceeded, so American culture and even its language changed too. American life might become a modern soap opera, but in a global age of television, America's opera was increasingly the world's opera, reflecting a developing, metamorphosing American economy that no longer seemed "real." As the historian and sociologist Stuart Ewen wrote, "a perceptual schizophrenia has become normalized in thinking about the economy." On January 8, 1987, the Dow Jones Industrial Average had topped 2,000 for the first time in its history, but by October 1987 the market had crashed. "Advertising, public relations, and other industries of image and hype are consolidating into global megacorporations," Ewen wrote. "Their prime role is to envelop a jerry-built material world with provocative, tenuous meanings, suggesting fathomable value, but occupying no clear time or space"—a triumph, as he called it, "of abstract value" in which "we listen to the ongoing celebrations of the "new prosperity" while bearing witness—in our lives—to industrial breakdown, widespread "hunger" and "homelessness" (New Age terminology for poverty), and the sacrificing of concrete social priorities upon an altar of economic exegesis, mammon."

America, Professor Ewen felt, was becoming an "economy made of empty air."

This was hardly a situation of Bill Clinton's making. Yet if the Arkansas governor were to have any chance of helping his country steer a conscionable path through the transitional jungle into the new global economy with honor, he needed to start in his own life. Repeatedly Betsey and Hillary urged him to do so in the aftermath of his 1987 withdrawal from the presidential race: to find honor in his most private domain lest he be attacked and eviscerated by Republican foes who, devoid of insight, compassion, or social conscience, would revel in hypocritical accusations.

Instead, Bill Clinton, like his hero JFK, did the opposite: enlisting his staff, or in his case his state troopers, who were sworn to secrecy and the preservation of the governor's life, to solicit for him and aid in his sexual liaisons. Brief oral sex in his state car (on the way to Chelsea's elementary school, for example, one of his state troopers was told to guard the entrance to the parking lot while a young beauty counter saleswoman from a Little Rock store slipped out and sat with the governor in his car, where "the lady's head" was observed to "go into his lap") alternated with wild, stylishly lingeried intercourse with girlfriends and mistresses of all backgrounds, classes, and colors. People might later sniff at Clinton's choice of women, but as Hillary's biographer Gail Sheehy remarked, Bill was ultrademocratic when it came to sex. "His tastes were ecumenical, covering all three branches of government and all social classes."

Perhaps the most heartrending comment on Bill's supposed rededication to "his family," however, and his sense of "what is right," was Hillary's *cri de coeur,* heard at this time by one of the governor's state troopers as Hillary remonstrated with her husband. "Look, Bill," Hillary yelled at him hysterically as he left the mansion, "I need to be fucked more than twice a year."

The Rules

"I wonder how history is going to note our marriage," Hillary puzzled one day, talking to a family friend. But she did not really want to know the answer, and her companion wisely volunteered none.

The bitter truth was that after the "traumatic decision not to run," as Bill afterward put it, the Clintons' marriage—ostensibly the reason for the governor's withdrawal—was disintegrating.

Blacks, Jews, Hispanics, homosexuals, women, and a thousand other categories of American citizen were also ineligible for the presidency by virtue of social and media prejudice, but this was no consolation to the grieving couple, denied a shot at the Democratic presidential nomination thanks to Bill's wayward urges and the temper of the times. As usual Bill blamed not himself but others. "Most rational people can deal with whatever rules they have to play by," he commented in August 1987. "But I think what most of the politicians felt was"—after the Gary Hart sinking—"What are the rules?" In this respect he blamed the media. "What are these people doing?" he complained. "Are they going to print rumors? Are they going to print rumors that are 10 years old or 15 years old? Am I going to have to spend the whole campaign dealing with that, and if they don't find anything will it still be debilitating?" He was not alone in this anxiety. "All the politicians talked about it—every time I went to Washington."

Hillary was even more hurt, for she felt not only that they'd had the chance "to run well" but that it was "certain that we would have been taken seriously, and it's entirely possible we could have won." If only, that was, Bill had "been able," as Dick Morris recalled Hillary's trenchant remark to her husband, "to keep your cock in your pants."

Losing the Way

In an interview in the *Arkansas Gazette* the week after Bill's withdrawal from the race for the White House, Hillary had complained about the way the media spotlight now subjected a candidate's whole life—private as well as public—not only to scrutiny but to open speculation. In England, a draconian law of libel protected rich people and politicians, but under America's more democratic laws there was no comparabale legal shield for "public figures." Exposure of the Bakkers' schemes, which had duped the

American public of millions of dollars, did not, in Hillary's view, authorize the press to subject well-meaning politicians to the same investigation. "Everybody knows when you're in public life, you're going to be giving up a lot of your privacy," she acknowledged, but did this give the press the right to print scurrilous stories and allegations? she asked. "This is one thing you learn in this business: People can say anything with total impunity because there is nothing you can do about it. You're not going to sue for libel. You just hope it will not have any effect."

Yet even Hillary, so clear in her aspirations and moralistic in how to achieve them, was aware that a sea change was taking place—and that the change went deeper than mere press titillation. "We've really lost our way," she acknowledged of modern American society; indeed, it had become, she lamented, "very tough to lead a satisfying life these days." In hoping to spend more time with Chelsea, she'd wished to "gain some balance. What's going on is real interesting," she remarked in an almost Arkansan lapse, "but no one is writing about it. Nobody understands it yet."

Hillary was thus as stumped as Ted Koppel—not yet recognizing that, like Tammy Faye Bakker, she was now caught up in the same late-eighties soap opera as the rest of celebrity America. She had told the press she and Bill were going to return to "a more balanced personal-public life," in which the decision over whether to run or not for the presidency had "forced us to say: What is really important to us right now?" Yet withdrawing—into a supposedly more balanced marital life in which parental responsibility for Chelsea came first—was clearly neither possible for them personally, nor would the "speculators" involved in America's soap-operatic mass entertainment let them rest there. The Bakkers, too, had attempted to denounce the press for invading their privacy and making up "lies" about their private life. By resigning from the PTL Ministry, they had hoped to sort out their personal lives. But doing so had merely left them powerless to avoid the predations, accusations, lawsuits, and Jim's eventual criminal trial and conviction—while losing their beloved homes, possessions, pensions, and copyrights of their own songs, as well as their privacy.

In thinking that she and Bill were, in this respect, different from Tammy Faye and Jim Bakker, Hillary Clinton was making an immense mistake. Such a distinction was based not merely on intellectual and social snobbery (she would tell one of Bill's state troopers not to talk in public because "You sound like a hick") but on her power of denial—ironically, the very quality that gave her own life such coherence, righteousness, and focus. Such denial, however, meant putting those of her husband's sexual transgressions that she knew of "into a box called lust," as Lucinda Franks later commented after interviewing Hillary, and hoping that the press and public would do likewise. But the press wouldn't—and in surveying the box called lust, journalists were increasingly drawn not only to the prospect of prurient, tabloid, circuslike entertainment but also to a mystery they did not themselves understand. In the potpourri of modern, indeed postmodern, America even Hillary could see that "all these stories or allegations or whatever" were "desperate attempts on the part of the press, frankly, to really figure out what's going on underneath."

Hillary was right. A whole host of *People*-type magazines and broadcast programs were now proliferating across America—journals and programs in which the sex lives of the stars, the rich and the famous, the luminaries and the infamous, wallpapered journals in various stages of undress from literal cover to cover. Such vaudeville-style, scurrilous entertainment, pivoting on human weaknesses and peccadilloes, had always characterized the "popular press" and for several centuries had been disdainfully ignored by the literate middle and upper classes. That distinction—indeed the very notion of "Distinction," as Pierre Bourdieu had shown in what would become his classic work of 1979, translated into English in 1984—was now past its sell-by date. Since the 1960s, the difference between broadsheet and tabloid, pop and classical, highbrow and lowbrow had been inexorably undermined in the interests of a more open, more upwardly mobile, more egalitarian, opportunistic society and counterculture. Big Bill Clinton, as the saxophone-playing, easygoing six-foot-three guy from a poor background in Hope and then Hot Springs, had himself been, at an amazingly young age, one of the chief beneficiaries of this blurring of distinctions—but the price for performing in the nation's top soap, or *télévérité,* as it might be called, clearly carried the danger that the genial young governor could, as part of the opera, be ritually garroted and hung if he messed up, to appease the public demand for colorful entertainment—all helping, in its strange way, the American reader and viewer to "figure out" what was going on underneath in society as the world approached the final decade of the millennium.

Hillary wanted Bill to reform, as did Betsey Wright, in order to avoid being in the soap opera altogether, rather than in the altogether. "One of the big problems right now in this country is that people are not paying enough attention to children," Hillary explained. "And it's pretty hard for us to go out selling that message and not pay attention to our own child. That's a contradiction we also weren't very comfortable with." Bill nominally agreed. Indeed, three weeks later, on a national television show, *Meet the Press,* in a discussion with the U.S. education secretary, William Bennett, Bill called for more sex education in schools with the proviso that he thought "it's a terrible mistake to teach sex education in schools without saying that young people should be restrained in their sexual activities."

Unfortunately, such restraint did not stretch to Bill Clinton's own private life. As Betsey Wright noted, he retreated into political indifference and personal dissolution. "He faltered; he was disinterested. It was very hard to pull him out. And it was in this kind of a dither that he then had the only serious affair, that I'm aware of, that he ever had."

First, however, he had seemingly put another nail in the coffin of his future presidential chances—at the Democratic National Convention in Atlanta.

Disaster in Atlanta

"I went through the traumatic decision not to run myself—and I was gone for six or seven months doing that," Bill later described his life from the beginning of 1987. "You know, you have an inevitable sort of letdown after that. I knew then that what I had to do was to really throw myself into this job"—he said of his governorship—"that I did not need any distractions."

For this reason, he claimed, he'd stood aside while the Democratic Party, in a series of primaries early in 1988, sought its best candidate to face Vice President Bush in the November 1988 election—without Bill Clinton. Nevertheless, in the summer of that year, as the nomination races reached their apogee, Governor Clinton was asked by Governor Dukakis, the clear Democratic favorite, to make the nominating speech at the party convention. With the possibility that he might be chosen for a high cabinet appointment, even vice president, the Arkansas governor embarked on his televised thirty-minute speech, the text of which had run to twelve drafts and had been agreed upon word for word with Dukakis.

It was a disaster. To Hillary's and Betsey Wright's horror, the auditorium lights were not dimmed, and overzealous supporters of the Massachusetts governor refused to be silent, volubly interrupting the nominating speaker, calling for the Arkansas governor to cut the bull and simply call for Dukakis's nomination. Clinton, misjudging the situation and loath to surrender his slot on national television, refused to be brief or silent. In perhaps the most embarrassing media moment of Clinton's entire career so far, the television producers were compelled to cease broadcasting his address halfway through. Meanwhile, on the floor of the convention, after thirty-three excruciating minutes, Clinton was finally booed off the stage.

Jesse Jackson had electrified the conference, Clinton had calcified it, Tom Shales caustically noted in *The Washington Post*. Bill's chances of national attention as a possible future presidential contender seemed now doubly dashed—so much so that conspiracy theories began to abound, with claims that Dukakis had deliberately sought to destroy Clinton as a rival. Bill Clinton himself recognized that he was out of touch and had mistaken the party's mood. "I just fell on my sword," he acknowledged afterward. "It was a comedy of errors." Invited to appear—and play his saxophone—on Johnny Carson's *The Tonight Show*, Bill retrieved some kudos by being able to laugh, in front of millions of television viewers, at his own poor performance in Atlanta. It was, however, as a comedian now, not a political hopeful. News broadcasters and commentators had dismissed him as a lightweight, and his own chief of staff, Betsey Wright, wept when recounting the episode to her staff back in Little Rock.

Dreams of Washington and the White House were once and for all, it seemed, at an end.

In Love with One's Wife and Another Woman

At one level Bill Clinton, for the first time in his life, didn't mind. Indeed, the cock-up in Atlanta merely affirmed the sense inside him that his life as a politician was over—as it would be, ironically, for Mike Dukakis who, branded as "soft on crime" by George Bush's negative-ad-producing PR staff, was routed in the November 1988 presidential election. Once again a Republican took possession of the presidency.

"Both Clintons developed a sense that his career was going to end," Dick Morris recalled. As Morris saw it, Bill was retreating into another mental breakdown, similar to that which he'd suffered after his defeat in 1980—only this time it became, at age forty-one, a full-blown midlife crisis. If he was not wanted by the people of America—indeed, was not wanted by the people of Arkansas, according to state legislators ("he appeared to have lost all influence with the Arkansas Senate and a fair percentage of the house," Meredith Oakley recalled of this period)—what was the point of continuing in politics?

It was in this mood that Bill Clinton's affair with a beautiful divorcée, related through her former marriage to "one of the wealthiest families in Arkansas," as Hillary's biographer Gail Sheehy described her, took off. "Tall, slim, blond, a striking divorcée in her early forties," Sheehy recorded, "the mystery woman began turning up at Clinton's political fund-raisers and receptions at the governor's mansion in 1988."

In truth Marilyn Jo Jenkins, née Denton, was the daughter of a railroad bookkeeper, her mother a teacher. Her ex-husband, whom she'd met as a fellow student at the local Henderson State College in Arkadelphia, had become an air force pilot and had served in Vietnam. They had moved seventeen times during his career before he had left the service, and they had both taken M.B.A.s in Massachusetts. The parents of two children, they had then divorced. Marilyn Jo had moved back to Arkansas, becoming first a customer service representative, then a marketing executive, with Middle South Utilities (later called Entenergy Arkansas).

Gail Sheehy thought Marilyn Jo allowed Clinton to feel "loved simply for what he was rather than for what he could be." One of Bill's state troopers considered Marilyn Jo to be "the only woman in my five years that I knew the governor really liked." Even Betsey Wright took the affair—and its potential ramifications—seriously, since it was profoundly disruptive in terms of Bill Clinton's performance as governor. The governor's telephone records said it all: three-minute calls to Hillary, ninety-three-minute marathons to Marilyn Jo. "It's tough to be in love with both your wife and another woman," Bill even confided to one of his state troopers in a moment of adolescent self-absorption.

From Hillary's bedroom in the governor's mansion and Marilyn Jo's in Sherwood, Bill shuttled backward and forward throughout 1989. In between he attempted to run the ship of state in his office in the capitol, infuriating Betsey Wright and his staff by his lack of concentration, his tardiness—and his endless phone calls to Marilyn Jo. His press secretary, Joan Roberts, resigned. Betsey Wright became so mad at him, she "told him she felt like boiling a pot of water and pouring it over his head." Sometimes the governor would speak to Marilyn Jo as many as *nineteen times* a day. It seemed as if he was torn in two, hoping that either Hillary or Marilyn Jo would cut the Gordian knot and decide his fate for him.

It was in this unfortunate limbo that, in the fall if 1989, he began to discuss with Dick Morris the political fallout from the Big D: divorce.

Divorce

Listening to the governor, Dick Morris was struck by Bill's lack of emotion—as if the decision to divorce were already made in Bill's heart.

It wasn't, of course—at least not unequivocally. As he explained years
later to another girlfriend, "By the time he reached the age of forty, he was
unhappy in his marriage and hated what he was doing to himself and others—the struggle between his religious upbringing and his natural proclivities ever more pronounced. He had," he confided, "considered divorcing
Hillary and leaving politics forever." He made no bones about his seriousness at the time: "If I had to become a gas-station attendant to live an honest life and be able to look myself in the mirror and be happy with who I
am, that's what I was prepared to do."

Bill Clinton would not have been Bill Clinton, however, had he been
able to make up his mind in politics without endless prevarication and pro-
crastination. In romance he was no different. People might mock him for
such shilly-shallying, but in part his dilemma stemmed from his very compassion. Hillary—"Hilla the Hun"—seemed so strong on the outside but
in reality was a deeply vulnerable woman, prone to delusion in a strangely
touching way, like a child who is perplexed when belief, as in, say, Father
Christmas, is revealed to be an illusion.

Bill had told Marilyn Jo he would marry her. But when he informed
Hillary of his decision, she seemed not to comprehend the reality for herself or for Chelsea—for whom they had, after all, supposedly sacrificed the
possibility of a White House race. Hillary instead became fixated on a
completely separate idea: namely that, if Bill was going to leave politics
"forever," then *she* would become the next governor of Arkansas!

Hillary's Turn

Hillary's fantasy was no less crazy than Bill's affair with Marilyn Jo.

"Hillary made it clear that she wanted to run if he didn't," Morris wrote,
recording the strangely surreal negotiations in which he now became embroiled. Indeed, Morris remembered her very words to Bill: "If you're not
going to be governor, I am."

The lovesick governor, according to Morris, was both contrite and ac-
commodating: "She feels," he recalled Bill explaining to him, "we've done
everything for me. My career and my needs have taken a front-row seat—
now it's her turn."

Governor Bill Clinton's response was, to Morris, a mark of just how deluded the two were becoming—not to speak of the havoc their psychodrama was playing on innocent and loyal staffers such as Betsey Wright.

Having driven his wife mad, Bill's anxiety to placate her, indeed to pretend she was not mad, was, in certain respects, touching in its naiveté: a superlative politician racked by personal guilt at having experienced real, adolescent happiness with another woman in approaching middle age—a guilt that in turn drove him to a lingering, intense, almost desperately genuine marital gratitude. It was, however, a gratitude that blinded him to what was obvious to everyone around him: that Hillary had "a tin ear" and no hope of winning a primary, let alone election as governor of the state of Arkansas.

Stricken by the Poll Results

As a midwesterner with eastern ideas, Hillary had never really been accepted in Arkansas, though her work in pressing for educational reform and certain programs for children was respected by many. Her status as a high-powered lawyer in the Rose Law Firm, benefiting from state contracts, particularly disturbed antifeminists, journalists, and political observers. Added to this difficult profile was the fact that she often just "didn't get it." Before the previous gubernatorial election, for example, she'd completely astonished Morris and others by insisting that a swimming pool be put in at the governor's mansion, claiming that her colleague at the Rose Law Firm, Vince Foster, had one.

Dick Morris, despite being an *echt* easterner, had found himself, for once in his life, completely speechless. "You'll get killed for that," he'd warned, incredulous that the governor's wife could talk of herself as leading the same life as the "lives of normal people"—when the numbers of "normal" people with a swimming pool in Arkansas could be counted in nanopercent! Sarcastically Morris had suggested doing a poll to confirm this. John Brummett, when he heard of the altercation, was equally incredulous. "It's like, 'Hey, we're in the second poorest state in the country, and lots of people hate my husband, but let's build a swimming pool anyway!'"

Bill had shot down talk of a poll on the idea of a governor's swimming pool. But to Morris's disbelief he now insisted that Morris carry out a new survey: a poll to determine Hillary's chances of winning a gubernatorial election under her own name and aegis.

Pocketing his fee, the stupefied Morris carried out the governor's instruction.

The conclusion, in Morris's view, was foregone.

To Be, or Not to Be Married

Utterly out of touch, Hillary, as Gail Sheehy put it, was "stricken by the poll results." Morris's polls proved that no one in Arkansas wanted Hillary to be governor.

Mortified on his wife's behalf, the lovesick, confused governor simply refused to accept Morris's survey results. Instead he now personally reworded Morris's poll questions to remind voters how much Hillary had done for the state through her education work and children's rights' struggle. Then he asked Morris to conduct the survey all over again.

The situation, to those who witnessed it, was risible to the point of comedy. To the Clintons' chagrin, Morris received the same response—indeed, an even worse one. Even *fewer* now wanted Hillary as governor of Arkansas!

Bill Clinton was as shocked as Hillary—indeed, shocked by both Hillary and her response to the poll. To divorce her after all she had done for his career and the daughter she had borne him was one thing. Divorce, after all, no longer carried the same stigma as of old—even President Reagan had divorced his first wife—as had also the man who'd beaten Bill for the governorship, Frank White. Even in his own family divorce was no stranger. Seeing Hillary so crushed and so devastated by the results of Morris's poll, however, was another matter. Could Bill, in all conscience, cast off a woman so respected yet so widely disliked in Arkansas; a woman he himself had brought to the state, having once set his cap for her and having inveigled her into moving to his home region and into a culture so foreign to her own? Virginia Kelley, four times married, might rejoice, never having taken to Hillary as a daughter-in-law. Yet for all his loyalty to his mother, this made Bill all the more sympathetic to his wife's cause. Hillary was down and bleeding. Nobody liked her, nobody would vote for her. Instinctively he felt he could not kick her out of his life just to marry Marilyn Jo.

This was crunch time in the life of a man from Hope who, since his failure to fulfill his ROTC contract, had so often failed to live up to his promises and undertakings. Martially. Politically. And now maritally.

Dropping the Pilot

Unable to carry out his decision to divorce, Bill Clinton had meanwhile driven his chief of staff, Betsey Wright, to desperation by his failures of focus in the governor's office, his underhanded dealings with politicians and interest groups, his insistence on maintaining a centrist, often conservative rather than liberal stance, his constant blaming of others for his woes rather than himself.

Thus Bill flunked, failed, foundered, and flailed. By November 1989, his long, inflammable relationship with Betsey Wright reached the flash point. Driven to despair, Betsey had already threatened to leave several times. Now, in an act of exasperation, the governor decided to ax not Marilyn Jo, his mistress, but instead his loyal deputy.

As Kaiser Wilhelm II had dropped Prince Otto von Bismarck, architect of Prussia's rise from a north German kingdom into the Second German Reich, so the governor of Arkansas now engineered and accepted the resignation of the chief of staff who had rescued him from political collapse and guided his political fortunes so selflessly thereafter.

"Betsey's life was Bill Clinton. Bill Clinton was her life! That's all there was to her life!" recalled the *Arkansas Gazette* editorial writer Ernie Dumas. "Betsey never married—and I don't know that she ever dated! She came here. She was a very quiet person. I don't know I ever saw her laugh—deadly serious. Very, very serious woman. She had a little house, tiny house she lived in, in Hill Crest. And she would stay at the governor's office till late at night, go home, get up the next morning and she would be at her work—whenever the first person arrived at work in the morning, Betsey would already be there. And she would go in on Saturday—she'd get up early on Saturday and go up to the capitol, to the governor's office! And she read every bit of mail that came through that office. She reviewed every document, every decision—when he ran for governor, when he was governor—every decision. She couldn't surrender any kind of function to anyone else. I mean, she had a lot of people work under her—but she reviewed *everything* that everybody did! That was my impression!"

As Clinton became more wayward, Betsey became "more dominant, more and more dominant—and obsessive." The governor's neglect of his duties was driving her crazy, and in turn "she's driving Bill Clinton crazy! She has fights, she screams, she cries, she carries on! And of course, Betsey's very unpopular among legislators—the legislators all hate Betsey! 'Cause she's kind of the gatekeeper: you've gotta kinda get past Betsey to see Bill—sort of 'What do you want?' She's very protective of him, she doesn't want Bill Clinton to get involved in any kind of shenanigans. Betsey's a pretty high-minded person. I think if she'd kept her wits about her and stayed with him all the time, I think [in the White House] Monica Lewinsky would have been out on her ass! She would have been outta there! Betsey would have spotted it and got her outta there!! Right away! Betsey wouldn't have put up with it a day! Or a lot of other stuff—the woman who came in flashing her boobs around, Clinton kinda rubbed on her—none of that would have got by!"

Bobby Roberts, Clinton's gubernatorial assistant, agreed. Bill Clinton was "one of the smartest tactical politicians you'd ever deal with. But Betsey gave him the discipline he needed to be a good politician. She was really good at it. Now, you know, she ran over a lot of people, she left a lot of bodies in the street doing that, and so she had a lot of enemies," he recalled. "She had very few friends, I think." Faced with Bill's affair with Marilyn Jo and his failure to run state government, Betsey had tried manfully to screw down the governor's lid. "Betsey was an absolutely controlling personality. I mean, you have to appreciate her and meet and work for her to understand how controlling she was. Did she have to be that way? Was that her personality? Or was that the only way she could get Bill to do right?"

Roberts shook his head sadly. "Probably a combination of both," he judged. "But let me give you an example of how she operated, and this will give you a little example of why, in the end, he might have gotten fed up with her, but why, also, it was necessary for her to do what she did.

"She had a long-standing rule when we were in the governor's office up there, particularly during the legislative session, but almost any other time, too, *Bill Clinton was to never have a meeting alone with anybody*—because he might promise something, or he might, you know, undo something, or make a statement that somehow didn't coincide with some bigger issue. So anytime there was a meeting going on in his office—his office desk like this, and there was a window behind it, and there was a door over there"—Roberts motioned—"And there was a little chair in the corner, and anytime there was a meeting going on, there was some staff member in that little chair. And if there wasn't a staff member in that little chair and Betsey found out about it, she would go get a staff member—I've had her do this to me!—and she'd say, 'Go get your ass in there, and get in that chair and tell me what he's saying!' "

It was not, moreover, simply a matter of what Bill was saying; it was what the governor might be doing. "I had to open up the door and go sit in the corner. Well, you can imagine, I mean, he felt he was being treated like a child. Betsey's view was: he *was* a child! And they're both right. He was being treated like a child, and he *was* a child in some ways. And so you can imagine after years and years of that sort of control, that you might get enough of it. And I think he just got enough of her. I mean, my description of it would be: it's like a bad marriage. I mean you just get to the point where—I don't know if you've ever been divorced. I have [from Joan Roberts]. You just think, 'I can't take another day of this, and I don't care if it's better or worse, I'm going to do something!' And I think that's what happened to him. And I think the root of the Monica Lewinsky issue rests in that decision that he made, to get rid of Betsey. I think he said to himself, 'I'm never going to have a baby-sitter again.' And he never did. And he ended up with that shit with Monica Lewinsky."

Out from Under the Iron Fist

"Betsey did her best down here," Dumas reflected, referring to the capitol, downtown. "O' course she couldn't watch over him all the time because she was trying to run the government—she was kind of the governor, she had to run all the nitty-gritty and make sure the time sheets were correct and everybody put in the hours they said they did in the governor's office, and I mean, she micromanaged everything!"

Betsey was, Dumas recalled, unable ever to take a vacation. She even forwent the $1,100 deposit she'd paid toward a group vacation going down the Colorado River in the Grand Canyon lest Bill get up to mischief in her absence—" 'Who knows what Bill would do?' " Dumas mimicked Betsey's genuine concern. "And so she never took one vacation, in all those years. Except right at the end.

"It was not a voluntary vacation," Dumas added tactfully. "Clinton told her she needed to leave for a while. Told her she had to get out. The story was, she'd become so obsessive that Bill and Hillary decided eventually she had to go! And she was told that she needed to resign and leave the staff. So she did. She's very bitter about it. She goes back to her little house up there, in Hill Crest, and becomes almost a recluse."

The pilot was thus dropped. "I don't think he was ever a very good governor after that, in terms of trying to do a lot," Bobby Roberts reflected sadly years later. At the time, however, the move had seemed imperative to Bill Clinton.

Taking Betsey's assistant, Gloria Cabe, as his executive secretary, Governor Clinton was like Henry II: finally freed of his Beckett. There would no longer be a palace gatekeeper. As Betsey recalled, when later she went to the White House to warn Nancy Hernreich, director of Oval Office Operations, about the need to ensure that the President was never left to his own devices, she was given short shrift. "Betsey," replied Ms. Hernreich, "we all promised him that he would never live under an iron fist like yours again!"

The Lowest Point

Getting rid of Betsey Wright, the governor's chief of staff, was one thing. Getting rid of Hillary Clinton, the governor's wife, was another. "When I left the governor's office, I left at a time when he had really . . ." Betsey Wright's voice trailed away. She took a deep breath. "It was really the lowest point of his relationship with Hillary—ever. And all growing out of an affair that was quite serious! And he had about busted his relationship with Hillary."

When Dick Morris stood up for Betsey, he was physically knocked down. The governor simply exploded, not only leveling the five-foot-six strategist and adviser but calling on him to resign as consultant. "I can't believe Clinton hit me!" Morris—who refused to resign—later moaned.

It was a literally as well as metaphorically tough time. "Mommy, why doesn't Daddy love you anymore?" little Chelsea was heard to ask Hillary as Christmas 1989 approached.

Seeing Hillary so humbled by Morris's two polls, however, Bill Clinton finally relented. He'd wanted to punish those who were oppressing him, instead of accepting him, as Marilyn Jo did. He'd forced Betsey Wright to resign, he'd clobbered Dick Morris. Yet for all his selfishness and yearning for Marilyn Jo's gentle, caring, maternal love—"She was somebody to be with and who'd soothe his troubled brow, right! And who probably never told him he'd been stupid over something he'd just done, which Hillary will do," Betsey reflected—William Jefferson Clinton found he simply could not watch his own wife, the mother of his only child, and for nearly twenty years his companion and political partner, be spurned by voters and her own political dreams thereby destroyed.

Marilyn Jo offered normality, ordinariness, simplicity, quiet and genuine affection, understanding, and a shared Arkansas heritage. Marilyn Jo, however, had simply come too late in Bill Clinton's life. He might slug Dick

Morris and banish Betsey Wright from his sight and conscience, *but he could not change reality.* He'd made his bed with Hillary, and though he might lie in those of others also, he was still bound to her: not only by his marital vows but by other, still more potent chains: his heart, his conscience—and his compassion.

The fact was, the more Hillary was disliked in Arkansas, the more Bill's heart—*caritas, agape,* conjugal, tender—went out to her. For all that she'd tried to throw herself into the spirit and ways of Arkansas, she'd remained a fish out of water: a social, cultural, and political misfit. People admired her, but almost no one liked her—and they would not vote for her. She was to them an alien with dark eyebrows and stout legs, an outsider from outer space. And Bill Clinton had always felt for outsiders like himself.

That image seethed within Bill Clinton's big and flabby breast. His troopers for the most part despised Hillary for her arrogance and intellectual condescension, which only made them more willing to help the governor "escape" from her marital prison. One night Hillary, waking in the night and finding her husband absent, had telephoned guardhouse security to find out where the governor was. Trooper Roger Perry had called Clinton posthaste and summoned him back from his tryst to face the marital music. The trooper had heard screaming in the mansion kitchen; afterward he saw that one of the doors of a kitchen cabinet had been kicked right off its hinges. Yes, Bill Clinton reserved the right to shout back at Hillary; in fact, in their small circle of friends the couple were famous for their screaming matches. But the knowledge that Hillary, who was so much his intellectual equal and his moral superior, could be so disliked by the people of Arkansas burned like acid within him. *He* reserved the right, as her husband, to shout back at her—but woe betide anyone else who did!

Christmas 1989 thus saw an amazing epiphany as Bill Clinton, archnarcissist, self-centered monster, seducer of women, and oral sex addict, found his selfish heart melting. Could he really, in all conscience, abandon Hillary Rodham, so unloved by the people of Arkansas? Could he *really* face the consequences of divorce for their beloved daughter, Chelsea?

Saying No

In the end Governor William Jefferson Clinton couldn't do it. Telling Marilyn Jo it was over, he asked Hillary early in 1990 if she would take him back. As he later recalled, "We thought that our lives were richer together, that for different reasons it was difficult for both of us to accommodate to other people—like it is for a lot of strong-willed people. And we love parenthood, and we're nuts about our kid in a wonderful way."

Hillary said yes—if he agreed to counseling with a Methodist minister, from her church.

After a model, goody-goody childhood Bill had made, in the course of his adult life, a series of strikes that, in the nature of the game called life, had ruled him out as a man of honor or even courage. He had never learned, as an adult, to say no, save when it suited him. Now, at last, he had finally said no to Marilyn Jo and had renewed his marriage vows to his defeated wife. He owed Hillary and had owned up to that most personal debt. It was, morally speaking, the supreme test of his adult life—his finest hour.

Whether he would or could be true to such vows remained to be seen. But to his own surprise the effect proved more invigorating than he could have dreamed possible when in the arms of Marilyn Jo. At the deepest level of his being, he recognized he had wrestled with his conscience and, out of loving compassion, had chosen the path of righteousness. He had thereby found, to his own amazement, self-respect.

Henceforth he might err and experience temporary weaknesses; but the knowledge that he had done the right thing would sustain him for the next decade. He had seen his wife humbled, broken in her self-esteem, like a bird with a broken wing; had picked her up and cradled her, and known in that moment that their bond was indissoluble. While the rest of America moved through serial divorce, he and Hillary had found a true fellowship of the ring that would sustain them, if they chose to remain in politics, for the rest of their political careers—whatever bricks, mudbats, allegations, accusations, lawsuits, or lassoes were thrown in their direction.

PART SEVEN

THE TURNING POINT

The Sun King, Arkansas

CHAPTER THIRTY-SIX

MOMENT
OF TRUTH

A Pathological Fear

Years after his disgrace, former senator Gary Hart mourned the loss of his political role in the United States. "There are only two places to be in American life," he lamented, "—on the sidelines or on the playing field." The California legislator Jesse Unruh was equally absolute: "Until you've been in politics you've never really been alive. It's the only sport for grown ups, all other sports are for kids."

In many ways Bill Clinton *was* still a kid, playing a grown-up sport: a kid hungry still for attention, desperate to be liked by everybody—something that was inherently impossible in such a high-profile occupation. "He wanted *everyone* to love him," Jim Blair mocked. "We had a county that's adjacent to Fort Smith that's called Crawford County. And it's full of sort of hill-type conservatives. And he could not carry it—he won election after election, and he never carried Crawford County!

"He was determined to carry Crawford County. I said, 'Bill, you know: most of those people down there are crazy. If you carry Crawford County, you're going to lose a bunch of other votes—*you might lose mine!*'

"But the sense that he had to . . ." Blair paused, shaking his head in exasperation. "You see, he wanted *everybody* to love him! And I think that comes from the dynamics of the absent father and the dynamics of the mother. He needs adoration like few people I've ever known! I mean, he *needs* it—and feeds off it. Now, he's certainly not the only political figure that way," Blair cautioned. "He's just been more obvious about it than a lot of 'em!"

Many stars of stage, screen, and the pop concert platform were, Blair acknowledged, prey to such need, while living in fear of its opposite: neglect, disdain, criticism. Bill Clinton was, in this sense, no different. "Anybody that wrote anything negative about him upset him," Jim Blair described this unfortunate trait in his friend. "I mean, things that *ought not get to you*! He always needed more love than any one person or any ten people or any thousand people could give him—I really think so."

"Character Flaw"

To Jim Blair, shaking his wise white mane, Bill Clinton's need for love and approval was a "character flaw" that would condemn him to a sort of never-ending purgatory; indeed, it stopped William Jefferson Clinton from achieving the sort of greatness to which his talents logically entitled him. Fearing rejection, the governor had often been reduced to political confusion, even impotence, in what Blair's wife, quoting a journalist, called "a pathological fear of offending anybody."

"Pathological," was a strong word but not irresponsible. Certainly Bill's lack of focus, after his 1987 decision to withdraw from the presidential running, had led to a disastrous failure to get the Arkansas legislature to raise taxes to pay for crucial state programs. "His further efforts in a special session to provide additional funding for education, prison problems, and the war on drugs through a temporary surcharge on personal and corporate income taxes produced little but talk of legislative gridlock and gubernatorial burnout," Diane Blair candidly chronicled, "and a widespread assumption that Clinton would and probably should move on to other pursuits."

What other pursuits than politics *could* Bill Clinton pursue, however? He was now middle-aged, hiding his graying hair with more and more dye, and had no employment experience outside political campaigning, elected office, and college teaching—to which, unlike the defeated Mike Dukakis in Massachusetts, he had *no* intention of returning.

Coming to a Decision

Governor Clinton thus procrastinated. He even summoned Betsey Wright from her enforced leave in Hillcrest. He had "decided he wanted to save the marriage," Betsey Wright recalled, "and that he wanted to patch up the relationship with me."

For Betsey it seemed typical that Bill Clinton should imagine he could just snap his fingers and smile to make things come right. "He never believed you had to choose," she reflected, for he'd "gotten so much of juggling that had worked out."

This time, however, the juggling would not work. Exhausted by the years of administrative peonage and assistant-principal duties, Betsey declined to work on Bill's team again, knowing it would take more energy, more fights, more vigilance than she had left at that stage in her life, as well as more resilience than Bill Clinton possessed, to reconstitute both his marriage and his chief of staff at the same time. "I made clear," she recalled, "that you can't do them both—it was going to take too much energy to fix the marriage, and that was where he needed to be. So I made the decision to leave the governor's office."

No party was scheduled for Betsey's farewell, however, not even a surprise one. "January of '90 was when I went off the payroll, but there had never been a governor's chief of staff who'd stayed in that position as long as I had. There was *nothing*! Not with his staff, not with the Cabinet—there was *nothing*! I was very hurt. Then I finally realized: Yeah, those farewells he did for others when they left—*I* did those, *he* didn't! *He* didn't do those things for people, *I* did those things!"

Meanwhile, Governor Clinton had promised, publicly, that he would decide by the end of January whether he would be a candidate for the state gubernatorial primary in May 1990 or would retire that year, at the end of his tenth year as governor of Arkansas. January came and went, however, without a decision by the governor.

February 1990 came—and went.

Finally, in one of the most "bizarre" press conferences in modern American political history, Governor Clinton called together five hundred staff, friends, supporters, and journalists for a convocation in the beautiful marbled hall of the Rotunda in the Arkansas State Capitol on March 1, 1990.

Governor Clinton had "asked if I would come and be there" to witness his momentous decision in person, Betsey Wright—soon to be appointed chairman of the state Democratic Party—recalled. Her response had been immediate: "I said, 'You bet! I'll be there!' "

Betsey was—and, having spoken to Bill in private before the announcement, she was quite, quite certain the governor was going to announce his retirement from the governorship. "When I talked to him that morning," Betsey later confirmed, "he told me that he *wasn't* going to run."

Life Without Power

Betsey Wright's enthusiastic approval of Governor Bill Clinton's "decision" *not* to run again in 1990 rested upon what she later called "a number of conversations with him about 'It would be very good for you to learn what life without power is before you moved on to something.' "

In declining to run for a fifth gubernatorial term, Bill Clinton could, like Governor Reagan in California in 1976, retire from politics with honor, Betsey felt—"that it didn't mean it was all over if he wasn't holding public office." Bill had, after all, balked at having to learn to embrace a career or activity other than politics after his defeat in 1980; now, a decade later, at only forty-three, he could—and perhaps should—seek and learn a new role, one that would empower him in a fresh, challenging way as a potential leader while he sought to reconstruct his marriage to Hillary—who was already earning more than four times his gubernatorial salary in the big, wide world.

Betsey Wright thus attended the governor's convocation/press conference expecting tears and lamentations, as in 1987. Bill had, after all, told a state senator to schedule his own press conference an hour later, so that the latter would be able to immediately announce his own candidacy for the governorship.

"And I don't know what happened!" Betsey later expostulated.

Agonizing Indecision

Agonizing over decisions had been the bane of Bill Clinton's life since becoming an adult. This time even Bill's mother, Virginia, had no idea what he was going to do; indeed, she told journalist Meredith Oakley that she had been "more confused than ever" after seeing Bill the night before the announcement, in the governor's mansion. On the previous occasion, when Bill had announced his withdrawal from possible entry in the presidential nomination race, Virginia confided that she had known "in advance," but "we didn't this time," she afterward told another reporter. "I don't think anybody knew about it this time."

Nobody did, leading to widespread speculation about what advice the governor was getting—and from whom. "Hillary thinks Bill ought to run for reelection," a Little Rock political consultant, Jerry Russell, had said in a speech in Hot Springs the previous November, "and Betsey doesn't think he ought to run for reelection." Since then little appeared to have changed—save that Betsey was no longer Bill's chief of staff.

Betsey might no longer be Bill's official amanuensis, but her opinion— and the argument behind her conviction—still carried great weight with him. Summoning so many hundreds of his friends and supporters from across the state, with three television stations to cover the event, was therefore Bill's weird way of forcing himself to make a choice one way or the other. To add to the confusion of his staff, he had no prepared text, only some scribbled notes, so that not even his aides and cabinet officers at the capitol had any idea what he was going to say—one state senator remarking that the decision must be the best kept political secret in decades.

An Amen Corner

In the governor's first high-pitched, hoarse words there seemed, initially, every intention to quit gubernatorial politics while the going was good. Only Hillary, perhaps, knew what struggle was going on in Bill Clinton's mind and conscience now as he wrestled with his conflicting agendas in the hopelessly audio-impaired yet magnificent white-marbled interior. "Many of those in the rotunda stood on tiptoe to see the governor," the journalists Rex Nelson and Philip Martin recalled. "Because of bad acoustics, most of them could not hear what he was saying."

It was no matter. Bill's contorted body language spoke volumes; indeed, the governor "played his audience composed primarily of longtime employees, supporters and contributors, like an amen corner on salvation Sunday," Meredith Oakley, attending on behalf of the *Arkansas Democrat,* later recalled. The governor "credited himself with dragging a backwater state kicking and screaming into the twentieth century," she sarcastically chronicled.

The governor was certainly not above self-congratulation. "When I took office in 1983," Clinton recounted his journey, "we were in deep trouble—economically, educationally, psychologically—and I set about then working with you to try to rebuild our state so that all our people could live up to their God-given potential. And in these last seven years and two months, the record we have made together is truly remarkable. By any measure, our schools are much better, our economy is much stronger, we've begun to tackle our serious drug problem and our other social problems. We've begun to face up to our environmental responsibilities of the future. We have begun to have a different view of ourselves and our future," he claimed, and "all over the country, people have begun to look at us in a different way." He did not take the credit for achieving this "alone"; indeed, he acknowledged that it had been done "with you." As Narcissist Extraordinary he gave, however, no names or honors to those who had guided, helped, and kept him afloat—least of all Betsey Wright. "It has been the most wonderful, rewarding experience of my life," he said—for this was his obituary, not theirs.

In speaking this way the governor "did not appear to be a happy man; rather he looked resigned to his fate," Meredith Oakley recalled. Certainly Clinton drew attention to "the personal toll that this feat had extracted." Droning on, the governor then announced that "the fire of an election no longer burns in me."

The words sounded like nails being driven into the governor's own coffin. It was, people assumed, all over, as the governor described in further detail his exhaustion: "The joy I once took at putting on an ad that answered someone else's ad, that won some clever little argument of the moment, is long since gone."

Answering ads? For most people, "answering ads" denoted the buying of a sofa, maybe even dating. For Bill Clinton, however, it clearly signified—or had signified till then—the excited slugfest of slogans, punches, and counterpunches that comprised electoral politics: the Rocky Balboa–like world of the political ring. And it was finished. It was over. The champ was through.

Or was he?

Great Theater

Twice defeated in his four earliest fights, Bill Clinton, pugilist, had become a veritable master of the ropes. As his friend Jim Blair recalled, electoral campaigns energized, challenged, and rewarded the governor more than any other young politician the poultry industry attorney and aficionado of politics had ever encountered. "There is a very brilliant, able political figure in this state named Dale Bumpers," Blair said as he explained the difference between Clinton and other talented Arkansas politicians. "And Dale Bumpers was governor back in the early '70s, and then United States senator for almost thirty years. He *hated* being governor! He hated dealing with all those people! I'm gonna tell you, Bill Clinton *loves* being governor! He loves being with all those people! He *loves* being governor—that's real, he *loves* it! Because of his need for . . . You know, you could sit up in the [U.S.] Senate and never see anybody you don't wanna see! That's almost impossible as governor—I mean, you just *gotta* be engaged. And a lot of these guys, these politicians, they want the power, and the influence. But they don't even *like* campaigns. I'm gonna tell you: *I think Bill Clinton enjoyed the campaign more than anything else!* In Arkansas you used to have to run every two years, which was absurd, and in time they changed it to four. But I don't think he minded! I mean, he *loved* campaigning!"

For a man who so loved campaigning to admit, now, in public, before friends, enemies, journalists, and the cameras that "the fire of an election" no longer kindled in him was therefore somehow shocking. The crowd, "convinced Clinton would not seek another term, let out a collective sigh," the journalists Rex Nelson and Philip Martin recalled.

John Robert Starr, to whom Bill had also confided he would be quitting state politics, was completely taken in. The governor's extolling of his own record and the description of his exhaustion were, Starr said in his column the next day, "99 and 44-100ths percent pure pap." Nevertheless, he added, "it was great theater."

The Sun King

There was, however, method in this performance, a psychologist might have observed. For in setting out the reasons why he might now retire from state politics rather than contest the 1990 gubernatorial election, Bill Clinton was playing not only the crowd but a psychological game: assembling an audience to witness and collectively contribute to the most important career decision, as well as personal commitment, of his life.

"Someday I hope Hillary or Bill will talk about what happened," Betsey Wright later remarked—yet the truth was simple. In his agonizingly narcissistic way, Governor Bill Clinton was seeking to prove *in public* to Betsey

Wright, standing in the audience, that she and those who agreed with her were wrong. If, reluctantly, he decided to put on his gloves again, he wanted Betsey to see with her own eyes, before cameras and a large audience, that it was being done not for selfish reasons but because *the people* wanted him to do so.

Dick Morris, pondering the governor's epiphany, did not understand it any better than Betsey or Meredith Oakley. The gnomelike strategist from New York saw it, rather, as a moral and psychological struggle: that Bill needed "some important, valiant fight for the good of the world to lend coherence and structure to his life," as Morris later speculated to David Maraniss, "and when he didn't have those fights he would turn on himself, he would eat away at himself, he would become depressed, paranoid, surly and, one suspects, escapist." Thus in Morris's eyes, the decision to run for the governorship again represented a way of avoiding a fate worse than high office—which "was the only way he could maintain any reasonable degree of psychological coherence."

In attempting to understand the governor's need to stay in office lest he become "depressed, paranoid, surly," and an "escapist," Dick Morris overlooked, however, a crucial fact: that Bill Clinton's sexual escapism was—however dangerously—actually enhanced and enabled as governor, as his state troopers would later reveal. A master multitasker, Governor Bill Clinton was certain he could combine the roles both of Houdini *and* chief executive—if the public could be seduced and persuaded to call for him to get back into the ring.

The ring promised, therefore, not only adulation, approval, and attention but sex—exciting, challenging, extramarital sex. However infatuated with Marilyn Jo Denton he had been, in his heart of hearts Bill Clinton knew he could never settle with her in an exclusive suburban marriage, any more than he could imagine fashioning an alternative life with any of the beauty queens, concubines, or royal mistresses who had consorted with him. Addicted to sexual seduction as self-challenge and self-approval, he could never seriously think of himself without that drug, any more than he could picture a future without the image of himself in the reflection of other people's eyes and expectations. Chief among those were those of Hillary, the person he respected more than any living individual. If he ditched Hillary, his lodestar, and her image of who he was and could become, who would he be? For almost his entire adult life he'd defined himself against Hillary's high expectations. At various times he'd hoped against hope—especially in view of his sexual behavior or misbehavior—that Hillary would ditch him and thus free him from the guilt that would churn inside him if he himself had to make the decision. Separation and divorce might have permitted him to find his own way to self-knowledge—even if it meant pumping gas or, like Shashi Kapoor's Siddhartha, poling his bamboo ferry across the Ganges in Conrad Rooks's bewitching film of Hermann Hesse's famous novel. Hillary, however, had refused to oblige, forcing him to be the one to decide. And when finally Bill had summoned the courage and actually asked her for a divorce, she'd responded by madness: determining to pursue their political ideals by running for governor herself—only to be utterly confounded, indeed crushed, by Morris's polls, causing his heart to break with compassion and guilt. He was then back to square one.

Thus, as he later confided to a girlfriend, "feeling miserable, downcast and directionless, he had made a momentous decision—it would, he believed, be better for his beloved daughter if he and Hillary stayed together and worked on their marriage." Doing this, Bill had concluded with some reluctance (since he feared the inevitable confrontation with Betsey Wright), would entail reentering the ring, not leaving it. But in making that determination, ironically, he would assure himself of the definite, dependable, dangerous, but exciting sexual rewards—*les droits de seigneur*—on which he'd come to rely and that Hillary tacitly permitted—rewards he could not ever willingly surrender, any more than JFK had done.

Doing the Best Job

One final reason to run—and a reason that was of critical importance in mapping out a coherent case against Betsey Wright's objections to his running—was the matter of other aspirants. If Bill Clinton stood for the governorship again, would he destroy the chances of other, worthier candidates?

Governor Clinton was certainly no paragon; indeed, his fear-laden "way of doing things" had often led to muddle and confusion as he'd sought to satisfy too many conflicting interests and constituencies to become a decisive, dependable leader. But politics is not simply the art of the possible, it is a matter of what is possible, *given the circumstances and the alternatives.* Economists and political theorists might weave their visions of modern society using the rider, "other things being equal," but they almost never were. One by one the "isms"—Marxism, communism, fascism—of the twentieth century had foundered on the anvil of the reality check. Winston Churchill had acknowledged the imperfections of democracy as an ideal form of human government—but had pointed out that it was the best *possible* in human circumstances. And this was true not only for democracy but for Democrats.

As he spoke to the assembled media, staff, and supporters, Governor Clinton therefore ran over the alternative candidates from his own and the Republican Party. Not one of them, in his opinion, was worthier than himself, for all that he himself came from a railside, rented house in Hope. He might be infuriatingly indecisive and hard to pin down in terms of issues, but were any of the other potential candidates any better? No other governor had ever appointed so many African Americans to state positions, or been so tireless in his cheerleading of minorities. His predecessors, Senators Bumpers and Pryor, had helped steer Arkansas away from its disastrous record on civil rights under Governor Faubus, but neither Bumpers nor Pryor was a charismatic personality, or comfortable around black people. Something in big Bill Clinton's beaming face—his blue eyes, his bulbous nose, his tendency toward allergies, his shock of fast-graying hair, his chalky voice, his empathy with ordinary folk, and his compassion—radiated a message of idealism and hope that outweighed the lapses, the compromises, the prevarications, the disappointments people felt about him, especially the gap between promises and reality. At least he *articulated,* as a leader, the promise of a better, more inclusive, and less divisive future. If the world, as Richard Schickel had claimed in *Intimate Strangers,* his 1985 treatise on celebrity, was now dominated by the electronic reality of television and the silver screen, big Bill Clinton was not only a star in person, but an electronic star: a star uniquely able to communicate his social and economic vision for Arkansas, even for America. President Reagan, the greatest of all actor-presidents, had done so on behalf of Republicans—why should not he, Bill Clinton, do so on behalf of Democrats?

"I believe in what you and I can do together," the governor of Arkansas therefore suddenly announced, looking at the sea of old friends and supporters—buoyed up by their "imploring looks." "And so I am here to say this. In spite of all my reservations about the personal considerations, I believe that more than any other person who could serve as governor, I could do the best job."

Turning Point

It was the turning point in Bill Clinton's life. David Leopoulos, Bill's childhood friend, claimed that "you could have knocked Hillary over with a feather" as the governor exhorted his congregation of apostles to "Go home and lift up the spirits of the people where you live. Tell them to vote for themselves and their children and the future of the state. Ask them to give me four more years. It will be the best years I ever gave, the best four years the state ever got."

This was preacher stuff, and completely untrue, but the relief of the crowd was palpable. *Bill Clinton would run again!* As Diane Blair had pointed out in a brilliant academic analysis of Arkansas politics, "In terms of public familiarity, media focus, political clout, and policy imprint, the governor is the sun around which many lesser planets revolve." The governor's staff were "considered uniquely the governor's own employees," so that "incoming governors, even when the transition is intraparty, sweep out the old staff and bring in an entirely new crew, whose only loyalty and accountability is to that particular incumbent."

With more than five hundred gubernatorial appointments and reappointments made every year, there was good reason for supporters to break out with almost ecstatic applause. Even Gennifer Flowers would ask for a state job—and get one! Under subsequent questioning, moreover, the governor assured skeptics he would serve out his full four years, if he won.

Reporters rushed out to file their stories as the announcement/press conference ended, while Bill and Hillary, who'd arrived hand in hand, kissed each other on the lips and hugged each other tight: their marriage saved, their new future before them.

CHAPTER THIRTY-SEVEN

PRIMARY TIME

"The Space of an Hour"

The public promise to serve out a four-year gubernatorial term was not, Betsey considered, the real problem. The real problem was, as in 1987, the business of women.

"I stood there when he shocked us all by saying he was running again—for governor!" Betsey recalled. "And I don't know what happened! I mean, there wasn't the space of an hour, clean, there!" she expostulated.

What was Bill *thinking*? Was he going to reform his private life? And what if he did *not* do so? It was, as Betsey had attempted to make Bill realize, no longer a matter of Bill Clinton alone: of Bill Clinton's self-gratification or his agreement with Hillary. "I mean, here's theoretically an adult human being, who should be allowed to make his own mistakes. Now, I used to argue with him, 'It's fine if they're your own private mistakes. But the problem is, you've got a lot of the rest of us in this with you! And it reflects on how much *we're* giving you, too, and how much *we're* lined up!' "

That argument—that the lives of others would be affected, even endangered, by Bill's further tempting of political and press fate—had cut no ice, or at any rate an insufficient amount. Betsey Wright was now on the outside, and her partial successor, Gloria Cabe, was incapable of performing the disciplinary role Betsey had undertaken for so many years. Would Bill stray once again—and put at risk all the hard work, the investment of time, money, faith, and goodwill, of the five hundred supporters crowding around "the candidate" and the thousands beyond them?

Betsey was nonplussed. It would be her painful duty, before long, to deal with what she would call "the bimbo eruptions" that she had so feared would surface. In the meantime, clearly, no one wanted to know the downside. Bill Clinton, the Sun King, had declared he would run again for the Arkansas crown and, given the lack of electable alternative candidates and the prospect of an "evil" Republican opponent, all—even skeptics like John Robert Starr—were swept by relief.

The Rope to Be an Adult

While Betsey Wright returned anxiously to her home in Hillcrest, Bill Clinton got into gear, aided and abetted by his consort. With Hillary added once again to the platform as a full-fledged but unticketed Democratic co-candidate, the team would be unbeatable, despite Betsey's departure.

Yet without Betsey Wright guarding the governor's inner sanctum, the decision not to hang up his gloves was, as would inevitably become apparent, a grave risk. "Hillary," Betsey later mused, "—part of the way that she loved Bill was to give him rope to be an adult and be responsible. I don't think she ever understood why I couldn't. But we're very different people in that regard. I mean, she obviously had a very different contract with him than I did."

Hillary did. Now that Bill had decided to opt for their marriage, or renewed marriage, she could not bring herself to police him, lest by her surveillance and nagging she drive him away again. "It's a different way of relating to her husband, as a smart, responsible adult human being who had been irresponsible at times but who always had enormous intention of learning from those mistakes and not making them again. But he always *did* make them again!" Betsey sighed—and shrugged. "I was like her—I always believed his intentions and his promises and his vows: 'We're gonna do better!' But he *didn't*!"

Survival of the Fittest

Former Congressman Jim Guy Tucker had watched Governor Clinton's press conference with a pounding heart. Assuming Bill Clinton would quit the governorship that year, Tucker had announced he would run for the post. Knowing better than to challenge Clinton, however, after their last encounter, Tucker wisely decided to negotiate a deal with Clinton. Instead of challenging the governor in the primary, Tucker would switch tack and run for lieutenant governor, a post that would allow him to become acting governor whenever Bill was out of state. If, as expected, Bill threw his hat into the presidential ring in 1991, this would be frequent. And if by some miracle, Clinton managed to win not only the Democratic nomination but the White House, too, the lieutenant governor would succeed him in Arkansas and move into the governor's mansion.

Jim Guy Tucker's decision was a wise one; indeed, Tucker's earlier decision to take time out from politics and gain experience of the "outside" world made him potentially a far more effective player than Clinton in the governor's office. For that very reason Betsey Wright had urged Bill to "retire" and learn executive and administrative skills in the nonpolitical world, as Jim Guy Tucker had done. But would such experience of "real life" necessarily have helped? Jim Guy Tucker's subsequent career, in retrospect, would lend little credence to the view that an alternative career would necessarily have made Bill Clinton a better, stronger person and, on his return into politics, a more successful politician. Defeated by Bill Clinton in the Democratic primary of 1982, the wildly handsome, Harvard-educated Tucker had become a senior law partner in Mitchell, Williams, Selig and Tucker in Little Rock, as well as chairman of a cable and television management company with interests worldwide. Such extension of Tucker's talents did him no permanent good; far from becoming the notable governor in the history of his state to which his talents and experience entitled him, the ex-marine, ex–Vietnam War correspondent, ex-congressman, media mogul, and successful prosecuting attorney would in due course be indicted in the wake of the Whitewater/S and L investigations, found guilty of fraud, forced to resign as governor of Arkansas, and be sentenced to prison!

The fact was, in the great postmodern melting pot of the late eighties and dawning nineties in America, with ever more clashing of cultural swords and profound economic changes taking place, life was becoming a matter of the survival of the fittest. Not the fittest moderns—men such as John F. Kennedy, Lyndon Baines Johnson, Richard M. Nixon, and Ronald Reagan—but the fittest *postmoderns:* individuals living in a nineties world where traditional morality had, essentially, gone out the intellectual, academic, social, religious, economic, financial, and political window. And in that arena Bill Clinton would be a survivor without parallel.

One Big Game

Three years before Bill Clinton's decision to continue in politics and not to quit, Gilman Louie, an amateur pilot, had invented a computer game called "Falcon." Simulating the flying skills required by an F-16 pilot, the game did it so vividly that U.S. Air Force pilots found themselves buying it. The next year, 1988, Louie had imported "Tetris" from the Soviet Union— a game that became the largest-selling computer game ever, with almost 80 million copies sold to customers, including Hillary Clinton, who played it on her Game Boy. Inevitably, after developing more games on the World Wide Web, Louie was recruited by the CIA, which considered his games background an asset. "I look at the world," Louie told *The New York Times,* "as one big system—one big game."

For those involved in politics rather than national security, this was a new slant on Machiavelli: not simply the lust for power and status on Earth at any price but the excitement of gambling—a survival game in which the game itself was as important as, perhaps more important than, the end; moreover, a game in which the crucial necessity was to remain in play and *not be dealt out.*

Without Hillary, Bill Clinton could not have stayed in the life game—or survived it. Even had he married Marilyn Jo Denton, there was no saying that he would have avoided the pitfalls that now peppered American life, from the lowliest to the highest. His mother's career as a trained anesthetist had ended in the ashes of a lawsuit—and, not long thereafter, cancer. His own brother's modest musical career had also come to grief before a prosecuting attorney and federal judge. From speeding fines to malpractice suits to felonies to rights abuses, lawyers controlled the country: defending, prosecuting, threatening, protecting, and upholding. Churned out by law schools in ever-increasing numbers, no one in America was safe from them; indeed, in a society increasingly devoted to the promotion of individualism rather than collective or government solutions, the United States was in danger of becoming a vast, rampant capitalist archipelago in which anybody who popped his or her head above the parapet of success, humble or highborn, was sueable or indictable—and even those who kept their heads down were not immune: liable to be hauled off to an American Lubyanka at the whim of a jealous neighbor or aggrieved colleague, injured motorist, irate patient, or political opponent. Money became no longer a capitalist dream but a means to pay inexorable, often exorbitant, legal bills in order to survive.

Bill Clinton could not step away from this plate, nor could he maintain the fiction of innocence or even the hard-and-fast liberal ideals of yesteryear. Almost everything he would touch would inevitably become tainted by compromise, caution, and canniness in the new struggle for survival: for he had decided to go forward. Going backward would not, of necessity, prove any better, he rightly reasoned—something Jim Bakker, handcuffed and hauled away to prison, was finding out.

From now on, *the game* would be all—and survival in it, everything. There would thus be no bill clinton, only Bill Clinton, or BC, a political design group, comprising policy wonks, operatives, strategists, lawyers, consultants, fashion consultants, fixers, fans, and fortune-tellers. This was, truly, the postmodern world of the nineties.

The Politics of Spectacle and Survival

Politics was now becoming, as Bill Clinton sensed far more clearly than Betsey or Hillary—indeed, probably more clearly than any politician of his generation—a matter of survival—but also a matter of survival in a new world of postmodern *spectacle.* Politics now offered roles no different from the popularity, fame, and comic destinies of televangelists: a *circus maximus,* a wild rodeo, a spinning wheel of fortunes, a parlor game watched on flickering screens in millions of homes: a soap opera played on a postmodern stage, amid a frenzy of "hogs at the trough," as Ted Koppel put it, involving hundreds of millions of dollars. Yet it was also a spectacle in which, as two of the smartest baby boomers of their generation, Bill and Hillary might just, *as a team,* brazen their way to the top, the Big Top, and across the "highwire"—as John Brummett would later describe the act—so that they might successfully reach national fame and, if lucky, the far side. And on the way, who knew? Perhaps they might do good, for they saw themselves, behind all the trappings, as basically good people, as had the unfortunate Bakkers.

The very first "fabrication" that was required of the BC tailoring brand, however, was that the governor should not simply promise he would run for the full four-year gubernatorial term in Arkansas but make that promise in public and on record. "Will you guarantee to us," Arkansas reporter-panelist Craig Cannon asked in a live televised gubernatorial campaign debate in 1990, "that if reelected, there is absolutely, positively no way that you'll run for any other political office and that you'll serve out your term in full?"

"You bet!" Bill Clinton responded, unfazed, like a dog promised a run in the woods. "I told you when I announced for governor I intended to run, and that's what I'm gonna do. I'm gonna serve four years. I made that decision when I decided to run. I'm being considered as a candidate for governor. That's the job I want. That's the job I'll do for the next four years."

Lying as a Matter of Degree

Everyone in 1990 knew the governor was lying.

Deliberate lying had always been a staple feature of southern politics, after all—like stuffing the ballot box or Orval Faubus's word to the President of the United States that he would not use the National Guard to stop black schoolchildren from attending Central High. But would standing for President in 1992 from a small, backward state in the South be such a terrible thing? Would it not bring prominence to Arkansas and its commerce, as the state became nationally better known as a direct result, even if he failed in his first bid? Besides, in the business of lying, Clinton lacked any motive of personal greed—he seemed genuinely to live for the fun, excitement, drama, and debate of politics. *Everyone* in politics lied, after all—it was only a matter of degree. Though he might not be rated a great governor, people did respond positively to the sort of warmheartedness, the politics of inclusion and empathy and human idealism, that Bill Clinton radiated. Less than 10 percent of a governor's time was now spent as an administrator, Diane Blair reckoned. "Now, especially with the explosive growth of federal aid to state and local governments in recent decades, the governor's responsibilities as chief lobbyist and negotiator for the state have multiplied astronomically," she reflected—a situation in which all southern governors were becoming "the de facto executive directors of the state chambers of commerce." The governor's responsibilities currently embraced "economic development, intergovernmental relationships, crisis management, and policy and opinion leadership"—responsibilities that had "all combined to give the governor unrivaled centrality in both politics and governance." In this often symbolic role Bill Clinton had proven a smart, user-friendly, tireless, and indelible presence in the governor's office. Hillary, his wife, might be more traditionally moral, more relentlessly focused, less given to prevarication and lying—but no one would elect *her,* the polls had indicated after all.

Given his faults and failures, Bill Clinton's polls were, for a four-time governor only forty-three years old, still amazingly high. If he ran hard

enough and Hillary stood behind, indeed alongside, him, he might answer
to a real national craving for an attractive younger politician who combined smartness with compassion, idealism with realism. In the real world,
one had to choose between evils—and Bill Clinton's kind of evil, in proclaiming an intention to serve out four years in Arkansas that he would
probably not fulfill, did not strike the majority of Arkansans as too
heinous, especially when set against Republican alternative governors for
the state of Arkansas—opponents who would have the backing of the nefarious chairman of the National Republican Party, Lee Atwater: a liar of
almost cosmic dimensions.

Home and Dry

Within the Democratic Party there was, thanks to the sudden resignation
on charges of fraudulent expense account claims, of Bill Clinton's hardworking successor as state attorney general, Steve Clark, only one serious
rival in the May 1990 Democratic primary: Tom McRae.

Bill Clinton simply refused to debate or be seen with McRae, a somewhat lofty and honorable director of the Winthrop Rockefeller Foundation who, like White in 1980, lacked frontline political experience but did
not have White's genial character—or his ability to use one-liners to characterize his opponent. Instead it was Hillary who went for the jugular. Pretending to be "passing by" when McRae was giving a news conference
shortly before the primary, she produced from her pocket, in front of astonished journalists and the all-important television cameras, a four-page
document the Clinton team had compiled from statements McRae had
made over the years, praising Clinton for the initiatives and stands he'd
taken—and for which McRae was now drubbing the governor. Like White
in 1982, McRae was completely shaken and caught wrong-footed by
Hillary, unable to respond to such humiliation at the hands of a woman.
His campaign collapsed.

Clinton thus sailed through the gubernatorial primary with a 14 percent
clear lead over the rest of the pack, avoiding a runoff. He was home and
dry—as long as he felled his Republican opponent in November.

Here Bill's mastery of political strategy came to the fore. As in the case
of the televangelists, his Achilles heel, he was well aware, was his "womanizing." He would therefore have to do his best to cauterize, then engineer,
the removal of the Republican who was most likely to use such smear am-

munition against him: Congressman Tommy Robinson, known as "Captain Hotdog."

Captain Hotdog

Tommy Robinson was the E.R. of America's ever-expanding *fin-de-siècle* soap opera, at least in Arkansas. A former Jacksonville police chief, then sheriff, then Democratic congressman, then Republican congressman, Tommy Robinson was straight out of Arkansas's checkered past: a charismatic, tub-thumping, telegenic folk hero, an eccentric who would have been a Pentecostalist preacher speaking in tongues had he not preferred guns. He featured in an Arkansas comic strip—and had greater name recognition than Governor Clinton. On switching parties in the House of Representatives so that he could challenge Clinton as a Republican without having to fight a Democratic primary battle, he had been assured of full national Republican Party backing; indeed, he had for a brief while become the Republican Party's star convert, photographed in the Rose Garden beside the Republican President, George Bush.

Bush was embarrassed to be seen in the company of a man like "Hotdog" Robinson, but Lee Atwater, Bush's campaign director and chairman of the National Republican Party, was, in extolling Robinson, out for bigger prey. Using the turncoat, Bush's team were prepared to go all out to destroy Clinton's chances of reelection and subsequent challenge for the presidency in 1992. As Atwater had earlier admitted, "What scares me is a southern moderate or conservative Democrat, and the scariest of all, because he's the most talented of the bunch, is Bill Clinton." On another occasion he had confided, "I ain't worried about Mario Cuomo. Bill Clinton *does* worry me."

Though Captain Robinson had been made director of the state Public Safety Department by Clinton himself in Clinton's first term as governor, the congressman was perfectly happy to turn against his former boss; indeed he relished the prospect. Through a network of gossiping colleagues "Captain Hotdog" had, he assured Atwater, assembled a veritable arsenal of antipersonnel mines with which to sabotage Governor Clinton in the election—as long as he first won the Republican primary. With Atwater's backing, this did not look difficult.

It was, however—and for a completely unexpected reason. Napoleon Bonaparte had always asked of a promising general, "Is he lucky?" Luckily for Bill Clinton, Lee Atwater suddenly fell ill in the spring of 1990, shortly before the Republican primary in Arkansas, with a brain tumor. And Bill's counterplay, in the aftermath of Atwater's removal to the hospital, was a stroke of genius.

Since Arkansas voters were permitted to cast ballots in both the Democratic *and* the Republican primaries, Clinton decided to urge a significant number of *Democrats* to vote against Robinson in the Republican primary—and Robinson failed to win the Republican nomination.

This left Governor Bill Clinton facing, in the November election, a political novice: the rags-to-riches multimillionaire Sheffield Nelson.

CHAPTER THIRTY-EIGHT

FIVE TIMES GOVERNOR

Shakespearean Malevolence

Sheffield Nelson's life before entering politics had been tough—and it became no easier once he did. As chairman of Arkla, Inc., his business talents had enabled him to forge a sweetheart deal with Jerry Jones, a colleague in the energy field, that had cost state energy consumers more than $100 million, permitting Jones in turn to buy the Dallas Cowboys football team and Nelson to oust the richest men in Arkansas, the Stephens brothers, from the board of their own energy firm, Arkla, Inc. This had understandably not endeared Nelson to the Stephens brothers; indeed, the subsequent Stephens-Nelson feud, the journalist Gene Lyons recorded, was of "Shakespearean malevolence."

For Bill Clinton this was, after the defeat of Lee Atwater's man, Congressman Robinson, a second stroke of good fortune. Not only did it deny Nelson the financial backing of either of the Stephens brothers, it had ensured that the Stephens brothers worked to help Clinton, not Nelson. Immediately after the primary, then—thanks to Jack Stephens's wife, Maryanne—Congressman Robinson's file of information on his fellow Republican rival made its way to Bill's office. These documents, Governor Clinton felt certain, would keep Nelson from making scandalous personal allegations during the election campaign that fall—and he was right. The governor, however, was taking no chances. From morning till late at night he barnstormed and glad-handed around the state with as much energy as before in his life—or more. Without the mantle of governor of Arkansas, he felt certain, he would simply lack the name recognition and credibility at such a young age to challenge Democratic rivals, let alone beat the incumbent President of the United States. "If I lose this race for governor," he maintained when hiring a new pollster, Stanley Greenberg, "I'll never get elected dog catcher."

Such energy seemed to pay off handsomely. The Clinton team ran what they thought would be their last poll on the Wednesday before the November 6, 1990, gubernatorial election. It showed Clinton running at 56 percent—more than enough to guarantee he could stay in the governor's mansion a further four years.

Knowing the Drill

Was Clinton counting his chickens—for which Arkansas had now become America's prime producing state—before they hatched? Nelson evidently thought so, for he had kept to the last moment a series of devastating anti-Democratic, antitax commercials, to be carried on all local television and radio stations.

Launched after "closing time" for responses to ads on the Friday afternoon before election day, Nelson's negative, "spend-and-raise" broadsides were deadly in their effectiveness. Indeed, they worried Dick Morris so much that he ran his own new poll on the Saturday morning. "They got their results back late Saturday night," Sheffield Nelson recollected, "and my understanding is that [Morris] had to call Clinton and get him out of bed at midnight Saturday night, which would have been early Sunday morning, to tell him that we had knocked him to 44 [percent] in the polls and he was in deep trouble, that the chances of coming back were slim, that they had to come out with something that was dynamite."

Nelson was right—but wholly ignorant of the campaigning professionalism that Bill Clinton had perfected over the previous decade. David Watkins, who had masterminded with Morris the last-minute negative advertising broadcasts that had clinched the Democratic primary against Governor Frank White in 1982, authenticated Nelson's account. "We got a call on Saturday night, before the election on Tuesday," he later recalled. The sudden 10 or 11 percent slump in the governor's poll was "a true aberration—no one would believe it, and there's still some skepticism that Morris didn't just do this for some reason, that he just made up the numbers. But it showed we were losing: that there had been a sea change and we were losing to Sheffield Nelson! So we did the same thing" as in 1982—except it was, this time, "a Saturday night, not a Friday. And Bill Clinton and I stayed up all night. And got us this little studio, and we do video, we do audio, we get volunteers. I mean, the drill, *we know the drill*! We do it again."

Television and radio station owners and managers were called whether at home or office, and slots were booked for Clinton's response. Messengers—some in cars, some even flying with the vital response tapes by air—assembled at headquarters. It was war—and war waged as ruthlessly as real war in certain respects. The drill involved a series of thirty- or sixty-second ads. "You threw in some negative and then the positive," Watkins recounted of the countercontent. "We did some negative on Sunday and Monday. Always on Tuesday it was positive: it was just 'Get out and vote!' "

For Clinton as a fighting politico-general, Watkins had the highest respect. "Bill Clinton would have been a great advertising man," the ex–advertising company chairman judged. "He was a great copywriter! He got it! He knew what appealed!"

A Great Copywriter

Not many months previously, Bill Clinton had claimed that the "joy" of answering an opponent's ad had worn off. If so, it was back. "Here's how it worked," Watkins explained the system. "Morris wrote most of the negative things—and Clinton approved them. After this, the positive things—Clinton always wrote almost all those! *Right there in the studio*. But he would write them at a minute and a half, and it would be my job to work with him to cut it down to a minute. Or from forty seconds to thirty. He was great, a *very, very* good writer. I mean, for him to be able to do it—it always amazed me how he was able to do it! Give me a blank piece of paper, and I'm still blank on it. If you put something on it, I can improve on it. Clinton was a master! A great writer—a great copywriter."

Nor did Clinton stop with counterads. On the Sunday morning, having stayed up all night, he called John Robert Starr, the columnist at the *Arkansas Democrat* who had begun to turn against him, saying he was in trouble. "There's no way you can be in trouble," Starr scoffed. "Yeah, the raise-and-spend commercials have got me dropping like a rock," Clinton maintained. "I'm below fifty percent and headed down. We gotta do something to reverse it." Anxious about the future of public education in Arkansas and the possibility of Nelson—who had no interest in education—winning, Starr went immediately to the newspaper office and on Clinton's behalf "pulled out the column I already had in the paper for Monday, and I wrote a column endorsing him, and then wrote another for Tuesday."

Overkill or not, the results were gratifying. Just under 400,000 Arkansans gave their vote to the incumbent governor and only 292,000 to the Republican challenger. Clinton garnered 59 percent of the vote, far above expectations. He would become governor of Arkansas for a *fifth* time, by a landslide.

Triumphant, Governor William Jefferson Clinton would be all set to run for the presidential nomination, two years later, from the imposing, gated grounds of the Arkansas governor's mansion in Little Rock.

Shadowy Silhouettes

Sheffield Nelson, by contrast, was so embittered by his defeat that he would spend subsequent years plotting revenge. What particularly irked him, as a successful businessman, was the fact that he'd been completely outmaneuvered. As Gene Lyons later chronicled, Nelson had been so convinced that his "raise-and-spend" antitax ads were succeeding over the final weekend, he'd made the decision not to use his second-line dynamite: a series of sex-smear commercials. These featured "shadowy silhouettes of anonymous women" with a Republican voice-over asking voters "to consider the 'character and moral judgment' " of the two candidates.

Ammunition for such a "poison gas attack" was certainly at hand. Tom McRae, for example, later acknowledged he'd already been approached during the Democratic primary by a man offering not only a fat check but also "a file of smutty opposition research on Clinton." The main topics were, according to Gene Lyons, "women and drugs." To his lasting credit, McRae—the great-grandson of a Democratic governor—had turned the offer down with the immortal words: "Has it ever occurred to you that there might be something more important than winning?"

Nelson, fighting as a turncoat Republican, evidently thought not. It was only a question of whether, as a candidate, he dared use such material—with the risk that it might blow up in his face or invite a riposte, especially in view of the fact that Clinton now had Congressman Robinson's file on Nelson.

People in glass houses would do well, in other words, not to throw bombs.

Scandal Bombing

Avoiding scandal bombs was now becoming, in the 1990s, the post-Hart obstacle course characterizing American political campaigns. Issues still counted; but behind the slogans and speeches it was the possibility of sexual scandal that kept the public entertained. Scandal had reached the point of satiation in every other area of human conduct; the public therefore looked for it in politics, too—yet appeared disgusted by it whenever it was provided!

"Americans do think there are certain standards of behavior, character and morality that a president must maintain," the columnist Sally Quinn would write a year later, "—and women, in general, seem to care more about the issue of presidential character than men." Uplifted by Jackie Kennedy's posthumous deification of the slain president as King of Camelot in the 1960s, the following two decades of disclosures had been almost unbearable for such women. "We expected better of Jack Kennedy, and that is why the revelations about him disturb us," Ms. Quinn commented, quoting Bill Clinton's own thoughtful analysis of JFK's philandering problem for good measure. "I think presidents are people, and I think there are lots of different flaws and shortcomings people have," Clinton prefaced his opinion. Kennedy was "obviously a man who thought he was ill, was in a hurry in life, grew up in a different time, was raised in a home where the rules were apparently different than most of us believe they should be now, and where the role of women in society was different than it is now."

But if the "rules" were now different, would the public—especially women—tolerate the governor's philandering, if it was documented?

Swaggart the Braggart

One clue to survival in the world of celebrity politics in the late twentieth century was to be found, Governor Bill Clinton knew, in his own Southern

Baptist church, the televangelist scandals of which had rocked the Christian ministry and the nation. The clue was Frances Swaggart—Mrs. Jimmy Swaggart.

In 1988, the year after the Bakkers' fall from grace, the Reverend Swaggart had made a widely televised confession, namely, that he had become a prey to the very sin he had so unsparingly denounced for decades: pornography. "I do not plan in any way to whitewash my sin," the reverend had explained. "And I do not call it a mistake, a mendacity. I call it a sin. I have no one but myself to blame. I do not lay the fault or the blame or the charge at anyone else but me. For no one is to blame but Jimmy Swaggart, I take the responsibility. I take the blame. I take the fault."

He hadn't, of course—or only a sliver of it. As a faith-healing, speaking-in-tongues charismatic Pentecostalist, he had built up one of the most successful television ministries in America, in Baton Rouge, Louisiana, employing fifteen hundred people on a payroll of $16 million per annum and involving a Bible college, churches, conventions, and publishing and broadcasting companies—his operation spending $32 million each year in the Baton Rouge area alone, where there was 11 percent unemployment. Through his ministry he'd brought in $128 million a year and contributed $3.3 million in Louisiana state taxes. Moreover, he was a preacher with a mission, "a commission" given to him personally "by God" to "reach the world by television." This was crucial. "TV will reach the millions and hundreds of millions," he had explained, "and reach them quickly," before the Second Coming—which, he claimed, was imminent. His appeal had been urgent. "That's what He's ordained me to do, and I'm trying to carry it out."

In carrying it out, Swaggart had had the support of an extraordinary wife. Frances Swaggart was the soul of rectitude. She had become the tough CEO of his operations and was rumored to have been behind not only the exposure of Jim Bakker but the hounding and defrocking of yet another rival evangelist: the Reverend Marvin Gorman, who'd reputedly seduced a parishioner. As if scripted by a television dramatist, the defrocked Gorman had then sought his revenge, arranging for his son to stake out the New Orleans apartment of a prostitute Swaggart was known to consort with. When Swaggart had reneged on his promise to recompense Gorman for the way he'd trashed his ministry, Gorman had shown the Assemblies of God—Swaggart's superior church elders—no less than *two hundred* color photographs of Jimmy Swaggart with the prostitute Debra Murphree.

Gorman's exposé had forced Swaggart to make a confession not only to the elders of the Assemblies of God but publicly, on television: a heartrending *apologia pro vita mea* on the small screen, asking each member of the Swaggart family in turn for their forgiveness for having engaged in a pornographic act with a prostitute—though not, he claimed, actual adultery.

In late February 1988, however, Debra Murphree had been tracked to West Palm Beach by WVUE Television and been interviewed. Her story was far more lurid than the tidied-up version to which Jimmy had publicly confessed. Far from the reverend's visit being a one-off affair, she revealed, Swaggart was addicted to sex and had sought out the dark-haired twenty-four-year-old constantly, in his tan Lincoln, cruising down Airline Highway. "I seen him drive down the street every week," she related, explaining what he asked her to do, as Swaggart's biographer Ann Rowe Seaman recounted: "Get naked, lie on the bed and pose, put on a dress with no underclothes and ride around, and in the evening, take her clothes off and get out of the car and then back in; this turned him on."

Had this been all, it would have been enough for a high-profile denouncer of "fornicators" and "sinners," a man whose wife who had once called *USA Today* to ask what dirt it had on Billy Graham—and had threatened to use what *she* possessed unless the journal used what *it* had on Graham. Now Debra Murphree added still more to the WVUE television reporter—as she would in the June 1988 issue of *Penthouse:* namely that Swaggart, who loved oral sex, had seen the framed photograph of her three children in her room and had asked if she would permit her ten-year-old daughter to watch them performing lewd acts.

The Assemblies of God, understandably, had been forced to defrock the Reverend Swaggart, despite the millions of dollars he was bringing in to the church. But Swaggart had then refused to accept their ruling! Instead, the now ex-reverend had left the Pentecostalist church and, with the help of his wife, set up his own. By confessing only to a small part of the alleged misconduct and blaming it on a lifelong temptation wrought by pornography (i.e., others), he was able to externalize the problem: to put it into the Devil's camp. When his cousin Cecil Beatty demanded to see him face-to-face and posed the question whether "all this I've heard is true," Swaggart had responded with apparent sincerity, "Cecil, I'm gonna tell you the truth. I got railroaded. I was framed."

Thanks to his wife's sterling support, Swaggart had avoided Bakker's fate—indeed, unlike Jim and Tammy Bakker, the Swaggarts made "a good team," their employees felt: Jimmy Lee Swaggart, the brilliant, charismatic, humorous, superbly musical (he had grown up with his cousin Jerry Lee Lewis), and empathetic performer on the stage; Frances, the "Dragon Lady," masterminding the operations behind it. "That's superwoman," a follower had once remarked when Frances mounted the stage to join her husband: a wife who excoriated the vast conspiracy of her husband's rivals and opponents, calling them liars, hypocrites, or tools of Satan; a woman of absolute moral rectitude who was not liked by many but was, as Ann Rowe Seaman described, so "very much right about what she said," both in her journal, *The Evangelist,* and elsewhere, "and so passionate" that it was "impossible not to admire her. The only impeaching factor was her absolute refusal to give any credence to her enemies."

Watching and reflecting on Jimmy Swaggart's seemingly miraculous survival, Bill Clinton had perceived what many didn't: that a terrier wife was, in the case of a man suffering from sex addiction, a must.

The Groin Demon

In her perceptive account of the Reverend Jimmy Swaggart's life saga, Ann Rowe Seaman later noted how Jimmy's "lapses" of morality went, like Bill Clinton's, hand in hand with his proselytizing—indeed, were an integral part of it. She pictured the reverend as a basically sincere Christian preacher beset by secret demons: demons "that no one in the house was ever to catch a glimpse of." If his "sinful urges" demanded "the things a groin demon has to have"—as she put it in an elegant euphemism—then such "things" were to confine themselves to tapping "a secret signal to him while he was alone praying or writing a sermon." In this way, Swaggart was supposedly able, for several years after his Airline Highway debacle, to hold his wicked serpents at bay while rebuilding his ministry, now called the World Evangelism Fellowship. Frances, his wife, helped him; indeed, she was his rod and guide. "What are you doing to my husband?" she'd screamed and bawled as she banged on the locked doors of the Assemblies of God Committee of Executive Presbyters—while inside, the thirteen male members had grilled Swaggart in a ten-hour investigation into of his misdeeds in 1988. Unwilling to accept that he was a pervert, she'd steadfastly maintained her faith in him thereafter. "She treated him like a little boy, and like a little boy he rebelled," one family member described the reverend's momentary lapse—a picture that was true in part but trite.

The Reverend Jimmy Swaggart *was* a little boy still—but a brilliant boy, too, inside an adult body assailed by adult demons, and having to operate in a Brave New World of investigative accountability—a world in which privacy was a thing of the past and sinful sprites and demons could no longer be permitted straightforward expression in whorehouses or private trysts, as they had been for millennia, lest such laxness mask something worse.

Swaggart was by no means alone among clergy. Even Catholic priests, who lacked domineering wives to treat them like little boys and cause them to rebel, were prone to sin—and were also coming under increasing press surveillance and accountability to the public, if not to the papal hierarchy. Already in 1985 the *National Catholic Reporter* had begun the process of bringing to light the issue of pandemic sexual abuse by clergymen, prefiguring a series of pedophile and homosexual sex scandals that would rock the Catholic Church in America at the beginning of the next century.

Swaggart's problem had not been homosexual, but it was characterized by wild, weird desires that bordered on pedophilia at times. Yet the fact remained that his extraordinary talent as a preacher seemed to issue from the very cloth of his struggle with those sinful desires—as his own wife somehow accepted, consciously or unconsciously. "Someone savvy about unconscious marital bargains might conclude that Jimmy was expected to deal with sex as best he could—as long as he delivered onstage," Ann Rowe Seaman later speculated. "If sexual tension was a big part of that, then let there be sexual tension. If that tension had to come from wickedness— prostitutes or pornography or working out some issues over childhood sexual trauma, then let that happen—but keep up appearances. Tension, after all, was the constant companion of a sex addict, from fear of being found out."

Even Swaggart himself admitted that temptation was a necessary ingredient of his teleministry. Had he not been assailed by demons, he later confided, "there was no anointing of the Holy Spirit. It was uncanny. It was as if Satan had left," he explained, "but it was as if the Holy Spirit had left as well."

Jimmy needed, Seaman concluded, "an essential contact with evil, and needed it regularly, in order to get up and do what he did onstage at the pace he did it—a pace," as she also pointed out, "largely set" by Frances, in the opinion of "a great number of observers."

Swaggart's sexual interest in children would be the least excusable of his sins. Yet even that could be seen—as Seaman saw it—as a product of his geography and his southern upbringing. Swaggart's child-bride story, like that of his cousin Jerry Lee Lewis, had been redolent of the South: the South of William Faulkner and Reynolds Price. "The child-bride phenomenon and its cousin pederasty are almost bred in the bone in some areas of the South," Seaman—a southerner herself—chronicled. "In frontier times, the physical boundaries of the delta states like Louisiana—swamps, rivers, waterways—kept populations isolated and the gene pools concentrated. Added to this was the basic clan structure of the South, which was supported by a long and intimate association with power differentials. From its long participation in slavery to its humiliation after the Civil War, Southern culture developed eddies that revolved around issues of control, appearances, and power."

As a child of the same Mississippi delta, it might be argued, Bill Clinton was in a similar, if not the same, paddleboat. Both men certainly wanted to do better. Both kept promising, in fact, to do better. But they didn't. Or couldn't—as Betsey Wright now learned.

Tumult in Personal Life

"I had a conversation with Bill one night out at the governor's mansion, when he and Hillary first started talking about running" for president, Betsey Wright recalled a decade later. "This was in 1991. And he said he didn't think—"

Betsey paused, as she summoned her memory of that fateful meeting. Chairman of the centrist Democratic Leadership Council, with a far more compliant new Arkansas legislature in place at the capitol in Little Rock—thanks both to the recent ethics law and Betsey Wright's procedural changes in charge of the state Democratic Party—the governor seemed to be riding high. *Why try to ride higher?*

Hillary had not been present, otherwise Ms. Wright would not have dreamed of tackling the subject—and attendant problems. Alone with Bill, however, Betsey put him to the test, she recalled. "We had an argument over whether it matters that you've had affairs. And I said, if it is really in the past and there have been no recurrences it probably doesn't. But an affair at the time [of running]—as in the case of Gary Hart—really reveals a certain amount of tumult in his personal life. Which means that that tumult isn't the steadying force you want to be elected."

Betsey was surprised by the governor's reaction. "I mean, it took Bill's breath away that I felt that way. But I do! I mean, I'm not a prude, but I do think that something is rocky in your personal life if you're running for president and having an affair!"

Betsey was being not moralistic but realistic. A man willing to cut such corners in an age of accountability was to her way of thinking myopic and incapable of the discipline required by the highest office on a world stage— "that you're taking risks that are ridiculous. I don't think that anybody thought that Gary [Hart] wanted to end his marriage—but I mean, there was something really rocky. . . . He wasn't a steady person then! He just wasn't steady! He was in some kind of tumult. And what I was saying to Bill was that if you behave that way, it will mean that you don't have your act together."

Was Betsey right? Or was she completely wrong—unable as a woman, and especially as a single woman and a dedicated feminist, to recognize the nature of Bill's age-old natural compulsion: a compulsion little different in its recurrent, endlessly tempting, taunting addiction from that of the Reverend Swaggart—or JFK?

The Right Messenger

On May 6, 1991, meanwhile, Governor Bill Clinton gave a crucial keynote speech to the national convention of the centrist Democratic Leadership Council in Cleveland, Ohio. He'd crisscrossed the West from Los Angeles to Colorado, setting up chapters of the council as chairman, but in order to show he was heading a party of New Democrats, not Old Democrats, he pointedly invited neither the Reverend Jesse Jackson nor the old presidential nominee, George McGovern, to speak.

Mike McCurry, a political consultant, had predicted at the time of Clinton's gubernatorial inauguration that "there are a lot of people who would like to see the Cleveland convention as the start of the 'Bill Clinton for president campaign.' " With no text save a few scribbled notes on a card, Governor Bill Clinton did not disappoint such people. Indeed, he gave before the eight hundred delegates and participants, who included Paul Tsongas, Al Gore, Sam Nunn, Richard Gephardt, and Jay Rockefeller, perhaps the best political speech of his life so far—an "address that energized the assembly," as the journalist Meredith Oakley recalled, "and elicited widespread encouragement that he seek the party's nomination."

Former senator Tsongas had already declared his candidacy five days before. Now, without declaring his own intentions, Bill Clinton had exploited to the full his opportunity to banish, in a twenty-two-minute address, memories of his Atlanta debacle, and to inspire a new following. He was, like the Reverend Jimmy Swaggart—or even the Reverend Pat Robertson, who had sworn to win the 1988 presidential election for "Christianity"—a preacher with a new take on an old gospel. The Democratic Party, Governor Clinton urged, *had* to turn around public perceptions of it as a tax-and-spend, soak-the-middle-class, soft-on-defense organization, otherwise "we won't continue as a national party," he warned.

"For once," Meredith Oakley described, "his voice was rested, untouched by the chronic hoarseness that dogged him throughout every heavy speaking schedule, and it was able to ebb and soar."

America, Clinton declared, "needs at least one political party that's not afraid to tell the people the truth and address the real needs of human beings. We're here to save the Democratic party, we're here to save the United States of America." Thinking of Ronald Reagan, of Reagan's successor George Bush, and of the social and economic problems America was still facing, Clinton claimed that for "more than a decade we have lived in a fantasy world in which it was bad form and terrible politics to admit that we have problems of this magnitude." Yet to imagine that the old Democratic Party would be able to address such problems if voted back into power was equally idle. "The Republican burden is their record of denial, evasion and neglect. But our burden is to give the people a new choice," he insisted, a choice "rooted in old values" but not in old ideologies or programs. "We've got to have a message that touches everybody, that makes sense to everybody, that goes beyond the state orthodoxies of 'left' and 'right.' "

As Oakley admitted—for she would bitterly contest Clinton's right to declare for the presidency himself, given his assurance to Arkansas voters—the "thunderous standing ovation that met the close of his remarks was not a mere courtesy. Many of the delegates came away persuaded that they had the right message and the right messenger."

They did. If, disregarding Betsey Wright's advice, he would run.

Some Folks from Washington

Among the fifty delegates from Arkansas who had traveled with Governor Clinton to the national convention of the DNC in Cleveland in May 1991 had been David Watkins. As Clinton's apolitical advertising and communications campaign manager, Watkins later felt Clinton was right to withdraw from the presidential race in 1987—a mark, he felt, of Clinton's gut instinct. "He made the right decision!" he commented in retrospect, certain that Clinton could not have fielded the character assassination squads at that time in American history—especially those operating under the notorious Lee Atwater, who had mercifully died in March 1991.

Back in Little Rock on the evening of May 7, 1991, after Bill's extraordinary speech in Cleveland, Watkins got a call: "David, we've got some folks from Washington coming, and we'd like to use your office to meet. They're going to discuss what Bill Clinton needs to do if he's going to run for President."

Paula Corbin

Elated, Watkins had obliged, making his office available to the "big shots": "Stan Greenberg, Frank Greer, Gloria Cabe, Mark Gearan, Bill Clinton, Hillary Clinton, and myself. I'm listening, 'cause these are guys from Washington, you know—particularly Greenberg, he's kinda conducting it. Anyway, we take a break about nine, sometime during the evening. Everyone goes to the bathroom except Clinton and I. We're sitting there. And he asks me what I think."

Both Clinton and Watkins—whose father had been a grocery salesman and had called on Clinton's grandfather when he ran his store—were from Hope. This time, in contrast to 1987, Watkins was gung ho. "I say, 'Absolutely! You should go for it!' This is a time, remember, when he has promised, when he ran, or agreed to go again, for governor, that he would remain as governor. He said, 'Well, how do we do it, how do I get out of *that*?' That was a true concern."

Watkins paused, remembering how they had then hit upon a solution, much like the one developed after his defeat in 1980: to go out and make it right with the people. "So the strategy was," Watkins recalled with retrospective pride, 'Well, you go out, you canvass the state, and you ask their permission.' " In the meantime, however, they would set up an "exploratory committee"—"a guy from Boston, who hires two or three guys, one of which is Gregg Smith, who I guess was really the first person in his presidential campaign."

History was now being made, by the participants. The next morning,

May 8, 1991, Governor Clinton had to give a speech to the Quality Management Conference, a state-sponsored affair by the Arkansas Industrial Development Council held at the Excelsior Hotel in Little Rock. Bill was excited—as were others. Supposedly he then lunched with Phil Price, a former aide currently working for the lieutenant governor, Jim Guy Tucker, who was also attending the conference. Then—if Price's subsequent version of events was accurate—Clinton must have returned to the conference, for at 1:15 P.M. he chatted with Jim Harrington, a management consultant from Ernst & Young, who was also about to address the conference.

Harrington remembered the occasion well. The newspapers that morning had been full of Clinton's "toe-tingling" speech in Cleveland, and the two men "talked about whether Clinton was going to run for president"—the $64,000 question. "He was there for my speech," Harrington subsequently confirmed to a *Washington Post* reporter without knowing the purpose of the journalist's inquiry, "and then he sort of drifted out." In the lobby Clinton was "just milling about" when he saw a small, mousy, but cute-looking woman with black hair at the registration desk, dressed in culottes.

The buxom brunette was Paula Corbin, the twenty-four-year-old fiancée of Steve Jones—who would make not only history but tragedy.

Making No Sense

What happened upstairs at the Excelsior Hotel—the governor of the state of Arkansas pulling his pants down and asking the registration secretary to perform oral sex—was, only two years later, unthinkable to the staff of the White House in Washington, D.C., at the helm of the most powerful state in the world. "When it was suggested," Sally Quinn wrote a few months later, describing a new press conference, "that, after Gary Hart, a candidate who ran around while running for the presidency would have to be psychotic, Hillary Clinton burst out laughing. 'That's a pretty fair estimate,' she said. Clinton did not respond."

Was Clinton psychotic? Even men like George Stephanopoulos, who had become an official aide to the President, would shake their heads in disbelief, Stephanopoulos berating Michael Isikoff, the *Washington Post* reporter charged with tracking down the Paula Jones story: "Did I realize when this encounter with Jones was supposed to have happened?" Isikoff afterward recounted Stephanopoulos's incredulity that a *Post* reporter would believe such garbage. "It was the day after Clinton had returned from giving the keynote speech at the Democratic Leadership Conference in Cleveland. Did I realize how significant that was?"

If Isikoff did not, he soon learned when he pulled up the press cuttings for the DLC convention, at which Bob Beckel, a party strategist, had gone on record saying that Clinton's was "the best Democratic speech I've heard in ten years." As Isikoff summarized Stephanopoulos's point, the DLC convention had been a historic occasion in modern American politics: the launchpad for one of the greatest political moon shots of the twentieth century. "Did I really think, Stephanopoulos asked, that Clinton would have been so crazy as to have done something like this right after Cleveland? To jeopardize everything he had worked for so many years. It just didn't make any sense, he said."

It didn't. At least not to innocent young Stephanopoulos, or indeed to young Isikoff at that moment—or to any of the dozens, hundreds, and ultimately thousands of staffers, supporters, and lawyers who would be induced to believe Clinton's denial of events. Clinton had not even attended the afternoon session of the management conference, his aides asserted, while Clinton himself could "not remember" having met Paula Corbin, despite his photographic memory for faces and names.

Paula remembered, however.

A Blow Job

Addiction doesn't make sense—afterward. At the time, however, the "groin demon," like the giant in "Jack and the Beanstalk," demanded his supper. A state trooper approached the diminutive Ms. Jones, telling her that the governor had asked if he might speak with her in his room upstairs. She wondered why but did not say no. Leaving her colleague from the Arkansas Industrial Development Council, Pamela Blackard, at the desk, young Paula Corbin accompanied the state trooper, in her culottes, to the governor's hotel room on the eleventh floor, to meet the blackguard.

When Paula returned ten minutes later, she was "shaking," Pamela recalled—as well as Paula's words: "You're not going to believe what happened."

Whether or not Paula had sensed what Clinton was up to would, as in the case of the televangelists and their prey, be known only to the participants—and perhaps not even to them, afterward. The trooper, Danny Ferguson, had made light of the governor's instruction, claiming, according to Paula herself, "that we do this all the time for the governor."

If so, what did the word "this" mean? And why did she go up? "Yes. I am very gullible and naive and I had a problem with that a lot," Paula later told "Izzy" Isikoff, reflecting on her life in Arkansas, coming from a small town and a Pentecostalist family in which to wear makeup or dance had been a sin. "But that's just my raising. I was brought up to trust people and especially of that statue [*sic*], you know, a governor."

The statue had come to life, however, when the diminutive Paula, alone in the hotel room with Clinton, found her hand being taken and the six-foot, three-inch governor backing her up against the windowsill. He had gone "beetroot red"—a sure sign, to those women who knew him intimately, that he was, like the Reverend Swaggart, struggling not only with high blood pressure but with his groin demon. "I will never forget the look on his face," Paula recalled. "I will never! His face was just red, beet red, I swear it was. Oh, it was horrible!"

Unaware what a fool he was making of himself, Bill had tried to slip his hand into Paula's shorts. "And I said, 'What are you doing? What is going on?' He was trying to nibble on my neck and I was trying to back off." The governor's unctuous words made his effort at seduction no better. "I was just noticing [you] downstairs." Clinton parlayed his excitement into speech, since action seemed premature. "I was looking at your curves and the way you walked around the front of the table," he remarked, "and I love the way your hair came down your back, the middle of your back and your curves."

If Clinton supposed that a new secretary at the AIDC, earning less than $10,000 a year, would be flattered and perform oral sex on him in the hope of promotion, he was to be very disappointed. Earlier in his career he had taken endless time over his seductions, in a leaf from Casanova's *Histoire de ma vie*. "Bill would never force himself on anyone—his need to be appreciated and loved is too great!" Betsey Wright would strenuously maintain, and for the most part she was right. Clinton was, moreover, afraid of female ire, as Betsey knew. "He wouldn't make anyone angry!" Betsey was certain. If so, why did Clinton then sit beside the trembling young woman, drop his pants, and start masturbating beside her? Power? Lust? Uncontrollable arousal?

David Maraniss, the biographer of Clinton's early years and a colleague of Michael Isikoff on *The Washington Post,* was nonplussed. "It didn't seem in keeping with Clinton's normal pattern to drop his pants like that without any indication that the other person was willing," Maraniss later told his newspaper's national editor, Karen DeYoung. Yet Paula would adamantly insist that she had neither spoken nor signaled any agreement to Clinton's flashing. "He had boxer shorts and everything and he exposed hisself with an erection to me on the couch. And I was literally scared, shocked," Paula narrated to Isikoff. The governor was "holding it . . . fiddling it or whatever. And he asked me to—I don't know his exact word—give him a blow job."

Isikoff had pressed her to be more specific. "I think he wanted me to kiss it . . . And he was saying it in a very disgusting way, just a horny-assed way that just scared me to death." Again, Isikoff pressed her to be more precise. "Disgusting way," she obliged, "he just, it was *please, I want it bad*—just that type of way, like he was wanting it bad, you know."

Isikoff pretended not to. Later, Paula would be more precise still, recalling the telltale mole that would prove that she had seen the governor's vital organ close up. Unlike the prostitute Debra Murphree or even Cathy Kampen (a "stripogram" performer who became involved with the Reverend Swaggart), however, Paula Corbin had denied, she asserted, the governor of Arkansas her mouth or even her hand—indeed, she got up to leave. "Well, I don't want to make you do something you don't want to do," Clinton had said as she left him—and he had told her to contact Dave Harrington if she got "in trouble" over her ten-minute absence from the registration desk. Presumably he had then finished the unblown job alone.

"I mean the man is just a pervert," Paula sniffed—though her own sexual development, after being raised the daughter of a fundamentalist lay preacher in Lonoke, Arkansas, had by many accounts been rebellious, wild, and woolly, leading to a reputation for exhibitionism—including the dissemination of nude photographs of herself—and for a great delight in "cock-teasing," her own brother-in-law later revealed. (He later said he believed her charges against Clinton.) Was Paula *really* so upset?

There was, however, a world of difference between a woman choosing to be a sexual exhibitionist on her own time and an employee being pressed by an employer to give him a blow job, on the job. If Paula had truly been "scared and shocked" on the eleventh floor of the Excelsior Hotel—and this was in all likelihood the truth—it was probably more from the notion of a man of her father's age and Clinton's gubernatorial authority demeaning himself and expecting her to satisfy his chauvinist wishes than from the sight of an erect and by all accounts not even very big, let alone scary, penis. When Paula told her friend Deborah Ballantine later that afternoon what had happened ("Debbie, he pulled his pants down to his knees and he asked me to suck his dick"), Ballantine had mocked her. "Paula, don't you know he does stuff like this?" Ballantine had then chided her for her naiveté. But Paula—"utterly guileless and unsophisticated" as Isikoff described her—apparently didn't.

Whether the governor realized what seeds of mischief, scandal, and, ultimately, international humiliation he had just sewn is doubtful. As Isikoff discovered when researching the story for *The Washington Post,* Clinton had shown no sign of being abashed or disappointed, let alone worried. He had told his trooper he hadn't scored; it was no big deal. In the statistics of such sexual encounters there was always an 80 to 90 percent chance of being turned down. At the White House even President Bush's political director, Mary Matalin, acknowledged that "the stature and trappings attendant to even the lowest White House job were addictive. One really gross guy used to brag how he could pick up girls with his White House baggage tag."

Clinton certainly did not feel he'd done wrong, since he hadn't proposed full sex nor had he harmed Paula, and he certainly did not see it as relevant to, or in any way connected with, his marital relationship with Hillary, whom he truly loved and admired. Like the Reverend Swaggart's problem, it was a temporary groin need that had surfaced at a moment in his life when he was tremendously elated—indeed, even Paula had asked if he was going to run for president! It simply hadn't worked out, mutually, requiring solitary release. He had then put it, like Satan, behind him.

Buoyed by the enthusiasm that people of every color and background were showing to his possible candidacy for the presidency, Bill Clinton was on top form. Just as the Reverend Swaggart tended to be, whenever he danced with the Devil—as, in October 1991, Swaggart did again.

Generational Change

George Stephanopoulos's later tone with Isikoff—his disbelief that a potential presidential candidate would risk his chances of success, at the very moment of jubilant reception by his peers, for a simple blow job—betrayed the innocent notion that "sex" was something consciously willed, or carefully considered, in terms of decorum and consequences. Disgusted,

Stephanopoulos—who had his own difficulties with women—would eventually resign from the White House staff, for he felt increasingly and cumulatively used: another pawn in Bill Clinton's selfish chess game, compelled to lie and prevaricate to defend a boss who simply could not tell the truth, especially about sex.

Who did, though? And if they did, would voters understand? In earlier years Hollywood studios had done everything possible to protect their stars from personal scandal, knowing that people tended to idolize their idols—and might spurn actors' movies if such idolization were offended. Those days were, however, long gone, to be replaced by their polar opposite, as studios gloried in the very scandals that kept their stars in the headlines. In 1995, Hugh Grant would cause oral sex with a prostitute to become a regrettable yet acceptable lapse for a box-office star—the vast majority of Americans no longer seeing sex or extramarital flirtation, whether playful, oral, or fully consummated, as a bar to high professional performance, save in politics. As Hillary Clinton would ask in 1991, "The fact that there was never a hint of any [sexual] misconduct about somebody else, like Richard Nixon, does that make him a better president [than JFK]? Who knows? These questions are simplistic in their intent that one area of a person's life—their sexual conduct—is their defining characteristic. And it may be for some people," she gave her own view, "and it may not be for others."

Time would tell. In the meanwhile, promiscuity and drugs in the entertainment industry had certainly come to be seen as inevitable accessories to success in popular music, filmmaking, theater, and television, with only rare exceptions. Sociobiologists were simultaneously making it clear why: namely, that sexual promiscuity was built into the genetic code of most natural life—indeed, according to research biologists, sexual competition and promiscuity had been from earliest times an integral part of human evolution, essential to the survival of human beings as a healthy species. As Matt Ridley would summarize in his classic account of evolutionary science, *The Red Queen,* in 1993, humans must outwit the predations of mutant diseases—and can do so only by effective reproduction that favors evolving genes, not traditional moralities, however noble and high-sounding these may be. AIDS might suggest that sexual loyalty is a guarantee of good health, but in the long history of the human species—as in almost all species—promiscuity has and will continue to be nature's primary way of ensuring genetic immunity and survival.

Despite this growing recognition, for reasons no political scientist could—or dared try to—explain, the area of political representation remained almost immune to more realistic public expectations of presidents and political leaders in America. The Gary Hart scandal suggested, in fact, that his country was still only at the very beginning of a difficult process of maturation. While 46 percent of married (or cohabiting) American men and 42 percent of American women now *admitted* having relationships outside their marriages, 80 percent of men and women characterized extramarital sex as "always wrong" and a further 14 percent as "almost always wrong."

Clearly, an adjustment was necessary that would bring expectation and reality—especially in the political arena—closer into line. Betsey Wright's concern was that this adjustment had not yet taken place. Meanwhile, she knew, the long-awaited generational trial of the century was inevitably approaching, with America about to face the prospect of its first baby-boom president in the White House—just as John F. Kennedy had been the first president born in the twentieth century to take the highest office, in 1961. That generational trial would inevitably lead to metaphorical bloodshed, and sex would be used to tar the candidate unless he were squeaky clean—which Bill was not, *nor was he willing to be.* "Listen," she snapped at Gene Lyons, "the guy represented generational change. He was a baby boomer. He'd been on campuses when birth control pills were first invented, and 'free sex' became a big deal. He had a brother who had gotten in trouble with drugs, and he was on campuses when drugs were used. He was attractive to women. There were a million rumors, and there were lots of people who would be willing to make allegations. I just knew," she added, "that there was no way we were going to make that kind of generational change in this country without a struggle. That was going to happen to the first baby boomer who got out there by himself."

Was it wise for Bill Clinton to be that "first baby boomer," given the likely "struggle"? Would any but a "squeaky-clean" candidate survive the media spotlight at the end of the twentieth century—unless public attitudes changed?

First Boomer

In Betsey Wright's view—a view that would be shared by many women in the months ahead—Governor Bill Clinton had no business tossing his hat into the ring, given his sexual promiscuity and his unwillingness to turn monogamous in middle age in order to conform with American hypocrisy. She didn't blame him for being a man and therefore promiscuous, but she did censure him for failing to see that, given the prurient interest of the press, he could no longer get away with adultery in the way so many of his predecessors had done.

If George Bush had been, as would be alleged, adulterous earlier in his career, as President of the United States he was nearing seventy and seemed, like his immediate predecessor President Reagan, to be able to manage without extramarital gratification. Bill Clinton, however, was a generation younger than Bush—not only in the prime of sexual life himself but powerfully attractive to women in the prime of *their* lives too.

If the merest White House baggage tag ensured sexual conquest, how would Bill Clinton be able to resist, even were he to reform? It would be like holding a red rag to a bull. A bull, moreover, who, as the half-orphaned stepson of an alcoholic, was simply too emotionally "needy" to decline, Betsey Wright could see.

Bill Clinton, however, thought otherwise. John F. Kennedy had been fueled by the high-octane prospect of becoming the nation's first Catholic president and the first to be born in the twentieth century. Bill Clinton was now irrevocably determined to become the first boomer. Campaigning speeded his adrenaline and sharpened his now-legendary political wits. As he had recently confided to his old girlfriend Gennifer Flowers, he'd out-foxed his Republican rival, Sheffield Nelson, and was proud of it. "I stuck it up their ass," he told her with delight, referring to Nelson's attempt to pin his butterfly. Nelson had tried to get inmates at a state prison "to trash me," he related—and boasted how he'd forced Nelson to pretend he was not behind the scheme. "I mean, I know he lied. I just wanted to make his asshole pucker."

Bill Clinton was entering LBJ's league. Dirt would be dished, he knew, but he would be ready. He had, after all, more brains than his opponents, more political experience, more popular support, more drive, more ambition. And more *wife*.

With Hillary beside him, Bill was certain, he was unbeatable—and the opposition knew it. A call from one of President Bush's advisers, Roger B. Porter, had recently proved it. "We've done a lot of looking at this race and your profile is one of a very few," Porter had explained, "that could cause us trouble. And we just want you to know if you get into this race, we will do everything we can to destroy you personally."

Governor Clinton had been warned. But nothing could have been more calculated to make the boy from Hope reaffirm his intention to seek the presidential crown. He would "stick it up their ass" and enjoy doing so— just as Jack Kennedy had once relished the idea of trouncing Republicans who despised his "trashy" Boston Irish roots. Bill would fight—if his fellow Arkansans would release him from his vow. And, God willing, he would win.

CHAPTER THIRTY-NINE

THE PERILS OF RUNNING FOR PRESIDENT

Exposure

Town by town, Governor Bill Clinton now toured his home state, asking constituents if he might run for President of the United States. Most were personally encouraging, though frankly dismissive of his chances.

The odds certainly seemed stacked against a successful Democratic challenge, for on January 16, 1991, in response to Saddam Hussein's seizure of Kuwait, a U.S.-led coalition had finally begun to attack Iraq by air, followed on February 23 by a land campaign under the overall command of General Norman Schwarzkopf. Four days later Kuwait City was liberated by triumphant Allied ground forces, and on March 3, 1991, the Iraqi military command capitulated, having suffered approximately 100,000 casualties against Allied losses of only 115. In polls taken, President Bush's popularity soared into the nineties.

Bill was unabashed. "I might get my brains beat out—probably will," he said to one reporter in his old university town of Fayetteville, from which he'd contested his first and unsuccessful election. If he did run for the presidency, he made clear, it would probably come to nothing, but it was worth it to the Natural State. "If I did all right," he argued, "I think there would be a lot of exposure given to the state. A lot of people would learn a lot of things about Arkansas."

More important for the governor in his bid to win the presidency one day, they would learn about him: "name recognition."

Dignified Lives

The Washington Post, noting Governor Clinton's eyes so obviously on the presidential nomination, decided to profile Hillary Clinton in July 1991: the first lady of Arkansas and wife of one of the Democratic Party's most charismatic possible contenders for the 1992 race.

President Bush's stratospheric poll rating might be insurmountable, yet Hillary seemed unperturbed. Despite the securing of the Middle East oil supply for the great engine of the global economy, the American economy itself remained moribund. Some economists had predicted not only a recession in the nineties, but another Great Depression. Dr. Ravi Batra, professor of economics at Southern Methodist University, for example, was one such prophet of doom. Ranked third in a group of forty-six academic "superstars" in North America. Dr. Batra, in terms that recalled the biblical Joseph in Egypt, had predicted that "an unprecedented depression will affect the American economy, and hence the world economy, around 1990 and last for seven years."

The year 1991 seemed to be proving Dr. Batra, Harvard's John Kenneth Galbraith, and MIT's Lester Thurow, as well as other doomsayers, right— but President Bush rarely talked about the economy or indeed domestic affairs. In relation to the major social, educational, and economic issues of the day, Hillary declared, she really didn't know "how much longer the country can wait for those issues to be part of the national debate." It was plain to The Washington Post and its readers that Hillary was a vital partner in the Clinton enterprise. Whatever Bill "decides to do," she claimed, "it is his decision." But few doubted that she would have a powerful part in it.

Though rumors of marital infidelity had begun to proliferate, Hillary was dismissive. "I think it's a sad diversion. Everybody, including public officials, deserves some zone of privacy. This is an intrusive and irrelevant issue. Bill and I have tried to lead dignified lives," she stated—though she quickly qualified her claim lest it attract the same stampede of investigative journalists that Gary Hart's claims had done. "I've never put Bill on a pedestal," she cautioned, "and said he's perfect."

For Hillary, it was "the issues" that should count—issues she hoped would "finally break through into the public consciousness and will be given the consideration they deserve," despite the trumpets of victory in the Middle East.

Certainly, whoever chose to attack Bill Clinton on grounds of marital impropriety would have Hillary Clinton to deal with—just as anyone messing with the Rev. Jimmy Swaggart had Frances, his wife, to fight.

Feeling the Pain

Hillary's participation in her husband's career and political fortunes did indeed mirror those of Frances Swaggart, who had become her husband's earthly savior. Before rising to preach his first ban-breaking sermon in defiance of his church's elders, Jimmy Swaggart had played two songs of his own on the piano but had then pointed to Frances as she stood on the podium, telling the five-thousand-strong congregation, "This is the greatest wife that God ever gave any preacher. I love you."

In her own address, Frances had thanked "the Lord for His grace and His love and His mercy. You know we have lived for the Lord Jesus many, many years but yet never has He been as real and as close as He has been these past few months," she'd declared. Now when she looked at people "and their hurting, I can not only sense their hurt; I can feel their hurt. I can actually feel the pain."

Here at last was the catchphrase or mantra for the nineties, the ultimate sign of compassion in what social scientists called "The Therapeutic State." Like Jim and Tammy Faye Bakker, the Swaggarts had learned to tap into the depth of this distinctively American religious well. Unlike the Bakkers, however, the Swaggarts had learned not only to feel people's pain but to survive the scandals and explosive allegations that caused much of it. Analyzing the way the Reverend Swaggart had parlayed his way back into the affections of his vast evangelical constituency after the Debra Murphree scandals of 1988, religious historian Michael Giuliano noted that Jimmy Swaggart had become by 1988 not only the top American television evangelist in terms of audience numbers but, according to journalist Dan Rather, the medium's "greatest communicator in the world": the master of "hot gospeling" whose musical and rhetorical skills—reflected in fifty-four albums with sales exceeding $200 million—were second to none.

It was an achievement that was not lost on the potential presidential candidate from Little Rock and his feisty northern wife. Certainly, without understanding the televangelist appeal and the brave but baffled American socioreligious stratum into which their preachers tapped, it would be impossible to understand the way a southern small-state governor was able, in the coming months, to step forward and snatch the presidential crown from a seemingly invincible Republican President only a year after Desert Storm.

Representing the American Dream

Bill Clinton, giving speech after speech, address after address across Arkansas in the spring and summer of 1991, certainly took televangelism seriously. He had, after all, been raised in the very soil of religious revivalism; President George Bush had not. In the 1988 election, Bush had had to fight with bare knuckles not only against Governor Dukakis on his left but also the Reverend Pat Robertson on his right—yet Bush's nodding appreciation of evangelicals had never been more than a courtesy by the nominal Texan, who seemed more at home in Kennebunkport, Maine, than in the evangelical South.

Big Bill Clinton, by contrast, was a Southern Baptist by birth and from the earliest age had attended evangelical church services, which he loved. Despite its tiny population, the state of Arkansas had grown more than its fair share of tented revivalists and preachers—in part, perhaps, because evangelism in America had always had a frontier character that worked well in Arkansas: a character that televangelists had now brilliantly transformed into a modern, technologically sophisticated missionary appeal. Old-fashioned church hymns had given way to crossover black gospel singing—emotive vocal music that reaffirmed a sense of community through its intensity, rhythm, and lyrics. The South *was* music—indeed, if Chicago-born Hillary Rodham had felt envious of Bill Clinton's sense of rootedness in the South, it was in part because the North has no equivalent church, unless it be the old-fashioned church rituals of Catholicism.

That Catholicism, however, owed its allegiance to a bejeweled Vatican pontiff far away in Italy; moreover, its rituals followed European styles of religious observance, with their accent on hierarchical pomp, ceremony, ritual, holy images, sanctified relics, saints, incense, and fine ecclesiastical robes and paintings. Evangelicals, by contrast, were vibrantly classless and distinctively American in language, style, ritual, and charismatic leadership ability, without the need of robes or uniforms. Moreover, it was the southern-based evangelicals who had seen the light of television in its infancy and, once FCC regulations were liberalized in 1960, had seized the opportunity to spread through the global ether the words, music, and celebratory tableaux of televangelism. Ted Koppel might mock their feeding habits, but the televangelist ministries were among the first multinational companies, and their grasp and use of modern technology were phenomenal. The government might sentence Jim Bakker to prison for forty-five years, George Bush might trounce his independent rival Pat Robertson, and the Assemblies of God might defrock both Marvin Gorman and his Judas, Jimmy Swaggart, but evangelism and televangelism continued to grow unchecked because, as Stanford professors George and Louis Spindler pointed out in a seminal socio-anthropological analysis of modern America in 1990, the televangelists had drawn inspiration from both Indians and blacks to produce a new synthesis: a cultural concoction that could not be erased by media scandal or mockery by easterners.

Puritan fundamentalism in the North was "duller, repressed, harsh, and withdrawn from sensual pleasures," the Spindlers pointed out. By contrast, the black Baptist Church "is often equally fundamentalist, but is expressive, exhibitionistic, joyous, ecstatic." The especial forte of televangelism, in this context, was that it could "make up for the pervasive sense of loss, of insecurity, of generalized anxiety, that is a part of the daily life in today's America. The palatial and colorful TV stages are no mean and paltry shacks inhabited by the poor. They represent and demonstrate material success. They are a special representation of the 'American dream' "—on a par with Hollywood.

"The fall of some of its most famous promoters occasioned by personal scandals and questions about fiscal matters" certainly "tarnished its image," the Spindlers acknowledged of televangelism. "Thousands have turned away from it," they admitted, "but thousands remain faithful. The need for the reassurance of orthodoxy and the search for affiliation are there." The PTL Ministry might fail, but another movement," they predicted, "will be cast up by our dynamic culture."

They were right, both in religion and in politics—as a Texan billionaire would demonstrate the following year. Meanwhile, the New Left movement was growing under its charismatic, centrist Arkansas preacher Governor Bill Clinton, accompanied on his revivalist crusade by his stalwart northern wife, Hillary, speaking not in tongues, but in politics: tapping into the rock and well of American individualism, pain and need with a new political message of prospective plenty—but also of the need for change in order to achieve it.

The Money Factor

Over the years Bill Clinton had constantly, indefatigably, even obsessively worked to build up his audience support. In the same way as an American televangelist, a modern American politician seeking high office had, Clinton recognized, not only to master the art of television performance and electronic voter persuasion, *but to raise the funds to put out that televised message.* For many politicians, as Bill Clinton's friend Jim Blair explained, such fund-raising, like campaigning, was the least pleasant aspect of political life. Yet for Bill Clinton, despite or because of his humble background, it rarely posed a problem. "I've never lost a race because of lack of money. I doubt it would be a factor," Clinton now declared during the summer of 1991 as he sought personal release from his "promise" to the voters of Arkansas—and he was not boasting.

How Bill Clinton managed to raise such prodigious sums from so many thousands of supporters, rich and poor, was certainly phenomenal. As the governor's longtime aide Bobby Roberts explained, it had its source not in any secret quid pro quo but derived, in large part, from the candidate's complete lack of inhibition in asking for funds. "He doesn't *mind* asking for money. He just doesn't *mind* asking you for money. And a lot of politicians *hate* that—you hear them bitching all the time about it. Not him. He didn't think anything about it." Jim McDougal's wife later recalled how, at college, she had been asked by Bill for a campaign contribution the first time he met her—and when she'd protested she was only twenty and a student, he had told Jim to give her the money to contribute!

Nor did Bill mind tailoring his political message to the electronic media. As religious cultural historian Quentin Schultze noted, "What is said— and how—must compete effectively with other programs on broadcast TV, cable and VCR. Televangelists face the competitive tyranny of the broadcast marketplace and the perceived needs of fickle viewers"—forcing preachers to become supercompetitive as well as emotionally articulate. As Professor Schultze noted, the mainline churches simply failed the test of television, in part because of their innate snobbery. They might permit the sale of candles, crucifixes, icons, and statuettes in church stores attached to cathedrals and places of worship, but in a larger sense they remained terri-

fied of giving "even the appearance of commercialism" and therefore refused to "solicit funds on air or to shape program content to be competitive in the commercial-TV ratings race. That philosophy has virtually
guaranteed that no mainline programs will ever rival the popularity of independent televangelists, just as public television attracts much smaller audiences than its commercial counterpart."

With his tremendous energy, empathy, photographic memory, and missionary zeal, Bill Clinton felt certain he could fashion a popular movement
that would knock the mainline program of the WASP prince, George
Bush, out of the ballpark. After almost ten years of being the incumbent,
defending his crown against all comers, moreover, Bill rather relished the
opportunity to run again as a contender—if the Democratic Party, riddled
with its own traditionalists, would only give him the chance.

The Blood Runs Faster

Bill Clinton might exaggerate the odds against success in ousting George
Bush from the White House, but not by much. He had done his homework.
"I don't know that ever in the history of the country," he told journalists,
"people have denied election or reelection to a war winner."

General Ulysses S. Grant, victor of the Civil War, had certainly won
two unbroken terms as President. So had General Dwight D. Eisenhower,
victor in Europe. Franklin D. Roosevelt, America's leader in World War II,
had won no fewer than four before an early death closed in on him. Even
President Harry Truman, Roosevelt's successor, who had dropped the
atomic bomb and forced the surrender not only of Germany but of Japan,
had confounded pollsters in the 1948 presidential election, beating off
New York Republican Governor Thomas Dewey's challenge and winning
against all predictions: empowering him to stand firm in Korea, to desegregate the armed forces by executive order, and to complete almost eight
years in the White House.

Four decades later, President Bush, in assembling an international
coalition early in 1991, gaining the support of Congress, and mounting
and executing Desert Storm, had certainly shown equal leadership skill to
that of Harry Truman—indeed, when asked whether he would have voted
in Congress for the President's war policy had he been a senator or congressman, Governor Clinton replied in the affirmative. Yet President
Bush's seeming invincibility in the summer of 1991 was, at a psychological

level, the very test run that made Bill Clinton's blood run faster. Years later an interviewer would note of Gary Hart (who studied for a late-life Ph.D. in philosophy at Oxford but wanted desperately to get back into politics) that "the problem, at bottom, is that Gary Hart never really liked politics very much, with all its pep rallies and elbow-grabbing; he liked the ideas, the big stuff." Bill Clinton, by contrast, liked both. Moreover, his elbow grabbing and love of campaigning could prove a priceless advantage in confronting a President who was a patrician and clearly did not relish such populist interaction.

The fact that his rivals in the Democratic Party seemed to be losing popular support only increased Bill's excitement. "Did you see the Cuomo and Bradley races?" he'd remarked proudly to a friend the night he'd won re-election as governor for the fifth time. The two easterners—Mario Cuomo, the governor of New York; Bill Bradley, senator for New Jersey—had only squeaked back into office, whereas he, Bill Clinton, had triumphed in Arkansas by a landslide. Like Rocky Balboa, he'd earned back the mantle of political success in 1982, and he'd never surrendered it again; indeed, his wins had become consistent knockouts. They might translate well to a larger national ring, given the chance.

"You know, I think that we can win in 1992," Hillary confided one day to a fellow parent, Skip Rutherford, a PR executive and Democratic volunteer in Little Rock, as they watched their daughters play softball.

"Now, if she's telling *me* that," Skip recalled his surprise, "you know she's telling the governor that."

A Court Summons

Beyond the humiliation of losing, there were other, perhaps far worse potential penalties for entering such a race, however. Hubris, in the ancient world, had always been punished by the gods. But even the Greeks had been more charitable than the American legal system, as Jim Bakker had found. Bakker had become president of the most successful of American televangelist ministries ever created, only to be literally thrown into chains and locked up in Rochester, Minnesota, where, as Tammy Faye Bakker later described, he was "given the dirtiest job in the prison": cleaning the toilets. They "were a filthy place, with urine, excrement, spit and vomit everywhere. And when there were fights, they would generally take place in the toilet, so add blood to the list of disgusting messes Jim would have to clean up."

The higher a televangelist preacher sought to rise, the lesson seemed to be, the harder he must be prepared to fall in the modern world if toppled—for celebrity seemed to attract a kind of counter–celebrity venom—people who were either jealous of the success of others or resentful over it for dark, psychological reasons. If celebrity reflected a popular need to idealize and project affection, even quasi worship, its matrix was the opposite: an ancient need to witness bloodshed in stonings, gladiatorial combat, public executions, lynchings—and now, in the last years of the twentieth century, to see punitive treatment meted out to certain individuals who, through weakness, were unable to fend off their rivals and opponents. The fact was that "Americans are not as much interested in ideas and perspectives, debates and dialogue," Professor Schultze commented, "as they are in people and personality"—and this personalization, writ ever larger by America's vast, advanced capitalist-consumerist, television-dominated society, meant that any man or woman arrogant enough to step up and file for candidacy as his party's nominee for President of the United States must be prepared for adulation on the one hand, ritual garroting on the other.

Such garroting had, traditionally, been done by skilled torturers. In the modern American world, such men had exchanged their leather vestments for lawyer's suits, lying in wait to pounce on a victim no matter how exalted or however public.

Jimmy Swaggart's mea culpa telesermon had, for example, been described by *Time* magazine as "without question, the most dramatic sermon ever aired on television," preached to more viewers than had watched Bush and Dukakis's presidential debates. It had proven, in its entirety as well as in the extracts aired on newscasts throughout the nation, to be "fabulous television," as Professor Schultze remarked—"more compelling than most made-for-TV films and more dramatic than any evening soap opera." Yet Swaggart's comeback sermon, after creating his own new church, had proved even more compelling. The guilt about his secret addiction to prostitutes and pornography was "like a cancer," he'd preached to tens of millions on television. "You can't escape it. It's there with you in the lonely hours of the night. It's there when the world is asleep and you remember. And it cuts. And it burns. And it sears. And you can't escape it and you cannot get away from it." He pointed out that "Millions of men and women today are holding a bottle of alcohol or a shot glass of liquor because of guilt. Millions today take drugs because of guilt. Psychiatry doesn't have an answer for it. Psychology doesn't have an answer for it.

Therapy doesn't have an answer for it," he'd asserted. The only answer was Jesus, who on the Cross had appealed to God: "My God, my God, why has Thou forsaken me?" The world had "never seen such power" as that exercised by Jesus when enacting miracles, such as the raising of Lazarus. "And you are talking about God Emmanuel manifested in the flesh who faced Hell's worst, who faced every demon and devil, who faced homosexuality, who faced lesbianism, who faced alcoholism, who faced drug addiction, who faced lying and cheating and thieving and stared Hell right square in the face and overcame—" Here the reverend had begun to speak in gibberish, while the church congregation, heeding the call of Jesus, literally rushed forward in their hundreds "to receive prayer for healing," Giuliano recorded, "and to speak in tongues" too.

But if Jimmy Swaggart had hoped that the forgiving example of Jesus could strategically resurrect him after the Debra Murphree scandal, he'd been cruelly disappointed. Among the members of the congregation pressing forward had been a man who had embraced Swaggart "in what seemed to be an act of admiration. As he'd let go, however, he'd simultaneously placed a document in Swaggart's hands." The document had been, as Michael Giuliano chronicled, neither a check nor a fan letter. Swaggart's Pentecostal heart froze when he realized it was "a court summons"—from his rival, the Reverend Marvin Gorman.

A New Generation

Here, beyond the risk of destruction of one's reputation, was yet another cost of ambition in America, whether on the political podium or in the telepulpit: a legal snake pit into which even the most successful preacher or politician could be pushed—usually by a rival. Swaggart was subsequently fined a staggering *$10 million* for unfairly ruining his rival Reverend Marvin Gorman's ministry, on top of prodigious legal fees.

Bill and Hillary, lawyers, were well aware of such dangers—and the extent to which Hillary's feminism might add further fuel to such hellfire and damnation. In her interview with *The Washington Post* early in July, Hillary had noted how the issue of professional spouses had—as in her own case—been played out and for the most part finally accepted at "the gubernatorial and congressional level. But apparently there's a whole different level of concern you would have to address in the presidential area," she warned presciently. As she added, "nobody has figured that out because it is a new generation."

Faced by a new generation, would the old generation of Americans countenance, let alone accept, a feminist first lady of Arkansas becoming potential First Lady of the United States? Would they use her as a stick with which to beat Bill—or use Bill's peccadilloes as a stick to beat her?

Dick Morris, Bill's alter ego and political strategist, frankly thought the dice were too heavily loaded against success. The politics of personal destruction were not over, he warned—and he strenuously advised Governor Clinton against a presidential run, echoing Betsey Wright's warning.

White America had, Morris also emphasized, turned more and more Republican—as Morris himself had, he later confessed. "I had built important relationships with Republicans, and frankly I didn't think much of his chances of winning," even if Bill got the Democratic Party nomination. Journalists in Bill's home state were skeptical, also, fearing that a failed bid, though it might draw attention to Arkansas, would distract the governor from his duties at a time when state and budgetary leadership was urgently required—an argument which Governor Mario Cuomo, embroiled in tough negotiations with the New York state legislature, would give as his own reason for sitting on the fence for the time being.

There was no shortage, then, of doomsayers and Jeremiahs discouraging Bill Clinton from running for president in the summer of 1991—just as in 1987.

It would be an interesting contest, played out on a level playing field but with no holds barred.

If, of course, he could get through the primaries.

PART EIGHT

DEMOCRATIC NOMINATION

WORLD EXCLUSIVE INTERVIEW

Star February 4, 1992 95¢ Canada 99¢

Dems' front-runner lied to America, says his former lover

MY 12-YEAR AFFAIR WITH BILL CLINTON

ONLY IN *Star*
FOUND! Ted Danson's forgotten first wife

ONLY IN *Star*
Delta Burke's television comeback —as a country singer

ONLY IN *Star*
I was Stevie Wonder's secret lover for 24 years

PLUS THE SECRET LOVE TAPES THAT PROVE IT!

MISTRESS TELLS ALL
We were lovers from 1977 to 1989

Gov. Clinton

Singer Gennifer Flowers

The scandal that made Clinton the "Comeback Kid"

CHAPTER FORTY

DECLARING

Power as Aphrodisiac

As the summer of 1991 ran its course, Governor Bill Clinton resigned as chairman of the centrist Democratic Leadership Council (committee membership in which precluded the backing of any specific candidate) and continued to crisscross Arkansas seeking further financial, political, and moral—even immoral—support for a possible presidential bid.

The more Bill Clinton articulated his vision of the future—with the implication that he himself might, as a national leader, contribute to America's metamorphosis from industrial to postindustrial information technology greatness—the more he was taken seriously as a candidate. In July 1991, however, Boris Yeltsin, a former carpenter and builder, became the first freely elected head of the Russian Republic in the USSR—followed, in August 1991, by the inevitable counterpunch: a putsch by hardliners. The plotters boldly arrested President Mikhail Gorbachev on vacation by the Black Sea and sought to effect a coup d'état in Moscow, the capital of both the USSR and the fledgling Russian Republic.

Was communism on its deathbed, rattling—or reviving? As the Cold War appeared to go up or into smoke, Governor Clinton panicked, calling his old "Rhodie" friend and Russia hand Strobe Talbott from a National Governors Association meeting in Seattle. The news from Russia was great for democracy, the governor acknowledged, but did it spell the end of his own chances of becoming the first post–Cold War president of the United States? President Bush had won the Gulf War, watched breathlessly on television by the larger part of the American electorate; now it looked as if the old combat pilot would be needed to keep watch over the final act of the Cold War, too.

Rumors of an Exotic Love Life

Strobe Talbott wisely cautioned Clinton against premature comment on the Russian putsch. Undaunted by the plotters, Yeltsin mounted a tank outside the Russian White House in Moscow and by his personal courage single-handedly decided the fate of nascent democracy in the once Communist stronghold. Russian communism would not be a threat to the United States any longer. American voters would be able to focus on home concerns—among which the moribund state of the economy, with its high unemployment, seemed intractable.

Bill Clinton's message of the need for change was well attuned to this concern. Outside of Arkansas, few had heard of Bill Clinton, however. Those who had, associated him with his disastrous nominating speech for Michael Dukakis in 1988. Political journalists were for the most part stationed in Washington, so that they tended to take seriously only those congressmen and senators with whom they were familiar. This territorial bias caused them to dismiss Clinton as a lightweight in comparison with the known quantities of the men of D.C.—and the fact that he had a smart, feminist wife did not help. Uninterested in Bill Clinton's politics or ideas, let alone his eleven years of experience in steering a conservative southern state toward change, they seemed fascinated only by rumors of his exotic love life.

Self-Indulgence

Jim Blair later reflected on his friendship with Bill Clinton, indeed their similarities: both Arkansans, of the same height and big build. Both came from the same poor social backgrounds, both had earned law degrees, both were blessed with superbrains, and both were married to smart, professional women, who became best friends. "The relationship was, you know, kind of very informal, almost like family."

Given such brotherly intimacy and identification, Jim Blair empathized with Bill in terms of his struggle to be moral. "What makes a man promiscuous?" he asked, rhetorically. For him, the reason was simple. "We're a close cousin of the primates, and the most promiscuous primate is the chimpanzee. It has the largest testicles. And the least promiscuous is the gorilla, who has the smallest. And human beings are almost in the middle of those." In Blair's opinion testosterone and genetics thus predestined humans to promiscuity—"less so than chimpanzees and more so than gorillas," he stated. "I think—and I'm just telling you my own view of the world—that men are genetically, *innately,* somewhat promiscuous. And they overlay that with a morality, for whatever purpose: community cohesion, civilization, or whatever."

Blair paused. "Now, I think," he added thoughtfully, "when you have somebody who is promiscuous when it is highly inappropriate, it is—I mean, it is self-indulgence. It is self-indulgence."

Civilization thus signified not the *curing* of men's natural trait, as Blair saw matters on behalf of his gender, but its *confinement* to "appropriate" circumstances. The giant, handsome, white-haired attorney, recently widowed, drew a deep breath, then threw up his hands. Bill's compulsion was all so human, so natural, if exaggerated to the point of inappropriateness for whatever reason! "I think some of it is a need for maybe this adoration, or whatever," he speculated, "but it is also a *drive!*" This drive could be seen in Bill Clinton's legendary ambition to succeed in politics, but its liquid propellant was clearly sex. Moreover, the fuel required oxygen to ignite— and in politics this chemistry was all too present—and all too tempting. "Again," Blair was at pains to point out from personal knowledge, "power is an *aphrodisiac* to women! Ever since I've known him," the millionaire attorney confided with a tinge of envy, "ever since he was attorney general, women have been *throwing* themselves at him!"

A Dime a Dozen

Aware that her husband was no more perfect than other energetic, driven men, and certainly no less promiscuous, Hillary Clinton had been forced to indulge Bill in his "distractions" for years—and could not, at heart, understand why others would not do the same. Had not Jackie Kennedy? Had not Lady Bird Johnson?

As the historian Robert Dallek judiciously noted, Lady Bird Johnson "was a large-hearted person whose generosity and sense of humor gave her some detachment from her husband's shortcomings." Such detachment had given rise to her immortal remark, when told of Texas Governor John Connelly's allegation of an affair between Lyndon Johnson and Alice Glass: "I would have thought that Alice Glass was a bit too plump for Lyndon."

Queen Victoria would not have been amused, but even as a late-twentieth-century feminist/postfeminist, Hillary sometimes despaired of America's refusal to be grown-up about such matters. At times it seemed as if the United States had become *less* mature sexually following the sixties revolution, women's lib, and Nixon's impeachment in the seventies than before; certainly this was true in politics. The media assumed that they were now legitimized in their prurient investigative reporting of politicians' private lives, on behalf of a public that applauded the peccadilloes of entertainers but affected to be outraged if the sinner was a politician! Privacy had gone out the window, while speculation now blew with gale force. "Rumors are a dime a dozen," Hillary snapped at one interviewer in Arkansas. "I could stand out here and start ten of my own. They are titillating, but the fact that they get into the mainstream media just amazes me." Thousands of fliers proclaiming revelations about Governor Clinton's numerous affairs had been posted, pasted, and tacked to telephone poles all across downtown Little Rock. Who could explain, she asked, why people took such things seriously? "It's pathetic."

It *was* pathetic—but it was also postmodern America. There had always existed an appetite for scandal in the nation since the time of the Founding Fathers; it was just that such scandal now entertained a country of 280 million people, instead of less than a million. "Maybe somebody will wake up and say, 'Hey, I believe in what Bill Clinton is saying and I'm going to run on that,'" Hillary snorted indignantly. Such an alternative candidate would save her the uphill struggle. "I might breathe a sigh of relief," she claimed. "I'm tired. I don't feel like running across the country."

Hillary didn't mean it, however. Since childhood, urged on by her father, she'd been a stranger to defeatism. Her weariness had been but a momentary lapse—especially since Governor Clinton's exploratory committee had begun reporting ever-growing enthusiasm for a Clinton bid for the party nomination.

In mid-September 1991, therefore, after a brief vacation in the Pacific Northwest, the Clintons flew to Washington, D.C., to attend what was known as the Sperling Breakfast, a traditional vetting ritual by the Fourth

Estate organized by the veteran correspondent of *The Christian Science Monitor,* Godfrey Sperling, Jr.: an opportunity for senior members of the national press to meet a potential presidential candidate and his wife.

It was, equally, a chance for the potential candidate to confront the scandalmongers of modern society directly, face-to-face, chest to chest, eyeball to eyeball—and for both parties to assess the prospects for a Clinton run.

"Screw 'Em"

Given the importance of the meeting, the Clintons spent the entire day before the breakfast rehearsing with a group of twenty political friends headed up by Los Angeles lawyer Mickey Kantor.

The advisory cabal raised the likely issue of sex with commendable frankness. Strategist Frank Greer's preferred spin on Clinton's "incredible reputation around town" was: meet the subject head-on. Serial divorce permitted politicians, such as former President Reagan, to move from woman to woman. By contrast, Bill and Hillary had decided to stick it out and stand by their spouses. Should they be hounded by the press for this? Surely the American people, in the 1990s, would respect them for working through their problems together, rather than running away from them and endangering the maturation of their child.

The assembly endorsed such an approach, alongside detailed discussion of policy issues and foreign affairs. Thereafter Bill and Hillary went out to dinner with their old friend Vernon Jordan, an experienced black lawyer in D.C.

Dinner with the lawyer proved a terrible mistake. To the consternation of PR strategist Frank Greer and the Kantor advisory group, when Bill and Hillary returned that night, they had changed their minds. "Hell, I just had dinner with Vernon Jordan," Bill explained to Greer, "and Jordan said, 'Screw 'em. Don't tell 'em anything!' "

The Sperling Breakfast

Hillary agreed. She was all for drawing a veil across their private lives at the crucial breakfast. Shaped by her twenty years at the secretive Rose Law Firm, she "showed a basic lack of understanding of the press," John Brummett, the *Arkansas Gazette* political reporter, later reflected.

Bill Clinton was aware of this—but extraordinarily loyal to Hillary as person and spouse, if not as a sexual partner. Accompanying the Clintons as they'd traveled across Arkansas, Brummett had on one occasion been tackled by Bill while Hillary slept. "You don't like Hillary, do you!" Bill had accused the hapless journalist, who hadn't denied it. "Well, let me tell you," Bill had remonstrated, the color rising in his cheeks, "Hillary's smart! She's the smartest person I have ever known in my life!"

On another occasion Brummett had even espied the couple secretly smooching on the plane while they thought Brummett was asleep. It was clear to the reporter that, whatever extramarital issues the Clintons might have, the marriage itself was still real—that while Bill deferred to his wife's extraordinary intellect, she still deferred to his physical embrace.

Could the press be trusted with such a modern, postfeminist marital arrangement, though? Would the public swallow such a complicated codependency? Hillary thought not—and thus, urged by Vernon Jordan, they decided to stonewall at the breakfast rather than take the hangout road.

The first questions, as the participants sipped Sperling's breakfast coffee and bit into the pastries, were about domestic political matters, about taxes and the economy, then about foreign affairs. Finally they came, as expected, to Bill's affairs.

"This is the sort of thing they were interested in in Rome when they were in decline," Bill pointed out, attempting to humble the journalists—predominantly men—who had their own rich histories of extramarital promiscuity.

The tactic proved a complete failure. "Those in the room continued to stare at him," Rex Nelson afterward wrote. "They wanted an answer, not a joke."

A Tour de Force

Clearly, Bill—or Hillary and Vernon—had miscalculated.

Fortunately, though Hillary might have a tin ear, Bill Clinton had magical antennae. Years later Jim Blair described his friend's astonishing intuitive ability: "Now, I have a sophisticated law practice, and I have known a lot of very successful people. And I have had two clients in my life who haven't had a lot of education [Don Tyson and Sam Walton]. One of them never finished college, the other never went to college. Both of them could read a balance sheet and tell more about it than the accountants that drew it up. And both of them made hundreds of millions of dollars. I can't explain that, 'cause I can't do that. In that framework," Blair went on, "Bill

Clinton can read a poll and tell more about it *than the people that took it*! He *knows* when a question is loaded! He *knows* when a question's not right. He *knows* when people are responding to a question, what they're trying to say. *How* he does that, I can't tell you."

Bill Clinton's empathy and ability to read people's minds and agendas were, in the hard-hearted world of high politics, truly extraordinary—and now came to his aid as, at the breakfast table, his attempt to shame the panel of journalists fell flat. Ranged around the table were newspaper reporters and columnists from *The Washington Post, The New Republic, Newsweek,* and other journals. They might each one be a personal hypocrite of the worst order—but collectively they represented constituencies of readers: voters who purchased their newspapers or magazines and would be curious to know certain things about the character of a presidential candidate. Wishing away such curiosity as irrelevant to the important "issues" facing America was naive, whatever Vernon Jordan, as a lawyer, might advise.

Hillary fell silent now as Bill returned to the previous day's prepping. It proved to be a tour de force. "I think the American people will have time to evaluate me and my character and my conduct," the governor remarked, "just the way voters have been doing for two centuries. What you need to know about me," he added, looking lovingly at Hillary beside him, "is we have been together almost twenty years and have been married almost sixteen, and we are committed to our marriage and its obligations, to our child and to each other. We love each other very much. Like nearly anybody that's been together twenty years, our relationship has not been perfect or free of difficulties. But we feel good about where we are. We believe in our obligations. And we intend to be together thirty or forty years from now, regardless of whether I run for president or not. And I think that ought to be enough."

He looked around the journalists' faces with his big smile, his shining blue eyes, his big southern heart infusing the "atmospherics" of the room. He had read their concern correctly *and given them the answer they wanted*. They were smiling back.

He was through.

Nothing Else to Say

It was now only a matter of days before Governor Clinton declared officially. Back in Little Rock, where he'd previously said he would not respond to any impertinent questions about his private life ("It's none of your business," he'd been quoted as saying, as well as accusing the press of being "the moral police of the country"), there was irritation among journalists that the governor had volunteered coded information on his marriage in Washington—information he'd denied journalists in his home state.

"I didn't volunteer anything." Bill denied the charge. "I didn't know for sure what they were going to ask," he explained in Clinton-speak—an answer avoiding an outright lie by subtle qualification. "My staff had nothing to do with that decision," he went on, bending but not travestying the truth. Inasmuch as he had decided *not* to follow Kantor's script yet had been forced to return to it once he'd seen the look on the national journalists' faces, he was telling the truth—a dramatic truth deeper than local journalists could ever know. "I have nothing else to say about this," the governor stated. "That's not what this election would be about and I have nothing else to say about it. It's not a very important thing. It's not important to most Americans. They haven't said anything to me about it. Most people in Arkansas haven't."

They would, however.

"Totally Crazy"

Jogging downtown in his running shorts in Little Rock on the morning of October 3, 1991, "Jell-O" Bill Clinton thought of the many times he'd nipped in to see Gennifer Flowers in the Quapaw Towers. Although their sexual relationship had ended in 1989, they were still friends, and they still spoke intimately on the telephone. Recently, when Geannie had asked for a job in state government, Bill had arranged it—able to dole out jobs not only to the boys, as for the past two centuries but, thanks to feminism, to the girls also. Compared with the favors dispensed by other governors and lawmakers throughout the land, it had seemed a simple and inexpensive form of gratitude—as well as insurance against future embarrassment that would surely begin the moment he mounted the special platform, or scaffold, that was being hastily erected outside the Old State House on East Markham.

Gennifer, naive and inexperienced, had always known this day would come but had no idea what ramifications it would have. John Brummett, however, had been amazed when Bill had confided to him in unforgettable words, "I think I'm gonna announce."

"I think you're totally crazy!" the veteran journalist had responded.
"Why? You don't think I can make it?"
"*Of course* I think you can make it!" Brummett had assured Clinton. "But why would you *want* to? Your life will be ripped apart, you'll be so exposed!"

Beside the Bush Colossus

While the workmen hammered at the makeshift podium, Governor Clinton had been up until the early hours of October 3, closeted with his closest advisers, crafting his tidings. The advisers did not include Betsey Wright. "I tried to get her back in the presidential campaign," David Watkins recalled, "and talked to her." But the previous month Betsey had fallen out again with Bill over his fund-raising for the DNC rather than the state Democratic Party, of which she was chairman, and she had thereupon, in disgust, resigned. "He needs to contact me and discuss my role," Betsey had replied to Watkins—but for the moment Bill was *on* a roll. He felt no need of his former nanny—especially knowing her views on whether or not he should run.

By midday nearly five thousand people had congregated outside the Old State House. CNN had arranged to broadcast the governor's announcement live, but the main terrestial channels had proved leery of giving Clinton too much play and thereby risking alienation of the Oval Office more than a year before the actual election. They had therefore decided not to televise the announcement of a minor candidate with little or no hope of winning his party's nomination, let alone dislodging a respected and popular president from his office. Even the local, deeply conservative *Arkansas Democrat* was contemptuous of Clinton's chances: "We don't for a moment believe that the Governor will see the inside of the White House this time around. George Bush bestrides next year's presidential horizon like a colossus."

"The Debris of a Broken Promise"

The *Arkansas Democrat* would, in due course, have to eat its words, but the negative sentiment was widely echoed among those who liked Bill Clinton and/or Hillary—and especially among those who didn't. "His word is dirt," Meredith Oakley, an admirer of Hillary, spat in her column, feeling betrayed. The governor was a "common, run-of-the-mill, dime-a-dozen politician" and could not be trusted. The spectacle of crowds cheering the governor's speech only irritated Oakley the more. "The bleaters who care more for celebrity than veracity are basking in a false and empty light," Ms. Oakley spat the words at her keyboard. "They trumpet the basest form of political expediency, for they revel amid the debris of a broken promise." Even Max Brantley, in the more liberal *Arkansas Gazette,* was censorious concerning the governor's broken pledge. "He can run for president," Brantley wrote. "But he can't hide from the people back home. They deserve straighter talk."

It was now no longer a matter of Arkansans' feelings, however, but of history: U.S. history. The moment had arrived: the culmination of a lifetime's dreams as, before a liberal congregation of baby boomers and enthusiasts, the governor gave a thirty-two-minute speech against the backdrop of the former state legislature building with its elegant white columns and sash windows suggesting another, even whiter house.

Fighting Words

Those who watched and listened to the speech on October 3, 1991, considered it to be one of Bill Clinton's very best. His allergies had flared up and his voice was once again hoarse, but the sentiments he expressed resonated with a new generation that looked forward to the future, and to change. "All of you, in different ways, have brought me here today, to a step beyond a life and a job I love, to make a commitment to a larger cause: preserving the American Dream, restoring the hopes of the forgotten middle class, reclaiming the future for our children," the governor announced. "I refuse to be part of the generation that celebrates the death of communism abroad with the loss of the American Dream at home. I refuse to be a part of a generation that fails to compete in the global economy and so condemns hardworking Americans to a life of struggle without reward or security. That is why I stand here today, because I refuse to stand by and let our children become part of the first generation of Americans to do worse than their parents. I don't want my child or your child to be part of a country that's coming apart instead of coming together."

These were both fighting and prophetic words. "The country is headed in the wrong direction fast, slipping behind, losing our way, and all we have out of Washington is status quo paralysis, no vision, no action, just neglect, selfishness and division," Clinton claimed. He spoke, moreover, not in a partisan spirit but as the leader of a new movement in America: a centrist movement comprising those who were tired of the internecine wars of right and left, liberal and conservative—for such divisiveness simply drew attention away from the more important issues: modernizing the American workplace, expanding trade, encouraging capitalist growth, discouraging malingering that set a poor example to the nation's youth—and investing more in education and affordable health care. Middle-class tax relief was a constant theme and, in a nation in which 80 percent of Americans saw themselves in that bracket, a popular one.

While the reaction in the newsrooms would be sour and skeptical, given President Bush's current poll ratings, in the crowd there was almost universal support: a microversion of the future. At the end of his speech the governor hugged his wife, kissed his daughter, and, to the sound of Fleetwood Mac's "Don't Stop," the grueling, grilling, historic, thirteen-month campaign now began.

CHAPTER FORTY-ONE

RETURN OF THE GENIE

The Old Paint Store

David Watkins remembered the presidential campaign's first headquarters vividly. Hoping to save money, "we discussed at one point having the headquarters in my office" in Little Rock, but the team decided it was "probably not right." They had put out a call for volunteers and fund-raisers. "I had a friend, and through him we rented the old paint store for eight hundred dollars a month, on a month-to-month rental"—lest the campaign abort at any point. "That was while they were trying to raise exploratory funds, just using three or four people and volunteers. We had a meeting—things are heating up, he's traveling a lot, and the Friday before Labor Day in '91 we have a meeting of the key people at the mansion. And Hillary, I recall, she was the one who said, 'Well, we really need an adult down at the paint store. David, would you be it for a while until Bill decides?' Well, on Clinton time that's going to be in a week. 'Sure,' I say. So on the Tuesday after Labor Day I go down to the paint store and start ordering in phones, getting more volunteers. It looks as if it's going to happen! Well, that week lasts until October 3, when he *does* announce that he's going to run for president!

"So I am running the campaign. There was some talk that Bruce Lindsey [a younger attorney who had worked with Bill Clinton in his law offices after the governor was defeated in 1980] would be the campaign manager, then there's talk that maybe I should be campaign manager. No one knew me as a politico or anyone of any political consequence, on a national basis. So they offered it to Skip Rutherford. And Skip turned it down, and I didn't want to do it. About the third week in October they finally hired David Wilhelm to be campaign manager."

Thus, in fits and starts, a national campaign fired up: a campaign that was to have profound consequences for the world, and for the individuals who were pulled aboard—many of them, in the course of the next months, years, and decade, being injured or ruined by the association against the cultural backdrop of a veritable civil war. And, like veterans of America's earlier Civil War, even those who returned from the struggle would always be scarred.

To See What Happens

Was this inevitable, given the culture wars that were finally coming to a sort of Götterdämmerung?

Only days after Bill Clinton's announcement, on October 11, 1992, the Reverend Jimmy Swaggart was pulled over by a police car in Indio, California, while driving a friend's Jaguar. As Michael Giuliano chronicled, "Inside the car were dozens of pornographic magazines, and one of the town's few prostitutes. The prostitute reported that Swaggart had picked her up, asking if she was 'working.' " Accused, the reverend refused to admit his addiction, however; instead he simply continued his Pentecostal-ist ministry, albeit canceling his "crusades" and preaching to vastly reduced telecongregations—only 39 stations carrying his broadcasts against 287 in 1988.

Swaggart's life story—in December 1995, he would again be stopped by police as he cruised up and down "the Strip" in Baton Rouge, claiming he was inspecting one of his ministry's remaining radio towers (which, unfortunately for him, had been sold a year before)—was, in its way, a paradigm for an American culture on trial, his Pentecostal drama sweeping his family and millions of adherents toward an ideal of faith while the personal foundations or props of his extraordinary success were relentlessly knocked away beneath him, as they had been in the case of Jim and Tammy Faye Bakker. The fact was, the new, postmodern, post–Cold War world now demanded but one thing, when seen *sub specie aeternitatis:* entertainment. And this Jimmy Swaggart had somehow known right from the beginning, in fact from the moment he'd fallen sick with envy of his cousin Jerry Lee Lewis, who was driving a Cadillac and pulling girls barely out of ankle socks: "Elvis Presley can have *Hound Dog,* Jerry Lee can have *Great Balls of Fire,* but I'll take the Holy Ghost and fire. Hallelujah!"

Fire, inevitably, had come. Mass entertainment, while it promised great rewards for those who prospered, had required, ever since the Minotaur ring of ancient Knossos or the gladiatorial arena of the Coliseum, victims. Performing as an entertainer like Elvis Presley or Swaggart's cousin Jerry Lee Lewis meant blazing a trail through music, drugs, sex, and celebrity. The list of those who fell in the course of feeding this public appetite for entertainment—from Jimmi Hendrix to Bob Marley, from Marilyn Monroe to Joe Orton—was becoming as long as the one on the Vietnam War Memorial, yet the cultural furnace was insatiable. Preachers and politicians might pretend they were superior to such a consuming American dynamic, but if they did so, they were being naive. Clearly, entering either the religious or the political profession was, in an age of soap opera entertainment with an insatiable public appetite for salacious gossip and a Fourth Estate licensed to report it, holding a red rag to a bull.

Disregarding the warning voices of people such as Betsey Wright and John Brummett, Bill Clinton had meanwhile obeyed the call to political arms—his vassals, liege men, retainers, hirelings, assistants, equerries, maids, stewards, and stewardesses unaware for the most part what was ahead of them.

Ironically, David Watkins—who would himself become a victim—recalled not only how modest were the organizational beginnings of the campaign but how modest were its goals. "David [Wilhelm] comes in. David is a politico who has no business knowledge, no knowledge of Arkansas, has only just met Clinton—he has no relationship with him yet. So David and I talk and I agree to stay on and run the business operations of the campaign. 'Cause the whole objective at that time is to make it as long as we can *and see what happens.* Ideally at least: hang on until the Michigan and Illinois primary, March 17, 1992. And if we hang on that long, by then probably somebody is going to be in the position to win the nomination. It will give Bill Clinton some national presence and publicity and get him ready for a *future* race. That was the objective!"

Even that limited objective appeared unlikely once the anti-Clintonites got to work, however.

Second-Line Candidates

President Bush's high poll numbers were, as it turned out, the very best possible news for Governor Clinton—for they scared off the Democratic Party's potential front-runners.

"The flight of the heavyweights from the Democratic field," as journalists Jack Germond and Jules Witcover chronicled, now "triggered the rush of second-line candidates"—among whom were Senator Paul Tsongas of Massachusetts, who had already declared in May 1991, and five more candidates who entered the starting boxes after Labor Day: Governor Doug Wilder, U.S. Senators Tom Harkin and Bob Kerrey, former Governor Jerry Brown—and Governor Bill Clinton.

Hillary Clinton was not even mentioned. But Hillary, everyone who knew anything in Arkansas was aware, was the key. A torch was being passed, yet the pundits in Washington seemed blissfully unaware of it. Like Frank White in 1982, they would get a rude shock.

Apart from the Iowa precinct caucuses—where Tom Harkin, the senator for Iowa, was bound to win as the favorite son—it would be the New Hampshire Democratic primary on February 18, 1992, that would signal the all-important initial race in the Presidential Nomination Stakes. A state small enough to ensure that candidates had to get out and canvass real people rather than rely on expensive advertising, New Hampshire was a litmus test—not least because, as a diminutive northeastern state, it was experiencing the worst of the economic recession.

For Bill Clinton, this was a perfect opportunity to demonstrate his prowess outside his home state, indeed in the North. If he and Hillary could make an impact on Democratic voters in New Hampshire who had never previously heard of them, then the Clintonistas had a real chance of applying Bill's magic right across the American tapestry. "I think when he came out in '92 to run," Bobby Roberts later reflected, "he was hell bent to *win*. And that kinda surprised me. I thought, 'Get your name out there! You're not going to beat George Bush—hell, he's at sixty-two percent positive rating! I mean, I didn't think Bill had got a chance. So I didn't take it very seriously, to be honest with you. And boy, did I misjudge that one!"

That Bill Clinton was a superlative campaigner, however, Bobby Roberts was in no doubt. Nor was David Watkins. At election tactics as well as communicating to large numbers of people, Bill Clinton was, in Watkins's view, without equal—even in comparison with his Yalie wife.

"Hillary has ideas," Watkins allowed, but she had nowhere like Bill's flair. "She was a critic, and she had some pretty good ideas. But she didn't have the sense of timing and political pulse that he did. Some people have it—I mean, he's a genius at that, he's a genius during a campaign. He had wonderful, wonderful political instincts related to a campaign, to running. And I think that's when he was happiest, as evidenced by his gubernatorial years. As far as governing, he did not have the same genius and some of the instincts that he has for campaigning. But no one's ever been better at campaigning. It's like seeing a great golfer, I would say, you know: you're seeing genius! Tiger Woods is terrific; he's head and shoulders above who's in second place. Bill Clinton's that way in a political campaign."

Bill's genius was, once again, his range—and his vision. He might mess up, as at the 1988 nominating convention, but such failures took place within an overall approach that could now encompass the odd, even repeated, setback. Like Ronald Reagan, he had consciously and unconsciously developed a mythology of self, one that allowed him to play the role of patient, dedicated baby-boomer agent of change in America: change that would not alienate or repel but would embrace Americans in a larger agenda—his so-called New Covenant.

Clinton's three speeches given at Georgetown University during the fall of 1991 had encouraged Washingtonians to witness at first hand the governor's grasp both of international and domestic issues; his speeches to the National Democratic Committee's executive meeting in September 1991 and some weeks later at the Association of Democratic State Chairs in Chicago, had, however, been masterly. Senator Harkin attributed the laudatory press accounts of such speeches as the work of Clinton's new spinmeister and campaign manager, David Wilhelm—"Wilhelm," Harkin memorably sneered, "got into my knickers big"—but the reporters sensed what Harkin did not: that Clinton's centrist message would tear a gaping hole in President Bush's otherwise impregnable citadel if the economy didn't pick up. Bush was now sixty-seven and had no clear economic program for recovery, let alone reducing the yawning national deficit. Among Democrats, Senator Harkin's liberal credentials were impeccable, and he was strong on medical insurance policy plans; beside Clinton, however, he looked a one-tune player, while Clinton seemed a veritable polymath. In Florida in December, the Clinton team spent $50,000 in a demonstration of his organizational strength alongside his stump skills. It was money well spent. Clinton's victory in the straw poll at the Florida State Democratic

Convention in Lake Buena Vista had resulted in an immediate infusion of further funding; indeed, his campaign war chest, after Florida, was rumored to be swelling by $700,000 *a week* in contributions. Clinton's form seemed so strong, in fact, that Senator Bob Kerrey's aides recommended that the Vietnam hero drop out of the straw-vote running altogether, lest he be shamed into last place.

David Watkins, as Clinton's business manager, was certainly proud of the ratio of spending to income during the campaign. "In so many campaigns you almost never match your incoming funds with what you spend—that had certainly always been the case." The cash flow of the 1992 campaign, by contrast, "was terrific—and I did that!" Watkins justly congratulated himself. "I signed every check, I knew where every dollar was! And that was as important as being able to have media dollars to spend on 'Super Tuesday' "—the day in March 1992 when eleven states would hold their primaries all at once.

In the meantime, as the New Hampshire primary approached in January 1992, all voting eyes were on Harkin, Kerrey, Tsongas—and the man from Hope. A man who, to the shock of liberals, had recently refused to show clemency to Rickey Ray Rector, a mentally impaired multiple murderer on death row in Arkansas.

The First Sacrifice

Some critics claimed that Governor Clinton acted purely out of political expediency—another example of "Slick Willie" at work: a man without principle whose word could not be trusted. But Bobby Roberts, Clinton's gubernatorial aide who dealt with the Department of Corrections, and Ernie Dumas, the legendary *Arkansas Gazette* political editor, later both acknowledged that Clinton had always supported the death penalty, since the 1970s. "Even when he was attorney general," Ernie Dumas recalled Steve Smith telling him, "they had this discussion about the death penalty, and Clinton said: 'Oh, no! I'm for the death penalty!' 'What? You're for the death penalty?' " Smith had queried, stunned. "And Clinton said—this is as close as you'll ever get to his political ideology—Smith said Clinton was adamant about it. ' *Yes!* Staunch supporter of the death penalty.' "

Dumas was correct. The Supreme Court's ruling on the constitutionality of capital punishment in 1986, for example, had been openly welcomed by Governor Clinton, in a statement to the press, as "the right decision." "I support our capital punishment law," he'd been quoted as saying, "and believe that it should be carried out in appropriate cases." As governor, he'd explained, his policy was "to set execution dates within 30 days of receiving a mandate from the appropriate court." Since then three convicted multiple murderers had been executed in Arkansas without clemency; the second had killed *fourteen* members of his own family. It was the execution of the fourth, Rickey Ray Rector, however, that posed a special problem in January 1992, as the New Hampshire primary approached.

Ten years before, Rector had mercilessly shot three men at a party in Conway, thirty miles from Little Rock, then killed the policeman who came to arrest him—shooting himself in the head thereafter and suffering such severe brain injuries that it became questionable whether he could stand trial. Sentenced to death and kept on death row for a decade, the Board of Corrections, the lieutenant governor, Jim Guy Tucker, and the Supreme Court had all ultimately recommended execution without clemency, but it was Bill Clinton, as governor, who had the last word. "We've talked about the death penalty since law school," Hillary explained to reporters. "We go back and forth on the issue of due process and the disproportionate number of minorities facing the death penalty, and we have serious concerns in those areas. We also abhor the craze for the death penalty. But we believe it does have a role."

Ignoring the potential backlash from liberals opposed to the death penalty, Governor Clinton's decision had been straightforward, given Rector's multiple killings while still compos mentis: "Die."

Many such liberal Democrats deplored Clinton's decision, seeing it as politically motivated: a sop to the Right. Certainly, to have exercised clemency for a black multimurderer in the midst of an election campaign would have seemed a sop to the Left, while providing ammunition to the armies of the Right, who were now known to be moving to attack and tar him with the same Willie Horton brush that had destroyed Dukakis. Rightly or wrongly, it revived journalist Paul Greenberg's question as to Bill Clinton's moral courage—but on the wrong issue.

Authorizing the execution of a black multiple murderer on January 24, 1992 (despite candlelight protest vigils outside the governor's mansion in Little Rock), was, however, only the first major hurdle of the campaign in New Hampshire. The next would involve a white female—a woman whom Bill Clinton had himself seduced, bedded, employed, and engaged in playful badinage over a period of twelve years, regardless of risk; a petite, blowsy-haired, big-bosomed, musically gifted ex-Republican: Gennifer Flowers.

"A Jingle Irony"

David Watkins vividly remembered the Gennifer Flowers fiasco. "It's a Sunday night, Clinton's dropping off a lot of the deadweight, and we have a strategy meeting, he's been about, campaigning. And he makes a statement to me—I'm not one of the guys, I don't do much of the talking at these meetings, I'm observing, I'm the operations guy, but I'm there because I'm a Clintonite too. And he feels comfortable with me—I have a longtime association. And he looks at me in this meeting, and he says, 'David—don't let these sons of bitches do this to you. Don't let 'em do it to you!' It was a crisis: 'Don't let them!' It wasn't *his* fault. It's always 'them.' "

Psychologically, this pattern of denial of personal responsibility was all too understandable, given Bill Clinton's childhood and upbringing. Indeed, it was a miracle, as Bobby Roberts maintained, that Bill had not turned out like his brother, Roger. But there was another reason for such refusal to bear responsibility for mess-up or failure: survival. As in Shakespeare's *Henry IV,* Bill Clinton's wayward life as a President in waiting was now coming to its climax. He had finally to show his mettle, on a national stage. And as Prince Hal had felt forced to deny Falstaff on his coronation as King Henry V, so Bill Clinton had to reject the fun-loving, wayward companion of his Arkansas years: Gennifer.

The beginning of this great act of public denial went back to the fall of 1991, when Gennifer, who'd been given a job as a supervisor on the Arkansas Appeals Tribunal on the instructions of the governor, was called to give evidence at a grievance committee hearing—since Charlette Perry, a black woman who'd been with the tribunal for five years and was well qualified for the post, had objected to Gennifer's hiring. Although Gennifer knew she'd gotten the job as a favor, it didn't worry her at all. This was, after all, the way things were done in America—in Arkansas just as it had been in LBJ's Texas or JFK's Massachusetts. When Ms. Perry filed a grievance, however, Gennifer became agitated—for it would mean she would have to appear before an investigative committee in the fall. "I called Bill in a panic," she related, unwilling to perjure herself. Bill, however, was unperturbed—indeed in his element. "Don't worry, Don [Barnes, head of the appeals agency] will take care of it."

Barnes, however, was overruled by the grievance committee—which decided in Ms. Perry's favor. Again, the governor told Gennifer not to worry: that Barnes had veto power over the committee's finding. "Don't worry about it," Gennifer was advised. Fortunately Ms. Perry backed off, considering that discretion might be the better part of valor. Nor had she sued for racial discrimination. Nevertheless the business had left a nasty taste—and once Governor Clinton ratcheted up the stakes by declaring he would run for the presidency, Gennifer had become fearful again. The rules of engagement—or protection—were changing. In Arkansas Clinton had been for almost a decade the governor, or king. As a presidential contender on a national stage, however, he knew he would be vulnerable to smears and investigations over which he would have little or no control.

Gennifer—who'd begun tape-recording their telephone conversations in case Bill double-crossed her—was initially pleased for him, so much so, in fact, that the fall of 1991, she had actually approached the campaign headquarters, not with a request for hush money but with a jingle. After all, Rat Packer Frank Sinatra had sung a widely used Kennedy campaign lyric to the catchy tune of "Rubbertree Plant"—why not a Gennifer Flowers' song?

"Back in his presidential primary campaign—it's sometime in that fall [of 1991]—I'd heard of Gennifer Flowers," Watkins recounted, "but then, I'm not a gossipmonger, those things don't interest me. A lot of talk of things happening—I've heard her name, and I'd heard some gossip of her connection with Bill Clinton. But she comes to the campaign! She comes and"—Watkins frowned, searching his memory for the details—"I don't know if somebody through Bill—or *he* called—or had someone call or say we oughtta see her, or *I* should see her, to listen. . . . Anyway, she had a jingle that she wanted to sell to the presidential campaign!"

Watkins paused, his friendly face breaking into a broad smile at the recollection. "Right! Well, I met with her, and two or three other people she brought with her. And this jingle was *awful,* in my opinion! And I turned her down! And I wondered later, had we bought that jingle, if things would have changed! That was November or December—early on, after he had decided to run. An irony! A jingle irony!"

The Second Sacrifice

Was Watkins right? If the campaign had purchased Gennifer's jingle and paid mush rather than hush money, might the whole Flowers scandal never have arisen?

The real irony, however, was that without Gennifer's histrionics, Bill Clinton might never have become President—for it was, paradoxically, the raising of the issue, and the manner in which Bill and Hillary Clinton dealt with it, that would allow the co-candidates finally to meet the nineties head-on, in all its postmodern, hodgepodge, soap opera craziness. Republicans hoping thereby to destroy the Democrats' most potent contender for the presidency would receive a rude, indeed devastating shock. The co-candidates, Bill and Hillary Clinton, would be winded, stagger, reel against the ropes, and hit the canvas—but they would not stay down for the count. Getting up, *they would look stronger than ever,* benefiting from the national—indeed, international—interest that the scandal, thanks to conservatives' and Republicans' wiles, had injected into the Democratic primary campaign.

"Regarding Gennifer Flowers," Bobby Roberts later commented, "let me say two things. One is, it made him a *household word.* So that wasn't so bad.

"And two, his *ability to overcome it* was tremendous, you know."

"Fish or Cut Bait"

The former aide, who later became director of Little Rock's main library and archives, looked for a moment out of his window at the downtown streets of the capital, and to the south, where an unsightly ramp rose to the main interstate highway.

"You know, you walk up to the ledge and you're not really going to jump over, you've got your parachute on, you're not really going to jump over. Then some son of a bitch shoves you over the edge, and then you've got to go. Once the Gennifer Flowers story got out, he had no choice! And I'm not saying he wasn't trying to win the presidency, but I have a sneaking suspicion that their strategy was 'Let's do as well as we can. Let's show what a bright young candidate I am, and when George Bush gets reelected, we will take his successor out in '96,' is what they really had in mind. But once the Flowers story got out, it was, as we say here in the South, fish or cut bait."

In other words, a campaign that had begun as a testing of the waters, with little to lose and much to gain, had suddenly turned into a matter of political life or death. Once Gennifer came clean, there was no going back. The soap opera of the nineties constantly required new actors, new color—the gaudier, the better—and fresh scripts. Politics, in this sense, was like evolution in the natural world: mutations spawning new variants, better adapted and able to amuse the operatic market, while bringing for the political performers the very thing they most sought: higher ratings.

Just as scientific observers of evolution were compelled to wonder at the sheer richness of mutant design in nature, so observers of American politics now watched, spellbound, as the overture to the grand postmodern political opera of the 1990s, was played—and in Act I a blond bombshell, a gifted and alluring singer, exploded onto stage.

Loud Rumour

William Shakespeare, in the second part of *Henry IV,* had posed the matter of scandal inimitably, asking his audience to "Open your ears; for which of you will stop / The Vent of hearing when loud Rumour speaks?"

Which indeed? This was the moment Clinton campaign workers had dreaded. John F. Kennedy, when confronted over his rampant promiscuity during the 1960 campaign and the possible harm it might do if exposed by reporters, had countered, "You want Richard Nixon to be your president?" Reporters at that time did not—and the stories of the presidential candidate's colorful love life duly went unrecorded by the press in his lifetime. But 1992 was different.

"I guess they hate us more than we hate them," Bill would sigh one day, talking to Jim Blair. "They" were Republicans. Certainly there were now, in the nineties, no campaign punches pulled or quarter given. If Democratic rivals would not bring the Clintons down, Republican strategists counseled, then Republicans must do the dirty work. Gennifer Flowers had known for some time to what lengths they would go. "I even received anonymous threats on the phone." Clinton, when declaring for the presidency, had "warned me again that our relationship would be scrutinized," she recounted, but had told her simply to lie. "Just deny everything" had been his instruction. They don't have any proof, and if you say it isn't true, they can't prove a thing."

Scrutiny was one thing, however, but dollar bills were another. Ron Fuller, a Republican legislator in Little Rock who was close to the Bush campaign, had called her, after Clinton's announcement, and had assured her he had friends in the Republican Party willing to pay her $50,000 just to confess she'd slept with Governor Clinton, without having to give any further details.

That politics in the nineties had descended to such a level was a dire reflection on the modern political process in the world's one remaining superpower after the fall of the Soviet Union. American democracy had, however, always been beaten out on the anvil of public debate, often fueled by scandal—indeed, it was the very modus operandi that made American democracy so vibrant compared to its paler, more circumscribed, cap-doffing European counterparts. The great themes, issues, and variations on postwar society, from pop music to civil rights, Vietnam to gay rights, drugs to feminism, had been played out in public media dramas, usually televised and giving rise to media frenzies that embarrassed Europeans, who found the process tacky.

It was. Yet for all this, it engaged the entire populace of the United States, from taxi drivers to churchgoers and scientists. Everyone in America had an opinion—on Lorena Bobbitt, the Kennedy rape trial in Palm Beach, the Clarence Thomas–Anita Hill sexual harassment scandal. . . . However sordid or scandalous the revelations might be in relation to each "trial"—a macho marine's penis severed and thrown away; arguably enforced inter-course on a Florida beach; a pubic hair supposedly left on a can of Coke in a senior government official's office—the exposure of such issues amounted to public or media trials in which a postmodern society constantly re-hearsed its prejudices and knee-jerk reactions and was forced by public clamor and discussion to review them. Justice was not always seen to be done—Bobbitt's penis was reinstated, despite the former marine's wife-bashing ways; yet another millionaire Kennedy was acquitted; Clarence Thomas, despite credible allegations of sexual harassment and a more than passing interest in pornography, was successfully appointed to the Supreme Court—but in the process Americans celebrated the value of free speech and the rights of lesser individuals to be heard, even if they were not ulti-mately validated. Anita Hill had, in Senate Judiciary hearings in October 1991, come to appreciate the savagery of the political system when her honor and integrity were deliberately trashed to ensure the promotion of President Bush's nominee. "It has become," she afterward acknowledged of the efforts to stop her from telling the truth in public, but also the symbolic nature of the effort, "bigger than Thomas—it's a crusade"—a political, gender, and cultural battlefield in which the participants' lives would irrev-ocably be altered, but as part of a social drama, a clash of cultures, conser-vative versus liberal. Testifying for only a part of a single day, October 11, 1991—the same day the Reverend Jimmy Swaggart was caught with a car full of pornography and a prostitute—Anita Hill had walked into a mael-strom—"a terrible experience" that left her psychologically ravaged and her career—despite a million-dollar book contract—effectively ruined.

The warning signs were thus plain to see. Individuals were mere pawns in a postmodern world: a jungle in which there was, as Anita Hill commented, no remaining "integrity in this whole context." Later, her bitterest denouncer, the journalist David Brock, would admit to having portrayed Anita Hill as a "deranged liar" specifically in order to "belong" to the young Republican "movement" by allowing himself to be "a perfect—and perfectly willing—instrument for the wishes of others." This, however, he would see in retrospect. At the time, as in the feeding frenzy of the televangelist scandals of the late eighties, the opera had to go on—and thus, inevitably and inexorably, "loud Rumour" of marital infidelity on the part of the charismatic Democratic front-runner in New Hampshire's looming primary was turned into an allegation with which to destroy him—that the charismatic governor had a mistress.

"Better Off Dead"

Governor Bill Clinton had hoped to keep Gennifer Flowers sweet after they had ceased having intercourse by getting her a state job, keeping her in it, and placing occasional phone calls in which, as her ex-lover, he would confide his most vexed political thoughts.

Did Clinton really think this postsexual attention would be enough to shield Gennifer from Republican predations? Hearing her story of a Republican dirty tricks offer, Bill asked if she would sign an affadavit that she'd been approached by someone acting on behalf of the Republican Party, but Gennifer balked—unsure whether, having turned down so much Republican money, she wished to be the political pawn of a Democrat who employed her, yet no longer had any rights to her heart, body, or tongue. She wanted, in other words, to remain independent.

The noose, though, was tightening, however much Bill Clinton hoped it wouldn't. One day the receptionist at the Flaming Arrow club (where Gennifer sang on certain evenings) told her that a reporter from *The Washington Post* was looking for her. The national press was clearly sniffing the air, like bloodhounds. Soon the *Dallas Morning News* joined the hunt, as well as TV sleuth-sleaze programs *Inside Edition* and *A Current Affair*—the latter all too appropriately named. Gennifer's mother, recovering from breast cancer surgery, was phoned in Missouri by a man who issued a scarcely veiled threat to Gennifer's well-being: "You should be real proud of your daughter. She'd be better off dead."

This was no idle warning; the list of beatings, suicides, and even murders of people connected with Bill Clinton would, over the years, become alarmingly long. Some connections were tenuous, to say the least, but others were more worrying. As in the case of the Boston Irish Kennedy mafia during the heyday of JFK and RFK, the candidate was surrounded not only by state troopers but by tiers of less visible staff: sponsors and supporters who, like Henry II's barons, were all too willing to rid the candidate of any potential threat—and willing to go to any lengths to do so. In this respect, Clinton was following a well-trodden path. Marilyn Monroe's suicide remained shrouded with mystery, thirty years later, as did JFK's assassination. In a world where Martin Luther King, Jr., John Lennon, Andy Warhol, Ronald Reagan, and Pope John Paul II had all been shot, attempts at assassination might be random—or not. She was, she recalled, becoming aware of the mortal, battering, and other fates that met many of those who defied or drew the wrath of Governor Clinton and his barons. However vague the stories, a host of articles and books would attest that she was not alone in this realization. People were not only threatened but could wind up—like the man falsely accused of raping a Clinton cousin— without testicles and in prison, or even dead, if they stepped out of line. Democratic stalwarts and "spinners" would dismiss such accounts as Republican concoctions, but the professional ruin and blood in all too many of them was real, whether or not the ultimate source was Clinton.

During his presidency, Clinton toyed with the idea of appointing an official biographer of himself, in the same way that Edmund Morris had been invited to sit in on White House meetings and write the official biography of Ronald Reagan. Clinton therefore invited the historian Taylor Branch, who'd worked with him on the McGovern campaign in the 1970s, to come and discuss the idea, indeed to rehearse salient episodes in his life for either a biography or autobiography. The result was disappointing. Clinton "tried to have him come once a week, I don't know how well that panned out, I only know there were a number of times when I was there when Taylor was also there, and tried to go over Bill's version of reality," Jim Blair later recalled. Like Branch, Blair was amazed at Bill's reconstruction of his past. "Although he does have an almost photographic memory, does he have the ability to remember things differently than the way they really happened? *Yes, he does!*" Blair noted emphatically. "My mentor in the law practice was that way. Unfortunately, I think I have a love for reality that doesn't let me do that—and it bothers me when other people do it." Whether, and if so to what extent,

Bill Clinton was aware of these murders, intimidations, and machinations may never be known.

Over the coming years, thousands and ultimately millions of people would become bothered by it. "Hey, somebody could have a tape-recording or a video of a speech he'd given where he had said something, and he would say, 'I didn't say that!' Well, *of course he said it. I was there. I heard* it! But he would convince himself that he hadn't said it," Blair scoffed indignantly, for he loved Bill Clinton—as did Bobby Roberts, Bill's longtime aide, who in his thoughtful analysis of his former boss had lamented this "character flaw," that "he's not quite dependable. His word's not quite good."

Money at the Root of Political Evil

With the stakes becoming so high—the presidency of the world's most powerful country—there was every reason, however, for lies, evasion, and skullduggery. From the Hell's Angels to the Triads, the Mafia to the cartels, America's underworld operated in a complex weave of menace, violence, threat, and homicide—and politics was inevitably involved and interwoven in such dealings. Dan Lasater had originally been introduced to Clinton by Governor Jimmy Carter. Clinton's connection with Lasater, convicted cocaine distributor and drug trafficker, whom Clinton had already pardoned as Arkansas governor in 1990, was a typical example of the inner machinations of power—as was his connection to Lasater's chief executive, Patsy Thomasson, erstwhile aide to Arkansas congressman Wilbur Mills, whose career had ended in scandal. Thomasson had held power of attorney over Lasater's entire drug money–laundering empire while Lasater was briefly imprisoned—yet was subsequently made executive secretary of the Arkansas Democratic Party! From all Lasater employees Ms. Thomasson enforced mandatory $500 minimum contributions to Clinton's campaign funds—and in due course would be promoted to a senior position in the White House, as *éminence grise.*

Among Republicans, the same nefarious networking and skullduggery went on. President Bush, a multimillionaire, had been head of the CIA and controlled a network of loyalists with access to vast campaign contributions—as had every previous president. JFK's campaigns had been largely financed by a multimillionaire father whose financial dealings had always been secretive and often shady, as well as reputedly, on occasion, mob-related. Yet even JFK, scion of such a shady house, had had to think twice during his electoral fight before asking Senator Lyndon Johnson to become his running mate lest LBJ be exposed for complicity in *murder.*

Lyndon Johnson's electoral victories and finances had always been suspicious, as one of his biographers, Robert Dallek, later chronicled. "His victory in 1948, when he had defeated former governor Coke Stevenson for the Democratic Senate nomination by eighty-seven votes, was particularly suspect. There were also questions about the Johnson family fortune," Dallek added. "Many folks wondered how a career politician could have accumulated radio, television, real estate, and bank holdings worth nearly $15 million. The Johnsons' 414-acre ranch in Texas, with a 6500-foot landing strip for two planes, and a sumptuous mansion in northwest Washington, 'The Elms,' purchased in 1961 from Perle Mesta, the 'hostess with the mostest,' added to the speculation. Although Johnson had cut numerous corners, engaged in various improprieties, and committed legal transgressions to win elections and become rich, he had escaped prosecution by cleverly obscuring his actions."

Politics, then, was an intrinsically dirty game: a continuous battle for office, a war in which cash was both grease and gunpowder. Money might be the root of all evil, but without it, power was unattainable—and unmaintainable. Even in those societies that eschewed money, or private money, such as the anticapitalist Soviet Union, society had fared no better in consequence. Indeed, the Soviet Union had now finally collapsed under its own lies, its exclusive Party member privileges, and its failure to deliver the comforts and entertainment people wanted. However flawed, American democracy was the best that Americans could come up with. In the main it worked—and for this reason, among others, it did not pay to peer too closely at its contradictions and imperfections.

The same, in a way, might be said—indeed *was* said—for monogamy: the next trial on Bill Clinton's journey.

Flaming Angel

"Be careful and just deny everything," Bill had told Gennifer— that as long as she did that, they'd be fine and dandy.

They weren't—indeed she was facing ruin in terms of her singing engagements. When her home in the Florence Place Apartments, to which she'd moved when she left the Quapaw Towers, was burglarized, she called Bill. Under increasing siege from investigative journalists, she now lost her singing engagement at the Flaming Angel, where the owner, anxious about reporters scaring away his more adulterous clients, asked Gennifer not to come back. At her apartment she found her place deftly ransacked. "So somebody broke into your apartment?" Bill asked disingenuously when she told him. "Somebody had gone through all your stuff? . . . You think they were trying to look for something on us? . . . You weren't missing any, any kind of papers or anything? . . . Well I mean did . . . any kind of personal records, or checkbooks or anything like that? . . . Phone records?" When Gennifer innocently asked if her own telephone records could be used to trace calls, Bill said "Yeah."

Gennifer was understandably perplexed. Did Bill already know of the break-in? *Had he ordered it?* Was this all a kind of domestic Watergate? Ironically, Hillary had used Nixon's audiotapes, with their suspicious "accidental" erasures, to incriminate the President and ensure his impeachment; now Gennifer was, for her own protection, using a tape recorder to ensure that Bill Clinton, Hillary's husband, and his circle could not have *her* erased.

Gennifer asked what Bill could do to help "if I decide I want to get the heck out of here"—meaning Little Rock. His words recorded on the turning tape, Bill nobly responded, "All you need to do is to let me know . . . I'll help you."

But how? How, in the midst of a presidential primary campaign, could Governor Clinton help Ms. Flowers without incriminating himself in the eyes of the scandalmongers?

Gennifer assumed that Clinton, complacent after almost twelve years of governing the state of Arkansas, was still under the impression he could have his way in all things, even defy gravity. If so, he was naive. He couldn't; indeed, the more his chances of winning the primary in New Hampshire rose, the more desperate his opponents would·become to fell him.

Cuomo Drops Out

Day by day as he campaigned across the Granite State and met voters face-to-face, Bill Clinton's chances of winning the primary improved. To Clinton's immense relief, Mario Cuomo had announced just before Christmas, on December 20, 1991, that he wouldn't run. "Most people think, you know, that except for Cuomo, I'm doing the best right now," Bill had told Gennifer in another taped conversation. "We're leading in the polls in Florida," he'd explained, but "Cuomo's at 87 percent name recognition," he'd acknowledged enviously, "and I have 54 percent so . . . I mean . . . I'm at a terrible disadvantage in name recognition still, but we're coming up."

With Cuomo finally and formally out, Bill now came up even faster. Indeed, by mid-January 1992, he was, according to Frank Greer's latest poll, more than ten points ahead of his nearest rival, Senator Paul Tsongas of Massachusetts, who was battling cancer and in all probability would not be nominated, yet had to be beaten for historical reasons. No presidential victor had ever *not* won New Hampshire's primary.

If reporters succeeded in getting to Gennifer and exposing an adulterous relationship, however, Bill Clinton would in all probability be torpedoed and sunk. Keeping Gennifer silent and out of Republican evildoers' way was thus essential.

Theft of Videotape

Would a prior confession of past adultery—a decision to own up to his sexuality and attractiveness to modern women, who liked a man who was "not intimidated by women who have a career"—have inoculated Bill Clinton against scandalous revelations in the campaign, as Gennifer later maintained?

Gennifer was not alone in thinking this. Bill Clinton's own advisers had, by a clear majority, favored early confession of past sins in order to get the subject out of the way. The admission of past infidelity at the Sperling Breakfast had gone some way toward this, with "no pretense, no hypocrisy." Beyond this, however, the Clintons had decided to run on issues and a political plan for addressing the domestic ills of recession and community in America. Once their political message was conveyed and a major primary victory was under their belt, Bill and Hillary Clinton argued, further revelations of actual past peccadilloes would look trite and Republican-inspired.

Thus it was that Bill might well have approved, perhaps even deliberately ordered, the ransacking of Gennifer's apartment before others—especially Republicans—could lay their hands on the innocent woman's crucial records. Gary Johnson, a neighbor who'd videotaped Clinton arriving at and departing from the parking lot of the Quapaw Towers—much as

Jimmy Swaggart had been videotaped visiting Debra Murphree in 1988—had, for example, been given the shakedown treatment: "visited" by thugs who broke into Johnson's apartment and smashed him almost to death, demanding to know where "the tape" was. Afterward, there was no sign of it.

Johnson had been foolish enough to let it be known he had such a tape. Gennifer was nowhere near as smart as Bill—but she was not stupid, either. To Bill she pretended to have no idea about such things as telephone records—but she took care to store the precious audiotapes of her conversations elsewhere. Bill, meanwhile, instructed her to lie about her state job—"If they ask you if you've talked to me about it, you can say no"—but Gennifer grew more and more apprehensive. She didn't think her lover was capable or willing to have her silenced, but wondered about his underlings and patrons. Complete denial, according to Bill, would lead back to peace and quiet, once reporters lost interest in the story. But would it? Bill was still behaving in his age-old manner: "so brazen I thought he believed himself to be bulletproof," Gennifer commented—aware that national journalists would not be so mealy-mouthed as those from the governor's home state.

She was right—for the better Bill did in the Democratic primaries, and the worse Bush, whose approval ratings were plummeting as the recession refused to bottom out, performed in Republican primaries, the more, not less, interest there would inevitably be in Bill Clinton the man—especially among worried Republicans.

The Star Threat

Ultimately it was the supermarket tabloid *The Star,* searching for smut, that hit pay dirt. For a mere $200 its salacious reporter got hold of Gennifer's unlisted phone number via an unsuspecting friend and proceeded to blackmail her. The journal intended, they informed her on the telephone, after taking unauthorized secret photos of her in the tribunal parking lot, to publish allegations of an affair with Bill Clinton, illustrated with the photos.

Instead of simply ignoring the threat, her attorney, having spoken to the tabloid's editor, recommended they fly to New York and counterthreaten a lawsuit—or broker a deal. Gennifer later claimed she had called Bill Clinton before she left but that he hadn't called back. (Two messages from Clinton were, however, later found on her answering machine.) "A lot of people will hate me for doing this," she confessed, "and to tell the truth, I feel sick to my stomach when I try to imagine what Bill thinks of me." She was, she claimed, done with "the deceit, the ducking and hiding from everybody"—indeed she'd called her family "before I decided to talk and I have their support. It's time to think of the future and get on with the rest of my life." She would, she felt, be liberated—able, after twelve long years of adultery and lying "to take off my dark glasses and face the world."

Doubtless this was true—though it overlooked the lure of considerable lucre. The fact was, this was modern America, where loyalty no longer predominated at work or at home and where the struggle for personal survival, in a recession, overrode all higher fidelity. To a now-middle-aged nightclub singer who had lost her job thanks to media hounds and held a day job only on the say-so of a governor who would be leaving Arkansas if he won the presidential election, the lure of significant money—or rather, the protection, for a single woman, that only money could buy—proved too much, as it already had for Jessica Hahn and Debra Murphree—and would for Paula Jones. The fact was, the dollar talked in elective politics as it talked in most other walks of American life, especially the news and entertainment industry. With her apartment being ransacked and telephone threats being made on her safety and life, selling her story to the tabloids seemed a good way not only to improve her bank balance (which was down to $1,000, she later claimed) but to raise her public profile to the point where she could not be quietly beaten up or even "erased." Had Clinton owned up to the affair already in 1990, when a certain Larry Nichols had briefly made public his allegations of a relationship, none of this would have happened, she later claimed. "I knew the wisest course for me was to come clean," she related, for "her days in Little Rock" were "over. Clubs won't book me." Had Bill allowed her to confess her sins, he too could have been saved. Instead, "he lied"— forcing them both to totter toward even greater shame and revelations.

Anything But a Snob

Gennifer's view overlooked, however, the American double bind of the 1980s and '90s: that, as columnist Mary McGrory would shortly point out, "women who wish to be modern and sophisticated about the Sixth Commandment still wonder if their husbands might misread their enlightenment for a generalized tolerance for roaming," quoting a young wife as saying, "I certainly wouldn't want Tom to get any idea that it would be okay for him."

American politicians were thus caught in the vise of a collective contradiction—and any voluntary confession of adultery would fall foul of that vise. For any serious politician posing as a leader in society, to have bucked such hypocrisy directly was to court political suicide. As *The New York Times* later put it, the fall of Senator Hart marked the moment when the power of the press to invade a politician's privacy was triumphantly demonstrated—"the moment when the boundaries between private and political lives came crashing down forever."

With Hart's slaughter, the press felt licensed to poke wherever they pleased. Four years after the Hart scandal, discretion over such matters was not an option for politicians, then, but a necessity.

In Gennifer Flowers's experience, however, the very opposite held true. Her very *life* was now and forever threatened, given Bill Clinton's bid for the presidency—and only by going public could she perhaps avoid violence, even murder. There was no going back to a life of privacy, whatever Bill Clinton might assure her in the way of "help." From obscurity she would therefore be forced to leap into a sort of stardom, like Hahn, Murphree, and others before her—tacky, perhaps, but then, Gennifer Flowers was anything but a snob. Moreover, the money, as a thousand would-be stars, starlets in Hollywood, or entertainers and models in New York had found, was enticing. Thus she flew to the Big Apple and in the less-than-imposing conference room of *Star* magazine was faced with a mocked-up forthcoming edition of the illustrated supermarket checkout journal—starring herself.

High Noon

The headline took Gennifer's breath away: DEM'S FRONT-RUNNER BILL CLINTON CHEATED WITH MISS AMERICA AND FOUR OTHER BEAUTIES—A FORMER MISS ARKANSAS, A SINGER, A REPORTER AND HIS OWN PRESS SPOKESWOMAN, the headline screamed. Inside, there were the parking-lot photographs of Gennifer and an interview, with photograph, of the Quapaw Tower manager, who confirmed having seen the governor arriving for his trysts.

Any notion of legal injunctions went out the window. Gennifer gave in. "I did not call Bill," she later confessed. "He was powerful in Arkansas, but his influence didn't reach much beyond the state line, so I didn't think there was anything he could do. Besides," she added, "I was pretty sure any advice he might give me would be in *his* best interest, not mine."

It was high noon, or gunfight on New York's OK Corral set, in the gathering new soap opera that would run for the next ten years. For $100,000 and the inevitable cold-shouldering by her appalled boyfriend Finis Shelnutt, Gennifer sold her intimate story—and, without realizing it, made Bill Clinton President of the United States.

Shit Hits the Fans

At the Clinton campaign headquarters, the prematurely balding, bullet-headed James Carville was bored. Carville and Paul Begala, his political strategist partner, had run Peace Corps founder Harris Wofford's special Senate campaign in the fall of 1991—helping him win it in a surprise victory against the former Republican governor of Pennsylvania and attorney general of the United States, Dick Thornburgh. Georgia governor Zell Miller had therefore highly recommended the pair to Governor Clinton, and in the absence of Dick Morris and Betsey Wright, Bill had duly taken them on as "consultants," along with a young deputy campaign manager for communications, George Stephanopoulos, who had considered working for Republican George Bush in 1979. Instead, Stephanopoulos had become a Democratic congressional legislative assistant as floor man to Dick Gephardt, the leader of the House of Representatives.

Carville was a man in the mold of Lee Atwater: an ex-marine taking no prisoners. He found the candidate so natural a campaigner and fund-raiser that he accepted the hiring, but then he found himself idle during the first weeks of the New Hampshire skirmish. Governor Cuomo's decision not to run had removed the one rival who would have challenged Clinton intellectually, politically, and in the field of battle. Senator Kerrey was a Vietnam hero but without a message; former senator Tsongas was local but underfunded; Senator Harkin was an old-style liberal; former California governor Jerry Brown's message was uninspiring. Clinton, by contrast, promised a middle-class tax cut, change, and a new, centrist confidence in America's future. His intelligence, fluency, and energy made him such an obvious winner that Carville's only job, as Betsey Wright's had been in 1982, was to help narrow the candidate's message to a few chosen topics that would define and distinguish him from the others. "What I need most of all from you guys is focus, is clarity. I don't know how to bring it down, to condense it," Bill had explained. This achieved, Carville watched Clinton's polls soar above the competition; indeed, by January 19, 1992, Clinton, according to

The Boston Globe, had led the pack with 29 percent against Tsongas's 17 and Kerrey's 16. The nomination seemed almost indecently assured.

Until, on January 23, 1992, the proverbial shit hit Bill Clinton's fan.

The Onslaught

> *. . . Rumour is a pipe*
> *Blown by surmises, jealousies, conjectures;*
> *And of so easy and so plain a stop*
> *That the blunt monster with uncounted heads,*
> *And the still-discordant wavering multitude,*
> *Can play upon it.*

As James Carville recalled, "there were rumors" aplenty long before the Flowers explosion, for the more Bill Clinton dominated the race for the Democratic Party nomination, the more reporters had descended on Little Rock, hunting for material to "flesh out" the man who would be president. "Reports of past affairs between the governor and various women had come up," Carville recounted, "and been explained away—'Oh, man, this is the same crap we've been hearing down here in Arkansas for years, it's all been flushed out before'—and, not to our credit, we accepted it without looking into the charges much deeper. Everybody operated on the Smoking Bimbo theory: No one had ever come forward, on fire and with passion, and said, 'We did it.' "

There had, it was true, been a week of tabloid reports, dredging up Larry Nichols's 1990 story of the governor's "Famous Five" mistresses, but since the five ladies had supposedly all denied the allegations, even Cokie Roberts of ABC television had been unable to generate any heat when she'd brought up the issue in a televised debate earlier in the week, and Carville had gone home. Since he himself was carrying on a passionate affair (which would lead to marriage) with a White House official who had become the political director of President Bush's campaign for reelection, Mary Matalin, Carville was not disposed to take the ethics of sexual affairs very seriously. As he afterward chided himself, "Illicit sex is a hot topic everywhere, particularly in political races. Clinton was a relatively young, good-looking guy with, deserved or not, a reputation. We should have investigated this line thoroughly and been prepared for any kind of onslaught, and we weren't."

Once rumor of an impending Flowers interview with *Star* magazine reached New Hampshire, however, Carville was advised by Clinton's right-hand man, young George Stephanopoulos, to get his ass to the Granite State (campaigners could not draw funding for a primary from national party funds if they remained in the primary state for more than three days at a time). A faxed press release from the tabloid said it all: Gennifer Flowers was saying not only "We did it" but that she and Bill had happily done "it" *for twelve years.*

Since Gennifer had previously denied the rumors of having had an affair with Clinton, Carville assumed they could crush the story on the grounds that she was being paid $100,000 for such nonsense. Gennifer's claim that she had actual audiotapes of telephone conversations with Bill Clinton, however, altered the entire landscape.

Carville's lover, Mary Matalin, was amused. "When the campaign opened we had begun a nice ritual: At the end of every day everybody would come into my office and drink red wine, watch the news, and just chatter," she recalled innocently. "Oh, my God, what would you do if you were in a campaign and something like this happened to you?" was now the buzz. Mary frankly "thought it was pretty funny." Here was a southern bimbo, a nightclub singer, whose revelations would surely destroy any hopes that Bill Clinton could ever look presidential, at least in the way that her revered sixty-seven-year-old boss George Bush did. "We made fun of her roots," Mary recalled, "and said, 'God, if that's Clinton's taste in women . . .' "

Like Ted Koppel airing the televangelists during the 1987 scandals five years before, Matalin assumed that the revelation would discredit the Clinton church beyond redemption. Indeed she even called her lover, who was rumored to be "a mess," not having "shaved in three days" and to be walking barefoot—to commiserate. Carville pretended nothing was happening. "Earth to James," Mary recalled the moment, as she shook her innocent head sadly. "That set the pattern for our communications through the entire campaign; there wasn't going to be any communication."

Lee Atwater had taught Mary: "Never interfere with your enemy when he's in the process of destroying himself." A veteran campaigner and spinmeisterin, Matalin therefore assumed the Clintonistas would react in the same way her Republican team would do—indeed how any self-respecting attorney would in court: "discredit the witness," then "discredit and humiliate the press."

Mary was being naive, however; she was as oblivious to the change in American culture as was her boss, President Bush, who would look amazed by simple, homey matters such as supermarket prices at the check-out, and had clearly never picked up *The Star* while waiting in the inevitable lines. It was not the interview but the *tapes,* as Carville and his colleagues knew, that threatened to be dynamite. Tapes had been the downfall of President Nixon—and unless a new kind of spinning was invented, it could be the end of would-be President Bill Clinton.

The Right Cojones

For the Louisiana consultant James Carville, the premature demise of his chosen candidate was sad. George Bush was unbeatable, Carville knew—except by a charismatic young Democrat with a popular and populist message. That Democrat was clearly Bill Clinton. He had the right *cojones* to challenge the incumbent president. The trouble was only, in Carville's view, his excess of *cojones.* Would he now go the way not only of all flesh but of Gary Hart?

Mary Matalin thought so. Indeed, like most modern women she welcomed the right of women to enjoy premarital sex—as she was—but not to indulge in infidelity. The difference of opinion between Matalin and Carville, in fact, symbolized the great American divide. Both sexes favored the right to multiple sexual partners in life—but whereas women confined such liberation to *serial* partners, in conformity with their evolutionary biology, men were biologically programmed to be *simultaneously* promiscuous. Matalin thus remained incensed by the picture of Lee Hart, the senator's "abused" wife, being humiliated in public. Gary Hart, in her book, was a heel: a no-good, two-timing philanderer. "The guy deserves whatever punishment he gets," she opined. "In Hart's case it was rabid scrutiny by the press, followed by the public execution of his presidential ambitions."

Matalin felt the same way about Bill Clinton—whatever political skills and compassion he might bring to bear in government. Moreover, women had 50 percent of the vote—in the one area, apart from religion, in which they could actually *dictate* an expectation of sexual fidelity, regardless of what men might feel. The gender bias of such a view did not lessen its visceral power. A man or woman who divorced and serially remarried—like President Reagan—was now deemed acceptable to most women, especially the newest wives. A man who strayed during marriage or a protracted part-nership was a pariah—and, in Matalin's words, "deserved" to be ruined.

Carville, as a man, felt the opposite: that Clinton did *not* deserve "what-ever punishment he gets," not only because he was, after all, a man like any other but because he was not humiliating his wife. On the contrary, Clin-ton was making gender history in American history by the way he was campaigning with Hillary as his veritable co-candidate—a wife intimately involved in both political strategy and decision making.

The prospect of a sex scandal destroying Clinton's candidacy, as it had destroyed Gary Hart's in the previous presidential campaign, thus reduced the ex-marine to despair: he kept breaking down and weeping. Yet the so-lution lay right in front of him and the whole team, without any of them realizing. She was in Atlanta at an event, while Gennifer was in New York working on her lascivious story ("They made love all over her apart-ment . . . 'not just in the bedroom, but on the floor, in the kitchen, on the couch, even in the shower' ") with the editors of *The Star.*

Telling Hillary

As Betsey Wright and Bobby Roberts best knew, Bill Clinton was a hero over some issues but a coward when called upon to relate bad news. Not daring to call Hillary in Atlanta himself, Bill asked Carville to do so.

"Mrs. Clinton, the governor wanted me to transmit to you, and it's im-portant that you know because you may get asked about it," Carville began, beating around the bush. Finally, though, he got to the point. "There's this paper called *The Star* and this woman named Gennifer Flow-ers . . ."

"Yes," she said, "I know Gennifer."

"She's claiming to have had an affair with the governor," Carville ex-plained sheepishly, "and it looks like the media might grab hold of this thing a little bit."

"Little" was a euphemism. The campaign was about to implode.

Smashing the Shit out of Gennifer

"How is Bill?" Hillary responded. And in that moment James Carville re-alized his mistake. The candidate and his wife might not have a perfect marriage, but *they cared for each other* before politics! For Carville, who put the winning of the campaign even before winning the hand of his lover, Mary Matalin, this was a revelation. And if it was a revelation to Carville, might it not also be for the voters of New Hampshire, and ultimately of America? Male infidelity was a given, however resented by the female sex; but modern male and female *love* could be made into a new weapon of campaign warfare—one that had never been used before in presidential politics.

In absolute secrecy, with no hint even to Matalin and her team, the Clintonistas now set to work fashioning a new warhead that would alter the face of political warfare. As in the case of Jimmy Swaggart, the key was not the medium of print but that of television. In a world that was being transformed by proliferating cable and satellite stations, political campaigning was now more than ever defined by the small screen.

"We brainstormed and came up with a coordinated strategy," Carville recalled. Ted Koppel's *Nightline* would provide the platform—except that, infuriatingly, bad weather kept Hillary in Atlanta, where the airport was closed. Hillary was essential to the plan. "We wanted them together, sitting next to each other. . . . If this was a real couple they wouldn't be facing accusations of infidelity separated by the entire Eastern Seaboard; they couldn't be separated in any way, it would have sent the wrong message."

Carville was in his element at last. "I kept thinking, 'Hey, I have a function now, I'm here, I'm thinking I'm earning a paycheck,' " he recalled. For the Vietnam vet this was action. Indifferent to the emotional pain or stress of such revelations to the candidate or his wife, Carville "actually felt good. 'I have a role,' " he told himself.

In the end it was arranged that Bill and Hillary would be interviewed not on *Nightline* but on CBS's *60 Minutes,* directly after the Super Bowl—the most watched sports event of the year. This would be a masterstroke if it worked, since a significant part of the population of the United States would be watching—an audience dominated by men, after an evening of male-male struggle and heroics. Instead of limiting the impact to the voters of New Hampshire, the campaign could suddenly reach out to tens of millions of viewers, achieving national name recognition for its candidate literally overnight.

Suddenly the opportunity seemed Heaven-sent—something "you and Hillary have been waiting for all along," Carville noted in a memo to his boss. Hillary was "the best thing you've got going for you. On camera, it's just you, Hillary, and interviewer Steve Kroft. We like those odds"—

indeed, "*She is our ace in the hole,*" Carville exulted. "Like you, she needs to be calm and confident. Unlike you, she can leap to your defense (and, more importantly, to your family's defense) if Steve goes across the line. Her bona fides as an attorney and children's advocate make her far more than some wounded little bride, dutifully sticking by you because she's got nowhere else to go. She holds the ultimate trump card."

"I was at war," Carville later acknowledged—and in war people get hurt, inevitably. Gennifer Flowers was to be fed to the dogs. "This is nothing but a trollop and we are going to smash the shit out of her in the news media," he declared when putting down a revolt of Clinton fund-raisers in Washington who "thought we were gone." On the contrary, he explained to them, the men and women of the Clinton campaign were girding themselves up for a no-holds-barred battle that might even decide the outcome of the war. It necessitated lying by Bill Clinton and a suspension of disbelief by the entire team. Mercifully, Betsey Wright, to whom Bill had confessed his catalogue of sins in 1987, was not part of the team, having accepted a fellowship at the Kennedy School of Government at Harvard. Newcomers such as Carville and Begala, "Boy" George Stephanopoulos, Frank Greer, and others could be won over by denials of wrongdoing, so that they would not need to go to Hell for lying. Bill and Hillary might, of course, but if all was fair in love and war, then they could genuinely rise above the fray, emphasize that they still loved each other, and, in the privacy of their consciences, accept they were fighting a hand-to-hand electoral battle where normal rules of polite behavior did not apply. "Bill Clinton did not have an affair with Gennifer Flowers," Carville later chronicled. "That was a given. I thought about it and the clear weight of evidence is that he didn't. First, he denied it—and I believed him."

Bill, possessed of a photographic memory, had even told Carville in advance what might be on Gennifer's tapes—spinning his version so that the Louisiana spinmeister was outspun. "He told me everything that was going to be on that tape before we heard it," Carville, completely taken in by Bill's account, later naively prided himself and his boss on doing. "What had he been doing talking to her in the first place? He didn't have to tell me; I knew," Carville convinced himself, unaware of Clinton's sex addiction. "She'd been a local newscaster. If you're the governor in a place like Little Rock, Arkansas, it's impossible *not* to know the local news people," he explained as a born-and-raised southerner. "I asked the governor about the calls. He said, 'I can assure you there's nothing to them. The only thing is, she told me something one time about oral sex and the only thing I can remember is I just laughed, I didn't really know what to say."

In the course of time such staff members—especially the young George Stephanopoulos—would feel betrayed by Bill Clinton's inability or unwillingness to tell them the truth, thus making them look like idiots for defending him against allegations he knew to be true. As Bobby Roberts, his gubernatorial aide, put it, Clinton "stuck me into doing stuff when I was working for him where I knew full well that I was not getting the whole truth, that I was only being told part of what was going on. But you would sort of . . . —because he's such a charming fellow and you want to believe him, you sort of fall into the game with him, you know."

This was no longer skirmishing in a small southern state, however; this was national war—or World War I, with the Germans encircling Paris. Being confessional about "Willard" and "Precious" would not save the capital; and protestations of innocence about mere sex, when in other respects—compared, say, to President Johnson or Richard Nixon—Bill Clinton was completely uninterested in personal wealth or status, seemed small beer. That Gennifer's reputation, indeed her job and livelihood, would have to be destroyed also seemed a small sacrifice. Lyndon Johnson had had people such as Henry Marshall assassinated, after all. Besides, what did Gennifer's "reputation" amount to, as a nightclub singer, and who had arranged her day job anyway?

Thus what had seemed like tragedy turned to media warfare, laced with American-spun farce. "Not only will we survive this but we will be strengthened," Carville predicted. "We've got them where we want them; we're surrounded, we can shoot in any direction and hit the bastards."

The CBS program was, indeed, sensational—in fact, it would become even more historic, in terms of America's cultural wars, than the great Koppel televangelist shows featuring Jim and Tammy Faye Bakker. Time and again in rehearsal the candidate and his wife were taken through the likely questions—questions that were more taxing than those of the later presidential debates. "We posed questions that we knew Steve Kroft would ask. 'Did you have an affair with Gennifer Flowers?' You've got to say no. The Governor was clear he had never had sex with Flowers. Clearly he and Mrs. Clinton had decided—and I don't think this was a bone of contention among the people in that room—that, with reference to the larger question, they were just going to say, 'We acknowledge that we have had difficulties in our marriage and we don't think that we have to say any more. Governor Clinton said, 'People get it.' "

Still, Carville was a bag of nerves on January 26, 1992, the day of the Super Bowl. The still relatively unknown governor from little Arkansas was about to get fifteen of CBS's *60 Minutes* of national fame—exactly as Warhol had specified. "History was going to judge us," Carville remembered thinking; "this was going to be in the books."

Producing a President

60 Minutes proved more exciting to most American viewers than the Super Bowl game it followed. "When it was over I ran to Clinton," Carville later recounted. "I couldn't stop crying."

Presidential adultery, or the tacit admission of such by a would-be president, had been aired on prime-time television for the first time in American history. Don Hewitt, the senior producer, had produced the legendary Kennedy-Nixon debates; kneeling beside Bill, Hewitt had begged the governor, on behalf of CBS, to admit to adultery. "It will be great television. I know. I know television. The last time I did something like this, Bill, it was the Kennedy-Nixon debates and it produced a president. This," he prophesied, "will produce a president, too."

Balking at such a direct admission, Clinton admitted "causing pain in my marriage" but said he was "not prepared tonight" to be more specific over matters "that any married couple" should ever have to discuss with anyone but themselves. "Are we going to take the reverse position now," Hillary then jumped in, "that if people have problems in their marriage and there are things in their past which they don't want to discuss which are painful to them, that they can't run?" And when Kroft attempted to portray the Clinton marriage as "very admirable" in that they had "stayed together—that you've worked your problems out and that you've seemed to reach some sort of understanding and arrangement—" Bill cut him off. "Wait a minute, wait a minute. You're looking at two people who *love* each other. This is not an arrangement or an understanding. This is a *marriage.*"

It was extraordinary television. And then Hillary, normally so uptight and private, burst out with the words "You know, I'm not sitting here, some little woman standing by my man like Tammy Wynette. I'm sitting here because I love him, and I respect him, and I honor what he's been through and what we've been through together, and you know, if that's not enough for people, then heck, don't vote for him." Millions blinked.

The one-hour interview, pared down to a quarter of an hour, had given the Clintons the national exposure they needed *as a couple*—and the result was beyond all expectations. Even Carville's Republican lover, Mary Matalin, had to admit that "the way they jujitsued the Flowers fiasco" was extraordinary; indeed, she said, it "gave us the heebie-jeebies." Carville, meanwhile, wiping his tears away, was triumphant.

The program had been watched by an estimated 34 million Americans, with up to 50 million more seeing and learning of its highlights on other programs. A national poll was taken by ABC television that night, with 80 percent of the respondents reported as saying that Clinton should stay in the race.

It was victory—until the next day, when came the counterblow.

In Classic Nineties Mode

The postmodern soap opera was now moving into its classic nineties mode, each day entertaining the public with a fresh and juicy personal revelation side by side with serious discussion of the issues foremost in people's minds: the continuing recession, high unemployment, concerns over health care . . .

Gennifer Flowers's answer to the tape-recorded and edited *60 Minutes* program was a live *Star* press conference in New York—with a tape recorder at hand. Some 350 journalists packed the room, in addition to the television cameras. Mary Matalin later confessed that although orders had gone out not to make any comment on the revelations, lest they appear to be a Republican plot, "all operations ceased and every television was turned to CNN."

Was this the "dumbing down" of America—or was it an acknowledgement, at least among younger people, that a new age had dawned?

Certainly the 1990s would be epitomized by television programs such as MTV and *The Jerry Springer Show,* launched in 1991, in which millions of viewers at home looked to the little screen for sexual revelation, titillation, and entertainment in a strangely symbiotic, virtual connection with the world beyond their own domestic walls. Such shows seemed wackier, tackier, and more surreal than real life—yet were real.

Was Rome burning? In journalism the boundary between fiction and factual reporting was so often becoming blurred that one could often only speak of "faction"—or "infotainment." The year before, in 1991, Professor Schultze had likened the success of televangelism to that of the circus in Western society a century before. Marx, Freud and Barnum had contributed "imperceptively but decisively to the ways that the Western World thinks," he quoted one cultural historian as saying; moreover, Barnum, who had died in 1891, was, in Schultze's view, by no means the least of the trio. His "greatest show on earth" had been a "colorful orgy of visual delight that combined the bizarre and the sublime, the beautiful and the gaudy, the outrageously humorous and the enormously terrifying, as well as the truly talent-filled show and the deceptively hyped spectacle." A century later it was a fitting description of televelangelism—and, increasingly, of political campaigning.

Modern Barnum was certainly the name of the new game as Gennifer Flowers now appeared on national cable television "in a bright red jacket with her brassy blond hair flowing from conspicuously dark roots" in yet another brilliantly gaudy act in America's postmodern circus.

The Star Press Conference

As James Carville noted, research among focus groups showed that each new act in the circus elicited a different audience reaction, according to its content and the age, gender, education, and cultural background of the viewer. For example, women were found to be far and away the more censorious about Bill Clinton's implied adultery, since the notion of adultery—"the A word," as Stephanopulos later described it—threatened them and their perceived evolutionary agenda, whereas Clinton's stock among men, who had hitherto been relatively immune to his "slick," "feminine," "narcissistic," and often prevaricating manner, were moved, suddenly, to identify with him in "the worst moment in my life" as he'd put it on *60 Minutes*. Hillary's response thus appealed to women, the victims of men's innate promiscuity, while men responded to Bill's male predicament.

Gennifer Flowers, unfortunately, appealed to neither constituency. When she appeared close up, live, on camera, women "reacted much more negatively," Carville recalled. "One woman took a look at her and said, 'She looks like a liar. And she ought to learn to dye her roots.' "

If Clinton threatened women in terms of "the A word," Gennifer, as the wild and attractive mistress of a "very married" man, paradoxically yet understandably threatened married women even more. Dimly, Gennifer became aware of this. "I was vilified," she later commented, "for having an affair with a married man. I freely admit I'm no saint. . . . But from all the finger pointing and accusations, you would think I was the first woman ever to get involved with a married man. Somehow the whole, sordid mess became *my* fault, and Bill was just an innocent victim. Being called a bimbo stirred up a volcano in me."

The CBS program had produced "drama and unprecedented personal revelation by a presidential candidate and his wife about their marriage," as campaign chroniclers Jack Germond and Jules Witcover wrote, but the subsequent broadcasting of Gennifer's live conference, with excerpts from Gennifer's audiotapes played to the assembled journalists, proved all the more spellbinding to national viewers and readers who, for the most part, had only just got to know the characters of Bill and Hillary the night before. It was, in its way, pure, adulterous, yet unadulterated comedy as, with utmost gravity, Gennifer announced, "I was Bill Clinton's lover for twelve years and for the past two years I have lied to protect him," after which the audiotapes were played. "The truth is, I loved him. Now he wants me to deny it. Well, I am sick of all the deceit and I'm sick of all the lies."

If Gennifer looked sore on the platform—she had a raging fever—she nonetheless sounded humorous, fun, and coconspiratorial in the tape extracts that were replayed to gawping reporters and their cameras. While Carville savaged CNN for daring to broadcast such tripe during a presidential election process, George Stephanopoulos watched the television transfixed. Looking for ammunition with which to sink her small, enemy ship, he later confessed to first thinking "*Maybe we can turn this into an 'anatomy of a smear' story instead of a morality play about Clinton's character.*"

Then, however, "came the tapes—scratchy but apparently authentic recordings of Clinton and Gennifer talking in intimate terms about their personal relationship and the presidential race," he later recounted—appalled that the governor had clearly been telephoning her, all too recently, from pay phones in the very sight of Stephanopoulos himself—yet had had the temerity to tell Stephanopoulos her story was a fabrication.

From Machiavelli, Stephanopoulos changed to Miss Manners as he listened carefully. In one taped conversation Gennifer told Bill he ought to go ahead and run, as he would make "a damn good" president, whereas President Bush was "a sneaky bastard." "He's two-faced. I'd love to see somebody get in there for a change, really make a difference"—indeed, she'd been disappointed when Bill hadn't run in 1987. At that time, she reminded him, he'd urged her "to be sure to say 'there's nothing to the rumor' " of their affair if questioned by reporters—to which she'd responded, tongue in cheek, that she would be sure, instead, to tell them that the governor "ate good pussy." Bill, in the recording, laughed and gave her permission, saying, "Well you can tell them that if I don't run for president."

Bill Clinton *was* running for president, however—and without his authorization Gennifer was telling the world his oral and other talents.

The Altar Boy

Watching and listening to the tapes, Stephanopoulos found himself stupefied. His father was a Greek Orthodox priest, as his grandfather had been, and though Stephanopoulos, as a former altar boy, currently lived or dated in premarital sin with his girlfriend, the young politico had a childlike reverence for others who did not, especially older folk. Marriage was not only an honorable but almost sacrosanct estate in George's mind. The thought that his boss had lied about his relationship with Gennifer filled him with fear. He later described his shock at the realization. "He lied," he remembered saying to himself. "Even if he didn't, what's he doing talking to her in the middle of the campaign? That must have been *her* Clinton and Lindsey called from that pay phone in Boston. How could he have been so stupid? So arrogant? Did he want to get caught? How come he let me hang out there? Never said a word the whole ride to Claremont while I swore to reporters her story was false—just sat there, pretending to read Lincoln."

Poor Stephanopoulos, a Republican turned idealistic Democrat and barely thirty, seemed to be in the wrong camp, as an Orthodox priest's boy: a warrior who in his heart of hearts would have been better suited to the right-wing Republican crusade in New Hampshire's Republican primary, tub-thumping Judeo-Christian values. At the time, however, he "kept my anger inside to avoid demoralizing the interns and volunteers." As he put it, self-ennoblingly, "I had to be strong for the kids who looked up to me."

"A Big Wet Splotch"

The result was an embarrassing, extraordinary, gaudy hodgepodge of conflicting moralities and values. Only months before, an august committee of all-male, white, white-haired old senators had leeringly interrogated a tiny, very beautiful black woman telling the bitter truth about a pornography-addicted candidate hoping for a place on the bench of the famed Supreme

Court. The nation had been transfixed. Now the same trial was being enacted in another form of court: trial directly by the media, with lecherous, leering, sin-sodden journalists on the panel, rather than senators, as they listened in New York to Gennifer Flowers's evidence. Instead of a black woman ranged against an ambitious black man this time, it was an attractive white woman ranged against an ambitious white male, Bill Clinton, who wanted a chance of a seat in the supreme, quasi-monarchical court: the White House.

Why was she doing it? Like Anita Hill's, Gennifer's motives were immediately suspect—and suspected. Why was she revealing her affair now, when earlier she had got her lawyer to deny it, even to suppress mention of it on Arkansas radio on pain of a lawsuit? Was it suddenly the lure of big lucre? Gennifer's rationale looked dubious—and, tapping into a general feeling of distaste at the idea that a presidential election could be dragged so low, James Carville and his colleagues had a field day. Even though Gennifer had opted to sell her story (which was soon followed by *Penthouse* photographs of her in the nude, with "Precious" on general display) for monetary gain and security rather than for nefarious political purposes, there was a sense that, despite President Bush's orders not to comment, the Republicans were somehow behind this. "Arkansas Governor Accuses Democratic Foes, 'Republican Attack Machine' of Character Assault" was the headline of Dan Balz and David Broder's campaign report in *The Washington Post*. The Republican spinmeisters had destroyed Governor Dukakis with their Willie Horton ad campaign in 1988, as well as fabricated rumors about his mental health; now they were going to destroy the Democrats' leading candidate by exposing his sex life in 1992, in order to play to America's lingering hang-ups about the subject. In this kill-or-be-killed situation, the Clinton team had little option but to strike back. "I was the first surrogate to go after her," Carville later admitted of the Clinton counterriposte. "By going with *Star,* taking the money, playing the aggrieved lover, she had put herself in the line of fire, she was fair game. I thought, 'Just don't call her a whore—but short of that, let 'er rip.' "

Instead of Gennifer destroying Clinton's candidacy, it was Gennifer who was now trashed: making Clinton look good, not bad, as the press came under withering fire from Clintonites seizing the high ground and declaring anyone who listened to such garbage a traitor to the honorable codes of their profession. On the campaign plane Carville held journalists captive, torturing them as mercilessly as a sergeant major after an orgy in Vietnam. " 'You people are like a bunch of drunks. Y'all get drunk in 1988 and then you dry out for four years and then you go up to Columbia, or wherever y'all have your little seminars, and promise yourself that you are not going to do it again. You dry out. And then Gennifer Flowers puts the first goddamn jigger of whiskey on the bar and you are all killing each other to get at it. You get drunk again and now you have a bad hangover. In fact you people are amazing. You went to college, you got a degree, you are a professional journalist, and you are letting someone like Gennifer Flowers dictate your coverage. What are you doing? This is the crack cocaine of journalism. Y'all are saying, 'I want to get off it, we don't want to cover this story. Gee, we hate this.' But look at your crotch and there's a big wet splotch there.' "

The Only Game in Town

As much as Carville might trash Gennifer and berate and humiliate attendant journalists, he was guilty of hypocrisy, as he himself well knew—and as Stephanopoulos, in his sinking heart of hearts, was painfully aware. Sex was the fuel on which men run—yet they were having to pretend the governor was a model of sexual probity if he was to stay in the race.

What, it might be asked, was going on? In the 1960s, sex had proved the liberating key to a new, post-Puritan culture, unlocking a closet out of which had tumbled hippies, gays, lesbians, transsexuals, and libertines. Thanks to AIDS and a countercounterculture bent upon reclaiming lost certainties, the closet appeared to be partially closing again.

The truth was that, in the final decade of the twentieth century, the cultural war was coming to a new climax, dividing the nation. In a recession-struck, fractious, postfeminist Western world human relations were still in transition: a moral and psychosexual puzzle. As sociologist professor Linda Rouse recorded, deceit was still endemic. "Most often, extramarital relations occur without the awareness of both parties," she noted. A 1991 survey showed an interesting difference between the genders, however: "men having affairs tended to like their wives better than their lovers, but women liked their lovers better than their husbands."

The puzzle, moreover, was now proving of profound interest to the *entire* population, not simply to teenagers, sophisticates, and perverts. As Carville himself put it, "The country and the media was [sic] riveted on us.

Our name recognition skyrocketed. We were the only game in town. A Southern babe, a Rhodes scholar presidential candidate, a compelling wife, a sleazy tabloid, sex, lies, audiotape—how could you care about another candidate?"

You couldn't. But the smirk on Carville's face was soon wiped off when the enemy launched yet another missile—a Scud that once again went straight beneath the Clinton team radar and hit the candidate in his guilty heart: Vietnam.

CHAPTER FORTY-TWO

THE DRAFT

Replaying the Sixties

In the late 1960s, while the sexual revolution continued to play havoc in traditional American communities, David Levine, in a play upon Queen Mary of England's legendary remark about the lost British port of Calais, whose seizure and occupation had cost so many English lives, had drawn a cartoon showing a tragic-looking Lyndon Johnson pulling up his shirt and examining the scar upon his chest, the outline of a familiar Southeast Asian peninsula: Vietnam.

Two decades later, presidential nomination contender Bill Clinton seemed to have weathered the Gennifer Flowers storm. But the Southeast Asian peninsula was different. Vietnam raised the specter of draft avoidance, of lack of patriotism, of insufficient apple pie and American flag waving.

"A Pretty High Negative"

Years before, Attorney General Bill Clinton had assumed that his letter from Oxford to Colonel Holmes had been removed from the ROTC files in Arkansas and the evidence destroyed.

He was wrong. Though he had infuriated his friends by his relentless determination to win over his enemies and even win their vote, his very success in politics was bound to arouse jealousy, and it did. Sheffield Nelson was busy mining the savings and loan financial scandals, which had beset Arkansas along with every other state, looking for a Bill Clinton, even a Hillary Clinton, connection. In due course he found what he thought might be buried gold in the McDougals' Whitewater Land Development investment. As Clinton's closest buddy, Jim Blair, reflected, "Sheffield is the source of the beginning of Whitewater. He is probably the source of a lot of these women originally coming out—he is the source of Clinton's grief. He has hated Clinton with a passion. Whether it's over what happened in that [1990 gubernatorial] political race or whether there are other factors, I don't know. But Jim McDougal went to him with some complaints about Jim Guy Tucker, not about Clinton. And Sheffield taped him and convinced him that his real betrayer was Clinton, and then Sheffield arranged for the guy from *The New York Times* that I always thought was incompetent, that broke that story. That was personal." Yet Blair also saw how it played into an even meaner, almost fanatical element that became braided into the postmodern American political tapestry. "There's always been the ideology thing," Blair sighed. "I mean, the conservatives at some level have always known that Clinton was their menace. And even on a national level the really smart ones worried about him long before anybody thought he could be effective. They saw that he was effective. And so I think there's always been some of that floating around there, with the idea 'Hey, let's stop Clinton before he gets started.' "

Ernie Dumas of the *Arkansas Gazette*—which had, to the chagrin of more liberal-minded Arkansans, been forced to close its doors and be swallowed by the conservative, right-wing *Arkansas Democrat*—agreed. "He's always had a pretty high negative in Arkansas. All the years he ran for office, he'd always had a pretty high negative. Part of that was the taxes—he raised some taxes—but a lot of it was, I think, always, this resentment of his open familiarity with and appointment of Blacks in great numbers to posts and committees—and talking about them!" In white Arkansas communities this was a no-no. "Some predecessors had similar attitudes," Dumas acknowledged, "but Clinton went farther, was far more open about it, *made no attempt to be subtle about it.* He was an ardent advocate of civil rights, made no bones about it, was open about it, *proud* of it." Indeed, one of his first acts as governor of Arkansas, in 1979, had been to "sign a bill that erases unconstitutional racial segregation laws from the state's law books," as the *Arkansas Gazette* had reported.

Bill Clinton's openness about civil rights and black issues thus produced a vivid red target for Republican sharpshooters in Little Rock. Rather than confront him over race, which was now a dead issue, however, or sexual revelations, which he had successfully parried, these opponents were all too willing to choose another with which to lambast and hopefully lynch him: the draft.

Give-And-Take

Bill Clinton's old Oxford University colleague Attorney Cliff Jackson, who'd arranged the all-important 1968 interview with the ROTC commander at Fayetteville, had for years kept silent over Bill's draft record, for he, too, was one of the millions of American college students who had gotten deferments or found ways out of having to serve in Vietnam. His beef was not Vietnam service but Bill himself: disappointment in Bill both as a human being and as a governor.

Bill's governance in the hillbilly state Jackson rated as "average to mediocre. I really didn't see any great success in Arkansas," he later explained. "And that's what we pointed out when I did decide to finally speak up. We had this little group named ARIAS—Alliance for the Rebirth of an Independent American Spirit—a political action committee. And we spent $40,000 to $45,000, which is nothing. But in New Hampshire, a little state, with newspaper and radio ads we made the point that when Bill Clinton was elected governor, Arkansas was at the fiftieth or forty-ninth position—we listed twelve or fourteen or fifteen categories. That during the time he was governor, taxes had increased from $900 million to $2.7 billion, about a threefold increase, and the increase was on the whole due to regressive taxation—gasoline taxes, sales tax increases, etc., on the backs of the very poor and middle class he was purporting to represent! And yet that, at the end of his tenure as governor, as he ran for president, Arkansas in each one of these categories, socioeconomic categories, was still forty-ninth and fiftieth! Now, how do you explain that? How do you explain *that*?" the trial lawyer demanded. "That, to me, is not effective governance, is it? I mean, should we not have had some progress in the various categories? I would think so," he answered his own question.

The ARIAS ads had been hard-hitting, always ending with "Please, Governor Clinton, don't do to America what you've done to Arkansas!" Yet even Jackson recognized how much tougher his old basketball sparring partner had become since Oxford days. Asked in a radio interview in New

Hampshire what his response was to the ARIAS ads, Bill described Jackson as a "long-time bitter Republican who has for years tried to bring me down."

Jackson was furious. "Every single adjective he used was wrong! I *was* a Republican in the past," he acknowledged, but "I mean, I've been an independent for years! I will vote Republican in Arkansas, all things being equal, because I believe in the two-party system, believe in competitive politics. By the same token, if I were in a Republican state, I'd vote Democratic on the same principles." Indeed, other things seldom being equal in Arkansas, "I *have* many times voted Democrat!" he pointed out. "Yet Bill's immediate response was 'long-time Republican who for years tried to bring me down'! Everything was untrue! I *hadn't* for years tried to bring him down. I did *nothing!* I wasn't Republican, I wasn't bitter, I wasn't longtime—there were some other adjectives in there, I don't remember what the other litany was."

Jackson's voice trailed away. He prided himself on being "a connoisseur of politics and political campaigning. I *enjoy* it—enjoy the give-and-take of it! And we packaged it [the ARIAS ads] to be effective and to garner some attention, because we were the only people from Arkansas at the time who were speaking out!"

Bill's response had been masterly, however, his portrayal of Jackson and his ARIAS colleagues as a group of embittered, wacky Republican outsiders far more effective than the ads of the Arkansas protest movement.

Until the draft issue resurfaced.

The Big "V"

Jackson was one of the few who knew the real truth behind Bill's failure to stand by his agreement to serve in the military, but he had hitherto not raised it during Clinton's campaigns for Congress, the attorney generalship, and the governorship. "*Millions* avoided the draft," Jackson pointed out—including himself, through a medical deferral. "And I *helped* him avoid the draft, for Pete's sake! So I'm not some holier-than-thou guy who's prowar, or pro–American involvement in Vietnam!" Even when an aggrieved retired air force colonel, Lieutenant Colonel Billy Geren, backed by a Republican politician, had drawn public attention to the missing "smoking letter" in 1978, during Bill's first gubernatorial race, Jackson had said nothing. Without access to the letter itself, Colonel Geren had simply been ignored—and Vietnam, as an issue, had been safely buried in Clinton's past.

Now, with Bill Clinton running for the presidency, the issue could legitimately be brought up and rehashed by others. The openly Republican *Wall Street Journal* was quietly furnished with the story, and in the aftermath of the Gennifer Flowers scandal, the plot thickened. Flowers's revelations had brought the "big A"—adultery—into the presidential circus arena for the first time in the twentieth century, an issue that exercised women. The "big V"—Vietnam—exercised men.

As in the case of adultery, hypocrisy would here be involved on a massive, if often unconscious, scale. Through deferments and alternative service, *almost the entire college population the United States* had avoided fighting in the tragic Kennedy-Johnson fiasco in Southeast Asia, leaving the prosecution of the war to working-class "grunts" and professional soldiers. Almost no historian, let alone journalist, supported the war in retrospect. But training or *service* in the armed forces was another matter—and in the Northeast, the home of the American Revolution, where local militia and volunteers had fought the British and inspired the War of Independence, Clinton's failure to honor his freely given contractual agreement with Colonel Holmes not only looked bad in hindsight, it was.

Holmes, a Republican, now decided to tell *The Wall Street Journal* the whole story for the first time. Bill's long-standing version—that he'd been given a draft deferment while at Oxford and had then voluntarily submitted to the draft lottery—was true, and Holmes had never contested it. Now, however, urged on by the Republicans' most prestigious national newspaper, Holmes explained the missing links: the fact that Clinton had made a prior, *binding* agreement with him to serve in the ROTC that had rescued him from imminent service in Vietnam—and had then *reneged* on it, as Clinton well knew.

That *failure to serve in the military,* not Vietnam, would now cost Clinton dearly. War and the military were, with religion and family values, bulwarks of the Republican agenda in America, despite the irony of Democratic presidents having prosecuted World War II, the Korean War, and the Vietnam War. Republicans therefore circled like vultures, eager for a kill. Senator Kerrey had won the Congressional Medal of Honor, as well as the Bronze Star—albeit for killing civilians, as would later be alleged—in Vietnam; but politically he was considered to be an easy candidate for President Bush to beat if he actually won the Democratic nomination. For the moment Kerrey's war record as a "behind-the-enemy-lines" navy Seal thus remained unexamined by proud Democrats and was kept under wraps by Republicans in the hope that Kerrey would smash the draft dodger's bid for the Democratic nomination. To facilitate this, Clinton's record was now scrutinized in fine detail, then passed to the journalists' "feeding frenzy"— where it was found wanting. Deeply wanting.

Stories that Clinton had participated—albeit merely as a marshal—in war demonstrations soon led to Republican canards such as one in which he had been seen in a tree in Fayetteville during a war protest or burning the American flag in England, even trying to renounce his U.S. citizenship in Europe. Josef Goebbels, a master of propaganda, had perfected the Big Lie—the notion that if trumpeted loudly enough, even a risible allegation will stick, to some extent. Fifty years later Republicans had, in the 1988 campaign, perfected this, but in reverse: small negative truths had led to louder, larger lies, which were ultimately, to some extent, believed by the credulous "masses."

Given that the political "assassination" of Governor Dukakis had proven so easy, Republican true believers argued that the same tactics should now be employed on Governor Clinton, even without the directing genius of Herr Atwater. The Arkansas governor was clearly wounded, and one more blow would put him out of his misery. Atwater's absence, however, left the Bush campaign without an executioner. As Sheffield Nelson, the apostate Republican whom Bill Clinton had beaten, later complained, President Bush's reelection campaign was "the worst-run campaign I've ever seen in my life. I gave them my entire [Clinton] file. I sent a box of stuff up there." Yet Nelson, in the absence of Atwater, found himself infuriatingly unable to "get them interested. They waited too late." Nelson's priceless warnings about Bill Clinton's political genius, like his salacious information, went unheeded. "I said, 'Let me tell you something, Clinton has an unbelievable ability to land on his feet, and if you ever give him a chance, he will come back. He's just like a rattlesnake. If you have a chance to cut his head off, you better do it or you're going to live to regret the day you didn't.'"

Falling Sick

In the meantime, knowing that he was vulnerable on the draft issue and had not told his own team the full truth, Bill Clinton faltered. *The Wall*

DEMOCRATIC NOMINATION · 631

Street Journal's arrow, quoting Colonel Holmes, had hit him in the chest, yet, without access to the original documentary proof, it had failed to kill him instantly, only knocking him to the ground, where the pain was excruciating. *Why had he not served in the ROTC, at least?* he raged at himself, knowing how he'd always been careful not to do anything, in his student years, that might later backfire or prejudice his ultimate ambition to become President. Yet he also knew the answer only too well: that ROTC service in Arkansas would have meant attending the University of Arkansas's second-line law school rather than going back to Oxford as a scholar and then to the world's most famous teaching and training institution for lawyers and high fliers: Yale. And thereby meeting a slew of future movers and shakers in the nation—prime among them being one Hillary Rodham . . .

Whether psychosomatically or coincidentally, Bill now fell sick and took to his bed, in the very midst of the campaign. Indeed, he felt so bad and so low that he insisted, against Carville's dire warnings, on flying back to Arkansas for the entire weekend to recuperate rather than continue to campaign.

It did no good, however.

Meltdown

Late on Sunday night Stan Greenberg got the results of his new poll. Around midnight he relayed them to Carville, using not "the A word" now, but "the M word": "Meltdown."

Carville, standing a few feet from the candidate, was dismayed. To Bill and Hillary Clinton and the inner campaign circle, Carville would say only that they needed to get a good night's sleep "'cause we are getting ready to go into the toughest fucking week of our lives."

The team demanded, however, to know the figures—and the language quickly degenerated.

"We're dropping like a turd in a well," Bill commented memorably—for Greenberg had recorded a twenty-point fall in Clinton's rating! It was equivalent to a nosedive only eight days before the primary.

Bill characteristically blamed his team. Jim Blair lamented his best friend's "unwillingness at times to accept responsibility for his own actions," as did David Watkins, who was running the business side of the 1992 campaign. Bill might be a genius campaigner, but "the other characteristic of Bill Clinton in his campaign: *it was never his fault!* If there was a mess-up, it was somebody else's fault that there was a mess-up, it really wasn't his. 'They' had done it to him, or somebody else had messed up. And he is totally capable of convincing himself that he didn't, wasn't at fault." Was it always that way? *"Always that way!"* Watkins emphasized. "When I knew him, he was *always* that way!" Even as governor, *"he* didn't mess up. *'They'* just didn't get it."

Now, as the New Hampshire primary election day approached, "they" had concentrated on advertisements instead of hard campaign labor. "The campaign isn't on top of things. *It's killing us!"* Bill wailed. "This campaign isn't working." He noted that 60 percent of voters in New Hampshire had a college education, yet the Clinton campaign was handing over the election on a plate to Paul Tsongas, who had far less of an education résumé than Clinton and way less experience in government. "All the work I've done, all the effort I've put into this—blown away because all you political people think all we have to do is run television spots," he berated his hapless subordinates, his face apoplectic with anger, pounding his thighs.

Carville and Begala knew, however, that it was the issue of the draft, not the inadequate efforts of the campaign staff, that was killing the candidate.

Hillary, however, knew her husband. Once Bill had finished his ranting, she spoke. "Okay, this is what we're going to do. We need to fly up there tomorrow and Bill needs to give a tough, passionate speech. Paul, you and George write it. 'Fight like hell.' You know, 'We're going to fight back.' We need radio commercials."

The co-candidate had taken charge.

The Smoking Letter

Landing at Nashua, New Hampshire, the next day, psyched up to fight yet still sick from his flulike symptoms, the candidate watched suspiciously as George Stephanopoulos was given a mysterious piece of paper by an ABC television producer.

Stephanopoulos, white-faced, handed the letter to Paul Begala. "We're through," he announced dramatically.

Paul Begala, reading the words "Thank you for saving me from the draft," later admitted that "my knees buckled." They'd weathered the "smoking bimbo," as Carville termed Gennifer. Now they had to confront the "smoking letter." It was a copy of the missing Clinton document—kept and provided to the press by Colonel Holmes's deputy, the aptly named Lieutenant Colonel Clinton Jones, who was living in retirement in Florida.

For a moment the letter seemed—with phrases like "loathing the military" and "maintain my political viability"—to sound, in forty-eight-year-old Carville's words, like "a death sentence to anyone who wanted to run for president," since the younger members of the team, most of them in their twenties, could read and see the world only in sound bites.

Hillary and Carville, however, were by nature, generation, and education readers. Studying the document carefully, sentence by sentence, paragraph by paragraph, page by page, they saw the matter differently. "This is terrific," Hillary—who had never read the correspondence—declared. She was bowled over by the sincerity and articulateness with which a twenty-two-year-old student had expressed his torment over the Vietnam War in 1969. "This is exactly what you were thinking at the time," she told her ashen-faced husband. "This proves everything that you were saying, Bill."

Carville was equally impressed. Indeed, he insisted they immediately buy ads in all the New Hampshire papers and print the letter *in its entirety.* Ted Koppel, meantime, was persuaded also to read aloud the entire letter, from beginning to end, on *Nightline,* while Bill now hit the campaign trail again but with a vengeance, declaring he was determined to "give this election back to the people, to lift the clouds off this election. For three weeks, of course, I've had some problems in the polls. All I've been asked about by the press are a woman I didn't sleep with and a draft I didn't dodge."

Both counterassertions were untrue. Clinton *had* slept with Gennifer Flowers, not once but many, many times; moreover, he *had* successfully dodged the draft—like virtually every college graduate in America! Thanks to Hillary's love, faith, and focus, however, the flu was banished and the big, hulking, charismatic candidate with the southern drawl was finally back on form. "From Wednesday on I have never seen anybody perform at anything near the level of Bill Clinton," Carville recalled in amazement. "He was giving his best speeches, he was reacting with crowds."

Campaign observers Jack Germond and Jules Witcover agreed. This was "the finest hour of the campaign to many of its campaign warriors," they judged, adversity forging a new "backs to the wall" camaraderie, a collective determination not to give in to the "enemy." The broader public were friends: anxious for a candidate with a credible solution to America's recessionary ills and the sort of charisma that promised energy, idealism,

634 · BILL CLINTON

and pride in what America could become, as the world's largest successful multiethnic, multicultural community, encompassing all faiths and diversity. Following ABC's *Nightline,* Bill did two more television programs in which he fielded open questions from voters, as well as a debate on the Saturday night before the primary and a Sunday-morning network interview. In between he raced around the Granite State in his campaign van, sitting beside the driver, seeking to be seen, heard, and hugged by as many people as possible. The nosedive began to level off, according to Greenberg's polls, but Clinton was too vexed and too energized now to care what his staff told or advised him. "Clinton's view was that he didn't want anybody standing between him and the voters, he wanted to meet them all," Carville recounted with disbelief. "He actually believed that he could win this thing hand to hand."

Bill couldn't, however—and the polls showed it. Of three surveys that were done on the eve of the primary, one showed him winning, possibly; the next showed Clinton running neck and neck with Tsongas. And the third—the campaign's own, based on a sample of some five hundred interviews—had him running third. "There was no question in my mind that if we ran third," Carville conceded, "we ran out."

Greer thought likewise: third place would be "disastrous."

The Comeback Kid

Once again Carville relayed the bad news to the candidate.

Gloom descended on the Clinton camp. Clinton blew up and blamed the team, his rival former Senator Tsongas, the cold weather, his allergies— and himself for not having pounded the pavements of New Hampshire harder, longer, earlier. It was Fayetteville 1974 all over again—but with ballot boxes that could not be stuffed without detection; also 1980, when Frank White had "kicked his butt" and he could not get back into the race in time.

Hillary, who had personally saved him after 1980, was a beacon of hope. She was like a calm, unshakable corps commander as the army commander fumed and raged. "I'm not going to listen to this," she eventually declared. "We'll know tomorrow. It could be right, it could be wrong," she shrugged, referring to Greenberg's disastrous poll. "I'm not going to lose any sleep over it."

Bill had wanted "to go out campaigning," as Carville recalled—or to savor red meat: McDonald's or female.

The next morning, though, Bill was out early. "There were some hands he hadn't shook, maybe some that needed shaking twice," Carville scoffed. But as the exit polls came in, the mood began to improve. Former Massachusetts senator Paul Tsongas would take first place, as the polls predicted, but Bill looked like taking second place—indeed, he was so far ahead of the rest of the pack that the others would, inevitably, fall by the wayside.

That night the counting confirmed the exits: Tsongas, from New England, first with 37 percent; Clinton, from the South, second with 25 percent; the rest 11 percent and below. "Bill Clinton had been given up for dead," Carville reflected later. "In the space of a month he'd taken every hit a politician could take. Now he'd made up ground, made a personal connection with the voters, and finished strong. Paul [Begala] came up with the line about the 'Comeback Kid.' It was perfect."

Lady Macbeth in a Business Suit

"Perfect" was an exaggeration or Carvillism, but Clinton's had certainly been an extraordinary performance. As the Arkansas governor remarked in his speech that night, he'd taken a lot of hits, but nowhere near as many as the people of the Granite State, who were still suffering from a bleak recession. For him politically there was, nevertheless, a silver lining, he pointed out prophetically. He had come in only second, but "at least I've proved one thing: I can take a punch."

Given his reputation as "Slick Willie"—for dissimulation, adultery, and draft dodging—this was the all-important factor. Bill Clinton, as a man, wasn't perfect, but as a campaigner he'd proven in open, electoral combat that he was tough—and had an even tougher wife beside him.

Meredith Oakley, who'd denounced the governor's "broken promise" to the voters of Arkansas, was awed by Hillary's latest display of firmness and focus—and her sheer aura, compared with the goggle-lensed first lady of Arkansas, barely thirty and in a headband, who'd entered the governor's mansion in 1978. "With the help of hairdressers, wardrobe advisers, and makeup artists, the degree of glamour she brought to the campaign stunned those who had known her in Arkansas," Oakley recalled Hillary's transformation, "and yet she spoke with the self-confidence and forcefulness of a full partner in the campaign."

The ABC interviewer, Steve Kroft, was equally bowled over by the co-candidate. "Hillary is tougher and more disciplined than Bill is, and she's analytical," Kroft remarked. "Among his faults," he remarked of Bill, "he has a tendency not to think of the consequences of things he says." Each time Bill had been tempted into vouchsafing more than was safe in the CBS interview, Kroft had noticed, Hillary had reined him in. "There isn't a person watching this," the co-candidate had declared at one point, "who would feel comfortable sitting on this couch detailing everything that ever went on in their life or their marriage, and I think it's real dangerous in this country if we don't have a zone of privacy for everybody," she'd said, cutting off further questions, while on every stump around New Hampshire "she persuasively articulated the Clinton agenda. The public adored her," Oakley gushed.

"Adored" was also an exaggeration, for many voters were put off by Hillary's apparent hardness, the feeling that she was Lady Macbeth in a business suit. But Hillary Rodham Clinton had certainly introduced a new strain into staid American politics: the first feminist would-be First Lady since Eleanor Roosevelt, and the first real co-candidate, campaigning alongside her partner. She and Bill were baby boomers, centrist in their politics, idealistic in their vision of America, and relentlessly hardworking in their determination not only to win the Democratic nomination—but to take a shot at the seemingly invincible President Bush.

Meanwhile, as their campaign television consultant, Mandy Grunwald, noted, something strange had been going on in the electoral mind. There had been "no meltdown after Gennifer Flowers," but "there had been after a weekend of the draft story. We did not understand what the alchemy between the two issues was, what long-lasting question it raised about Clinton."

Nobody did. But Clinton having survived, it was clear that new chemical compounds were developing in the great American unconscious, even conscious—and that Bill and Hillary Clinton were the catalysts, in a way that no other Democratic candidate at the time was or even promised to be. Even in his own party Clinton was fast becoming the Antichrist to some on the left of center, a breath of younger, fresher air to others who were tired of twelve uninterrupted years of Republican presidency.

Political analysts and observers, however, had witnessed only a hint of the Clinton potential. With virtually no black voters in New Hampshire—one of the whitest states in America—Clinton's greatest strength was yet to be seen. Moreover, the skirt-'n'-draft issues were only the first dramas in the unfolding '92 soap opera. Despite his high polls as the victor of Desert Storm, President Bush stunned his party faithful in New Hampshire by failing to trounce Pat Buchanan—a mere newspaper columnist and white, gun-lobby-supported bigot—in the Republican primary. Moreover, with the President only scraping through the primary, a new billionaire candidate, fed up with gridlock in Congress and a federal deficit of $4 trillion and still rising, suddenly entered the race—challenging both Republican and Democratic contenders as an Independent: a ploy that would split the vote in ways no one could predict.

Overnight the President's reelection, once deemed a certainty, looked far, far from inevitable.

CHAPTER FORTY-THREE

ENTER PEROT

A New Turn

Judging by the presidential primary in New Hampshire, it was clear that a new turn in America's "culture wars" was taking place. As Germond and Witcover observed, voters were "mad as hell" over the state of the economy and the apparent failure of politicians in Washington to improve matters. In such a "mad" condition, it became obvious to the veteran observers, voters might well forsake *both* traditional parties.

How much could a President *do*, however? Like governors in individual American states, the President of the United States held a largely symbolic position. He might propose, but Congress for the most part disposed. In a culture of celebrity, however, it was that symbolism, as Professor Diane Blair had noted of the Arkansas governorship—and Professor Schultze had noted of top televangelists—that remained powerfully real for people. Voters still wished to *identify* with their President, even in hard times. In the aftermath of President Reagan—the Great Communicator—the public had come to admire President Bush for his prosecution of the Gulf War, with its small number of American casualties, its securing of future oil supplies from the Middle East, its proof of Allied solidarity, and its demonstration in the field of battle that the debacle of Vietnam could finally be set aside. However, in a time of ongoing—and seemingly unending—recession, voters no longer identified with him. The First Family of George Herbert Walker Bush seemed well off, comfortable, and shielded from the difficulties that several hundred million Americans were facing.

Bill Clinton's message of economic redemption and a middle-class tax cut was thus calibrated to appeal to "the people of America," as candidates liked to call voters. Clinton's skirt-'n'-draft past, however, raised serious questions about his trustworthiness, especially in view of the somewhat elusive way he dealt with questions about that past. His voice, on the Flowers tapes, sounded very much like the candidate's real voice, and his countercharges—that the tapes had been doctored, that Gennifer was a moneygrubbing tart, and that no affair had ever taken place—seemed robust yet not *entirely* truthful. Ditto Vietnam.

H. Ross Perot, by contrast, rode into the American circus arena like a genuine Texan cowboy: an innocent, determined to clean up government and sort out America's economic ills, just as he had demonstrated in his extraordinary career in information technology, the land of America's future, its new economic West. Promising to become a onetime cleanup candidate for the presidency if enough supporters wrote him onto the ballot in all fifty states, Perot's protest movement now swept the nation. By concentrating the public mind on economic issues rather than foreign policy in a time of recession, Perot would stir up the presidential pot, even if he, Ross Perot, was not the man the majority of the nation wished to see in the White House.

Fear in the Party Corridors

The political director of Bush's reelection campaign, Mary Matalin, later admitted that they had misjudged Perot's appeal "from the very beginning"—because, she claimed, "we knew in real life he was certifiable."

Certifiably insane or not, in the wake of Pat Buchanan's strong showing in New Hampshire Ross Perot's mounting polls soon jolted Matalin's team out of their complacency. In the Democratic and Republican primaries in Oregon, Ross Perot siphoned off 13 percent of Democratic votes and 15 percent of Republican—*simply on write-in ballots*! It was not this, however, that sent fear cascading down the party corridors as much as the exit polls. They looked astounding: no fewer than 45 percent of Democratic voters and 41 percent of Republicans said they would vote for Perot in the November election if he stood as an independent!

In California, a *Los Angeles Times* poll was equally ominous: it showed Perot nudging 40 percent—with Clinton down at 26 percent, and President Bush below Governor Clinton even, at 25! Suddenly, the whole 1992 election looked up in the air.

Inspector Perot

Given the Atwater nature of modern political warfare, the Republican response was predictable if tardy. "Over the course of a single weekend, drug czar Bob Martinez, Second Lady Marilyn Quayle, Marlin Fitzwater and Rich Ball all attacked Perot," Matalin recounted—a broadside that, in turn, licensed the press to do so, especially when Perot, riding a surge of public support for his antiestablishment, antigovernment stance, appointed a team of professionals to run his campaign.

"Well, shoot," many jaded journalists thought as they now sharpened their quills and prepared their arrows, "amateur night in Dixie is getting pretty serious." Perot had become, they argued, "fair game," subject to the same media Calvary to which all political contestants had, in the view of the modern Fourth Estate, to submit.

Until then Perot had seemed a specimen of quintessential Americana: a crew-cut, can-do Texan entrepreneur who would get the American economy back on its feet, cutting the Gordian knots and entanglements of Washington, D.C., with its towering Babel or babble enmeshing the American people. As the press began to pick over Perot's past, however, a new picture emerged: "Inspector Perot," a security freak who even had his own children's friends checked out by his secret police; a moral dictator of frightening prejudices, meannesses—and irrational, wacky decisions. On an *ABC News* talk show Perot declared he would not appoint homosexuals or adulterers to his cabinet. Given 1980 and 1988 campaign rumors that George Bush had for many years enjoyed the pleasures of a mistress (another Jennifer, though spelled with a "J," Bush's longtime aide Jennifer Fitzgerald), this was seen as an attack on both the President and the would-be President, since Bill Clinton, too, was deemed to have tacitly admitted to past adultery in his CBS interview.

Perot's Taliban-like political views sounded fine to born-again Christian moralists but looked bleak to most other sinners, even hack reporters—and in consequence they revolted. *The Dallas Morning News* soon published a story that Perot had broken into a tenant's house because the tenant was nine days late paying his huge $7,500 monthly rent. There were stories of Perot's hiring private detectives to spy on extramarital and other behaviors of employees, competitors, *even his own and other people's families*—indeed, that he had even investigated Vice President Bush's four sons in 1986, sending the Vice President a note warning him, as *The Washington Post* reported, that two of them "were said to be involved in improper activities."

Almost overnight the American cowboy innocent was recast by the media: this time reportrayed not as Tom Mix but as a mix of the nefarious Senator Joseph McCarthy and the odious J. Edgar Hoover—with the incumbent Republican Vice President of the United States openly warning the American people, "Imagine Ross Perot having the IRS, the FBI and the CIA under his control."

Act I of the American electoral soap opera thus had a new villain: "Inspector" Perot.

Nuclear Bombing

Having initially ignored the Perot phenomenon, the Bush team had now convinced themselves that Inspector Perot was the main threat to their man. Governor Clinton, beaten into second place in the Democratic primary in New Hampshire, would inevitably, they argued, self-destruct as more stories leached from the Arkansas tomb. Perot's clear, forceful, moralistic message on the economy was, however, a new monster, and must be met in the only way Republicans knew how to. Thus, instead of urging the President's campaign team to work with the White House to address the need for a new American economic agenda to beat the recession, Bush played Henry II once more. As Mary Matalin confided, Bush "literally said, 'You guys get paid to worry about this, so do what you have to do'— something like that." As campaign observers Jack Germond and Jules Witcover recorded, "it was the same old George Bush, holding his nose while others did something he said was distasteful to him—but not distasteful enough for him to call off the dogs."

The dogs proved to have razor-sharp teeth. Candidates had "positives" and "negatives." Despairing of improving Bush's sliding positives, the Republican campaign team set about "improving" Perot's negatives: "a spontaneous eruption" that rippled across Washington, as Matalin recalled. The "Republican community inside the Beltway takes it as a signal, and they start shooting away, and it just got out of control," she later acknowledged, ashamed. "We were not supposed to nuclear bomb the guy," she confessed. "It was supposed to be a little bit of Death by a Thousand Cuts."

Faced with war on two fronts, Bush had chosen to adopt a Churchill/Roosevelt-type "Germany First" campaign strategy, with American bombers first raining TNT on Hitler's rather than Hirohito's evil empire: in this case, the nefarious Ross Perot, as Bush's B-17 daylight raids homed in on the Wolf's Lair in Texas, laying waste to the ultimate source of Führer Perot's popular power: Perot himself.

Perot would never forgive the Republican "dirty tricks" campaign, which finally caught him in his private bunker. As Perot's aide Ed Rollins, former National Republican Congressional Committee member and manager of Ronald Reagan's landslide reelection campaign in 1984, confided, Perot was mortally offended; indeed, he called Tom Luce, his other ex-Republican chief campaign aide, on the night of July 10, 1992, almost a dozen agitated times. Perot was "really worked up over ABC was going to go with a story about one of his daughters [and] a college professor," Rollins recounted. Perot had apparently ordered his daughter and her beau to be kept "under surveillance"—the jilted college professor claiming, in the media interview, that Perot had "confronted him and said, 'My daughter's never going to marry a Jew.' "

Perot was furious—as well he might be.

Governor Clinton had said, after losing the tough New Hampshire primary, that the experience had proved he was able to take a punch. Ross Perot now proved he could not.

Invasion of Privacy

It was not simply the Jewish vote Perot seemed, thanks to his gung ho, gun-toting maverick approach, destined to lose. Addressing the NAACP in Nashville, Perot had referred to "you people" and "your people"—a patronizing way of speaking to blacks that had alienated the entire audience. "Your people?" one outraged young member of the audience had shot back. "*Our* people!"

Perot had not listened, nor had he understood. Inclusiveness had now vanished from his vocabulary as he warred with the world, intending to communicate his message via the American media. With his vast personal wealth he had thought he could simply buy media time and approval, but, like almost every successful billionaire, Perot was a miser. His heart, broken by the scurrilous personal allegations in the press, balked at the $150 million budget that his campaign advisers now estimated to be the cost of an all-out presidential bid. To their chagrin he fired Rollins, architect of Reagan's victory, telling Hamilton Jordan that he was not going to "hand over" the campaign to professionals. "You should also know that I may just decide to pull the plug on this whole thing," he added ominously. To Jordan's disbelief, Perot then gave his reason: "This thing is unbelievable. My family's privacy has been invaded."

His family's privacy? It was clear Perot was living in a nineteenth-century world, for all his grasp of late-twentieth-century information technology. Jordan could not credit Perot's naiveté as the would-be president then asked, 'What is it like if you make it to the White House?' "

Jordan's response was to tell Perot the truth: "I said, it just gets worse."

Perot Pulls Out

Negative Republican campaigning and the press invasion of Perot's privacy—with newspaper stories coming out about three of his own children, plus another quasi son about whom Perot cared deeply—had crushed him. That night the Texan decided it was not worth the candle.

"He just said," Jordan recalled, "he saw no need to put his family through this."

Ignoring the extraordinary groundswell of public support and volunteerism he'd inspired, and with a strange excuse about not wanting to give rise to a dead heat that would be bad for the nation, Perot suddenly quit.

The Manhattan Project

For one brief moment Ross Perot had mounted the boards of modern American politics—then had balked at the cost, not only in dollars but in terms of the invasions of his privacy. One could only feel compassion for a man suffering such *ad hominem, ad familiam* tactical attacks using—as Mary Matalin acknowledged—nuclear-tipped warheads.

Warned by Betsey Wright that his own armor had weak spots and could not withstand such a Republican-directed onslaught, Bill Clinton had himself balked in 1987, suffering the midlife crisis that had brought him to the very edge of divorce, even an exit from politics, his ultimate true love. This time, however, another soldier had bravely taken the brunt of the enemy attack. Using daily public denunciations by senior Republicans and faxed derogatory information about Perot's past on Republican Party letterheads, the Republicans had blitzed the Inspector and had thereby brought the cowboy to his knees. As Tom Luce noted, "All that stuff was being fed by the Republicans," inciting a media "feeding frenzy."

This Republican concentration on Perot, however, as ex-Republican Tom Luce later reflected, proved fatal for the Republican campaign, for it led to the press making "a conscious decision to take their guns off Bill Clinton," allowing the Arkansan to "get off the ground." It was, Luce added, the "fatal mistake" of his former colleagues, for Clinton was "winded, he was down for a nine count and they let him go to a neutral corner and get well, because they turned all these guns off of Clinton onto Perot, and concentrated on Perot for three weeks. In doing so, they let Bill Clinton completely withdraw from the front pages of the papers, get out of the vortex of the negative press that Bill Clinton was in. In that time he redid his economic plan, people quit talking about Gennifer Flowers, and he came back with the democratic convention and his economic plan . . . It enabled him to sound substantive while Bush was throwing rocks at Perot."

Though it overlooked Clinton's extraordinary survival story in the tough and often grueling primary campaigns after New Hampshire, Bill's core team agreed. Although, with the support of Georgia governor Zell Miller, Bill won Georgia's primary as well as the "Super Tuesday" ballot of southern states, garnering impressive support from southern blacks, Bill's negatives—particularly his problem telling the simple, unvarnished truth—raised grave questions about his ultimate electability. The cover of the April 8 issue of *Time* magazine encapsulated the problem. Across the forehead of Bill Clinton's face, photographed like an X ray, the headline read: "Why Voters Don't Trust Clinton."

"I think that was one of the key periods of the campaign," David Wilhelm recalled," because we were teetering after the California primary, and I actually think that if George Bush had gone on the attack during that period, we might have suffered nicks and cuts that we could never have recovered from."

George Stephanopoulos was certainly grateful for the respite. The Republicans, he acknowledged, "made a fatal mistake turning their howitzers on Ross Perot. It gave us an opportunity to come up the middle." Nevertheless, Bill Clinton's resurrection was not achieved without considerable hand-wringing. While the Bush team engaged the Perot colossus, the Clinton team tried by interviewing politicians, academics, pollsters, and focus groups to work out what was going wrong—or, as Germond and Witcover put it, to "crack the enigma of candidate Clinton" who now seemed charismatic enough to win his party's nomination in July, yet not reliable enough to win the popular vote in November.

Why were voters experiencing such "tremendous unease" about Clinton, as the Democratic governor of Pennsylvania, Robert Casey, openly asked? Clinton had, after all, beaten off the Democratic opposition—including ruthlessly trouncing Paul Tsongas in Florida, where the Clinton team surgically extracted from Tsongas's past platform the proposals that would most hurt Florida residents (increased gas taxes and cuts in Medicare) and pasted them across the state's television screens as warnings. "You can tell when somebody has a glass jaw," James Carville pitilessly described Tsongas, "and after three days of TV his jaw was shattered. He had nothing to come back with; we'd smacked him with his own bad news."

Tsongas had dropped out after Illinois and Michigan, leaving only Jerry Brown for Clinton to beat—yet there was little sign as yet that the electorate was taking Bill Clinton to its heart. His positives might be high—but his negatives seemed even higher. During the Connecticut campaign, for example, Clinton went to play nine holes of golf at a whites-only golf club, a lapse that made his civil rights record look suspect. Then, in an act of stupendous stupidity, he admitted to having smoked marijuana at Oxford—yet claimed he had not inhaled!

This faux pas provided, as Carville noted, "fodder to every stand-up comedian in America"—and epitomized Bill's problem.

Ironically, as Betsey Wright later pointed out, having read Clinton's Oxford diaries, Clinton *hadn't* inhaled—at least in his first year at Oxford—thanks to his allergies. But the way in which Bill had mentioned the fact, during a simple Sunday interview show, admitting that he had smoked but saying he hadn't liked it, adding "I didn't inhale," *sounded* so phony it was risible. As Carville recalled, Clinton had not needed to mention Oxford at all, let alone go into such detail. It was a typical example of Clinton "overkill": the determination to add, and go on adding, to an exam paper, in order thereby to convince the examiner he knew the subject at every level and in every facet; also, in Connecticut, of the need to give skeptical Sunday voters one extra proof that he was a good, moral person and worth voting for.

The reaction was, as it had been when Clinton was a small child in Hope attempting to inveigle other children to like him by inviting them to test his new swing, counterproductive. "Instead of talking about how to get drugs off the streets of New York we were talking about Bill Clinton smoking pot at Oxford," Carville fumed. The candidate came across as dishonest—indeed, two days later a *Los Angeles Times* poll showed 39 percent of Americans as being of the opinion that Clinton did not have the honesty and integrity to serve as president—outnumbering those who thought he did.

The Clinton campaign not only reflected on this, it also reflected it. "There was nobody in charge," Carville described the Clinton headquarters. "It was kind of like a floating crap game with different players getting their hands on the dice."

Though Clinton ultimately beat Brown in the June New York primary—thanks to an unintendedly tough criticism by the Arkansas governor of the black rap singer SoulJay, as well as a widely discussed photo of former governor Brown schmoozing with the Reverend Jesse Jackson, who had made anti-Semitic remarks—those closest to the ground knew it was a hollow victory. With Kansas, Minnesota, and Wisconsin also falling to Clinton, Bill was assured of the Democratic nomination at the summer convention in New York in terms of delegates—but had scant chance of beating Bush once Bush turned his formidable Republican forces back from Perot onto Clinton. "We were about to catch the fish, but the fish was going to be dead," Carville memorably summed up the looming Democratic Party nomination: a fate that had met every Democratic contender for the presidency since LBJ, save, briefly, Jimmy Carter's win over Ted Kennedy and then President Ford, almost two decades earlier.

Thus began the Manhattan Project: the quest for a scientifically controlled reconstruction of the candidate, in time for the nomination. "Bill Clinton," the campaign team was clear, was a label in urgent need of redefinition. "What we found," Carville confessed after the results of audience research came in, was that "people didn't know who Bill Clinton was, and what they thought they knew," he added, "they didn't much like." One voter, polled by the focus group operatives, said it for them all, Frank Greer recalled, "by observing that if Clinton was asked what his favorite color was, "he'd say, 'plaid.' "

It was high time, then, for a makeover, while the Republican armies were otherwise engaged. And for those who in 1982 had watched Bill Clinton's comeback, who better than Hillary to effect that change in voter response?

It was high time, they argued, to unveil Hillary as their atomic weapon, as once she had been used to blast Frank White out of the Arkansas gubernatorial waters.

The Los Alamos Experiment

Excited, Bill and his inner circle, like technicians at Los Alamos, sat down to assess Hillary's nuclear capability as a feminist and passionate debater of the "issues."

This time the political scientists crowded before a television monitor in the Holiday Inn in Charleston, West Virginia, where they were to look at the experimental mushroom cloud: the results of a new polling technique that tracked people's responses to video film—in this case, their responses to the candidate and his wife politicking.

As in 1989, when Dick Morris had been asked to run a poll of potential voters in Arkansas for Hillary as candidate, Bill, as a lifelong political junkie, was agog with anticipation.

"He was aware of her intelligence, her ability, her importance to the campaign," Carville acknowledged of his boss, for Hillary had been involved in every major strategic decision of the campaign, even minor tactical ones. Her resolution and focus had saved the day when the Gennifer Flowers story had broken and when the draft letter had surfaced. She had a record of accomplishments as a lawyer, a children's rights activist, and a leading figure of educational reform that regularly put her among the top fifty professional women in America.

Holding his can of Coke, Bill Clinton beamed as he listened to the scientists' explanation of the new polling procedure. "Once we had tabulated the results," Carville recalled of the innovation, "we superimposed them as a line on the screen and ran the tape [of Bill and Hillary speaking] for Clinton. He had never seen the technique and was fascinated."

According to the "Manhattan Project" scientists, this new technique would lead to the harnessing of an awesome new power. As in 1989, however, the results were stunning: stunningly bad.

Hillary's Hair

"Hillary was not particularly popular at this moment in the campaign," Carville later admitted, "and when she appeared on the screen the dials just plunged. All of them. I mean they just dropped into a trench."

Bill's jaw also dropped. "Clinton looked at the chasm line and said, 'You know, they just don't like her hair.' "

Carville's first impulse was to burst out laughing.

"No one could talk, no one could even make eye contact. There was this stifled silence." Carville himself had dropped under the table, "pretending to tie my shoe. No way I was standing up. Finally Clinton left the room."

"They don't like her hair!" the team chanted, collapsing. People were almost literally splitting their sides. And yet this was perhaps the most touching and revealing moment of the entire campaign so far, akin to the moment when, during filming of the crucial CBS interview, a red-hot arc light had been inadvertently toppled and Bill, unseen by any camera, had snatched his little wife from its path.

"They don't like her hair!" Once again, unseen by the American public, Bill had betrayed his most honest feeling, however risible to others. "This was a man who desperately loved his wife," Carville recalled with amazement. "He could not deal with the fact that, at the time, Hillary was unpopular." Carville paused. "Couldn't deal with it? He couldn't see it!" he recalled, astonished.

Taking Bill for Granted

The plunging public response to Hillary denoted that the Manhattan Project as a nuclear weapons program would have to be abandoned.

It was 1990 all over again. Bill would have to fight the battle himself. But how, when people were so suspicious of his slickness?

Belatedly the "best and the brightest" brains of 1992 looked around—and realized that the answer lay directly before them; indeed, it needed no knowledge of nuclear physics to discern. *They had taken Bill Clinton himself for granted,* overwhelmed by his drive, energy, intelligence, education, distinctions, and political savvy.

The fallout from earlier Republican hits—Gennifer, marijuana, Vietnam War draft evasion, Slick Willie—was still radioactive, and it might be difficult to change the minds of voters who were convinced by them, even though Bill would probably campaign, as was his wont, to the eleventh hour and fifty-ninth minute in an attempt to do so. Yet the larger part of the American population *had never even heard of him,* coming as he did from a tiny southern state. It was time, then, to construct a new image. With his illustrious academic record—Georgetown, Rhodes Scholarship at Oxford, Yale University Law School, professor at the University of Arkansas by the age of twenty-six, governor at thirty-two—there was, the focus groups revealed, a widespread assumption that Bill had been born with a silver spoon in his mouth. By contrast, Ross Perot had come across as refreshingly straightforward: a simple peasant reformer in the manner of Wat Tyler, legendary leader of the peasants' revolt in 1381.

Bill's television and Hollywood friends thus got down to work. The result would be not an atom bomb—but a hydrogen bomb.

CHAPTER FORTY-FOUR

NOMINATION

"Bimbo Eruptions"

While the Manhattan team labored to invent a secret weapon that would work, Betsey Wright, brought back from the John F. Kennedy School of Government at Harvard, was employed to ensure that Republican weapons of mass destruction would not.

Using Jack Palladino, a San Francisco private eye whom Hillary had gotten to know when working as an intern on the Black Panther defense in 1970 and who had supposedly disproven the authenticity of the Flowers tapes, Wright organized what became known in Little Rock as "Scandal Control": a unit specifically set up to deal with what Betsey coined, in what became a legendary term, "the bimbo eruptions." Researching the backgrounds of potential "gold diggers" who might offer compromising information about Bill Clinton, Wright and her team threatened to expose the diggers' *own* private lives if they dared try to make money out of the candidate.

"I don't think anybody besides Betsey and I will ever know how hard the Republicans tried to destroy him," recalled Betsey's aide Kathie Ford frankly. Sadly, she was not exaggerating. Palladino's $100,000 fees were paid out of federally subsidized campaign funds, but they were dwarfed by the amounts being offered to dredge up dirt on Governor Clinton. Tabloid reporters were openly offering, as *The Washington Post* confirmed in July 1992, "top dollar"; indeed, "juicy sums of up to $500,000 a pop" were being touted "to tell embarrassing stories about the Arkansas governor," *Washington Post* reporter Michael Isikoff later recalled.

Half a million dollars? The entire democratic electoral system of the United States was now being compromised by Isikoff's colleagues in the so-called serious press in the search for trash: trash that could be used for competitive advantage over their rivals in the war of modern media. By contrast, the sums expended on trying to keep the press out of the garbage bins and to maintain a level political playing field, in the interests of American democracy, were modest—and, in terms of the survival of democratic politics in America, vital.

Wright's work—she even had visiting journalists followed, to watch what they were up to in Arkansas—proved 100 percent successful, without her once needing to resort to more than the threat of countersmear. As in the Cold War, mutual extermination was a horrific danger, but effective in avoiding hostilities. Not one of Wright's nineteen possible "eruptions" was permitted to erupt.

To Wright's chagrin, however, her very triumph in cauterizing the infected area of Clinton's candidacy would make her, in due course, a liability. As she later lamented, "After he got to the White House I became an untouchable because his association with me was 'someone who knew about the women'! Appointments that I was up for the call would come at the last minute: 'After all, we think it'll look like a payoff or hush money!' 'What?' Betsey remembered expostulating, 'I didn't steal anything!' It was, you know," she reflected bitterly, "an interesting and ironic twist, in the way things went—all I did for him in the '92 campaign in trying to protect his reputation and character ended up being what made me an untouchable by him and the White House staff!"

Choosing a Vice President

For months prior to the New York convention Bill Clinton had mulled over the question of an appropriate vice presidential candidate.

Bill's preferred option, General Colin Powell, met with no positive response from the general, just as President Truman had sought vainly to co-opt General Eisenhower in 1948. Some sixty alternative vice presidential candidates had thereupon been reviewed by a committee under the chairmanship of the black Washington lawyer Vernon Jordan and directed by a lawyer, adviser, and quintessential "public servant," the former deputy secretary of state Warren Christopher, who had advised Presidents Lyndon Johnson and Jimmy Carter.

In the end Clinton defied the pundits who argued for a ticket balancing North and South, age and youth. Instead, he chose—together with a promise of an office in the West Wing and "meaningful policy assignments that would draw on his special talents," as Christopher later chronicled—a man his own age, indeed a year younger, and also from the South: Senator Al Gore.

Mark Grobmeyer, a political insider, had introduced Clinton to Gore five years before and had recently urged Clinton to take the Tennessee senator as his running mate, despite the same-South constituency they represented. Gore was well grounded in Washington and in foreign as well as environmental policy, Clinton in domestic economic, educational, and social issues, suggesting a good team. The one had gubernatorial experience, the other senatorial. Above all, however, they represented the "best and the brightest" of a new generation of baby boomers—and they got along well from the moment they began rehearsing their political beliefs and aspirations.

In the making of a President, image is crucial, for upon it the prejudices and intuitive expectations of a nation can depend. Image can, of course, be created out of nothing, but it is better when it arises out of something—and Clinton and Gore definitely had something. Grobmeyer witnessed the moment in Little Rock when Bill announced his decision. "It was a beautiful day," Grobmeyer recalled the almost royal moment as he sat in the front row outside, waiting beneath the specially constructed podium at the rear of the governor's mansion, ringed by century-old trees, and "here they come out," he reconstructed the historic occasion, "Bill and Hillary, with Chelsea, Al and Tipper and their kids—it was a powerful, powerful thing. And I knew at that point that he was going to be president and Al was going to be vice president. I thought 'No way Bush could win against them.' It was real. It wasn't just an image made up for TV. They're both real people. Their families are real people and there's nothing phony about them. What you see is what you get."

The selection of Al Gore proved an inspired choice. But it would need more than a handsome young running mate to turn the presidential tide, as delegates to the 1992 Democratic Convention in New York were well aware.

Priming the Convention

In Chicago 1968, uniformed police had been employed to combat Vietnam War protesters outside the Democratic convention hall—images that not only tarnished the party's reputation for decades but contributed to the fall of Vice President Hubert Humphrey, the party's nominee, and his running mate, Senator Muskie. Save for the one-term election of Jimmy Carter, subsequent nominations had proven fruitless and often contentious. Nineteen ninety-two, the Democratic National Convention organizers determined, would be different.

To the chagrin of Republicans, they were. Thanks to the extraordinary skills of party chairman Ron Brown and the Hollywood-based producer Gary Smith, the nomination process worked like clockwork, following a coherent, well-planned script. Given the clear results of the primaries, only those rivals and delegates willing to endorse Bill Clinton were allowed to speak at the four-day event. Adherence to the new party mantra of centrism was also promulgated—for this was a convention not to choose a presidential candidate but to invest him.

Bill and Hillary Clinton began by walking through Manhattan, followed by cameramen and reporters—but they did not speak until Clinton was officially nominated on the night of Wednesday, July 16, 1992, and even then it was not in person but telecast from Madison Square Garden to "thank you all for being here and loving your country and to tell you that tomorrow night I will be the comeback kid. Good night and God bless you all."

Thus for three days and nights the Democratic convention was pumped up in what communications professor Larry Smith saw as a "two-phased narrative strategy that cast their presidential ticket in terms acceptable to a diverse constituency and"—now that the Bush team had destroyed Perot—"established a narrative posture capable of withstanding the much-anticipated Republican attacks on Clinton's character."

Delegate after delegate primed the convention as Democrats derided Bush and the Republican Party, then called for change—the "us-versus-them" grammar of revivalist-style, tented bonanzas. From "the need for change" to the "agents of change" on Wednesday, the narrative of the convention took delegates (and reporting media) though a tribute to Robert F. Kennedy and even an extraordinary segment where AIDS sufferers were brought onto the stage, complete with a mega–video screen backcloth, in an almost televangelist ritual of personal witness to the trials of American life and the need for a personal messiah. It was political theater—but performance art, too, and of the highest quality: moving, sincere, idealistic, and imbued with hope. Mark Miller of *Newsweek* observed, fascinated, as the party nominee and Hillary—who had been out campaigning for Bill all day—sat with TV dinners in a side room and watched on a small screen as Bob Hattoy and Elizabeth Glaser addressed the convention. "Bill was overcome. He wept at each speech as did Hillary and it was just an amazing moment," Miller recalled. Clinton literally put the phone down on Jerry Brown, who was complaining about the treatment he was getting, and cut him off with the words "Bob Hattoy is about to speak. I've got to go." Afterward, Miller recalled, "Chelsea came in, and she had been crying. We were all crying."

It was risible yet real: schlock yet stirring. Infuriated Republicans watched in awe as the Democrats, seemingly without warning, appropriated Ronald Reagan's mastery of televised drama. Mary Matalin was particularly incensed, especially at the thought that her lover was involved in this moving *trompe l'oeil.* "This was the most flagrant, revolting hypocrisy of all time," she raged in retrospect, "*and they got away with it*"—seemingly unaware of the irony not only that Reagan's pioneering methods were now being employed by Democrats rather than Republicans but that she and her lover were, in their diametrically opposed camps, primary stagehands in a surreal yet endlessly entertaining new soap opera that was fast becoming as enthralling to many Americans as the other soaps they watched obsessively, day after day, on television.

The Nomination

Al Gore's speech to the New York convention, as vice presidential nominee, had meanwhile been particularly effective, with a moving reference to his life-threatened son. It was Governor Mario Cuomo, however, who formally nominated the presidential candidate—and in ringing terms. "Bill Clinton," the New York governor declared, "believes, as we all here do, in the first principle of our Democratic commitment: the politics of inclusion, the solemn obligation to create opportunity for all our people, not just the fit and the fortunate—for the aging factory worker in Pittsburgh and the schoolchild in Atlanta, for the family farmer in Des Moines and the eager immigrants sweating to make their place alongside of us here in New York City and in San Francisco. For all the people," Cuomo continued, "from wherever, no matter how recently, of whatever color, of whatever creed, of whatever sex, of whatever sexual orientation, all of them equal members of the American family, and the neediest of them, the neediest of them, deserving the most help from the rest of us. That is the fundamental Democratic predicate."

Cuomo's words were prophetic—for perhaps more than any President in American history, Bill Clinton would come to stand for the politics of inclusion in America, an approach that, unlike so much else in the soap-operatic and soap-advertising business of politics in modern America, was utterly genuine—indeed, the most genuine part about Bill Clinton. "I think that what is said about Bill Clinton—that he became 'the first black president'—is really true," Joycelyn Elders, a black pediatrician who had known Bill Clinton since he was attorney general, had served as his director of Arkansas Health Services from 1987, and later became the surgeon general of the United States, reflected. "I really think that, you know, when he goes to black churches he's more comfortable than I am! And I think his heart was in the right place, and he really wanted to do good things. But by the same token, we also knew Bill Clinton was a consummate politician. And whatever he did, he was not going to push so far that he would hurt himself politically!"

Above all, as Dr. Elders recognized, Bill Clinton was both competitive and goal-oriented. "Ever since I've known Bill Clinton, Bill Clinton has wanted to be President of the United States," she recalled. "You didn't have to talk to him long, he'd tell you that! And he'd tell you how he went and met Kennedy and all—he knew from then he wanted to be President. But the Kennedys: they were these liberals. So he knew he couldn't be a Kennedy in terms of his actions, thoughts, and politics and stay in Arkansas! It's such a conservative state!"

Watching Clinton's rise to political power, Dr. Elders not only marveled at the dexterity with which he had played the different interest groups in such a conservative southern state, after his 1982 comeback, but the absoluteness of his ambition. "He could have gone to Washington, joined a big law firm, but he would have been just one of many lawyers in a big law firm. Bill Clinton's aim was never to make a lot of money. It was never to run a big business. He was always after power," the pediatric endocrinologist and sharecropper's daughter considered. "He felt that the power to control was in politics. And he wanted to make a difference." In her view he had, especially by his emphasis on education, which in some respects

preceded health. "I believe you can't keep people healthy if they're ignorant," Dr. Elders memorably remarked, having fought for early childhood
education as hard as she had for rural clinics. Bill Clinton had "a really
keen mind—whatever you went over with him, he really focused on it, he
really made sure he understood it." But in the end it was, always, a matter
of control, of remaining top dog. "He didn't like to lose anything," she
mused. "You know, like you don't even know what you want—but you
don't want to lose! And I think that's what drove him—he *never* wanted to
lose!"

Since 1982 he hadn't, despite all the odds. After enthusiastic recommendations by Clinton's earlier rivals Paul Tsongas, Tom Harkin, and Bob
Kerrey, even Governor Wilder of Virginia, and after winning the nomination with 3,372 votes to 596 for his nearest rival, Jerry Brown—who was
not permitted to speak—the stage of the Democratic convention was literally set for Clinton's acceptance.

It was now that Governor Ann Richards launched the secret weapon: a
thirteen-minute documentary film. "Bill Clinton is not a creation of the
media or of this party," Governor Richards declared. "He's not a card-
board cut-out candidate. He is a real human being: a son, a father, a husband and a friend. And those of us who know and respect Bill Clinton
want you to know that this Democratic party has a presidential nominee
that you would be proud to call your friend."

The lights dimmed—and the triumph of the Democratic will flickered
into life.

The Man from Hope

The Bill Clinton who bestrode the huge screen was adorable: deeply
human, and all-American. "I was born in a little town called Hope,
Arkansas, three months after my father died," Bill Clinton started the film
in a narrative voice-over. "It was a wonderful little small town, you know,
where it seemed everybody knew everybody else."

Through the critical moments of his life—the confrontation with his
abusive stepfather, the meeting with President Kennedy, the impact of the
civil rights struggle, his romance with Hillary, his presence at the birth of
his daughter—the autobiographical film painted through interviews, back-
drops, and archival film a hypnotic, Horatio Alger–like story of an American dream being realized. It was intensely emotional, intimate, and
poignant, unfolding with bewitching images that anchored viewers in a

collective small-town American past. Only this one was not—at least not ostensibly fictionalized, it was *real:* every snapshot, every amateur film clip, every interviewee's recollection a genuine historical artifact.

Communications professors would later marvel—and balk—at the way the brief biographical documentary married art and ideology, creating, as Leni Riefenstahl had done in her famous film *Triumph of the Will* in 1935, a "central figure as one both 'destined'—perhaps for the presidency—and as one embodying certain beliefs and values." It drew on "one of the most venerable and potent American cultural myths"—the notion of the self-made man or "rags-to-riches" rise, using the power of archival evidence and witness-testimony to verify the mythic portrait.

Linda Bloodworth-Thomasen shrugged off the accolades as well as subsequent academic criticism. For her portrait of Hitler at the 1934 Nuremberg Nazi Party rally—which followed the "Night of the Long Knives" assassination of Ernst Roehm and his senior storm trooper staff— Leni Riefenstahl had been given the Third Reich's most coveted film prizes, only to be excoriated in America and denied, after World War II, the possibility of making further films. Bloodworth-Thomason was no Riefenstahl; yet like Riefenstahl she had instinctively measured the public pulse and had responded to the need for a new image of a man she deeply admired and who was currently misunderstood, his image tarnished by a series of allegations and revelations that were maliciously destroying his credibility and thus electability. Like the Führer in 1934, Clinton had given her carte blanche, had "just said: 'Show the American people who we are,' " and she had—but not through the adoring lens of the masses.

Rather, in the most American of ways, she had sought to humanize a character who, like a deer from out of state, had been caught in the glare of the media spotlight and daubed with splashes of paint—labeled an adulterer, draft dodger, marijuana smoker, Slick Willie . . . "The Man from Hope" was not intended to be "slick," Linda later explained, but the very opposite: "You put a camera two inches from a man's face, and you ask him about the most painful and the happiest moments of his life, he has nowhere to go, and nowhere to hide. He just has to be exactly who he is."

The hastily constructed film single-handedly recast Bill Clinton for the Democratic Party and the American electorate. It included Bill's reflections on the political system—"I was raised to believe in this country, to believe in this system, to believe that elections were good things that gave people a chance to have their say and change the course of events"—and a moving account of the death of Bill's stepfather; shots of Bill and Chelsea playing softball; his thoughts on the CBS *60 Minutes* interview about his marriage; Chelsea's response to that interview. Finally it closed with a reverse of Riefenstahl's famed opening.

Whereas *Triumph of the Will* had begun with Hitler's silver-colored, twin-engine aircraft flying through the clouds above Nuremberg in 1934, below which hundreds of thousands of expectant Nazis were massing in antlike columns for their annual jamboree, *The Man from Hope* ended with Clinton's plane crossing the American sky, upon which home-video images played with current campaign footage and Bill Clinton's voice could be heard saying softly, "Sometimes late at night on the campaign I'll look out the window and think how far I am from that little town in Arkansas. And yet in many ways I know that all I am or ever will be came from there. A place and a time when nobody locked their doors at night, everybody showed up for a parade on Main Street, and kids like me could dream of being a part of something bigger than themselves. I guess there'll always be a sadness in me that I never heard the sound of my father's voice or felt his hand around mine. But all of us have sadness and disappointments in our lives, and hopefully we grow stronger for it. I know every day that I'm alive I hope I'm a better person than the day before. I hope that every day from this day forward we can be a nation coming together instead of coming apart. And I hope that we as a people will always acknowledge that each child in our country is as important as our own. [Home movie shots of Chelsea] I still believe these things are possible. I still believe in the promise of America. And I still believe in a place called [black-and-white photo of railway station] Hope."

As the documentary, projected onto the huge screen, finally came to an end, Bill Clinton walked onto the rostrum and waved to the delegates. The celluloid biography, as Professor Rosteck noted in a retrospective analysis, had, unlike a fictional film, deliberately left the audience hanging, just as Riefenstahl had done in her portrait of Hitler—inviting the audience "to help the 'hero' achieve his goal."

A Masterpiece of Political Advertising

Leaving out (after considerable argument with the campaign team) the story of Vietnam, the brief film proved, as one commentator wrote, a "triumph of suggestive compression." Another remarked how the candidate appeared as "a fine, decent American, manly but sensitive, firm in his ideas of right and wrong yet compassionate, a devoted husband and doting father, a man who has had his share of troubles in life but prefers to talk about the troubles of others. Bill Clinton, the film seems to say, represents the best that small-town America can produce." And yet another perceived a "recurrent subliminal message: here is a man who has nothing to hide, who can look Americans straight in the eye and bare his soul."

The audience was stunned. As William Grimes wrote in *The New York Times,* the film "won the heart of every delegate"—indeed, *Time* afterward reported, even Bush campaigners were "wowed." In the words of Jonathan Raban, the distinguished *Los Angeles Times* critic, *The Man from Hope* was "a masterpiece, perhaps *the* masterpiece, of political advertising."

To James Carville's disappointment, however, the acceptance speech that followed was as long as Hitler's in 1934, lasting almost an hour. It was, Carville believed, the product of too many cooks—Paul Begala, Roy Spence, David Kusnet, George Stephanopoulos, Carville himself, and the Greens: Green, Greenberg, Grunwald . . . It "could have been more focused and shorter," Carville reflected. Instead Governor Clinton "spoke for fifty-four minutes and twenty seconds. Too long. I give the speech B-minus. I wouldn't count it as a disaster, but I felt with a sharper focus and less duration we could have brought it up to an A-minus."

It did not matter, though. Perot had that very day, July 16, 1992, announced he was pulling out of the race, and the telephones were hot with competing calls from Republican and Democratic headquarters to Perot's campaign staff and supporters, inviting them to join the race on one or other side, now that the cowboy had thought better of it. The networks meanwhile identified and rebroadcast Bill's crucial lines, beaming him to the largest audience he had ever enjoyed in his life. "The most important family policy, urban policy, labor policy, minority policy and foreign policy America can have," Governor Clinton was heard to say by more than 100 million Americans, "is an expanding entrepreneurial economy of high-wage, high-skilled jobs. And so in the name of all those who do the work and pay the taxes, raise the kids and play by the rules, in the name of the hardworking Americans who make up our forgotten middle class, I proudly accept your nomination for president of the United States."

"The Most Stunning 180"

Suddenly, somehow, a campaign that had lurched from crisis to crisis and had lacked definition now coalesced into a seamless, triumphant flow: the most professional nominating event since that of the Republican former governor of California, Ronald Reagan. By choosing Al Gore as his running mate and with almost military orchestration of the televised national convention agenda, official Democratic nominee William Jefferson Clinton's national polls soared to a *20* point lead over those of incumbent President George Bush: the biggest single rise in political annals and the largest margin over an opponent at this point in a presidential campaign for half a century. It was a stunning achievement.

Best of all, perhaps, was the timing—for Bill Clinton's triumphant nomination in New York now served as a giant magnet to Perot supporters left in the lurch by their Texan hero. As Mary Matalin described it, "In addition to the normal bump Clinton was going to get from his convention, that giant sucking sound we heard was all those Perot change votes moving en masse to Clinton."

For Republicans who had worked so hard to destroy Perot, it was a heartbreaking sight. "Clinton," Matalin sighed, "went in there on his knees and sprinted out as America's panacea. It was the most stunning 180 I'd ever seen in politics."

PART NINE

THE 1992 ELECTION

Flying toward victory, 1992

CHAPTER FORTY-FIVE

ON THE CAMPAIGN TRAIL

A Whistle-Stop Bus Tour

From Madison Square Garden the Clinton team immediately boarded a line of eight buses. They then headed out the city to meet more Americans, just as FDR had done by train sixty years before, at the nadir of the Depression.

Carville, promoted to campaign supremo in an effort to ensure that all the actors, even in minor parts, sang to a single new tune, had counseled against the bus tour but had been overruled by the governor—a further example of Bill Clinton's extraordinary political instincts outshining those even of his top advisers. Campaign time, Carville believed, would be better spent proselytizing in swing states, but Bill had always drawn inspiration from one-on-one "retail politics" with voters. No other form of campaigning could show up the difference between contender and incumbent, he felt—and he was right.

Something of JFK's youthful vigor, energy, and sheer attractiveness was on local and national display as the young man from Hope, buoyed up by his nomination for the presidency, met, embraced, and talked to ordinary Americans in bars, coffee shops, and fast-food restaurants, on the street and in stores. Here was a candidate and his running mate, both in their midforties, together with their attractive young wives, on the road;

not quite Jack Kerouac in search of speed, drugs, sex, and mysticism but spontaneous and willing to listen, literally, to the multifarious voices of America.

The press, which had fed only months before on what it thought to be the rotting corpse of a fallen gladiator, now watched in amazement as the Clinton-Gore Ensemble was welcomed by voters of every color, class, background, and profession. While appearing on the Larry King show earlier that spring, Bill had told his host he had no need of commiseration over the arduous business of campaigning, for he loved the business. Now, on a symbolic road trip across America and in an astonishing display of indefatigable hand shaking, stump speaking, listening, and talking, he proved it to be true. He'd been doing this almost all his adult life, and the excitement and challenge of it had never palled, his restless curiosity and intelligence both piqued and flattered by the attention ordinary voters gave him. It was narcissistic, yet by no means did it depend on flattery—on the contrary, to the chagrin of those who thought him their close friend, he still paid more attention to those with ambivalent or even hostile opinions, reveling in confrontational debate and discussion.

The whistle-stop bus tour took the Clintons and Gores across New Jersey into West Virginia, Pennsylvania, and Ohio for over a thousand miles to Saint Louis, Missouri, picking up and dropping off local journalists and broadcasters whose companies could not afford the expense of jet travel. "Change is the key to your security," Clinton hammered home his message at factory after factory. "The other side is saying 'we've been in charge for twelve years and if you want change, vote for more of the same.' That approach doesn't make sense. Their approach has failed."

Despite the attractive young Democratic contenders' wives, Republicans ridiculed Bill and Al, in a quasi-homophobic smear, as "a team of pretty boys." This time, however, the smear didn't stick. Clinton had sensed the mood of the country, and as more and more people turned out to greet the strange caravan of vehicles, crossing the continent like a Bedouin tribe, even Clinton's staff was amazed. "Something's going on here," Mark Gearan was heard to say, puzzled. "We just rolled out of there hoping for the best." Where hundreds were predicted, thousands appeared. Clinton drove his own vehicle, with Al Gore beside him, and the two men formed a bond and partnership perhaps unique in the annals of presidential and vice presidential candidates on the stump. Both were "policy wonks" with a passionate, indeed obsessive, interest in the issues of the day, from abortion to education, health care to the environment, employment to taxation.

Infected by the easy camaraderie of Clinton and his staff, Senator Gore lost something of his stiffness, inventing a routine where he would warm up the crowd at each stop like a preacher. "Bush and Quayle have run out of ideas," the famed environmentalist senator would shout. "They've run out of energy. They've run out of gas, and with your help come November, they're going to be run out of office!"

The contrast with President Bush—who had won the 1988 election in part by taking as running mate an unknown younger man who would avoid the geriatric pall that had clouded the Reagan administration in its final days, but who now kept his spelling-impaired Vice President at arm's length—was palpable. Signs by the roadside began to appear, addressed by and to the Clinton-Gore team: "Give us eight minutes and we'll give you eight years." It was as if history was being made and people wished to be a part of it. In Vandalia, Illinois, on the last night of the trip, the crowd was twice the size of the population, and in Saint Louis, some thirty thousand people jammed the streets to welcome the caravan.

So successful was the whistlestop bus tour that in all, seven such caravan-campaigns were conducted in the months between the July convention and the November election. One Iowa legislator watched the Clinton-Gore team at work and remarked kindly of Clinton: "He's made two fabulous choices. First he picked this guy, and then this bus thing. People love it. They have to come out and see these two young guys who look and act like they're ready to go." As Mort Engelberg, the busmeister, reflected afterward, the whistle-stop tour of America "became sort of a metaphor—symbolic of this campaign: this is for everybody."

Hillary as Symbol

Clinton's soaring polls after the Democratic National Convention—the Democratic nominee leading Bush by 55 percent to 31—made it imperative that the President mount a counterattack if he were to win a second term. Knowing this full well, the Clinton team prepared themselves in the paint store in Little Rock for the inevitable Republican counterblast—Hillary even setting up a "war room."

As the election campaign now moved toward its climax, it did indeed begin to resemble the sinews of war, with its strategies, tactics, choice of ground on which to fight, armies, wagon trains, advance scouts, vanguards, hangers-on, war correspondents, and camp women—the last no longer there to cook, sew, and comfort the men, but in a feminist age to fight as fellow warriors for the cause, a development epitomized in the star-crossed lovers Matalin and Carville.

If the Democrats had been weighed down for twelve years by the ideological baggage of their liberal past, the Republicans were equally weighed down by the increasingly burdensome conservative wing of their party, the religious Right. Though President Bush had ultimately beaten off Pat Buchanan's challenge in the primaries, it was considered wise to allow Buchanan, as his former party rival, to speak at the Republican National Convention in Houston in August—and this Buchanan did, his opening-night address being broadcast on prime-time television.

The moment Buchanan opened his mouth, however, it became clear Bush had made a mistake. Instead of being a celebratory fest of those in power following one of the most successful Allied military operations in history, the Republican gathering launched into revivalist hate-rally mode, its speakers defiantly opposed to change of any sort, in the manner of many evangelical sects that gloried in traditional interpretations of the Bible and moral denunciation of those other sects they saw as evil.

Staunch Republican Sandra Goodall, political director in a communications consultancy, remembered her growing sense of fear as she watched the Houston convention unfold beneath the city's great stadium. "As the cameras scanned the vast expanse of the Houston Astro Dome, what I noticed first was the huge number of vacant seats," she recalled, recalling the ominous feeling in the pit of her stomach. The crowd, she wrote, "looked sparse and dead compared to the lively, young, standing-room-only crowd at the Madison Square Garden. The second thing I noticed was that the venom began to flow from the minute the first speaker walked onto the stage. Each speaker spoke with an exclusionary vengeance that built into a hatred for everything that wasn't Republican, white-washed, ultraconservative, and Christian. And at the very center of the hatred was a symbol of everything that was wrong with America, everything that was bad and evil." It was, she noted, "a symbol that rolled AIDS, homosexuality, child abuse, condoms, sex outside of marriage, the decline of the white male, all into one neat package": namely, Hillary Clinton.

Religious War

The wisdom of the decision to keep Hillary under wraps, after the results of the new Greenberg polling survey had come in, was now proven—in spades.

Ignoring not only 9 million unemployed Americans but a yawning national deficit and seemingly unending recession, a succession of speakers ranted about "family values," abortion, and homosexuality. "The agenda Clinton and Clinton would impose on America," Buchanan sneered, "abortion on demand, a litmus test for the Supreme Court, homosexual rights, discrimination against religious schools, women in combat units—that's change all right. That's not the kind of change America needs, it's not the kind of change America wants, and it is not the kind of change we can abide in a nation that we still call God's country," he shouted to applause from the party and religious faithful. Buchanan excoriated Clinton for sitting in a "dormitory in Oxford, England" figuring out "how to dodge the draft" and questioned Clinton's "moral authority to send young Americans into battle." Moreover, he foresaw divisive battles at home—and welcomed them. "There is a religious war going on in this country for the soul of America. It is a cultural war as critical to the kind of nation we shall be as the Cold War itself. And in that struggle for the soul of America," he declared, "Clinton and Clinton are on the other side and George Bush is on our side."

The delegates cheered as Pat Robertson, in the same vein, denounced the Arkansan governor and his wife. "When Bill and Hillary Clinton talk about family values," he declared, "they are not talking about either families or values. They are talking about a radical plan to destroy the traditional family and transfer its functions to the federal government."

One middle-aged Bush supporter from the Farm Belt, a vice president of a corporation, burst into tears at the sound of the delegates cheering deliriously while Buchanan was saying such things. "What's happened to my party?" she sobbed. "I can't believe what's happening here."

Runaway Train

What was happening was articulated by the Vice President of the United States of America. "The gap between us and our opponents is a cultural divide," Dan Quayle declared. "It is not just a difference between conservative and liberal. It is a difference between fighting for what is right and refusing to see what is wrong."

As the veteran campaign observers Germond and Witcover noted, there was something different here that had not been there before—at least in the way it seemed to dominate the Republican convention in oil-rich Houston and completely mask the economic plight of the country. "This moral element was something new at this level of American politics," the reporters afterward wrote. "In the past, extremists on both ends of the ideological spectrum had demonstrated hard edges of hostility and anger," but it had "usually been possible for conservatives and liberals to behave with civility and even good humor towards those with whom they totally disagreed." Now, beneath the tentlike cover of the Astrodome, "the delegates of the religious right were a different breed of activists who believed those who disagreed with them were not just wrong, but evil."

"That's pitiful, they're getting pitiful," remarked Bill Clinton in Pittsburgh when he heard of the latest assault on Hillary by the aptly named Rich Bond, the chairman of the Republican National Committee, who had claimed that Hillary had "likened marriage and the family to slavery." The Republicans were descending to gutter tactics, and it was not only demeaning but a travesty of a woman Bill Clinton loved and admired. "This comment by Bond is pathetic," Bill remarked. "It's going to be very difficult for the American people to take them seriously if they can't do any better than that."

As Bush's acceptance speech demonstrated, however, they couldn't. Bush had himself photographed on the podium with Barbara, his wife, his five children, and his twelve grandchildren, but he looked uncomfortable with his running mate and, above all, had no specific economic revival plan to offer the nation other than his recent assurance that heads were going to roll in his cabinet. None had, save for the campaign chief, John Sununu, who would be replaced by Secretary of State James Baker.

There followed a 10-point rise in President Bush's polls from 31 percent to 41—nowhere near enough, however, to catch the runaway Clinton-Gore bus.

Enter Muhammad Ali

Perplexed, Bush nevertheless decided to stay with the strategy he'd agreed upon with Buchanan: to "take apart" Bill Clinton, in Buchanan's own words, just as the Bush team had once destroyed Michael Dukakis. Clinton's Achilles heel was clearly his women—but Hillary had closed off that avenue of attack by standing by her man in the spring, and Betsey Wright had ensured that there would be no further "bimbo eruptions." Therefore Hillary must be further demonized—the Bush team strategized—just as

Perot had been successfully destroyed, by marking him as a dictator, invading his privacy and ruthlessly select-targeting and "exposing" members of his family.

Unfortunately for such strategies, they backfired. The whistle-stop Democratic bus tour had created an image in the public eye of two eager, good-looking, and highly educated young Democrats who shared more than thirty years' experience of state and national government, hand in hand with two handsome and also highly educated young wives, both of them mothers, *both of whom were leaving the microphones to their husbands.* As Gail Sheehy, who accompanied the caravan on behalf of *Vanity Fair,* later recalled, Hillary had learned "from her counterpart how to melt into the backdrop as part of the blond blur of supportive wives, she wore only dresses and little makeup. Her headband was becoming her signature, like Jackie Kennedy's pillbox hats. She and Tipper would sit under a tent in their long-skirted milkmaid dresses circa 1958, their ankles crossed, spooning fruit cup and chatting about nothing of consequence while the hunks tossed a football." In such feminine camouflage, Hillary proved impossible for Republican snipers to get into their sights, let alone hit, forcing the Republicans back into carpet bombing: attacking Bill Clinton's vague "character" problem.

With Bush trailing in the polls, however, this strategy also backfired. "If you can't run with the big dogs, stay under the porch," Bush had sneeringly told a crowd in Woodstock, Georgia—but the macho, Willie Horton–style tactic of 1988 was history; it no longer worked. Clinton had learned the lesson and responded immediately to each and every attack, ensuring that his riposte would be quoted along with the accusation.

Republican campaign director Mary Matalin, unused to her own remarks rebounding onto herself and the President's team, was soon taken to task for the gutter level of the campaign's vituperative personal attacks. Meanwhile, Bill Clinton seemed like Muhammad Ali in his greatest days, standing close to the incumbent champion and taunting him with challenging words. When Bush addressed the National Guard Association in Salt Lake City in November, Clinton changed his schedule to speak there the same day. Hundreds of reporters assembled for the expected "bloodletting" only to find Bush, this time, cowering under the porch. There had been, the President declared, "a great deal of speculation" that he was "going to come out here and use this forum to attack Governor Clinton." Though he felt "very strongly about certain aspects of the controversy swirling around Governor Clinton," he announced, he was backing off. "I didn't come here to attack him," the President declared.

Bill Clinton, it was clear, was not going to suffer the kind of hammering Dukakis had received, or he would punch back—in person.

Trading Blows

Muhammad Ali, four years older than Bill Clinton, had also changed his name, refused to serve in Vietnam ("I ain't got no quarrel with them Vietcong"), supported civil rights, known many women carnally (including four in marriage), sired nine children—and transformed boxing in a series of fights in the 1960s and early '70s that would never be matched. He'd knocked out reigning world champion Sonny Liston and later Joe Frazier, but it was in taking the punches of his opponents that he had become legendary—until chronic encephalopathy, or *dementia pugilistica,* finally felled him in the 1980s.

Meantime, in September 1992, President Bush was confined to long-distance barking from the White House porch. Since the New York *Post* had published allegations that Bush had had a long-standing adulterous affair with Jennifer Fitzgerald, it was considered advisable not to try to raise Gennifer Flowers's *Titanic,* lest other newspapers run with the *Post* story. Instead, in a radio interview with Rush Limbaugh, the loudmouth right-wing bigot and talk-show host, in New York, Bush focused on Clinton's draft record. "I have a very different concept of military service," the World War II veteran began. "I'm sure I would never call the military immoral," he continued, misquoting from Clinton's letter to Colonel Holmes. "Now, maybe he's changed his view on that. . . . Let's find out. Let's let him level with the American people"—a challenge that Clinton, campaigning at that very moment with the former chairman of the Joint Chiefs of Staff, Admiral William J. Crowe, Jr., was able to strike down with ease, since he had never used the word "immoral." Pointing to Admiral Crowe beside him, Clinton remarked that the former chairman of America's armed services "has more credibility on truth-telling than George Bush" and would certainly not have endorsed the Clinton-Gore candidacy if he shared Bush's view.

Seven weeks shy of the November election, President Bush was found still to be trailing 15 percent in the latest *Washington Post/ABC News* poll. Instead of taking the time to develop and communicate a Republican blueprint for economic recovery, the Republican team had relied on negative campaigning. It was clearly not working, and President Bush was going down.

Clutching at straws, Floyd Brown, the man who had produced the Willie Horton 1988 television ads, announced he was going to provide a toll-free phone number where voters could hear the entire Gennifer Flowers audiotapes, but AT&T balked at permitting such dirty tactics so close to a national election, especially when Governor Clinton looked set to become the next President of the United States. Simultaneously the Bush team attempted a last-ditch assault on Clinton's gubernatorial record in Arkansas and his patriotism, excoriating Clinton's failure to stop the pollution of Arkansas rivers through chicken-farming effluent, as they had once tainted Governor Dukakis with allowing the pollution of Boston's harbor. The team also raised sniggers and suspicions by focusing on Clinton's visit to Moscow while at Oxford. Instead of leaving it there, however, the Republican spinmeisters yet again overplayed their hand. It was suggested that Clinton had tried to apply for foreign citizenship to avoid the draft, and a rumor was planted that whole pages were missing from Clinton's passport file at the State Department. Lest the mud stick, James Carville pinned a poster on the wall of the Clinton War Room, to keep his colleagues focused on the real issues—paramount among which was the soon-to-be-legendary reminder: "The economy, stupid." George Stephanopoulos, running Clinton's communications office, responded to Bush's latest smear as "a sad and pathetic ploy by a desperate politician. If he worried as much about what most Americans are going through in 1992 as he does about what Bill Clinton did in 1969," Stephanopoulos sighed, "we'd all be in better shape."

However, it was at this point in what increasingly resembled a Sonny Liston–Muhammad Ali fight, only five weeks before the election, that the battle between Democrats and Republicans was once again thrown into utter turmoil.

Ross Perot suddenly reappeared in the ring—not as referee but as a third boxer!

Perot: The Eight-Hundred-Pound Gorilla

Since July 1992, the Texas billionaire had lain low. His supporters, calling themselves United We Stand America, had not, however. In a laudable display of volunteerism they had ensured enough signatures to put Perot onto the ballot in all fifty states.

Perot himself had used the intervening time to recover from his campaign wounds. Now, on October 1, 1992, at the very moment when the Republican team sharpened their knives in preparation for the final hand-to-hand combat with the Clinton gang in the last few weeks of the fight, as they had done with Michael Dukakis, Perot stunned the world by his reentry into the postmodern American soap opera.

How would Perot's presence affect the election, pundits wondered? His ratings had gone down appreciably since the summer; indeed, a new *USA Today*/CNN survey of voters currently gave Clinton a 17 percent lead over President Bush—52 to 35 percent—with the absent Perot down to a mere 7 percent after having nudged 40 percent back in June. Would Perot's blitz-focus on the economy, analysts asked, gradually take votes away from Clinton as the candidate most concerned with beating the recession? Or would Perot's passionate obsession with the American deficit and economy further validate Clinton's message that it was "the economy, stupid"—diminishing and marginalizing an increasingly elderly-looking, ex-CIA "foreign affairs" President who could talk only of presidential "character" and the need to send American boys to war and possibly death?

With such question marks hanging over their heads, both the Bush and Clinton teams sent their top executives to Texas to befriend the "eight-hundred-pound gorilla," as Perot called himself, assuring the Inspector they would share the upcoming limelight of the 1992 presidential debates with him, now that he was on the ballot—if the format and frequency of such debates could be agreed upon.

Programming the Debates

By successfully dictating the style of the two presidential debates in the 1988 election, James Baker had helped George Bush win the White House that year, for he had insisted that the candidates respond to questions from a panel of filtering reporters, in the manner of a press conference—overriding the Democrats, who wanted a single moderator, channeling *audience* questions in the manner of a debate rather than a press conference. Baker had got his way in 1988, but 1992 was different. Bill Clinton was leading every national poll by at least 10 percentage points; he had no *need* to debate at all, though he was certainly keen to do so.

Had Baker compromised, the three debates—scheduled by the independent Commission on Presidential Debates to begin in September—would already have been under way. James Baker's refusal to debate the debate formats, however, lost his candidate the election, for the lingering disagreement between the two campaign managers meant that by October 1992, when Perot reentered the race, the Texas independent would be able to participate in all three contests, hammering at the issue of the recession and further diminishing the stature of an incumbent President who had no program to revive the economy.

Backing down, Baker now agreed that the first debate would take place in Saint Louis on October 11, in front of a panel of three reporters—Bush's preferred style. The second would take place on October 19 in Richmond, Virginia, in the town meeting format that Bill Clinton had personally suggested—*his* forte. The Clintonistas had assumed that Baker would never countenance a town meeting format. "My view was they'd never accept this, they'd never give Bill Clinton a chance to deal with real people in an open forum," Mickey Kantor, the chairman of Clinton's campaign, recalled—and his fellow negotiators were of like mind. "They all said, 'They'll never agree to that, they'd be crazy to do that.'"

With a new poll showing Clinton's lead moving inexorably toward 20 percent, however, President Bush had but little option. The third and final debate was programmed to be held in East Lansing, Michigan, on October 23, 1992—the latest that the Clinton team would agree to before the November 3 election.

The curtain on the final act of the 1992 presidential soap opera was thus ready to go up—but with three, not two, protagonists.

The Final Act

All across America tens of millions of dollars were being spent on radio and television advertising—$35 million by the Clinton team, $45 million by Ross Perot—but it was in the gladiatorial arena of the presidential debates that the votes of "don't knows" would finally be decided. After weeks of being called "chicken" for not debating, Bush would have a chance to show his colors—or at least to discolor those of his opponents.

Prepped aboard *Air Force One* by Roger Ailes, the media consultant who'd advised Bush in the 1988 debates, Bush launched straight into the "character question" in the first debate in Saint Louis, attacking Clinton for participating in demonstrations against Vietnam as a student in Oxford. "Maybe, they say, well, it was a youthful indiscretion," the President allowed before boasting, "I was nineteen or twenty flying off an aircraft carrier and that shaped me to be a commander in chief of the armed forces. And I'm sorry, but demonstrating—it's not a question of patriotism, it's a question of character and judgment."

Senator David Pryor had, however, been doing his own research, and had discovered that President Bush's father, Senator Prescott Bush, had bravely stood up to the arch-anti-Communist in the Cold War, Senator Joe McCarthy. That morning *The Boston Globe* had therefore published an article calling attention to *père* Bush and his stand against McCarthy's evil ways in the Senate. Using this, Bill Clinton's counterpunch was masterly. "You *have* questioned my patriotism," he quietly acknowledged Bush's attack, before reminding the audience of McCarthy's similar tactics. But when "Joe McCarthy went around this country attacking people's patriotism," he warned the President—and tens of millions of viewers—McCarthy was "wrong," deliberately intimidating honorable Americans until "a senator from Connecticut stood up to him named Prescott Bush."

At the mention of his father and his stand against McCarthy, President Bush looked stunned. "Your father was right to stand up to Joe McCarthy," Clinton said, punching him again, relentlessly. "You were wrong to attack my patriotism," the southpaw punched again. "I was opposed to the war, but I love my country."

Bush's attempt to cut down his young adversary had failed.

Stumped for Ideas

Ross Perot, meanwhile, also dodged the issue of his own credibility, at least in terms of Washington service. Those who criticized him for lack of political experience had "a point," he allowed. "I don't have any experience in running up a $4 trillion debt. I don't have any experience in gridlock government. I have experience in not taking ten years in solving a ten-minute problem."

The issues of deficit and recession, rather than the triumph of Desert Storm, were relentlessly held in play; indeed, the recession resulted in yet more embarrassment for Bush when, stumped for ideas on how to revive the flagging economy, the President announced that he would, after the campaign, appoint James Baker to look into the matter—an extraordinary abdication of responsibility by an incumbent president.

From there, the Republican debate strategy, based upon undermining Clinton's "character," rolled back downhill. Ross Perot's blistering focus on the economy provided brilliant one-liner entertainment but ultimately little conviction that, as President of the United States, the wacky billionaire could be entrusted with the nation's helm. Someone, however, would have to take charge of that—and the fact was, the President no longer gave people confidence that he was man to do it.

Round one, in the President's favored format, had thus not provided the hoped-for presidential knockout.

Admiral Stockdale Falls

A knockout certainly did occur, however, in the next debate. Unfortunately for President Bush, it was in the vice presidential debate in Atlanta—and it only removed the independent vice presidential nominee, Admiral James Stockdale.

Taking his cue from the President, Vice President Dan Quayle immediately attacked Governor Clinton, in absentia, in the single vice presidential debate. Senator Gore simply ignored "Q"'s taunts, steadfastly standing his ground on the economy, domestic issues, foreign affairs, and the environment. Perot's chosen running mate, Admiral Stockdale, however, proved wholly out of his depth, indeed out of ideas—finally confessing that on the subject of health care, he was "out of ammunition."

Admiral Stockdale was clearly out of the running. But with the first round of presidential debates inconclusive in terms of the main party nominees, and the one vice presidential debate over, all eyes turned to the crucial second presidential debate in Richmond, Virginia, once the capital of the Confederacy. Would Governor Clinton, a left-hander, be able to produce a punch that would flatten the President while holding off the Inspector?

What Do We Want to Watch, Honey?

"No matter what I read, what I watched, what I overheard, what I overtly heard," communications professor H. L. Goodall later recounted, "this election was clearly coming down to a generational and cultural clash. A clash of values. Of visions. Of histories. Of herstories. Of power. The lines were indelibly etched into every conversation, every cartoon, every editorial. It was the sixties again, lived here in the nineties. And like the sixties, it was messy. Very messy."

It was. As the political ad war heated up, "our mainstream media-nation merged into the high-velocity lanes of hyperreality," Goodall recounted, amazed at the way a country, his own country, was changing before his very eyes. In this sense, as in 1960, the election marked not only a changing of the guard but a gigantic cultural shift, expressed in a new cultural language, no longer confined to the edges of American society but spoken at its very center. "What was only months before considered alternative media—the talk shows, the music channels, the popular magazines—became virtually indistinguishable from any other form of commercial—or communicative—appeal."

It was no longer, in 1992, a question of who would "win" the debates as of who promised the best infotainment if elected: the future of America was thus reduced to a question not of "what you can do for your country," Goodall noted humorously yet in absolute clinical seriousness, "but instead what do we want to watch tonight, honey, for the next four years?"

For the first time in American history, certainly since Ronald Reagan, the choice of presidential candidate was boiling down to the buttons on Everyman's television remote.

The Defining Moment

What took place on October 19, 1992, in Richmond, Virginia, would certainly go down in presidential campaign history. In the town meeting format, a young black woman, Marisa Hall, stood up before the cameras and asked, "How has the national debt personally affected each of your lives? And if it hasn't, how can you honestly find a cure for the economic problems of the common people if you have no experience in what's ailing them?"

Ross Perot answered first, stating that it was the very worsening of the national debt that had forced him to put aside his business career and become a presidential candidate. As such, he wanted to rebuild a strong American economy that his children and grandchildren could inherit.

The moderator, ABC television's Carole Simpson, then turned to President Bush. Though uncertain what the questioner meant, Bush seemed shy of asking the questioner, as a black woman, to articulate her question more clearly. Like Perot, he misunderstood the real question, responding lamely that "the national debt affects everybody. Obviously it has a lot to do with interest rates" and asking for more time to think about the issue, like a schoolboy in a class for which he hadn't prepped. When Carole Simpson pressed him, however, to give a fuller response, the President dug his own grave. Instead of addressing Ms. Hall directly, he defensively asked the white moderator whether the black questioner was suggesting that "if somebody has means, the national debt doesn't affect them?" Ms. Hall then attempted to rephrase or explain her question.

"Well, I've had friends that have been laid off from jobs," the twenty-six-year-old single woman declared. "I know people who cannot afford to pay the mortgages on their homes, their car payment. I have personal problems with the national debt. But how has it affected *you*?" she queried. "And if you have no experience in it, how can you help us, if you don't know what we're feeling?"

Here was the single most telling and compelling question of the 1992 campaign, put to a President who was widely respected, but who was felt to be out of touch with the ordinary citizens of his country. The Bush team, watching in their communications room, held their breath. The moderator attempted to make it easier for the President, who still seemed puzzled. "I think she means more the recession—the economic problems today the country is facing, rather than the deficit," Ms. Simpson paraphrased.

President Bush appeared to understand and to relax. "Well, listen, you ought to be in the White House for a day and hear what I hear and see what I see," he now told Ms. Hall. "But I don't think it's fair to say, 'You haven't had cancer, therefore you don't know what it's like,' " the President went on, digging his trench even deeper.

Bush's team, in their room, also "didn't get it"; indeed, they were still as mystified by the black lady's question as the President had been. "Everybody in our room was saying, 'What's the question? What is she talking about?' We had the same reaction President Bush did, which was literal," Mary Matalin later admitted—and then gave the most telling explanation of Washington arrogance. "Beyond the Beltway, normal people mentally translated 'national debt' to 'recession.' We didn't," she explained, as if talking about a different species of Americans—a species who didn't struggle with 10 million unemployed neighbors, relatives, and whole families—40 percent of whom were, after being laid off, unable to find a new job, while their home equity values continued to plummet.

It was indisputably the "defining moment" of the debates, of the election, and of the nation at the end of the Reagan-Bush era. "I would have *paid* to have that question asked," James Carville later remarked—concerned that, for all the campaigning of the past few months, Bush's air of aristocracy, of having rich friends who "didn't understand what real people were going through," had never quite been addressed or exposed.

Rich Bond, the chairman of the Republican Party, had recently claimed, on behalf of Republicans, "We are America; those other people are not America." It was an unfortunate claim: exclusionary, self-insulating, and complacent—the voice of the haves to the have-nots. Now, finally, a voter—female and black—had asked the President of the United States whether he understood. And to the consternation of some 90 million Americans, the President responded that he did not. "I think it's sad," Bush acknowledged the plight of the unemployed, "but I think in terms of the recession, of course you feel it when you're president of the United States. And that's why I'm trying to do something about it by stimulating the exports, investing more, better education system. Thank you. I'm glad to clarify it."

But Bush had *not* clarified it for Ms. Hall.

Each of the three candidates had a wireless radio microphone attached to his clothing. It was now Governor Clinton's turn to respond to the question. Whereas both Perot and Bush had remained at their stools, as if anchored to them, Bill Clinton first established eye contact with Ms. Hall, then addressed her, directly, as if no one else in the hall existed. "I've been governor of a small state for twelve years," he began—and, before the tracking cameras, moved from his stool and stepped across the stage to speak more closely to the questioner, only a few feet from her. "I'll tell you how it's affected me," he continued. "I've seen what's happened in the last four years when in my state, when people lose their jobs, there's a good chance I know them by their names. When a factory closes, I know the people who ran it. When the businesses go bankrupt, I know them."

Tall, his hair prematurely gray, his eyes bright, blue, and intelligent, and his manner easy, the big Arkansas governor seemed genuinely interested in the plight of the questioner and Americans like her. "I've been out here for thirteen months meeting in meetings just like this ever since October [1991], with people like you all over America—people that have lost their jobs, lost their livelihood, lost their health insurance. What I want you to understand is the national debt is not the only cause of that," he went on. "It is because America has not invested in its people. It is because we have not grown. It is because we've had twelve years of trickle-down econom-ics . . . It is because we are in the grip of a failed economic theory. And this decision you're about to make better be about what kind of economic the-ory you want . . ."

Standing alone and in command, Governor Bill Clinton looked and sounded like the sort of man who *would* address the issue if elected Presi-dent—would "invest in American jobs, American education, control American health care costs, and," as he ended his response, "bring the American people together again."

Clinton had taken over. He "commanded the atmospherics" in his role of would-be commander in chief of the economy, as Jeff Greenfield re-marked on *ABC News,* while President Bush had looked mortified and out of place. Indeed, seeming to want to get out of the town meeting as swiftly as possible, President Bush "looked at his watch three times," Dale Her-beck, a professor of communications and forensics, later noted. Ross Perot's stool, meanwhile, looked too high for the little Texan—and by the time of the closing statements President Bush had symbolically almost re-treated behind his.

It was presidential meltdown.

Throwing Up

Next door, in the holding room, Mary Matalin and her colleagues were in-censed by the way the moderator had appeared to respond positively to Clinton's "body language" and his "jumping bean act" of empathy and connection with the questioner, while forcing the President of the United States to "raise his hand like a schoolboy and ask could he please have a comment on that. When you're watching in the holding room, that's the kind of stuff that curdles your blood."

Matalin's lover, by contrast, was undergoing a kind of religious ecstasy in *his* holding room, where the Clinton team was jubilant over its gladia-tor's performance. Referring to the Republican camp, James Carville re-marked cruelly, "I'll bet you they're throwing up over there now."

Carville was correct. A CBS poll conducted immediately after the de-bate indicated that 54 percent of viewers felt Clinton had "won" the de-bate, with Bush and Perot dividing the rest.

Bill had only to hold his own in the final debate, the team felt, and they were home and dry.

Life on Main Street, U.S.A.

Meanwhile, Jack Germond and Jules Witcover, covering the proceedings as journalists, were impressed by the way journalists were no longer the public's sole conduit to the consciences of the candidates. Not only was "the whole campaign taking place on the nation's television screens," they noted, but *more and more people were participating.* "What was new," they pointed out, "was the voice of the people speaking out loud and clear, calling directly for answers. . . . All these voices, for the first time since the end of World War II and the start of the Cold War, were talking almost exclusively about the condition of life on Main Street, U.S.A. They had been quiet long enough."

Dale Herbeck agreed. Snobs might scoff at the "debasement" of the debates as "political spectacles virtually devoid of substance," he later commented, but they were missing the point. For decades viewers had watched the debates, waiting for the candidates to make mistakes and be tripped up by reporters, as a stylized rehearsal for high office in the presidential palace—the White House. Now, however, by involving real and ordinary citizens, Clinton had expanded the format and thereby altered the "ritual" forever. "Candidate Clinton's approach to the 1992 presidential debates was unique," Herbeck considered, "largely because it attempted to transcend the spectacle by directly engaging the viewer as participant."

For good or ill, Main Street, U.S.A., wanted *a part in the campaign* as well as in the anonymous balloting process—something that seemed to frighten the President yet was welcomed by "Candidate Clinton." The "main thing is," Clinton reminded voters during the third debate, that the President clearly "still didn't get it, from what he said the other night to that fine woman on our program, the 209 people in Richmond." Tens of millions of Americans felt likewise.

In that third and final presidential debate President Bush attempted to goad both Clinton and Perot into losing their composure, thus sullying their chances of looking "presidential"—as had happened with Michael Dukakis, especially when Dukakis failed to respond aggressively or passionately to a theoretical question about his likely response if his wife was raped. To middle America he'd looked a wimp.

The demolition of Dukakis in 1988 was, however, now a matter of campaign history, its lessons clear for all to see—and avoid. Republican attempts to repeat that strategy had, throughout the campaign, simply come to grief as Clinton and Gore both responded immediately and emphatically to the least implication or allegation that they were soft on crime or in character.

Still smarting from the Republicans' "dirty tricks" efforts in August, Ross Perot fell into the President's trap, losing his composure and venting his spleen over the invasion of his family's privacy—but in the process providing a public window onto his embittered inner world and thereby raising the question whether, when taxed with matters beyond management of the economy and America's frightening deficit, he would prove a solid President or commander in chief.

By contrast Governor Clinton never lost his composure at Michigan State University in East Lansing, despite the final, traditional "trial by journalists" format. Constantly needled by the President on the matter of trust, Clinton saw his task as looking potentially presidential—and to the relief of his handlers, he did just that. His favorable polls remained steady at 42 percent. Bush trailed at 32 percent, 10 points behind him, with Perot at 18.

Perot now had little chance, for all the money he was belatedly throwing into his campaign. For President Bush, however, there were two weeks left in which to claw his way back and save the White House from the Arkansas hordes.

Trashing "Those Bozos"

Several days after the final presidential debate, on the same CBS *60 Minutes* program on which Bill Clinton had saved himself, Ross Perot dug his own grave deeper. Yet again he blamed Republicans for a "dirty tricks" operation, this time claiming that Republicans had attempted to ruin the wedding of his daughter the previous August by circulating a defamatory picture of her in advance—and adding charges that Republicans had planned to bug his telephones in Dallas.

Responding, the White House press spokesman ridiculed Perot's "fantastic stories about his daughter and disrupting her wedding and the CIA. It's all loony," he commented, adding that Perot was a "paranoid person who had delusions." The President himself, having refused to see Perot personally to discuss such "dirty tricks," agreed that the whole incident was "crazy." Perot's *ABC News* polls, instead of going up, dropped from around 20 percent to 16 the week before election day.

With Perot more or less trashed as a "loony," President Bush seemed at last to come to his senses. Recognizing he had one last opportunity to get back into the race by personal barnstorming, he now went on a trans-American "trash Clinton and Gore" spree, referring to them openly as "those bozos" and to Gore in particular as "the Ozone Man."

Here was a return to an older tradition of simplistic circus spectacle, full of clowns, mudslinging, and humor—but with all three candidates spending prodigious sums on television and radio advertising. By the last week of the campaign, Perot alone had spent almost $60 million, mostly on commercials.

Would it work? As the day of the election approached, the static over America seemed to turn into northern lights, with charges and counter-charges lighting up the Halloween skies.

A Night to Remember

For a moment, President Bush's polls seemed to go up, drawing from Perot's plummeting popularity as the gap between himself and front-runner Clinton narrowed.

Once again James Carville and his colleagues became spooked, terrified that victory, so seemingly close, would slip through their endlessly spinning fingers. Would American voters, in the end, vote for the Devil they knew rather than the one they didn't—yet? "We lost 14 points in Ohio in one night. Bush spent the whole day there," Carville recalled. "Scared the hell out of us. Then we showed a huge drop in Pennsylvania." This was serious, potentially fatally so. "We had a scenario where we could lose Ohio," Carville admitted in retrospect, "but never Pennsylvania."

History had seemed, tantalizingly, to be in the making, not only thanks to a new kind of centrist Democratic candidate, but thanks to a new, more inclusive Democratic appeal to voters to become involved in the political process and to embrace change. Would that prospect now fade?

Bush a Liar—Officially

On Halloween, the very last day of October 1992, however, President George Herbert Walker Bush, hero of World War II and victor of Desert Storm, found himself mortally wounded politically, hit by a stray missile in what amounted to "friendly fire."

Caspar Weinberger, former secretary of defense and Bush's former cabinet colleague, was suddenly reindicted by a stalwart Republican: the government's special prosecutor or independent counsel in the "Irangate" inquiry, Larry Walsh.

Weinberger had donated his official papers to the Library of Congress. An examination of these papers now indicated that George Bush had lied in his account of the arms-for-hostages deal in testimony he had given to the Irangate hearings in Congress.

The President attempted to pooh-pooh the new information, even though it emanated from a reputable, indeed Republican, source, but at a moment when he was trying to tar Clinton as a "bozo" of untrustworthy character, the Weinberger revelation not only put Bush back on the defensive but suggested that he was as deceitful as Clinton. Bush's campaign strategist, Charlie Black, confided later that he didn't actually "verbalize" the sinking feeling in his heart as "Well, I know this race is over," but, as he recalled, "I knew that was about it."

Taking home the Associated Press story, campaign chairman Bob Teeter "laid it on my dresser" as a campaign "memento"—the last "true smoking gun," as Senator Gore called it.

President Bush was a liar—officially.

A Clash of Generations

The 1992 election, Mary Matalin continued to believe, was not about issues and still less about the economy. It was, as she later characterized it, a "referendum on two men." With the smoking Weinberger gun, it became clear that President Bush was as much a master of fudging the past as Governor Clinton was.

Mary Matalin, moreover, was wrong about the referendum. The election was no longer about two men but about two generations—as in 1960.

As journalist Michael Ventura wrote in the *Los Angeles Weekly* a few days before the election, he had "no complaints." He was, he confessed, "one of the few people I know who genuinely like Bill Clinton"—and this was not because he believed a word that Clinton said! President Bush had impugned Governor Clinton's character as being a matter of trust; but in a postmodern, deconstructed world, "trust" was a term that encompassed whatever you invested in it. In lying to Congress over Irangate, had Bush evidenced trustworthiness, save to Weinberger and the indicted members of the CIA he would thereafter pardon?

Clinton, Ventura acknowledged, was slick—but slick in an extraordinarily disciplined way. Day after day he'd faced the onslaught over Gennifer Flowers, the draft, marijuana, his patriotism, "without flinching or fading." Whereas Bush was good when the numbers were on his side, "Bill Clinton was good when nothing was on his side. What Bush does poorly, Clinton does well: I'm talking about the mix of equivocation, obfuscation, outright lies, shadowy maneuvers and smarmy style with which politicians survive."

In this sense, there was nothing unusual in Bill Clinton as a politician—save in the brilliance with which he performed in a postmodern age. "Clinton has proved his mastery of fundamental political craft as practiced by Jefferson, Jackson, Lincoln, both Roosevelts, Eisenhower and Johnson—our most effective presidents. Blessed are the slick," Ventura added, "for they shall get things done."

Moreover, though Clinton's private life and ethical missteps might be a red rag to the bull of righteous Republicans, Ventura knew that such men, and often their women, were, for the most part, hypocrites. He was unfazed. Yes, Clinton *was* "a draft evader with a messy sex life and character flaws bordering on the schizophrenic," he acknowledged as the November election loomed—but would Bill Clinton, if elected president, be any worse than his predecessors? "We've had rapists, philanderers and, to put it delicately, out-of-the way sexual preferences in the White House from the start. We've had killers, slavers, crooks, alcoholics, gamblers—addicts of every description. (When President Kennedy was asked by a friend why he allowed his lust to engender the security of the nation, he replied: 'I can't help it.') We've had crack-ups: Woodrow Wilson, Lyndon Johnson and Richard Nixon were in states of severe mental collapse during the last months of their presidencies. The White House," Ventura remarked sagely, "is a dark place. Clinton will bring it no darkness that hasn't been there before."

Last Lap

As Clinton and Gore zigzagged across the nation in the final days of the campaign, it became clearer and clearer that Michael Ventura was right. It was not a question of "believing" in Bill Clinton but of believing in his energy, dynamism, and commitment to trying to improve America's ailing economy, its inequitable health care system, and its public education in time for a new, electronic information age century, on the one hand, while accepting his willingness to be slick, to compromise, and even to lie as the sadly necessary qualities to achieve this agenda in modern, indeed post-modern, America on the other.

By contrast, elements of President Bush's campaign, to the end, remained riven with negative, smearing, disparaging, name-calling—and counterpro-ductive skullduggery. In the hope of finding a smoking gun, Bush's staff, under James Baker, had recently authorized a Watergate-style break-in to obtain records belonging to the State Department, namely Governor Clinton's personal passport files, the story of which had been published in *The Washington Post* on October 14, 1992—the day before the second debate. The stakes had thus been raised still further, though there was egg splattered all around the Bush campaign headquarters once it was learned that Elizabeth Tamposi, a Republican activist who'd been made assistant secretary of state for consular affairs, had ordered her State Department subordinates—supposedly without White House authority—to search not only Clinton's but also Clinton's *mother's* passport files! Tamposi had hoped that the files, stored in Suitland, Maryland, outside Washington, D.C., might reveal in-criminating evidence relating to Vietnam, the draft, and the trip through Eu-rope and the Soviet Union—as well as confirmation of a rumor Republicans were spreading that Clinton had sought at one point in his career to obtain foreign nationality rather than serve in the armed forces.

Officials in Suitland had secretly searched the files after business hours on September 30 and again on October 1, 1992—not only finding nothing in the least incriminating in them but leaving a trail of phone calls to the White House that incriminated *themselves,* not Governor Clinton.

The excuse that it had all been done in response to a press request under the Freedom of Information Act had quickly fallen apart when it was re-vealed that there was no FOI request regarding Virginia Kelley, who was currently undergoing radiotherapy for breast cancer. Senator Gore had im-mediately protested that it was "part of a McCarthyite smear effort" by the Republican Party, reaffirming Clinton's remark to President Bush in the first debate. The Bush administration, Governor Clinton himself com-mented, was panicking—"not only rifling through my files but actually in-vestigating my mother, a well-known subversive," he mocked. "It would be funny if it weren't so pathetic."

Virginia Kelley, characteristically, had been more direct. "I'm insulted, I'm indignant. You know I'm at the age that I lived through Hitler and his

Gestapo. I lived through the police state. I do not want this to happen to my country."

Though President Bush had called the act "most reprehensible" and apologized, as well as ordering an inquiry that eventually led to the dismissal of Tamposi, it had placed him in an invidious position if he hoped to raise the "character issue" yet again. He was left, ultimately, only with invective. "Governor Clinton and Ozone, all they do is talk about change. If I want foreign policy advice, I'd go to Millie"—Bush's dog—"before I'd go to Ozone and Governor Clinton" was a typical Bush remark to crowds in Columbus, Ohio, who lapped it up.

The election was turning into a farce. In a last hurrah, a new charge—that Clinton was having an affair with a wire service reporter assigned to his campaign—was faxed by the chairman of the National Republican Congressional Committee to every newspaper office across the nation. But it was too late.

Clinton's indefatigable goodwill, vitality, stamina, and sheer love of campaigning had shone through. The press, sensing a winner, had finally warmed to him, for all his evasions. He was the Secret Service's nightmare as he plunged into crowds of strangers to shake hands and trade views across the country. From 9 A.M. to 11 P.M. on the final day before the election, he led a flight of three aircraft to the seven key midwest and southwestern states where the outcome was known to be close: Pennsylvania, Ohio, Michigan, Kentucky, Missouri, Colorado, and New Mexico. Finally, in darkness, the governor's plane flew him back to Arkansas and the governor's mansion in Little Rock, where the journey had all begun.

It was all over, at last, bar the voting.

CHAPTER FORTY-SIX

VICTORY

Election Day

Early on the morning of November 3, 1992, polling stations across the continent opened.

However much pundits had decried the standard of electoral debate—the descent of political campaigning into tabloid sloganeering, the gargantuan sums expended on negative advertising, the endless mudslinging—in the end the voter turnout showed the opposite: the nation was aware that it had reached a cultural crossroads, a turning point, a moment of generational change. The Soviet Union had already experienced it; now it was America's turn.

Since 1960, the trend had been toward greater and greater electoral apathy, with fewer and fewer voters casting the ballots so crucial to the survival of democracy. Now, in the wake of one of the most acerbic yet colorful, accusatory yet circuslike electoral campaigns of the twentieth century, the trend was triumphantly reversed. Voting numbers rocketed to 104 million votes cast in a country of 230 million voters—an increase of more than 10 percent over the previous election, only four years before. With Ross Perot's entry, then departure, then reentrance, the soap opera of 1992 had become all the more riveting, the ebb and flow of allegations and counter-allegations keeping viewers on the edge of their seats—and involved.

Which way the pendulum would swing was intoxicating to Carville and Stephanopoulos at the War Room in Little Rock, who had both given way to first-night nerves and predicted defeat for Clinton. To their ecstatic relief, however, Ohio tipped the electoral chamber votes beyond the 270 necessary for a Democratic win, officially announced at 9:45 P.M. Central Standard Time that evening.

Half an hour later George Bush conceded defeat; indeed, by the next day it would be clear that the President, so victorious in the Persian Gulf War, had lost by more than five and a half million votes in the largest turnout for three decades, when in 1960 John F. Kennedy had squeaked past Richard Nixon by less than a few thousand ballots. As predicted by the polls, Governor Clinton had won 43 percent of the votes cast, President Bush only 38 percent, and Ross Perot a respectable 19 percent—not far off the figures of those polled after the second, crucial debate.

For George Herbert Walker Bush it was a historic demise: he was only the fourth incumbent President in the twentieth century to fail to be reelected. Instead, Bill Clinton, five times governor of one of the smallest and poorest states in the Union, would become the next President of the United States of America, aged only forty-six.

At the Gates of Rome

For Mary Matalin in Houston, the result was a catastrophe. For some time she'd been, as she later confessed, "in denial," convinced that her President was going to win. She'd therefore gone for a jog and afterward a massage, steambath, and manicure, "secure we were in the middle of one of the great election comebacks of all time."

The comeback, however, had been proved a go-back—with Matalin and scores of her companions losing their cherished jobs.

Margaret Tutweiler, the White House press spokeswoman, seemed, for example, paralyzed by shock, as well as psychosomatic back pain. "She was transfixed by Clinton's image on the four TVs in front of her. She just kept saying over and over, 'I can't believe this man is President. I can't believe this man is President.' " It was as if the age of Republican elegance was about to end, with barbarians at the gates of Rome.

Matalin ended the night drunk and despondent, she later confessed, in her Texas hotel bed. But to tens of millions of others, President Bush's defeat was Bill Clinton's victory. Joan Duffy, reporter for the *Memphis Com-*

mercial Appeal, considered that the big Arkansan was "the best politician I've ever seen in my life. He never ceases to amaze me. There's nobody who can work a crowd like he can, it's just silly to compete with it because there's just nobody better, and it's genuine when he's campaigning. He loves to campaign."

Anyone who underestimated Bill Clinton, as President Bush's staff had done, was making a big mistake. "This is the toughest son of a bitch I've ever seen in my life," James Carville had remarked after the Gennifer Flowers scandal—a born "policy wonk," a political dynamo, a forty-second President of the United States of America, and a cat with nine lives—who, to survive on the next stage of his life's journey, would need all nine.

NOTES

1. The Walls of Hope

4 nobody knows: William Cassady was born in Ireland circa 1700. His son Zachariah had come to America circa 1755, settling in Chesterfield County, South Carolina, and had taken part in the Revolutionary War. The Cassadys had then migrated first to Henry County, then to Covington County, Alabama. George Washington, born in 1830, had there sired twelve children by his wife, Nancy Ann Snelgrove, whom he married circa 1852. Of their eight daughters and four sons, James Monroe was the eldest male: Floris Tatom (niece of William Jefferson Clinton's grandfather, James Eldridge Cassidy), "Cassady & Russell Family History," privately assembled and annotated genealogy shown to the author by Mrs. Tatom, March 14, 2001.

4 in Alabama: James Monroe Cassady is buried in the old Fairmont Cemetery, Red Level, Covington, Alabama. His wife survived him by almost half a century.

4 "The debt-ridden": Harry Ashmore, *Arkansas: A Bicentennial History,* 1978, 120.

5 his name to Cassidy: To conform, it is said, with his uncle Noah Cassidy, who had changed the family spelling when enlisting in World War I; Floris Tatom, "Cassady & Russell Family History," privately assembled and annotated genealogy shown to the author by Mrs. Tatom, March 14, 2001. See also genealogical files in Arkansas State Historical Commission Archives, Little Rock; *Nexus: The Bimonthly Newsletter of the New England Historic*

Genealogical Society 9, no. 6 (December 1992); and *Hempstead Trails,* Hempstead County Genealogical Society, 8, no. 1 (April 1993).

5 "eking out": Quoted in *Hempstead Trails,* Hempstead County, Arkansas, October 1992.

5 Hope had: Virginia Kelley, with James Morgan, *Leading with My Heart,* 1994, 20. The town of Hope had begun in 1873, in the midst of a "beautiful little prairie" about 350 feet above sea level, with the offering of building lots by representatives of the St. Louis, Iron Mountain & Southern Railroad, halfway between Dallas and Memphis. The town was named after the daughter of the Land Commissioner of the railroad company, Hope. All streets ran parallel and perpendicular to the railway line. The first tracks were laid by the Cairo & Fulton Railway (which became the St. Louis, Iron Mountain & Southern Railroad in 1874, and later the Missouri Pacific), but after the turn of the century the Frisco and Louisiana & Arkansas Railroads laid their own tracks (and stations) to take passengers, by 1908, as far as Oklahoma, and between Hope and Shreveport, Louisiana, ninety miles away, and beyond there to New Orleans. Another line, the Arkansas & Louisiana Railway (better known as the Nashville Branch of the Missouri Pacific) took passengers and freight to nearby Washington and Nashville; Harry W. Shiver, ed., *Hope's First Century: A Commemorative History of Hope, 1875–1975,* 1974.

5 "Cotton Row": Hope was known for its long-staple, high-quality cotton. South Walnut Street from Division Street to Second Street comprised "Cotton Row," where the big cotton buyers lived. Prices had leaped from seven cents per pound before World War I to forty cents per pound during the war, and five or six buyers became millionaires briefly, before prices tumbled; Shiver, *Hope's First Century.*

5 "a rough, busy": Tom McMath, "When I Was a Barefoot Boy," in Shiver, *Hope's First Century,* 32.

5 Ivory Handle Company: The Ivory Handle Company had been founded in Hope in 1900. It was sold to W. E. Bruner in 1933, becoming the Bruner-Ivory Handle Company, making walking canes, ladder rungs, prod poles, barbecue chips, show sticks, and shepherd crooks; Shiver, *Hope's First Century,* 71. A photograph of Eldridge Cassidy in white overalls, white cap, and thick gloves and holding a huge furnace shovel in front of one of the company's twenty-foot-high furnaces, was reproduced in Kelley with Morgan, *Leading with My Heart.*

6 "Cotton remained": Ashmore, *Arkansas.*

6 "The state government": Ben F. Johnson, *Arkansas in Modern America, 1930–1999,* 2000, 20.

7 on farms and plantations: C. Calvin Smith, *War and Wartime Changes: The Transformation of Arkansas, 1940–1945,* 1986, 20.

7 The state's roads: "Most of the U.S. highway mileage in the state remained graveled surface and numerous local roads were designated 'impassable' " in an audit revealing that at least 11.5 percent of minimal investment had been criminally skimmed. Ben Johnson, *Arkansas in Modern America*, 14.

7 "as a benighted land": Ibid., 29.

7 "By 1924": Mark Robert Schneider, "*We Return Fighting*": *The Civil Rights Movement in the Jazz Age*, 2002, 216.

8 "No official action": Ibid.

8 "asylum for the emigrant": S. Fountain, ed., *Authentic Voices: Arkansas Culture, 1541–1860*, 1986, 187.

9 "watermelons": C. Calvin Smith, *War and Wartime Changes*, 20.

9 "When we get": Donald Holley, *Uncle Sam's Farmers: The New Deal Communities in the Lower Mississippi Valley*, 1975, 3.

9 "Red Cross headquarters": *Arkansas Gazette*, January 4, 1931.

10 "There ain't no ladies": Holley, *Uncle Sam's Farmers*, 86.

10 "Fundamentalist": Michael B. Dougan, *Arkansan Odyssey: The Saga of Arkansas from Prehistoric Times to Present*, 1995, 442.

10 "I have traveled": Ashmore, *Arkansas*, 168–9.

10 "Hundreds of thousands": Ibid., 173.

11 "cruelest acts": Kelley with Morgan, *Leading with My Heart*, 25.

12 "proved to be": Quoted in Loren Baritz, *The Good Life: The Meaning of Success for the American Middle Class*, 1989, 140.

12 "had better chances": Ibid., 115.

12 "Families whose": Ibid., 141–2.

13 "flourishing mythology": Ibid., 145.

13 "The major obligation": Ibid.

13 "as Americans": Ibid., 146.

13 "The need for": Ibid., 151.

14 "The soap's": Ibid., 157.

14 "what we call": Joe Purvis, interview with the author, February 7, 2001.

14 "even this classic": Baritz, *The Good Life*, 159.

15 "the practice of": Margaret Jones Bolsterli, *Born in the Delta: Reflections on the Making of a Southern White Sensibility*, 1991, 8–9.

15 Delta belles: Ibid., 10.

15 "The Drunken": Ibid., 58–9.

16 "your place on": Ibid., 13.

16 "bright-colored clothes": Jim Morgan, interview with the author, February 9, 2001.

16 "Common people": Bolsterli, *Born in the Delta*, 12–13.

17 "the peculiar quality": Ibid., 53.

18 "major and lifelong": Kelley with Morgan, *Leading with My Heart*, 30.

18 "a house of": Quoted in Baritz, *The Good Life,* 140.

18 "wasn't necessarily": Kelley with Morgan, *Leading with My Heart,* 32.

19 "Everybody here": Interview with the author, March 16, 2001.

19 "Virginia liked": Ibid.

19 "You'd get in": Ibid.

20 "Oh yes": Ibid.

20 "eventually transcend": Bolsterli, *Born in the Delta,* 13.

21 "Honey, *everybody's*": Ibid.

2. Tug-of-War

23 "way out on": Shiver, *Hope's First Century,* 87.

24 "If I ever": Kelley with Morgan, *Leading with My Heart,* 36.

25 "We're not married": Jim Morgan, interview with the author, February 9, 2001.

26 "that all the rules": Ibid.

26 "Yes, she's lying": Kelley with Morgan, *Leading with My Heart,* 43.

26 "so in love": Jim Morgan, interview with the author, February 9, 2001.

26 "Willie" Jefferson Blythe II: Mary Nell Turner (Hope, Arkansas, historian and genealogist), interview with the author, March 15, 2001. See also *Nexus: The Bimonthly Newsletter of the New England Historic Genealogical Society* 9, no. 6 (December 1992), and *Hempstead Trails,* Hempstead County, Arkansas, April 1993, Vol. VIII, No. 1. Since the "second" William Jefferson Blythe (1918–46) was named after an uncle, William "Willie" Jefferson Farr Blythe (1882/4–1935), genealogists concluded that William Jefferson Blythe, born on February 27, 1918, in Sherman, Texas, was really William Jefferson Blythe III, not II.

27 "to keep from": Meredith L. Oakley, *On the Make: The Rise of Bill Clinton,* 1994, 21.

28 "She loved to": Ibid., 21.

28 "new and daily": C. Calvin Smith, *War and Wartime Changes,* 49.

28 "as waitresses": Ibid.

28 "The infection rate": Ibid., 50.

29 "Victory girls": Ibid., 55.

29 "the war's impact": Ibid.

29 more than 10 percent: Ibid., 29.

29 "a bustling city": Shiver, *Hope's First Century,* 61.

30 "had been through hell": Obituary, *Hope Star,* May 18, 1946.

31 Sixteen million: Baritz, *The Good Life,* 176, 179.

31 "The non-sexual female": Ibid., 171–2.

31 "emasculated males": Ibid., 173.

31 "in war": Ibid., 176.

31 "Her cooking mattered": Ibid., 181.

32 "Honorably discharged": Certificate of Honorable Discharge, copy kindly furnished to author by Mary Nell Turner, March 15, 2001.

32 "before Christmas 1945": Jim Morgan, interview with the author, February 9, 2001.

32 Studies would show: For a scholarly discussion of paternity studies and sperm competition in humans and mammals, see Tim Birkhead, *Promiscuity: An Evolutionary History of Sperm Competition,* 2000, Chap. 2, "Paternity and Protection." Matt Ridley, *The Red Queen: Sex and the Evolution of Human Nature,* 1993 (Chap. 6, "Polygamy and the Nature of Men," and Chap. 7, "Monogamy and the Nature of Women"), gives an exceptionally clear summary.

33 The car ran off: Jim Morgan, interview with the author, February 9, 2001.

33 "my own opinion": Jim Blair, interview with the author, March 23, 2001. The story was told to Blair by his friend Lewis Eppley, who passed it on to Bill Clinton's factotum, Bruce Lindsey, "and that's the last I heard of it," Blair commented.

34 "small-town gossip": Wilma Rowe Booker, interview with the author, March 15, 2001.

35 "He was a big": Ibid.

35 the most intelligent: No scholarly or scientific comparison between presidents has yet been made. Interestingly, shortly into the presidency of George W. Bush, in July 2001, a preliminary report on the IQ quotients of the twelve most recent U.S. presidents was released on the Internet, where a number of sites rate historical figures. Put out by the Lovenstein Institute of Scranton, Pennsylvania, this assessed presidents on scholarly achievements, writings produced without the aid of staff, ability to speak with clarity, and several other psychological factors, which were then scored in the Swanson/Crain system of intelligence ranking. Within an error margin of five percentage points the results were, in order of intelligence: William J. Clinton (D), 182; James E. Carter (D), 175; John F. Kennedy (D), 174; Richard M. Nixon (R), 155; Franklin D. Roosevelt (D), 147; Harry S Truman (D), 132; Lyndon B. Johnson (D), 126; Dwight D. Eisenhower (R), 122; Gerald R. Ford (R), 121; Ronald W. Reagan (R), 105; George H. W. Bush (R), 98; George W. Bush (R), 91. The list, which seemed to accord with academic and popular conceptions at that time, especially abroad, was published in the London *Guardian* on July 19, 2001, but was later revealed to be a hoax.

35 "The birth certificate": To the chagrin of astrologers worldwide, the exact time of William Jefferson Blythe's cesarean-section birth is disputed. For many years it was reputed to be 3:44 A.M. Central Standard Time, based on a copied version of his birth certificate. However, when asked during the 1992 election, Virginia Kelley, his mother, gave a time of 8:51 A.M. CST. See, among others,

Edith Hathaway, "Which Chart for Bill Clinton?," *The Mountain Astrologer,* October–November 1996.

36 "just a poor": Falba Lively, interview with the author, February 15, 2001.

36 "pursuit of her": Stanley A. Renshon, *High Hopes: The Clinton Presidency and the Politics of Ambition,* 1996, 159ff.

36 "He always seemed": Wilma Rowe Booker, interview with the author, March 15, 2001.

37 "This was probably": Baritz, *The Good Life,* 205.

37 "locked in": Bolsterli, *Born in the Delta,* 34.

37 "Arkansas was": C. Calvin Smith, *War and Wartime Changes,* 31.

37 "Mrs. Blythe will be": Quoted in Kelley with Morgan, *Leading with My Heart,* 68.

37 "it was all": Ibid., 69.

37 "I'm sure": Interview with the author, February 16, 2001.

38 "a pretty wild critter": Joe Purvis, interview with the author, February 7, 2001.

38 "wild and woolly": Ibid.

39 "sinful city": Shirley Abbott, *The Bookmaker's Daughter,* 1991, 52.

39 "The American Carlsbad": *The Chicago 400* 3 (February 1895), quoted in F. J. Scully, *Hot Springs, Arkansas and Hot Springs National Park: The Story of a City and the Nation's Health Resort,* 1966, 167.

39 "a haven for": Abbott, *The Bookmaker's Daughter,* 57.

40 "He liked expensive": Roy Reed, *Faubus: The Life and Times of an American Prodigal,* 1997, 316.

41 "We had glamour": Abbott, *The Bookmaker's Daughter,* 51.

41 "On the farm": Jim Johnson, interview with the author, March 23, 2001.

41 "The police were": Abbott, *The Bookmaker's Daughter,* 57.

41 "He was in": Wilma Rowe Booker, interview with the author, March 15, 2001.

42 "and a lot more": Kelley with Morgan, *Leading with My Heart,* 71–2.

42 "appearance rather than": Renshon, *High Hopes,* 162.

42 "less enthralled": Kelley with Morgan, *Leading with My Heart,* 77.

43 "Any mother": Roxie Lawrence, interview with the author, March 16, 2001.

43 "In essence": Joe Purvis, interview with the author, February 7, 2001.

44 "to count and": Charles F. Allen, interview with Bill Clinton, February 5, 1991, quoted in Charles F. Allen and Jonathan Portis, *The Comeback Kid: The Life and Career of Bill Clinton,* 1992, 5. Also Kelley with Morgan, *Leading with My Heart,* 83.

44 "wear good on one": Carolyn (Yeldell) Staley, interview with the author, January 19, 2001.

45 crying his heart out: Beckie Moore (director, Clinton Birthplace Center), interview with the author, February 16, 2001.

45 "became confused": Falba Lively, interview with the author, February 15, 2001.

45 "never to be": Ernest Dumas, ed., *The Clintons of Arkansas: An Introduction by Those Who Know Them Best,* 1993, 27.

46 "Roger": Kelley with Morgan, *Leading with My Heart,* 73.

47 "Mother remained": Ibid., 83.

48 "Everybody in town": Ibid., 85–6.

48 "but the blackness": Ibid.

49 "fixin' to marry": David Maraniss, *First in His Class. A Biography of Bill Clinton,* 31.

50 "a little white": Floris Tatom, annotation to photo of Virginia Clinton with her two sons, in "Cassady & Russell Family History" album, compiled by Floris Tatom and presented to the Clinton Birthplace Trust, Hope, Arkansas, 1999.

3. From Hope to Hot Springs

52 "He loved to be": Donna Taylor, interview with the author, March 16, 2001.

52 "We had a": Ibid.

52 "flamboyant mother": Interview with the author, March 16, 2001.

53 "He didn't have": Ibid.

53 "Bill nearly always": Dumas, *The Clintons of Arkansas,* 27.

53 "I remember": Joe Purvis, interview with the author, February 7, 2001.

53 "It upset him": Dumas, *The Clintons of Arkansas,* 28.

54 "but you always knew": Donna Taylor, interview with the author, March 16, 2001.

55 "kept stealing from himself"': Jim Morgan, interview with the author, February 9, 2001.

55 "I heard a": Kelley with Morgan, *Leading with My Heart,* 92.

55 As Virginia: Jim Morgan, interview with the author, February 9, 2001.

56 "running down": Ibid.

56 Suddenly Roger: Maraniss, *First in His Class,* 1995, gives the sale of the Buick dealership as September 1952 and the move to Hot Springs as "a few months later," but all records confirm that the move took place in the fall of 1953.

57 "In Arkansas": Jim Johnson, interview with the author, March 23, 2001.

58 "I equate it": Ibid.

59 "that would also": Ibid.

60 It boasted: *Polk Directory,* 1953, Arkansas State Historical Commission Archive; also R. Hanley and S. Hanley, *Hot Springs, Arkansas,* 2000.

61 "Why there's no real problem": Allen and Portis, *The Comeback Kid,* 6.

61 "I was too young": Robert E. Levin, *Bill Clinton: The Inside Story,* 1992, 10–11.

62 The near tragedy: Kelley with Morgan, *Leading with My Heart,* 102.

63 "At times like": Ibid., 111.

63 "just bedlam": Ibid., 110.

64 "I couldn't wait": David Lauter of the *Los Angeles Times,* "Need to Forge Consensus Strength and Weakness for Clinton," *The Morning News,* January 17, 1992.
64 "Let carousing": Kelley with Morgan, *Leading with My Heart,* 125.
65 The next morning: Jim Morgan, interview with the author, February 9, 2001.
65 "a corrupter of morals": James H. Jones, *Alfred C. Kinsey: A Public/Private Life,* 1997, 773.
66 "It is impossible": David Halberstam, *The Fifties,* 1993, 280.
66 "a prevailing degradation": Ibid.
66 "driven more": Jones, *Alfred C. Kinsey,* 773.
66 The truth: Birkhead, *Promiscuity;* also, for an overview, see David B. Barash and Judith E. Lipton, *The Myth of Monogamy: Fidelity and Infidelity in Animals and People,* 2001.

4. Domestic Strife

68 "a wonderfully antiseptic": Halberstam, *The Fifties,* 508.
68 "no serious sickness": Ibid., 509.
69 "the moms never worked": Ibid., 511.
69 "a deep illness": Ibid., 590.
69 "Let's face it": Ibid., 592.
69 "controlled the": Kelley with Morgan, *Leading with My Heart,* 112.
70 "As Bill slept": Ibid.
70 "unreliable and childish": C. K. Davis, *Two-Bit Culture: The Paperbacking of American Culture,* 1984, 255.
71 "dunghill of Arkansas": Jim Morgan, interview with the author, February 9, 2001.
71 "Self-destruction": Kelley with Morgan, *Leading with My Heart.*
73 "the Age of": Baritz, *The Good Life,* 202.
73 "I think it": Allen and Portis, *The Comeback Kid,* 9.
73 "left a lasting": Levin, *Bill Clinton,* 12.
73 "pretty weird": David Gallen, *Bill Clinton: As They Know Him: An Oral Biography,* 1994.
73 "family was good": Levin, *Bill Clinton,* 15.
75 *The Ed Sullivan Show:* Earlier called *The Toast of the Town,* name had been changed in 1955.
75 "It was one thing": Halberstam, *The Fifties,* 479.
75 "but he's my taste": Kelley with Morgan, *Leading with My Heart,* 130.
75 "whenever Roger gave": Ibid.
76 "If I could find": Halberstam, *The Fifties,* 471.
77 "I never once": Kelley with Morgan, *Leading with My Heart,* 130.

77 "I'd start slapping": Ibid., 131.
78 "We had most": Levin, *Bill Clinton*, 12, and David Leopoulos, interview with the author, March 19, 2001.
78 "He was the cultural": Eleanor Clift, "Political Ambitions, Personal Choices: Bill Clinton Talks About Work, Love and Faith," *Newsweek*, March 9, 1992.
78 "Elvis Presley is": Halberstam, *The Fifties*, 456–7.
78 "Before Elvis": Ibid., 457.

5. Learning Right from Wrong

79 "thievery in broad daylight": Halberstam, *The Fifties*, 465.
79 This declaration pledged: A. J. Badger, "The White Reaction to *Brown:* Arkansas, the Southern Manifesto, and Massive Resistance," in *Understanding the Little Rock Crisis*, ed. E. Jacoway and C. Fred Williams, 1999, 88.
80 "that indicated": Ibid., 89.
81 "What went wrong?": Badger, "The White Reaction to *Brown*," 84.
82 "He did not want": Thelma R. Engler, in *Civil Obedience: An Oral History of School Desegregation in Fayetteville, Arkansas, 1954–1965*, eds. Julianne L. Adams and Thomas A. DeBlack, 1994, 148.
82 "Integration in Little Rock": Reed, *Faubus*, 184–5.
84 "The anger and": Halberstam, *The Fifties*, 666.
84 "We were dedicated": Reed, *Faubus*, 192.
84 "We had Blossom": Ibid., 192, 213.
85 "Jim": Ibid., 193.
85 "What are your orders?": Halberstam, *The Fifties*, 674.
85 "a profound personal effect": Bill Clinton, "A Deep Debt of Gratitude for a Valuable Lesson," *Crisis*, October 1997.
86 "I am sure": Quoted in Daisy Bates, *The Long Shadow of Little Rock*, 1987, 77–8.
86 "disgraceful political hoax": Dougan, *Arkansas Odyssey*, 500.
86 "they are trying": Reed, *Faubus*, 361.
86 "a microcosm": Clinton, "A Deep Debt of Gratitude."
86 "After the attack": Bates, *The Long Shadow of Little Rock*, 77.
87 "Just because": Reed, *Faubus*, 219.
87 "Just let those niggers": Bates, *The Long Shadow of Little Rock*, 89.
87 "Extremists often": Dougan, *Arkansas Odyssey*, 497.
88 "I hope they bring": Reed, *Faubus*, 497.
89 "For the first time": Bates, *The Long Shadow of Little Rock*, 104.
89 His wife, Alta Faubus: Reed, *Faubus*, 239.
89 "I can probe him": Reed, *Faubus*, 221. Brooks Hays was beaten by a last-minute write-in candidate, a known racist by the name of Dr. Dale Alford.

89 "The governor's weak spot": Ibid., 189.

89 "Thus it was": Ibid.

90 "tossing and squirming": Ibid., 239.

90 "tried to explain": Clinton, "A Deep Debt of Gratitude."

91 "I felt then": David Leopoulos, interview with the author, March 19, 2001.

91 "You're right": Jim Morgan, interview with the author, February 9, 2001.

92 "He's just different": Falba Lively, interview with the author, February 15, 2001.

6. Divorce

93 "When I was a small": Levin, *Bill Clinton,* 11, 13.

93 Henry J: The legendary industrialist Henry J. Kaiser had wanted an inexpensive car to sell alongside the more costly automobiles his Kaiser-Frazer company produced, resulting in the 1951 "K513": "the most important new car in America," as its advertisements claimed; "smart, tough, thrifty." In a special contest a college student's wife from Denver chose the winning name. The Henry J was produced from 1951 to 1954. Total manufactured: approximately 130,000.

94 "It really was": Levin, *Bill Clinton,* 15.

94 "But at times": Ibid.

94 "everything in the world": Kelley with Morgan, *Leading with My Heart,* 137.

95 Years later: Anne Moir, producer, *Why Men Don't Iron,* three-part documentary series, 1998; Anne Moir and Bill Moir, *Why Men Don't Iron: The Science of Gender Studies,* 2000, *inter alia.*

96 "father, brother": Kelley with Morgan, *Leading with My Heart,* 137.

97 "Oh, what a": Gallen, *Bill Clinton,* 31.

97 "make each other": Jerry Oppenheimer, *State of a Union: Inside the Complex Marriage of Bill and Hillary Clinton,* 2000, 109.

98 "My mother was": Glenda Cooper, interview with the author, March 25, 2001.

99 "marked us out": Ibid.

100 "a lot of racial": Ibid.

100 "You know, that's": Ibid.

101 "I was aware": Ibid.

101 "a substitute for": Alice Miller, *The Drama of the Gifted Child: The Search for the True Self* (originally titled *Prisoners of Childhood*), 1981, 4.

101 "I was raised": Eleanor Clift and Jonathon Alter, "You Didn't Reveal Your Pain: Clinton Reflects on the Turmoil of His Childhood," *Newsweek,* March 30, 1990.

102 "I never felt": Eleanor Clift, "Political Ambitions, Personal Choices: Bill Clinton Talks About Work, Love and Faith," *Newsweek,* March 9, 1992.

102 "a lot of adversity": Quoted in Gallen, *Bill Clinton,* 25–6.

102 In 1957: Priscilla Painton, "Clinton's Spiritual Journey," *Time,* April 5, 1993.

102 "I spent most": David Shribman, "Clinton, Arkansas's Best-Known Overachiever, Widens His Horizons to Include the White House," *The Wall Street Journal,* October 8, 1991.

102 "violent": Kelley with Morgan, *Leading with My Heart,* 133.

103 "was the beginning": Ibid., 135.

103 Its lower half: Originally built in 1896 as a Queen Anne Revival house, it had been converted in 1938 to Tudor Revival, with a hodgepodge of features from Swiss chalet porch to Victorian massing and craftsman-style windows; Audrey Burtrum-Stanley, letter to the author, December 2002.

104 "I kept moving": Kelley with Morgan, *Leading with My Heart,* 134.

104 "I just broke": Bill Clinton, quoted in Joe Klein, *New York,* January 20, 1992.

104 "And of course": Kelley with Morgan, *Leading with My Heart,* 134.

104 "*I may be*": Ibid.

105 "Billy never said": Christopher Andersen, *Bill and Hillary: The Marriage,* 1999, 58.

105 "I was raised": Clift and Alter, "You Didn't Reveal Your Pain."

105 "an alcoholic family": *Time,* June 8, 1992.

105 "That was a dramatic": Ibid.

106 "reconciliations, relapses": Ibid.

106 "intermittent hell": Clift and Alter, "You Didn't Reveal Your Pain."

106 "I came to see": "Bill Clinton's Hidden Life," *US News & World Report,* July 20, 1992.

107 "I grew up": Clift and Alter, "You Didn't Reveal Your Pain."

107 "his mother's baby": Kelley with Morgan, *Leading with My Heart,* 159.

107 "For the last four": Deposition by Virginia Cassidy Clinton, *Virginia C. Clinton v. Roger M. Clinton,* May 15, 1962.

107 "The last occasion": Ibid.

108 "protect me when": David Maraniss, "Clinton's Life Shaped by Early Turmoil," *The Washington Post,* January 26, 1992.

108 "I am afraid": Deposition by Virginia Cassidy Clinton, *Virginia C. Clinton v. Roger M. Clinton,* May 15, 1962. Also in Maraniss, "Clinton's Life Shaped by Early Turmoil." Also in Oakley, *On the Make,* 30.

108 "sat down warily": Kelley with Morgan, *Leading with My Heart,* 145.

108 "a wonderful new": Ibid.

7. The Sixties

111 "I decided it was": Maraniss, *First in His Class,* 41.

111 "The name doesn't matter": Oakley, *On the Make,* 31.

111 "I was the father": Maraniss, *First in His Class,* 40.

111 "I never regret": Eleanor Clift and Jonathon Alter, "You Didn't Reveal Your Pain."

112 "Mother, you're making": Maraniss, *First in His Class,* 40.

112 "the instrument of": Lauter, "Need to Forge Consensus Strength and Weakness for Clinton."

112 "in those days": Paul Root, interview with the author, March 16, 2001.

113 "I don't think": Ibid.

114 "disgustingly responsible": *Time,* June 8, 1992.

114 "That was the dumbest": Maraniss, "Clinton's Life Shaped by Early Turmoil."

114 "Bill has this thing": David Leopoulos, interview with the author, March 19, 2001.

115 "devastated": Ibid.

115 "a duck can": Oppenheimer, *State of a Union,* 109.

115 "but certainly": Ibid.

115 "I used to tease": Ibid.

115 "Don't you ever": Carlyn Wilson, quoted in Jim Moore, *Clinton: Young Man in a Hurry,* 1992, 27.

115 "Bubba! Bubba!": Kelley with Morgan, *Leading with My Heart,* 161.

116 "We could hear": Ibid.

116 "blocking out": Maraniss, "Clinton's Life Shaped by Early Turmoil."

117 "The Boys State": Joe Purvis, interview with the author, February 7, 2001.

117 "podgy": Ibid.

118 "It's the biggest thrill": *Hot Springs Sentinel-Record,* June 1963.

118 action committee: See Sarah Alderman Murphy, *Breaking the Silence: Little Rock's Women's Emergency Committee to Open Our Schools, 1958–1963,* 1997.

118 "The school was desegregated": Paul Root, interview with the author, March 16, 2001.

118 "If you look at that": Ibid.

119 "People say": Maraniss, "Clinton's Life Shaped by Early Turmoil."

119 "end to the violence": Lauter, "Need to Forge Consensus Strength and Weakness for Clinton."

119 "It seems like": Maraniss, "Clinton's Life Shaped by Early Turmoil."

119 "racial discrimination": *Senior Scholastic,* September 23, 1963.

119 "didn't need": Maraniss, *First in His Class,* 16.

121 "When he came back": Moore, *Clinton,* 25; Allen and Portis, *The Comeback Kid,* 10.

121 "never seen him": Moore, *Clinton,* 25.

121 "He came into": Gallen, *Bill Clinton,* 33.

121 "Suppose they don't": Carolyn (Yeldell) Staley, interview with the author, January 20, 2001.

122 "good. In fact": Gallen, *Bill Clinton,* 35.

123 "I went to his church": Paul Root, interview with the author, March 16, 2001.

123 "the opportunity": *Arkansas Democrat,* September 27, 1977.

123 "Looking at American": Jim Blair, interview with the author, March 23, 2001.

124 "He'd go to band camp": Maraniss, *First in His Class,* 46–7.

125 "It was personal": Quoted in Kelley with Morgan, *Leading with My Heart,* 154.

125 "Now, Virginia, typically": David Leopoulos, interview with the author, March 19, 2001.

126 "Mother, can I": Maraniss, "Clinton's Life Shaped by Early Turmoil."

127 "I remember where": "Bill Clinton's Hidden Life."

127 "He was totally": Maraniss, *First in His Class,* 44.

128 "you could feel": Phil Jamison, quoted in ibid.

128 "daily barrages": Bill Clinton, "A Deep Debt of Gratitude."

129 "Leave within us": Mayra Irvin copy, in Maraniss, *First in His Class,* 49.

8. Georgetown Years

130 "one of the best": Carroll Quigley, *The Hoya,* November 16, 1967, Georgetown University Library, Special Collections Division.

131 "Don't worry, Mother": Maraniss, *First in His Class,* 51.

131 fathers would later regret: As one Georgetown student would put it, Bill Clinton was later "impeached because he lacked the moral compass that we are quick to assume that our university will instill in us. . . . 'Honor' is a word that just doesn't belong in the same sentence with 'Bill Clinton' "—lamenting that both "President Clinton and the United States are mired in relativism, and neither is capable of articulating truth"; Dan Szy, Commentary, Georgetown University *Independent,* November 20, 2000, Georgetown University Library, Special Collections Department. The Jesuit priest Father James Walsh disagreed, however, feeling it "dishonorable to talk about sexual intimacy. It's something no one has the right to know. . . . It's not only a dangerous but a ridiculous notion that leadership is dependent upon a person's moral personal qualities"; "Alma Mater Hates Sin, Loves Sinner," *USA Today,* October 4, 1998.

131 "amiable farm boy": *The Courier,* December 1964, Georgetown University Library, Special Collections Division.

132 "How could the only": Maraniss, *First in His Class,* 61.

132 "a school with curfews": Robert Devaney, *The Georgetowner,* May 28, 1998, Georgetown University Library, Special Collections Department.

133 "Bill Clinton was not": J. Emmett Tyrrell, *Boy Clinton: The Political Biography,* 1996, 51.

134 "Bill, you've got": Maraniss, *First in His Class,* 70.

134 "flim-flamming you": Ibid., 62.

135 "If I go": Bill Clinton, letter to Denise Hyland, quoted in Maraniss, *First in His Class,* 67.

136 "I think the heat": Bill Clinton, letter to Denise Hyland, quoted in Maraniss, *First in His Class,* 79.

136 "I never took orders": Bill Clinton, letter to Denise Hyland, quoted in Maraniss, *First in His Class,* 77.

136 "I would give anything": Bill Clinton, letter to Denise Hyland, quoted in Maraniss, *First in His Class,* 79.

137 "hand-picked": Maraniss, *First in His Class,* 75.

137 "ability to take": Lyda Holt, quoted in Maraniss, *First in His Class,* 78.

138 "You're gonna hear": Maraniss, *First in His Class,* 79.

139 two part-time salaries!: Gallen, *Bill Clinton,* 37.

139 "Someday, this is": Maraniss, *First in His Class,* 86.

140 "basic instinct": Ibid., 89.

141 "merely administers": *The Hoya,* March 2, 1967, Georgetown University Library, Special Collections Department.

141 "A Realistic": March 8, 1967, William J. Clinton, FS 196, item 181-3, Georgetown University Library, Special Collections Department.

141 "About three-fourths": *The Hoya,* March 16, 1967, Georgetown University Library, Special Collections Department.

142 "Instead of handbills": Maraniss, *First in His Class,* 91.

9. Turning Twenty-One

143 "have a prejudiced bone": Glenda Cooper, interview with the author, March 25, 2001.

144 "There was not": Norvill Jones, in Maraniss, *First in His Class,* 85.

144 "the good Americans": Bill Clinton, letter to Denise Hyland, in Maraniss, *First in His Class,* 94.

145 "like a guy": Maraniss, *First in His Class,* 95.

146 "one man per lifetime": Beth Bailey, "Sexual Revolution(s)," in D. Farber, ed., *The Sixties: From Memory to History,* 1994, 249.

147 "He had met women": Jim Moore, quoted in Maraniss, *First in His Class,* 95.

148 "been much help": Kelley with Morgan, *Leading with My Heart,* 165.

148 "Don't be ashamed": Ibid.

148 "To have his father": Ibid., 169.

149 "I want you to": Gallen, *Bill Clinton,* 42.

150 "Well, Mother": Ibid.

10. The End of an Era

155 "and they are experimenting": *The Hoya,* March 7, 1967, Georgetown University Library, Special Collections Division

156 "It may sound": Arthur Marwick, *The Sixties: Cultural Revolution in Britain, France, Italy, and the United States, c. 1958–c. 1974,* 1998, 659.

156 "in public view": Ibid., 661.

157 "I would be": Maraniss, *First in His Class,* 109.

161 "I want you to know": Letter of January 8, 1968, in "Clinton, Wm" file, Georgetown University Library, Special Collections Department.

162 "great. We'll drive": Maraniss, *First in His Class,* 111.

11. On the Fulbright Trail

163 "Why not?": Tom Campbell, quoted in Dumas, *The Clintons of Arkansas,* 51.

164 "a part of Bill Clinton": William T. Coleman III, quoted in Dumas, *The Clintons of Arkansas,* 60.

164 "fashionable theories": Said in 1982, quoted in Marwick, *The Sixties,* 40.

165 As the cultural sociologist: Pierre Bourdieu, *Distinction: A Social Critique of the Judgement of Taste,* 1984.

166 "Affable and obviously smart": Jim McDougal, *Arkansas Mischief: The Birth of a National Scandal,* 1998, 110.

167 "I never heard him": Ibid.

167 "out of control": Maraniss, *First in His Class,* 115.

168 "Fuck you": Jim McDougal, *Arkansas Mischief,* 115.

169 "I don't know": Maraniss, *First in His Class,* 116.

169 "I walked out": Ibid., 117.

169 "good on one shoulder": Carolyn (Yeldell) Staley, interview with the author, January 20, 2001.

169 "Bill had the need": Dumas, *The Clintons of Arkansas,* 51.

169 "He hadn't ever said": Maraniss, *First in His Class,* 117.

170 "I turned around": Ibid.

170 "The woman I marry": Ibid.

171 "put Bill Clinton's": Ibid., 119.

12. Rhodes Scholar

172 given an introduction: The introduction was arranged, at Clinton's request, by Hoyt Purvis, who was working for Senator Fulbright in Little Rock but had also spent time at Oxford; Gallen, *Bill Clinton,* 43.

172 "women and love": Willie Morris, *New York Days,* 1993, 138.

173 "down to earth": Maraniss, *First in His Class,* 124.

173 "She and I": Robert B. Reich, *Locked in the Cabinet,* 1997, 15.

173 "The ocean is choppy": Ibid., 4.

174 "Rhodes Scholars who": Tyrrell, *Boy Clinton,* 83–5.

176 "I remember meeting": Maraniss, *First in His Class,* 124.

177 "pledge ourselves": Ibid., 127.

177 neither Reich nor Talbott: Ultimately Strobe Talbott would serve as assistant secretary of state (1993–99) and Reich as secretary of labor (1993–96). Reich would also unsuccessfully stand in the 2002 Massachusetts primaries for Democratic nomination for governor of Massachusetts.

177 "I am happy": Maraniss, *First in His Class,* 132.

177 "The sun seldom": Gallen, *Bill Clinton,* 45.

177 "Did I feel": Cliff Jackson, interview with the author, July 27, 2002.

178 "The pace is": Gallen, *Bill Clinton,* 45.

179 "I'm continuously": Ibid.

179 "always the character": Maraniss, *First in His Class,* 133.

179 "now get my tail": Nigel Hamilton, *JFK: Reckless Youth,* 1992, 171.

179 "Stouthearted Kennedy": Ibid., 168.

179 "got fucked": Ibid., 166.

180 "Women weren't supposed": Cliff Jackson, interview with the author, July 27, 2002.

180 "Bill and I": Reich, *Locked in the Cabinet,* 6.

181 "certified dwarf": Maraniss, *First in His Class,* 142.

182 "I never had": Oakley, *On the Make,* 65.

182 "He and I had": Cliff Jackson, interview with the author, July 27, 2002.

183 "Certainty is precluded": Maraniss, *First in His Class,* 139.

185 "most dramatic success": Tom Dillard, quoted in T. P. Donovan et al., eds., *The Governors of Arkansas: Essays in Political Biography,* 1995, 242.

185 "finally put the kibosh": Kelley with Morgan, *Leading with My Heart,* 173.

185 the backdrop: Ibid.

186 "where we are": Maraniss, *First in His Class,* 147.

186 "how you move": Ibid., 114.

186 "Arkansas Senator": Reich, *Locked in the Cabinet,* 15.

187 "one of the most": David Bourdon, *Warhol,* 1989, 14–16.

188 "No!": Maraniss, *First in His Class,* 147.

189 "Time to get back": Bill Clinton, letter to Denise Hyland, quoted in Maraniss, *First in His Class,* 149.

189 "Times are getting tough": Ibid.

13. Avoiding the Draft

195 "put his head": Maraniss, *First in His Class,* 166.

196 "this room at Univ": Ibid., 170.

196 Pulitzer Prize–winning book: John F. Kennedy, *Profiles in Courage,* 1955.

196 "just a mess": Maraniss, *First in His Class,* 170.

196 "My friends just don't": Ibid., 162.

197 "I'm going to be": Bill Clinton, letter to Denise Hyland, quoted in Maraniss, *First in His Class,* 172.

198 "He is feverishly": Maraniss, *First in His Class,* 172.

198 "I have also arranged": Ibid., 172.

199 "On the 17th": Bill Clinton, letter to Denise Hyland, quoted in Maraniss, *First in His Class,* 174.

199 "of not being": Maraniss, *First in His Class,* 175.

199 "a sick man": Bill Clinton, letter to Rick Stearns, quoted in Maraniss, *First in His Class,* 179.

199 "not a particularly": Cliff Jackson, interview with the author, July 27, 2002.

200 "because his actions": Cliff Jackson, interview with the author, July 27, 2002.

200 "I went on the hook": Cliff Jackson, interview with the author, July 27, 2002.

200 "Nothing could be": Bill Clinton, letter to Rick Stearns, quoted in Maraniss, *First in His Class,* 179.

200 "It seemed really": Bill Clinton, letter to Denise Hyland, quoted in Maraniss, *First in His Class,* 174.

201 "My mind is": Bill Clinton, letter to Rick Stearns, quoted in Maraniss, *First in His Class,* 179.

201 "most of them": Ibid.

201 "I know one": Ibid.

201 "I want so much": Ibid.

201 "I knew it by July 26": Cliff Jackson, interview with the author, July 27, 2002.

201 "No. And I": Ibid.

202 "A lot of people": Maraniss, *First in His Class,* 180.

202 "left and been drafted": Ibid., 185–6.

203 "I didn't really know": Ibid., 171.

203 "Bill has succeeded": Ibid., 181.

204 a war criminal: *The New York Times Magazine,* April 29, 2001.

205 "We thought we were": Ibid.

205 "I liked Bill Clinton": Jim Johnson, interview with the author, February 19, 2001.

205 "Clinton, the out-of-control": Eli Zaretsky, in L. Berlant and L. Duggan, eds., *Our Monica, Ourselves,* 2001, 10.

14. The Fugitive

207 "taking me in": Maraniss, *First in His Class,* 196.

207 "You're right": Maraniss, *First in His Class,* 186.

208 "an absolute slum": Ibid., 196–7.

208 "Oxford at the end": Martin Walker, *The President We Deserve: Bill Clinton, His Rise, Fall and Comeback,* 1996, 65.

209 "was successful with girls": Maraniss, *First in His Class,* 196.

209 "Bill liked female company": Oakley, *On the Make*, 63, 8.
210 *Lady Chatterley's Lover*: "Is it a book that you would even wish your wife or your servants to read?" the counsel for the prosecution, Mervyn Rees-Jones, had famously asked the jury, aghast that the book might give Englishwomen "ideas" and unaware that members of the jury might not actually have servants.
210 "In case you ever": Oakley, *On the Make*, 84.
211 "very cuddly": Ibid., 69; Maraniss, *First in His Class*, 153.
211 "but he was a very": Oakley, *On the Make*, 69.
211 Red Queen syndrome: See Matt Ridley, *The Red Queen*, among others.
216 "the best known essay": Maraniss, *First in His Class*, 199. The "essay" was published in every major newspaper in the United States in February 1992.
216 "extraordinary letter": Jim Myers, *World* Washington Bureau, "Ex-ROTC Employee Lauds Clinton Letter," February 20, 1992.

15. The End of the Sixties

220 "our soldiers": Tyrrell, *Boy Clinton*, 64, 70.
221 "Socialists" with: Ibid., 71–2.
221 "sentimental Left": Ibid., 75.
221 "I can see them": Ibid., 77–8.
221 "The irrefutable fact": Ibid., 76.
222 Oxford degree: Almost a third of the class of 1968 Rhodes Scholars did not bother to take Oxford degrees, "the highest percentage in the post–World War II period"; Maraniss, *First in His Class*, 223.
223 "Ellsberg, according to Henry": H. R. Haldeman, *The Ends of Power*, 1978, 155.

16. Atonement

228 "more positions": Maraniss, *First in His Class*, 232.
229 The Heroic Period: Carl Oglesby, "Notes on a Decade Ready for the Dustbin," in Mitchell Goodman, ed., *The Movement Toward a New America: The Beginnings of a Long Revolution*, 1970, 737.
229 "this messianic sense": Tom Hayden, *Reunion: A Memoir*, 1998, 74.
230 "somewhere between": Eric Rennie, *From a Campaign Album* (1973), quoted in Maraniss, *First in His Class*, 232.
230 "lost boys and girls": Peter Collier and David Horowitz, *Destructive Generation: Second Thoughts About the '60s*, 1989, 17.
230 "amorality": Tyrrell, *Boy Clinton*, 58.
230 "Coat and Tie Radicals": Ibid.
230 "Politics gives guys": Maraniss, *First in His Class*, 218.

17. Bill and Hillary

232 "asked if": Gallen, *Bill Clinton,* 48.

233 "There were all": Ibid., 49.

233 "Mr. Aura": Gail Sheehy, *Hillary's Choice,* 1999, 76.

234 "went through law school": Jim Blair, interview with the author, March 23, 2002.

234 "He did not": Sheehy, *Hillary's Choice,* 77.

234 "to overcome fears": Maraniss, *First in His Class,* 156.

234 "Bill was cool": Walker, *The President We Deserve,* 64.

234 "Man, don't you know": Dumas, *The Clintons of Arkansas,* 54.

235 "fitting them all": Sheehy, *Hillary's Choice,* 77.

235 Edward Brooke: Senator Brooke, the first black person ever to be elected to the U.S. Senate by popular vote, had remarked, "Whatever romantics may say about violence in our national life, the use of force is repugnant to the spirit of American politics. So long as society retains a capacity for nonviolent political change, resort to violent political action is anathema." To this, Hillary Rodham had responded, "We feel that for too long our leaders have used politics as the art of the possible. And the challenge now is to practice politics as the art of making what appears to be impossible, possible. We feel that our prevailing acquisitive and competitive corporate life . . . is not the way for us. We're searching for more immediate, ecstatic . . . modes of living. . . . We're not interested in social reconstruction, it's human reconstruction"; Hillary Rodham, commencement address, May 31, 1969. The speech was picked up by *Life* magazine, which published excerpts.

235 "tall guy with": Nancy Bekavac, quoted in Gallen, *Bill Clinton,* 50.

235 "Look, if you're": Sheehy, *Hillary's Choice,* 76.

236 "pulsing hormones": Ibid., 62, 69.

236 "I never stated": Ibid., 74.

237 "You're not a Republican": Ibid., 63.

237 "wasting" her time: Ibid., 73.

238 "junk everywhere": Gallen, *Bill Clinton,* 50.

238 "Listen, don't bother": Ibid., 44.

238 "Five of us": Maraniss, *First in His Class,* 218.

239 "They were trying": Norman King, *Hillary: Her True Story,* 1993, 29.

239 "was regarded": David Brock, *The Seduction of Hillary Rodham Clinton,* 1996, 38.

239 "probably considered": Ibid., 39.

239 "They hated him": Joyce Milton, *The First Partner: Hillary Rodham Clinton,* 1999, 51.

240 "was too ready": Ibid.

240 "It was considered": Brock, *The Seduction of Hillary Rodham Clinton*, 38.

240 "This tall, rather imposing": Ibid., 24.

241 "a mind conservative": Sheehy, *Hillary's Choice*, 83.

241 "Total experimentation": Quoted in Walker, *The President We Deserve*, 73.

242 "I loved being with her": King, *Hillary*, 45.

242 "They were both": Ibid., 43.

242 "look-like-shit": Brock, *The Seduction of Hillary Rodham Clinton*, 26.

243 "wild shrub of hair": Sheehy, *Hillary's Choice*, 75.

243 "Don't forget": Ibid., 72.

243 "I was afraid": Ibid., 76.

243 "one was run": Gallen, *Bill Clinton*, 51.

244 "what became of": Hillary Rodham Clinton, *It Takes a Village*, 1996, 22.

245 "washed out": Milton, *The First Partner*, 50.

246 " 'No,' ": Sheehy, *Hillary's Choice*, 82.

18. Living in Sin

247 "in newspapers": Beth Bailey, "Sexual Revolution(s)" in Farber, *The Sixties*, 251.

248 "openly flaunting": Ibid., 252.

248 "an issue of": Ibid., 250.

248 "rock and roll": Ibid., 256.

249 "sex is not so much": Ibid., 254.

251 "Look at this": Brock, *The Seduction of Hillary Rodham Clinton*, 41.

251 "You know, I'm really": Sheehy, *Hillary's Choice*, 85.

252 "Bill and Hillary": King, *Hillary*, 44.

252 "She is very articulate": Milton, *The First Partner*, 50.

252 "She is much more": Brock, *The Seduction of Hillary Rodham Clinton*, 42.

252 "It was a tough time": Maraniss, *First in His Class*, 263.

253 "He said his professor": Jim Blair, interview with the author, March 23, 2001.

253 "Can't say I look": Letter, November 17 [1971], communicated to the author by Cliff Jackson.

254 "Khrushchev couldn't read": Ibid.

254 "were not meant": Letter, undated (but probably mid-December 1971), communicated to the author by Cliff Jackson.

255 "You could never": Maraniss, *First in His Class*, 239.

255 "Come off it": Ibid., 247.

256 "Hillary is not": Oakley, *On the Make*, 103.

256 "afraid of me": Sheehy, *Hillary's Choice*, 76.

256 "He's more complex": Maraniss, *First in His Class*, 248.

256 "She saw past": Oakley, *On the Make*, 103.

257 "basking in each other's": Brock, *The Seduction of Hillary Rodham Clinton*, 41.

19. On the Texas Titanic

259 "I just had": Sheehy, *Hillary's Choice*, 84.

259 "It would make": Gallen, *Bill Clinton*, 50.

259 "young men without legs": Gordon L. Weil, *The Long Shot: McGovern Runs for President*, 1973, 14.

260 "leftie": Nixon aide Charles Colson "rushed to the president's office, and the two men quickly hatched a bizarre plot that far surpassed in its base criminality anything of which Nixon subsequently was accused in the Watergate-inspired articles of impeachment"; Stephan Lesher, *George Wallace: American Populist*, 1994, 484.

261 Wallace's running: Ibid., 489.

261 "hellfire and brimstone": Oakley, *On the Make*, 110.

261 "I looked at him": Ibid., 115.

263 "One of them": Maraniss, *First in His Class*, 265.

263 "say what he thought": Weil, *The Long Shot*, 220.

263 "McGovern cannot tell": Ibid.

264 "I felt": Theodore H. White, *The Making of the President, 1972*, 1973, 319.

264 "weeping as Hart": Sheehy, *Hillary's Choice*, 84.

264 "At the beginning": Jim Blair, interview with the author, March 23, 2001.

264 "Yeah, a lot": Ibid.

265 "Stories of who": Bebe Champ, quoted in Maraniss, *First in His Class*, 276.

265 "Not a day": David Broder, *Changing of the Guard: Power and Leadership in America*, 1980, 259.

266 "run 'Hillary' off": Sheehy, *Hillary's Choice*, 113.

266 "*Nobody* had met": Ibid., 85.

266 "the ethical and pure": Maraniss, *First in His Class*, 277.

266 "been working in Texas": Betsey Wright, interview with the author, March 23, 2001.

266 "Bill gets into": Ibid.

267 "far more intrigued": Ibid.

268 "the most brutal reality": White, *The Making of the President*, 343.

268 "every time a war": Maraniss, *First in His Class*, 281–2.

269 "As soon as": Ibid., 280–1.

269 "He came back": King, *Hillary*, 46.

269 "We always had": Ibid.

20. Law Professor

273 "few hundred that": White, *The Making of the President*, 333.

274 "was very enthusiastic": Al Witte, interview with the author, February 13, 2001.

274 "I kind of assumed": Ibid.

275 "Bill, are you": Maraniss, *First in His Class,* 288.

275 "I've thought a lot": Al Witte, interview with the author, February 13, 2001.

276 it was glacial: Virginia, before her death, remembered the encounter happening during the McGovern campaign, the previous year, when Roger was fifteen and her third husband, Jeff Dwire, was still in good shape, before his heart attack; but about the nature of the encounter, both women were crystal clear.

277 "A mahogany brown": Kelley with Morgan, *Leading with My Heart,* 192.

277 "the minute Hillary went": Ibid., 191–2.

278 "Talk about being": Ann Henry, interview with the author, February 14, 2001.

279 "dowdy-looking woman": Quoted in Milton, *The First Partner,* 69–70.

279 "I mean": Bobby Roberts, interview with the author, February 7, 2001.

280 "I was very unsure": Quoted in King, *Hillary,* 47.

21. Campaign for Congress

282 "There's a beautiful": Al Witte, interview with the author, February 13, 2001.

282 "a sort of minor": Ibid.

283 "As I say": Ibid.

283 "I didn't even know": Milt Copeland, interview with the author, February 13, 2001.

283 "I think many lawyers": Ann Henry, interview with the author, February 14, 2001.

283 "for a party": Ibid.

283 "He did not get": Al Witte, interview with the author, February 13, 2001.

284 "I kept hearing": Ibid.

284 "Money has never": Ann Henry, interview with the author, February 14, 2001.

284 "There's not a bitch": Oppenheimer, *State of a Union,* 136.

285 "surreal, unbelievable": Norman King, *The Woman in the White House: The Remarkable Story of Hillary Rodham Clinton,* 1996, 47.

285 "I worked with her": Ibid., 138.

286 "plumbers": So dubbed because they were assigned to fix leaks; Haldeman, *The Ends of Power,* 158.

287 "If I run": "In Possible Congressional Race: Clinton Emphasizes Issues," *Arkansas Traveler,* February 18, 1974.

287 nuclear bombs: See, among others, Stanley K. Kutler, ed., *Abuse of Power: The New Nixon Tapes,* 1997; and Daniel Ellsberg, *Secrets: A Memoir of Vietnam and the Pentagon Papers,* 2002.

287 "Actually, what tends": Al Witte, interview with the author, February 13, 2001.

288 "from the time": Ann Henry, interview with the author, February 14, 2001.

288 "and he made": Ibid.

288 "Some felt that": Jim Blair, interview with the author, March 23, 2001.

289 "Then, when Clinton": Ann Henry, interview with the author, February 14, 2001.

289 "He doesn't mind": Bobby Roberts, interview with the author, February 7, 2001.

289 "It was her": Maraniss, *First in His Class,* 320.

290 "all of a sudden": Oppenheimer, *State of a Union,* 123.

290 "The most extraordinary thing": Robert Sack was a lawyer colleague of Hillary on the Doar staff: Maraniss, *First in His Class,* 312.

290 "Bill, if you're going": Paul Fray, interview with Jerry Oppenheimer, quoted in Oppenheimer, *State of a Union,* 124.

290 "Don't keep a diary": Maraniss, *First in His Class,* 311.

291 "It was an unbelievable": King, *The Woman in the White House,* 48.

292 "I mean, people": Cliff Jackson, interview with the author, July 27, 2002.

292 "I always thought": Ibid.

292 "In 1974": Ibid.

293 "I mean, this is": Ibid.

293 "*I* found out": Ibid.

294 "It was clear": Betsey Wright, interview with the author, March 23, 2001.

294 "He was always": Ibid.

294 "He was careless": Ibid.

294 "Rumors were flying": Mary Lee Fray, interview with Gail Sheehy, quoted in Sheehy, *Hillary's Choice,* 112–13.

295 " 'Look,' I told her": Paul Fray, interview with Gail Sheehy, quoted in Sheehy, *Hillary's Choice,* 111.

295 "That was Hillary's": Ibid., 110.

296 "the goals we've set": Oppenheimer, *State of a Union,* 2.

296 "Thanks—somehow": Ibid., 129.

296 "You just don't know": Ibid., 149.

296 "special friends": Sheehy, *Hillary's Choice,* 112.

297 "You know, Tom Bell": Maraniss, *First in His Class,* 313.

297 "evil" president: Sheehy, *Hillary's Choice,* 90.

298 "is going to cost": Maraniss, *First in His Class,* 325.

298 "She nixed it": Ibid., 336.

299 "He was literally": Sheehy, *Hillary's Choice,* 119.

299 "lost from the start": Betsey Wright, interview with the author, March 23, 2001.

22. The Wedding

300 "He didn't win": Jim Blair, interview with the author, March 23, 2001.

300 Dale Bumpers: A poll conducted by Arkansas political scientists Cal Ledbetter and C. Fred Williams in 1998, based on a perfect score of 5, ranked Dale Bumpers as by far the greatest modern governor of Arkansas—indeed,

the only governor to rank in the 4.5-to-5-point "great" category (4.536), in "Arkansas Governors in the 20th Century: A Ranking and Analysis, 1979 and 1998," extracted in the *Arkansas Times,* August 28, 1998.

301 "Bumpers and Clinton": Al Witte, interview with the author, February 13, 2001.

301 "David Pryor was": Ibid.

301 "I think there was": Ibid.

302 "Mother," he'd told Virginia: Sheehy, *Hillary's Choice,* 120.

302 "and I don't know": Marla Crider, interview with Jerry Oppenheimer, quoted in Oppenheimer, *State of a Union,* 130.

303 "She challenges me": Ibid.

303 Hillary had threatened: Maraniss, *First in His Class,* 321.

303 "gone out with": Paul Fray, interview with Jerry Oppenheimer, quoted in Oppenheimer, *State of a Union,* 131. According to many evolutionary psychological studies, such hypocrisy is "natural": men seem genetically programmed to be more promiscuous, yet more sexually jealous, than women. See, among others, Joann Ellison Rodgers, *Sex: A Natural History,* 2001, 8. Recent studies and publications, however, contend that females are just as naturally promiscuous but have different agendas and strategies for getting their way—"both sexes in state of dynamic flux," as Professor Tim Birkhead commented in *Promiscuity.* See, among others, Carol Cruzan Morton, "Girls Gone Wild: In the Animal Kingdom, Female Promiscuity May Be More the Rule than the Exception," *The Boston Globe,* March 11, 2003. Olivia Judson pointed out, in *Dr. Tatiania's Sex Advice to All Creation,* 2002, that "the female potential for promiscuity may curb a male's caddish behavior," as Carol Morton summarized. Professor Birkhead cautioned that, while promiscuity for men enhances their reproductive potential in almost all species, in "sexually monogamous species, promiscuity either confers no benefits or imposes a cost on females"— possibly explaining the differential; Birkhead, *Promiscuity,* 231.

303 "he would really": Betsey Wright, interview with the author, March 23, 2001.

304 "I would grind": Kelley with Morgan, *Leading with My Heart,* 199.

304 "Look," she stated: Sheehy, *Hillary's Choice,* 126.

305 "Making the decision": Ibid., 121.

305 "in the middle": Ibid., 108.

306 "a normal, healthy": Marla Crider, interview with Jerry Oppenheimer, quoted in Oppenheimer, *State of a Union,* 130.

306 "She is quick": William Wilson, Jr., quoted in King, *The Woman in the White House,* 48.

307 "But, Hillary": Ann Henry, interview with the author, February 14, 2001.

307 " 'Hmm, wine' ": Marla Crider, interview with Jerry Oppenheimer, quoted in Oppenheimer, *State of a Union,* 130.

307 "mess everywhere": Kelley with Morgan, *Leading with My Heart,* 219.

308 Holiday Inn: Sheehy, *Hillary's Choice,* 122.

308 "Whoever heard": Ann Henry, interview with the author, February 14, 2001.

308 "I said, you know": Ibid.

309 "Hillary Rodham": Sheehy, *Hillary's Choice,* 122.

309 "I might want": Ann Henry, interview with the author, February 14, 2001.

309 "Fuck this shit": Oppenheimer, *State of a Union,* 219.

23. Strike Two

310 "the psychological man": Christopher Lasch, *The Culture of Narcissism: American Life in an Age of Diminishing Expectations,* 1978, xvi.

311 "Bumpers, you know": Ann Henry, interview with the author, February 14, 2001.

313 "a background in": "Bill Clinton to Seek Attorney General Post," *Grapevine,* March 17, 1976.

314 "Geannie": Gennifer Flowers, *Passion and Betrayal,* 1995, 6.

314 "womanizing": Ibid., 15.

314 "lazy, sexy smile": Ibid., 31.

314 "didn't try": Ibid., 28.

315 "other people began": Gennifer Flowers interview, 'My 12-Year Affair with Bill Clinton,' *Star,* February 4, 1992.

315 "and we'd talk": Ibid.

315 "We held hands": Ibid.

315 "consciously manipulated": Flowers, *Passion and Betrayal,* 4.

315 "master of his game": Ibid., 31.

315 "a public figure": Ibid., 2.

315 "We both knew": Flowers interview, *Star.*

316 "He was such": Ibid.

316 "Everything about": Flowers, *Passion and Betrayal,* 32.

316 "not particularly": Ibid.

316 "This man made me": Ibid.

316 "His stamina": Ibid.

318 "casual about": Ibid., 36.

318 "he didn't think": Ibid., 37.

318 "he'd talk about": Flowers interview, *Star.*

24. Attorney General

324 "From humans' earliest days": Rodgers, *Sex,* 489.

324 "True monogamy": Judson, *Dr. Tatiana's Sex Advice to All Creation,* 153.

324 "energetic, enthusiastic": Burl Rotenberry, interview with the author, February 6, 2001.

324 "I remember going": Joe Purvis, interview with the author, February 7, 2001.

324 "a great administrator": Ibid.

325 "tended to keep": Burl Rotenberry, interview with the author, February 6, 2001.

325 "I don't mean this": Ibid.

326 "I mean, after all": Ibid.

326 "I would say": Ibid.

326 "Historically": Ibid.

327 "In the entire": Ibid.

327 "He had an enormous": Ibid.

327 "This is probably": Ibid.

327 "vague recollection": Ibid.

328 "I had never before": Richard Morris, *Behind the Oval Office: Winning the Presidency in the Nineties,* 1997, 45.

329 "Eventually Washington": Ernie Dumas, interview with the author, February 8, 2001.

329 "With his liquid": Susan McDougal with Pat Harris, *The Woman Who Wouldn't Talk,* 2003, 24.

329 "Bumpers has already": Ernie Dumas, interview with the author, February 8, 2001.

329 "Do you think Pryor": Ibid.

330 "Clinton was really torn": Ibid.

330 "Heretofore in Arkansas": Ibid.

330 "He's always had": Ibid.

332 "Is it for sale?": Rex Nelson with Philip Martin, *The Hillary Factor: The Story of America's First Lady,* 1993, 204.

332 "pied piper": Ibid.

332 "old-fashioned": Ibid., 209–10.

333 "He has extraordinary": *Arkansas Gazette,* May 31, 1978.

333 "David's too nice": Richard Morris, *Behind the Oval Office,* 46.

333 "It is one": Ernie Dumas, interview with the author, February 8, 2001.

333 "Clinton and I": Richard, Morris, *Behind the Oval Office,* 49–50.

334 "I'm Easy": Flowers, *Passion and Betrayal,* 51.

336 "suggested to one": Jeffrey Toobin, *A Vast Conspiracy,* 1999, 383. Also Joe Conason and Gene Lyons, *The Hunting of the President: The Ten-Year Campaign to Destroy Bill and Hillary Clinton,* 2001, 60–64.

336 "she always covered": Sean Hannity, interview with Juanita Broaddrick, Fox News Channel, June 10, 2003.

336 "Diamonds and Denim": Arkansas has, in its Crater of Diamonds State Park, the only diamond mine in the United States where members of the public can mine and keep their gemstone findings.

25. Youngest-Ever Governor of Arkansas

337 "My theories": Richard Morris, *Behind the Oval Office,* 50.

337 "When he fired me": Ibid.

337 "the Boy Scout": Ibid., 13.

338 "Clinton's Cabinet": Howell Raines, "Clinton Among New Governors in South Making Bold Changes," *Arkansas Gazette,* March 4, 1979.

339 "When he first gets": Ernie Dumas, interview with the author, February 8, 2001.

339 "never known another": Susan McDougal with Harris, *The Woman Who Wouldn't Talk,* 33.

339 "There's a terrible": Betsey Wright, interview with the author, March 23, 2001.

339 "Clinton has also": Howell Raines, "Clinton Among New Governors in South."

340 "I discovered": Jim Blair, interview with the author, March 23, 2001.

340 "was in an Eagle Scout": Richard Morris, *Behind the Oval Office,* 50.

340 "small business": Donovan et al., *The Governors of Arkansas,* 263.

341 "one of the most": Ibid., 263–4.

341 "had an extraordinary": Betsey Wright, interview with the author, March 23, 2001.

341 "I mean, it's hard": Jim Blair, interview with the author, March 23, 2001.

342 "plunge himself into": "Clinton Talks with Carter," *Arkansas Gazette,* September 22, 1979.

343 "restoration of trust": "Clinton Critical of President in Address at Georgetown," *Arkansas Gazette,* May 26, 1980.

346 "bittersweet arrangement": Joe E. Barnhart, *The Southern Baptist Holy War: The Self-Destructive Struggle for Power Within the Largest Protestant Denomination in America,* 1986, 1–2.

346 "breaking down": Quoted in Maraniss, *First in His Class,* 383.

346 "The middle ground": Bobby Roberts, interview with the author, February 7, 2001.

347 "There's the race thing": Ernie Dumas, interview with the author, February 8, 2001.

347 "would have been": Frank White, interview with the author, March 22, 2001.

347 "I just thought": Ibid.

348 "many of the young": Susan McDougal with Harris, *The Woman Who Wouldn't Talk,* 54.

348 "I had never voted": Frank White, interview with the author, March 22, 2001.

348 "Well, I decided": Ibid.

349 "He raised the license": Ibid.

350 "When people started": Ibid.

350 "Car taxes": Ibid.

351 "Like I said": Ibid.

351 "so easy to": *Passion and Betrayal,* 57.

352 "like he'd invented": Sheehy, *Hillary's Choice,* 133.

352 "I think they knew": Betsey Wright, interview with the author, March 23, 2001.

352 "No, he didn't": Frank White, interview with the author, March 22, 2001.

353 Legal Services Corporation: For a full account of Hillary's chairmanship and the misfortunes of her protégé Dan Bradley, who died in 1988, see Milton, *The First Partner,* 125–36.

353 "and the level": Susan McDougal with Harris, *The Woman Who Wouldn't Talk,* 54.

353 "more to life": Mandy Merck, quoted in Maraniss, *First in His Class,* 375.

354 "I remember feeling": Susan McDougal with Harris, *The Woman Who Wouldn't Talk,* 32.

354 "We may not be": Carolyn (Yeldell) Staley, quoted in Maraniss, *First in His Class,* 375.

354 "You know what": Frank White, interview with the author, March 22, 2001.

355 "The culture of Arkansas": Ibid.

355 "The only way": Ibid.

355 "Rudy, they're killing me": Maraniss, *First in His Class,* 379.

355 "His aunt Floris Tatom": Floris Tatom, interview with the author, March 14, 2001.

356 "panicked": Frank White, interview with the author, March 22, 2001. White was correct, as John Brummett revealed in "Clinton Studies, Discards Session Call," *Arkansas Gazette,* November 18, 1980.

356 "The conservative": Ernie Dumas, interview with the author, February 8, 2001.

356 "Bill couldn't tell": Ibid.

356 "Steve and Bill": Ibid.

356 "We probably did": David Osborne, quoted in Allen and Portis, *The Comeback Kid,* 62.

357 "The falling-out": Ernie Dumas, interview with the author, February 8, 2001.

357 "Basically, all": Ibid.

358 "he was called": Ibid.

358 "They were their dearest": Ibid.

358 "So Rudy had to go": Ibid.

358 "Bill Clinton can't": Ibid.

358 "a desperately human trait!": Ibid.

359 "Here's a poser": "Godzilla Versus the Hollow Man," *Arkansas Times,* August 1982.

359 "Oh, absolutely": Bobby Roberts, interview with the author, February 7, 2001.

359 "I mean, it is": Ibid.

359 "About six days before": Frank White, interview with the author, March 22, 2001.

359 "That told me": Ibid.

360 " 'Hey,' they said": Ibid.

360 "I said, '$70,000' ": Ibid.

360 "Well hey!": Ibid.

360 "I hit him hard": Ibid.

361 "showed him beatin' ": Ibid.

361 "At ten o'clock": Ibid.

361 "He *never* conceded": Ibid.

26. Recovery

362 like a baby: Frank White, interview with the author, March 22, 2001.

362 "My recollection of that": Jim Blair, interview with the author, March 23, 2001.

363 "We kept apple pie": Michael Schaller, *Reckoning with Reagan,* 1992, 36.

363 "You're so goddamned": Deb Reichmann, "Nixon Discussed Nuclear Strike in Vietnam," *The Boston Globe,* March 1, 2002.

363 "level Vietnam": Schaller, *Reckoning with Reagan,* 14.

364 "The message is clear": Ibid., 22.

364 "You need to go": Jim Blair, interview with the author, March 23, 2001.

364 "I mean, he's never": Ibid.

367 "whacked between the eyes": Nelson with Martin, *The Hillary Factor,* 227.

367 "The thing I remember": Jim Blair, interview with the author, March 23, 2001.

367 "I mean, the biggest": Betsey Wright, interview with the author, March 23, 2001.

368 "I don't know why": Ibid. Governor Winthrop Rockefeller had commuted the sentences of all prisoners on death row in the final hours of his governorship.

368 "Mr. Clinton has been": *Arkansas Gazette,* November 12, 1980.

368 chairing the national: John C. White, the national chairman, was not seeking a second four-year term and called "to ask if Mr. Clinton would be interested in the national chairmanship"; "Clinton Being Considered for Democratic Chairman," *Arkansas Gazette,* November 12, 1980.

368 "We didn't elect": Schaller, *Reckoning with Reagan,* 5.

369 milked taxpayers: Ibid., 70, 115.

369 "We will mine": Ibid., 100.

370 "After he lost": Jim Blair, interview with the author, March 23, 2001.

370 "You sonofabitch!": Maraniss, *First in His Class,* 389.

370 "I said, 'Bill' ": Jim Blair, interview with the author, March 23, 2001.

371 "He called me": Betsey Wright, interview with the author, March 23, 2001.

371 "I listened to this": Ibid.

371 "I was just stunned": Ibid.

372 If he wished: See letter of December 28, 1980, to William Fulbright in J. William Fulbright Postsenatorial Papers, Special Collections Division, University of Arkansas Libraries, Fayetteville, Arkansas.

372 "stayed in the basement": Betsey Wright, interview with the author, March 23, 2001.

372 "stayed up late": Audrey Burtrum-Stanley to author, November 4, 2002.

372 "I thought I was": Flowers interview, *Star.*

372 "Honey, she's": Flowers, *Passion and Betrayal,* 41.

372 "I want": Maraniss, *First in His Class,* 394.

373 "I found him": Richard Morris, *Behind the Oval Office,* 51.

373 "I saw that it": Ibid.

373 "pretending to practice": Jim Blair, interview with the author, March 23, 2001.

373 "screwed up": Maraniss, *First in His Class,* 392.

374 "But Clinton didn't": Richard Morris, *Behind the Oval Office,* 53.

374 "Wake up!": Sheehy, *Hillary's Choice,* 139.

374 "There's not a father": Jim Blair, interview with the author, March 23, 2001.

374 "This guy has evolved": Quoted in Sheehy, *Hillary's Choice,* 136–7.

375 "Had Clinton been": Quoted in Allen and Portis, *The Comeback Kid,* 61.

376 "As we watched": Richard Morris, *Behind the Oval Office,* 55.

27. The Comeback

377 "a spin": Sheehy, *Hillary's Choice,* 134.

378 "As God is my witness": Ibid., 148.

378 "The frustrations": Ibid., 149.

378 "You got to go": Ibid., 148.

378 "Bill was always": Ibid., 149.

379 "Hillary denied": Ibid., 132.

379 "It was awful": Ibid., 135.

379 "smartest woman": John Brummett, interview with the author, March 2001.

380 "There was always": Betsey Wright, interview with the author, March 23, 2001.

380 Scopes I: Expert testimony had been denied by the judge in "Scopes I."

381 "The Creation-Science": "Clinton the Choice," *The Arkansas Traveler* 76 (75), October 29, 1982.

381 "apple pie": Stephen Jay Gould, *Rocks of Ages: Science and Religion in the Fullness of Life,* 1999, 129–31.

NOTES · 721

381 "What would you do": Ibid., 144–5.

382 "a fiasco": "Clinton the Choice."

382 "said in a local": Gould, *Rocks of Ages*, 145.

382 "I had so much": Betsey Wright, interview with the author, March 23, 2001.

383 "what I call": Ibid.

383 "Clinton didn't want to": Richard Morris, *Behind the Oval Office*, 53.

383 "I'll do it": Ibid., 54.

383 "Many of you": Ibid.

384 "The line about": Ibid.

384 "bunker mentality": Susan McDougal with Harris, *The Woman Who Wouldn't Talk*, 56.

384 "Personnel management": Burl Rotenberry, interview with the author, February 6, 2001.

385 "Bill, you're out": Sheehy, *Hillary's Choice*, 141.

385 "If someone turns out": Ibid., 136.

385 "She thinks everyone": Ibid., 137.

386 "the ideals and": Schaller, *Reckoning with Reagan*, 6.

386 "I don't know": Ibid., 14.

386 "enjoyed the most generous": Ibid., 55.

387 "Hillary is beautiful": Anne Henry, interview with the author, February 14, 2001.

388 "I feared I had": Richard Morris, *Behind the Oval Office*, 55.

388 "The primary was": Betsey Wright, interview with the author, March 23, 2002.

388 "attacked him on": Richard Morris, *Behind the Oval Office*, 55.

389 "So out of that": Betsey Wright, interview with the author, March 23, 2002.

389 "good and hot": Jim McDougal, *Arkansas Mischief*, 186.

389 "We had geared": Betsey Wright, interview with the author, March 23, 2002.

389 "We want Frank!": Nelson with Martin, *The Hillary Factor*, 230.

390 "hint of guilt": Jim McDougal, *Arkansas Mischief*, 186.

390 "unprepared to hail": Ibid., 187.

390 "more restrained": Nelson with Martin, *The Hillary Factor*, 227.

391 "as the ideal": Jim McDougal, *Arkansas Mischief*, 186.

391 sexual McCarthyism: Alan Dershowitz, *Sexual McCarthyism: Clinton, Starr, and the Emerging Constitutional Crisis*, 1998.

392 raised still more: Already in May 1982, the campaign finance figures were: Bill Clinton $547,466.20, Frank White $531,381.93; "Clinton's Total Contributions Beat Every Other Candidate's," *Arkansas Gazette*, May 19, 1982.

392 "She ambushed me": Sheehy, *Hillary's Choice*, 146–7.

393 "eviscerate him": Ibid., 147.

393 "My little wife": Frank White, interview with the author, March 22, 2001.

394 "that women impose": Carol Gilligan, *In a Different Voice: Psychological Theory and Women's Development*, 1982, 105.

394 "You're either useful": Carolyn Staley, quoted in Sheehy, *Hillary's Choice*, 126.

396 "Haven't you people": Schaller, *Reckoning with Reagan*, 53.

396 "His first term": Ernie Dumas, interview with the author, February 8, 2001.

396 "When Clinton decided": Ibid.

397 "Bill Clinton used": Ibid.

398 "If Frank's smart": *Arkansas Gazette*, September 5, 1983, quoted in Oakley, *On the Make*, 271.

398 "Chelsea could": *Arkansas Gazette*, September 5, 1983.

398 "He knew that": Maraniss, *First in His Class*, 402.

399 "We felt like": Ibid., 403.

399 "run anything in": *Arkansas Gazette*, September 16, 1983, quoted in Oakley, *On the Make*, 231.

399 "We worked": Maraniss, *First in His Class*, 403.

399 "blacks in that": Rodney Slater in Dewayne Wickham, *Bill Clinton and Black America*, 2002, 151.

399 "My little old town": Ibid., 151–2.

400 "most powerful": Ibid.

400 "a defining moment": Ibid.

400 "See, if he": Ibid., 25–6.

400 Orval Faubus: Governor White had appointed the former governor director of veterans affairs.

401 "I think for the rest": "Clinton Thanks, Praises AEA; Vows Support," *Arkansas Gazette*, November 7, 1982.

401 "And it became clear": Betsey Wright, interview with the author, March 23, 2001.

402 "veritable lovefest": Meredith Oakley, *Arkansas Democrat*, January 12, 1982. Also Oakley, *On the Make*, 273.

402 "Today is Easter": Meredith Oakley, *Arkansas Democrat*, January 12, 1982. Also Oakley, *On the Make*, 274.

28. On the A Team

405 "In Arkansas": "Clinton's Triumph," *Arkansas Gazette*, November 4, 1982.

405 *doppelgänger:* Sheehy, *Hillary's Choice*, 144.

406 "This might sound": Nelson with Martin, *The Hillary Factor*, 235.

406 "A person who marries": Ibid.

407 "quiet and bureaucratic": Susan McDougal with Harris, *The Woman Who Wouldn't Talk*, 32.

407 "I mean, it's not": Betsey Wright, interview with the author, March 23, 2001.

408 "His budget provided": "The Choice Is Clinton," *Arkansas Gazette*, October 17, 1982.

408 "Over the long run": Quoted in Moore, *Clinton,* 70.

410 "Folks either loved": Nelson with Martin, *The Hillary Factor,* 243.

410 "She visited one": Quoted in ibid., 245.

410 "more important to me": *Arkansas Gazette,* October 8, 1983.

410 "I think we elected": Nelson with Martin, *The Hillary Factor,* 248.

411 "war": Moore, *Clinton,* 86.

411 "always able to make": Susan McDougal with Harris, *The Woman Who Wouldn't Talk,* 26–9.

411 "I feel," he remarked: *Arkansas Gazette,* October 27, 1983.

411 "From 1982": Ernie Dumas, interview with the author, February 8, 2001.

412 "has three groups": *Arkansas Gazette,* February 5, 1984.

413 "I know I sound": Nelson with Martin, *The Hillary Factor,* 250–2.

414 "our entire social": Ibid., 252.

414 "I watched Hillary": Sheehy, *Hillary's Choice,* 146.

414 "He had two": Quoted in ibid., 149.

414 "They were intellects": Betsey Wright, interview with the author, March 23, 2001.

414 "the ones that": Ibid.

415 "have misinterpreted": Max Brantley, quoted in Oppenheimer, *State of a Union,* 183.

415 several hundred: Ibid., 182, among others.

415 "He knows human": Sheehy, *Hillary's Choice,* 149.

415 "we had no future": Flowers, *Passion and Betrayal,* 59.

415 "Bill fix": Ibid., 60.

416 "ready and eager": Ibid., 62.

417 "Of course, all": Betsey Wright, interview with the author, March 23, 2001.

417 "it always struck": Susan McDougal with Harris, *The Woman Who Wouldn't Talk,* 33.

417 "*nothing* to do": Betsey Wright, interview with the author, March 23, 2001.

417 "smelled kind of": Susan McDougal with Harris, *The Woman Who Wouldn't Talk,* 29.

417 "concept of industrial": Lasch, *The Culture of Narcissism,* 137.

418 "If I didn't": Sheehy, *Hillary's Choice,* 136.

418 "the ruling power": Ibid., 153.

418 "locked in adolescence": Ibid., 142.

418 "best I've ever seen": Frank White, interview with the author, March 22, 2001.

418 "He's an incredible": Ibid.

418 "I have never": Betsey Wright, interview with the author, March 23, 2001.

419 "*never* work for": Ibid.

419 "I was always struck": Bobby Roberts, interview with the author, February 7, 2001.

419 "opened so many": Betsey Wright, interview with the author, March 23, 2001.

420 "I think Hillary": Jim Blair, interview with the author, March 23, 2001.

420 "When you play": Nelson with Martin, *The Hillary Factor,* 249.

422 "She was so deadly": Susan McDougal with Harris, *The Woman Who Wouldn't Talk,* 32.

423 "Of course, Hillary": Betsey Wright, interview with the author, March 23, 2001.

423 "intellectual, political": Ibid.

423 "soul mates": Sheehy, *Hillary's Choice,* 151.

423 forbade even her closest: Betsey Wright, interview with the author, March 23, 2001.

29. A Bad Apple

425 "You mean you don't": Kelley with Morgan, *Leading with My Heart,* 249.

425 "I was told": Roger Morris, *Partners in Power: The Clintons and Their America* 1996, 327.

425 "bad-apple brother": Bobby Roberts, interview with the author, February 7, 2001.

426 "I mean, essentially": Ibid.

426 "You've got to go": Ibid.

426 "really in anguish": Ibid.

427 "only that each of us": Nelson with Martin, *The Hillary Factor,* 252.

427 more prominent cases: For example, JFK's brother Teddy Kennedy was caught cheating and thrown out of Harvard. LBJ's brother Sam had troubles, as did Don Nixon, brother of Richard Nixon. President G. W. Bush's brother Neil also got into trouble with the Silverado Savings and Loan scandal.

427 Billy Bulger: Billy Bulger, president of the University of Massachusetts and former president of the Massachusetts Senate for seventeen years, testified secretly before the federal grand jury in 2001 but took the Fifth Amendment rather than testify in open court before the congressional committee investigating FBI corruption and the disappearance of his brother "Whitey" Bulger in 2002; *The New York Times,* December 7, 2002, among others. For an account of "Whitey" Bulger's merciless crimes and misdemeanors, see Edward J. MacKenzie, Jr., and Phyllis Karas with Ross A. Muscato, *Street Soldier: My Life as an Enforcer for Whitey Bulger and the Boston Irish Mob,* 2003.

428 "Why did he let": Roger Morris, *Partners in Power,* 327.

428 "It was a very sad": Bobby Roberts, interview with the author, February 7, 2001.

428 "That's what's so": Ibid.

429 "was always defending": Betsey Wright, interview with the author, March 23, 2001.

429 "I'm just calling": Kelley with Morgan, *Leading with My Heart*, 248.

429 "There was a deafening": Ibid., 249.

429 "Never once had I": Ibid.

429 "It *hurt* her": Betsey Wright, interview with the author, March 23, 2001.

430 "breakdown in shared": Nelson with Martin, *The Hillary Factor*, 239.

431 "According to friends": Roger Morris, *Partners in Power*, 329.

431 Documented testimony: Ibid.

431 "I think we're all": Sheehy, *Hillary's Choice*, 186.

431 "an illusory shortcut": Gary Zukay and Linda Francis, *The Heart of the Soul: Emotional Awareness*, 2002, 235.

432 "While he and I": Flowers, *Passion and Betrayal*, 63.

433 "You son of": Ibid., 65.

433 "I'll be over": Ibid.

433 "anguish in his soul": Account of May 24, 1997, meeting ("D-Day or Dump Day"); Andrew Morton, *Monica's Story*, 1999, 113–14.

434 "Sometimes the two": Ambrose Evans-Pritchard, *The Secret Life of Bill Clinton*, 1997, 243–4.

435 "because he didn't": Kelley with Morgan, *Leading with My Heart*, 252.

435 "screaming fits": Susan McDougal with Harris, *The Woman Who Wouldn't Talk*, 97.

435 "He cowered a bit": Sheehy, *Hillary's Choice*, 149.

436 "authorities about cocaine": "Roger Clinton Files Motion to Change Plea in Drug Case," *Arkansas Democrat*, November 9, 1984.

436 "I guess I'm": Roger Morris, *Partners in Power*, 329.

436 "We watched till": Kelley with Morgan, *Leading with My Heart*, 254.

436 "with respect": *The Arkansas Gazette*, January 29, 1985.

436 "experienced the death": Kelley with Morgan, *Leading with My Heart*, 254.

437 "He hit a low": Allen and Portis, *The Comeback Kid*, 104.

437 "clear that Clinton": Oakley, *On the Make*, 303.

437 "Many times if": Betsey Wright, interview with the author, March 23, 2001.

438 "Part of the role": Ibid.

438 "I do know": Ibid.

438 "See, I didn't": Roger Clinton speaking to Rodney Myers, an undercover informant, in Evans-Pritchard, *The Secret Life of Bill Clinton*, 140.

439 "Almost a quarter": Roger Morris, *Partners in Power*, 290.

439 "Our lovemaking": Flowers interview, *Star*.

439 "You know women": Flowers, *Passion and Betrayal*, 68.

439 "Bill treated": Flowers interview, *Star*.

439 "have pinned him": Flowers, *Passion and Betrayal*, 68.

439 "I knew she": Flowers interview, *Star*.

439 "after he hung": Flowers, *Passion and Betrayal*, 69.

440 Ivan Boesky: In 1986 Ivan Boesky pleaded guilty to illegal insider trading, was sentenced to three years' imprisonment, paid $100 million in fines and illegal profits, and was barred from the securities industry for life.

440 Michael Milken: Michael Milken "earned" a $550 million paycheck in 1987 but pleaded guilty to securities violations and filing false income tax returns. In 1990 he was sentenced to ten years in jail and $600 million in fines.

440 "scandal and": Marvin Kalb, *One Scandalous Story: Clinton, Lewinsky, & 13 Days That Tarnished American Journalism,* 2001, 7–8.

441 "She works eighteen": Ernie Dumas, interview with the author, February 8, 2001.

441 "I doubt if": Ibid.

441 "I mean, we were": Betsey Wright, interview with the author, March 23, 2001.

442 "He did some good": Frank White, interview with the author, March 22, 2001.

442 "Your dominant newspaper": Frank White, interview with the author, March 22, 2001.

442 "Stop—Or My": *National Review,* March 30, 1992.

443 "by now taken": Oakley, *On the Make,* 308.

443 "I cannot ask": Ibid., 312.

445 "the most negative": Ibid., 319.

30. Heart of Darkness

448 landslide: In 1984, Bill Clinton had received 554,561 votes to his opponent, Woody Freeman's, 331,987, but the election was far less dramatically contested, and as it had been a presidential reelection year, voter turnout had been significantly greater.

448 "He beat me": Frank White, interview with the author, March 22, 2001.

449 "has seen two men": Quoted in Nelson with Martin, *The Hillary Factor,* 279.

449 "Someone needs to": Ibid.

449 "By election day": Nelson with Martin, *The Hillary Factor,* 279.

451 "I think his adult life": Betsey Wright, interview with the author, March 23, 2001.

452 "Oh, yes, I'd": Allen and Portis, *The Comeback Kid,* 121.

452 "Governor, you're gonna": James B. Stewart, *Blood Sport: The President and His Adversaries,* 1996, 171.

453 "He was absolutely": Flowers, *Passion and Betrayal,* 72.

453 "even more inventive": Ibid., 74.

454 "He kind of": Ibid.

454 "spank him during": Ibid.

454 "dildo-shaped vibrator": Ibid., 75.

455 "Even though": Flowers interview, *Star.*

456 "intensity": Flowers, *Passion and Betrayal,* 75.

456 "Jim promised": Jim McDougal, *Arkansas Mischief,* 213.

457 Bill had confessed: "I was born at sixteen and I'll always feel I'm sixteen. And Hillary was born at age forty"; Stewart, *Blood Sport,* 121.

458 "Personally, I think": Nelson with Martin, *The Hillary Factor,* 281.

458 "Two chronic complaints": Oakley, *On the Make,* 333.

458 "I wonder how many": Ibid., 337.

458 "learned his lessons": Betsey Wright, interview with the author, March 23, 2001.

459 "The key": Bobby Roberts, interview with the author, February 7, 2001.

459 "Compassion": Robert Caro, "The Compassion of Lyndon Johnson," *The New Yorker,* April 1, 2002.

460 "Bill Clinton is not": Allen and Portis, *The Comeback Kid,* 121.

461 "I am basically": Paul Greenberg, interview with the author, March 22, 2001.

462 "changed his tactics": Ibid.

462 "I think he does": Bobby Roberts, interview with the author, February 7, 2001.

463 "the greatest champion": Caro, "The Compassion of Lyndon Johnson."

463 "took the risk": Paul Greenberg, interview with the author, March 22, 2001.

463 "In Arkansas": Ibid.

464 "As for the nature": Ibid.

465 "something interesting there": Betsey Wright, interview with the author, March 23, 2001.

465 "have it all": Ibid.

466 "His dealing with": Ibid.

466 "Don't commit": Sheehy, *Hillary's Choice,* 174–5.

467 "We can't continue": Richard Morris, *Behind the Oval Office,* 61.

467 "bombarding kids": Nelson with Martin, *The Hillary Factor,* 271.

467 "Adults are not": Ibid.

467 "It's not birth control": Ibid.

468 "We've all done": Sheehy, *Hillary's Choice,* 174; also Judith Warner, *Hillary Clinton: The Inside Story,* 1993, 145.

468 sex survey statistics: See, e.g., Linda Rouse, *Marital and Sexual Lifestyles in the United States: Attitudes, Behaviors and Relationships in Social Context,* 2002, 126, quoting a 1984 study that noted that "Forty-two percent of the females and 46 percent of the males indicated some form of intimate involvement outside of their married or cohabiting relationships."

468 "tremendous terror": Maraniss, *First in His Class,* 440.

468 Even academics: Marian Schlesinger, interview with the author.

469 "a dismal array": Richard Morris, *Behind the Oval Office,* 61.

31. The Meeting That Never Happened

473 "I have never": Ann Henry, interview with the author, February 14, 2001.

473 "She was so angry": Ibid.

474 "I called Diane": Ibid.

474 "I think you need": Ibid.

474 "Diane would never": Betsey Wright, interview with the author, March 23, 2001.

474 "and I was told": Ann Henry, interview with the author, February 14, 2001.

474 "I was the bad-news": Betsey Wright, interview with the author, March 23, 2001.

475 "What Bill thought": Ibid.

475 "He pulled out": Ibid.

475 "It just knocked": Ibid.

475 "The way Maraniss": Ibid.

476 "He has made": Ibid.

476 "minimize the importance": Ibid.

476 "I had to be": Ibid.

32. Saying No

477 "I don't think": Betsey Wright, interview with the author, March 23, 2001.

478 "There was such": Ibid.

478 "We talked about it": Ibid.

478 "He said, 'but' ": Ibid.

478 "said he couldn't run": Ibid.

478 "I saw a lot": Bill Clinton, "Political Ambitions, Personal Choices: Bill Clinton Talks About Work, Love and Faith," *Newsweek*, March 9, 1992.

479 "a loosening of": Quoted in E. J. Dionne, Jr., "Clintons See Difficult Decision as Public Version of a Common Dilemma," *Arkansas Gazette*, August 17, 1987.

479 "I've been around": Ann Henry, interview with the author, February 14, 2001.

479 "It's the women": Ibid.

480 withdrawing from: Oakley, *On the Make*, 347.

480 "I hope I will have": Sheehy, *Hillary's Choice*, 178.

481 "Oh, it was": Ibid.

481 "convinced no decision": "Clinton Says the Word: No," *Arkansas Gazette*, July 15, 1987.

482 "Bernie," Hillary: Sheehy, *Hillary's Choice*, 178.

33. Televangelist Preview

485 "When it came time": Oakley, *On the Make*, 347, and *Arkansas Gazette*, July 16, 1987.

485 "In the '70s": Quoted in E. J. Dionne, Jr., "Clintons See Difficult Decision as Public Version of a Common Dilemma," *Arkansas Gazette*, August 17, 1987.

485 "I think something": Bobby Roberts, interview with the author, February 7, 2001.

486 *"I don't know"*: Ibid.

486 "I think he maybe": Ibid.

486 "It's a very": Bill Clinton, "Political Ambitions, Personal Choices: Bill Clinton Talks About Work, Love and Faith." *Newsweek,* March 9, 1992.

487 "By the end": Charles E. Shepard, *Forgiven: The Rise and Fall of Jim Bakker and the PTL Ministry,* 1989, 538–9.

487 "Nancy and I": Joe E. Barnhart with Steven Winzenburg, *Jim and Tammy: Charismatic Intrigue Inside PTL,* 1988, 6.

488 "It is extremely": Shepard, *Forgiven,* 347.

489 "Why don't you hire": Ibid., 279.

489 "You can't trust": Barnhart with Winzenburg, *Jim and Tammy,* 162.

490 "I'll see ya": Ibid.

490 "Jim is a shepherd": Ibid., 163.

490 "You had a good": Ibid., 164.

490 $1 million: Shepard, *Forgiven,* 287, 548.

491 "call him home": Ibid., 487.

491 "Television news ratings": Ann Rowe Seaman: *Swaggart: The Unauthorized Biography of an American Evangelist,* 1999, 20.

491 "pastiche of the religious": Susan Harding, "The Born-Again Telescandals," in Nicolas B. Dirks et al., eds., *Culture/Power/History: A Reader in Contemporary Social Theory,* 1994, 542.

492 "voice of modernity": Ibid., 541.

492 "pigs at the trough": Ibid., 542.

493 "I don't see": Shepard, *Forgiven,* 547.

493 "soap opera": *Nightline,* ABC, May 27, 1987.

493 "After every barrage": Harding, "The Born-Again Telescandals," 552.

494 Once behind bars: The IRS suspected the Bakkers of having pocketed $4.8 million from PTL between 1984 and 1987 to support their flamboyant lifestyle. IRS investigations led to Bakker and his attorney, the Reverend Richard Dortch, being indicted for fraud in 1988 on charges relating to the sale of $1,000 partnerships guaranteeing three days a year of free lodging at Heritage USA for life. In 1986 too many had been sold, resulting in some 1,500 "lifetime partners" per month being refused their three-day entitlements because of accommodation overcommitments—invoking accusations of fraud. The sale of such holiday partnerships had netted $158 million for PTL, $4 million of which had been diverted for personal use. In 1989, Dortch was sentenced to eight years' imprisonment and a $200,000 fine. Bakker was convicted on all twenty-four counts and sentenced to forty-five years in prison with a fine of $500,000. He served five years. By way of comparison, "junk bond king" Michael Milken pled guilty in 1990 to six counts of securities fraud and paid a $600 million

penalty—$50 million more than his earnings for 1987. Plea bargaining had led to the dropping of ninety-two charges of racketeering and insider trading. He was sentenced to ten years in prison, with parole expected in three. He was still left with about $1 billion. Arbitrageur and insider trader Ivan Boesky, his accomplice, was sentenced to three years' imprisonment but was let out after eighteen months, in 1989, still hanging on to $100 million. See Haynes Johnson, *Sleepwalking Through History: America in the Reagan Years,* 1991.

34. The Face of America's Future

495 "production, hard work": Susan Harding, "The Born-Again Telescandals," 547.

496 "believe in redemption": Bill Clinton, "Political Ambitions, Personal Choices: Bill Clinton Talks About Work, Love and Faith," *Newsweek,* March 9, 1992.

496 "a kind of postmodern": Harding, "The Born-Again Telescandals," 547–8.

497 "an irrepressible sense": Ibid., 549.

497 "the opening up": Ibid., 555.

497 "somewhat lower class": Ibid., 547.

497 "a whole host": Ibid., 552.

35. The Specter of Divorce

499 "a statute": Bill Armstrong, quoted in Maraniss, *First in His Class,* 440.

499 "When we got": Hillary Clinton, July 16, 1987, quoted in Oakley, *On the Make,* 348.

500 "See, he thought": Betsey Wright, interview with the author, March 23, 2001.

500 "That was his worst": Ibid.

500 "It hurt so bad": Quoted in E. J. Dionne, Jr., "Clintons See Difficult Decision as Public Version of a Common Dilemma," *Arkansas Gazette,* August 17, 1987.

500 "at least five": Milton, *The First Partner,* 190.

501 "Clinton assigned": Ibid.

501 "view among some Britons": Alan Cowell, "A Big Secret Wallis Simpson Kept from Her Royal Lover," *The New York Times,* January 30, 2003.

501 "a perceptual schizophrenia": Stuart Ewen, *All-Consuming Images: The Politics of Style in Contemporary Culture,* 1988, 159.

502 "economy made of": Ibid.

502 "the lady's head": Milton, *The First Partner,* 191.

502 "His tastes were": Sheehy, *Hillary's Choice,* 181.

502 "Look, Bill": Milton, *The First Partner,* 191.

503 "I wonder how": Maraniss, *First in His Class,* 426.

503 "traumatic decision": Oakley, *On the Make,* 357.

503 "Most rational people": Dionne, "Clintons See Difficult Decision as Public Version of a Common Dilemma."

503 "to run well": Nelson with Martin, *The Hillary Factor,* 284.

503 "been able": Dick Morris's version of Bill and Hillary Clinton's dialogue in Sheehy, *Hillary's Choice,* 187.

504 "Everybody knows": Nelson with Martin, *The Hillary Factor,* 287.

504 "We've really lost": Ibid.

504 "a more balanced": E. J. Dionne, Jr., *New York Times News Service,* "Clintons See Difficult Decision as Public Version of a Common Dilemma."

504 "You sound like": Milton, *The First Partner,* 192.

505 "into a box": *Larry King,* quoted in Sheehy, *Hillary's Choice,* 182.

505 "all these stories": Nelson with Martin, *The Hillary Factor,* 287.

505 "Distinction": Bourdieu, *Distinction.*

505 "One of the big": Dionne, "Clintons See Difficult Decision as Public Version of a Common Dilemma."

506 "it's a terrible": Judy Galman, "Clinton, on TV, Stresses Funding, 'Value' Teaching," *Arkansas Democrat,* September 7, 1987.

506 "He faltered": Betsey Wright, interview with the author, March 23, 2001.

506 "I went through": Oakley, *On the Make,* 357.

507 "I just fell": Allen and Portis, *The Comeback Kid,* 127.

507 "Both Clintons": Sheehy, *Hillary's Choice,* 179.

507 "he appeared": Oakley, *On the Make,* 354.

508 "one of the wealthiest": Sheehy, *Hillary's Choice,* 182–3.

508 "loved simply": Ibid., 185.

508 "the only woman": Ibid., 183.

508 "It's tough": Ibid., 185.

508 "told him she felt": Maraniss, *First in His Class,* 451.

509 "By the time": Morton, *Monica's Story,* 114.

509 "Hillary made it clear": Sheehy, *Hillary's Choice,* 186.

509 "She feels": Ibid.

510 had one: Ibid., 172.

510 "You'll get killed": Ibid.

510 "It's like": Ibid. Also, John Brummett, interview with the author, March 2001.

511 "stricken by": Sheehy, 186.

512 "Betsey's life": Ernie Dumas, interview with the author, February 8, 2001.

512 "more dominant": Ibid.

513 "one of the smartest": Bobby Roberts, interview with the author, February 7, 2001.

513 "Probably a combination": Ibid.

514 "I had to open": Ibid.

514 "Betsey did her best": Ernie Dumas, interview with the author, February 7, 2001.

514 'Who knows what': Ibid.

515 "I don't think": Bobby Roberts, interview with the author, February 7, 2001.

515 "Betsey," replied: Betsey Wright, interview with the author, March 23, 2001.

515 "When I left": Ibid.

515 "I can't believe": Gloria Cabe, letter to David Maraniss, in Maraniss, *First in His Class,* 455.

515 "She was somebody": Betsey Wright, interview with the author, March 23, 2001.

516 off its hinges: Milton, *The First Partner,* 191.

517 "We thought that": Clinton, "Political Ambitions, Personal Choices: Bill Clinton Talks About Work, Love and Faith."

36. *Moment of Truth*

521 "There are only": Quoted in Matt Bai, "The Outsider: Gary Hart Wants to Become the Democrats' Elder Statesman," *The New York Times Magazine,* February 2, 2003.

521 "Until you've been": Quoted in Diane Blair, *Arkansas Politics and Government: Do the People Rule?,* 1988, 158.

521 "He wanted *everyone*": Jim Blair, interview with the author, March 23, 2001.

522 "Anybody that wrote": Ibid.

522 "character flaw": Ibid.

522 "a pathological fear": Donovan et al., *The Governors of Arkansas,* 266.

522 "His further efforts": Diane Blair, in Donovan et al., *The Governors of Arkansas,* 271.

523 "decided he wanted": Betsey Wright, interview with the author, March 23, 2001.

523 "He never believed": Ibid.

523 "I made clear": Ibid.

523 "January of '90": Ibid.

523 "asked if I would": Ibid.

524 "When I talked": Ibid.

524 "a number": Ibid.

524 "that it didn't": Ibid.

524 "And I don't know": Ibid.

524 "more confused than ever": Nelson with Martin, *The Hillary Factor,* 306.

525 "Hillary thinks Bill": Ibid., 304.

525 "Many of those": Ibid., 305.

525 "played his audience": Oakley, *On the Make,* 414.

525 "When I took office": Ibid., 415.

526 "the fire": Quoted in Nelson with Martin, *The Hillary Factor*, 305.

526 "The joy": Ibid.

527 "There is a very brilliant": Jim Blair, interview with the author, March 23, 2001.

527 "convinced Clinton": Nelson with Martin, *The Hillary Factor*, 305.

527 "99 and 44-100ths": *Arkansas Democrat*, March 2, 1990.

527 "Someday I hope": Betsey Wright, interview with the author, March 23, 2001.

528 "some important": Maraniss, *First in His Class*, 452.

529 "feeling miserable": Morton, *Monica's Story*, 114.

529 JFK had done: See Seymour M. Hersh, *The Dark Side of Camelot*, 1997; Laurence Leamer, *The Kennedy Men 1901–1963: The Laws of the Father*, 2001; and Robert Dallek, *An Unfinished Life: John F. Kennedy 1917–1963*, 2003, among others.

530 "I believe in what": Oakley, *On the Make*, 417.

531 "you could have knocked": Ibid., 418.

531 "In terms of public": Diane Blair, *Arkansas Politics and Government*, 137–8.

531 "considered uniquely": Ibid., 154.

37. Primary Time

532 "I stood there": Betsey Wright, interview with the author, March 23, 2001.

532 "I mean, here's": Ibid.

533 "Hillary," Betsey: Ibid.

533 "It's a different way": Ibid.

535 "I look at the world": Jeffrey Rosen, "Silicon Valley's Spy Game," *The New York Times Magazine*, April 14, 2002.

537 "Will you guarantee": Quoted in Oakley, *On the Make*, 419.

537 "You bet!": Ibid.

537 "Now, especially": Blair, *Arkansas Politics and Government*, 150, 151, 1156.

539 "I ain't worried": Conason and Lyons, *The Hunting of the President*, 2001, 2.

38. Five Times Governor

541 "Shakespearean malevolence": Conason and Lyons, *The Hunting of the President*, 8.

541 file of information: Ibid., 11.

542 "If I lose": Maraniss, *First in His Class*, 456.

542 "They got their results": Oakley, *On the Make*, 424.

542 "We got a call": David Watkins, interview with the author, February 16, 2001.

543 "You threw in some": Ibid.

543 "Here's how it worked": Ibid.

544 "There's no way": Oakley, *On the Make,* 423–4.

544 "shadowy silhouettes": Conason and Lyons, *The Hunting of the President,* 10.

545 "Americans do think": Sally Quinn, "Tabloid Politics, the Clintons and the Way We Now Scrutinize Our Potential Presidents," *The Washington Post,* January 26, 1992.

546 "I do not plan": Seaman, *Swaggart,* 291.

546 Through his ministry: Ibid.

546 "a commission": Ibid., 286.

547 "Get naked, lie on": Ibid., 327.

547 on Graham: Ibid., 295.

547 "all this I've heard": Ibid., 344.

548 "That's superwoman": Ibid., 297.

548 demons "that no one": Ibid., 385.

548 "What are you doing": Ibid., 348.

548 "She treated him": Ibid., 352.

549 "Someone savvy": Ibid., 348.

549 "there was no anointing": Ibid.

549 "an essential contact": Ibid.

550 "The child-bride phenomenon": Ibid., 371–2.

550 "I had a conversation": Betsey Wright, interview with the author, March 23, 2001.

551 "I mean, it took": Ibid.

551 "that you're taking": Ibid.

551 "there are a lot": Oakley, *On the Make,* 448.

551 "an address that energized": Ibid., 449.

552 "For once": Ibid.

552 "needs at least": Ibid.

552 "thunderous standing": Ibid., 449–50.

553 "He made": David Watkins, interview with the author, February 16, 2001.

553 "David, we've": Ibid.

553 "Stan Greenberg": Ibid.

553 "I say: 'Absolutely' ": Ibid.

553 "So the strategy": Ibid.

554 "talked about whether": Michael Isikoff, *Uncovering Clinton: A Reporter's Story,* 1999, 48.

554 "When it was suggested": Sally Quinn, "Tabloid Politics, the Clintons and the Way We Now Scrutinize Our Potential Presidents."

555 "Did I realize": Isikoff, *Uncovering Clinton,* 37.

555 "Did I really think": Ibid., 38.

556 "You're not going": Ibid., 20–1.

556 "I will never forget": Ibid., 21.

556 "And I said": Ibid., 22.

556 "Bill would never": Betsey Wright, interview with the author, March 23, 2001.

557 "It didn't seem": Isikoff, *Uncovering Clinton,* 52.

557 "He had boxer shorts": Ibid., 22.

557 "I think he wanted": Ibid.

557 Cathy Kampen: Swaggart apparently seduced Kampen, whom he first met at a gas pump, by offering to give her personal counseling and even to finance a store she wished to open; but he never had full intercourse with her, preferring her to pose, like Debra Murphree, in provocative clothing such as a French maid's outfit, without underwear. "I told you you have to help me," he overruled her protests, using the same argument as his archrival, the Reverend Jim Bakker. "This helps me. You're the only person who can help me with this. And I want to make things nice for you, too. You deserve it. God wants you to have it. God loves you." Swaggart had then gotten Kampen to wear a black leather outfit, handcuff him, and with a small whip "lay him over a chair and whip his buttocks while he masturbated." He would urge her to be firmer: "Harder, harder. Beat me harder." Then, when he spurted, he would tell her it was "wonderful, but that next time, she needed to beat him harder. 'You have to tell me I'm scum,' he said. 'I'm no good. I need to be beaten.' " Mrs. Kampen had also to masturbate him, herself, and masturbate herself, using a dildo Swaggart brought with him. He also urged her to bring her young teenage daughter into the counseling sessions, "you know, to teach her" about sex. When she refused and also turned down the suggestion that he watch her having sex with her daughter or with another woman, which she claimed was "against God's law," the reverend smacked her down. "Not if you're only playing," he responded. "Not if it's not real. If it's an act." Then, turning the tables, he asked, "You act, don't you?"—referring to her stripogram work. To Mrs. Kampen, the relationship became increasingly sick, and so, she felt, was the reverend—especially when he made her, a married woman, strip naked on the Mississippi River levee several times and pretend he was going to run her over in his car—apparently a threat his father had used in his own early childhood. "He always reminded me of a miserable, sad little boy," Mrs. Kampen commented in her deposition for a lawsuit that year. When she hesitated or declined to obey his orders, such as to urinate on him, Swaggart would become menacing. "It was almost like the devil would"—she struggled to describe the weirdness of Swaggart's two selves—"one day—one minute, he was just as sweet with honey dripping. Then it was like the Exorcist." When Kampen ended the relationship, the Reverend Swaggart's colleagues threatened her with "trouble"—even her life—should she squeal, thus forcing her to go public in an interview in *Penthouse* and obtain a sworn legal deposition, lest she be "erased." Swaggart, meanwhile, once more

went into denial mode, claiming that there had never been "anything in my life at any time that has been deviant or aberrant, whether it be psychological, spiritual, sexual, domestic, or physical." His denial had, moreover, worked—at least in temporal terms. By 1991, Swaggart was back at number six in terms of American religious broadcast viewing figures and fund-raising among televangelists; Hunter Lundy, *Let Us Prey: The Public Trial of Jimmy Swaggart*, 1999, 147.

557 "Well, I don't want": Isikoff, *Uncovering Clinton*, 22.

557 "I mean the man": Ibid., 42.

558 "the stature and trappings": Mary Matalin and James Carville, *All's Fair: Love, War, and Running for President*, 1994, 49.

559 "The fact that": Quoted in Quinn, "Tabloid Politics, the Clintons and the Way We Now Scrutinize Our Potential Presidents.

559 Matt Ridley: Matt Ridley, *The Red Queen.*

560 "always wrong": Rouse, *Marital and Sexual Lifestyles,* 126, 122.

560 "Listen," she snapped: Conason and Lyons, *The Hunting of the President,* 51.

561 "I stuck it up": Isikoff, *Uncovering Clinton,* 56.

561 "We've done a lot": David Maraniss, *The Clinton Enigma: A Four-and-a-Half-Minute Speech Reveals This President's Entire Life,* 1998, 93. Porter did not later deny making the phone call but disputed the content.

39. The Perils of Running for President

563 "I might get": Allen and Portis, *The Comeback Kid,* 150.

563 "If I did": Nelson with Martin, *The Hillary Factor,* 318.

564 "an unprecedented depression": Ravi Batra, *The Great Depression of 1990: Why It's Got to Happen—How to Protect Yourself,* 1987, 26.

564 "how much longer": Nelson with Martin, *The Hillary Factor,* 319.

564 "I think it's a sad": Ibid., 320.

565 "This is the greatest": Quoted in Michael J. Giuliano, *Thrice-born: The Rhetorical Comeback of Jimmy Swaggart,* 1999, 125.

565 "the Lord for His grace": Ibid.

565 audience numbers: An estimated worldwide viewership of a 100 million via 3,200 stations in 143 countries; Giuliano, *Thrice-born,* 4.

565 "greatest communicator": Ibid., 15.

566 "duller, repressed": George and Louise Spindler, *The American Cultural Dialogue and Its Transmission,* 1990, 92.

566 "The fall of some": Ibid., 92–3.

568 "I've never lost": Oakley, *On the Make,* 465.

568 "He doesn't *mind*": Bobby Roberts, interview with the author, February 7, 2001.

568 "What is said": Quentin J. Schultze, *Televangelism and American Culture: The Business of Popular Religion,* 1991, 30.

569 "I don't know": Oakley, *On the Make,* 462–3.

570 "the problem": Matt Bai, "The Outsider: Gary Hart Wants to Become the Democrats' Elder Statesman," *The New York Times Magazine,* February 2, 2003.

570 "Did you see": John Brummett, *Highwire: From the Back Roads to the Beltway: The Education of Bill Clinton,* 1994, 17.

570 "You know, I think": Oakley, *On the Make,* 458, and John Brummett, interview with the author, February 2001.

570 "given the dirtiest": Tammy Faye Messner, *Tammy: Telling It My Way,* 1996, 275.

571 "Americans are not": Schultze, *Televangelism and American Culture,* 32–3.

571 "without question": *Time,* March 7, 1988.

571 "fabulous television": Schultze, *Televangelism and American Culture,* 39.

571 "like a cancer": Giuliano, *Thrice-born,* 45.

572 "in what seemed": Ibid.

572 "the gubernatorial": Nelson with Martin, *The Hillary Factor,* 319.

572 "I had built": Richard Morris, *Behind the Oval Office,* 68.

40. Declaring

578 "The relationship": Jim Blair, interview with the author, March 23, 2001.

579 "What makes a man": Ibid.

579 "Now, I think": Ibid.

579 "I think some of it": Ibid.

580 "was a large-hearted": Robert Dallek, *Flawed Giant: Lyndon Johnson and His Times,* 1998, 187.

580 "Rumors are a dime": Nelson with Martin, *The Hillary Factor,* 320.

580 "Maybe somebody": Ibid.

581 "incredible reputation": Maraniss, *First in His Class,* 460.

581 "Hell, I just had": Ibid., 461.

581 "showed a basic lack": Brummett, *Highwire,* 23.

582 "You don't like Hillary": John Brummett, interview with the author, March 2001.

582 "This is the sort": Nelson with Martin, *The Hillary Factor,* 321.

582 "Those in the room": Ibid.

582 "Now, I have a": Jim Blair, interview with the author, March 23, 2001.

583 "I think the American": Nelson with Martin, *The Hillary Factor,* 321; Maraniss, *First in His Class,* 461; Allen and Portis, *The Comeback Kid,* 151.

584 "It's none": Allen and Portis, *The Comeback Kid,* 148.

584 "the moral police": Ibid.

584 "I didn't volunteer": Ibid., 151.

585 "I think you're": John Brummett, interview with the author, March 2001.

585 "I tried to get her": David Watkins, interview with the author, February 16, 2001.

585 "We don't": *Arkansas Democrat,* extra edition, October 3, 1991.

586 "His word is dirt": Ibid.

586 "He can run": Allen and Portis, *The Comeback Kid,* 156.

41. Return of the Genie

588 "we discussed": David Watkins, interview with the author, February 16, 2001.

589 "Inside the car": Giuliano, *Thrice-born,* 114.

589 a year before: Ibid., 116.

590 "Elvis Presley can": Steve Chapple, "Whole Lotta Savin' Goin' On," *Mother Jones,* July–August 1986, 41, quoted in Giuliano, ibid., 15.

590 "David [Wilhelm] comes in": David Watkins, interview with the author, February 16, 2001.

591 "The flight of": Jack Germond and Jules Witcover, *Mad as Hell: Revolt at the Ballot Box,* 1993, 92.

591 "I think when he": Bobby Roberts, interview with the author, February 7, 2001.

592 "Hillary has ideas": David Watkins, interview with the author, February 16, 2001.

593 "In so many": Ibid.

593 Rickey Ray Rector: See Allen and Portis, *The Comeback Kid,* 182–3.

593 "Even when he was": Ernie Dumas, interview with the author, February 8, 2001.

593 "the right decision": "Clinton Says Ruling on Juries Right, Sees Duty to Set Execution Dates," *Arkansas Gazette,* May 7, 1986.

594 "We've talked about": "Clinton's Record on Issues in Arkansas Gets Mixed Reviews," *The Washington Post,* February 1992.

595 "It's a Sunday night": David Watkins, interview with the author, February 16, 2001.

595 "I called Bill": Marion Collins and Steven Edwards, "Gennifer Flowers bombshell: I won't go to jail for Bill Clinton," *Star,* February 11, 1992.

596 "Back in his": David Watkins, interview with the author, February 16, 2001.

596 "Right! Well": Ibid.

597 "Regarding Gennifer Flowers": Bobby Roberts, interview with the author, February 7, 2001.

597 "You know, you walk": Ibid.

598 "Open your ears": William Shakespeare, *The Second Part of Henry IV,* Introduction.

598 "I guess they hate": Jim Blair, interview with the author, March 23, 2001.

598 "I even received": Flowers interview, *Star.*

599 "It has become": Jane Mayer and Jill Abramson, *Strange Justice: The Selling of Clarence Thomas,* 1994, 3.

600 "integrity in this": Ibid.

600 "deranged liar": David Brock, *Blinded by the Right,* 2002, 102.

600 "You should be": Flowers, *Passion and Betrayal,* 93.

601 articles and books: Pritchard-Evans, *The Secret Life of Bill Clinton,* 1997; Alexander Coburn and Ken Silverstein, *Washington Babylon,* 1996; and Roger Morris, *Partners in Power,* among others.

601 "tried to have him" Jim Blair, interview with the author, March 23, 2001.

602 "Hey, somebody": Ibid.

602 "character flaw": Bobby Roberts, interview with the author, February 7, 2001.

602 *éminence grise:* Pritchard-Evans, *The Secret Life of Bill Clinton,* 297–8.

603 complicity in *murder:* The "suicide" in 1962 of Henry Marshall, an official of the Agriculture Department investigating the dealings of Billie Sol Estes in Texas, was murder not only most foul but telling: a clear message to snoopers not to find dirt on LBJ. Estes later cited LBJ as having been behind the murder, but to no avail, the judge's ruling of "suicide" remaining on file for a further quarter century and only being overturned a decade after LBJ's death.

603 "His victory in 1948": Dallek, *Flawed Giant,* 38–9.

603 *was* said: Barash and Lipton, *The Myth of Monogamy,* 2001, 190.

603 "Be careful": Flowers interview, *Star.*

604 "So somebody broke": Quoted, in, among others, Floyd G. Brown, *"Slick Willie": Why America Cannot Trust Bill Clinton,* 1992, 156–7.

604 "if I decide": Quoted, in, among others, ibid.

604 "Most people think": Quoted, in, among others, Brown, *"Slick Willie,"* 158.

605 "not intimidated": Collins and Edwards, *Star.*

605 "no pretense, no hypocrisy": Sally Quinn, "Tabloid Politics, the Clintons and the Way We Now Scrutinize Our Potential Presidents," *The Washington Post,* January 26, 1992; also Rowland Evans and Robert Novak, "Media 'Feeding Frenzy,' " *The Washington Post,* January 29, 1992.

606 "If they ask you": Quoted in, among others, Brown, *"Slick Willie,"* 158.

606 "so brazen": Flowers interview, *Star.*

606 "A lot of people": Ibid.

607 "I knew the wisest": Ibid.

607 "women who wish": Mary McGrory, "The Front-Runner Stumbles," *The Washington Post,* February 11, 1992.

608 "the moment when": Matt Bai, "The Outsider: Gary Hart Wants to Become

the Democrats' Elder Statesman," *The New York Times Magazine,* February 2, 2003.

608 DEM'S FRONT-RUNNER: Flowers, *Passion and Betrayal,* 103.

608 "I did not call": Ibid., 106.

609 "What I need most": Matalin and Carville, *All's Fair,* 84.

610 "Rumour is a pipe": William Shakespeare, *The Second Part of Henry IV,* Introduction.

610 "Reports of past": Matalin and Carville, *All's Fair,* 100.

610 "Illicit sex": Ibid.

611 "When the campaign": Ibid., 115.

611 "thought it was": Ibid., 114.

611 "Earth to James": Ibid., 116.

611 "Never interfere": Ibid., 114.

611 "discredit the witness": Ibid., 116.

612 "The guy deserves": Ibid., 115.

613 "They made love": "My 12-Year Affair with Bill Clinton, Plus the Secret Love Tapes That Prove It!," *Star,* February 4, 1992.

613 "Mrs. Clinton": Matalin and Carville, *All's Fair,* 102.

614 "We brainstormed": Ibid., 103.

614 "I kept thinking": Ibid., 103–4.

614 "you and Hillary": Ibid., 105–6.

615 "I was at war": Ibid., 107, 102.

615 "He told me everything": Ibid., 101–2.

616 "stuck me into": Bobby Roberts, interview with the author, February 7, 2001.

616 "Not only will we": Matalin and Carville, *All's Fair,* 107.

616 "We posed questions": Ibid., 109.

617 "History was going": Ibid.

617 "When it was over": Ibid., 111.

617 "It will be great": Germond and Witcover, *Mad as Hell,* 185.

617 "causing pain in": Ibid., 185–6.

617 "You know, I'm not": Ibid., 186.

618 "the way they jujitsued": Matalin and Carville, *All's Fair,* 116.

618 "all operations ceased": Ibid., 115.

619 "imperceptively": Schultze, *Televangelism and American Culture,* 99.

619 "in a bright red": Germond and Witcover, *Mad as Hell,* 187.

619 "the A word": George Stephanopoulos, *All Too Human,* 1999, 65.

619 "the worst moment": Germond and Witcover, *Mad as Hell,* 187.

619 "reacted much more": Matalin and Carville, *All's Fair,* 112–13.

619 "I was vilified": Flowers, *Passion and Betrayal,* 123.

620 "drama and unprecedented": Germond and Witcover, *Mad as Hell,* 186–7.

620 *"Maybe we can":* Stephanopoulos, *All Too Human,* 68.

620 "He's two-faced": Quoted in, among others, Brown, *"Slick Willie,"* 153–4.

621 "He lied": Stephanopoulos, *All Too Human,* 68.

622 "Arkansas Governor": Dan Balz and David S. Broder, "Clinton Pledges to 'Fight like Hell' for Victory," *The Washington Post,* February 11, 1992.

622 "I was the first": Matalin and Carville, *All's Fair,* 113.

623 "Most often, extramarital": Rouse, *Marital and Sexual Lifestyles,* 127.

623 "The country and": Matalin and Carville, *All's Fair,* 113.

42. The Draft

626 "Sheffield is the source": Jim Blair, interview with the author, March 23, 2001.

626 "He's always had": Ernie Dumas, interview with the author, February 8, 2001.

626 "sign a bill": "Clinton Visits Civil War Capital, Signs Bill Erasing Segregation Laws," *Arkansas Gazette,* February 23, 1979.

627 "average to mediocre": Cliff Jackson, interview with the author, July 27, 2002.

628 "long-time bitter": Ibid.

628 "Every single adjective": Ibid.

628 "a connoisseur": Ibid.

628 "*Millions* avoided": Ibid.

630 "the worst-run": Oakley, *On the Make,* 492–3.

631 "'cause we are getting": Matalin and Carville, *All's Fair,* 135.

631 "unwillingness at times": Jim Blair, interview with the author, March 23, 2001.

632 "the other characteristic": David Watkins, interview with the author, February 16, 2001.

632 "Okay, this is": Matalin and Carville, *All's Fair,* 136.

632 "Thank you for": Germond and Witcover, *Mad as Hell,* 197.

633 "a death sentence": Matalin and Carville, *All's Fair,* 137.

633 "This is terrific": Germond and Witcover, *Mad as Hell,* 197–8.

633 "give this election": Matalin and Carville, *All's Fair,* 138.

633 "From Wednesday on": Ibid.

633 "the finest hour": Germond and Witcover, *Mad as Hell,* 205.

634 "Clinton's view was": Matalin and Carville, *All's Fair,* 138–9.

634 "disastrous": Germond and Witcover, *Mad as Hell,* 208.

634 "I'm not going to": Matalin and Carville, *All's Fair,* 140.

635 "There were some": Ibid.

635 "Bill Clinton had been": Ibid., 141.

635 "at least I've": Germond and Witcover, *Mad as Hell,* 209.

635 "With the help": Oakley, *On the Make,* 510.

636 "Hillary is tougher": Ibid., 513.

636 "There isn't a person": Ibid., 512.

636 "she persuasively": Ibid., 510.

636 "no meltdown": Germond and Witcover, *Mad as Hell,* 209.

43. Enter Perot

639 "we knew in real": Matalin and Carville, *All's Fair,* 148.

640 "Over the course of": Ibid., 149.

640 "Well, shoot": Sal Russo, California political consultant, quoted in Germond and Witcover, *Mad as Hell,* 317.

641 "were said to be": Germond and Witcover, *Mad as Hell,* 318.

641 "Imagine Ross Perot": Ibid., 318–19.

641 "it was the same old": Ibid., 351.

641 "a spontaneous eruption": Ibid., 352.

642 "We were not": Ibid.

642 "really worked up": Ibid., 366.

642 "you people": Ibid., 367.

643 "You should also know": Ibid., 369.

643 "I said, it just": Ibid.

643 "He just said": Ibid., 369–70.

644 "All that stuff": Ibid., 353.

644 "I think that was": Ibid., 354.

645 "made a fatal": Ibid.

645 "crack the enigma": Ibid., 282.

645 "You can tell": Matalin and Carville, *All's Fair,* 159.

645 "fodder to every": Ibid., 167.

646 "Instead of talking about": Ibid., 169–70.

646 "We were about": Ibid., 171.

646 "What we found": Ibid., 172.

647 "by observing that": Germond and Witcover, *Mad as Hell,* 283.

647 "He was aware": Matalin and Carville, *All's Fair,* 173.

647 "Once we had tabulated": Ibid., 174.

648 "Hillary was not": Ibid.

648 "You know, they": Ibid.

648 "No one could": Ibid.

648 *"They don't like":* Ibid.

648 "This was a man": Ibid.

44. Nomination

650 "I don't think anybody": Gallen, *Bill Clinton,* 272.

651 "top dollar": Isikoff, *Uncovering Clinton,* 31.

651 "After he got to": Betsey Wright, interview with the author, March 23, 2001.

652 "meaningful policy assignments": Warren Christopher, *Chances of a Lifetime*, 2001, 153.

652 "It was a beautiful day": Gallen, *Bill Clinton*, 252.

653 "thank you all": Larry D. Smith, "The New York Convention," in Stephen Smith, ed., *Bill Clinton on Stump, State and Stage*, 1994, 212.

653 "two-phased narrative": Ibid., 204.

654 "Bill was overcome": Gallen, *Bill Clinton*, 253.

654 "Bill Clinton," the New: Quoted in Germond and Witcover, *Mad as Hell*, 345.

655 "I think that what": Dr. Joycelyn Elders, interview with the author, February 5, 2001.

655 "Ever since I've known": Ibid.

655 "He could have gone": Ibid.

656 "Bill Clinton is not": Smith, "The New York Convention," 213.

657 "central figure": Thomas Rosteck, "The Intertextuality of the Man from Hope," in Stephen Smith, ed., *Bill Clinton on Stump, State and Stage*, 237.

657 "You put a camera": *Los Angeles Times*, July 25, 1992.

658 "to help the 'hero' ": Rosteck, "The Intertextuality of the Man from Hope," 240.

659 "recurrent subliminal": Ibid.

659 "won the heart": *The New York Times*, July 17, 1992.

659 "wowed": *Time*, July 27, 1992.

659 "a masterpiece": *Los Angeles Times Magazine*, August 30, 1992.

659 "could have been": Matalin and Carville, *All's Fair*, 239–40.

659 "The most important": Quoted in Germond and Witcover, *Mad as Hell*, 346.

660 "In addition to": Matalin and Carville, *All's Fair*, 239.

660 "Clinton," Matalin: Ibid., 240.

45. On the Campaign Trail

664 "Change is the key": Germond and Witcover, *Mad as Hell*, 381.

664 "Something's going on": Ibid., 382.

665 "He's made two": Ibid., 387.

665 "became sort of": Ibid., 388.

666 "As the cameras": Sandra Goodall, "De/Reconstructing Hillary," in Stephen Smith, ed., *Bill Clinton on Stump, State and Stage*, 181.

667 "The agenda Clinton": Germond and Witcover, *Mad as Hell*, 410.

667 "When Bill and Hillary": Ibid., 412.

667 "What's happened": Ibid., 413.

667 "The gap between": Ibid., 415.

668 "This moral element": Ibid., 412–13.

668 "That's pitiful": Ibid., 408.

668 "take apart": Ibid., 412.

669 "from her counterpart": Sheehy, *Hillary's Choice*, 216.

669 "a great deal": Germond and Witcover, *Mad as Hell*, 429.

670 "I have a very": Ibid., 430.

673 "My view was": Ibid., 472–3.

674 "Maybe, they say": Ibid., 474.

674 "You *have* questioned": Ibid., 474–5.

674 "a point": Ibid., 476.

675 "out of ammunition": Ibid., 477.

675 "No matter what": H. L. Goodall, "Living in the Rock N Roll Campaign," in Stephen Smith, ed., *Bill Clinton on Stump, State and Stage*, 397.

676 "What was only": Ibid., 400.

676 "what you can do": Ibid., 404.

676 "How has the national debt": Germond and Witcover, *Mad as Hell*, 9.

677 "Well, I've had": Ibid., 10; also in John Hohenberg, *The Bill Clinton Story: Winning the Presidency*, 1994, 201–2.

677 "I think she": Germond and Witcover, *Mad as Hell*, 10; and Hohenberg, ibid., 202.

677 "Well, listen, you ought": Ibid.

677 "Everybody in our room": Matalin and Carville, *All's Fair*, 415.

678 "I would have *paid*": Ibid., 416.

678 "We are America": Ibid., 306.

678 "I think it's sad": Hohenberg, *The Bill Clinton Story*, 202.

678 "I've been": Germond and Witcover, *Mad as Hell*, 11.

678 "I've been out here": Ibid.

679 "commanded the atmospherics": Dale Herbeck, "Presidential Debate as Political Ritual," in Stephen Smith, ed., *Bill Clinton on Stump, State and Stage*, 258.

679 "body language": Matalin and Carville, *All's Fair*, 418.

679 "I'll bet you": Ibid.

679 A CBS poll: Herbeck, "Presidential Debate as Political Ritual," 259.

680 "the whole campaign": Germond and Witcover, *Mad as Hell*, 516.

680 "political spectacles": Herbeck, "Presidential Debate as Political Ritual," 250.

681 "fantastic stories": Hohenberg, *The Bill Clinton Story*, 224.

682 "We lost 14 points": Matalin and Carville, *All's Fair*, 441.

683 "verbalize": Germond and Witcover, *Mad as Hell*, 498.

683 "referendum on two men": Ibid., 504.

683 "no complaints": Michael Ventura, quoted in Goodall, "Living in the Rock N Roll Campaign," 406.

684 "without flinching": Ibid.

684 "Clinton has proved": Ibid.

684 "a draft evader": Ibid.

686 "not only rifling": Quoted in Germond and Witcover, *Mad as Hell,* 481.

686 "I'm insulted": Ibid.

686 "most reprehensible": Ibid.

686 "Governor Clinton": Ibid., 496.

686 was faxed: Ibid., 505.

46. Victory

688 "secure we were": Matalin and Carville, *All's Fair,* 462.

688 "She was transfixed": Ibid., 467.

689 "the best politician": Gallen, *Bill Clinton,* 274.

689 "This is the toughest": Ibid., 275.

BIBLIOGRAPHY

Abbott, Shirley. *The Bookmaker's Daughter.* New York: Ticknor & Fields, 1991.

Adams, Julianne L., and Thomas A. DeBlack, eds. *Civil Obedience: An Oral History of School Desegregation in Fayetteville, Arkansas, 1954–1965.* Fayetteville: University of Arkansas Press, 1994.

Allen, Charles F., and Jonathan Portis. *The Comeback Kid: The Life and Career of Bill Clinton.* New York: Birch Lane Press, 1992.

Andersen, Christopher. *Bill and Hillary: The Marriage.* New York, William Morrow, 1999.

Ashmore, Harry. *Arkansas: A Bicentennial History.* New York: W. W. Norton, 1978.

Badger, A. J., "The White Reaction to *Brown*: Arkansas, the Southern Manifesto, and Massive Resistance," in *Understanding the Little Rock Crisis,* ed. E. Jacoway and C. Fred Williams, Fayetteville: University of Arkansas Press, 1999.

Barash, David B., and Judith E. Lipton. *The Myth of Monogamy: Fidelity and Infidelity in Animals and People.* New York: W. H. Freeman, 2001.

Baritz, Loren. *The Good Life: The Meaning of Success for the American Middle Class.* New York: Knopf, 1989.

Barnhart, Joe E. *The Southern Baptist Holy War: The Self-Destructive Struggle for Power Within the Largest Protestant Denomination in America.* Austin: Texas Monthly Press, 1986.

Barnhart, Joe E., with Steven Winzenburg. *Jim and Tammy: Charismatic Intrigue Inside PTL.* Buffalo, N.Y.: Prometheus Books, 1988.

Bates, Daisy. *The Long Shadow of Little Rock*. Fayetteville: University of Arkansas Press, 1987.

Batra, Ravi. *The Great Depression of 1990: Why It's Got to Happen—How to Protect Yourself*. New York: Simon & Schuster, 1987.

Berlant, L., and L. Duggan, eds. *Our Monica, Ourselves*. New York: New York University Press, 2001.

Birkhead, Tim. *Promiscuity: An Evolutionary History of Sperm Competition*. Cambridge, Mass.: Harvard University Press, 2000.

Blair, Diane. *Arkansas Politics and Government: Do the People Rule?* Lincoln: University of Nebraska Press, 1988.

Bolsterli, Margaret Jones. *Born in the Delta: Reflections on the Making of a Southern White Sensibility*. Knoxville: University of Tennessee Press, 1991.

Bourdieu, Pierre. *Distinction: A Social Critique of the Judgement of Taste*. Cambridge, Mass.: Harvard University Press, 1984.

Bourdon, David. *Warhol*. New York: H. N. Abrams, 1989.

Brock, David. *Blinded by the Right*. New York: Crown Publishers, 2002.

———. *The Seduction of Hillary Rodham Clinton*. New York: Free Press, 1996.

Broder, David. *Changing of the Guard: Power and Leadership in America*. New York: Simon & Schuster, 1980.

Brown, Floyd G. *"Slick Willie": Why America Cannot Trust Bill Clinton*. Annapolis, Md.: Annapolis Publishing Company, 1992.

Brummett, John. *Highwire: From the Back Roads to the Beltway: The Education of Bill Clinton*. New York: Hyperion, 1994.

Christopher, Warren. *Chances of a Lifetime*. New York: Scribner, 2001.

Clinton, Hillary Rodham. *It Takes a Village*. New York: Simon & Schuster, 1996.

Coburn, Alexander, and Ken Silverstein. *Washington Babylon*. New York: Verso, 1996.

Collier, Peter, and David Horowitz. *Destructive Generation: Second Thoughts About the '60s*. New York: Simon & Schuster, 1989.

Conason, Joe, and Gene Lyons. *The Hunting of the President: The Ten-Year Campaign to Destroy Bill and Hillary Clinton*. New York: St. Martin's Press, 2001.

Dallek, Robert. *Flawed Giant: Lyndon Johnson and His Times*. New York: Oxford University Press, 1998.

———. *An Unfinished Life: John F. Kennedy 1917–1963*. Boston: Little, Brown, 2003.

Davis, C. K. *Two-Bit Culture: The Paperbacking of American Culture*. Boston: Houghton Mifflin, 1984.

Dershowitz, Alan. *Sexual McCarthyism: Clinton, Starr, and the Emerging Constitutional Crisis*. New York: Basic Books, 1998.

Dirks, Nicholas B., et al., eds. *Culture/Power/History: A Reader in Contemporary Social Theory*. Princeton: Princeton University Press, 1994.

Donovan, T. P., et al., eds. *The Governors of Arkansas: Essays in Political Biography.* Fayetteville: University of Arkansas Press, 1995.

Dougan, Michael B. *Arkansan Odyssey: The Saga of Arkansas from Prehistoric Times to Present.* Little Rock, Ark.: Rose Publishing Company, 1995.

Dumas, Ernest, ed. *The Clintons of Arkansas: An Introduction by Those Who Know Them Best.* Fayetteville: University of Arkansas Press, 1993.

Ellsberg, Daniel. *Secrets: A Memoir of Vietnam and the Pentagon Papers.* New York: Viking, 2002.

Evans-Pritchard, Ambrose. *The Secret Life of Bill Clinton.* Washington, D.C.: Regnery Publishing, 1997.

Ewen, Stuart. *All-Consuming Images: The Politics of Style in Contemporary Culture.* New York: Basic Books, 1988.

Farber, D., ed. *The Sixties: From Memory to History.* Chapel Hill: University of North Carolina Press, 1994.

Flowers, Gennifer. *Passion and Betrayal.* Del Mar, Calif.: Emery Dalton Books, 1995.

Fountain, S., ed. *Authentic Voices: Arkansas Culture, 1541–1860.* Little Rock: University of Central Arkansas Press, 1986.

Gallen, David. *Bill Clinton: As They Know Him: An Oral Biography.* New York: Gallen Publishing Group, 1994.

Germond, Jack, and Jules Witcover. *Mad as Hell: Revolt at the Ballot Box.* New York: Warner Books, 1993.

Gilligan, Carol. *In a Different Voice: Psychological Theory and Women's Development.* Cambridge, Mass.: Harvard University Press, 1982/1993.

Giuliano, Michael J. *Thrice-born: The Rhetorical Comeback of Jimmy Swaggart.* Macon, Ga.: Mercer University Press, 1999.

Goodman, Mitchell, ed. *The Movement Toward a New America: The Beginnings of a Long Revolution.* Philadelphia: Pilgrim Press, 1970.

Gould, Stephen Jay. *Rocks of Ages: Science and Religion in the Fullness of Life.* New York: Ballantine Books, 1999.

Halberstam, David. *The Fifties.* New York: Villard, 1993.

Haldeman, H. R. *The Ends of Power.* New York: Dell, 1978.

Hamilton, Nigel. *JFK: Reckless Youth.* New York: Random House, 1992.

Hanley, R. and S. Hanley. *Hot Springs, Arkansas.* Charleston, S.C.: Arcadia Publishing, 2000.

Hayden, Tom. *Reunion: A Memoir.* New York: Random House, 1998.

Hersh, Seymour M. *The Dark Side of Camelot.* Boston: Little, Brown, 1997.

Hohenberg, John. *The Bill Clinton Story: Winning the Presidency.* Syracuse, N.Y.: Syracuse University Press, 1994.

Holley, Donald. *Uncle Sam's Farmers: The New Deal Communities in the Lower Mississippi Valley.* Urbana: University of Illinois Press, 1975.

Isikoff, Michael. *Uncovering Clinton: A Reporter's Story.* New York: Crown Publishers, 1999.

Jacoway, E., and C. Fred Williams, eds. *Understanding the Little Rock Crisis.* Fayetteville: University of Arkansas Press, 1999.

Johnson, Ben F. *Arkansas in Modern America: 1930–1999.* Fayetteville: University of Arkansas Press, 2000.

Johnson, Haynes. *Sleepwalking Through History: America in the Reagan Years.* New York: W. W. Norton, 1991.

Jones, James H. *Alfred C. Kinsey: A Public/Private Life.* New York: W. W. Norton, 1997.

Judson, Olivia. *Dr. Tatiana's Sex Advice to All Creation.* New York: Metropolitan Books, 2002.

Kalb, Marvin. *One Scandalous Story: Clinton, Lewinsky, & 13 Days That Tarnished American Journalism.* New York: Free Press, 2001.

Kelley, Virginia, with James Morgan. *Leading with My Heart.* New York: Simon & Schuster, 1994.

Kennedy, John F. *Profiles in Courage.* New York: Harper, 1955.

King, Norman. *Hillary: Her True Story.* New York: Carol Publishing Group, 1993.

———. *The Woman in the White House: The Remarkable Story of Hillary Rodham Clinton.* New York: Birch Lane Press/Carol Publishing, 1996.

Kutler, Stanley K., ed. *Abuse of Power: The New Nixon Tapes,* with an introduction and commentary by Stanley I. Kutler. New York: Free Press, 1997.

Lasch, Christopher. *The Culture of Narcissism: American Life in an Age of Diminishing Expectations.* New York: Warner Books, 1978.

Leamer, Laurence. *The Kennedy Men, 1901–1963: The Laws of the Fathers.* New York: William Morrow, 2001.

Lesher, Stephan. *George Wallace: American Populist.* Reading, Mass.: Addison-Wesley, 1994.

Levin, Robert E. *Bill Clinton: The Inside Story.* New York: S.P.I. Books/Shapolsky Publishers, 1992.

Lundy, Hunter. *Let Us Prey: The Public Trial of Jimmy Swaggart.* Columbus, Miss.: Genesis Press, Inc., 1999.

MacKenzie, Edward J., Jr., and Phyllis Karas with Ross A. Muscato. *Street Soldier: My Life as an Enforcer for Whitey Bulger and the Irish Mob.* South Royalton, Vt.: Steerforth Press, 2003.

Maraniss, David. *The Clinton Enigma: A Four-and-a-Half-Minute Speech Reveals This President's Entire Life.* New York: Simon & Schuster, 1998.

———. *First in His Class. A Biography of Bill Clinton.* New York: Simon & Schuster, 1995.

Marwick, Arthur. *The Sixties: Cultural Revolution in Britain, France, Italy, and the United States, c. 1958–c. 1974.* Oxford: Oxford University Press, 1998.

Matalin, Mary, and James Carville. *All's Fair: Love, War, and Running for President.* New York: Random House, 1994.

Mayer, Jane, and Jill Abramson. *Strange Justice: The Selling of Clarence Thomas.* Boston: Houghton Mifflin, 1994.

McDougal, Jim. *Arkansas Mischief: The Birth of a National Scandal.* New York: Henry Holt and Company, 1998.

McDougal, Susan, with Pat Harris. *The Woman Who Wouldn't Talk.* New York: Carroll & Graf Publishers, 2003.

Messner, Tammy Faye. *Tammy: Telling It My Way.* New York: Villard, 1996.

Miller, Alice. *The Drama of the Gifted Child: The Search for the True Self.* New York: Basic Books, 1981.

Milton, Joyce. *The First Partner: Hillary Rodham Clinton.* New York: William Morrow, 1999.

Moir, Anne and Bill. *Why Men Don't Iron: The Fascinating and Unalterable Differences Between Men and Women.* New York: Citadel Press, 1999.

Moore, Jim. *Clinton: Young Man in a Hurry.* Fort Worth, Tex.: The Summit Group, 1992.

Morris, Richard. *Behind the Oval Office: Winning the Presidency in the Nineties.* New York: Random House, 1997.

Morris, Roger. *Partners in Power: The Clintons and Their America.* Washington, D.C.: Regnery Publishing, 1996.

Morris, Willie. *New York Days.* Boston: Little, Brown, 1993.

Morton, Andrew. *Monica's Story.* New York: St. Martin's Press, 1999.

Murphy, Sarah Alderman. *Breaking the Silence: Little Rock's Women's Emergency Committee to Open Our Schools, 1958–1963.* Fayetteville: University of Arkansas Press, 1997.

Nelson, Rex, with Philip Martin. *The Hillary Factor: The Story of America's First Lady.* New York: Gallen Publishing Group, 1993.

Oakley, Meredith L. *On the Make: The Rise of Bill Clinton.* Washington, D.C.: Regnery Publishing, 1994.

Oppenheimer, Jerry. *State of a Union: Inside the Complex Marriage of Bill and Hillary Clinton.* New York: HarperCollins, 2000.

Pritchard-Evans, Ambrose. *The Secret Life of Bill Clinton: The Unreported Stories.* Washington, D.C.: Regnery Publishing, 1997.

Reed, Roy. *Faubus: The Life and Times of an American Prodigal.* Fayetteville: University of Arkansas Press, 1997.

Reich, Robert B. *Locked in the Cabinet.* New York: Knopf, 1997.

Renshon, Stanley A. *High Hopes: The Clinton Presidency and the Politics of Ambition.* New York: New York University Press, 1996.

Ridley, Matt. *The Red Queen: Sex and the Evolution of Human Nature.* New York: Macmillan, 1993.

Rodgers, Joann Ellison. *Sex: A Natural History.* New York: W. H. Freeman, 2001.

Rouse, Linda. *Marital and Sexual Lifestyles in the United States: Attitudes, Behaviors and Relationships in Social Context.* New York: Haworth Clinical Practice Press, 2002.

Schaller, Michael. *Reckoning with Reagan.* New York: Oxford University Press, 1992.

Schneider, Mark Robert. *"We Return Fighting": The Civil Rights Movement in the Jazz Age.* Boston: Northeastern University Press, 2002.

Schultze, Quentin J. *Televangelism and American Culture: The Business of Popular Religion.* Grand Rapids, Mich.: Baker Book House, 1991.

Scully, F. J. *Hot Springs, Arkansas, and Hot Springs National Park: The Story of a City and the Nation's Health Resort.* Little Rock, Ark.: Pioneer Press, 1966.

Seaman, Ann Rowe. *Swaggart: The Unauthorized Biography of an American Evangelist.* New York: Continuum, 1999.

Sheehy, Gail. *Hillary's Choice.* New York: Random House, 1999.

Shepard, Charles E. *Forgiven: The Rise and Fall of Jim Bakker and the PTL Ministry.* New York: Atlantic Monthly Press, 1989.

Shiver, Harry W., ed. *Hope's First Century: A Commemorative History of Hope, 1875–1975.* Hope, Ark.: Hope Centennial Committee, 1974.

Smith, C. Calvin. *War and Wartime Changes: The Transformation of Arkansas, 1940–1945.* Fayetteville: University of Arkansas Press, 1986.

Smith, Steven, ed. *Bill Clinton on Stump, State and Stage.* Fayetteville: University of Arkansas Press, 1994.

Spindler, George, and Louise Spindler. *The American Cultural Dialogue and Its Transmission.* Bristol, Pa.: The Falmer Press/Taylor & Francis, 1990.

Stephanopoulos, George. *All Too Human.* Boston: Little, Brown, 1999.

Stewart, James B. *Blood Sport: The President and His Adversaries.* New York: Simon & Schuster, 1996.

Tyrrell, J. Emmett. *Boy Clinton: The Political Biography.* Washington, D.C.: Regnery Publishing, 1996.

Walker, Martin. *The President We Deserve: Bill Clinton, His Rise, Fall and Comeback.* New York: Crown Publishers, 1996.

Warner, Judith. *Hillary Clinton: The Inside Story.* New York: Signet, 1993.

Weil, Gordon L. *The Long Shot: McGovern Runs for President.* New York: Norton, 1973.

White, Theodore H. *The Making of the President, 1972.* New York: Atheneum Publishers, 1973.

Wickham, Dewayne. *Bill Clinton and Black America.* New York: Ballantine, 2002.

Zukay, Gary, and Linda Francis. *The Heart of the Soul: Emotional Awareness.* New York: Simon & Schuster, 2002.

INDEX

Blair, Jim (*cont'd*):
    of interest in money, 364; and
    Clinton's morality, 579; and Clinton's
    multitasking, 419–20; and Clinton's
    need to be loved, 521–22; on Clinton's
    official biography, 601–2; on Clinton's
    paternity, 33–34; and Clinton's politi-
    cal sensitivity, 582–83; and Clinton's
    post-1980 plans, 363, 364, 365, 373;
    and Clinton's promiscuity, 434, 579;
    and Clinton's reactions to elections of
    1980, 362, 370; Clinton's relationship
    with, 578; and Clinton's unwilling-
    ness to accept responsibility, 341,
    370, 374, 385, 631; and elections of
    1972, 264–65; and elections of 1974,
    289, 300; and elections of 1980, 369;
    and elections of 1982, 400; and
    Fulbright's 1974 campaign, 283, 288;
    and fund-raising, 568; and Hillary's
    stock market trades, 353; personal
    and professional background of, 578;
    and Republican-Democratic rela-
    tions, 598; and saxophone playing of
    Clinton, 123–24; as Tyson Foods
    counsel, 283; on Whitewater, 626
blame. *See* responsibility, Clinton taking
Bloodworth-Thomason, Linda, 657
Blossom, Virgil, 81, 82, 83, 84
Blythe, Bill (William Jefferson III), 24,
    25–29, 30–32, 33–35, 38, 49, 77,
    242
Blythe, Earnest, 28
Blythe, Henry Leon, 27
Blythe, Sharron, 27
Blythe, Virginia. *See* Clinton, Virginia
    Dell
Blythe, William Jefferson II "Willie," 26
Blythe, William Jefferson IV. *See* Clinton,
    Bill (William Jefferson)
Bobbitt, Lorena, 599
Boesky, Ivan, 440, 497
Bolsterli, Margaret Jones, 15–16, 17, 20,
    21, 37, 55
Bolt, Robert, 464
Bond, Rich, 668, 678
Booker, Wilma Rowe, 34–35, 41
The Boston Globe, 610, 674
Bourdieu, Pierre, 165, 505
Bouvier, Jack, 421, 422
Boys Nation, 117–20, 121, 132
Boys State, 116–18
Bradley, Bill, 570
Branch, Taylor, 262, 266, 267, 601
Brandley, Ellen, 252
Brando, Marlon, 126
Brantley, Max, 385, 397, 414, 468, 469,
    481, 586
Brezhnev, Leonid, 287, 297

Broaddrick, Juanita, 336
Brock, David, 239, 600
Broder, David, 622
Brooke, Edward, 235
Brookwood Elementary School (Hope,
    Arkansas), 54, 58
Brown, Floyd, 671
Brown, Helen Gurley, 146
Brown, Jerry, 368, 591, 609, 645, 646, 654,
    656
Brown, Minnijean, 89
Brown, Ron, 653
Brown v. Board of Education (1954), 79,
    80, 81, 84
Browning, Dolly Kyle, 279, 500
Brummett, John, 378, 435, 458, 460, 510,
    536, 581, 582, 584–85, 590
Buchanan, Pat, 637, 639, 666, 667, 668
Bulger, Billy, 427–28
Bulger, James J. "Whitey," 427–28
Bumpers, Dale, 300–301, 311, 314, 329,
    331, 341, 449, 452, 527, 530
Burns, Bob, 302
Burnstein, Malcolm, 245–46
Busby, Horace, 263
Bush, Barbara, 668
Bush, George H. W.: acceptance speech in
    1992 of, 668; and Bakkers, 488; cam-
    paign contributions for, 602; as CIA
    head, 301; and Clinton's Soviet trip,
    220; and Clinton's speech at DLC
    convention, 552; and Cold War, 578;
    defining moment in elections of
    1992 for, 676–77, 678, 679; and elec-
    tions of 1984, 450; and Gennifer
    Flowers story, 611–12, 622; invinci-
    bility of, 569–70; Morris works for,
    469; negative campaigning by, 507;
    and Perot candidacy, 637; Perot's in-
    vestigation of, 641; polls about, 563,
    564, 587, 591, 606, 636, 668, 669,
    670, 682; promiscuity of, 561, 640,
    670; and public identification with
    president, 638; and Robinson, 539;
    speeches of, 669–70; underestima-
    tion of Clinton by, 689; as vice presi-
    dent, 450; and Vietnam, 142. *See
    also* elections of 1988; elections of
    1992
Bush, George W., 147
Bush, Prescott, 674
busing, 260
Butte, George, 172
butting story, 61–62

Cabe, Gloria, 515, 532, 553
Calabresi, Guido, 252
California: elections of 1992 in, 640, 644;
    Proposition 13 in, 344, 363

Meyers, Mary Pinchot, 159
The Miami Herald, 452
Michigan: elections of 1992 in, 590, 645
midlife crisis of Clinton, 500, 501, 502, 506, 507, 508–9, 643–44
Milken, Michael, 440
Miller, Alice, 98, 101
Miller, John, 355
Miller, Mark, 654
Miller, Zell, 609, 644
Mills, Wilbur, 80, 261, 325, 602
Milton, Joyce, 500, 501
Minnesota: elections of 1992 in, 646
minorities, 209, 369, 530, 594. *See also* blacks
Miss Marie Purkins' School for Little Folks (Hope, Arkansas), 52
mistresses: as socially acceptable, 318–19
Mitchell, Bill, 102
Mitchison, Naomi, 10
Modglin, Terry, 139–40, 141
Moloy, Paul, 134
Mondale, Walter, 413
money: Clinton's lack of interest in, 284, 364, 415; and feminism, 69–70; and Flowers-Clinton relationship, 319; importance of, 535; and politics, 438–39; and power, 74, 603; as root of political evil, 602–3; and televangelism, 492. *See also* fund-raising
"Monica complex," 293
Monroe, Marilyn, 318, 601
Moore, Jim, 145, 147, 160, 161–62, 163
Moore, Rudy, 338–39, 355, 356, 357–58, 375
morality: in Arkansas, 10; and Bill and Hillary's intentions, 413; Blair's views about Clinton's, 579; change in, 247–48; and Clinton's ambitions and goals, 462, 463; and draft, 320; and Flowers' pregnancy/abortion, 320; gender approaches to, 394; of Hillary, 537; Hillary's views about, 467; in Hope, 42; in Hot Springs, 59; in 1930s, 10; and religion, 17, 44, 46; and Roger Jr.'s drug addiction, 436–37; and survival of the fittest, 534; and white conservative backlash, 451. *See also* cohabitation; courage
Morgan, Jim, 92
Morris, Dick: and apology of Clinton, 382–83, 388; and Bush (George H. W.), 469; and Clinton as copywriter, 543; and Clinton as governor, 340, 406; Clinton knocks down, 515–16; and Clinton's comeback, 377, 379, 382–83, 384, 388, 389, 399, 445; Clinton's firing of, 337, 340,

341, 350; and Clinton's midlife crisis, 507, 508–9; and Clinton's post-1980 plans, 373–74, 375, 376; and Clinton's promiscuity, 503; and Clinton's thoughts of divorce, 508–9; and Clintonspeak, 384; and Dukakis-King race, 382; and elections of 1978, 328–29, 330, 333; and elections of 1980, 350, 360; and elections of 1982, 388, 389, 399; and elections of 1988, 466–67, 468, 469; and elections of 1990, 528, 542, 543; and elections of 1992, 609, 647; and Hillary's fantasy to be governor, 509–11, 515; and negative campaigning, 333, 334, 379; as part of new triumvirate, 375; and perils of running for presidency, 572; and politics of personal destruction, 334, 572; and swimming pool at governor's mansion, 510; and Wright, 375, 515–16
Morris, Edmund, 601
Morris, Roger, 426, 431, 439
Morris, Willie, 172
Morrison, Toni, 92
Mount Pine Camp (Hot Springs, Arkansas), 134
Moyers, Bill, 368
"Mr. Aura": Clinton as, 233
Murphree, Debra, 546–47, 557, 565, 572, 606, 607, 608
music, 76, 79, 122–24, 157, 233, 334. *See also* Presley, Elvis; saxophone
Muskie, Edmund, 261, 653
My Lai massacre, 214

name recognition, 443, 450, 457, 564, 605, 623
narcissism, 310–11, 416, 417, 421
Nash, Bob, 399
Nasser, Gamal Abdel, 74
National Association for the Advancement of Colored People (NAACP), 83, 642
National Catholic Reporter, 549
National Governors Association, 444, 448, 457, 478, 577–78
National Guard, 189, 195, 197, 198, 223
National Guard Association: Bush address to, 669–70
National Republican Congressional Committee, 686
National Reserve, 459
National Review, 443
Natural and Scenic Rivers Commission, 340–41
NBC, 412

Sixteenth Street Baptist Church
(Birmingham, Alabama), 128
sixties: change as characteristic of, 154;
Clinton as child of, 164, 206, 219,
231, 321, 454, 461; Clinton as personification of best of, 228; as decade of
change, 391; disintegration of
promise of, 229–30; elections of 1972
as death knell of, 268; end of, 218–24;
LeClair case as symbol of change in,
247–48; legacy of, 249; paying for,
191–93; sex as liberating in, 623; as
turning point for American society,
186
60 Minutes (CBS-TV), 614–15, 616–18,
619, 620, 636, 640, 648, 658, 681
Slater, Rodney, 399, 400
slick/"Slick Willie": Clinton as, 132, 140,
206, 413, 443, 460–61, 465–66, 635,
648, 684, 685; Greenberg coins term,
205
Smith, C. Calvin, 9, 28–29, 37
Smith, Gary, 653
Smith, Gregg, 553
Smith, Larry, 653
Smith, Maurice, 437, 439, 442
Smith, Stephen A.: as chief of staff, 325,
338; and Clinton as attorney general,
325, 326; and Clinton as governor,
338–39; and Clinton's political future,
326; Clinton's relationship with,
356–57, 462; and death penalty, 593;
and elections of 1974, 298; and elections of 1980, 462; firing of, 356–57,
375; functions of, 326; as part of
Bearded Troika, 338–39; and
Whitewater, 390
Smoking Bimbo theory, 610
"smoking letter," 628–29, 632–34, 647, 670
social class: and Bill and Hillary's relationship, 302–3; fall of, 164–65; in
Hope, 16–19, 20–21, 49–50, 51–52,
228; in Hot Springs, 59, 99; in 1960s,
164–65; and Presley, 76; in South,
15–19, 20–21; and television, 76–77;
at Yale, 239–40
Sorenson, Theodore, 109
SoulJay, 646
South: Clinton's sense of rootedness in,
566–68; feminism in, 37; and Hillary's
image, 394–95; segregation in, 22;
and sexual activities, 550; social class
in, 15–19, 20–21; violence in, 17
Southern Governors Conference, 86
Southern Manifesto, 80–81, 87, 119,
165
Southern Tenant Farmers Union, 9–10
Southwestern Proving Grounds (Hope,
Arkansas), 29–30, 54

Soviet Union: and Carter, 343; Clinton's
desire to go to, 183; Clinton's paper
about political pluralism in, 182–83,
225; Clinton's trip to, 218–19, 220,
225, 233, 238, 255, 671, 685; collapse
of, 603; as "evil empire," 369; and
Nixon, 287. *See also* Prague Spring;
Russia
Spain: Clinton's trip to, 222
special interests, 346, 389
spectacle: politics of, 536–37
speech(es) of Clinton: and acceptance
speech in elections of 1992, 659; to
Association of Democratic State
Chairs, 592; and Clinton's declaration
for presidency, 586–87; Clinton's first
political, 137–38; at Democratic
Leadership Council (Cleveland),
551–52; at Democratic National
Convention in 1980, 346; drafted for
Holt, 137; for Dukakis's nomination
in 1988, 506–7, 578, 592; in elections
of 1978, 330; in elections of 1992,
592, 633, 635; at Georgetown, 141;
Greenberg's analysis of, 461; guber-
natorial inaugural, 408; in high
school, 121, 128, 129; to National
Democratic Committee, 592; to New
Hampshire Democratic Committee,
451; to Quality Management
Conference, 554
Spence, Roy, 659
Sperling, Godfrey, Jr., 581
Sperling breakfast, 580–83, 605
Spindler, George, 567
Spindler, Louis, 567
sports, 114, 124, 146, 334, 409, 410
Spurlin, Virgil, 122, 123, 129
St. John's Catholic School (Hot Springs,
Arkansas), 61, 70, 74
St. Joseph's Catholic Church (Hot
Springs, Arkansas), 61
St. Joseph's Hospital (Hot Springs,
Arkansas), 59
staff, governor's, 531. *See also specific per-
son*
Staley, Carolyn: and Bill and Hillary's re-
lationship, 304; and Clinton as ath-
lete, 115; and Clinton as go-between,
44; and Clinton as musician, 124; and
Clinton's application to Georgetown,
121–22; and Clinton's comeback, 377;
and Clinton's image, 105; and
Clinton's promiscuity, 124, 305;
Clinton's relationship with, 114, 154,
156, 157, 159, 168, 169–70, 186–88,
191; and Clinton's secrecy, 105; and
Clinton's views of addictions, 431;
hospital visit with Virginia by, 125;

and riots in Washington, 154, 156; and song for Chelsea's birth, 354

Stallone, Sylvester, 387–88

The Star: and Gennifer Flowers story, 606–7, 608, 610–12, 613, 618, 619–21

Starr, John Robert, 352, 375, 396–98, 411–12, 527, 533, 543–44

State Department, U.S.: Clinton's records in, 685

State Land Bank, 341

Stearns, Rick, 172, 176, 191, 200, 201, 202, 206, 207, 208–9, 261

Steinem, Gloria, 242

Stephanopoulos, George: and Bush campaign of 1979, 609; and Bush smear campaign, 671; and Clinton's acceptance speech in elections of 1992, 659; Clinton's relationship with, 293; and draft story, 632; and election day in elections of 1992, 688; as feeling betrayed, 615–16; and Gennifer Flowers story, 610–11, 615–16, 619, 620, 621; and lying by Clinton, 615–16, 621; and Paula Jones story, 554–55, 558–59; and Perot in elections of 1992, 644–45; and primaries in elections of 1992, 554–55, 558–59, 609, 610–11; professional background of, 609; and promiscuity in politics, 623; resignation of, 559

Stephens, Jackson, 313, 541–42

Stephens, Maryanne, 541

Stephens, Witt, 136, 313, 332, 541–42

Stephens family, 331, 342

Stevenson, Adlai, 469

Stevenson, Coke, 603

Stewart, David, 288

Stockdale, James, 675

Stother, Ray, 466–67

structuralism, 391

Student Non-violent Coordinating Committee, 144

Sturgis High School (Tennessee), 76

success, 462–65

Sullivan, Ed, 75, 76, 77, 84

Sununu, John, 668

"Super Tuesday": in elections of 1992, 593, 644

Supreme Court, U.S.: and busing, 260; and death penalty issue, 593; and Rector death penalty, 594; and Scopes II, 380; and segregation issues, 79, 80, 81, 87, 89; and teacher testing, 437. *See also specific ruling*

survival: and Bill and Hillary's relationship, 435, 535; in celebrity politics, 545–58; and Clinton as new man, 211; and Clinton's childhood and youth, 95, 102, 105; and deceit,

212–13; and Gennifer Flowers story, 595–96; and Great Depression, 12; and Greenberg's comments about success, 463, 464; of media, 469; money as essential to, 535; and politics as a game, 535–36; politics of, 534, 536–37; and Red Queen syndrome, 211; Wright as central to Clinton's, 441, 459

Swaggart, Frances, 546, 547, 548, 549, 565

Swaggart, Jimmy: arrest of, 589–90; and Bakker, 491, 546, 589; as braggart, 545–48; Clinton compared with, 552, 556, 614; as Clinton model, 565–66; Gorman's "court summons" for, 572; mea culpa telesermon of, 571–72; and Murphree, 546–47, 565, 572, 605–6; and pedophilia, 549 50; and pornography, 546, 547, 549, 571–72, 589, 599; and power of evangelism, 567; and prostitutes, 549, 557, 589, 599; sex addiction of, 258, 548–49, 551, 558, 571–72; as televangelist, 565–66; videotape of, 606

swimming pool story, 510

Talbott, Strobe, 172, 177, 208, 211, 218, 245, 250, 254, 259, 577–78

Tamposi, Elizabeth, 685, 686

Tatom, Floris, 355

Taunton, Larry, 118, 120

taxes: in Arkansas, 8, 522, 626, 627; and Bumpers as governor, 341; and Carter administration, 343; and Clinton as governor, 337, 338, 345, 349, 350, 410, 449, 499; and Clinton's comeback, 384, 388, 394; and Clinton's declaration for presidency, 587; and elections of 1982, 388, 394; and elections of 1992, 609, 627; in Hot Springs, 60; and Reagan administration, 499, 501; and White as governor, 363

Taylor, Donna, 52, 54

teacher testing, 409, 410, 411, 437

Teeley, Pete, 488

Teeter, Bob, 683

televangelism, 486–88, 489–94, 495, 497, 566–71, 611, 616, 618–19, 653–54. *See also specific minister*

televangelists: as symbolic, 638

television, 73, 74–75, 76–77, 84, 88, 137, 411, 449, 479, 680. *See also* televangelism

terrorism: and Carter administration, 343

Texas: elections of 1972 in, 263, 264, 265, 266–67, 268

Thatcher, Margaret, 164–65, 344, 391, 395, 409

NIGEL HAMILTON was born in England in 1944 and studied at Munich University and the University of Cambridge, England, where he took an honors degree in history. His first major biography, *The Brothers Mann,* was critically acclaimed both in Britain and the United States, as was *Monty,* his three-volume official biography of the legendary World War II commander Field Marshal Bernard Montgomery, which won the Whitbread Prize for Biography and the Templer Medal for Best Contribution to Military History. His television film *Monty—In Love and War* also won the New York Blue Ribbon Award for Best Documentary-Profile.

In 1992 Nigel Hamilton published the first volume of his biography of President John F. Kennedy, *JFK: Reckless Youth,* which became an international bestseller and was dramatized for ABC television. As director of the British Institute of Biography and professor of biography at De Montfort University, England, Mr. Hamilton has made it a life task to advance the understanding and teaching of biography. Mr. Hamilton is currently a fellow of the John W. McCormack Graduate School of Policy Studies, University of Massachusetts, Boston, where he is researching and writing the second volume of *Bill Clinton: An American Journey.*

ABOUT THE TYPE

This book was set in Times Roman, designed by Stanley Morison specifically for *The Times* of London. The typeface was introduced in the newspaper in 1932. Times Roman had its greatest success in the United States as a book and commercial typeface, rather than one used in newspapers.